Psychotherapies

Psychotherapies
A Comparative Casebook

Edited by
Stephen J. Morse
Law Center
University of Southern California

and

Robert I. Watson, Jr.
Institute of Advanced Psychological Studies
Adelphi University

With the Editorial Assistance of Gary E. Schwartz

HOLT, RINEHART AND WINSTON
New York   Chicago   San Francisco   Atlanta
Dallas   Montreal   Toronto   London   Sydney

Library of Congress Cataloging in Publication Data
Main entry under title:

Psychotherapies.

    Includes bibliographies and index.
    1. Psychotherapy.   I. Morse, Stephen J.   II. Watson,
Robert I., 1947–
RC480.P818   616.8'914   76–46353
ISBN 0-03-017826-6

Preface

In the fall of 1972 the two editors assisted Gary Schwartz in teaching a course on abnormal personality to students at Harvard University. We wished to teach the students some basic aspects of psychotherapy, but we were continually frustrated by the lack of a book that would demonstrate the differences and similarities in *therapeutic process* of different schools of psychotherapy. Students found theoretical readings about psychotherapy arid. What clearly seemed needed was a collection of cases that would show what and why a psychotherapist did what he or she did during the actual conduct of psychotherapeutic treatment. Most of the available materials were either too theoretical or included too few schools at a time when so many psychotherapeutic approaches were available. Therefore, we decided to edit this book to meet the need for a volume that would enable students to compare psychotherapeutic process across many different psychotherapeutic schools. Because of other pressing commitments, Gary Schwartz was unable to continue his participation, but he played an active role in the original planning and organization of the book.

It was decided to break the book down into three sections: dynamic psychotherapies, humanistic psychotherapies (third force), and behavior therapies. There is a general introduction to psychotherapy, and each section of cases is preceded by an historical and technical overview of the schools represented in that section so that the novice can attain sufficient background to understand the cases. Although the editors have preferences among the various psychotherapeutic schools, we have tried to be impartial in writing these introductions. Further, each case is preceded by a brief introductory note that should guide the reader's understanding of some of the unique or noteworthy features of the individual cases. Only individual psychotherapy cases are included because group psychotherapy is such a diverse and expanding field that including representative group therapy cases would have lengthened the book unconscionably.

"Classic" cases as well as more modern ones have been included in order to give readers an appreciation of the evolution of techniques, and an appreciation of current ones. The editors have tried in *Psychotherapies* to include cases with widely varying and interesting patient pathology and treatment settings so that the reader may see the broad applicability of the psychotherapies. Because such a broad sample of psychopathology is presented, the volume may also be used as a casebook in psychopathology.

Given the large number of psychotherapeutic techniques and schools available today, naturally it was impossible to approach completeness in the selections. We have tried in our selections to be representative of the major schools of therapy, however, and to avoid including therapies that seemed simply "faddish." We apologize to those who feel that an important therapy has been unfairly excluded.

We should like to thank the staff of the University of Southern California Law Center for their assistance and support in completing this volume. Special thanks are due to Ms. June Massa, and also to Ms. Elaine Hadley and Ms. Freda Maltin of the Law Center. Part of the work on this book was done while one of us (S. J. M.) was visiting with the Psychology Department of Boston University, to which thanks are due for its support. Ms. Elaine Evans was particularly helpful in Boston. We should also like to express our thanks to the staff of the Institute of Advanced Psychological Studies, Adelphi University, for their aid in the final preparation of the book. A special note of thanks is due to Grace Watson for her assistance on the humanistic section. Finally, Professor Gary E. Schwartz, now of Yale University, must be thanked for his original contributions and continuing encouragement.

Los Angeles, Ca.   S. J. M.
Garden City, N.Y.   R. I. W., Jr.
November 1977

Contents

Chapter 1
An Introduction to Psychotherapy

ROBERT I. WATSON, JR. and STEPHEN J. MORSE

It is useful to describe the basic nature of and the current issues in individual psychotherapy so the new student of psychotherapy will be able to begin this volume with some understanding of the nature and problems of psychotherapy, and so the sophisticated reader will be able to see some of our prejudices. We begin by defining therapy and then go on to its goals, practitioners, and process. Next we turn to an analysis of the most important current issues in psychotherapy.

WHAT IS PSYCHOTHERAPY?

Our preliminary definition of individual psychotherapy is *a special form of interaction between two individuals, the patient and the therapist, in which the patient initiates the interaction by seeking psychological help and in which the therapist structures the interaction using psychological principles to aid the patient in gaining more control over his or her life through changing thoughts, feelings, and actions.* The therapist's role is to help the patient learn new behavior. The techniques for facilitating this learning process are quite different from one form of therapy to another, but all therapy is essentially a learning experience for the patient.

The actual interaction and relationship in psychotherapy is superficially very similar to other human interactions. But two crucial variables differentiate the therapeutic interaction: the way in which the interaction is structured and the goals of the interaction. Using the specific framework in which he or she has been trained, the therapist plans and structures the therapeutic situation to facilitate the learning of new behavior. The dynamic

1

and humanistic schools consider the interaction therapeutic in itself; behavior therapists, however, place less emphasis on the interaction per se.

Psychotherapy is not defined by the academic degrees or the training of the therapist, nor by the setting in which it takes place. Except in those states that restrict therapeutic practice exclusively to certain professional groups such as psychologists and physicians, psychotherapy can be carried out by anyone, with any other individual, in any setting. In our society there are certain professionals (psychiatrists, clinical psychologists, social workers) who are recognized as having special knowledge about how the psychotherapeutic learning process should be structured and about how human problems may be understood psychologically. Individuals, therefore, are more likely to turn to these professionals when they feel they need help.

The individual's desire for help is an important part of the process of psychotherapy. In most instances, the procedure must be initiated by a person who desires some form of personal change, for it is questionable whether change can be forced upon a patient while at the same time preserving respect for the individual's dignity. We believe that effective and respectful psychotherapy ought to involve the voluntary cooperation of two free agents.

WHAT ARE THE GOALS OF PSYCHOTHERAPY?

Although different therapies may focus on different aspects of human behavior, the ultimate goal in all therapies is to bring about change in maladaptive behavior and thus to relieve the patient's self-perceived or socially perceived suffering, pain, or unhappiness.[1] While the ultimate goal of psychotherapy is the relief of unhappiness, the specific focus of psychotherapy is to help the individual gain more control over his or her own life by changing the behavior that seems to be causing the unhappiness. The person entering psychotherapy feels somewhat powerless to change the acts, thoughts, and feelings that stand in the way of achieving his life goals. One person cannot fly because he is afraid; another person cannot stop thinking certain thoughts that make her profoundly uncomfortable; another person is always too "down" to function optimally. In all cases, behavior that the patient seems unable to control appears to direct him or her in ways that create unhappiness. Psychotherapy then attempts to aid the patient become

[1] Although the emphasis of all psychotherapy is on changing behavior, the influence of innate or constitutional factors is not denied. Persons are biological beings, and the basis for any learning is their biological endowment. Although biological factors do limit the extent to which and in what manner the patient may learn, by their very nature such factors are impervious to change by psychological means. In treating certain types of patients, such as retarded or senile persons, therapy must directly consider biological factors. And despite the limit biology places on the process of psychotherapy, as the recent biofeedback literature demonstrates, it is clear that factors that were once considered to be wholly biological have a definite psychological component and can be influenced through psychological means.

more competent in pursuing life goals by stimulating mastery over the thoughts, feelings, and actions that hinder this competence.

Why is gaining control of one's life the specific focus of therapy? Here we must return to the common-sense truth of human behavior that people nearly always feel better if they feel that they have more control over their own lives. Since most people enter into therapy because they are unhappy, the raison d'être for psychotherapy is to help them feel happier. Although feeling happier is often seen by the patient as the goal of psychotherapy, the most that therapy can do is to help the patient learn those behaviors that give one more control over one's own life. Through this process, the patient has the greatest chance of feeling happier.

Although the patient should gain control over his own life, it is important to be aware to what extent the therapist's values play a role in the psychotherapeutic process. The therapist brings to the relationship his or her own value preferences, while the patient may adhere to a different set of values. Thus values and moral judgments will always play a role in therapy, no matter how much the therapist attempts to push them to the background. The therapist's task, however, is neither to make the patient into a mirror image nor to exert influence toward accepting one particular set of values. Rather than doing such a disservice to the patient, the therapist should both attempt to have the patient gain control over his or her own problems and to leave the patient free to make private value judgments.

WHO PERFORMS PSYCHOTHERAPY?

In our society, the mode of becoming a psychotherapist is to undergo established training procedures that lead to certification in certain professions. These trained professionals fall into four broad groups: psychiatrists, psychoanalysts, clinical psychologists, and psychiatric social workers. *Psychiatrists* are medical doctors who have specialized in psychiatry, the branch of medicine that deals with the treatment of mental disorders. Closely allied to the psychiatrists are the *psychoanalysts*. They are usually psychiatrists who have undergone special training in the theory and practice of psychoanalysis at institutes specifically established to provide this training. Not all psychiatrists are psychoanalysts, however, because not all psychiatrists have taken specialized psychoanalytic training. And not all psychoanalysts are psychiatrists because some psychoanalysts, known as lay analysts, have not had medical training. Psychotherapy is also practiced by *clinical psychologists*, whose basic graduate training is in psychology, and who often do diagnostic work as well as therapy. *Psychiatric social workers*, who compose the group that produces the largest number of psychotherapists, practice independently and as members of teams in hospitals and clinics. Other professionals, such as physicians, who are not trained specifically in psychotherapy may also use psychotherapy to aid their patients, sometimes without recognizing it. In addition, there are proliferating programs that train non-professionals and paraprofessionals in a number of psychotherapeutic-like counseling techniques.

Behavior is multidetermined, and all theories and abstract conceptualizations are impositions on the data of human behavior. Yet knowledge of certain personality theories and conceptualizations does seem to be useful in understanding other individuals. A theory of human nature and behavior is certainly held by each person, whether or not it is explicitly formulated, and, at some level, is used constantly to guide behavior when interacting with others. What differentiates psychotherapy from other human interactions is that the psychotherapist has a tutored, conscious knowledge of the laws or regularities that seemingly govern human behavior. Furthermore, the professional psychotherapist is more able than the average person to discern which of these laws, applied in what manner, may be of most assistance to a particular patient. Finally, the therapist intervenes in ways suggested by those laws (i.e., performs therapy) in a manner supposedly *proven* to yield the highest probability of successful therapeutic outcome. This does not mean, of course, that the therapist simply imparts these laws to the patient. Learning in depth or assimilation or practice—such processes must take place on the part of the patient.

Which type of professional or nonprofessional treats a given patient depends greatly on the referral channel used by the patient, on the individual's resources and on available local facilities. The agencies utilized as well as the individual's ability to pay for psychotherapy will influence the source of counseling. Similarly, although every therapist will see a wide range of problems in a typical career or even in one day, there are limitations placed on the range of patients by the work setting and contact with specific referral channels. For example, a therapist working in a state mental hospital is highly likely to see large numbers of psychotic and alcoholic patients, while one who works in a social service agency will see more patients with neurotic and marital difficulties.

HOW ARE THE GOALS OF PSYCHOTHERAPY REACHED?

As we have noted, all the various forms of psychotherapy attempt to change individual behavior by helping the patient gain control over his or her life. Different forms of therapy concentrate on different aspects of behavior— some deal with actions, others more with thoughts and feelings; some concentrate on verbal interactions, while others explore nonverbal behavior; some place their emphasis on exploring the past, while others deal almost exclusively with the present.

Besides concentrating on different aspects of behavior, different psychotherapies employ different techniques. These techniques vary because of the philosophical, social, cultural, historical, educational, and theoretical differences among the psychotherapists who apply them. Some attempt to aid the patient by being directive, while others are predominantly nondirective. Some see the best method of gaining control as emotional and intellectual insight; others believe the best means is by counterconditioning or modification of the patient's schedules of reinforcement.

There are three major classes of schools of psychotherapy—the dynamic, the humanistic, and the behavioral. Although there is great variation within each of these classes, the schools of psychotherapy within a class do share common theoretical viewpoints.

The roots of the dynamic school of therapy are found in the psychoanalytic theory and work of Sigmund Freud. The dynamic school emphasizes the thoughts, feelings, and past life of the patient and the need for insight into them. The humanistic therapies are much more diverse and have their basic foundation in a phenomenological view of man. Emphasizing the unique qualities of each individual patient's vision of the self in the various life settings, the humanistic techniques are quite varied. Typically, they range from the relational and insight-oriented techniques used by existential analysts (similar to dynamic therapies) to the directive rational-emotive techniques used by Albert Ellis (claimed by some to be behavioral techniques).

The behavior therapies have their basis in the learning theories and work of Ivan Pavlov, John B. Watson, Edward L. Thorndike, B. F. Skinner, Albert Bandura, and others. Concentrating their techniques mainly on the specific, overt actions of the patient, the behavior therapies differ from others, which regard such behavior as only symptomatic. Using techniques derived largely from principles of learning discovered in the psychological laboratory, behavior therapists attempt to bring about change by modifying these actions in a more adaptive way.

As one facet of its commonality with other sciences, psychotherapy is constantly developing. As will be shown, each of the three major schools of psychotherapy is undergoing an evolution of theory and technique in an effort to ensure that new goals can be reached and that these therapies remain applicable to specific patient populations and problems.

Among the dynamic therapists, a major innovation has been increased reliance on and manipulation of the present, here-and-now relationship between therapist and patient. A primary tool for behavior change, such methods work well with patients with severe character disorders. The increasing treatment of so-called narcissistic and borderline personalities (Kernberg, 1968; Kohut, 1971) is one aspect of this development. While such individuals have a stable personality organization, they are infantile characters whose internalized object-relations and defenses are primitive: Treatment of such persons requires adjustment of traditional modes of managing the therapeutic relationship. Some therapists encourage deep regression in the therapeutic situation while attempting to provide the type of relationship that the patient lacked in his or her formative years (Balint, 1968).

The humanistic psychotherapies, in all their forms, are moving toward a better definition of the techniques they employ and are, in some cases, redefining their major emphases. This redefinition is particularly true of rational-emotive therapy, which is presently laying much more emphasis upon the "cognitive restructuring" of the individual. The patients learn how to "cognitively restructure" their environment, in turn giving them a new way to view themselves and their world. This approach has recently proved useful in aiding women to be more assertive.

Behavior therapies are changing as well. Since behavioral techniques have become more generally accepted, behaviorists have been able to concentrate more upon clinical elements, especially the interaction between therapist and patient. Newer learning techniques such as modeling have also been applied to therapeutic situations. Other new forms of behavior therapy which attempt to deal with various forms of psychopathology are multimodal therapy, which promotes general goals rather than attempts to change only highly restricted behaviors, and biofeedback, which works on problems previously considered to be only physical.

A discussion of how the goals of psychotherapy are reached would be incomplete without brief mention of the view, propounded by experts such as Hans H. Strupp (1973, 1975), that there are certain common ingredients in all psychotherapies that account for the behavior changes produced by all therapies. Strupp (1973, p. 1) has described three "basic ingredients of therapeutic change." First, the therapist creates a "helping relationship patterned after the parent–child relationship." Second, the therapist creates a power base from which he or she influences the patient, using common psychological techniques such as suggestion, interpretation, and the manipulation of reward. Third, Strupp notes that the first two ingredients are "crucially dependent on a client who has the capacity and willingness to profit from experience."[2]

Although many experts (e.g., Garfield, 1973) would not agree that the same basic ingredients in all therapies account for the changes within each, Strupp's view is provocative. And Strupp's position might help explain the observation that most individual therapies seem to have similar success rates despite supposed differences in theory and technique. As the reader studies the cases in this volume, it will be productive to note if the three basic ingredients seem to be present and whether the change-producing variables in the different therapies are, in actuality, identical.

CURRENT ISSUES IN PSYCHOTHERAPY

There are five major issues presently affecting the field of psychotherapy: (1) the patients' rights movement; (2) women in psychotherapy; (3) the proliferation and popularization of psychotherapy; (4) the provision of psychotherapeutic service; and (5) the efficacy of psychotherapy.

[2] Strupp admits that these criteria are vague but, in the article from which they are taken, he explicates them at some length.

The patients' rights movement began with a twofold concen for the civil liberties of involuntarily hospitalized mental patients and for the plight of those labeled mentally ill. Thomas Szasz (1960, 1961), a psychiatrist who is highly critical of psychiatric theory and practice, gave this movement its intellectual impetus by claiming that mental illness is a "myth." He believes that to conceptualize maladaptive behavior as an "illness" is to use a dangerous metaphor that is unjustified scientifically. The medical metaphor for maladaptive behavior is dangerous, Szasz argues, because it authorizes, in pseudoscientific guise, the moral labeling and social control of deviant individuals. Although the alleged goal of this labeling and control is benevolent paternalism, for Szasz the only behavior that authorizes unwanted state intrusion into a person's life is the commission of a crime. Any other intrusion is an impermissible infringement on liberty.

Although Szasz's critique is too radical for many persons, there is force in his thesis and in related arguments. The patients' rights movement arose because the specter of possible misuse of psychiatric labels and power raised serious questions for many concerned with the mental health system.

Psychotherapists are now faced with at least two important questions arising from this movement: first, When is the involuntary application of psychotherapy to an unwilling patient justified, and second, When is the label of mental illness used to mask a therapist's social value preferences? In other words, can such categorization lead to harmful labeling of the patient and to therapy that fosters the therapist's value preferences rather than the patient's autonomy?

A recent example that raises both questions for mental health professionals involves the rights and treatment of homosexual patients. Davison (1976), a noted behavior therapist, is concerned with the coercive forces exerted on homosexuals to begin treatment. He believes, as most therapists do, that the patient must enter therapy voluntarily. The treatment of any patient forced into a therapeutic situation, whether by law or by private pressures, raises ethical issues for the potential therapist. For instance, granted a person's unwillingness to change, we may ask if such measures unduly infringe on the dignity of the individual.

Regarding homosexual behavior, social pressures, insidious and otherwise, may be a primary motivating force for the homosexual's desire to change sexual orientation. Davison suggests that all therapies aimed at changing the sexual orientation of homosexuals be stopped, even with voluntary patients, because the existence of any therapeutic program lends credence to the view that homosexuality in itself is pathological, which Davison does not believe. The important point to recognize, however, is that the question of whether homosexuality per se is pathological is not answerable by scientific methods alone. As with all questions concerning behavior, the therapist's position will also be a product of his value preferences.

Other therapists disagree with this position while still believing in the voluntary nature of therapy. For example, Halleck (1976) would still treat the homosexual, engaging in a dialogue with the person in an attempt to clarify the motivation for the desired change and giving enough information to enable the potential patient to make an informed choice in this matter.

Related to the issue of patients' rights is a second area of concern, the question of women and psychotherapy. Some practitioners and some members of the women's movement feel that the theory and practice of psychotherapy are sexist (e.g., Chesler, 1972). In many instances they see psychotherapy as a repressive force narrowing the options of women patients instead of allowing them a greater diversity in their lives. As in the treatment of homosexuals, the therapist's values play a major role in what he or she sees as the goal of treatment for the patient, namely, what behavior should be changed through therapy. How should a therapist treat a woman patient who, because of social pressure, has been made, first, to feel uncomfortable with a nontraditional female role and, second, to seek therapy promoting conformity to the traditional female role? Similarly, should the focus of treatment for an unhappily married patient ever be an acceptance of traditional marital roles, even if such treatment would ameliorate the immediate marital tensions? The values of the therapist are extremely important in answering these questions.

Many women presently feel that they can receive more understanding and less prejudicial treatment from a female therapist. Some women's organizations have approved lists of therapists, both male and female, who they feel have a positive, less stereotyped orientation toward female patients, seeing women as active and striving for themselves. Therapeutic programs presently are being developed to deal with problems that especially confront women in our society. Some of these, such as the work being done on assertiveness, are in direct conflict with stereotyped views of women. Even with such therapies, however, the psychotherapist has to decide when and with whom to use these techniques.

Within the professions of psychotherapy there has been some effort to train more women therapists. Over the last ten years there has been a realization that many roles, even within the helping professions, have been closed to women. Presently more opportunities have arisen for women as therapists, yet they are hampered in their work by the conservative nature of many of the professions involved in psychotherapy. Overall, the position of women in psychotherapy both as therapists and patients mirrors the role of women within our society—both are in a state of change.

A third area of concern for many members of the profession is the growth and popularization of psychotherapy. More available and more accepted, psychotherapy has grown with new techniques based on established principles that have been developed to deal with more individuals in a shorter period of time. In many cases, the new techniques have met with great success. Simultaneously, less established forms of psychotherapy have been popularized by media emphasis on relatively untested and faddish forms of therapy. Many individuals seek out these forms without adequate knowledge of the range of options in psychotherapy. Several of these new forms worry members of the profession because they are often based on very tenuous theoretical concepts and because very little has been done to study their effectiveness. The concern is that these therapies may prove ineffective and discourage individuals who might have been aided by therapy based on more established methods. At the same time there is a realization that new methods must be tried if psychotherapy is to progress and make more contributions to human welfare.

A fourth issue facing the profession of psychotherapy is the problem of limited psychotherapeutic resources. There are simply not enough trained, competent therapists to treat the growing numbers of persons who need and want psychotherapeutic treatment. Neither the expansion of traditional training programs nor the proliferation of newer therapies is able to meet the demand for services.

The problem of limited therapeutic resources is largely caused by the length of time required by many traditional therapies and by the inability of psychotherapists to treat more than a small number of individual patients at any one time. Further, because psychotherapy training is limited and because psychotherapy itself is often lengthy, therapists are too few and quite expensive.

There have been many responses to the demand for therapeutic services. First, the growth of behavior therapy is attributable in part to the need for services. On the average, behavior therapy treatment is shorter and less expensive than dynamic or humanistic treatment. Second, the community mental health movement and clinic care in general have attempted to provide services to the substantial numbers of people who cannot afford private psychotherapy. The increasing use of paraprofessionals, briefer therapies, and group methods, especially in clinics, is a third response to the need for services. Many studies have shown that both briefer and group methods can be as efficacious as intensive psychotherapy (Avnet, 1962; Luborsky et al., 1975), and we may expect to see more use made of these modalities.

We might take note here of the ethical dilemma of inequality in the provision of services that faces the psychotherapeutic profession. Wealthier persons can "shop around" until they find a therapist or therapy they like. Having done so, they can afford the luxury of long-term intensive treatment. Poor persons, however, usually must accept the therapist and type of treatment offered by a clinic that is often staffed with professionals drawn largely from a social stratum different from their own. Further, clinics rarely can offer intensive, long-term treatment; there are too few therapists and too many needy clients. Inequality in the provision of services is an intractable problem that plagues not only psychotherapists but all professionals.

Another factor that will greatly affect the practice and provision of psychotherapy services is the increasing use of insurance to pay for therapy. Insurers demand evidence of therapeutic efficiency when they develop compensation schemes; typically they place a maximum on the amount they will pay for a particular course of treatment. Thus, psychotherapists may be forced by economic necessity to employ briefer and group methods, even if they would prefer to offer other types of therapy. If therapists wish to be reimbursed for intensive, long-term treatment, they will certainly have to prove its comparative efficacy for particular problems. If psychotherapeutic services are included, as they almost certainly will be, in a comprehensive scheme of national health insurance, we can expect increased pressure on psychotherapists to offer only efficient modes of treatment.

The fifth issue facing psychotherapists is the question of the efficacy of psychotherapy. As all psychotherapy researchers would attest, psychotherapy process and outcome studies are notoriously difficult to perform. For example, it is very hard to operationalize the relevant variables such as "improvement," especially where the patient presents nonspecific problems (e.g., "existential crisis"). Further, because psychotherapy is an extremely private relationship and because patients are often embarrassed to be receiving mental health services, it is hard to gain the cooperation of a research population.

Despite the prodigious difficulties there have been numerous studies, some of which are methodologically acceptable and which can lead to some tentative conclusions. In a long review of studies of the traditional therapies, Bergin (1971) discovered that they do produce success more often than spontaneous remission (see also Meltzoff & Kornreich, 1970), although the 15 to 45 percent success rate reported is not very high. We should add that Bergin also found that therapy could lead to patient deterioration, an outcome previously denied by many therapists. Such a finding is clearly disturbing and emphasizes the need for further psychotherapy research.

Behavior therapists claim that behavior therapy is particularly efficacious as well as efficient. Early outcome studies of behavior therapy (Wolpe, 1958) did demonstrate astonishing success rates. Recent evidence (Lazarus, 1971; Luborsky et al., 1975; Yates, 1975) has been less encouraging, although behavior therapy is as successful as other types of therapy. A major recent and careful study (Sloane et al., 1975) found little outcome difference between traditional psychotherapy and behavior therapy. For certain types of disorders such as phobias, however, where there are specific symptoms, behavior therapy is often the treatment of choice.

The most provocative issue in the area of psychotherapeutic efficacy is the comparative success of various types of therapies. Luborsky et al. (1975), after a thorough review of studies that compared the efficacy of different therapies, reached the following conclusions:

1. Most comparative studies of different forms of psychotherapy found

insignificant differences in proportion of patients who improved by the end of psychotherapy.

2. The controlled comparative studies indicate that a high percentage of patients who go through any of these psychotherapies gain from them. . . .

4. There are only a few especially beneficial matches of type of treatment and type of patient (pp. 1003–1004).

Although, as noted, there are grave methodological problems in studying psychotherapy, this review and its conclusions are probably the most reliable current "statement of the art."

The last conclusion of Luborsky et al. is especially relevant to psychotherapeutic efficacy. The only beneficial matches they found were that, first, psychosomatic symptoms are treated more successfully by psychotherapy-plus-medical regimen than by medical regimen alone; and second, behavior therapy is especially suited to treatment of "circumscribed phobias."[3] The findings are disheartening because more beneficial matches would produce correspondingly greater success rates. We can respond to this finding only by noting that psychotherapy is an infant science, and by hoping that future research will demonstrate the particular therapists and techniques appropriate for each type of patient, problem, and condition. Until such data are available, psychotherapy practice will tend to be an empirical process dominated by trial and error.

In the future it is hoped that therapists will be trained in a large number of techniques. Lacking psychological investment in a particular therapy, therapists would be more inclined to notice that it was not working with a particular patient. Further, if therapists had broad training they could change techniques readily with a given patient in an attempt to find the therapist–therapy–patient mix that would be most beneficial for the patient.

Having completed our general review of the field of psychotherapy, let us now turn to the questions of why and how the study of cases can aid our understanding of psychotherapy.

WHY READ CASE STUDIES IN PSYCHOTHERAPY?

There are a number of reasons to read case studies of different psychotherapies. Going beyond theory, case studies show what a therapist actually does with a patient. As many therapists have pointed out, what theory says to do and what is actually done are often quite different.

In addition, psychotherapists of different schools sometimes believe that

---

[3] In their review, Luborsky et al. did not include behavior therapy studies that focused on removing "specific habit disturbances" such as smoking. They used only behavior therapy studies that dealt with pervasive personality and adjustment disorders.

their practice has nothing in common with the practice of therapists of other schools, a belief reinforced by the wide theoretical differences between schools. By reading cases one can see the differences in techniques among the various schools. But by reading closely, one can also discern the similarities, especially in the therapist–patient interaction. By reading comparative case studies, one can decide for oneself how wide is the gulf between the schools.

The reader of psychotherapy literature must distinguish a large number of factors: the therapist's theory of psychopathology, the actual pathological behavior, the therapist's theory of therapeutic change, and the actual therapeutic practice. A therapist's theories of pathology and change may be wrong, yet therapy may succeed. The relationship between practice and theory may be tenuous, even if the theory is correct. Again, therapy may succeed despite the weak link. By reading cases rather than theory, one can get a clearer perspective on these issues and a more accurate picture of the methods used in the various forms of therapy.

Case studies can aid the aspiring therapist by conveying an idea of the breadth of treatment techniques available, and thus by motivating aspiring therapists to increase the breadth of their training.

Unfortunately, no case report is as useful as direct observation of therapy or actual supervised work with patients, and while the study of therapy through case reports is beneficial, it is nonetheless limited. Much therapeutic interaction occurs nonverbally, and such interactions are very difficult to capture in a written report. Therefore, unless one actually views a therapeutic interaction, the student will always miss crucial parts.

Case studies also demonstrate what Kiesler (1966) has termed the two "myths of uniformity" in psychotherapy. The first myth is that all *therapists* of the same school are alike, practice in the same setting, use similar techniques, or are interchangeable in other ways. The second myth is that all *patients* are alike.

In reality, both patients and therapists are individual human beings. Being of the same school does not necessarily indicate identical forms of treatment, for individual differences in personality affect considerably the way any two therapists of the same school conduct psychotherapy. Because each therapist must be comfortable with how he or she practices therapy, techniques will be modified accordingly. Therapists are rarely so rigid that they treat every patient in exactly the same manner. Patients differ both as individuals and in the problems they present to the therapist, but even when different patients present ostensibly the same problem, it will be presented quite differently. While a general outline from one patient to another may be followed, wittingly or unwittingly the therapist will modify the technique to aid particular patients.

Case studies are an excellent way to be introduced to the workings of the various forms of psychotherapy. They should lead to useful learning experiences for those who are interested in practicing psychotherapy and for those who are simply curious about what occurs between a therapist and a patient in the privacy of the consulting room.

REFERENCES

Avnet, H. H. *Pyschiatric insurance.* New York: Group Health Insurance, 1962.

Balint, M. *The basic fault: Therapeutic aspects of regression.* London: Tavistock, 1968.

Bergin, A. The evaluation of therapeutic outcomes. In A. Bergin & S. Garfield (Eds.), *Handbook of psychotherapy and behavior change.* New York: John Wiley, 1971.

Chesler, P. *Women and madness.* New York: Doubleday, 1972.

Davison, G. C. Homosexuality: The ethical challenge. *Journal of Consulting and Clinical Psychology,* 1976, *44,* 157–162.

Garfield, S. Basic ingredients or common factors in psychotherapy. *Journal of Clinical and Consulting Psychology,* 1973, *41,* 9–12.

Halleck, S. L. Another response to "Homosexuality: The ethical challenge." *Journal of Consulting and Clinical Psychology,* 1976, *44,* 167–170.

Kernberg, O. The treatment of patients with borderline personality organization. *International Journal of Psychoanalysis,* 1968, *49,* 600–619.

Kiesler, D. J. Some myths in psychotherapy and the search for a paradigm. *Psychological Bulletin,* 1966, *65,* 110–136.

Kohut, H. *The analysis of the self.* New York: International Universities Press, 1971.

Lazarus, A. A. *Behavior therapy and beyond.* New York: McGraw-Hill, 1971.

Luborsky, L., Singer, B., & Luborsky, L. Comparative studies of psychotherapy. *Archives of General Psychiatry,* 1975, *32,* 995–1008.

Meltzoff, J. & Kornreich, M. *Research in psychotherapy.* New York: Atherton, 1970.

Sloane, R. B., Staples, F., Cristol, A., Yorkston, N., & Whipple, K. *Psychotherapy v. behavior therapy.* Cambridge, Massachusetts: Harvard, 1975.

Strupp, H. H. On the basic ingredients of psychotherapy. *Journal of Consulting and Clinical Psychology,* 1973, *41,* 1–8.

Strupp, H. H. Psychoanalysis, "focal" psychotherapy, and the nature of the therapeutic influence. *Archives of General Psychiatry,* 1975, *32,* 127–135.

Szasz, T. Myth of mental illness. *American Psychologist,* 1960, *15,* 113–118.

Szasz, T. The uses of naming and the origin of the myth of mental illness. *American Psychologist,* 1961, *16,* 59–65.

Wolpe, J. *Psychotherapy by reciprocal inhibition.* Stanford, California: Stanford University Press, 1958.

Yates, A. *Theory and practice in behavior therapy.* New York: John Wiley, 1975.

Section One
DYNAMIC PSYCHOTHERAPY

Chapter 2
An Introduction to Dynamic Psychotherapy

STEPHEN J. MORSE

The psychodynamic psychotherapies are based upon the premise that human behavior is determined largely by unconscious psychological forces. Therefore, the general goal of dynamic therapy is to make the patient aware of the unconscious psychological forces that are causing him or her difficulty.

Psychodynamic psychotherapy began with Sigmund Freud's (1856–1939) development of psychoanalysis as both a theory of human behavior and as a technique for treating disordered behavior. Current schools of dynamic therapies are either direct heirs to Freud's psychoanalysis, or they have developed in reaction to it. Despite theoretical differences, however, the therapeutic practice of the various schools is quite similar. In this chapter, we shall trace the origins of the different psychodynamic theories and therapies, and then we shall consider the common techniques of dynamic psychotherapy.

HISTORICAL OVERVIEW

Psychoanalysis refers to both the theory and the technique that Sigmund Freud developed and refined while working as a practicing neurologist, neuropathologist, and then psychiatrist in Vienna from the 1880s until his death in 1939. Confronted by the perplexities of neurotic behavior, Freud found that the physical and psychological theories and treatment methods of his time were inadequate for understanding and curing his patients. Although the existence of the unconscious had been recognized for centuries by artists and others, Freud was the first person to explore systematically the unconscious determinants of behavior in an attempt to understand and cure his patients. Psychoanalysis, the new technique that he discovered, was the first dynamic psychotherapy and it is the foundation for all future ones. Freud's theory and technique revolutionized the understanding and treatment of mental disorders.

Sigmund Freud's Early Career

Freud was born in a small town in the Austro-Hungarian empire to Jakob and Amalie Freud, who were of Jewish and middle-class background. Freud was Amalie's first child and she was his father's third wife. He often noted that being the firstborn of a young, beautiful, and doting mother gave him a sense of confidence that was a great spur to his later success. The family moved to Vienna when Freud was a young boy, and he remained there until forced to flee the Nazis in 1938. Although he originally planned to study law and to enter politics, a chance reading of an essay by Goethe propelled him toward the natural sciences and a career in medicine. Always at the top of his class, Freud entered medical school at the University of Vienna in the fall of 1873. Scientific education was then under the influence of the mechanistic philosophy of men such as Helmholtz who believed that all phenomena could be reduced ultimately to basic physical and chemical-energic laws. The influence of this philosophical background remained prominent in Freud's thought throughout his life.

Early in his studies, recognizing that he was more interested in basic research than in the clinical care of patients, Freud entered training for a research career in neurology. The financial necessities of an impending marriage and the bleak opportunities for advancement in his laboratory, however, made it necessary for him to receive clinical training and to enter private practice in clinical neurology. Neurology was dominated then by physical theories of the causation of neurosis and by physical treatment methods such as electrical stimulation of hysterically paralyzed limbs. Freud learned these theories and methods, but he was exposed also to other influences in the course of his training. He visited Paris to study with Charcot, the great French neurologist, who was developing a psychological theory of the origin of hysteria and using hypnosis to simulate hysterical symptoms and to cure hysteria. Thus, Freud entered private practice with knowledge of physically oriented neurology but with an enthusiasm for psychological theory and treatment.

In clinical practice, Freud found that his background did not help him understand or cure the wide range of neurotic problems presented by his patients. In his early years, however, he collaborated with an experienced physician named Joseph Breuer, who had successfully treated a neurotic woman in an unusual manner that impressed Freud greatly. This was the case of Anna O., which was later written up in *Studies on Hysteria* (1895/ 1955, 1–305), co-authored by Breuer and Freud. Anna O. was a young woman with a variety of psychopathological symptoms, but the most interesting aspect of her treatment was that if she remembered and talked about the context or circumstances during which a symptom developed, the symptom disappeared. Breuer used this "talking cure" to remove one symptom after another. Breuer's success led Freud to use hypnosis, suggestion, questioning, and other methods in an attempt to induce his patients to speak of the painful memories and feelings that seemed to be at the root of their symptoms. Freud used these techniques throughout the late 1880s and early 1890s.

Freud's Discovery of Psychoanalysis

Between 1892 and 1895 Freud "discovered" the technique of *free association*,[1] which is still the basic tool for exploring the unconscious determinants of behavior. Freud found that some of his patients could not be hypnotized or did not respond to suggestion or questioning, and thus he wished to find another method to induce the recovery of memories and feelings. During the treatment of Elisabeth von R. in 1892 (also reported in *Studies on Hysteria)*, Elisabeth told Freud that questioning interfered with the free flow of her thoughts. Freud thus "discovered" free association and learned to be silent, allowing the patient to talk without direction from him. In 1896 Freud finally abandoned all interventions to help the patient associate. Psychoanalysis as a method of psychotherapy may be dated from the first use of free association.

From Charcot, Breuer, and others, and from his own clinician experience when he encouraged and allowed his patients to speak without censorship, Freud learned much about the psychology of neurotic behavior. First, he learned that neurotic symptoms and behavior were psychologically meaningful and seemed to be causally related to thoughts, feelings, memories, and impulses that were a source of conflict for the patient. Second, neurotic conflict seemed to be caused by childhood experiences. Third, because these thoughts and feelings were conflictual the patient was not presently aware of them—the thoughts and feelings were unconscious. Free association allowed these conflictual, unconscious mental contents to become conscious.

Fourth, irrational and maladaptive neurotic symptoms were found covertly to express unconscious conflicts in disguised form. For instance, one of Freud's patients had an hysterical paralysis of her legs; although she

---

[1] Free association is the process whereby the patient is told to tell the therapist without censorship whatever thought, feeling, or memory enters his or her mind. Considerations of shame, impropriety, triviality, and so on are to be abandoned, and absolutely anything that comes into one's mind is to be related. In one of his few papers on technique (1913/1958, 123–144), Freud wrote that he would say the following to a patient: "So say whatever goes through your mind. Act as though, for instance, you were a traveller sitting next to the window of a railway carriage and describing to someone inside the carriage the changing views which you see outside. Finally, never forget that you have promised to be absolutely honest, and never leave anything out because, for some reason or other, it is unpleasant to tell it (p. 135)."

had no organic disability, she was unable to walk. Freud unraveled the following meaning of the symptom: The woman had been sexually attracted to a gardener but was unable to admit these feelings to herself because she considered them immoral. She thus suffered a conflict between her sexual feelings and her ethical standards. She "resolved" the conflict by becoming unable to walk, and thus unable to go into the garden where her sexual feelings would be aroused by the gardener. Rather than face the conflict, she developed a neurotic symptom. Naturally, she was not conscious of this process, but the symptom symbolically expressed both her sexual wishes and fears.

Fifth, Freud discovered that many unconscious thoughts, feelings, memories, and impulses seemed to be concerned with sexuality (which he had defined broadly to mean "sensuality"). Finally, neurotic conditions could be alleviated if the patient became conscious, through free association and therapeutic interventions (e.g., interpretations, which we discuss later), of the pathogenic conflict that was expressed and hidden by the neurotic behavior.

Although the rudimentary theory and technique of psychoanalysis were developed in the middle 1890s, the great breakthrough in Freud's personal life, career, and theory was his self-analysis (which he began in the summer of 1897 when he was forty-one years old). His biographer, Jones (1953), remarks that this "Herculean" effort, which Freud continued until he died, could only have been motivated by Freud's complete devotion to truth, especially the deepest truths about himself. During the course of self-analysis, Freud discovered the importance of the Oedipus complex, the repressed simultaneous loving and rivalrous feelings that each person feels for both parents. The decisive importance of infantile sexuality for the future course of psychological life was revealed primarily during the course of Freud's self-analysis and was later elaborated through observations of his patients. From self-analysis came the thrust for all the later discoveries that were to continue until Freud's death. It is not unfair to state that later discoveries were increasingly sophisticated elaborations of early discoveries.

Freud developed his technique empirically as he worked with various patients. In all cases, however, the goal of psychoanalysis was insight into unconscious motivation, a cognitive and affective achievement. At first psychoanalysis was concerned exclusively with "classic" neurotic behavior (hysteria, obsessive-compulsive states, phobias—all neuroses with defined symptoms) and with the direct alleviation of symptoms by the recovery of unconscious thoughts, feelings, and memories. Although psychological causes and cures were posited, the conditions treated were considered "diseases" whose physical causes would be discovered when further scientific sophistication was achieved.

In this volume we have included a long excerpt from the "Rat Man" case, one of Freud's early (1909) and most famous cases. The case study shows in detail Freud's psychoanalytic method of understanding and analyzing an obsessive-compulsive neurotic.

By 1900 the basic concepts and the "fundamental rule" (free association) of dynamic treatment were discovered. Let us review, therefore, the general principles that were Freud's legacy to later dynamic therapists. First and foremost is the hypothesis of unconscious motivation. All dynamic therapists, whatever they consider the substance of the unconscious to be, use the concept of unconscious motivational forces as a working hypothesis. Second is the hypothesis of psychological determinism, which states that all behavior has causes, is meaningful, and is never random. Thus all behavior can ultimately be "explained" by discovery of its causes. A third hypothesis, developed by Freud and common to all dynamic therapists, is that the events of the past exert a sustained influence upon the present. It is true that dynamic therapists of different schools vary in the extent to which they emphasize the past, yet all would agree that the past is of fundamental importance. Freud's two most important contributions to therapeutic technique were first, the development of free association as a tool for understanding unconscious motivation and the lawfulness of behavior, and second, the usefulness of insight into one's own motivations for helping the patient overcome psychological distress.

We shall return to a more specific discussion of the techniques of dynamic psychotherapy after we complete our historical survey.

Later Developments in Psychoanalysis and Psychoanalytic Technique

During the first decade of the twentieth century psychoanalysis concentrated on the contents of the unconscious and the pathogenic instinctual conflicts contained therein. From 1910 on, however, and especially after 1920, the focus of psychoanalysis shifted. Freud became more interested in the ego, the executive structure of the personality, and how it dealt with the stresses from both the person's inner psychological reality and the outer environmental reality. Emphasis was placed on anxiety and defense mechanisms, rather than on the instinctual substance of the conflicts. Interest in the "repressed" was replaced by interest in the superego, the "repressing agency"; that is, theorists became increasingly concerned with the question of how and why wishes, impulses, and feelings became unconscious. Study of the ego's adaptation to the variety of environments it faced led to a corresponding change in therapeutic technique. Rather than being primarily concerned with the etiology of specific symptoms, psychoanalysis emphasized the analysis of the ego and *character,* the sum total of the person's reactions to his inner and outer world. Psychoanalysis became less concerned with the person's "disease" and more concerned with the nature of the individual and how he or she adapted and coped with various facets of life.

Freud's psychoanalytic theorizing spanned nearly fifty years during which his theory underwent many significant changes. Although those therapists that would consider themselves Freudians have continued to modify Freud's original theories, Freud's work is still the bedrock of later psychoanalytic theory. Despite the modifications in theory, however, the practice of psychoanalysis has remained quite stable procedurally over the years. In addition, some therapists who remained committed to Freudian principles of psychology have modified their techniques by extending psychoanalysis proper to new types of patients or by using Freudian psychoanalytic principles in a more abbreviated, less comprehesnive form of therapy that we shall call "psychoanalytic psychotherapy" or therapy to distinguish it from its progenitor, psychoanalysis.

The first major innovation within the mainstream of Freudian therapy was the extension of psychoanalytic treatment to children. The psychoanalytic theory of psychological development was not developed by working with or directly observing infants and children. Rather, it was the product of the creative genius of Freud who developed his theory by reconstructing the course of childhood mental life from his self-analysis and from the free associations of his adult patients. In fact, Freud never treated a child patient, although he did publish one child case study, "Analysis of a Phobia in a Five Year Old Boy," the case of "Little Hans" (1905/1955, 5–149). Little Hans was a phobic five-year-old whose physician father was an adherent of Freud's new school of psychology. The father told Freud of the boy's problems, and Freud suggested that the *father* treat the little boy psychoanalytically under Freud's guidance. Freud did see the boy once during the course of the treatment, but it was primarily the father who treated Hans and kept the records of the case. The major treatment modality used was interpretation; when Little Hans would present a dream, fantasy, or action that seemed involved in the neurosis, it would be interpreted to him. Hans' phobia was eliminated, and Freud learned a great deal about the dynamics of phobias and neuroses, but Freud never again "treated" a child despite this success.

The attempt to extend psychoanalytic principles to the treatment and education of children and to the reformation of delinquents began in earnest in the 1920s. These attempts were pioneered by Freud's daughter Anna, August Aichhorn, and Melanie Klein (who also developed a variant of Freudian theory that is still popular among British and South-American psychoanalysts). Like many of the great early analysts, these therapists were not medically trained, but in those earlier days medical training was not a prerequisite for psychoanalytic training.

Unlike Freud, who developed his theory of child development from adult analyses, the child analysts developed their theory and technique from direct observation of and therapeutic contact with children. For instance, instead of simply talking with very young children, Melaine Klein encouraged them to play with toys and with her in the consulting room. She hypothesized that although children cannot verbalize conflicts and life-themes as fluently as adults, they can act them out for the therapist if they are free to play in the consulting room. Thus, free associations became

replaced by free "play-associations." In the play situation the child demonstrates to the analyst the fears, anxieties, and conflicts that are causing the
maladaptive behavior. Then, in common-sense language appropriate to the
level of the child's cognitive development, the child analyst tries to make
the child aware of the source of the problem.

We have included in this book one of the most famous child psychoanalytic cases ever published, the case of Frankie by Dr. Berta Bornstein, which
gives the reader a complete overview of the child-analytic process.

In addition to treating children, psychonalysts also began to psycho-
analyze patients who were more severely disordered than the neurotics with
whom the early psychoanalysts had worked. Some therapists attempted to
use psychoanalysis with psychotic patients, but these efforts generally
failed and today few therapists would consider psychoanalysis the treatment of choice for psychotic patients. Furthermore, psychoanalysis has been
used to treat patients with character disorders or with "borderline" personality organizations. While some minor modifications may be made of strict
psychoanalysis in working with these types of patients, the technique
employed is psychoanalysis and not a variant. Included in this volume is a
very rich case of a woman with a severe character disorder who displayed
schizophrenic symptoms and underwent treatment by Dr. L. Bryce Boyer,
a well-known psychoanalyst.

Psychoanalysis is a lengthy, costly therapy that aims to restructure radically the patient's personality organization. However, not all patients wish
to undergo such massive amounts of treatment, nor is psychoanalysis an
appropriate method for all patients. Some patients may benefit greatly from
less deep and comprehensive insight into their problems and/or they may
desire restricted or symptomatic relief rather than substantial personality
restructuring. For these patients, psychoanalytic psychotherapy may be indicated. Psychoanalytic psychotherapy employs psychoanalytic psychology
to formulate and understand the patient's difficulty and as a basis for treatment technique. It is a less intense form of therapy than psychonalysis;
patients are usually seen less frequently and need not necessarily free associate. At present, psychoanalytic clinicians in the United States and Britain
are experimenting with extremely brief (e.g., 12- to 20-session) forms of
therapy that focus intensively on the patient's core or nuclear conflict.
These clinicians claim that the new, brief, analytic therapies are highly
effective. Psychoanalytic psychotherapy has become increasingly popular,
even among those trained to practice psychoanalysis, and today considerably more patients are treated with psychoanalytic psychotherapy than
with psychoanalysis.

We have included a few brief psychoanalytic psychotherapy cases from
the classic *Psychoanalytic Therapy* by Franz Alexander and Thomas French,
who report the work of the Chicago Psychoanalytic Institute, whose analysts were pioneers in analytic psychotherapy.

Among the large number of practicing dynamic psychotherapists, the majority are still allied with Freudian principles and techniques. There have been many theoretical variations from Freudian theory, and many dynamic therapies cannot be considered Freudian, but alternative theories and therapies account for many fewer therapists than the Freudians. Furthermore, even though the alternatives are important, they have had less impact on psychological and psychiatric theory than has Freudian theory.

Alternatives to Freudian Theory and Technique

The psychodynamic alternatives to Freudian therapies may be categorized into two classes: the early rebels and the neo-Freudians. The first group, best exemplified by Carl G. Jung (1875–1961) and Alfred Adler (1870–1937), separated from Freud because they felt that his basic theory of human behavior was incorrect. The neo-Freudians such as Erich Fromm (1900–   ), Karen Horney (1885–1952), Harry Stack Sullivan (1892–1949), and Erik Erikson (1903–   ) did not dissociate themselves from Freud but, instead, attempted to correct what they thought was Freud's misplaced emphasis on intrapsychic factors. While overtly or covertly accepting large parts of Freud's work, they argued that Freud placed insufficient emphasis on the sociocultural and interpersonal factors involved in the cause and treatment of disordered behavior.

At the outset we should note that for the most part these innovators in dynamic psychotherapy were far more original in substantive theory than they were in theapeutic method. Few of the innovators wrote systematic papers exploring the therapeutic ramifications of their theoretical divergences. Comments on therapeutic method (as opposed to the substantive focus of therapy) are scattered and random. As we have noted, although these therapists were prolific and creative, they have not had an impact proportionate to the amount of their disagreement and writing. Many have founded their own schools and a few have founded independent training and study institutes, but they still do not exert a major influence upon psychotherapeutic services. Since we are discussing therapeutic process, their work will be examined only briefly.

JUNG AND ADLER   Freud's discoveries which emphasized the sexual life of infants and small children were met with shock, disdain, and repudiation in late Victorian Vienna [although a later historian, Ellenberger (1970), claims that this repudiation has been overstated and overemphasized, beginning with Freud himself]. Despite this reaction, Freud consistently adhered to the primacy of the libido theory of motivation. In fact, adherence to this concept was the sine qua non for remaining within the Freudian fold, and it was disagreement with the concept that led Jung and Adler to rebel against Freud and to be expelled from the fold.

Carl Jung, one of Freud's earliest adherents, was groomed to become the leader of the psychoanalytic movement after Freud died. Jung, a charismatic Swiss-Protestant physician, was especially favored because Freud felt that his leadership would alter the conception that psychoanalysis was a "Jewish" science. But Jung never accepted fully the theory of infantile sexuality that Freud considered the touchstone of psychoanalysis. By 1912 Jung reformulated Freud's libido theory, emphasizing that libido was the undifferentiated energy that accounted for mental life; sexual libido was only one form of this energy. This reformulation led to the final break between the two men, and from then on Jung systematically developed his own theory.[2]

A central hypothesis in Jung's theory was that the parents' neurotic difficulties unconsciously create a conflict-ridden and pathogenic environment for the child. Freud had claimed originally that deformations in libidinal development were the source of psychopathology, but Jung argued that the hidden interaction between parent and child caused behavior disorders. Unlike Freud, Jung believed that adulthood was an important period of psychological growth and that spiritual development was vital to the healthy personality. Jung theorized that positive and negative parts of the personality could be repressed, and that one task of therapy was to allow the positive factors to reemerge. Jung emphasized the principle of complementarity, which held that the personality is a composite of opposite tendencies or aspects. Whichever aspect of the personality is consciously or overtly expressed will be mirrored by its opposite in the unconscious. For instance, all persons have a masculine (animus) side and a feminine (anima) aspect of their personalities. In most men the anima will be repressed, whereas in women the animus will be repressed. Jungian theory posits four dominant behavioral characteristics in all people: thinking, feeling, sensation, and intuition. These are arranged as pairs of opposites in the personality; thinking-feeling is one polarity and sensation-intuition is the other. The well-adjusted individual should be able to integrate and develop both aspects.

Jung also developed a character typology, the extrovert–introvert dimension. As always, all persons have tendencies toward both ends of the continuum but one will be dominant and the other will be repressed. In addition, all persons have a "Persona" which is the outer attitude that the person adopts in response to cultural expectations. Although not really part of the true character, the Persona is a protective armor around the true character of the person that is difficult to remove. Finally, let us take note of Jung's concept of the "collective unconscious," the mental repository of the significant memories of human racial experience held in common by all humans. Freud partially accepted this concept in *Totem and Taboo* (1913), but for Jung the collective unconscious was a crucial psychological force which explained the similarities in myths and symbols across different historical eras and different cultures. Jung claimed that the patient needed

[2] Freud's conception of this break, and of the break with Alfred Adler, may be found in Freud's book, *On the History of the Psychoanalytic Movement* (1914/1957, 7–66). The fascinating Freud–Jung letters have also been published (1974).

to become aware of the contents of his collective unconscious to achieve psychological health.

Jung led a long, productive life, founding a school known as Analytical Psychology. He was an extraordinarily creative writer, but he did not exert much influence on psychiatry or psychology outside a small number of followers. Jung's impact may be seen in the work of Herman Rorschach, the founder of the projective inkblot test that bears Rorschach's name, and in the character typological work of psychologists such as Eysenck (although Eysenck's emphasis is quite different). The Jungians were and are primarily located in Switzerland and London, although other Jung training groups have been founded elsewhere. Today there is a renaissance of interest in Jung that accompanies a renewed interest in mysticism and Far-Eastern philosophy and religion. Jung training institutes seem to be revitalized and gaining adherents. It is too early to tell whether the interest in Jung's theory and therapy will continue, but it has yet to exert much general influence on the teaching of psychotherapy. Jungian psychology is a creative scheme, however, that emphasizes very different aspects of human experience from Freudian psychology. It is a more optimistic view of human nature and potential. Our selection of a case of Jungian treatment of a homosexual man by Jolande Jacobi, a leading Jungian before her recent death, will illustrate many of the theoretical and practical aspects of the analytical psychological school.

Alfred Adler broke with Freud at the same time as Jung, but he was fundamentally different from Jung. He was not personally attractive or charismatic, and he did not write well. Ellenberger (1970) claimed that Adler has not been given sufficient credit as a seminal and creative thinker because he was personally and intellectually unexciting. Like Jung, however, Adler broke from Freud because he rejected the theory of the sexual etiology of the neuroses. Adler thought neuroses were the result of attempts to compensate for the inferiority feelings that were caused by every person's childhood feelings of weakness and helplessness. To compensate, people strive for power over others and for unrealistic goals that Adler called "fictive" goals. Striving for power and superiority may be achieved by becoming ill and thus manipulating the environment or by openly struggling for power for its own sake.

Adler was simultaneously pessimistic and optimistic. Inferiority feelings were inevitable, and thus the neurotic struggle to overcome them also was inevitable. On the other hand, he felt that persons were more malleable and changeable than Freud thought, and that constructive social changes would lead to less debilitating parent–child interactions. Adler was a committed socialist who felt that in order to be healthy a person needed to be unselfishly committed to the good of others, a quality he called "social interest."

Adler did make some enduring contributions. By emphasizing the person's attempt to overcome uncomfortable feelings, he focused attention on ego defenses and the adaptive functions of the ego. Adler was arguably the first therapist to consider character structure and the whole person as the proper province for dynamic therapy. Furthermore, he considered the future goals one set for oneself as crucial guiding aspects of one's life. Thus, Adler, like many modern therapists, emphasized the purposive or intentional aspects of human existence.

Today Adlerian theory is part of the public domain. Striving for superiority, the inferiority complex, and other Adlerian concepts are part of common parlance. Indeed, Adler has been criticized for being too simplistic and superficial. But he supplied needed emphasis on the ego in dynamic psychology. Despite his contributions, Adler has had little independent influence on psychotherapy outside the small circle of his followers. There are few Adlerian training institutes, and there does not seem to be an Adlerian renaissance. It seems that the contribution of Adler has been absorbed mainly into the mainstream of the other therapeutic schools.

THE NEO-FREUDIANS   The neo-Freudians, a large and diverse group, have become influential since the 1930s. They emphasize that social and cultural factors are more important than biological or intrapsychic factors in explaining human behavior. They consider libido and instinct theories to be outdated; the individual's adaptation to his or her environment is the crucial behavioral variable. Concepts such as the Oedipus complex, formation of the superego, and the inferiority feelings allegedly held by many women are seen as products of our culture. Interpersonal relationships are emphasized when describing the formation of character and the causation of anxiety and disordered behavior. Finally, sexuality is considered a result of character rather than the *cause* of character. In neo-Freudian psychotherapy emphasis is placed on a person's distorted interpersonal relationships and relationship to society.

The work of Erik Erikson is a good example of the neo-Freudian approach. Although he allies himself with Freudian theory, Erikson has expanded Freudian theory significantly. Whereas Freud emphasized the psychosexual ramifications of each stage of development (e.g., oral, anal, phallic), Erikson also considers crucial the psycho*social* tasks appropriate to each stage. For instance, in the first year of life oral sexuality is not all important; equally important is the infant's experience of the first rudimentary interpersonal modalities such as "getting what is given," or "taking," or "holding on to" things. Furthermore, according to Erikson the experience of the first year of life inculcates a fundamental attitude toward the world that may be characterized as basic trust or mistrust. Finally, the first stage of life leads to the feeling of hope, which finds its cultural institutional expression in organized religions.

All the developmental stages are similarly expanded, taking into account the interpersonal and cultural aspects of each stage of life. In addition to this first stage of trust versus mistrust, Erikson postulated seven other stages:

(2) autonomy versus shame and doubt; (3) initiative versus guilt; (4) industry versus inferiority; (5) identity versus identity confusion; (6) intimacy versus isolation; (7) generativity versus stagnation; (8) ego integrity versus despair. The first four stages correspond quite well to the classic Freudian stages (oral, anal, phallic, latency, genital), but the last four stages, which concern adolescence and adulthood, are Erikson's new contribution.

There can be doubt, however, that Erikson's most influential theorizing has been about adolescence, the stage during which he claims that the formation of a stable identity is the crucial task. In his theorizing about adolescence, Erikson demonstrates the neo-Freudian emphasis on the relationship of the person to his society. Erickson's conception of the *identity crisis,* the need to piece together for oneself a stable configuration of who one is as an independent person and how one fits in to his society and its expectations, has considerably affected current views of adolescence. Not only must a final psychosexual identity be forged in adolescence, but an historical, occupational, and psychosocial identity must be achieved as well.

The neo-Freudians differ widely in the extent to which they adhere to Freud's belief in the determinative influence of biology on behavior. They all believe, however, that biology determines behavior less than culture, which is seen as quite malleable. The neo-Freudians tend to be more optimistic than Freud; as persons can perfect society, so can they perfect themselves. This type of optimism is seen throughout neo-Freudian writings (e.g., Erikson's *Gandhi's Truth*). Furthermore, neo-Freudians believe that the first five years of life are important but not totally dispositive of the person's later development. Like Erikson, most view adolescence as a time of great importance for new development, and many would also stress the growth potential of the adult stages of life.

The influence of the neo-Freudians is varied. Their cultural orientation has had a major effect on the Freudians, helping the Freudians to correct their overemphasis on intrapsychic factors. Individually they have had variable influence on therapeutic practice. Neither Erikson nor Fromm has founded independent training institutes or journals devoted to his theories. Erikson is often considered to be in the mainstream of Freudian theory, but he does merit attention as a separate theorist. His work is profoundly influential, and it is probably used to some extent by nearly all Freudians and neo-Freudians. We have included a fragment of one of Erikson's cases in which he demonstrates his more interpersonal and culturally oriented neo-Freudian approach to dynamic psychotherapy.

Erich Fromm's work contains few clinical examples and is mainly centered on sociopolitical theory and criticism. Although many therapists quote and refer to Erikson, whose work is full of rich clinical examples, clinicians rarely quote or refer to Fromm. Karen Horney and Harry Stack Sullivan both founded training institutes and journals dedicated to the dissemination of theory and practice founded upon their work. Sullivan has had considerable influence on dynamic psychotherapy in the United States, especially dynamic psychotherapy with schizophrenics. Horney, whose work is usually considered a minor offshoot from Freud, has had less influence.

This completes our overview of the development of dynamic psychotherapy. We shall now turn to a general discussion of the technique of these therapists.

THE TECHNIQUE OF DYNAMIC PSYCHOTHERAPY

In our discussion of the technique of dynamic psychotherapy, we shall draw most of our terminology and examples from psychoanalysis and psychoanalytic psychotherapy. The Freudians and the neo-Freudians share the same therapeutic language and follow quite similar therapeutic practice. Many neo-Freudians call their standard procedure psychoanalysis and its less intense form, psychoanalytic psychotherapy. Differences between Freudians and neo-Freudians are greater on issues of theory than on issues of practice. Because Jungian therapy and child psychoanalysis are somewhat different, these differences will be explored in the notes that introduce the cases that demonstrate these methods.

Psychoanalysis began as a method of treating neurotic symptoms that were thought to be caused mainly by conflict about sexuality. At first, as in the Case of Anna O., the aim of treatment was to uncover the unconscious causes of underlying symptoms, and thus to remove the symptoms. As the focus of theory shifted from drive theory to a more adaptational psychology, therapy also changed. Patients not only had symptoms, but more fundamentally, they had "problems in living"; they were unhappy about their loving and their working (as Freud put it). Rather than being methods for ameliorating only specific neurotic symptoms, psychoanalysis and psychoanalytic psychotherapy became treatments for character disorders and the wide range of global problems in living from which people suffer.

Psychodynamic Procedure

Freud's patients, and patients receiving psychoanalysis today, would lie on a couch with Freud sitting in a chair behind them, out of sight. The use of the couch has three purposes. First, by lying down and not looking at the analyst, the patient is able to be as relaxed and as free as possible from any distractions that would occur if he or she perceived the analyst's overt or covert responses. The removal of external distractions also allows the patient to delve more deeply into his or her own self. Second, Freud noted that it was too difficult to look patients in the eye for eight hours per day. Third, this procedure leaves the analyst free to assume the proper listening attitude, which Freud termed "free-floating attention." This attitude allows the patient's associations to resonate in the analyst's own unconscious. In sum, the use of the couch allows both patient and analyst to be less distracted and more relaxed.

Freud's patients would come to him six days per week for an hour per day, and treatment rarely lasted more than six months to one year. Today psychoanalytic patients are more likely to come four or five days each week, and a complete psychoanalysis will rarely be completed in less than two to three years. Often it will take as many as five or six years. In psychoanalytic psychotherapy[3] there is no set frequency of consultations, but once or twice per week is probably average. Also, the patient will usually sit up facing the therapist.

In psychoanalysis the patient is instructed initially about the fundamental rule of free association, and then is left to talk about whatever comes into his or her mind without direction from the psychoanalyst. In therapy, the patient may or may not be encouraged to attempt free association, but almost certainly he will be encouraged to be spontaneous and to speak about whatever he chooses. Generally, in therapy the therapist is more likely to direct one's attention to certain topics or to question one about topics left unexplored. This is not done so frequently in psychoanalysis. In all cases, the therapist treats the patient's productions with a nonjudgmental, caring objectivity.

The therapist usually intrudes into the interaction as little as possible. This is obviously truer in psychoanalysis where the therapist is out of the patient's sight and is less directive. By remaining unobtrusive and unassertive the therapist becomes like a "screen" onto which the patient can transfer or project various feelings and fantasies about significant people from the past. If the patient knows little of the therapist's life and personality, the patient's feelings and fantasies about the therapist are more clearly a product of the patient's psychology.[4] Although the blank-screen image and the silence of the analyst may be caricatured, analysists and other therapists are more active than popular opinion portrays them. But as Freud discovered in 1892, if the therapist intrudes too much he or she interferes with the patient's free associations and spontaneity.

Transference, Therapeutic Relationship, and Countertransference

In his earliest analytic cases, Freud discovered an unusual result of his nondirective and unobtrusive method. Patients began to behave with Freud in much the same way that they had behaved with significant persons, such as their parents, in the past. Patients began to develop with the therapist the same neurotic patterns that dominated their lives and that had led them to treatment in the first place. This unavoidable process of treating the thera-

---

[3] Which we shall call "therapy" for purposes of abbreviation in the rest of this section.

[4] Conversely, as the introduction to humanistic therapies will demonstrate, some humanistic therapists believe that "knowing" the therapist is crucial.

pist like other significant persons was called *transference*, and the neurosis that developed in the relationship to the therapist was called the *transference neurosis*.

More intensive treatment usually leads to more intensive transference phenomena, and the transference is usually, although not invariably, stronger in analysis than in therapy. Neurotic patterns are recreated in vivo in the treatment sessions where they can be examined, and where insight can be gained into them with the therapist's help. Dynamic therapists became aware of the ubiquity and importance of the distorted, unrealistic recreation of past relationships in the patient's relationship with the therapist. This led them to focus their interventions primarily on the examination of the relationship to the therapist.

The concept of the *therapeutic* or *working alliance* must be distinguished from the transference. The transference is the result of infantile needs, conflicts, and feelings; it is not a presently realistic relationship to the therapist (even though it is existing in the present in the treatment situation). Despite the magnitude of the transference, the patient must take responsibility for his or her treatment. Even during the times of most intense regression, it is hoped that the patient will maintain the capacity for observation, synthesis, and understanding. The patient should tacitly form a treatment contract wherein he agrees to undergo the anxiety, sacrifice, and assumption of responsibility for himself which, with the therapist's help, are necessary for change. This agreement, whereby the patient trusts the therapist to help him or her despite the intensity and frequency of irrational feelings that may and must arise, is known as the "therapeutic alliance." It is a real-world current trust and contract that is necessary before the treatment can work. It is the patient's agreement with the therapist that the patient will continue to assist himself and the therapist in the treatment process.

A critical factor the therapist must also take into account is *countertransference*. Not only does one transfer conflicts with past figures onto one's relationship with the therapist, but also the therapist does likewise with the patient. These feelings of the therapist for the patient are called countertransference, and ideally the therapist should be totally aware of them so that they do not interfere with the treatment. All persons have some conflicts and pains in common. Thus, the patient's explorations of his conflicts, as well as his real-world personality, are bound to revive some of the therapist's own conflicts. To help avoid this, formal psychoanalytic training requires that the future analyst undergo a personal analysis, called a didactic or training analysis.[5]

[5] Neither psychiatric, psychological, social work, nor psychiatric nursing training require that the future practitioner undergo any form of personal therapy. Some particular training programs in these professions may encourage it or require it, but it is not a formal requirement for certification in any of the four major psychotherapeutic professions. Only formal psychoanalytic training, which is gained at independent psychoanalytic institutes, requires a personal analysis as a formal requirement (and, in fact, the fundamental requirement) for certification.

The negative aspect of countertransference is that the therapist is not able to understand the patient objectively (or at least as much as is possible within human limits) because of his or her own conflicts and needs. But countertransference can have a positive aspect if the therapist is well aware of his own conflicts. By monitoring the feelings the patient elicits in him, the therapist can often gain an understanding of the fundamental conflicts facing the patient and thus can better appreciate how the patient affects other people.

While the centrality of transference is still accepted today, there is much more emphasis on the therapist being a "real person" to the patient, even among quite "orthodox" Freudians. It is doubtful that a therapist could successfully work with a patient toward whom she did not feel fundamentally "friendly." This does not mean that therapist and patient become friends in the sense of chums; it does mean that the therapist will be more willing to emerge from the blank-screen therapeutic stance, and to show her real feelings on occasion.[6]

Friendship is probably curative, and, for some patients, the therapist may be the only friend (in any sense) that they have in the world. However, it must be remembered that the fundamental goal of dynamic treatment is understanding and insight. Dynamic psychotherapy is undeniably a real human relationship. But if the therapist allows the relationship to become "too real" by overly injecting his own personality, then he will tend to lose the precious objectivity he strives for. Free association will be interfered with, and it will be difficult to see the patient's conflicts in a desirably pure state. The patient will react to the therapist rather than demonstrating productively her uncontaminated unconscious motivation. There are many ways, including friendship, to help emotionally distressed people feel better. But insight is the goal of dynamic treatment and, paradoxical as it may seem, friendship may interfere with this process.[7]

Resistance

Freud recognized a perplexing fact from the beginning of his psychoanalytic treatment of patients. Although patients willingly came for treatment because they were suffering, and although there was only one fundamental rule of the treatment, free association, patients continually "broke" this rule. They censored thoughts, feelings, and memories; sometimes they did not want to talk, and sometimes nothing came to the patient's mind although he or she was trying to associate. Patients wanted to be helped but, paradoxically, they would not consistently free associate, the one necessary input into the treatment from the patients that would allow Freud to help them.

This behavior, termed *resistance*, is hypothesized to have many motiva-

---

[6] The reader should also consult Matarazzo's insightful discussion of this issue (1971).

[7] In his classic work on the subject of friendship and its role in psychotherapy, Schofield disputes this conclusion (1965).

tions. Patients resist primarily because they feel anxious, and anxiety was the reason that a thought or feeling was originally repressed. In treatment these same "unacceptable" thoughts and so on still make patients anxious, and they do not want to allow these thoughts to be conscious or to allow the therapist to be aware that they think such thoughts. Patients thus resist either consciously or unconsciously; they "hold back," even though expressing the thoughts is necessary to the treatment. All patients resist during the course of all dynamic therapies. Like transference, resistance is ubiquitous. The frequency and intensity of resistance depends on many factors. Among the most important are the intensity of the tratment (how much it threatens to "uncover") and the intensity of the patient's anxiety.

The following is an example that relates the idea of resistance to transference. Suppose that for good reason a therapist is five minutes late for an appointment one day. The patient may be understanding but then is unwilling to talk. It is possible that unconsciously the patient experienced the slight tardiness as a rejection and was angry at the therapist. To admit her thought and feeling to consciousness, however, the patient would have to realize that she is quite dependent on the therapist (a painful discovery) and that she harbors "irrational" needs and feelings. Thus, without knowing why she is silent, the patient resists because she is unconsciously angry at the therapist and would feel emotional distress if she recognized that she had such irrational reactions (which we assume are based on childhood learning experiences).

Silence may not be the only resistance. For example, the patient may enter into a lengthy discourse on the rules of politeness for being late (intellectualizing to avoid the painful feeling) or may comment admiringly on the analyst's attire ("undoing"[8] the angry feeling by a complimentary remark). The repertoire of behaviors that persons have developed for resistant and defensive uses is ingeniously infinite.

Resistance is constant throughout the course of dynamic psychotherapy. It is both normal and the main hindrance to alleviating the patient's distress. Indeed, a major goal of dynamic treatment is systematically to help the patient gain insight into the particular resistances used. Resistance interferes with the ultimate success of the treatment only if it is unanalyzable. The patient is helped to comprehend how he misperceives and misunderstands his own experience by gaining insight into his defense processes and resistance.

The Therapeutic Work

After the patient elucidates these misperceptions and misunderstandings and attends to them, the therapist turns to the "why" questions—the moti-

[8] *Undoing* is a psychological defense mechanism whereby the individual tries to counteract the real or fantasized effect or even the occurrence of a thought, word, or deed. This is done by using another thought, word, or deed that "takes back" the original, anxiety-producing behavior. The reader who wishes full definitions of psychoanalytic terms, including their histories, is referred to Laplanche and Pontalis (1967/1973).

vations for the misperceiving and misunderstanding. The patient explores why she misperceives, because it is assumed that if she can understand why, and if the reason no longer makes sense in her adult living, then she can now discard the maladaptive behavior.

Dynamic therapists hypothesize that the difficulties in a person's present life are a result of debilitating past experiences. The person maintains behaviors that may have served to prevent anxiety in childhood but which are now maladaptive. Motivations for behavior are unconscious and often a person is unaware of how he sabotages his attempts to achieve own satisfaction. Dynamic theorists assume that in response to the imagined and real threats of significant persons, primarily the parents, the child represses conflictual thoughts, feelings, memories, and actions that he or she fears will result in punishment. A small, weak child cannot realistically assess threats to himself and usually judges himself far more harshly than he is judged by those around him.

Freud felt that the prime threats were helplessness, separation, castration, and guilt (1926/1959, 87–174). Other theorists posit different threats as crucial but most agree with Freud's basic view of the development of maladaptive behavior. The child develops a varied repertoire of behaviors and defenses in order to prevent unacceptable thoughts, impulses, feelings, or memories from reaching consciousness. While defensive maneuvers ward off overt anxiety, they do restrict the range of a person's understanding and insight into his or her own motivations and the motivations of others.

Defensive behavior seems to have "survival" value for a child although in most cases the "threat" is not so dangerous as the child fantasizes. Unconscious conflict may be reflected in overt symptomatology or in characteristic patterns of behavior that prevent the person from reaching desired goals. The defensive behavior that once seemed to have survival value thus results in later debilitation.

Many of the same wishes and fears that were operative with significant others and led to defensive and maladaptive behavior will now be directed toward the therapist. In the nonjudgmental atmosphere of the therapeutic relationship, the unconscious wishes, fantasies, feelings, and impulses may emerge into consciousness. Now there is no judgment or punishment of these behaviors; there is only the attempt to understand them. The therapist helps the patient to understand his conflictual unconscious motivations, which can now be assessed more realistically and less judgmentally.

Previously we saw how the patient might resist because she was angry at the therapist for being late to an appointment. At the same time she would use defenses to avoid becoming aware of this anger. Assuming that the patient through insight was able to be aware of her resistance and mode of defense, she would then have to face squarely the issue of why she was inhibited or afraid to express her anger directly. Typically the patient might argue that it is not polite and/or rational to be angry with the therapist, especially since the therapist had a good excuse. While this is probably true in the polite company of general social interaction, it is not true in the therapeutic situation, an environment tailored to facilitate the expression of "irrational" and "impolite" feelings and thoughts. Thus, this answer on the patient's part would probably be seen quickly as further resistance and defense (rationalization). The patient knows cognitively and rationally that irrational anger can be safely expressed in the therapeutic setting. This is the substance of dynamic therapy. The reason one enters into therapy is to understand the persistence of the irrational in one's "rational" adult living. Thus our patient is still left with the question of why she is afraid to express anger or even to be aware of it.

Let us assume that unconsciously she fears that if she expresses the anger she feels toward the therapist, upon whom she has transferred feelings of dependency similar to those she felt toward her parents, then the therapist will reject her. Admission at a "gut level" that one is dependent and afraid of being rejected is quite threatening. In this case, it would be the task of the therapist's interpretation to help the patient to be aware of these dependency needs and fears of rejections. Of course, the therapist does not simply tell (i.e., interpret to) the patient about the motive for repressing anger as soon as the therapist can reasonably determine what the motive is. When a therapist communicates information to a patient is a matter of tact and timing; information is conveyed when the patient can "hear" the information and make use of it in a therapeutic way.

Working Through and Termination

Any and all resistances or motives do not arise only once in therapy (no matter how brief), become interpreted, and then magically disappear. Patterns of behavior, memories, and feelings occur repeatedly throughout the therapy. Yet each time the behavior is expressed differently, and each time a bit more is learned about the nature of the patient's life and functioning. By means of the *working-through* process the patient is able to integrate new insights, to attempt new patterns of behavior, and to restructure his or her personality functioning.

During this aspect of the therapy, given the protective context of the therapeutic relationship and the patient's greater control over his life as an adult, the patient should learn that his motives, thoughts, and feelings are not so "bad" and frightening as initially feared. He or she is then able safely to express repressed thoughts and feelings to the therapist. The patient is able to be more honest with himself and with the therapist without undue anxiety. In learning theory terms, the patient is reinforced for new behavior; and then new honesty, spontaneity, and insight can be generalized to life outside therapy. As the maladaptive behavior patterns recur in the treatment or are described to the therapist, each time somewhat differently from previous times, the patient learns more about the preconditions for and permutations of his difficulties.

As he or she learns more and continues to practice new behavior (new modes of expressing himself), the relationship with the therapist becomes less a reenactment of earlier patterns and more realistic. The recreated neurotic feelings toward the therapist, the transference neurosis, is said to be dissolved. There is less distortion, less defensiveness, and less misperception. As the patient begins to behave in new ways with the therapist and learns that it is safe and appropriate to act in these new ways, she can then begin to practice them outside the therapeutic situations where she can again be reinforced for these new behaviors. It is hoped that by having made sense out of feelings, thoughts, and actions she formerly felt were nonsensical, by understanding herself better, the patient will then feel and be more in control over her own life and will be able to love and work more successfully.

There are no set rules governing when dynamic therapy terminates. Analysis is generally not considered complete until the transference neurosis is cured. Ideally, dynamic therapies end when the working through is complete. What this tautology means is dependent upon the goals of the patient, the goals of the therapist, the theoretical orientation of the therapist, and the fact that, as Freud pointed out (1937, 216–253), analysis (or therapy) is interminable. What Freud meant by this is that because conflict is always a product of civilization, and defense always accompanies conflict, it is impossible for the therapy to be completely over. Most basically put, therapy ends optimally when a patient has insight into the core difficulties that interfered with his loving and working, and when he has integrated this insight fully enough into his character to then have the choice about whether or not he wishes to change.

Therapeutic Intervention Techniques

The discussion of the intervention techniques used by therapists will rely directly on the classification and analysis proposed by the noted psychoanalyst, Edward Bibring (1954). Bibring suggested that there are five classes of dynamic therapeutic tools: *suggestion, abreaction, manipulation, clarification,* and *interpretation.* At any time in any therapy, one or more of the five techniques may be employed. It should be emphasized that these are formal classes of technique and none of them is tied to any particular psychological content area. Each is applicable to all schools of dynamic therapy and has different uses which shall be elucidated below. Although there may be some overlap among the five classes, Bibring's classification is useful because it helps order the mass of data produced in any therapeutic interaction by helping the student to understand why the therapist acted in a certain way. The therapist's choice of a technique modality should lead to reasonable inferences about what he or she thought was transpiring in the therapeutic situation, and about what the therapist thought would be most useful for the patient. As the reader considers the cases in this section, it will be useful to try to decide which particular type of intervention the therapist was using and why.

Bibring defined *suggestion*, the first technique, as the induction of ideas, impulses, emotions, actions, or various other mental processes in the patient, independent of or to the exclusion of, the patient's rational or critical realistic thinking. Curative suggestion, the use of suggestion to effect a direct change (the paradigm of which is hypnosis), is rarely used in dynamic therapy.

When suggestion is used it is usually "technical" suggestion, which aims to promote the treatment process. For example, telling a depressed person that she will no longer feel depressed because there is nothing wrong with her would be a curative suggestion (and partially a manipulation). Asking a patient to fantasize about a particular topic ("What do you think would happen if you got angry at your boss? Have a fantasy about it?") would be a technical suggestion whose aim is not to cure the patient directly but to facilitate the treatment. In general, suggestion rarely is used consciously in dynamic therapy, and curative suggestion is so rarely used that it is not considered part of the dynamic therapist's therapeutic armamentarium.

Abreaction, the second technique, was quite important in the early development of psychoanalysis (e.g., the cathartic talking cure of Anna O.), and it is now associated mainly with the treatment of traumatic neuroses. The therapist encourages the recollection of affect-laden experiences or thoughts that are beyond the patient's awareness and cannot be remembered (hypnotic drugs such as sodium amytal may be used in this process). Then the patient transforms strong emotions into weak ones by discharging the affect associated with the idea or memory. Drained of its emotional tension, the idea or memory becomes more manageable. Except in the treatment of traumatic neuroses, this technique is rarely therapeutic by itself, but in conjunction with the other techniques it may give the person more control over the distressing content of his or her psyche.

For example, if a person's parent dies and the person consciously experiences little sadness, anger, or grief, in therapy the experiencing of the repressed grief may become possible and the patient may have the "good cry" that was too painful to have when the death occurred. Theoretically, the patient should then see that the pain is not unbearable, some tension is discharged, and the pathologically inhibited mourning process may be recommenced. Today the status of abreaction is in question, and it is doubtful that the hydraulic model of emotion implied in its use (i.e., allowing built-up pressure to be discharged as through a valve, making the reservoir more manageable) is very helpful in understanding human behavior.

Manipulation, the third technique, was defined by Bibring as the employment of the patient's preexisting potential for the purpose of achieving therapeutic change either technically, by promoting treatment, or curatively, by direct inducement of change. Crude types of manipulation, such as giving advice or guidance to tell the patient what to do, are excluded. The dynamic therapist does not take responsibility for the life of the patient nor attempt to run his or her life. Such manipulation is considered disrespectful.

"Technical" manipulation may be used either to produce favorable attitudes toward therapy or to remove obstructive trends. For example, a person who believes that anger should never be vented may be told that any emotion may be expressed in therapy. This technical manipulation promotes treatment by encouraging the expression of feeling.

"Curative" manipulation is used to provide a new learning experience directly to the patient; a nonjudgmental environment may be a curative manipulation. For instance, one may adjust one's real-world behavior to the fantasized punitive moral judgment of others, which naturally constrains one's range of experiencing. Not being judged by the therapist is a new learning experience. As a consequence the patient may not judge a thought or feeling of his own but only try to understand it. When he does this without adverse effect, the patient has had a new learning experience. At times latent tendencies will be reinforced; at other times, new behaviors will be elicited and then reinforced.

The crucial distinction that must be made between suggestion, abreaction, and manipulation on the one hand, and clarification and interpretation on the other hand, is that the former three effect change without directly providing or increasing the patient's self-understanding. The positive learning experience furnished by the nonjudgmental environment of the analytic situation may indeed help the patient to judge himself less, and it may enhance his opportunity to understand the nature and source of his punitive self-judgments, but by itself, this environment will not substantially increase insight.

A perplexing issue is the mechanism by which non–insight-oriented techniques allow new learning to take place. We have noted the central role of unconscious conflict in causing maladaptive behavior. The puzzle is how interventions not aimed directly at the unconscious can further resolution of unconscious conflict. Other questions are, which kinds of patients and what types of problems are most helped by non–insight-oriented interventions, and whether the resulting changes are lasting or temporary, superficial or deep. We cannot answer these questions here, but they should be noted.

Insight into unconscious determinants of behavior is gained through the techniques of *clarification* and *interpretation*. Clarification aims to make the patient aware of behavior that she does not attend to, but which she can readily attend to if it is pointed out to her. It may be said that clarification focuses the patient's attention on her preconscious mode of experiencing. It is a commonplace that patients will express contiguously two related thoughts without recognizing the relationship. For instance, a patient may come into an appointment complaining of feeling depressed. The next thing she may mention is that she had a fight with her husband that morning. Although it may be apparent to an observer that the depressed mood and the fight are related, the patient may be totally unaware of it; yet if the therapist simply points out that perhaps they are related, the patient will often be able to recognize the connection.

Generally patients do not make connections, are vague about their feelings and complaints, and distort reality in innumerable ways. Clarification attempts to elucidate the distortions, to repair the broken connections, and to delineate obscure thoughts and feelings. The goal is to demonstrate to the patient the behaviors that cause problems without (necessarily) showing the reason for the behavior. For instance, if a patient's usual response when he is angry at someone is to pay the object of the anger a compliment, a clarification might simply point this out. Clarification assists the patient in attaining a greater measure of self-awareness and self-observation so that he can now verbalize his preconscious behavior to himself and to the therapist. In our example, if the patient finds himself paying someone an undue compliment, he will be sensitized to the possibility that he feels angry and he will then be able to verbalize his feelings to himself and the therapist.

Thus, clarification elucidates the person's relationship to herself and the world around her. Awareness and verbalization of maladaptive thoughts, feelings, actions, and impulses allow the patient to become distant from them, to view them in a more detached and coolly appraising manner, to become less identified with them, and to feel less overwhelmed by them. Ideally, the patient begins to feel that his or her maladaptive behavior is not an integral part of his existence.

Clarification is only the first step to complete insight. It aims at description and awareness of behavior, not at understanding of the unconscious, conflicted *reasons* that underlie the behavior. If a person begins to be aware of maladaptive behavior, one could ask why he or she would not then simply decide to act differently. The answer is that he could, but it is assumed that he would be imposing a stern and difficult task on himself, and that the action would not be integrated with his underlying feelings. Theoretically, the new behavior might become habitual but at the posssible cost of a split in his integrated wholeness as a person. Thus, we may teach someone not to undo anger and even to express it, but if the underlying conflict and fear about anger is not resolved, confrontations will still leave one feeling anxious and upset. Or, alternatively, the underlying feelings may be repressed at the cost of feelings of emptiness or depersonalization.

Ordering meanings is the fundamental goal of *interpretation*, the last of our techniques. Even after a person becomes aware of maladaptive behavior patterns, typically they still do not make sense to him or her. One does gain understanding into *how* one is an agent of one's own suffering, but not into *why*. Until persons can satisfactorily answer the "why" questions that plague them, they tend to remain uneasy. Interpretations make sense of non-sense. Through interpretation the therapist attempts to make coherent sense of the patient's past and present behavior, to help him or her understand the reason for this behavior.

In dynamic therapy interpretation refers only to interventions aimed at unconscious material. That is, the therapist tries to elucidate unconscious defenses, connections, wishes, and meanings. Whereas clarification usually remains at the descriptive-phenomenological level, interpretation is based on inferences about underlying reasons for the patient's manifest behavior. From the material the patient communicates during his or her therapeutic hours, the therapist forms what essentially are hypotheses about underlying motives and he then communicates these hypotheses to the patient. Interpretations are working hypotheses that seek to create a meaningful system of explanation to the patient about her own behavior. Rarely are interpretations made once. Interpretation continues throughout therapy in an attempt to confirm and disconfirm the hypotheses more precisely. Bibring noted that unlike clarification, which aims at ego-detachment, interpretation tends to increase ego-involvement because it reactivates painful unconscious tendencies, memories, and conflicts by making them conscious. It is painful to learn that part of the reason one fears to express anger toward one's therapist is because such anger revives conflict over angry feelings felt toward one's father. One may become more invovled in an old love–hate relationship with one's father, expressing the involvement in the transference relationship with the therapist.

The working-through process allows for repeated and increasingly precise interpretation of similar behavior as it recurs. If an interpretation is valid, its repeated working through allows the patient to integrate it into his understanding of himself to become part of his behavorial repertoire. Thus the patient may come to achieve full emotional and cognitive insight. The patient will then feel differently about himself and his life and will be able to try new behavior and to abandon the behaviors based on unrealistic conflicts.

Interpretations are usually delivered in common-sense, everyday language, not in jargon. The therapist does not say to the patient, "Your super-ego is punishing your ego because of the regressive reactivation of oedipal conflicts with authority figures." Rather, he or she is more likely to say, "You were afraid to be angry with me because you feel guilty about being angry with anyone who is like a father to you." Interpretations should involve feelings. The former interpretation will encourage the patient to intellectualize and avoid his feelings. But intellectual insight is generally useless, because it does not have affective meaning. The patient should reexperience various conflicts and work them through with emotional insight in order to change his behavior.

A type of interpretation that deserves special mention is the "construction" (Freud; 1937/1964). A construction is different from other interpretations not only because the therapist attempts to elucidate unconscious determinants of behavior but also because he or she attempts to hypothesize about the way things were (or seemingly must have been) in the past. There is usually no sound empirical evidence with which to verify a construction, but the construction is communicated to the patient as if it were the way things must have happened. For example, in addition to interpreting a patient's relationship to the therapist in terms of the patient's childhood relationship with his or her father, the therapist may hypothesize that the father must have reacted always or nearly always in a given way when the son or daughter expressed ambivalence. From scanty clues, sometimes a therapist will hypothesize how one particular, important event must have occurred. The goal is always to show the patient how these events affect current living, a goal which is partially accomplished by making coherent sense of past events.

Timing is a key factor in the usefulness of an interpretation (or any other intervention). Usually the proper timing for an interpretation is (1) when the patient's defenses are strong enough to hear it without the interpretation producing undue anxiety; and (2) when the patient is almost ready to have the insight himself. If the therapist gives an interpretation when the patient still has no insight into the problem, it will be experienced as intrusive or wrong; or the patient may use it to intellectualize, and thus it will interfere. An interpretation should be the last small push that integrates the patient's growing awareness.

Tact and respect are also critical. Since interpretations are often about matters that are painful, they should be phrased and communicated so as to do the least amount of violence to the patient's self-esteem. The narcissistic injury involved in an interpretation should be minimized. Although interpretations should be thought out and carefully delivered, they should not be stilted. To be therapeutic, interpretations should be given at the right time and in the right manner.

A major problem is knowing when an interpretation is correct. Sometimes, the facts upon which an interpretation is based can be externally, empirically verified (such as whether or not the patient wet his or her bed during childhood), but these facts should not be confused with the interpretation itself. The important facts are really the psychological facts because dynamic therapists believe that psychical reality is as "real" as material reality. For example, the person who always feels she is a failure despite achieving success in most endeavors has a very different psychical and material reality. Pointing to her success is not going to make her feel better —her friends do that all the time and it does not help. Interpretations must be correct in terms of psychical reality even if they are incorrect in terms of material reality.

Yet we still have not said how we know that an interpretation is correct, no matter which kind of reality it deals with. The usual answer is that an interpretation is correct if it feels right to the patient and makes sense to him or her. A therapist tries to judge the usefulness of an interpretation from the totality of the patient's response to the interpretation. During the long working-through process, if an interpretation repeatedly elicits feelings and new associations and makes sense of the patient's psychological life, then it is likely that it is correct. If a patient thoughtfully rejects an interpretation, the therapist is more likely to think it is wrong than if the patient protests too much. Similarly, when an interpretation (which is nearly always tied to painful material) is too readily accepted, the therapist will be wary. Interpretations are "correct" if they work.

Why Therapy Changes Behavior

A major disagreement that has arisen among dynamic theorists is the conceptualization of how, primarily, patients change. One school of thought holds that change is a result of the cognitive, intellectual understanding that occurs, including understanding of feelings. The other school of thought believes that change is a result of the nature of the relationship that arises between the therapist and the patient. Probably, both are true because both cognitive and noncognitive factors are involved in the development and modification of all behavior.

The theory one holds about the mechanism of change will clearly affect therapeutic practice. The therapist with a cognitive orientation will place more weight on making the correct interpretation—making sure it is as precisely accurate as possible. The therapist with a more relational orientation will worry less about the substance of the interpretations, and will worry more about the type of relationship he or she is providing for the patient. Typically, the former orientation is associated with orthodox analysts who make few changes in the basic analytic setting. The latter orientation is associated with more flexible approaches to treatment, with more allowance made for the therapist to intrude his own personality into the therapeutic relationship.

Although there is quite heated disagreement about the process of therapeutic change, probably both orientations are correct. Different types of patients require different approaches for maximum therapeutic results. For instance, disturbed analysands might benefit more from a "real" relationship, whereas "healthier" neurotics might achieve greater success with a more orthodox approach. In addition, an individual patient may benefit from the use of different approaches during different phases of his or her therapy. It is impossible to achieve any closure on this issue at the present time, but it is important that the reader be aware of the difference of opinion about therapeutic change.

As Freud pointed out (1900/1953), behavior is overdetermined, which means that every behavior has many causes. Different theorists probably are approaching similar problems not from mutually exclusive directions,[9] but simply from differing directions. Many insights may apply to any one piece of behavior. Different therapies have differing appeal to various patients and therapists depending on their fundamental conflicts, life history, and cognitive-intellectual styles. The question of which therapy should be used is a question of effectiveness, not a question of right or wrong. Dynamic therapy should not lead to fanaticism or belief in a therapeutic dogma, because one of its chief premises is that there are no "answers."

[9] Even if they make opposite predictions—dialectic process seems fundamental in man's use of symbolic process (Ricoeur, 1971).

Thus, the person who undergoes dynamic therapy and is a "true believer" in that therapy, has not had successful therapy, and the therapist is deceiving himself if he thinks otherwise.

CONCLUSION

In the safety of the therapeutic situation, feelings can be expressed and become part of the conscious awareness of the patient. One now has more data about oneself with which to order one's life. The individual can learn what types of situations make him more upset than he wants to be and in what situations it is appropriate and safe to act as he feels. As similar situations occur over and over again, the lesson is learned at an ever more integrated level—the lesson becomes part of him or her. At the same time the patient learns the limits of change and the limits of insight. These lessons about limits may be the most important lessons learned. Therapy should ideally give one more choice. The goal is *not* that the patient necessarily should act differently; all that is required is that he be able to act differently if he so chooses. For Freud, adaptive living was a matter of renunciation, of choosing to give up our most infantile desires, and of accepting the deformation of one's past. Freud (1895/1955) ended his early work, *Studies on Hysteria*, with the following passage:

> When I have promised my patients help or improvement by . . . treatment I have often been faced by this objection: "Why you tell me yourself that my illness is probably connected with my circumstances and the events of my life. You cannot alter these in any way. How do you propose to help me then?" And I have been able to make this reply: "No doubt fate would find it easier than I do to relieve you of your illness. But you will be able to convince yourself that much will be gained if we succeed in transforming your hysterical misery into common unhappiness. With a mental life that has been restored to health you will be better armed against that unhappiness (p. 305)."

Although Freud might have used different language later on, it is probably the same answer he would have given to his last patient.

REFERENCES

Bibring, E. Psychoanalysis and the dynamic psychotherapies. *Journal of the American Psychoanalytic Association,* 1954, *2,* 745–770.

Breuer, J., & Freud, S. Studies on hysteria. In *The standard edition of the complete psychological works of Sigmund Freud* (Vol. 2). London: Hogarth, 1955. (Originally published, 1895.)

Ellenberger, H. *The discovery of the unconscious.* New York: Basic Books, 1970.

Erikson, E. H. *Gandhi's truth.* New York: W. W. Norton, 1969.

Freud, S. The interpretation of dreams. In *The standard edition of the complete psychological works of Sigmund Freud* (Vols. 4 & 5). London: Hogarth, 1953. (Originally published, 1900.)

————. Analysis of a phobia in a five year old boy. In *The standard edition of the complete psychological works of Sigmund Freud* (Vol. 10). London: Hogarth, 1955. (Originally published, 1905.)

————. On beginning the treatment (further recommendations on the technique of psycho-analysis I). In *The standard edition of the complete psychological works of Sigmund Freud* (Vol. 12). London: Hogarth, 1958. (Originally published, 1913.)

————. Totem and taboo. In *The standard edition of the complete psychological works of Sigmund Freud* (Vol. 13), pp. 1-161. London: Hogarth, 1953. (Originally published, 1913.)

————. On the history of the psychoanalytic movement. In *The standard edition of the complete psychological works of Sigmund Freud* (Vol. 14). London: Hogarth, 1957. (Originally published, 1914.)

————. Inhibitions, symptoms and anxiety. In *The standard edition of the complete psychological works of Sigmund Freud* (Vol. 20). London: Hogarth, 1959. (Originally published, 1926.)

————. Analysis terminable and interminable. In *The standard edition of the complete psychological works of Sigmund Freud* (Vol. 23). London: Hogarth, 1937.

————. Constructions in analysis. In *The standard edition of the complete psychological works of Sigmund Freud* (Vol. 23). London: Hogarth, 1964. (Originally published, 1937.)

Jones, E. *The life and work of Sigmund Freud* (Vol. 1). New York: Basic Books, 1953.

Laplanche, J., & Pontalis, J.-B. *The language of psycho-analysis* (Donald Nicholson-Smith, Trans.). New York: W. W. Norton, 1973. (Originally published, 1967.)

Matarazzo, J. The practice of psychotherapy is art and not science. In A. R. Mahrer & L. Pearson (Eds.), *Creative development in psychotherapy*. Cleveland: Case Western Reserve Press, 1971.

McGuire, W. (Ed.) [*The Freud/Jung letters: The correspondence between Sigmund Freud and C. G. Jung*] (Ralph Manheim & R. F. C. Hull, trans.). Princeton, N.J.: Princeton University Press, 1974.

Ricoeur, P. *Freud and philosophy*. New Haven, Conn.: Yale University Press, 1971.

Schofield, W. *Psychotherapy: The purchase of friendship*. Englewood Cliffs, N.J.: Prentice-Hall, 1965.

Chapter 3
Classical
Psychoanalysis

The young, "classically" neurotic patient in this case, who is known as "Rat Man" because of the content of one of his obsessions, was treated successfully by Freud in the course of just over a year between 1907 and 1908. Thus, it is a very early case that comes from the period when psychoanalytic treatment focussed on symptoms and uncovering the repressed contents of the unconscious ("id psychology") rather than on problems in living and the patient's adaptation to his or her external as well as internal world. Except in a short series of papers written between 1912 and 1915, Freud rarely wrote systematically about technique, and this case is no exception. However, the case is a good description of the course of an analysis, is full of comments on technique, and gives the reader some indication of the enormous complexity of the psychodynamics of just one person. The reader should note the vast amount of material presented to Freud. The Rat Man's symptoms and life are an infinite and seamless web of interlocking meanings, patterns, and connections that Freud unravels psychoanalytically. The seemingly irrational and nonsensical neurotic behavior made good, if maladaptive, sense after all. Freud was quite didactic in his approach to the treatment. He explained various aspects of the psychoanalytic theory of behavior to Rat Man, as well as apprising him of how the treatment worked. The whole treatment seems very cognitive, but we may surmise that insights were affectively as well as intellectually experienced by the Rat Man. Also of note is Freud's attention to the opening communication as previewing the important theme of Rat Man's relationship to men, especially his father. Today we would especially mark the transference implications of such an opening, but in these early years the full importance of the transference was only gradually being recognized. Thus, there is much more emphasis in the case on the details of Rat Man's past and present life and less attention to transference. However, the reader should be attentive to transference implications that are not overtly attended to. In general, however, the case is paradigmatic in its attention to unconscious motivation, conflict, the importance of the past, resistance, and other key elements of psychoanalytic theory and treatment.

Notes upon a Case
of Obsessional Neurosis

The Rat Man

SIGMUND FREUD

A youngish man of university education introduced himself to me with the statement that he had suffered from obsessions ever since his childhood, but with particular intensity for the last four years. The chief features of his disorder were *fears* that something might happen to two people of whom he was very fond—his father and a lady whom he admired. Besides this he was aware of *compulsive impulses*—such as an impulse, for instance, to cut his throat with a razor; and further he produced *prohibitions*, sometimes in connection with quite unimportant things. He had wasted years, he told me, in fighting against these ideas of his, and in this way had lost much ground in the course of his life. He had tried various treatments, but none had been of any use to him except a course of hydrotherapy at a sanatorium near ——; and this, he thought, had probably only been because he had made an acquaintance there which had led to regular sexual intercourse. Here he had no opportunities of the sort, and he seldom had intercourse and only at irregular intervals. He felt disgust at prostitutes. Altogether, he said, his sexual life had been stunted; masturbation had played only a small part in it, in his sixteenth or seventeenth year. His potency was normal; he had first had intercourse at the age of twenty-six.

Chapter III, "Notes upon a case of obsessional neurosis (1909)," from *Collected papers*, Volume 3, by Sigmund Freud, authorized translation by Alix and James Strachey, edited by Ernest Jones, M.D. Published by Basic Books, Inc., by arrangement with The Hogarth Press Ltd. and The Institute of Psycho-Analysis, London. Reprinted by permission of Sigmund Freud Copyrights Limited, in *The standard edition of the complete psychological works of Sigmund Freud*, revised and edited by James Strachey.

He gave me the impression of being a clear-headed and shrewd person. When I asked him what it was that made him lay such stress upon telling me about his sexual life, he replied that that was what he knew about my theories. Actually, however, he had read none of my writings, except that a short time before he had been turning over the pages of one of my books[1] and had come across the explanation of some curious verbal associations which had so much reminded him of some of his own "efforts of thought" in connection with his ideas that he had decided to put himself in my hands.

(A) THE BEGINNING OF THE TREATMENT

The next day I made him pledge himself to submit to the one and only condition of the treatment—namely, to say everything that came into his head, even if it was *unpleasant* to him, or seemed *unimportant* or *irrelevant* or *senseless*. I then gave him leave to start his communications with any subject he pleased, and he began thus:[2]

[1] *The Psychopathology of Everyday Life* [1901*b*].

[2] What follows is based upon notes made on the evening of the day of treatment, and adheres as closely as possible to my recollection of the patient's words.—I feel obliged to offer a warning against the practice of noting down what the patient says during the actual time of treatment. The consequent withdrawal of the physician's attention does the patient more harm than can be made up for by any increase in accuracy that may be achieved in the reproduction of his case history. [This point is enlarged upon in Freud's first paper of technical "Recommendations" (1912*e*), Sections *b* and *c*.]

He had a friend, he told me, of whom he had an extraordinarily high opinion. He used always to go to him when he was tormented by some criminal impulse, and ask him whether he despised him as a criminal. His friend used then to give him moral support by assuring him that he was a man of irreproachable conduct, and had probably been in the habit, from his youth onwards, of taking a dark view of his own life. At an earlier date, he went on, another person had exercised a similar influence over him. This was a nineteen-year-old student (he himself had been fourteen or fifteen at the time) who had taken a liking to him, and had raised his self-esteem to an extraordinary degree, so that he appeared to himself to be a genius. This student had subsequently become his tutor, and had suddenly altered his behaviour and begun treating him as though he were an idiot. At length he had noticed that the student was interested in one of his sisters, and had realized that he had only taken him up in order to gain admission into the house. This had been the first great blow of his life.

He then proceeded without any apparent transition:—

(B) INFANTILE SEXUALITY

"My sexual life began very early. I can remember a scene during my fourth or fifth year. (From my sixth year onwards I can remember everything.) This scene came into my head quite distinctly, years later. We had a very pretty young governess called Fraulein Peter.[3] One evening she was lying on the sofa lightly dressed, and reading. I was lying beside her, and begged her to let me creep under her skirt. She told me I might, so long as I said nothing to any one about it. She had very little on, and I fingered her genitals and the lower part of her body, which struck me as very queer. After this I was left with a burning and tormenting curiosity to see the female body. I can still remember the intense excitement with which I waited at the Baths (which I was still allowed to go to with the governess and my sisters) for the governess to undress and get into the water. I can remember more things from my sixth year onwards. At that time we had another governess, who was also young and good-looking. She had abscesses on her buttocks which she was in the habit of pressing out at night. I used to wait eagerly for that moment, to appease my curiosity. It was just the same at the Baths—though Fräulein Lina was more reserved than her predecessor." (In reply to a question which I threw in, "As a rule," the patient told me, "I did not sleep in her room, but mostly with my parents.") "I remember a scene which must have taken place when I was seven years old.[4] We were sitting together one evening—the governess, the cook, another servant-girl, myself and my brother, who was eighteen months younger than me. The young women were talking, and I suddenly became aware of Fraulein Lina saying: 'It could be done with the little one; but Paul' (that was I) 'is too clumsy, he would be sure to miss it.' I did

---

[3] Dr. Alfred Adler, who was formerly an analyst, once drew attention in a privately delivered paper to the peculiar importance which attaches to the *very first* communications made by patients. Here is an instance of this. The patient's opening words laid stress upon the influence exercised over him by men, that is to say, upon the part played in his life by homosexual object-choice; but immediately afterwards they touched upon a second *motif*, which was to become of great importance later on, namely, the conflict between man and woman and the opposition of their interests. Even the fact that he remembered his first pretty governess by her surname, which happened to be a man's first name, must be taken into account in this connection. In middle-class circles in Vienna it is more usual to call a governess by her first name, and it is by that name that she is more commonly remembered.—[In the original (1909) version, the first words of this footnote ran: "My colleague Dr. Alfred Adler . . ." They were changed to their present form in 1913.]

[4] The patient subsequently admitted that this scene probably occurred one or two years later.

not understand clearly what was meant, but I felt the slight and began to cry. Lina comforted me, and told me how a girl, who had done something of the kind with a little boy she was in charge of, had been put in prison for several months. I do not believe she actually did anything wrong with me, but I took a great many liberties with her. When I got into her bed I used to uncover her and touch her, and she made no objections. She was not very intelligent, and clearly had very strong sexual cravings. At twenty-three she had already had a child. She afterwards married its father, so that to-day she is a Frau Hofrat.[5] Even now I often see her in the street.

"When I was six years old I already suffered from erections, and I know that once I went to my mother to complain about them. I know too that in doing so I had some misgivings to get over, for I had a feeling that there was some connection between this subject and my ideas and inquisitiveness, and at that time I used to have a morbid idea *that my parents knew my thoughts; I explained this to myself by supposing that I had spoken them out loud, without having heard myself do it.* I look on this as the beginning of my illness. There were certain people, girls, who pleased me very much, and I had a very strong wish *to see them naked.* But in wishing this I had *an uncanny feeling, as though something must happen if I thought such things, and as though I must do all sorts of things to prevent it.*"

(In reply to a question he gave an example of these fears: "For instance, *that my father might die.*") "Thoughts about my father's death occupied my mind from a very early age and for a long period of time, and greatly depressed me."

At this point I learnt with astonishment that the patient's father, with whom his

obsessional fears were, after all, occupied now [p. 45], had died several years previously.

The events in his sixth or seventh year which the patient described in the first hour of his treatment were not merely, as he supposed, the beginning of his illness, but were already the illness itself. It was a complete obsessional neurosis, wanting in no essential element, at once the nucleus and the prototype of the later disorder,— an elementary organism, as it were, the study of which could alone enable us to obtain a grasp of the complicated organization of his subsequent illness. The child, as we have seen, was under the domination of a component of the sexual instinct, the desire to look [scopophilia], as a result of which there was a constant recurrence in him of a very intense wish connected with persons of the female sex who pleased him—the wish, that is, to see them naked. This wish corresponds to the later obsessional or compulsive idea; and if the quality of compulsion was not yet present in the wish, this was because the ego had not yet placed itself in complete opposition to it and did not yet regard it as something foreign to itself. Nevertheless, opposition to this wish from some source or other was already in activity, for its occurrence was regularly accompanied by a distressing affect.[6] A conflict was evidently in progress in the mind of this young libertine. Side by side with the obsessive wish, and intimately associated with it, was an obsessive fear: every time he had a wish of this kind he could not help fearing that something dreadful would happen. This something dreadful was already clothed in a characteristic indeterminateness which was thenceforward to be an invariable feature of every manifestation of the neurosis. But in a child it is not hard to discover what it is that is veiled behind an indeterminateness of this

---

[5] [The Austrian title of '*Hofrat*' was awarded to prominent physicians, lawyers, university professors, civil servants, etc. It was perhaps equivalent to a knighthood in modern England.]

[6] Yet attempts have been made to explain obsessions without taking the affects into account!

kind. If the patient can once be induced to give a particular instance in place of the vague generalities which characterize an obsessional neurosis, it may be confidently assumed that the instance is the original and actual thing which has tried to hide itself behind the generalization. Our present patient's obsessive fear, therefore, when restored to its original meaning, would run as follows: "If I have this wish to see a woman naked, my father will be bound to die." The distressing affect was distinctly coloured with a tinge of uncanniness and superstition, and was already beginning to give rise to impulses to do something to ward off the impending evil. These impulses were subsequently to develop into the *protective measures* which the patient adopted.

We find, accordingly: an erotic instinct and a revolt against it; a wish which has not yet become compulsive and, struggling against it, a fear which is already compulsive; a distressing affect and an impulsion towards the performance of defensive acts. The inventory of the neurosis has reached its full muster. Indeed, something more is present, namely, a kind of *delusion* or *delirium*[7] with the strange content that his parents knew his thoughts because he spoke them out loud without his hearing himself do it. We shall not go far astray if we suppose that in making this attempt at an explanation the child had some inkling of those remarkable mental processes which we describe as unconscious and which we cannot dispense with if we are to throw any scientific light upon this obscure subject. "I speak my thoughts out loud, without hearing them" sounds like a projection into the external world of our own hypothesis that he had thoughts without knowing anything about them; it sounds like an endopsychic perception of what has been repressed.

7 ["Delirium" is here and elsewhere in this paper used in a special sense. . . . In French and German psychiatry, the term often corresponds to the English "delusion."]

For the situation is clear. This elementary neurosis of childhood already involved a problem and an apparent absurdity, like any complicated neurosis of maturity. What can have been the meaning of the child's idea that if he had this lascivious wish his father would be bound to die? Was it sheer nonsense? Or are there means of understanding the words and of perceiving them as a necessary consequence of earlier events and premises?

If we apply knowledge gained elsewhere to this case of childhood neurosis, we shall not be able to avoid a suspicion that in this instance as in others (that is to say, before the child had reached his sixth year) there had been conflicts and repressions, which had themselves been overtaken by amnesia, but had left behind them as a residuum the particular content of this obsessive fear. Later on we shall learn how far it is possible for us to rediscover those forgotten experiences or to reconstruct them with some degree of certainty. In the meantime stress may be laid on the fact, which is probably more than a mere coincidence, that the patient's infantile amnesia ended precisely with his sixth year [see p. 46].

To find a chronic obsessional neurosis beginning like this in early childhood, with lascivious wishes of this sort connected with uncanny apprehensions and an inclination to the performance of defensive acts, is no new thing to me. I have come across it in a number of other cases. It is absolutely typical, although probably not the only possible type. Before proceeding to the events of the second session, I should like to add one more word on the subject of the patient's early sexual experiences. It will hardly be disputed that they may be described as having been considerable both in themselves and in their consequences. But it has been the same with the other cases of obsessional neurosis that I have had the opportunity of analysing. Such cases, unlike those of hysteria, invariably possess the characteristic of premature sexual activity. Obsessional neuroses make it much more obvious than hysterias that the factors which go to form a psychoneurosis are to be found in the patient's *infantile* sexual life and not in his present one. The current sexual life of an obsessional neurotic may often appear perfectly normal to a superficial observer; indeed, it frequently offers to the eye far fewer pathogenic elements and abnormalities than in the instance we are now considering.

(C) THE GREAT OBSESSIVE FEAR

"I think I will begin to-day with the experience which was the immediate occasion of my coming to you. It was in August, during the manœuvres in ——. I had been suffering before, and tormenting myself with all kinds of obsessional thoughts, but they had quickly passed off during the manœuvres. I was keen to show the regular officers that people like me had not only learnt a good deal but could stand a good deal too. One day we started from —— on a short march. During a halt I lost my pince-nez, and, although I could easily have found them, I did not want to delay our start, so I gave them up. But I wired to my opticians in Vienna to send me another pair by the next post. During that same halt I sat between two officers, one of whom, a captain with a Czech name, was to be of no small importance to me. I had a kind of dread of him, *for he was obviously fond of cruelty.* I do not say he was a bad man, but at the officers' mess he had repeatedly defended the introduction of corporal punishment, so that I had been obliged to disagree with him very sharply. Well, during this halt we got into conversation, and the captain told me he had read of a specially horrible punishment used in the East . . ."

Here the patient broke off, got up from the sofa, and begged me to spare him the recital of the details. I assured him that I myself had no taste whatever for cruelty,

and certainly had no desire to torment him, but that naturally I could not grant him something which was beyond my power. He might just as well ask me to give him the moon. The overcoming of resistances was a law of the treatment, and on no consideration could it be dispensed with. (I had explained the idea of "resistance" to him at the beginning of the hour, when he told me there was much in himself which he would have to overcome if he was to relate this experience of his.) I went on to say that I would do all I could, nevertheless, to guess the full meaning of any hints he gave me. Was he perhaps thinking of impalement?—"No, not that; . . . the criminal was tied up . . ."—he expressed himself so indistinctly that I could not immediately guess in what position— ". . . a pot was turned upside down on his buttocks . . . some *rats* were put into it . . . and they . . ."—he had again got up, and was showing every sign of horror and resistance—". . . *bored their way in* . . ."

Into his anus, I helped him out.

At all the more important moments while he was telling his story his face took on a very strange, composite expression. I could only interpret it as one of *horror at pleasure of his own of which he himself was unaware.* He proceeded with the greatest difficulty: "At that moment the idea flashed through my mind *that this was happening to a person who was very dear to me.*"[8] In answer to a direct question he said that it was not he himself who was carrying out the punishment, but that it was being carried out as it were impersonally. After a little prompting I learnt that the person to whom this "idea" of his related was the lady whom he admired.

He broke off his story in order to assure me that these thoughts were entirely foreign and repugnant to him, and to tell

---

[8] He said "idea"—the stronger and more significant term "wish," or rather "fear," having evidently been censored. Unfortunately I am not able to reproduce the peculiar indeterminateness of all his remarks.

me that everything which had followed in their train had passed through his mind with the most extraordinary rapidity. Simultaneously with the idea there always appeared a "sanction," that is to say, the defensive measures which he was obliged to adopt in order to prevent the phantasy from being fulfilled. When the captain had spoken of this ghastly punishment, he went on, and these ideas had come into his head, by employing his usual formulas (a "but" accompanied by a gesture of repudiation, and the phrase "whatever are you thinking of?") he had just succeeded in warding off *both* of them.

This "both" took me aback, and it has no doubt also mystified the reader. For so far we have heard only of one idea—of the rat punishment being carried out upon the lady. He was now obliged to admit that a second idea had occurred to him simultaneously, namely, the idea of the punishment also being applied to his father. As his father had died many years previously, this obsessive fear was much more nonsensical even than the first, and accordingly it had attempted to escape being confessed to for a little while longer.

That evening, he continued, the same captain had handed him a packet that had arrived by the post and had said: "Lieutenant A.[9] has paid the charges[10] for you. You must pay him back." The packet had contained the pince-nez that he had wired for. At that instant, however, a "sanction" had taken shape in his mind, namely, *that he was not to pay back the money* or it would happen—(that is, the phantasy about the rats would come true as regards his father and the lady). And immediately, in accordance with a type of procedure with which he was familiar, to combat this sanction there had arisen a command in the shape of a vow: "*You must pay back the* 3.80 *kronen*[11] *to Lieutenant A.*" He had said these words to himself almost half aloud.

Two days later the manoeuvres had come to an end. He had spent the whole of the intervening time in efforts at repaying Lieutenant A. the small amount in question; but a succession of difficulties of an apparently *external* nature had arisen to prevent it. First he had tried to effect the payment through another officer who had been going to the post office. But he had been much relieved when this officer brought him back the money, saying that he had not met Lieutenant A. there, for this method of fulfilling his vow had not satisfied him, as it did not correspond with the wording, which ran: "*You* must pay back the money to Lieutenant A." Finally, he had met Lieutenant A., the person he was looking for; but that officer had refused to accept the money, declaring that he had not paid anything for him, and had nothing whatever to do with the post, which was the business of Lieutenant B. This had thrown my patient into great perplexity, for it meant that he was unable to keep his vow, since it had been based upon false premises. He had excogitated a very curious means of getting out of his difficulty, namely, that he should go to the post office with both the men, A. and B., that A. should give the young lady there the 3.80 *kronen*, that the young lady should give them to B., and that then he himself should pay back the 3.80 *kronen* to A. according to the wording of his vow.

It would not surprise me to hear that at this point the reader had ceased to be able to follow. For even the detailed account which the patient gave me of the external events of these days and of his reactions to them was full of self-contradictions and sounded hopelessly confused. It was only when he told the story for the third time that I could get him to realize its obscuri-

---

[9] The names are of little consequence here.

[10] [The charges in question were for the cost of the new pince-nez. In Austria a system of "cash on delivery" operated through the post office.]

[11] [A sum at that time equal to about *cs. 2d.* or 75 cents.]

ties and could lay bare the errors of memory and the displacements in which he had become involved. I shall spare myself the trouble of reproducing these details, the essentials of which we shall easily be able to pick up later on, and I will only add that at the end of this second session the patient behaved as though he were dazed and bewildered. He repeatedly addressed me as "Captain," probably because at the beginning of the hour I had told him that I myself was not fond of cruelty like Captain N., and that I had no intention of tormenting him unnecessarily.

The only other piece of information that I obtained from him during this hour was that from the very first, on all the previous occassions on which he had a fear that something would happen to people he loved no less than on the present one, he had referred the punishments not only to our present life but also to eternity —to the next world. Up to his fourteenth or fifteenth year he had been devoutly religious, but from that time on he had gradually developed into the free-thinker that he was to-day. He reconciled the contradiction between his beliefs and his obsessions by saying to himself: "What do you know about the next world? Nothing *can* be known about it. You're not risking anything—so do it." This form of argument seemed unobjectionable to a man who was in other respects particularly clear-headed, and in this way he exploited the uncertainty of reason in the face of these questions to the benefit of the religious attitude which he had outgrown.

At the third session he completed his very characteristic story of his efforts at fulfilling his obsessional vow. That evening the last gathering of officers had taken place before the end of the manoeuvres. It had fallen to him to reply to the toast of "The Gentlemen of the Reserve." He had spoken well, but as if he were in a dream, for at the back of his mind he was being incessantly tormented by his vow. He had

spent a terrible night. Arguments and counter-arguments had struggled with one another. The chief argument, of course, had been that the premise upon which his vow had been based—that Lieutenant A. had paid the money for him—had proved to be false. However, he had consoled himself with the thought that the business was not yet finished, as A. would be riding with him next morning part of the way to the railway station at P——,[12] so that he would still have time to ask him the necessary favour. . . . As a matter of fact he had not done this, and had allowed A. to go off without him; but he had given instructions to his orderly to let A. know that he intended to pay him a visit that afternoon. He himself had reached the station at half-past nine in the morning. He had deposited his luggage there and had seen to various things he had to do in the small town, with the intention of afterwards paying his visit to A. The village in which A. was stationed was about an hour's drive from the town of P——. The railway journey to the place where the post office was [Z——] would take three hours. He had calculated, therefore, that the execution of his complicated plan would just leave him time to catch the evening train from P——to Vienna. The ideas that were struggling within him had been, on the one hand, that he was simply being cowardly and was obviously only trying to save himself the unpleasantness of asking A. to make the sacrifice in question and of cutting a foolish figure before him, and that that was why he was disregarding his vow; and, on the other hand, that it would, on the contrary, be cowardly of him to *fulfil* his vow, since he only wanted to do so in order to be left in peace by his obsessions. When in the course of his deliberations, the patient added, he found the arguments so evenly balanced as these, it was his custom to allow his actions to be

[12] [Freud's Original Record shows that this place was Przemysl.]

decided by chance events as though by the hand of God. When, therefore, a porter at the station had addressed him with the words, "Ten o'clock train, sir?" he had answered "Yes," and in fact had gone off by the ten o'clock train. In this way he had produced a *fait accompli* and felt greatly relieved. He had proceeded to book a seat for luncheon in the restaurant car. At the first station they had stopped at it had suddenly struck him that he still had time to get out, wait for the next down train, travel back in it to P——, drive to the place where Lieutenant A. was quartered, from there make the three hours' train journey with him to the post office, and so forth. It had only been the consideration that he had booked his seat for luncheon with the steward of the restaurant car that had prevented his carrying out this design. He had not abandoned it, however; he had only put off getting out until a later stop. In this way he had struggled through from station to station, till he had reached one at which it had seemed to him impossible to get out because he had relatives living there. He had then determined to travel through to Vienna, to look up his friend there and lay the whole matter before him, and then, after his friend had made his decision, to catch the night train back to P——. When I expressed a doubt whether this would have been feasible, he assured me that he would have had half an hour to spare between the arrival of the one train and the departure of the other. When he had arrived in Vienna, however, he had failed to find his friend at the restaurant at which he had counted on meeting him, and had not reached his friend's house till eleven o'clock at night. He told him the whole story that very night. His friend had held up his hands in amazement to think that he could still be in doubt whether he was suffering from an obsession, and had calmed him down for the night, so that he had slept excellently. Next morning they had gone together to the post office, to dispatch the 3.80 *kronen* to the post

office [Z——] at which the packet containing the pince-nez had arrived.

It was this last statement which provided me with a starting-point from which I could begin straightening out the various distortions involved in his story. After his friend had brought him to his senses he had dispatched the small sum of money in question neither to Lieutenant A. nor to Lieutenant B., but direct to the post office. He must therefore have known that he owed the amount of the charges due upon the packet *to no one but the official at the post office,* and he must have known this before he started on his journey. It turned out that in fact he had known it before the captain made his request and before he himself made his vow; for he now remembered that a few hours *before* meeting the cruel captain he had had occasion to introduce himself to another captain, who had told him how matters actually stood. This officer, on hearing his name, had told him that he had been at the post office a short time before, and that the young lady there has asked him whether he knew a Lieutenant L. (the patient, that is), for whom a packet had arrived, to be paid for on delivery. The officer had replied that he did not, but the young lady had been of opinion that she could trust the unkown lieutenant and had said that in the meantime she would pay the charges herself. It had been in this way that the patient had come into possession of the pince-nez he had ordered. The cruel captain had made a mistake when, as he handed him over the packet, he had asked him to pay back the 3.80 *kronen* to A., and the patient must have known it was a mistake. In spite of this he had made a vow founded upon this mistake, a vow that was bound to be a torment to him. In so doing he had suppressed to himself, just as in telling the story he had suppressed to me, the episode of the other captain and the existence of the trusting young lady at the post office. I must admit that when this correction has been made his behaviour becomes even more senseless and unintelligible than before.

After he had left his friend and returned to his family his doubts had overtaken him afresh. His friend's arguments, he saw, had been no different from his own, and he was under no delusion that his temporary relief was attributable to anything more than his friend's personal influence. His determination to consult a doctor was woven into his delirium in the following ingenious manner. He thought he would get a doctor to give him a certificate to the effect that it was necessary for him, in order to recover his health, to perform some such action as he had planned in connection with Lieutenant A.; and the lieutenant would no doubt let himself be persuaded by the certificate into accepting the 3.80 crowns from him. The chance that one of my books happened to fall into his hands just at that moment directed his choice to me. There was no question of getting a certificate from me, however; all that he asked of me was, very reasonably, to be freed of his obsessions. Many months later, when his resistance was at its height, he once more felt a temptation to travel to P——after all, to look up Lieutenant A. and to go through the farce of returning him the money.

(D) INITIATION INTO THE NATURE OF THE TREATMENT

The reader must not expect to hear at once what light I have to throw upon the patient's strange and senseless obsessions about the rats. The true technique of psychoanalysis requires the physician to suppress his curiosity and leaves the patient complete freedom in choosing the order in which topics shall succeed each other during the treatment. At the fourth session, accordingly, I received the patient with the question: "And how do you intend to proceed to-day?"

"I have decided to tell you something which I consider most important and which has tormented me from the very first." He then told me at great length the story of the last illness of his father, who had died of emphysema nine years previously. One evening, thinking that the condition was one which would come to a crisis, he had asked the doctor when the danger could be regarded as over. "The evening of the day after to-morrow" had been the reply. It had never entered his head that his father might not survive that limit. At half-past eleven at night he had lain down for an hour's rest. He had woken up at one o'clock, and had been told by a medical friend that his father had died. He had reproached himself with not having been present at his death; and the reproach had been intensified when the nurse told him that his father had spoken his name once during the last days, and had said to her as she came up to the bed: "Is that Paul." He had thought he noticed that his mother and sisters had been inclined to reproach themselves in a similar way; but they had never spoken about it. At first, however, the reproach had not tormented him. For a long time he had not realized the fact of his father's death. It had constantly happened that, when he heard a good joke, he would say to himself: "I must tell Father that." His imagination, too, had been occupied with his father, so that often, when there was a knock at the door, he would think: "Here comes Father," and when he walked into a room he would expect to find his father in it. And although he had never forgotten that his father was dead, the prospect of seeing a ghostly apparition of this kind had had no terrors for him; on the contrary, he had greatly desired it. It had not been until eighteen months later that the recollection of his neglect had recurred to him and begun to torment him terribly, so that he had come to treat himself as a criminal. The occasion of this happening had been the death of an aunt by marriage and of a visit of condolence that he had paid at her house. From that time forward he had extended the structure of his obsessional thoughts so as to include the next world. The immediate consequence of this development had been that he became seriously incapacitated from working.[13] He told me that the only thing that had kept him going at that time had been the consolation given him by his friend, who had always brushed his self-reproaches aside on the ground that they were grossly exaggerated. Hearing this, I took the opportunity of giving him a first glance at the underlying principles of psycho-analytic therapy. When there is a *mésalliance*,[14] I began, between an affect and its ideational content (in this instance, between the intensity of the self-reproach and the occasion for it), a layman will say that the affect is too great for the occasion—that it is exaggerated—and that consequently the inference following from the self-reproach (the inference that the patient is a criminal) is false. On the contrary, the [analytic] physician says: "No. The affect is justified. The sense of guilt is not in itself open to further criticism. But it belongs to some other content, which is unknown (*unconscious*), and which requires to be looked for. The known ideational content has only got into its actual position owing to a false connection. We are not used to feeling strong affects without their having any ideational content, and therefore, if the

content is missing, we seize as a substitute upon some other content which is in some way or other suitable, much as our police, when they cannot catch the right murderer, arrest a wrong one instead. Moreover, this fact of there being a false connection is the only way of accounting for the powerlessness of logical processes to combat the tormenting idea." I concluded by admitting that this new way of looking at the matter gave immediate rise to some hard problems; for how could he admit that his self-reproach of being a criminal towards his father was justified, when he must know that as a matter of fact he had never committed any crime against him?

At the next session the patient showed great interest in what I had said, but ventured, so he told me, to bring forward a few doubts.—How, he asked, could the information that the self-reproach, the sense of guilt, was justified have a therapeutic effect?—I explained that it was not the information that had this effect, but the discovery of the unknown content to which the self-reproach was really attached.—Yes, he said, that was the precise point to which his question had been directed.—I then made some short observations upon *the psychological differences between the conscious and the unconscious*, and upon the fact that everything conscious was subject to a process of wearing-away, while what was unconscious was relatively unchangeable; and I illustrated my remarks by pointing to the antiques standing about in my room. They were, in fact, I said, only objects found in a tomb, and their burial had been their preservation: the destruction of Pompeii was only beginning now that it had been dug up.— Was there any guarantee, he next enquired, of what one's attitude would be towards what was discovered? One man, he thought, would no doubt behave in such a way as to get the better of his self-reproach, but another would not.—No, I

---

[13] A more detailed description of the episode, which the patient gave me later on, made it possible to understand the effect that it produced on him. His uncle, lamenting the loss of his wife, had exclaimed: "Other men allow themselves every possible indulgence, but I lived for this woman alone!" The patient had assumed that his uncle was alluding to his father and was casting doubts upon his conjugal fidelity; and although his uncle had denied this construction of his words most positively, it was no longer possible to counteract their effect.

[14] [The following account of displacement of affect is closely modelled on the one given in Freud's first paper on "The Neuro-Psychoses of Defence" (1894a), Section II, where the term "false connection" is used in the same special sense as in the passage below.]

said, it followed from the nature of the circumstances that in every case the affect would be overcome—for the most part during the progress of the work itself. Every effort was made to preserve Pompeii, whereas people were anxious to be rid of tormenting ideas like his.—He had said to himself, he went on, that a self-reproach could only arise from a breach of a person's own inner moral principles and not from that of any external ones.—I agreed, and said that the man who merely breaks an external law often regards himself as a hero.—Such an occurrence, he continued, was thus only possible where a *disintegration of the personality* was already present. Was there a possibility of his effecting a re-integration of his personality? If this could be done, he thought he would be able to make a success of his life, perhaps more of one than most people.—I replied that I was in complete agreement with this notion of a splitting of his personality. He had only to assimilate this new contrast, between a moral self and an evil one, with the contrast I had already mentioned, between the conscious and the unconscious. The moral self was the conscious, the evil self was the unconscious.[15]—He then said that, though he considered himself a moral person, he could quite definitely remember having done things in his *childhood* which came from his other self.—I remarked that here he had incidentally hit upon one of the chief characteristics of the unconscious, namely, its relation to the *infantile*. The unconscious, I explained, *was* the infantile; it was that part of the self which had become separated off from it in infancy, which had not shared the later stages of its development, and which had in consequence become *repressed*. It was the derivatives of this repressed unconscious that were responsible for the involuntary thoughts which constituted his

illness. He might now, I added, discover yet another characteristic of the unconscious; it was a discovery which I should be glad to let him make for himself.—He found nothing more to say in this immediate connection, but instead he expressed a doubt whether it was possible to undo modifications of such long standing. What, in particular, could be done against his idea about the next world, for it could not be refuted by logic?—I told him I did not dispute the gravity of his case nor the significance of his pathological constructions; but at the same time his youth was very much in his personality. In this connection I said a word or two upon the good opinion I had formed of him, and this gave him visible pleasure.

At the next session he began by saying that he must tell me an event in his childhood. From the age of seven, as he had already told me [p. 47], he had had a fear that his parents guessed his thoughts, and this fear had in fact persisted all through his life. When he was twelve years old he had been in love with a little girl, the sister of a friend of his. (In answer to a question he said that his love had not been sensual; he had not wanted to see her naked for she was too small.) But she had not shown him as much affection as he had desired. And thereupon the idea had come to him that she would be kind to him if some misfortune were to befall him; and as an instance of such a misfortune his father's death had forced itself upon his mind. He had at once rejected the idea with energy. And even now he could not admit the possibility that what had arisen in this way could have been a "wish"; it had clearly been no more than a "train of thought."[16]—By way of objection I asked him why, if it had not been a wish, he had repudiated it.—Merely, he replied, on account of the content of the

---

[15] All of this is of course only true in the roughest way, but it serves as a first introduction to the subject.

[16] Obsessional neurotics are not the only people who are satisfied with euphemisms of this kind.

idea, the notion that his father might die. —I remarked that he was treating the phrase as though it were one that involved *lèse-majesté;* it was well known, of course, that it was equally punishable to say "The Emperor is an ass" or to disguise the forbidden words by saying "If any one says, etc., . . . then he will have me to reckon with." I added that I could easily insert the idea which he had so energetically repudiated into a context which would exclude the possibility of any such repudiation: for instance, "If my father dies, I shall kill myself upon his grave."—He was shaken, but did not abandon his objection. I therefore broke off the argument with the remark that I felt sure this had not been the first occurrence of his idea of his father's dying; it had evidently originated at an earlier date, and some day we should have to trace back its history.—He then proceeded to tell me that a precisely similar thought had flashed through his mind a second time, six months before his father's death. At that time[17] he had already been in love with his lady, but financial obstacles made it impossible to think of an alliance with her. The idea had then occurred to him that *his father's death might make him rich enough to marry her.* In defending himself against this idea he had gone to the length of wishing that his father might leave him nothing at all, so that he might have no compensation for his terrible loss. The same idea, though in a much milder form, had come to him for a third time, on the day before his father's death. He had then thought: "Now I may be going to lose what I love most"; and then had come the contradiction: "No, there is some one else whose loss would be even more painful to you."[18] These thoughts surprised him very much, for he was quite certain that his father's death could never have been an object of

his desire but only of his fear.—After his forcible enunciation of these words I thought it advisable to bring a fresh piece of theory to his notice. According to psycho-analytic theory, I told him, every fear corresponded to a former wish which was now repressed; we were therefore obliged to believe the exact contrary of what he had asserted. This would also fit in with another theoretical requirement, namely, that the unconscious must be the precise contrary of the conscious.—He was much agitated at this and very incredulous. He wondered how he could posssibly have had such a wish, considering that he loved his father more than any one else in the world; there could be no doubt that he would have renounced all his own prospects of happiness if by so doing he could have saved his father's life.—I answered that it was precisely such intense love as his that was the necessary precondition of the repressed hatred. In the case of people to whom he felt indifferent he would certainly have no difficulty in maintaining side by side inclinations to a moderate liking and to an equally moderate dislike: supposing, for instance, that he were an official, he might think that his chief was agreeable as a superior, but at the same time pettifogging as a lawyer and inhuman as a judge. (Shakespeare makes Brutus speak in a similar way of Julius Caesar: "As Caesar loved me, I weep for him; as he was fortunate, I rejoice at it; as he was valiant, I honour him; but, as he was ambitious, I slew him."[19] But these words already strike us as rather strange, and for the very reason that we had imagined Brutus's feeling for Caesar as something deeper.) In the case of some one who was closer to him, of his wife for instance, he would wish his feelings to be unmixed, and consequently, as was only human, he

---

[17] That is, ten years ago.

[18] There is here an unmistakable indication of an opposition between the two objects of his love, his father and the "lady."

[19] [These same words from *Julius Caesar* (III, 2) played an important part in the associations to one of Freud's own dreams. Cf. *The Interpretation of Dreams* (1900a), Chapter VI, end of Section F; *Standard Ed.,* 5, 424.]

would overlook her faults, since they might make him dislike her—he would ignore them as though he were blind to them. So it was precisely the intensity of his love that would not allow his hatred—though to give it such a name was to caricature the feeling—to remain conscious. To be sure, the hatred must have a source, and to discover that source was certainly a problem; his own statements pointed to the time when he was afraid that his parents guessed his thoughts. On the other hand, too, it might be asked why this intense love of his had not succeeded in extinguishing his hatred, as usually happened where there were two opposing impulses. We could only presume that the hatred must flow from some source, must be connected with some particular cause, which made it indestructible. On the one hand, then, some connection of this sort must be keeping his hatred for his father alive, while on the other hand, his intense love prevented it from becoming conscious. Therefore nothing remained for it but to exist in the unconscious, though it was able from time to time to flash out for a moment into consciousness.

He admitted that all of this sounded quite plausible, but he was naturally not in the very least convinced by it.[20] He would venture to ask, he said, how it was that an idea of this kind could have remissions, how it could appear for a moment when he was twelve years old, and again when he was twenty, and then once more two years later, this time for good. He could not believe that his hostility had been extinguished in the intervals, and yet during them there had been no sign of self-reproaches.—To this I replied that whenever any one asked a question like that, he was already prepared with an answer; he needed only to be encouraged to go on talking.—He then proceeded, somewhat disconnectedly as it seemed, to say that he had been his father's best friend, and that his father had been his. Except on a few subjects, upon which fathers and sons usually hold aloof from one another—(What could he mean by that?)—, there had been a greater intimacy between them than there now was between him and his best friend. As regards the lady for whose sake he had sacrificed his father in that idea of his, it was true that he had loved her very much, but he had never felt really sensual wishes towards her, such as he had constantly had in his childhood. Altogether, in his childhood his sensual impulses had been stronger than during his puberty.—At this I told him I thought he had now produced the answer we were waiting for, and had at the same time discovered the third great characteristic of the unconscious [p. 55]. The source from which his hostility to his father derived its indestructibility was evidently something in the nature of *sensual desires*, and in that connection he must have felt his father as in some way or other an *interference*. A conflict of this kind, I added, between sensuality and childish love was entirely typical. The remissions he had spoken of had occurred because the premature explosion of his sensual feelings had had as its immediate consequence a considerable diminution of their violence. It was not until he was once more seized with intense erotic desires that his hostility reappeared again owing to the revival of the old situation. I then got him to agree that I had not led him on to the subject either of childhood or of sex, but that he had raised them both of his own free will.—He then went on to ask why he had not simply come to a decision, at the time he was in love with the lady, that his father's interference with

[20] It is never the aim of discussions like this to create conviction. They are only intended to bring the repressed complexes into consciousness, to set the conflict going in the field of conscious mental activity, and to facilitate the emergence of fresh material from the unconscious. A sense of conviction is only attained after the patient has himself worked over the reclaimed material, and so long as he is not fully convinced the material must be considered as unexhausted.

that love could not for a moment weigh against his love of his father.—I replied that it was scarcely possible to destroy a person *in absentia*. Such a decision would only have been possible if the wish that he took objection to had made its first appearance on that occasion; whereas, as a matter of fact, it was a *long-repressed wish*, towards which he could not behave otherwise than he had formerly done, and which was consequently immune from destruction. This wish (to get rid of his father as being an interference) must have originated at a time when circumstances had been very different—at a time, perhaps, when he had not loved his father more than the person whom he desired sensually, or when he was incapable of making a clear decision. It must have been in his very early childhood, therefore, before he had reached the age of six, and before the date at which his memory became continuous; and things must have remained in the same state ever since.— With this piece of construction our discussion was broken off for the time being. [Cf. p. 69.]

At the next session, which was the seventh, he took up the same subject once more. He could not believe, he said, that he had ever entertained such a wish against his father. He remembered a story of Sudermann's, he went on, that had made a deep impression upon him. In this story[21] there was a woman who, as she sat by her sister's sick-bed, felt a wish that her sister should die so that she herself might marry her husband. The woman thereupon committed suicide, thinking she was not fit to live after being guilty of such baseness. He could understand this, he said, and it would be only right if his thoughts were the death of him, for he deserved nothing less.[22]—I remarked that it was well known to us that patients derived a certain satisfaction from their sufferings, so that in reality they all resisted their own recovery to some extent. He must never lose sight of the fact that a treatment like ours proceeded to the accompaniment of a *constant resistance*; I should be repeatedly reminding him of this fact.

He then went on to say that he would like to speak of a criminal act, whose author he did not recognize as himself, though he quite clearly recollected committing it. He quoted a saying of Nietzsche's:[23] 'I did this,' says my Memory. 'I cannot have done this,' says my Pride and remains inexorable. In the end— Memory yields." "Well," he continued, "my memory has *not* yielded on this point."—"That is because you derive pleasure from your self-reproaches as a means of self-punishment."—"My younger brother—I am really very fond of him now, and he is causing me a great deal of worry just at present, for he wants to make what I consider a preposterous match; I have thought before now of going and killing the person concerned so as to prevent his marrying her—well, my younger brother and I used to fight a lot when we were children. We were very fond of each other at the same time, and were inseparable; but I was plainly filled with jealousy, as he was the stronger and better-looking of the two and consequently the favourite."—"Yes. You have already given me a description of a scene of jealousy in connection with Fräulein Lina [p. 46]."—"Very well then, on some such occasion (it was certainly before I was eight years old, for I was not going to school yet, which I began to do when I

---

21 [Sudermann's novel *Geschwister*.]
22 This sense of guilt involves the most glaring contradiction of his opening denial that he had ever entertained such an evil wish against his

father. This is a common type of reaction to repressed material which has become conscious: the "No" with which the fact is first denied is immediately followed by a confirmation of it, though, to begin with, only an indirect one. [Cf. Freud's much later paper on "Negation" (1925h) and the first two sections of his "Constructions in Analysis" (1937d).]
23 *Jenseits von Gut und Böse*, iv. 68.

was eight)—on some such occasion, this is what I did. We both had toy guns of the usual make. I loaded mine with the ramrod and told him that if he looked up the barrel he would see something. Then, while he was looking in, I pulled the trigger. He was hit on the forehead and not hurt; but I had meant to hurt him very much indeed. Afterwards I was quite beside myself, and threw myself on the ground and asked myself how ever I could have done such a thing. But I *did* do it." —I took the opportunity of urging my case. If he had preserved the recollection of an action so foreign to him as this, he could not, I maintained, deny the possibility of something similar, which he had now forgotten entirely, having happened at a still earlier age in relation to his father.—He then told me he was aware of having felt other vindictive impulses, this time towards the lady he admired so much, of whose character he painted a glowing picture. It might be true, he said, that she could not love easily; but she was reserving her whole self for the one man to whom she would some day belong. She did not love him. When he had become certain of that, a conscious phantasy had taken shape in his mind of how he should grow very rich and marry some one else, and should then take her to call on the lady in order to hurt her feelings. But at that point the phantasy had broken down, for he had been obliged to own to himself that the other woman, his wife, was completely indifferent to him; then his thoughts had become confused, till finally it had been clearly borne in upon him that this other woman would have to die. In this phantasy, just as in his attempt upon his brother, he recognized the quality of *cowardice* which was so particularly horrible to him.[24]—In the further course of our conversation I pointed out to him that he ought logically to consider himself as in no way responsible for any of these

traits in his character; for all of these reprehensible impulses originated from his infancy, and were only derivatives of his infantile character surviving in his unconscious; and he must know that moral responsibility could not be applied to children. It was only by a process of development, I added, that a man, with his moral responsibility, grew up out of the sum of his infantile predispositions.[25] He expressed a doubt, however, whether all his evil impulses had originated from that source. But I promised to prove it to him in the course of the treatment.

He went on to adduce the fact of his illness having become so enormously intensified since his father's death; and I said I agreed with him in so far as I regarded his sorrow at his father's death as the chief source of the *intensity* of his illness. His sorrow had found, as it were, a pathological expression in his illness. Whereas, I told him, a normal period of mourning would last from one to two years, a pathological one like this would last indefinitely.

This is as much of the present case history as I am able to report in a detailed and consecutive manner. It coincides roughly with the expository portion of the treatment; this lasted in all for more than eleven months.

(E) SOME OBSESSIONAL IDEAS AND THEIR EXPLANATION

Obsessional ideas, as is well known, have an appearance of being either without motive or without meaning, just as dreams have. The first problem is how to give them a sense and a status in the subject's mental life, so as to make them comprehensible and even obvious. The problem

---

[24] This quality of his will find an explanation later on.

[25] I only produced these arguments so as once more to demonstrate to myself their inefficacy. I cannot understand how other psychotherapists can assert that they successfully combat neurosis with such weapons as these.

of translating them may seem insoluble; but we must never let ourselves be misled by that illusion. The wildest and most eccentric obsessional ideas can be cleared up if they are investigated deeply enough. The solution is effected by bringing the obsessional ideas into temporal relationship with the patient's experiences, that is to say, by enquiring when a particular obsessional idea made its first appearance and in what external circumstances it is apt to recur. When, as so often happens, an obsessional idea has not succeeded in establishing itself permanently, the task of clearing it up is correspondingly simplified. We can easily convince ourselves that, when once the interconnections between an obsessional idea and the patient's experiences have been discovered, there will be no difficulty in obtaining access to whatever else may be puzzling or worth knowing in the pathological structure we are dealing with—its meaning, the mechanism of its origin, and its derivation from the preponderant motive forces of the patient's mind.

As a particularly clear example I will begin with one of the *suicidal impulses* which appeared so frequently in our patient. This instance almost analysed itself in the telling. He had once, he told me, lost some weeks of study owing to his lady's absence: she had gone away to nurse her grandmother, who was seriously ill. Just as he was in the middle of a very hard piece of work the idea had occurred to him: "If you received a command to take your examination this term at the first possible opportunity, you might manage to obey it. But if you were commanded to cut your throat with a razor, what then?" He had at once become aware that this command had already been given, and was hurrying to the cupboard to fetch his razor when he thought: "No, it's not so simple as that. You must[26] go and kill the old

[26] The sense requires that the word "first" should be interpolated here.

woman." Upon that, he had fallen to the ground, beside himself with horror.

In this instance the connection between the compulsive idea and the patient's life is contained in the opening words of his story. His lady was absent, while he was working very hard for an examination so as to bring the possibility of an alliance with her nearer. While he was working he was overcome by a longing for his absent lady, and he thought of the cause of her absence. And now there came over him something which, if he had been a normal man, would probably have been some kind of feeling of annoyance with her grandmother: "Why must the old woman get ill just at the very moment when I'm longing for *her* so frightfully?" We must suppose that something similar but far more intense passed through our patient's mind—an unconscious fit of rage which could combine with his longing and find expression in the exclamation: "Oh, I should like to go and kill that old woman for robbing me of my love!" Thereupon followed the command: "Kill yourself, as a punishment for these savage and murderous passions!" The whole process then passed into the obsessional patient's consciousness accompanied by the most violent affect and *in a reverse order*—the punitive command coming first, and the mention of the guilty outburst afterwards. I cannot think that this attempt at an explanation will seem forced or that it involves many hypothetical elements. . . .

(F) THE PRECIPITATING CAUSE OF THE ILLNESS

One day the patient mentioned quite casually an event which I could not fail to recognize as the precipitating cause of his illness, or at least as the immediate occasion of the attack which had begun some six years previously and had persisted to that day. He himself had no notion that he had brought forward anything of importance; he could not remember that he had ever attached any importance to the event; and moreover he had never forgotten it. Such an attitude on his part calls for some theoretical consideration.

In hysteria it is the rule that the precipitating causes of the illness are overtaken by amnesia no less than the infantile experiences by whose help the precipitating causes are able to transform their affective energy into symptoms. And where the amnesia cannot be complete, it nevertheless subjects the recent traumatic precipitating cause to a process of erosion and robs it at least of its most important components. In this amnesia we see the evidence of the repression which has taken place. The case is different in obsessional neuroses. The infantile preconditions of the neurosis may be overtaken by amnesia, though this is often an incomplete one; but the immediate occasions of the illness are, on the contrary, retained in the memory. Repression makes use of another, and in reality a simpler, mechanism. The trauma, instead of being forgotten, is deprived of its affective cathexis; so that what remains in consciousness is nothing but its ideational content, which is perfectly colourless and is judged to be unimportant. The distinction between what occurs in hysteria and in an obsessional neurosis lies in the psychological processes which we can reconstruct behind the phenomena; the *result* is almost always the same, for the colourless mnemonic content is rarely reproduced and plays no part in the patient's mental activity. In order to differentiate between the two kinds of repression we have on the surface nothing to rely upon but the patient's assurance that he has a feeling in the one case of having always known the thing and in the other of having long ago forgotten it. . . .[27]

[27] It must therefore be admitted that in an obsessional neurosis there are two kinds of knowledge, and it is just as reasonable to hold that the patient "knows" his traumas as that he does *not* know" them. For he knows them in that he has

But I must now return to a more detailed examination of the precipitating cause of our present patient's illness. His mother was brought up in a wealthy family with which she was distantly connected. This family carried on a large industrial concern. His father, at the time of his marriage, had been taken into the business, and had thus by his marriage made himself a fairly comfortable position. The patient had learnt from some chaff exchanged between his parents (whose marriage was an extremely happy one) that his father, some time before making his mother's acquaintance, had made advances to a pretty but penniless girl of humble birth. So much by way of introduction. After his father's death the patient's mother told him one day that she had been discussing his future with her rich relations, and that one of her cousins had declared himself ready to let him marry one of his daughters when his education was completed; a business connection with the firm would offer him a brilliant opening in his profession. This family plan stirred up in him a conflict as to whether he should remain faithful to the lady he loved in spite of her poverty, or whether he should follow in his father's footsteps and marry the lovely, rich, and well-connected girl who had been assigned to him. And he resolved this conflict, which was in fact one

not forgotten them, and he does not know them in that he is unaware of their significance. It is often the same in ordinary life. The waiters who used to serve Schopenhauer at his regular restaurant "knew" him in a certain sense, at a time when, apart from that, he was not known either in Frankfurt or outside it; but they did not "know" him in the sense in which we speak to-day of "knowing" Schopenhauer.—[In *Inhibitions, Symptoms and Anxiety* (1926d; Chapter XI, A (c)), Freud proposed that the term "repression" should be restricted in its use to the mechanism found at work in hysteria, and he re-introduced the term "defence" to cover *all* the various techniques employed in dealing with psychical conflicts. He would accordingly have written later "two kinds of *defence*" in the sentence in the text above instead of "two kinds of *repression*."]

between his love and the persisting influence of his father's wishes, by falling ill; or, to put it more correctly, by falling ill he avoided the task of resolving it in real life.[28]

The proof that this view was correct lies in the fact that the chief result of his illness was an obstinate incapacity for work, which allowed him to postpone the completion of his education for years. But the results of such an illness are never unintentional; what appears to be the *consequence* of the illness is in reality the *cause* or *motive* of falling ill.

As was to be expected, the patient did not, to begin with, accept my elucidation of the matter. He could not imagine, he said, that the plan of marriage could have had any such effects: it had not made the slightest impression on him at the time. But in the further course of treatment he was forcibly brought to believe in the truth of my suspicion, and in a most singular manner. With the help of a transference phantasy, he experienced, as though it were new and belonged to the present, the very episode from the past which we had forgotten, or which had only passed through his mind unconsciously. There came an obscure and difficult period in the treatment; eventually it turned out that he had once met a young girl on the stairs in my house and had on the spot promoted her into being my daughter. She had pleased him, and he pictured to himself that the only reason I was so kind and incredibly patient with him was that I wanted to have him for a son-in-law. At the same time he raised the wealth and position of my family to a level which agreed with the model he had in mind.

---

[28] It is worth emphasizing that his flight into illness was made possible by his identifying himself with his father. The identification enabled his affects to regress on to the residues of his childhood. [See Section G.—The phrase "flight into illness" had already been used by Freud in "Some General Remarks on Hysterical Attacks" (1909*a*), Section B.]

But his undying love for his lady fought against the temptation. After we had gone through a series of the severest resistances and bitterest vituperations on his part, he could no longer remain blind to the overwhelming effect of the perfect analogy between the transference phantasy and the actual state of affairs in the past. I will repeat one of the dreams which he had at this period, so as to give an example of his manner of treating the subject. He dreamt that *he saw my daughter in front of him; she had two patches of dung instead of eyes.* No one who understands the language of dreams will find much difficulty in translating this one: it declared that *he was marrying my daughter not for her "beaux yeux" but for her money.*

(G) THE FATHER COMPLEX AND THE SOLUTION OF THE RAT IDEA

From the precipitating cause of the patient's illness in his adult years there was a thread leading back to his childhood. He had found himself in a situation similar to that in which, as he knew or suspected, his father had been before *his* marriage; and he had thus been able to identify himself with his father. But his dead father was involved in his recent attack in yet another way. The conflict at the root of his illness was in essentials a struggle between the persisting influence of his father's wishes and his own amatory predilections. If we take into consideration what the patient reported in the course of the first hours of his treatment, we shall not be able to avoid a suspicion that this struggle was a very ancient one and had arisen as far back as in his childhood.

By all accounts our patient's father was a most excellent man. Before his marriage he had been a non-commissioned officer, and, as relics of that period of his life, he had retained a straightforward soldierly manner and a *penchant* for using downright language. Apart from those virtues which are celebrated upon every tombstone, he was distinguished by a hearty sense of humour and a kindly tolerance towards his fellow-men. That he could be hasty and violent was certainly not inconsistent with his other qualities, but was rather a necessary complement to them; but it occasionally brought down the most severe castigations upon the children, while they were young and naughty. When they grew up, however, he differed from other fathers in not attempting to exalt himself into a sacrosanct authority, but in sharing with them a knowledge of the little failures and misfortunes of his life with good-natured candour. His son was certainly not exaggerating when he declared that they had lived together like the best of friends, except upon a single point (p. 57). And it must no doubt have been in connection with that very point that thoughts about his father's death had occupied his mind when he was a small boy with unusual and undue intensity (p. 47), and that those thoughts made their appearance in the wording of the obsessional ideas of his childhood; and it can only have been in that same connection that he was able to wish for his father's death, in order that a certain little girl's sympathy might be aroused and that she might behave more kindly towards him (p. 55).

There can be no question that there was something in the sphere of sexuality that stood between the father and son, and that the father had come into some sort of opposition to the son's prematurely developed erotic life. Several years after his father's death, the first time he experienced the pleasurable sensations of copulation, an idea sprang into his mind: "This is glorious! One might murder one's father for this!" This was at once an echo and an elucidation of the obsessional ideas of his childhood. Moreover, his father, shortly before his death, had directly opposed what later became our patient's

dominating passion. He had noticed that his son was always in the lady's company, and had advised him to keep away from her, saying that it was imprudent of him and that he would only make a fool of himself. . . .

Starting from these indications and from other data of a similar kind, I ventured to put forward a construction to the effect that when he was a child of under six he had been guilty of some sexual misdemeanor connected with masturbation and had been soundly castigated for it by his father. This punishment, according to my hypothesis, had, it was true, put an end to his masturbating, but on the other hand it had left behind it an ineradicable grudge against his father and had established him for all time in his role of an interferer with the patient's sexual enjoyment.[29] To my great astonishment the patient then informed me that his mother had repeatedly described to him an occurrence of this kind which dated from his earliest childhood and had evidently escaped being forgotten by her on account of its remarkable consequences. He himself, however, had no recollection of it whatever. The tale was as follows. When he was very small—it became possible to establish the date more exactly owing to its having coincided with the fatal illness of an elder sister—he had done something naughty, for which his father had given him a beating. The little boy had flown into a terrible rage and had hurled abuse at his father even while he was under his blows. But as he knew no bad language, he had called him all the names of common objects that he could think of, and had screamed: "You lamp! You towel! You plate!" and so on. His father, shaken by such an outburst of elemental

[29] Compare my suspicions to a similar effect in one of the first sessions (p. 57).—[The importance of "constructions" such as this in the technique of psycho-analysis was discussed by Freud in one of his last papers (1937d).]

fury, had stopped beating him, and had declared: "The child will be either a great man or a great criminal!"[30] The patient believed that the scene made a permanent impression upon himself as well as upon his father. His father, he said, never beat him again; and he also attributed to this experience a part of the change which came over his own character. From that time forward he was a coward [p. 59]—out of fear of the violence of his own rage. His whole life long, moreover, he was terribly afraid of blows, and used to creep away and hide, filled with terror and indignation, when one of his brothers or sisters was beaten.

The patient subsequently questioned his mother again. She confirmed the story, adding that at the time he had been between three and four years old and that he had been given the punishment because he had *bitten* some one. She could remember no further details, except for a very uncertain idea that the person the little boy had hurt might have been his nurse. In her account there was no suggestion of his misdeed having been of a sexual nature.[31]

[30] These alternatives did not exhaust the possibilities. His father had overlooked the commonest outcome of such premature passions—a neurosis.

[31] In psycho-analyses we frequently come across occurrences of this kind, dating back to the earliest years of the patient's childhood, in which his infantile sexual activity appears to reach its climax and often comes to a catastrophic end owing to some misfortune or punishment. Such occurrences are apt to appear in a shadowy way in dreams. Often they will become so clear that the analyst thinks he has a firm hold of them, and will nevertheless evade any final elucidation; and unless he proceeds with the greatest skill and caution he may be compelled to leave it undecided whether the scene in question actually took place or not. It will help to put us upon the right track in interpreting it, if we recognize that more than one version of the scene (each often differing greatly from the other) may be detected in the patient's unconscious phantasies. If we do not wish to go astray in our judgement of their historical reality, we must above all bear in mind that people's "childhood memories" are

A discussion of this childhood scene will be found in the footnote, and here I will only remark that its emergence shook the patient for the first time in his refusal to believe that at some prehistoric period in his childhood he had been seized with fury (which had subsequently become latent) against the father whom he loved so much. I must confess that I had expected it to have a greater effect, for the incident had been described to him so often—even by his father himself—that there could be no doubt of its objective reality. But, with that capacity for being illogical which never fails to bewilder one in such highly intelligent people as obsessional neurotics, he kept urging against the evidential value of the story the fact that he himself could not remember the scene. And so it was only along the painful road of transference that he was able to reach a conviction that his relation to his father really necessitated the postulation of this unconscious complement. Things soon reached a point at which, in his dreams, his waking phantasies, and his associations, he began heaping the grossest and filthiest abuse upon me and my family, though in his deliberate actions he never treated me with anything but the greatest respect. His demeanour as he repeated these insults to me was that of a man in despair. "How can a gentleman like you, sir," he used to ask, "let yourself be abused in this way by a low, good-for-nothing fellow like me? You ought to turn me out: that's all I deserve." While he talked like this, he would get up from the sofa and roam about the room,—a habit which he explained at first as being due to delicacy of feeling: he could not bring himself, he said, to utter such horrible things while he was lying there so comfortably. But soon he himself found a more cogent explanation, namely, that he was avoiding my proximity for fear of my giving him a beating. If he stayed on the sofa he behaved like some one in desperate terror trying to save himself from castiga-

Footnote 31 continued

only consolidated at a later period, usually at the age of puberty; and that this involves a complicated process of remodelling, analogous in every way to the process by which a nation constructs legends about its early history. It at once becomes evident that in his phantasies about his infancy the individual as he grows up *endeavours to efface the recollection of his auto-erotic activities*; and this he does by exalting their memory-traces to the level of object-love, just as a real historian will view the past in the light of the present. This explains why these phantasies abound in seductions and assaults, where the facts will have been confined to auto-erotic activities and the caresses or punishments that stimulated them. Furthermore, it becomes clear that in constructing phantasies about his childhood, the individual *sexualizes his memories*; that is, he brings commonplace experiences into relation with his sexual activity, and extends his sexual interest to them—though in doing this he is probably following upon the traces of a really existing connection. No one who remembers my "Analysis of a Phobia in a Five-Year-Old Boy" [1909*b* . . .] will need to be told that it is not my intention in these remarks to detract from the importance which I have hitherto attached to infantile sexuality by reducing it to nothing more than sexual interests at the age of puberty. I merely wish to give some technical advice that may help to clear up a class of phantasy which is calculated to falsify the picture of infantile sexual activity.

It is seldom that we are in the fortunate position of being able, as in the present instance, to establish the facts upon which these tales of the individual's prehistoric past are based, by recourse to the unimpeachable testimony of a grown-up person. Even so, the statement made by our patient's mother leaves the way open to various possibilities. That she did not proclaim the sexual character of the offence for which the child was punished may have been due to the activity of her own censorship; for with all parents it is precisely this sexual element in their children's past that their own censorship is most anxious to eliminate. But it is just as possible that the child was reproved by his nurse or by his mother herself for some commonplace piece of naughtiness of a non-sexual nature, and that his reaction was so violent that he was castigated by his father. In phantasies of this kind nurses and servants are regularly replaced by the superior figure of the mother. A deeper interpretation of the patient's dreams in relation to this episode revealed the clearest traces of the presence in his mind of an imaginative production of a positively epic character. In this his sexual desires for his mother and sister and his sister's premature death were linked up with the young hero's chastisement at

his father's hand. It was impossible to unravel this tissue of phantasy thread by thread; the therapeutic success of the treatment was precisely what stood in the way of this. The patient recovered, and his ordinary life began to assert its claims: there were many tasks before him, which he had already neglected far too long, and which were incompatible with a continuation of the treatment. I am not to be blamed, therefore, for this gap in the analysis. The scientific results of psycho-analysis are at present only a by-product of its therapeutic aims, and for that reason it is often just in those cases where treatment fails that most discoveries are made.

The content of the sexual life of infancy consists in auto-erotic activity on the part of the dominant sexual components, in traces of object-love, and in the formation of that complex which deserves to be called *the nuclear complex of the neuroses*. It is the complex which comprises the child's earliest impulses, alike tender and hostile, towards its parents and brothers and sisters, after its curiosity has been awakened—usually by the arrival of a new baby brother or sister. The uniformity of the content of the sexual life of children, together with the unvarying character of the modifying tendencies which are later brought to bear upon it, will easily account for the constant sameness which as a rule characterizes the phantasies that are constructed around the period of childhood, irrespective of how greatly or how little real experiences have contributed towards them. It is entirely characteristic of the nuclear complex of infancy that the child's father should be assigned the part of a sexual opponent and of an interferer with auto-erotic sexual activities; and real events are usually to a large extent responsible for bringing this about.

[The distinction between childhood memories and childhood phantasies preoccupied Freud throughout his career. See, for instance, his paper on "Screen Memories" (1899*a*). . . . His doubts as to the validity of childhood memories go back to 1897 (see his letter to Fliess of September 21, Letter 69 in Freud, 1950*a*), though his conclusions on this point were not published till many years later (Freud, 1906*a*). On the other hand, in some of his very last writings he insists that there is always a grain of historical truth behind apparently mythological phantasies. See, e.g., *Moses and Monotheism* (1939*a*), III, 2, *g*.—The term "nuclear complex" had already been used by Freud, but in another sense, in his paper on "The Sexual Theories of Children" (1908*c*). The term "Oedipus Complex" seems to have been first used by him in his published writings a little later, in the first of his "Contributions to the Psychology of Love" (1910*h*).]

tions of terrific violence; he would bury his head in his hands, cover his face with his arm, jump up suddenly and rush away, his features distorted with pain, and so on. He recalled that his father had had a passionate temper, and sometimes in his violence had not known where to stop. Thus, little by little, in this school of suffering, the patient won the sense of conviction which he had lacked—though to any disinterested mind the truth would have been almost self-evident.

And now the path was clear to the solution of his rat idea. The treatment had reached its turning-point, and a quantity of material information which had hitherto been withheld became available, and so made possible a reconstruction of the whole concatenation of events.

In my description I shall, as I have already said, content myself with the briefest possible summary of the circumstances. Obviously the first problem to be solved was why the two speeches of the Czech captain—his rat story [p. 49], and his request to the patient that he should pay back the money to Lieutenant A. [p. 50] —should have had such an agitating effect on him and should have provoked such violently pathological reactions. The presumption was that it was a question of "complexive sensitiveness,"[32] and that the speeches had jarred upon certain hyperaesthetic spots in his unconscious. And so it proved to be. As always happened with the patient in connection with military matters, he had been in a state of unconscious identification with his father, who had seen many years' service [p. 62] and had been full of stories of his soldiering days. Now it happened by chance—for chance may play a part in the formation of a symptom, just as the wording may help in the making of a joke—that one of his father's little adventures had an important element in common with the

captain's request. His father, in his capacity as non-commissioned officer, had control over a small sum of money and had on one occasion lost it at cards. (Thus he had been a *"Spielratte"*.[33]) He would have found himself in a serious position if one of his comrades had not advanced him the amount. After he had left the army and become well-off, he had tried to find this friend in need so as to pay him back the money, but had not managed to trace him. The patient was uncertain whether he had ever succeeded in returning the money. The recollection of this sin of his father's youth was painful to him, for, in spite of appearances, his unconscious was filled with hostile strictures upon his father's character. The captain's words, "You must pay back the 3.80 *kronen* to Lieutenant A.," had sounded to his ears like an allusion to this unpaid debt of his father's. . . .

In elucidating the effects produced by the captain's rat story we must follow the course of the analysis more closely. The patient began by producing an enormous mass of associative material, which at first, however, threw no light upon the circumstances in which the formation of his obsession had taken place. The idea of the punishment carried out by means of rats had acted as a stimulus to a number of his instincts and had called up a whole quantity of recollections; so that, in the short interval between the captain's story and his request to him to pay back the money, rats had acquired a series of symbolic meanings, to which, during the period which followed, fresh ones were continually being added. I must confess that I can only give a very incomplete account of the whole business. What the rat punishment stirred up more than anything else was his *anal erotism*, which had played an important part in his childhood and had been kept in activity for many years by a con-

32 [A term borrowed from the word-association experiments of Jung and his school (Jung, 1906). . . .]

33 [Literally, "play-rat." Colloquial German for "gambler."]

stant irritation due to worms. In this way rats came to have the meaning of *"money."*[34] The patient gave an indication of this connection by reacting to the word *"Ratten"* ["rats"] with the association *"Raten"* ["instalments"]. In his obsessional deliria he had coined himself a regular rat currency. When, for instance, in reply to a question, I told him the amount of my fee for an hour's treatment, he said to himself (as I learned six months later): "So many florins, so many rats." Little by little he translated into this language the whole complex of money interests which centered round his father's legacy to him; that is to say, all his ideas connected with that subject were, by way of the verbal bridge *"Raten—Ratten,"* carried over into his obsessional life and brought under the dominion of his unconscious. Moreover, the captain's request to him to pay back the charges due upon the packet served to strengthen the money significance of rats, by way of another verbal bridge *"Spielratte,"* which led back to his father's gambling debt [p. 66].

But the patient was also familiar with the fact that rats are carriers of dangerous infectious diseases; he could therefore employ them as symbols of his dread (justifiable enough in the army) of *syphilitic infection.* This dread concealed all sorts of doubts as to the kind of life his father had led during his term of military service. Again, in another sense, the *penis* itself is a carrier of syphilitic infection; and in this way he could consider the rat as a male organ of sex. It had a further title to be so regarded; for a penis (especially a child's penis) can easily be compared to a *worm,* and the captain's story had been about rats burrowing in some one's anus, just as the large round-worms had in his when he was a child. Thus the penis significance of rats was based, once more, upon anal erotism. And apart from this, the rat is a dirty animal, feeding

upon excrement and living in sewers.[35] It is perhaps unnecessary to point out how great an extension of the rat delirium became possible owing to this new meaning. For instance, "So many rats, so many florins" could serve as an excellent characterization of a certain female profession which he particularly detested. On the other hand, it is certainly not a matter of indifference that the substitution of a penis for a rat in the captain's story resulted in a situation of intercourse *per anum,* which could not fail to be especially revolting to him when brought into connection with his father and the woman he loved. And when we consider that the same situation was reproduced in the compulsive threat which had formed in his mind after the captain had made his request [p. 50], we shall be forcibly reminded of certain curses in use among the Southern Slavs.[36] Moreover, all of this material, and more besides, was woven into the fabric of the rat discussions behind the screen-association *"heiraten"* ["to marry"].

The story of the rat punishment, as was shown by the patient's own account of the matter and by his facial expression as he repeated the story to me, had fanned into a flame all his prematurely suppressed impulses of cruelty, egoistic and sexual alike. Yet, in spite of all this wealth of material, no light was thrown upon the meaning of his obsessional idea until one day the Rat-Wife in Ibsen's *Little Eyolf* came up in the analysis, and it became impossible to escape the inference that in many of the shapes assumed by his obsessional deliria rats had another meaning still—namely,

---

[34] See my paper on "Character and Anal Erotism" (1908*b*).

[35] If the reader feels tempted to shake his head at the possibility of such leaps of imagination in the neurotic mind, I may remind him that artists have sometimes indulged in similar freaks of fancy. Such, for instance, are Le Poitevin's *Diableries érotiques.*

[36] The exact terms of these curses will be found in the periodical *Anthropophyteia* [2, (1905), 421 ff.], edited by F. S. Krauss.

that of *children*.[37] Enquiry into the origin of this new meaning at once brought me up against some of the earliest and most important roots. Once when the patient was visiting his father's grave he had seen a big beast, which he had taken to be a rat, gliding along over the grave.[38] He assumed that it had actually come out of his father's grave, and had just been having a meal off his corpse. The notion of a rat is inseparably bound up with the fact that it has sharp teeth with which it gnaws and bites. But rats cannot be sharp-toothed, greedy and dirty with impunity: they are cruelly persecuted and mercilessly put to death by man, as the patient had often observed with horror. He had often pitied the poor creatures. But he himself had been just such a nasty dirty little wretch, who was apt to bite people when he was in a rage, and had been fearfully punished for doing so. He could truly be said to find "a living likeness of himself" in the rat. It was almost as though Fate, when the captain told him his story, had been putting him through an association test: she had called out a "complex stimulus-word," and he had reacted to it with his obsessional idea.

According, then, to his earliest and most momentous experiences, rats were children. And at this point he brought out a piece of information which he had kept away from its context long enough, but which now fully explained the interest he was bound to feel in children. The lady, whose admirer he had been for so many years,

but whom he had nevertheless not been able to make up his mind to marry, was condemned to childlessness by reason of a gynaecological operation which had involved the removal of both ovaries. This indeed—for he was extraordinarily fond of children—had been the chief reason for his hesitation.

It was only then that it became possible to understand the inexplicable process by which his obsessional idea had been formed. With the assistance of our knowledge of infantile sexual theories and of symbolism (as learnt from the interpretation of dreams) the whole thing could be translated and given a meaning. When, at the afternoon halt (during which he had lost his pince-nez), the captain had told him about the rat punishment, the patient had only been struck at first by the combined cruelty and lasciviousness of the situation depicted. But immediately afterwards a connection had been set up with the scene from his childhood in which he himself had bitten some one. The captain—a man who could defend such punishments—had become a substitute for his father, and had thus drawn down upon himself a part of the reviving animosity which had burst out, on the original occasion, against his cruel father. The idea which came into his consciousness for a moment, to the effect that something of the sort might happen to some one he was fond of, is probably to be translated into a wish such as "You ought to have the same thing done to you!" aimed at the teller of the story, but through him at his father. A day and a half later,[39] when the captain had handed him the packet upon which the charges were due

[37] Ibsen's Rat-Wife must certainly be derived from the legendary Pied Piper of Hamelin, who first enticed away the rats into the water, and then, by the same means, lured the children out of the town, never to return. So too, Little Eyolf threw himself into the water under the spell of the Rat-Wife. In legends generally the rat appears not so much as a disgusting creature but as something uncanny—as a chthonic animal, one might almost say; and it is used to represent the souls of the dead.

[38] It was no doubt a weasel, of which there are great numbers in the Zentralfriedhof [the principal cemetery] in Vienna.

[39] Not that evening, as he first told me. It was quite impossible that the pince-nez he had ordered could have arrived the same day. The patient shortened the interval of time retrospectively, because it was the period during which the decisive mental connections had been set up, and during which the repressed episode had taken place—the episode of his interview with the officer who told him of the friendly conduct of the young lady at the post office [p. 52].

and had requested him to pay back the 3.80 *kronen* to Lieutenant A. [p. 50], he had already been aware that his "cruel superior" was making a mistake, and that the only person he owed anything to was the young lady at the post office. It might easily, therefore, have occurred to him to think of some derisive reply, such as, "Will I, though?" or "Pay your grandmother!" or "Yes! You bet I'll pay him back the money!"—answers which would have been subject to no compulsive force. But instead, out of the stirrings of his father-complex and out of his memory of the scene from his childhood, there formed in his mind some such answer as: "Yes! I'll pay back the money to A. when my father and the lady have children!" or "As sure as my father and the lady can have children, I'll pay him back the money!" In short, a derisive affirmation attached to an absurd condition which could never be fulfilled.[40]

But now the crime had been committed; he had insulted the two persons who were dearest to him—his father and his lady. The deed had called for punishment, and the penalty had consisted in his binding himself by a vow which it was impossible for him to fulfil and which entailed literal obedience to his superior's ill-founded request. The vow ran as follows: "*Now you must really pay back the money to A.*" In his compulsive obedience he had repressed his better knowledge that the captain's request had been based upon erroneous premises: "Yes, you must pay back the money to A., as your father's surrogate has required. Your father cannot be mistaken." So too the king cannot be mistaken; if he

addresses one of his subjects by a title which is not his, the subject bears that title ever afterwards. . . .

We should not be justified in expecting such severe obsessional ideas as were present in this case to be cleared up in any simpler manner or by any other means. When we reached the solution that has been described above, the patient's rat delirium disappeared. . . .

REFERENCES

Freud, S. 1894a: "The Neuro-Psychoses of Defence," *Col. Papers*, 1924–1950, *1*, 59; *Stan. Ed.*, 1953, *3*.
1899a: "Screen Memories," *Col. Papers*, 5, 47; *Stan. Ed.*, 3.
1908b: "Character and Anal Erotism," *Col. Papers*, 2, 45; *Stan. Ed.*, 9.
1908c: "On the Sexual Theories of Children," *Col. Papers*, 2, 59; *Stan. Ed.*, 9.
1909a: "Some General Remarks on Hysterical Attacks," *Col. Papers*, 2, 100; *Stan. Ed.*, 9.
1909b: "Analysis of a Phobia in a Five-Year-Old Boy," *Col. Papers*, 3, 149; *Stan. Ed.*, 10, 3.
1910h: "A Special Type of Choice of Object Made by Men," *Col. Papers*, 4, 192; *Stan. Ed.*, 11.
1912e: "Recommendations to Physicians Practising Psycho-Analysis," *Col. Papers*, 2, 323; *Stan. Ed.*, 12.
1925h: "Negation," *Col. Papers*, 5, 181; *Stan. Ed.*, 19.
1926d: *The Problem of Anxiety*, New York, 1936; *Stan. Ed.*, 20.
1937d: "Constructions in Analysis," *Col. Papers*, 5, 358; *Stan. Ed.*, 23.
1950a: *The Origins of Psycho-Analysis*, London & New York, 1954. Partly, including "A Project for a Scientific Psychology," in *Stan. Ed.*, 1.
Jung, C. G., Ed. 1906: *Studies in Word-Association*, London.

[40] Thus absurdity signifies derision in the language of obsessional thought, just as it does in dreams. See my *Interpretation of Dreams* [1900a, Chapter VI, Section G; *Standard Ed.*, 5, 444–445].

Chapter 4
Modern Psychoanalysis

Dr. Boyer presents a case of the psychoanalysis of a young woman with a disorder more severe than the type of condition usually treated by psychoanalysis. The patient exhibits severe and distinct symptoms and also has more general problems in her life. She is very prone to regressive and self-destructive behavior. For many years Dr. Boyer has psychoanalyzed people with such severe disorders, and it may be said fairly that he is a leader among those attempting such treatments. The reader will note that the treatment focussed on providing a good object-relationship for the patient as a precondition for ego change. With such a difficult case, only after the early developmental issues are worked through sufficiently does attention turn to classic oedipal issues. Dr. Boyer offers himself (and his attitude of realistic, nonjudgmental, cautious optimism) as a figure with whom to identify. He appeals to the adult, realistic capacities of the patient. Especially noteworthy is his emphasis on the patient's aggression rather than her sexuality, which follows from his hypothesis that this is the major source of difficulty. Some further technical points of interest are his facilitation of the patient's curiosity about herself, his care to avoid activating undue psychotic anxiety in the patient, and his emphasis on her ability to be active and to analyze (i.e., "take care of") herself. At the end of the analysis, although it is technically incomplete, Dr. Boyer is satisfied because the patient is functioning much better, the primary symptom is understood, and the patient can analyze herself. The follow-up, however, demonstrates that some of the issues that Dr. Boyer felt were completely resolved at the end of the first treatment, were, indeed, still a source of difficulty. This case demonstrates well Freud's observation that even if analysis is successful, it is an "interminable" process.

Psychoanalytic Technique in the Treatment of Certain Characterological and Schizophrenic Disorders

L. BRYCE BOYER

In this communication a case fragment will be used to delineate a technique used in the treatment of certain characterological and schizophrenic disorders. It has evolved as a result of almost 20 years' use of psychoanalysis within the framework of the structural theory in the treatment of such conditions, without essential modification of procedures employed customarily with neurotics. I have avoided role-playing and resisted consistently patients' attempts to make me change my analytic stance. I have interpreted the psychotic and neurotic transference in their positive and negative aspects without the use of reassuring or formal educative techniques, never attempting to foster the so-called positive transference.

The case study which is abstracted here was chosen for two reasons. First, its course was smooth and the technique used demonstrates the most recent of an ever-developing series of modifications. In a sense this study is misleading because the progress of the patient was unusually even and the apparently successful result followed unusually quickly, the psychoanalysis having occupied just less than three years. No cure can be claimed because the analysis was terminated but a few months ago. Second, the patient presented an uncommon symptom complex, a variant of that described by Greenacre (1947) under the

From *International Journal of Psycho-Analysis*, 1971, *52*, 67–78, 83–85. Copyright © 1971 by the International Journal of Psycho-Analysis. Reprinted by permission.

rubric "vision, headache and the halo," which served the same defensive and adaptive purposes, the analysis of which was crucial to the therapeutic outcome.

CASE REPORT

The principal although not initial complaint of an attractive, highly intelligent 25-year-old woman was terrifying black sensations in her head, which had begun during her puberty. She had kept the symptom secret, fearing its discovery would lead to her being hospitalized as mad. The sensations did not make her dizzy but she always lay down while experiencing them, being apprehensive she might otherwise become lightheaded, fall, scream, babble, lose excretory control and reach a state of helplessness, requiring permanent care as if she were an infant. Although they were not mentioned during the first months of her analysis, she also had a number of phobias, some of which will be noted below.

General Information

She had gone through life smitten with guilt for infractions of an exceedingly high internal moral code and aspiring to be angelic in thought and deed. She had placed various people on pedestals, inevitably choosing individuals who disappointed her by being morally less than perfect, and had from her earliest memory felt unwanted and unloved and despised her parents, ostensibly because they argued, drank and lacked respect for one another.

During her high-school years she had considered herself to be fat and ugly and avoided opportunities for dates. She left her parents' home at nineteen for the first time to attend a university. While there, she could not concentrate on her studies. During her first term she became progressively withdrawn. She made no friends and felt the world to be unreal. She attended a few classes but became inexplicably frightened and soon found herself spending her days in women's rest rooms. There she would lie on sofas in a thoughtless trance-like state until other girls entered; then she would sit on a toilet seat cover until she was again alone. She was afraid if she were seen lying on the sofas, she would be reported and hospitalized as insane.

She failed a term and was placed on probation. During the next semester, a man who strongly resembled her father physically asked her to go on an automobile ride and she accepted her first date. She passively submitted to a kiss but was frightened when he sought to be more intimate. He became angry and excited and masturbated before her. She experienced the black sensation in her head and felt guilty because she had not permitted intercourse. She readily accepted a second date on which she refused intercourse but performed fellatio, being careful to remove her mouth before ejaculation. She experienced disgust and gagged. Soon thereafter she permitted intercourse and became pregnant. The gestation was greeted ambivalently. Her mother had expected her to become a school teacher, a career towards which she had sharply mixed feelings. She now had an excuse to marry and avoid further pursuit of that profession. At the same time, she feared her mother's wrath and abandonment. Once married, she studied subjects she enjoyed and was able to complete her college work with excellent grades, despite many hardships.

She found all sexual contact repugnant. Although before the marriage she found fellatio less disgusting than intercourse, now she could not tolerate oral-genital activities and usually refused intercourse. She was grossly but unwittingly exhibitionistic and seductive, but when her husband sought sexual relations she taunted him until he either raped or slapped her. Most frequently he responded to her provocation by masturbating before her; her observations of his manipulations produced the terrifying blackness in her head. She gradually slept less often with her husband and, although she was tall and their bathtub was short, chose to sleep in the tub, holding her arms about her as she was curled in a near-foetal position. When she held herself so, she entered a trance-like, thoughtless state and drifted to sleep.

It was later learned that her provocations of fights before sexual relations imitated what she either assumed or observed to be frequent actions of her parents when she was four to 13 years of age. During that period, her father often came home late at night intoxicated. Her mother responded by provoking a fight which the patient thought to have been followed by sexual relations during which her mother complained that she was disgusted.

When the patient's son was born, she transiently believed his birth to have been the result of parthenogenesis. Although the marriage pattern did not change, she felt she could not divorce "for religious reasons." Two years later, three events coincided. Her father died. His death came after a long illness and she felt nothing concerning his demise. During the course of her analysis, she maintained he had died for her years before and consistently denied grieving when he factually became deceased. A daughter was born and she once again believed briefly the birth to have been parthenogenetic. Soon thereafter, marital life became so miserable that her husband left the home and went to a different state to continue his education. Although she was relieved, she soon became depressed and, although she was a devoted mother, was sure she was neglecting her children. Concurrently appeared nightmares in which she was beaten or raped by her husband, a Negro or some middle-aged white man; they were followed by the black sensations. She progressively provoked strife with her mother-in-law, based on a conviction that mother-surrogate would take her children from her. Fearful she would go insane and harm her children psychologically, she sought treatment. Although the mother-in-law was paying for the analysis, she could not believe such largess was evidence of good will toward her, preferring to think it was a gift to her children. She considered herself to be schizophrenic and had heard that during treatment for that disorder, patients sometimes regressed. She reasoned that her mother-in-law thought she would become hopelessly insane during her treatment and then have reason to take the children.

Course of Treatment

The patient was referred for analysis by a colleague who had diagnosed her to be schizophrenic. She had seen him for marital counseling, complaining that her husband was brutal and preferred masturbation to intercourse. That analyst suggested that she might have provoked some of her husband's behaviour and she had responded with righteous indignation, needing to believe that she had been an innocent victim of his psychopathology. Yet when leaving that therapist's care in an apparent rage, she had requested analysis by me, having been told by a former patient that I treated schizophrenics and was "tough." I understood from this information that she feared she was insane, feared her capacity to act unwisely or impulsively and craved a strong superego and ego surrogate who would care enough for her to insist that she behave.

In the first interview, she spoke under pressure and her sentences were so disconnected that I understood much of what she meant only because of my knowledge of the products of primary-process thinking. She complained that she had been wronged by her husband and former therapist. Before I speak of my response to her, I shall present some of my ideas concerning what must be accomplished in the initial stages of dealing with such patients and the techniques I have developed to accomplish those goals.

In previous communications I have suggested that the primary task in treatment is to restore and/or develop within the patient a reasonable ego and superego, and that this can be accomplished by modifying or replacing cold, unloving and archaic introjects (Boyer, 1961, 1965a, 1966a, b; Boyer & Giovacchini 1967, Ch. 4). I have expressed the opinion that therapy must be directed towards the growth of intrapsychic and interpersonal communication techniques. I have come to believe that the most important initial step is the presentation to the analysand of a calm, patient, objective, implicitly optimistic attitude with which to identify, that of a person who does not respond with anxiety to reactions of panic or attempts at manipulation, but who treats each production of the patient, whether verbal or otherwise, as though it is important enough to heed, and who does not believe that the immediate satisfaction of urges is necessary. Although it is my viewpoint that the role of interpretation in the structuralizing of the ego (Boyer & Giovacchini, 1967, Ch. 6; Giovacchini, 1969) is the most important contribution psychoanalytic treatment has to make in the treatment of these conditions, I do not think that interpretation can be optimally effective until the cathexis of maladaptive introjects has lessened and healthier ones have begun to replace them.

Loewenstein (1956) has differentiated among three functions of speech: the cognitive, the expressive and the appeal functions. In the psychotic the second two functions predominate and it is the task of the analyst to respond to the appeal function only by interpretation, to transform the appeal function to the expressive function, by demonstrating to the patient that he expresses something about himself when he speaks of other persons or things. The analyst attempts to exclude both the functions of expression and appeal from his own speech. In my experience this effort on the part of the analyst should begin immediately and his using the cognitive mode which appeals to the patient's ego rather than his id reduces immediately the tenuousness of contact between analyst and analysand. Technically, I thus make contact through interpretation and direct my interpretative efforts to the surface, stressing the defensive nature of the patient's productions.

Believing that the patient craved control and feared herself to be insane, I appealed to her rationality by responding in the cognitive mode. Having understood her complaint that she was wronged by her husband and previous analyst to mean she feared she had provoked their behaviour, I told her that it seemed she was worried that she had a problem related to provocativeness for which she feared she should feel guilty. She was indignant and threatened not to return. I ignored this irrationality and again appealed to her ego, saying we could begin regular interviews the next day.

My instructions concerning the conditions of her treatment were that I would expect her to make a sincere effort to tell me whatever came to her mind and to keep me informed about emotional and physical experiences which occurred during the interviews, that I did not send statements but expected to be paid accurately during a specific interview of the month, that she would be charged for any cancellations unless her time were filled by another patient, and that I was generally absent several times yearly for short periods and once for an extended time. I have found with such patients that specific conditions offer needed ego and superego support.

In the second interview she was obvi-ously calmer and reassured. She said she should talk about her sexual problem, a problem previously unmentioned, but she could not do so. Therefore she would tell me about her past. During the next five interviews she recounted many dreams and events from early childhood and complained bitterly that she had never been loved. Her sentences were fragmented and frequently involved a series of loosely related subjects. There was a tendency towards clang associations. The material was laden with massive denials and contradictions. When she was confronted gently with obvious contradictions, she acknowledged them briefly and proceeded as though I had made no intervention. Highly cathected black and white oversimplifications were rife. The dreams all involved the themes of falling or flying and her associations were regularly of being abandoned. At the same time she said she had hated her parents. She complained that she had never been held even as an infant, and simultaneously said she could never tolerate being touched by either parent. She claimed that her mother and father had always drunk immoderately but also talked of her father's having been a successful businessman except for a short time and of her mother's puritanism. She claimed her parents had always argued loudly but remembered with scorn her mother's enjoyment in doing things for father. She averred she had feared that one parent would murder the other, although there were no physical fights, and yet had hoped for the death of either to spare her the terror she experienced while hearing their arguments. She maintained that her parents had no love for each other or any of their six children. She was the second, preceded by a brother two years older and succeeded by a sister one year younger and brothers three, five and seven years her junior. She complained that her sister and youngest brother had been parental favourites. Early memories also included scenes in which her elder brothers were beaten by the father for disobedience and one in which mother whipped her when she was about five years old because of exhibitionistic and voyeuristic play with the eldest brother.

In the sixth interview she said she would never lie on the couch, which had not been mentioned previously. Since she had presented so much material negatively, I understood this communication to mean she now felt sufficiently secure that she meant to lie on the couch. During those interviews I had been generally passive. Sometimes when she became very tense and was silent for some minutes, I suggested that she might be feeling embarrassment because of her awareness that some of her denials and gross contradictions were logically inconsistent. On three occasions, after I had made some simple, clear remarks, she asked me to repeat what I had said. I understood this to mean in part that she was testing to see whether I would humiliate her by responding as though she were truly incompetent and responded that she seemed to feel the need to view me as someone who didn't believe she could remember and make use of her memory (Hoedemaker, 1967). Each time she was obviously relieved, demonstrated she knew very well what I had said and temporarily relinquished speaking confusedly.

In the seventh interview she lay on the couch. She was frightened, blushed, alternately pressed her thighs tightly together and spread her legs slightly and manipulated the buttons and zippers on her modest dresses. She was frightened and complained for the first time of the black sensations in her head. It was obvious that she was having fantasies, whether conscious or unconscious, of sexual attack and seemed probable that the black sensations were associated with fantasies of seeing an erection. However, I chose to ignore the phallic or genital fantasies, merely asking for elaboration of her experience of the black sensations and obtaining some factual historical data pertaining to them.

Over the years I have come to the conclusion that to deal early with genital sexual material in the psychoanalysis of such patients is contra-indicated. With Rosenfeld (1966a, p. 353), I do not interpret apparently oedipal material on a libidinal level. Such a procedure is usually understood by the patient to be a seductive invitation from the analyst and stirs up acute psychotic excitement. The patient's anxiety increases regularly and frequently results in defensive regressive manoeuvers whenever he believes he has forced the therapist out of his analytic role. If I refer to such material, I do so from the standpoint of its aggressive and manipulative aspects, or interpret upwards, using a technique learned from Loewenstein in a seminar he conducted for candidates of the San Francisco Psychoanalytic Institute some 20 years ago. Thus, as an example, if the patient relates that he has open fantasies of intercourse with his mother, I respond that he must love her very much. I believe the patient who suffers from a severe characterological or schizophrenic disorder has massive fears of the vicissitudes of his aggressive impulses and that analysis proceeds smoothest when attention is directed gently but consistently towards the analysis of the protective manoeuvres he employs to defend against his fear that his hostility will result in the analyst's death or his own.

Thus after the patient lay down and manifested such fears of sexual involvement with the analyst as a parent surrogate I made no comment relating to this theme. When she remained silent for long periods and challenged me to prove that my silence did not mean I hated her, my remarks pointed at the projective aspects of her own hostility as manifested by her self-devaluation.

After the first few weeks, she no longer spoke of her past. Long periods of shivering silence were broken by highly emotional accounts of her present interpersonal difficulties, all of which she attributed to the ill-will of whichever adults she contacted. She assumed that the alleged hostile treatment afforded her was due to her physical ugliness. She admitted no positive feelings towards anyone but her children and was sure they preferred their paternal grandmother to her. At the same time, preparing for possible future divorce, she quickly learned the necessary skills and found a fine job as a private secretary in an office where it appeared to the analyst that she was treated with deference and trust, but in which she felt she was slighted and scorned. It was impossible to obtain coherent information from her concerning any current event. A combination of causes contributed to the distorted reporting. She was apparently unaware of her provocativeness, misinterpreted others' gestures and expressions to indicate adverse opinions towards her and was terrified of reporting fantasies directly. Of course, she also was simultaneously convinced that the analyst read her mind and that his silence indicated his disgust with her; yet she consciously withheld information. It became apparent that she generally believed herself to be reporting actual occurrences accurately but that her perceptions of external events were grossly distorted because she projected unconscious sadomasochistic, voyeuristic and exhibitionistic wishes on to others. Before I speak of the technical procedure I chose to use at this time, I shall summarize its rationale.

By this time, although still frightened, the patient had begun to introject some degree of the analyst's attitude of calm and patient optimism and to feel that she might be worth saving. Whereas she had spoken previously only of despair concerning her future, she now uttered occasional words of hope. Earlier, she had felt panicked by frustration either within or outside the consultation room, but now she queried herself with the analyst's words, "What do you fear might happen if you do not get immediately what you want?" and was able to avoid a temper tantrum or withdrawal into a state of apparently thoughtless inactivity. Yet she still sought to have the analyst do all of her thinking and it was obvious she ascribed omniscience and omnipotence to him. The major problem which seemed to confront her analysis was the need to reach a therapeutic alliance. The development of such an alliance requires the patient to develop some distance from his problems and emotions, so that he can think about them as well as experience them. This woman was engaged in three principal kinds of behaviour which she did not understand. She massively projected parts of her own identity into others, she grossly misperceived external as well as intrapsychic events and she provoked hostility on the parts of others which she could then use to rationalize her own anger. It was obvious that she was re-enacting childhood behaviour, both living out and acting out. I use the words living out to mean repetitions of earlier behaviour which are not connected directly with the analytic situation and acting out to mean behaviour which attempts to solve through action transference problems. Rosenfeld (1966b) has recently discussed the relationship between acting out and the aggressive drive.

As stated above, I have concluded that in dealing with such patients interpretations should during the early stages of treatment be directed towards aggressive drive derivatives and that oedipal libidinal interpretations are generally useless if not actually damaging to treatment. I have also learned that gentle, consistent confrontations of the patient with his inconsistencies and misperceptions makes him curious about the meanings of his behaviour and thinking. On reviewing the case histories of my patients of recent years, I find I have been confronting them more and more with their misperceptions, inconsistencies and distortions of events in the consultation room and less with external events (Boyer, 1967a, pp. 192–4). Where the events are known to the analyst who can then remind the patient of what actually transpired, it is more difficult for the analysand to maintain the validity of his altered presentations. Simultaneously, the patient is in general eager to use the psychoanalyst as an ego and superego model. However, in this case, there was a special situation which made it seem optimal to direct the analysis toward the understanding of her defences against aggressive impulses, without focusing on her hostility towards the analyst.

From the outset there had been a split transference of grand proportions. She had almost no awareness of hostility towards me and the principal focus of her anger was her mother-in-law, so clearly a substitute for her mother. Lesser and more diffuse aggression was directed to other relatives and work colleagues. As stated previously, in general I believe interpretations to be most effective when they are directed towards the surface, i.e. towards what is closest to the patient's consciousness, in direct opposition to the viewpoint of many members of the Kleinian school (Avenburg, 1962; Segal, 1967). Ordinarily in my treatment of such cases, I focus from the beginning on the defensive aspects of aggressive drive behaviour which manifest themselves in the transference situation, by directing attention primarily to what transpires in the consultation room. In the present case, too, initially I thus focused my remarks. However, they were met with little more than ridicule and the patient's responses were usually directed towards the hostility of her mother-in-law. The bulk of that hostility, as I understand the situation, was projected from the patient, although some resulted as well from her provocative behaviour towards that rather unusually

kindly woman. I decided to follow her lead and exploit the split transference.

For the development of a therapeutic alliance, the patient must develop curiosity about himself. This woman seemed for some time to have very little. She maintained that she was and had been mistreated because of the innate hostility of others, their greed and desires to use her, and her imagined physical ugliness. I decided to direct our attention simultaneously in two directions. I mentioned her slips of the tongue, gestures, leaving the door ajar, periodic muscular tensions and manipulations of her clothes. Initially she was infuriated that I should call attention to such apparent trivia but then became interested in possible meanings of such phenomena and was pleased with herself when she could analyse them. Yet she did not extrapolate from her experience inside the consultation room to events outside. Thus I began to reconstruct aloud what I guessed might actually have occurred and then been misperceived in her encounters with relatives, work colleagues and especially her mother-in-law. She was at first outraged and panicked when I suggested that external events occurred in manners other than she had reported. Then, however, she checked my guesses and was amazed to find them to have been generally accurate. At the same time, she was relieved to discover that I could make errors. She thus began to view me as fallible and to know that her active cooperation was required for developing self-understanding. I also used another technical manoeuvre I have found to be of value.

A task of the treatment of such cases is to assist the patient in improving intrapsychic and interpersonal communication. In any psychoanalysis, betterment of intrapsychic communication is implicit. Not infrequently, with these patients, there is a lag in the improvement of the understanding of interpersonal messages. When a patient presents data in a manner which is influenced heavily by the primary process, in general I understand a large part of his message. Even when I think I comprehend all of what he has told me, I tell him I think I understand what he has sought to convey but ask him to tell me more about it in different words. He is simultaneously reassured that I have gleaned some of his meaning and frightened by my implicit statement that his message is obscure. He presents the material in a somewhat more logical manner. After some time, he begins to test his new manner of communication with people outside the office and is pleased to observe that he is better understood and has fewer interpersonal difficulties.

To return to the present case: subsequently, during a period of a few months, I reconstructed past events from her current actions both in the consultation room and from her interactions with others. She then began to consider the possibility that her past perceptions also had been awry and began to admit that she might have been treated less badly than she remembered. Thereupon her provocative livings out and actings out diminished and a solid working alliance was established. From the end of the first year, she actively conducted her treatment. One example of the correction of a current ongoing interaction follows.

As we noted earlier, during the first few months she was convinced that her mother-in-law was trying to take her children from her and that they preferred their paternal grandmother to her. When I guessed that she had been unwittingly provocative and then misinterpreted the mother-in-law's contributions to the strife between them, she gradually validated my notions positively. As she did so, she remembered how as a child of seven or eight she played secretly with her young brother, trying to nurse him on her body and investigating his genitals. With her typical use of denial and reversal, she recalled she had believed a brother to have

been her own child whom her mother had stolen. With the recollection of these memories, she gradually shifted her attitude towards her mother-in-law. They became friendly and cooperative. Simultaneously her fear that her children preferred their grandmother disappeared. As she renounced the previous attitude toward the older woman, she also repressed once again the memories of her activities with her youngest brother.

As the hostile components of her relationship with her mother-in-law were analysed, she was able gradually to focus on some hateful aspects of her behaviour towards me and the split transference disappeared, both positive and negative aspects being centred on me.

Let us turn to the vicissitudes of the black sensations in her head. When she first lay on the couch she behaved like a frightened girl who expected sexual attack. Although the temperature of the consultation room was fairly constant, she frequently became suddenly cold and complained bitterly that the analyst was secretly manipulating the heater and the air-conditioner in such a way to cause her physical sensations. A blanket was on the couch but she avoided touching it. I always worked in my shirt-sleeves. She was incredulous that I was not uncomfortable when she perceived the room to have become insufferably cold. When she entered the office, she looked only at my face and on many occasions it became obvious that while she knew in detail the contents of the room which she could see while lying down, she was consciously unaware of items in what she termed my half of the office. Her dreams provided information that she had registered unconsciously details of my dress and all of the office accoutrements. On various occasions, when she felt suddenly cold, she also experienced the black sensations. Interpretations indicating her to have romantic thoughts concerning the analyst were dismissed with indignation. Then the black sensations and experiences of sudden changes of temperature stopped. Because her symptoms had ceased without their having been understood I assumed she was engaging in some unreported acting out. Therefore I asked whether she was withholding information concerning her behaviour outside the office and she reported that she was having an affair but she could not bring herself to supply detailed information. She vigorously denied that she was attempting to protect herself from disturbing thoughts concerning the analyst but ceased the affair and had no further social engagements with men. She then became consciously aware of the contents of my half of the office. For some months there was no recurrence of the black sensations or the perceived temperature changes. During this period she rarely mentioned her husband except to complain when he was tardy in sending child support money. After she renounced her affair she said she had decided on divorce but then she did not mention further relations with her husband or whatever actions she might be taking pertaining to legal separation or divorce. Just before the cessation of the black sensations, she described them visually, saying the sensation was "like a ball of collected black strings, with the ends sticking out everywhere." Later she would say that each of the strings was the surface manifestation of a fantasy which had to be unravelled. From this time forward, she made the black sensations and their visualization a conscious focus of her analysis, attempting to relate most major associations to them.

During the first half of the second year of analysis she had a consistent pattern of activities preceding sleep. She lay on her side, knees drawn up, and hugged herself. Then she rocked herself, while visualizing being held and rocked in the analyst's arms like a baby. She felt blissful at such times and denied awareness of any sexual sensations or thoughts. The trance-like state formerly experienced without consci-

ous thought or feeling in the bathtub of the marital home was relived, but now with satisfying thought content and intense physical sensations of warmth and comfort in the upper half of her body. Gradually she began to have fantasies of nursing on the analyst's penis and she savoured the sensations of fullness in her mouth and the milk she sensed drinking from his penis. With no suggestion from the analyst, she consciously equated the penis with her mother's breast. She said she should be experiencing jealousy of her younger sibs, but that she could not recall them as nursing babies nor could she remember having ever seen her mother's breasts except in adult years, when they were flat and sagging. She said she thought she should also be experiencing some sexual feelings while visualizing sucking on the analyst's penis, but that she did not and she voluntarily steadfastly denied sexual desires directed at father, mother or analyst. She was happy and contented and the former feelings of having been discriminated against at work and elsewhere outside the consultation room, while conscious at times, were but superficially cathected. She often withheld information and recognized her behaviour as illogical but said it was her intention to prolong the analysis as long as she could, because she was happy for the first time in her life. She volunteered the information that the money she got from her mother-in-law to pay for her coming to see me was also equated with mother's milk and permission to be held by father but said she needed to have the experience of being loved and prized, even though she was aware that the fantasies and actions were entirely unreal in terms of actual expectations from the analyst or any other persons in her adult life. During this approximately six-month period the analyst waited and was almost totally silent, beyond responding to her greetings at the beginnings and ends of hours. Then came a change. However, before that alteration in behaviour and content is reported, I shall explain my rationale for remaining passive during the six-month period.

Hartmann (1939a) stressed the need of the presence of an average expectable environment for the unfolding of innate maturational tendencies and the differentiation of id and ego. We are accustomed to think of the serial development of the oral, anal, phallic and genital phases of psychosexual and psychosocial development.

The patients suffering from severe characterological or schizophrenic disorders whom I have analysed or am analysing number thirty. All had undergone obvious regressions, usually phenomenologically psychotic, at puberty, or subsequent periods when unresolved oedipal conflicts had been reawakened. Thus they had had environments which were sufficiently favourable to have permitted unfolding of the innate maturational phases. The predominant symptomatology reflected strong fixations, perhaps combined with developmental failures. In the analytic situation identificatory processes and the structuralizing effects of interpretations had resulted in the replacement of unhealthy introjects by more mature ones in the large majority of these patients. When pregenital problems had been more or less satisfactorily resolved, they were able to analyse phallic and genital conflicts with at least moderate success. These data suggest the optimistic but unproven supposition that such patients may in the therapeutic situation achieve a controlled and adaptive regression (Hartman, 1939b; Lindon, 1967; Winnicott, 1955) to a period which has attributes of a more optimal mother-infant relationship than existed when the patient was an infant; when such a relationship has developed, innate maturational tendencies can continue to unfold accompanied by alterations of the far-reaching effects of early learning, provided ill-timed actions of the psychoanalyst do not interfere. I hesitate to suggest that the

same may be true with patients who have remained autistic from infancy or had childhood psychoses which can be traced to failure of separation-individuation (Mahler, 1963; Mahler & Furer, 1960, 1963; Mahler & Settlage, 1959; Mahler & LaPerriere, 1965). I have no clinical material from which to draw conclusions.

The patient whose analysis provides the data for this communication appeared to have established a therapeutic alliance. She had the capacity to simultaneously regress and to observe and was curious to learn about herself. Her regressive behaviour was limited largely to her pre-sleep activities and the analytic room. Interpersonal relationships were steadily improving and she was handling family problems more realistically. She was being promoted rapidly in her work and had achieved a responsible position. I was comfortable with her continuous period of regression and thought it to be advisable for her to have time to experience the sense of well being she seemed to need, inasmuch as there was continuous evidence of improvement.

Although during the analysis until this time she had avoided touching the blanket which lay on the couch at her side, she now began to contemplate covering herself to experience in the office the pre-sleep experiences she had so repetitiously described. As she did so, the black sensations recurred, but with diminished intensity and scant fright. Rather, they were viewed as interesting and to be investigated. She finally braved covering herself with the blanket and for a period relished the comfort of lying on the couch, visualizing being held by the analyst and sucking on his penis, which for the first time she pictured clearly as erect and circumcized as had been her brothers' and her husband's. She recognized the absurdity of her fantasy, since it involved her lying on the analyst's lap and she was but a little shorter than he. Then she began to feel sensations of bladder fullness, whether covered by the blanket or not. This was confusing to her. She had always urinated at home just before coming to the office and now she began also to use the toilet provided for patients. Then occurred episodes of watery diarrhoea for which no medical explanation was found, when she checked her fantasy that she had belated symptoms of amoebic dysentery from childhood trips to the tropics with her parents. She had always been mildly curious about the analyst's other female patients but now she became moderately interested in both male and female sibling surrogates. Then she became aware that while she had either sensations of urinary or faecal urgency while on the couch she was also sexually excited.

It will be recalled that previously, when she had the pre-sleep experiences in her home, she had felt warmth only in the upper half of her body. Genital sensations remained repressed. Apparently the experiencing and analysis of her period of regression had served the purpose of removing repressions and structuralizing some needs. Whereas bladder, anal and vaginal sensations had previously remained at least in part fused, now she was able to separate them.

There had been no conscious sexual excitation for many months. She now revealed that she had never knowingly touched herself between her legs from the age of five or six years except to cleanse herself or care for menstrual discharge. Before analysis she had suffered from dysmenorrhoea and profuse flow, but while she was living out the fantasy of being held and nursed she had felt no menstrual discomfort and excessive flow had been rare. Now the menstrual symptoms recurred. She found herself tempted to explore her genitals with her hands. In contrast to her previous blissful serenity while in the analyst's presence, she became fearful that he disliked her and would abandon her were she to touch her genitals. For months she had not reported dreams. Now recurred nightmares in which there were violent attacks performed on her by men, with mutilation and bleeding. The manifest content gradually changed so that genital mutilation took place, at first caused by knives and then the insertion of huge instruments. She thought that as a child she must have feared sexual assault by her eldest brother, but she could remember only their handling each other and exhibiting themselves. Eventually she decided that she should explore her genitals. She said: "The ends of the strings are sticking out and I want to see whether I can unravel them."

She began to explore her genitals and rectum with her fingers. She found herself putting all of the fingers of both hands into either orifice and stretching it. She remembered in detail much sexual play during her third to sixth years, principally actions which took place while she was alone in the bathtub. She was convinced that she had then stretched both the vagina and rectum and inserted various objects, including the nursing bottle of her younger brother, a cream bottle, a lipstick and a tube of toothpaste, the contents of which she alternately squeezed into her vagina or rectum or ate. Always aware of hatred and envy for her younger sister, whom she felt to be favoured by both parents, now, via highly cathected fantasies of the analyst's sexual involvement with his other female patients, she remembered intense childhood jealousy and an attempt at murdering her rival.

One of the phobias with which she had come to analysis was that of going into dark places either while alone or with a man. During the early weeks of analysis she had recalled that at the age of six her father had been angry with her because she was afraid to go to the basement to get food for her mother and had dragged her into the cellar over her screaming protests, presumably to show her there was nothing to fear. In the version then presented, father had been drunk and mother had stood by while he buffeted the child.

This memory now recurred but in a different light. She recalled that prior to that time she had eagerly gone to the basement and had enjoyed sitting on the washing machine while it was hot and vibrating. On one occasion she had taken with her a lipstick, painted her genital area and then been spanked by her mother. In her reconstruction of what might have led to this behaviour, she supposed that she had used the lipstick to make her genitals more attractive to father, equating mouth and vagina, and that the red colouring had also been a substitute for blood which she had supposed was the result of some activity between her parents. After she presented these data which preceded her father's taking her to the basement, she remembered that her father had been listening to a romantic opera, one of his favourites, and she had disturbed him to request that he help her look for a toy she thought she had left in the basement. He had reluctantly agreed, whereupon she became panicky he would beat or sexually attack her. Because he was angry that she had interrupted him, he insisted she go with him.

She could not recall having ever seen her mother naked or pregnant, or evidence of menstruation. Her father had been a successful businessman during her early years and apparently respected by mother. However, when she was four or five, he became an inveterate drinker for some years. Mother during that period had been the efficient member of the household. The patient now hypothesized, but did not remember, that she had equated mother's efficiency with the acquisition of father's penis and had thought babies to have been transformations of the stolen penis, which could emerge either in the form of faecal sticks or infants. She finally wondered whether she had ever seen either of her parents naked.

During the next few interviews black sensations recurred frequently but were accompanied by little anxiety. At times the black strings were visualized as the heads of snakes which could bite and swallow. She then recalled with embarrassment having at three or four years of age tried to nurse on a bitch, shoving the puppies aside, and got black hair in her mouth. Thereupon she spoke for the first time of lifelong fears of snakes and spiders in terms of oral-genital fantasies in which she equated pubic hair and penises which could bite. She said those fears were gone and I never heard of them again. Then, while she was visualizing the black mass in her head, it began to jump up and down and assumed the form of a huge black phallus.

She had mentioned rarely that there had been a Negro maid in the family all during her childhood. Now she said she had wondered whether that woman were her true mother and remembered having seen the maid's pubic hair while she was urinating and been awestruck. She remembered also that throughout her analysis at various times when she was not in the office she had visualized an erection and experienced the black sensations. She had meant to inform me but had forgotten. Finally she said she thought she recalled walking into her parents' bedroom and seeing her father alone, in profile and naked. She had been four years old at the time and her mother was pregnant with her second youngest brother. The interview which will now be related in detail occurred a week later.

She entered the office looking amused and said she thought she now understood the meaning of the black sensations in her head. She remembered a dream which had surprised her because she'd not thought of her husband for several weeks. Their divorce had become final some months previously. She said:

My husband had a baby, probably literally had a baby. He carried it around as a little girl would a doll she liked. I talked to him or to you as I stood before a mirror. I squeezed blackheads out of my face and each time one came out I'd say: "This is to show you that I'm not afraid of such and such." He carted the baby around. I was somehow in the picture. He also had an enormous penis, at least twice as big as his erection, that is, twice as long.

At this point in the interview she wrapped a facial tissue around her index finger like a bandage.

There were about 20 of me and I remember having intercourse over and over again. No. I just remember the feeling of his penis outside of me while he held me. His penis was white and shining and there were no hairs. It was like Jesus' would be if He had one. I was as surprised and awestruck as those three little girls must have been in Portugal when they saw the Virgin Mary. It was a miracle. I can't remember actually seeing the erection so much as seeing it glow. I was really astonished the first time I saw and felt my husband's erection, it was so long and hard.

She now found herself tearing the tissue to shreds, and continued:

I feel like an animal in a cage. I wish the hour would end so I wouldn't have to use another piece of tissue and make a bandage of it and tear it up, too. I think I'm playing with it instead of masturbating. Now I have to go to the bathroom. I couldn't masturbate here and I dislike even wanting to. Now I want to put my hands in my mouth. It would feel good to make my mouth bigger and take all of that huge penis inside. Now I want to spit. When he shoved his penis in my mouth I gagged and gagged. I was trying to get all of it inside me and swallow it. Maybe I wanted to have a penis after my brother was born, and then believed I'd had my brother all by myself. I'm not confused about my father and his penis any more. I'm confused about my mother. How did I grad-

uate from wanting to suck on a breast to wanting to suck on a penis? My mother was so capable that I thought she must have a penis, too, and that both men and women could have babies all by themselves. I'm glad I no longer believe I *am* a penis and I want to lose the idea I have a penis somewhere. I've always feared my clitoris would grow into a real penis. I was afraid my mother would catch me in the bathtub when I'd rub on it and make it hard. Maybe she'd see it and take it away and then I couldn't have babies all alone.

During the interviews of the next two weeks her productions were limited largely to attempts to understand the dream. She saw the blackheads as representing the black ends which stuck out from the ball of tangled strings. She recalled vividly and with much abreaction her invasion of the parental bedroom. Her father had been alone, standing in the lighted closet of an otherwise darkened room. She was convinced she had seen his erection in profile and was awestruck. As she spoke of the experience she had to urinate and saw light in her head. She was sure she had experienced the sensation of a great light in her head when she had viewed father, had felt dazed and intense urinary urgency. She had groped her way to the toilet and "almost blacked out." She had as an older child seen a brother masturbating. Now she thought that she had then decided unconsciously her father had been masturbating and subsequently tried to provoke men to masturbate before her, hoping that they, as father-surrogates, would rape her. When the son with whom mother was pregnant was born, the patient believed the child to be her own. She thought but did not clearly remember that when mother was big with pregnancy, the patient had become seriously constipated and that she finally had a large bowel movement when mother went to the hospital to have the baby. When her own son was born her experience had been that of having a large bowel movement. She had thought that girls were born with penises but that some injury cut the penis off, leaving only an internal stub which might grow into large penis once again. An alternative hypothesis had been that a woman could obtain the penis during intercourse, by biting it off either with her mouth or her vagina.

During this period she did not mention some ideas she had presented as theoretical during earlier interviews. However, she presented all the recollections from childhood with vividness and conviction. Other data were offered but their presentation here would be redundant. One item perhaps deserves emphasis. During the time when she had been living contentedly in the fantasy of nursing on my penis, there had occurred a series of interviews in which she found herself lying rigidly on the couch. She then had dreams the manifest content of which had been a little girl sitting on her father's lap and gradually standing erect and stiff. She now offered the interpretation, with no hesitation or even wonderment, that she must have imagined that she was father's penis. She thought she recalled that while she lay on the sofas while a freshman in college, she must have been trying to allay her fears she was displeasing her father through failing at school, by imagining she was his erection and therefore his prized possession.

In adolescence she had grown very fast and was quite tall. She had also suffered from acne and was especially ashamed of blackheads. From her early teens she had been convinced a reason she was disliked and mistreated was because she was fat and her skin was ugly. After the acne disappeared, her skin remained a bit oily. While she was analysing the dream she admitted she had never been overweight. She decided that she had equated being tall with father's erection and had displaced her concern about her height on to being fat, equating obesity and pregnancy. The blackheads were equated with the snake-

penises and were also evidence that she was pregnant. After this bit of analysis, she was no longer unduly concerned about her physical appearance.[1]

The recovery of the visual trauma of seeing father's erection was the last major step in this woman's analysis, which lasted only a few months more. There were few and barely cathected recurrences of the black sensations, her self-depreciation disappeared, she increased even further her capacity to perceive correctly events in which she became involved and became a happy and confident woman. A last fear was recognized and resolved. As noted earlier, when she began analysis, upon entry into the consultation room she looked only at the analyst's face and did not consciously record office accoutrements in his "half of the room." Although she gradually became able to see those objects, before the recovery of the visual trauma she remained able to look only at the analyst's face. During the analysis, on various occasions interruptions during her interviews had required the analyst to walk past her and on each occasion she had sat up as he arose to go to the door. When her actions had been questioned, she had responded vaguely. Now another interruption took place and she remained supine. She became consciously aware that she had been avoiding looking at the front of his trousers and then that she had gone through life afraid to satisfy a wish to look for evidence that a man had an erection.

As mentioned before, during one period of her analysis she had had a brief affair with a man of the age of her father when he died [and as she thought her analyst to have]. Subsequently she had accepted no dates although she had opportunities. After

---

[1] This fantasy of childbirth through the skin in the form of blackheads resembles that of a former patient, who believed his mother bore children through blisters induced by the applications of suction cups in the treatment of pneumonia (Boyer, 1959) and that of an author who had babies come from carbuncles (White, 1949).

the recovery of the memory of having viewed father naked, she continued to work through her transference neurosis in oedipal terms. Then she established a highly pleasing alliance with a man who was eminently suitable to be her children's foster-father. Their sexual relations were very gratifying to her.

Throughout her treatment there had been frequent, usually brief interruptions due to the analyst's absence. In the first two years her anxiety was analysed in terms of oral-sadistic fears and impulses. Her relationship with the new partner had its beginning two months before another planned absence of the analyst, of two months' duration. Just before the separation, she tried to provoke the lover to leave her, using what seemed to me to have been largely voluntary misperceptions of his communications to her. I suggested she was seeking to get him to leave her because she had wanted me to be jealous and to have punished her through means of my absence. During the separation she got along well with her lover. On my return, we analysed further the meaning of her behaviour. Her use of regression was understood as a defence against the separation and an attempt to deny that some aspects of her love for the analyst were based principally on transference elements.

During the analysis of the transference neurosis in oedipal terms it became clear that the visual trauma at the age of four had resulted in an attempt to master the psychic injury through the simultaneous use of a number of manoeuvres. Regression, denial, repression and reversal had been used to defend against hostility pertaining to genital sensations and desires. Simultaneously that erotized aggression was discharged unsatisfactorily and guiltily through repetitious reenactments of the original trauma with her eldest brother who became her father-surrogate. There had been an uneven and precocious development of a sadistic superego. While engaging in much voyeuristic and exhibition-

istic behaviour, she had provoked punishments from her mother. At the same time she had identified both with the phallus of the father and the pregnancy of the mother. Her fears the mother had stolen her baby were now understood as a denial and reversal of her wish to steal mother's babies and supplant mother as the wife of father. Scant material emerged which could lead to convincing awareness of a theme which was implicit in much of the data, her wish to supplant her father in his relations with mother.

During the last months of her analysis, yet another vicissitude manifested itself with regard to the black sensations in her head. While resolving the oedipal aspects of her transference neurosis, she spoke of fantasies of having intercourse with the analyst while in fact having sexual relations with her fiancé. Previously her preoccupation with the analyst's penis had been concerned with its use as a substitute breast. Now, while visualizing the analyst as a genital father-surrogate, the black sensations recurred, although with scant emotional involvement. Over a period of some weeks she repeatedly saw the skein of black threads and as she divested herself of unwanted ego and superego traits she had introjected from various family members, she saw herself pulling out individual black threads and discarding them. Thus the black threads were seen as introjects.

Her relationship with her fiancé seemed to be solid. She felt secure and had scant impetus to continue her analysis. Marriage arrangements were set and she wanted to enter into the new nuptial state without interference from a continued relationship with her analyst. It seemed fruitless to continue the analysis, although likely that there had been inadequate actual recall of primal scene and toilet-training experiences, and of her implied prolonged fantasy that she had been the analyst's penis. My reasoning was that she would return for further analysis should further difficulties prove to be particularly troublesome.

One phenomenon which has evidenced itself led me to be optimistic. She had given evidence that she either had an unusual capacity to analyse consciously without reporting the steps of her analytic activity, or preconsciously. It will be remembered that she had reported certain fears or phobias only after they had disappeared.

DISCUSSION

The material which has been offered could be discussed from many viewpoints. However, the principal aim of this communication is to illustrate a technique for treating certain patients who suffer from characterological, schizophrenic and schizoaffective disorders. A technical approach depends upon a theoretical orientation. . . .

SUMMARY

A technique for the treatment within the framework of the structural theory of certain characterological, schizophrenic and schizoaffective disorders has been presented through the presentation of a fragment of an analysis in which have been interpolated explanatory remarks. Problems pertaining to diagnosis have been discussed. The analysand had a symptom complex, a visual trauma followed by sensations of blackness in the head and the development of a figurative halo, strongly reminiscent of the syndrome described by Greenacre: vision, headache and the halo. The symptom-complex had similar origins and psychological uses as that of Greenacre's patients. Its analysis was crucial to the apparently satisfactory result which was achieved in an unusually short time.

REFERENCES

Abraham, K. (1913). Restrictions and transformations of scoptophilia in psychoneurotics; with remarks on analogous phenomena in folk-psychology. *Selected Papers on Psychoanalysis*. London: Hogarth Press, 1948.

Aray, J. (1968). Discussion of present paper. (Meeting of Grupo Venezolano de Estudios Psicoanaliticos, Caracas.)

Arlow, J. A. & Brenner, C. (1964). *Psychoanalytic Concepts and the Structural Theory*. New York: Int. Univ. Press.

Avenburg, R. (1962). Modificaciones estructurales en un paciente esquizofrénico a través del primer mes de análisis. *Rev. Psicoanál.* 19, 351–365.

Bellak, L. & Hurvich, M. (1969). A systematic study of ego functions. *J. nerv. ment. Dis.* 148, 569–585.

Bergman, P. & Escalona, S. K. (1949). Unusual sensitivities in very young children. *Psychoanal. Study Child* 3–4.

Boyer, L. B. (1956). On maternal overstimulation and ego defects. *Psychoanal. Study Child* 11.

Boyer, L. B. (1959). An unusual childhood theory of pregnancy. *J. Hillside Hosp.* 8, 279–283.

Boyer, L. B. (1961). Provisional evaluation of psycho-analysis with few parameters employed in the treatment of schizophrenia. *Int. J. Psycho-Anal.* 42, 389–403.

Boyer, L. B. (1965a). Tratamiento ambulatorio de pacientes esquizofrénicos. *Acta psiquiát. psicológ-América Latina* 11, 147–154.

Boyer, L. B. (1965b). Desarrollo historico de la psicoterapia psicoanalitica de las esquizofrenias: contribuciones de Freud. *Cuad. Psicoanál.* 1, 355–381.

Boyer, L. B. (1966a). Office treatment of schizophrenic patients by psychoanalysis. *Psychoanal. Forum* 1, 337–356.

Boyer, L. B. (1966b). Tratamiento de pacientes esquizofrénicos en consultorio: el uso de la terapia psicoanalitica con escasos parámetros. *Rev. Psicoanál.* 23, 287–317.

Boyer, L. B. (1966c). Desarrollo histórico de la terapia psicoanalítica de la esquizofrenia: contribuciones de los discipulos de Freud. *Rev. Psicoanal.* 23, 91–148.

Boyer, L. B. (1966d). La terapia psicoanalítica della schizofrenia. *Riv. Psicoanal.* 12, 3–22.

Boyer, L. B. (1967a). Author's reply. *Psychoanal. Forum* 2, 190–195.

Boyer, L. B. (1967b). Freuds Beitrag zur Psychotherapie der Schizophrenie. *Psyche* 21, 869–894.

Boyer, L. B. & Giovacchini, P. L. (1967). *Psychoanalytic Treatment of Schizophrenic and Characterological Disorders*. New York: Science House.

Fromm-Reichmann, F. (1939). Transference problems in schizophrenics. *Psychoanal. Q.* 8, 412–426.

Fromm-Reichmann, F. (1950). *Principles of Intensive Psychotherapy*. Chicago: Univ. of Chicago Press.

Frosch, J. (1964). The psychotic character: clinical psychiatric considerations. *Psychiat. Q.* 38, 81–96.

Garma, A. (1958). *El Dolor de Cabeza*. Buenos Aires: Nova.

Garma, A. (1968). Discussion of present paper. (Asociación Psicoanalítica Argentina, Buenos Aires.)

Giovacchini, P. L. (1958). Some effective meanings of dizziness. *Psychoanal. Q.* 27, 217–225.

Giovacchini, P. L. (1969). The influence of interpretation upon schizophrenic patients. *Int. J. Psycho-Anal.* 50, 179–186.

Glover, E. (1955). *The Technique of Psychoanalysis*. New York: Int. Univ. Press.

Greenacre, P. (1947). Vision, headache and the halo. *Trauma, Growth and Personality*. New York: Int. Univ. Press, 1952.

Greenacre, P. (1967). Discussion of present paper. (Meeting of Am. Psychoanal. Ass., New York.)

Grinker, R. R., Sr., Werble, B. & Dryf, R. C. (1968). *The Borderline Syndrome: A Behavioral Study of Ego-Functions*. New York and London: Basic Books.

Hartmann, H. (1939a). *Ego Psychology and the Problem of Adaptation*. New York: Int. Univ. Press, 1958.

Hartmann, H. (1939b). Psychoanalysis and the concept of health. *Essays on Ego Psychology*. New York: Int. Univ. Press, 1964.

Hoedemaker, E. D. (1967). Intensive psychotherapy of schizophrenia: an initial interview. *Can. Psychiat. Ass. J.* 12, 253–261.

Kernberg, O. (1967). Borderline personality organization. *J. Am. psychoanal. Ass.* 15, 641–685.

Lindon, J. A. (ed.) (1967). On regression: a workshop. *Psychoanal. Forum* 2, 293–316.

Little, M. (1958). On delusional transference (transference psychosis). *Int. J. Psycho-Anal.* 39, 134–138.

Little, M. (1966). Transference in borderline states. *Int. J. Psycho-Anal.* 47, 476–485.

Loewenstein, R. M. (1956). Some remarks on the role of speech in psychoanalytic technique. *Int. J. Psycho-Anal.* 37, 460–468.

Long, R. T. (1968). Discussion of present paper. (Meeting of Psychoanalysts of Southwest, San Antonio, Texas.)

Mahler, M. S. (1963). Thoughts about development and individuation. *Psychoanal. Study Child* 18.

Mahler, M. S. & Furer, M. (1960). Observations on research regarding the "symbiotic syndrome" of infantile psychosis. *Psychoanal. Q.* 29, 317–327.

Mahler, M. S. & Furer, M. (1963). Certain aspects of the separation-individuation phase. *Psychoanal. Q.* 32, 1–14.

Mahler, M. S. & LaPerriere, K. (1965). Mother–child interaction during separation-individuation. *Psychoanal. Q.* 34, 483–498.

Mahler, M. S. & Settlage, C. (1959). Severe emotional disturbances in childhood: psychosis. In S. Arieti (ed.), *American Handbook of Psychiatry,* vol. 1. New York: Basic Books.

Modell, A. H. (1963). Primitive object relationships and the predisposition to schizophrenia. *Int. J. Psycho-Anal.* 44, 282–292.

Paz, C. (1963). Ansiedades psicóticas: complejo de édipo y elaboración de la posición depresiva en un borderline. (Read to Associación Psicoanalítica Argentina, Buenos Aires.)

Pichon Rivière, E. (1951). Algunas observaciones sobre la transferencia en los pacientes psicóticos. *Rev. Psicoanál.* 18 (1961), 131–138.

Rangell, L. (1955). Panel report: The borderline case. *J. Am. psychoanal. Ass.* 3, 285–298.

Rosenfeld, H. A. (1954). Considerations regarding the psycho-analytic approach to acute and chronic schizophrenia. *Int. J. Psycho-Anal.* 35, 135–140.

Rosenfeld, H. A. (1966a). Discussion of paper by L. Bryce Boyer. *Psychoanal. Forum* 1, 351–353.

Rosenfeld, H. A. (1966b). Una investigación sobre la necesidad de "acting out" en los pacientes neuróticos y psicóticos durante el análisis. *Rev. Psicoanál.* 23, 424–437.

Schechtmann, J. (1968). Discussion of present paper. (Asociación Psicoanalítica Argentina, Buenos Aires.)

Schmideberg, M. (1959). The borderline patient. In S. Arieti (ed.), *American Handbook of Psychiatry,* vol. 1. New York: Basic Books.

Searles, H. F. (1963). Transference psychosis in the psychotherapy of chronic schizophrenia. *Int. J. Psycho-Anal.* 44, 249–281.

Segal, H. (1967). Melanie Klein's technique. *Psychoanal. Forum* 2, 197–227.

Simmonds, C. (1968). Discussion of present paper. (Meeting of Psychoanalysts of Southwest, San Antonio, Texas.)

Teruel, G. (1968). Discussion of present paper. (Meeting of Grupo Venezolano de Estudios Psicoanalitícos, Caracas.)

Wallerstein, R. S. (1967). Reconstruction and mastery in the transference psychosis. *J. Am. psychoanal. Ass.* 15, 551–583.

White, E. L. (1949). Lukundoo. In P. v. S. Stern (ed.), *The Pocket Week-End Book.* New York: Pocket Books.

Winnicott, D. W. (1955). Metapsychological and clinical aspects of regression within the psychoanalytical set-up. *Int. J. Psycho-Anal.* 36, 16–26.

FOLLOW-UP[4]   L. Bryce Boyer

The patient returned for further treatment after a period of five years and has been seen twice weekly for three months at the time of this writing. Although she has ample money to do so, she does not want to reenter psychoanalysis, saying "I'm worried about what I might find out about myself."

Following the termination of her analysis, there had been no catatonic-type or even reverie states, no further episodes of black spots, and no recalled phobic episodes.

When she married, she felt some conscious guilt because she knew she was more intelligent and forceful than her husband and wanted to belittle him. She fought this desire by giving up her work and devoting her life to being an efficient and loving housewife and mother. After four years, her husband's income had become too little to support the family and, with his encouragement, she sought work, promptly attaining an executive position of prestige, authority, and a salary larger than her husband's. She became responsible for the actions of a score of male employees and received rapid promotions because of her excellence.

She soon found herself retrospectively resenting her previous relatively passive marital life and began more overtly to dominate her husband. She took umbrage at his willing acceptance of her increasing authoritativeness and began to spend more and more time at her work. She started to have minor anxiety attacks, no doubt caused by a combination of unconscious fear that she might become physically hostile and damage her husband and concern lest she corporally change into a man.

Her relations with her mother had become intimate following her marriage; she learned that her mother had been unfaithful to her father and that she continued to be somewhat promiscuous in addition to having a lover. She began to have occasional sexual encounters with men who were older or more forceful than her husband. She felt no conscious guilt about the adultery per se, but only because she found exquisite pleasure in oral-genital relationships—activities her husband had never offered and she had told herself she did not want.

When she began to seek work, she dreamed overtly of me, although she did not remember what actions transpired in her dreams. She was surprised, because previously she very rarely had conscious thoughts about me and recalled no dreams in which I figured in the manifest content.

Soon after she reentered treatment, she unconsciously engineered a situation in which she and her mother got drunk in a bar, picked up men, and shared a motel suite where they awoke relatively amnesic about the night's orgy. During a subsequent interview, she recalled that when she had encouraged her partner to have intercourse a tergo, she had had a fantasy that he was a combination of her father and me and had interrupted sexual relations with her mother to come to her.

During the three months of her treatment, it has become apparent that she is seriously worried about her tendency to act out rather than to analyze. She has established an ongoing affair with a man my age and seems quite conscious of the transference meanings of her behavior. She feels that she must either stop her affair or her treatment and has not as yet decided what she will do.

At this time, I am uncertain about why she is reliving her oedipal rivalry with

---

[4] Prepared by L. Bryce Boyer for inclusion in this volume.

her mother but suspect that her actions consist of defensive behavior to avoid awareness that she seeks to become a man in order to take her father's place with her mother. Unconsciously she reasons that if she can gratify her mother sexually, she will have her mother all to herself, and that her mother will satisfy every pregenital wish she may have.

Within a few weeks after the Follow-Up was [originally] written, she opted to stop treatment after deciding she had been acting out with her mother, but preferred to work on her problems without "You're making me face what I'm doing." I did not hear from her during the next four years. Then I received a letter from her, stating she had divorced her passive second husband and entered into an ongoing affair with a married man who was clearly a substitute for me and her father. Her relations with her mother and children were said to be warm and nonconflictual. She had continued to be promoted in her work and had "bumped" several men from their positions of authority. She said her life was entirely satisfactory to her.

Chapter 5
Psychoanalytic Psychotherapy

Beginning in 1938 under the direction of Franz Alexander and Thomas French, members of the Chicago Psychoanalytic Institute embarked upon a project whereby they attempted to treat patients with a form of psychotherapy that was more flexible and brief than psychoanalysis. In fact, after only two interviews with a depressed fifty-one-year-old man, they achieved a striking therapeutic success that led to experimentation with new forms of psychotherapy based upon psychoanalytic theory and experience.

The first case is taken from literature, but it demonstrates the fundamental principle of psychoanalytic psychotherapy—a "corrective emotional experience." As in psychoanalysis, the goal is the relief of subjective suffering through insight and through such an "experience." It should be noted that in these cases patients were seen less frequently, a transference neurosis was not always allowed to develop, the intensity of the transference relationship was manipulated and controlled by interpretation, the couch was not necessarily used, and the treatments were planned and had a specific focus. Thus, these therapists made fewer attempts to obtain a complete unravelling of all the strands of the personality structure than Freud and standard psychoanalysis. Psychotherapy in these cases is more flexible, less all encompassing. Treatment is focussed on identified problems, and a wide range of problems are capable of being ameliorated. One should consider, as one reads through these cases, how and why standard psychoanalytic procedures are being modified to suit the patient's difficulty and the goals of the treatment. The cases, which are followed by comments about them, demonstrate the flexibility and efficacy of psychoanalytic psychotherapy. Present methods of brief analytic psychotherapy are quite similar to those described in these cases.

The Principle of Corrective Emotional Experience

FRANZ ALEXANDER and THOMAS MORTON FRENCH

In all forms of etiological psychotherapy, the basic therapeutic principle is the same: to reexpose the patient, under more favorable circumstances, to emotional situations which he could not handle in the past. The patient, in order to be helped, must undergo a corrective emotional experience suitable to repair the traumatic influence of previous experiences. It is of secondary importance whether this corrective experience takes place during treatment in the transference relationship, or parallel with the treatment in the daily life of the patient.

The simplest example of such a corrective experience is offered by the procedure called narcosynthesis. The patient in narcosis re-lives in fantasy the dangers of combat which he had been unable emotionally to master in reality. Because the narcotic and the presence of the therapist in whom he has confidence reduce the intensity of his anxiety, the patient becomes more capable of facing the situation to which he had succumbed.

The character of the transference relationship is unique in that the patient has an opportunity to display any of a great variety of behavior patterns. It is important to realize that the mastery of an unresolved conflict in this relationship becomes possible, not only because the transference conflict is less intense than the original one, but also because the analyst assumes an attitude different from that which the parent had assumed toward the child in the original conflict situation.

From *Psychoanalytic Therapy*, 66–70, 155–157, 234–244, 320–324, by Franz Alexander and Thomas Morton French et al. Copyright 1946, Renewed © 1974 The Ronald Press Company, New York.

While the patient continues to act according to outdated patterns, the analyst's reaction conforms strictly to the actual therapeutic situation. This makes the patient's transference behavior a one-sided shadow-boxing, and thus the therapist has an opportunity to help the patient both to see intellectually and to *feel* the irrationality of his emotional reactions. At the same time, the analyst's objective, understanding attitude allows the patient to deal differently with his emotional reactions and thus to make a new settlement of the old problem. The old pattern was an attempt at adaptation on the part of the child to parental behavior. When one link (the parental response) in this interpersonal relationship is changed through the medium of the therapist, the patient's reaction becomes pointless.

In the formulation of the dynamics of treatment, the usual tendency is to stress the repetition of the old conflict in the transference relationship and to emphasize the similarity of the old conflict situation to the transference situation. The therapeutic significance of the *differences* between the original conflict situation and the present therapeutic situation is often overlooked. And in just this difference lies the secret of the therapeutic value of the analytic procedure. Because the therapist's attitude is different from that of the authoritative person of the past, he gives the patient an opportunity to face again and again, under more favorable circumstances, those emotional situations which were formerly unbearable and to deal with them in a manner different from the old.

This can be accomplished only through actual experience in the patient's relationship to the therapist; intellectual insight alone is not sufficient. It is, however, vitally necessary for the therapist to have a clear understanding of the genetic development of the patient's emotional difficulties so that he may revive for the patient the original conflict situations from which he has retreated. The patient's intellectual understanding of the genetics has only an accessory significance. The more precisely the therapist understands the dynamics and is thus able to reactivate the early attitudes, the more adequately can he provide, by his own attitude, the new experiences necessary to produce therapeutic results.

A completely neutral psychoanalyst does not exist in reality, nor would he be desirable. While it is necessary that the therapist maintain an objective, helpful attitude at all times, within this attitude lies the possibility of a great variety of responses to the patient. Spontaneous reactions to the patient's attitudes are frequently not desirable for the therapy, since they may repeat the parents' impatience or solicitude which caused the neurosis and cannot, therefore, constitute the corrective experience necessary for cure.

THE CASE OF JEAN VALJEAN

Every reader is familiar with the classic example of a corrective emotional experience in Victor Hugo's "Les Miserables." In his account of Jean Valjean's conversion, Hugo anticipated the fundamental principle of every psychotherapy which aims to establish a profound change in the patient's personality. It will be recalled that Jean Valjean, the ex-convict, underwent a dramatic change in his personality because of the overwhelming and unexpected kindness of the bishop whom he had tried to rob. While he was still stunned by being treated for the first time in his life better than he deserved, Valjean met little Gervais playing a hurdygurdy on the road. When the little boy's two-franc piece fell to the ground, the ex-convict put his foot on the coin and refused to give it back. Although the little boy cried and

pleaded desperately, Valjean remained adamant. In a paralyzed and utterly confused state of mind he was unable to remove his foot from the coin. Only after Gervais left in despair did Valjean awake from his stupor. He ran after the boy in a frantic effort to make good his evil act, but could not find him. This was the beginning of his conversion.

Hugo writes: "He felt indistinctly that the priest's forgiveness was the most formidable assault by which he had yet been shaken; that his hardening would be permanent if he resisted this clemency; that if he yielded he must renounce that hatred with which the actions of other men had filled his soul during so many years, and which pleased him: that this time he must either conquer or be vanquished; and that the struggle, a colossal and final struggle, had begun between his wickedness and that man's goodness. One thing which he did not suspect is certain, however, that he was no longer the same man; all was changed in him, and it was no longer in his power to get rid of the fact that the bishop had spoken to him and taken his hand."

Jean Valjean did not know why he had robbed the boy. He felt clearly, however, that "if he were not henceforth the best of men he would be the worst, that he must now ascend higher than the bishop or sink lower than the galley-slave, that if he wished to be good he must become an angel, and if he wished to remain wicked that he must become a monster." Here the author interrupts his dramatic narration and goes into a psychodynamic discussion of Valjean's emotional processes in an attempt to explain his sudden conversion.

HUGO'S DYNAMIC PERCEPTION.—Were it not for the episode with Gervais and Hugo's psychological explanation of Valjean's emotional state, the story of Valjean's conversion would not deserve our attention. The scene with the bishop which demonstrates the effect of kindness upon unfortunate and maltreated pariahs is anything but novel. The encounter with the boy, however, shows not only that Hugo instinctively understood the emotional metamorphosis but also that he was acquainted with the dynamic process in all its details. Hugo shows us explicitly—and no better explanation could be given today—why Valjean behaved in such an inhuman manner toward little Gervais, robbing the helpless boy just after he had been overwhelmed by the bishop's generosity.

For Hugo the concept of disturbed emotional balance was not a mere phrase but a fully understood psychological reality. He raised the question why Valjean committed such a brutish act just at this moment and he answered it with another question, "Was it a final and, as it were, supreme effort of the evil thought he had brought from the Bagne, a remainder of impulse, a result of what is called in statics 'acquired force'?" Hugo understood that the bishop's act was a violent attack upon Valjean's precarious emotional equilibrium, which consisted in being cruel toward a cruel world, and Hugo saw that Valjean in response had to reestablish his balance in a spiteful insistence upon being bad.

In this, Hugo describes an experience well known in psychoanalysis; that whenever a symptom or neurotic attitude is attacked by the treatment, a recrudescence of the symptom usually occurs before the patient is able to give it up altogether. The experienced psychoanalyst knows this storm before the calm, this exacerbation of the morbid condition which precedes improvement, and he watches with eager expectation for its occurrence.

MODEL OF BRIEF PSYCHOTHERAPY.—We might question that one favorable experience could undo the cumulative effects of lifelong maltreatment. We are justified, however, in assuming that Valjean, although a hardened criminal, had a conscience which was rendered ineffective only by the hardships of his emotional development. He had to emphasize to himself his

adverse fate in order to feel free to act destructively. This equilibrium was disturbed by the bishop's unexpected and extraordinary kindness.

Valjean's conversion took place within a few hours; it is a model of brief psychotherapy. This masterpiece of psychodynamic analysis was written in 1862, about sixty years before Freud introduced his concept of the super-ego and its compelling influence upon human behavior.

That Hugo's story is no mere creation of fantasy has been proved by many clinical examples. Aichhorn's reports on his delinquent patients present similar occurrences. The author of this section has also observed the tremendous effect upon young delinquents of the mere fact that the therapist's attitude was not critical and moralistic but rather that of a benevolent and helpful friend. In some patients, the pronounced contrast between the patient's own self-critical superego reactions and the analyst's permissive attitude alone may produce profound results.

Franz Alexander, M.D.

The second case to be discussed is another of those which first claimed our interest because of the satisfactory result achieved in a short time.

CASE C

(Reactive Depression)

A physician, a German refugee 45 years old, came for psychotherapy because of an intense depression resulting from extreme irritation with his son. He was seen for a single consultation with excellent results. The therapist (a man) was also a recent immigrant.

The patient had had no serious neurotic difficulties before. He had been in this country for ten months, and his wife and only child, a nine-year-old boy, had only recently joined him. His chief complaint was that he felt extremely irritated by his son, that he could not concentrate on his work in the boy's presence, that he was annoyed by his demanding attitude and his constant need for attention. He was now so discouraged over his inability to adjust himself to the child that he had become exceedingly depressed and decided to consult a psychiatrist.

In the course of the discussion, the patient's attention was distracted from his complaints about his son with a few questions about the way he had lived before his family joined him. He then talked freely about the circumstances of his immigration and about his first attempts to reconstruct his life in the new environment. Although he had had a hard time in the beginning, he had been fairly successful in getting established in his profession.

As he talked it became clear to him that his son and wife had joined him "too soon," that they had come before he was ready to offer them the security they needed. With considerable emotion—at first hesitantly, then with conviction—he said he realized that life would be easier now if his son and wife were not with him. He saw that the demands of his son were really not exaggerated but seemed so because he himself felt insecure—not only within himself but also in his economic adjustment. He felt guilty and responsible, and even saw some justification for his son's behavior, since his own difficulties in the new environment did not allow him to be the ideal father his standards demanded. As he talked the whole situation over, he gained more and more insight into these feelings (which were not far under the surface) and with this insight he experienced marked relief.

But insight alone was not enough. It was necessary also to help this patient make some practical arrangement whereby he could adjust his way of working to the American style of life—chiefly through having an office outside the home. This made it possible for him to divide his energies; he could be a hardworking doctor part of the time, and an attentive father and husband the rest of the time.

When he was seen by the therapist two years later, the patient referred to himself as a "week-end father." He expressed his gratitude for the insight he had gained in this one interview, and added that not only his relationship to his son but the relationship to other aspects of his family life and to the American scene in general had greatly improved.

Comments on Case C

It might be argued that a confidential talk with a friend would have helped this patient as much as the psychiatric interview. The evidence, however, is against this assumption since the patient had often talked over his difficulties with his refugee friends, many of whom had difficulty in adjusting themselves to new ways and conditions.

The therapeutic success in this case consisted mainly in bringing into consciousness conflicting emotions which were preconscious but still suppressed. This man had become rebellious against too much responsibility in a trying situation and was depressed as a result. Insight into his unconscious reaction to immigration in general, and to his family situation in particular, facilitated his emotional readjustment. He had a strong, efficient ego and its powers of integration were readily mobilized and set to work.

The fact that the patient was seen in only one interview precludes any analysis of the transference situation. We surmise, however, that the patient saw in this analyst who, he knew, had also gone through the trying experience of immigration a few years before, a good object for identification. This in itself speeded the rapport necessary for any successful therapy and served as a support of the patient's ego which had begun to fail under the heavy load of responsibility.

Another reason for this therapist's being

especially suitable for this patient was the fact that he had already learned the ways of American doctors and could give the patient concrete advice and help in establishing himself in the medical profession.

Martin Grotjahn, M.D.

CASE K

(Phobia)

A senior in a coeducational college, an attractive, friendly twenty-one-year-old girl, requested treatment for a severe generalized anxiety and confusion which was most troublesome when she was away from home and particularly acute in the classroom and at dances. This anxiety had recently become so extreme that the patient insisted on staying at home and refused to let her mother leave her side. Excellent results were brought by a treatment which extended over a period of two months (interviews twice a week for the first month and once a week for the second), followed by two interviews a month apart to assure the therapist that the healing process continued.

Although the patient remembered that she had always been anxious and uncomfortable in social situations, these acute manifestations had developed suddenly about six months before, during a Christmas visit to the parents of a male friend. Her distress had increased so greatly that, upon her return from the visit, she ceased going to classes and regularly refused to attend dances or other parties. She had been thrown into acute panic upon several occasions—once in a large class with a male instructor, the other times at college parties.

Other symptoms of interest were anorexia, nausea with occasional vomiting, insomnia, and amenorrhea. She had been under endocrine treatment for amenorrhea for several months, but since there had been no improvement she had voluntarily stopped treatment. She had lost eleven pounds and was very slender.

During psychotherapy (with a woman analyst) the symptom picture of this case showed progressive improvement. The patient went back to her classes within the second week, and before treatment was concluded was able to take her final examinations, graduate, and enter into the gaieties of dances, parties, and other college activities—without symptom return and with the reestablishment of regular menses.

Sufficient historical material was freely given by the patient in the first interview to furnish a background from which to reconstruct the causes of the conflict responsible for the presenting symptoms. The patient was an only child. Her mother had been widowed when the patient was two and from the time of her husband's death had devoted most of her life to her child. The mother and daughter had lived with the maternal grandparents who were also very devoted to the patient. She spoke of her grandmother as being very dependent upon her mother, and of her grandfather as a gentle, lovable man who played a very unimportant role in the planning for the family—which was of definite matriarchal organization. She remembered having always been a very obedient child, although she had been told that, when very young, she had indulged in severe temper tantrums which had ceased suddenly at about four years.

At about ten, the patient was taught masturbation by an older girl in the neighborhood and had practiced it occasionally since then, but with a severe sense of guilt. She could remember no childhood curiosity about sex, but she was unusually ignorant of such matters and had felt embarrassed when she heard other children discussing them.

Being an intellectually precocious and musically talented girl, she was pushed in school and was expected to practice her music for long hours. She had planned to be a concert musician, but two years previous to her illness she had taken an aversion to her instrument and became anxious whenever she considered returning to her music. Socially, she had always had a circle of acquaintances, but during her school years her work schedule offered little time for them. Her main recreation as she was growing up was visiting adult friends of her mother, an occasional concert, and moving pictures.

When she went to college, her mother left the grandparents' home and established an apartment for the two of them near the college. Although the patient joined a sorority, she had little social life with the other girls for fear that her mother might be lonely during her absence. When boys visited her, she always included her mother and even took her on all dates other than college dances. Consciously she considered her mother as a "pal," but she admitted that because her mother was gay and good company she had often thought the boys liked her only because of her mother. One boy, however, who had been devoted to her for over a year, insisted upon omitting the mother from their dates. He proposed marriage to the patient and was accepted. Since she considered herself engaged, she had indulged in "necking" with him before the onset of her illness. Although she enjoyed it, she had felt guilty and was sure her mother would disapprove.

Her fiancé had invited her to his home for the Christmas holidays to meet his parents. During this visit, which was the first trip on which she had ever been away from her mother, she developed the severe symptom picture described. It started with insomnia the second night of her visit, after he had given her an engagement ring. She became fearful during the night that something dreadful might happen to her mother, and the next day became so ill that she insisted upon returning home.

It was evident from this history and from the symptom content that the girl had been precipitated, by the realization of the nearness of her approaching marriage, into a conflict between her dependent wish toward her mother and the more adult sexual wish toward her fiancé; this conflict was near the surface but not yet in consciousness. Fear of injury to her mother suggested also a stirring of unconscious hostility toward her mother who had always directed and shared her life, who stood in the way of her interest in sexuality and its coincident independent life, and who might also win away her fiancé as she had taken away the father, the grandfather, and (more recently) the other boys who had been attentive to the patient.

Guilt and anxiety thus played a role in producing the symptoms, the secondary gain of which was to solve the conflict temporarily by renouncing sexuality and an independent life. When she was so ill, she need not consider marriage or independent activity—as classes, dances, companionship and so forth. At the same time, she intensified her dependence upon her mother through her illness. Her mother dared not leave the patient, even in the home, for fear symptoms would develop in her absence.

In the first interview, the patient was given insight into her hostility toward her mother, with an explanation of how it grew from her mother's restriction of her independence and self-expression—a result of her mother's ambitions for her—and from the consequent restrictions of her social life. The therapist discussed with her the fact that all children develop such hostilities toward their parents, and showed the patient how, from fear of losing love, she had formed defenses against her own childhood hostility by exaggerated obedience, shyness, and avoidance of tabooed activity. An explanation was given to her of how the conflict had been intensified into severe symptom formation during her first trip away from home, because she was really deserting her mother in choosing to be with her fiancé and yet was enjoying herself. A hint was also offered her about guilt reactions to any enjoyment because of her training to sacrifice so much for achievement in work. This guilt in turn made her even more dependent upon her mother, the childhood disciplinarian whose presence could protect her from indulging her wishes for pleasure.

These interpretations were followed with a permissive suggestion that she might try to refrain from repressing angry feelings toward her mother when critical thoughts occurred, with an explanation of the naturalness of such feelings in spite of the traditional teaching that one should love one's parents under all circumstances. It was then suggested that some mild self-indulgence such as lunch with her sorority sisters or an after-class drink in the drugstore with them if she felt the inclination might aid in her recovery, and that she go to classes or begin to study again only when she felt comfortable and wished to. But, in order to protect her from losing prohibitions too rapidly, she was urged not to indulge herself beyond her feeling of comfort.

In this first interview, the sexual component in her conflict relative to pleasurable indulgences was not touched upon. Since this element seemed to be much more deeply repressed than her conflict between her dependent and independent wishes, and since it was emotionally charged, it could be handled only after some freedom from the mother had been achieved and the dependent transference to the more permissive therapist had gained strength.

In the second interview, three days later, the patient's manner was less tense and she reported that she had begun to feel that she would recover. She had not been back to classes but had spent her days at the sorority house studying. In the afternoons, she had worried lest her mother be lonely and had returned home early for dinner. She had not seen her fiancé although he had telephoned daily.

Tears came when the patient reviewed in detail memories of deprivation as a child, when she had longed to play with other children and had been made to practice or to visit adults with her mother. Occasional excursions with her grandfather, to the circus and to the zoo in particular, were marred by her mother's criticisms of the grandfather who kept her out too long. On these trips she was happy and felt her grandfather was like Santa Claus, but her pleasure was always tempered by fear of eventual criticism. Sympathy for her deprived childhood was offered by the therapist, and again the hostile feeling of any child toward a parent in such a situation was discussed with her. In order to soften the guilt resulting from the anger which was obviously reaching consciousness, she was helped to recognize the fact that parents, meaning well, often deprive children unwisely in an attempt to do the best they can for their training. Her response expressed relief. "I feel better to think that mother wasn't really mean, and maybe wanted me to have the best of things."

At this point the therapist asked permission to talk with the mother in order to explain the patient's need for freedom and to warn her that her daughter might occasionally be irritable at home during the treatment period. The patient was assured that there would be no discussion of confidential information.

In the resultant interview, the mother proved quite willing to cooperate, both because she was truly distressed by her daughter's symptoms and because she suffered some personal discomfort from the patient's intensified dependence upon her. Not only was the mother able to be tolerant of the girl's whims but, following the therapist's suggestion, she also began to develop a richer social life for herself and to renew old friendships. At the same time, she did not withdraw her "mothering" completely and the patient's dependent satisfactions were not cut off abruptly as she experimented with greater freedom in satisfying her own wishes. That this gradual change of attitude on the part of the mother had a profound influence on the patient's progress could be seen with increasing clarity as the therapy proceeded.

In the third interview, the patient

brought the information that she had been sleeping well, had gone to classes, and, although there were sudden moments of anxiety, had not had to leave the classroom. She had lunched daily with friends; and the previous day she had taken a walk along the lake with her fiancé which both had enjoyed, but after about half an hour she had begun to worry about leaving her mother alone and had gone home. A new symptom, however, had developed which was frankly hostile to her mother. She had impulsive wishes to hit her mother when away from her, and when she was with her she heard what her mother said but could not see her clearly. Although these symptoms had not really frightened her, they were startling and convinced her of the intensity of hostility toward her mother.

In this interview, insight was offered in two realms. The transference relationship was discussed in detail and it was suggested that in indulging herself now she was doing it partly to please the therapist, who was momentarily a parent-figure, just as she had always inhibited herself previously to please her mother. And she was shown the split which had occurred in the parent-image—the therapist as the good parent and her own mother as the bad one who could be hated. At this point, an explanation was given of her conscious and unconscious need for dependence, and of her use at the moment of the therapist as the person upon whom she depended. Again she was encouraged to enlarge her social experiences by the use of opportunities as they presented themselves. In giving advice of this kind it is, of course, essential for the therapist to be quite sure not only of the needs of the patient, but of both the external situation and the patient's capacity to act independently without an increase of anxiety. It would be highly traumatic, naturally, to a patient if in trying to be friendly he were met with rejection.

The second point in this interview was her attitude toward sexuality. This subject was introduced easily by the discussion of possible reasons for the precipitation of the anxiety symptoms at a time when she was with her fiancé and away from her mother and girl friends. She was encouraged to talk freely of her fiancé and of her concept of marriage. She revealed fear of sexual intercourse and a puritanical attitude as well, saying that she had thought of it as an evil to be endured because of the "base nature of man." For a person of her generation, her general sexual information was very vague. As is often true of persons brought up by persons with strong sexual taboos, she did not remember ever having been curious about birth, sex differences, and so forth, nor did she remember masturbating as a child. She admitted having indulged in masturbation as an adolescent after she had been taught by an older girl, but she had done this only rarely and with tremendous guilt and fear.

Sex information was therefore given to this patient as part of the treatment procedure, just as one often teaches a child in the course of psychotherapy. As with the child, answering the sex questions of an adult whose information is confused or incorrect has a two-fold therapeutic result. It tends to relieve unconscious guilt connected with sexual curiosity and (through the transference) it tends to bring sexual wishes to consciousness, since the good parent in the form of the therapist does not condemn interest in sex.

At the beginning of the fourth interview, the patient was again tense and cried while she told that her fiancé was begging her for dates and was urging her to go to a dance the following week. She had been preoccupied since the last interview with sexual thoughts, and had felt that marriage would be impossible since the idea of sexual relations with him revolted her. She told a fragment of a dream she had had the previous night: She was running from a large man along a dark street; then she found herself in a small basement room and just as the man was going to grab her she saw that he had no arms. She awoke screaming and trembling.

She offered two enlightening associations to this dream. One was that the fiancé had a slight limp as a result of childhood poliomyelitis, and the second was a memory of seeing a man expose himself in an alley when she was a small child. Her recollection was of seeing an enormous penis and of running home in terror, but of being afraid to tell her mother of the experience.

The patient then confessed that she had recently doubted her love for her fiancé and thought that perhaps she was sorry for him, although his paralysis had not been severe enough to handicap him in athletics or other activities. She wondered if she did not cling to him for fear that other men would not love her if they knew her well. The therapist interpreted only the safety which she felt with the man in the dream when there were no arms, which was similar to her previous feeling of safety with her fiancé when she had thought of him as also injured. It was suggested that her fear arose only after he gave her the ring which might assure marriage and make her face relations with a real man. Her reaction to this was a smiling admission that her fiancé was certainly much more dominating than she had first thought him.

The next three interviews covered details of her doubts about her fiancé, her decision that she really did not love him, her plans to move to the sorority house while her mother visited friends in another city, and questions concerning possibilities of seeing other men. She also reported active classwork and weekly parties.

In the following interview she reported another dream fragment: She was in the woods and started to take hold of a tree trunk when she noticed that she was holding a penis which was attached to herself. In telling the dream she laughed and said

it reminded her of the time when as a little girl she tried to urinate standing up and the urine went over the toilet cover. She had no memory of seeing a boy urinate, but admitted that she must have. The therapist told her of penis-envy in little girls and the hostility which sometimes developed toward boys as a result. She admitted then the despair she had always felt in her musical achievement because she believed that men would always be more successful.

Little fresh insight came with further interviews. There was repetition and elaboration of the material of the previous hours, and much of the time was consumed by reports of her activities and requests for detailed suggestions about how to meet certain social situations, such as dates with men other than her fiancé or the correct behavior as bridesmaid at a wedding in which she decided to take part although she had previously refused for fear her old symptoms would reappear. Her menses had been reestablished, and except for some insecurity socially her symptoms had ceased. Plans for the summer were also worked out with her and her mother so that she could spend half the time with friends and half in a resort with her mother.

Seven months after the termination of treatment, the patient was seen again in a friendly visit, and she appeared as a charming, self-reliant young woman. She had returned to her music; was engaged to be married but to another man, this time with inner conviction of success; and was working temporarily in an office while making plans for her marriage. She had encouraged her mother to return to the grandparents and was living in an apartment with a college chum who was also working. She stated that she saw her mother about once a week and enjoyed her as a companion. She could now feel amused at both her previous dependence on her mother and her hostility toward her.

Three years after the last treatment interview, her marriage of two years' duration was still obviously happy and there had been no symptom return.

Comments on Case K

Several factors operated to bring about a therapeutic change in this patient. Of greatest importance was the opportunity for a dependent relationship to a mother-figure (the therapist) who was neither demanding of love nor ambitious for success, and who was permissive of the patient's sexual interests and of her wish for pleasure with friends of her own age. Insight concerning her sexual and independent wishes made the relationship with the therapist clearer and more acceptable. But insight alone was not the curative factor; it was rather the new relationship, a framework in which she felt free to experiment emotionally and socially.

The absence of transference repetition in this case was accomplished by the mother's changed attitude toward the girl. Because of this and because she was still living with her mother, the patient was able to re-live the disturbing feelings with the original object rather than to transfer them to the therapist. In this way, the patient experienced a corrected mother-daughter relationship, not only within the therapy but in her life situation as well. This accelerated the therapy and made it possible in a short treatment to reach a deeper conflict, her fear of men.

This conflict, her fear of men and her castrative wishes against them, was brought out as the repression of her sexual wishes was relaxed. Insight into the meaning of the two dreams which showed a deepseated masculine identification made it possible for her to identify herself still further with the permissive therapist and to accept as normal the passive feminine wishes which had been thwarted by her mother's (and thus her own) earlier attitude of contempt and aversion.

Margaret W. Gerard, M.D.

CASE T

(Potential Psychosis)

The patient was a young man of nineteen, a brilliant student in engineering at a nearby university. After much hesitation and long talks with gifted friends of his who had been helped by analysis, he finally came for treatment with a great longing for help and, by that time, almost *too little* resistance to therapy. He was seen over a period of a year with interviews first every week and then at intervals of every two or three weeks. The results, although limited in scope, were highly satisfactory.

The patient's major complaint was that, although he knew he was capable of brilliant creative work in his field of mathematics and architecture, he would for weeks at a time become so anxious and depressed that he would stay away from school. He also recognized that he had much anxiety in regard to any close association with girls. Having read and talked much about psychoanalysis before he came to treatment, the patient in the first interview literally "poured out" his life story, making many complicated and *correct* interpretations of the dynamics of his underlying conflicts, especially those dealing with oedipal material. The therapist (a woman) was relatively noncommittal.

In the second interview, the patient revealed that in the first session he had withheld a dream which he now wished to relate. This proved to be an oedipal dream, the elements of which were complexly disguised. In reality, he already knew of his strong love for his mother and resentment toward his father. The fact that he had withheld the dream before, a dream much disguised, should have served as more of a warning to the therapist than it did. The patient was allowed to bring associations to the disguised elements, and did so with eagerness.

No marked anxiety was evident during

this interview, but a few days later the patient called the therapist for an appointment, obviously very much disturbed. In this interview, it was learned that the patient had stopped both his schoolwork and his job—by which he earned money to pay for the treatment. He had stayed away from school and work because he felt his men teachers and his employer were hostile to him, and he remained in his room because he felt they would follow him on the street "to see what I was up to." Obviously, a paranoid reaction had followed the mobilization and deeper analysis of his oedipal conflict.

The therapist knew from his history that his mother had always protected him from his authoritative, harsh father, and it was felt that this had only served to intensify his attachment to her and deepen the conflict. At once the therapist told the patient, therefore, that she knew he was upset and guilty and fearful of these men, but that since he had ended his job what were his plans for paying for his treatment? The patient appeared startled and then visibly relaxed as he seemed to be thinking. The therapist felt that, at this point, the patient would only become worse if she protected him from his employer and charged no fee—this was exactly what his mother had always done. It seemed he not only had become guilty from the analysis of the dream, but also had the unconscious intention of pushing the therapist into taking part in his deeper impulses.

After some thought, the patient ventured, "You could not see me for a while and excuse the fee?" The therapist assured him the issue was *not* the fee but what it meant, and she briefly pointed out to him that he seemed to have some wish to push her into exactly the same position his mother had held, in indulging him and protecting him against the father. The therapist said no more, and at the end of the hour the patient said he felt far less anx- and would return to school and work.

The next hour he returned, calm and pleased with himself for having resumed work but also resenting the fact that the therapist had withheld help. He was able, however, to see that intellectually her point was well taken.

From that time on, the patient brought in very few dreams, but talked mostly about his studies, in which he was astonishingly brilliant. Personal contact with some of his professors before this had revealed to the therapist the amazing gifts of this boy. The therapist decided to encourage him and to show her appreciation for all his creativeness, in no way to mobilize any erotic attachment to her, to decrease his interviews gradually, and to attempt to stabilize this nineteen-year-old at a creative level. It was thought possible that some years later, with the added self-esteem which productivity would bring, the patient's ego might be better able to stand analysis.

During the rest of the year of treatment, the patient became increasingly sure of himself and pleased by the realization that he possessed true genius. That the therapist knew she was inferior to him intellectually could be conveyed to him easily by the nature of her questions and by her evident respect. His own mother was a woman of only average intelligence and vision, whose capacity to appreciate his intellectual gifts was extremely limited. The therapist could at least follow his ideas closely enough to give him real gratification from seeing that her admiration was not superficial flattery but true appreciation. He proceeded to win her approval and admiration on an intellectual level, and repressed—or possibly sublimated, in part—his erotic feelings.

His earlier relationship to his gifted father changed to mutual admiration and a productive exchange of ideas. The patient became deeply absorbed in his studies and research, received many awards for his achievements and rarely mentioned any interest in girls.

After a year, treatment was terminated except for a rare communication as to his progress. A year later he entered one of the armed services, and now (three years after the therapy was terminated) he is functioning well in a highly specialized technical group in that branch of the service. Occasional letters have expressed his intense gratitude for what he is able to accomplish.

Comments on Case T

What the eventual effectiveness of this young man's intellectual sublimations will be, remains a question. Certainly at the time he was first seen, before he had achieved the unusually high professional status that is now his, to have pursued an analysis of his pregenital and oedipal conflicts might well have precipitated a psychosis. Had he been several years older, the therapist would have been more confident of a safe outcome in a psychoanalysis.

This young man is fortunate in having within him the elements of genius. His tremendous intellectual gifts make it possible for him easily to outrank most of the men with whom he deals so that for the present, at least, he has no great threat from men. It is to be hoped that he will continue to function chiefly in the intellectual realm, where he will surely gain unusual recognition. At some later time, perhaps, he may again succumb to emotional pressure and need help. At that time his security and self-regard through achievement, added to his increased age, should be sufficient to carry him through analysis if it becomes necessary. At present, in an entirely unexhibitionistic manner, he recognizes his rare gifts and wins the praise of men and women.

This case demonstrates the need to deal immediately and specifically with the clinical picture as presented and to avoid any routine or usual mode of procedure.

It emphasizes the necessity of stabilizing a patient, if possible, at a level at which his gifts and emotional defenses can be productive. Those therapists who treat adolescents or late adolescents often must formulate such a plan. A *complete* intellectual and emotional life cannot be achieved for everyone. If the therapist has such an aim, in many instances he may destroy the patient's opportunities for achievement in *any* area. This fact applies to any form of treatment; it is not peculiar to the briefer psychotherapy. In this particular case, it might have been catastrophic to have seen the patient in daily interviews and to have analyzed unconscious material. (In fact, much *conscious* material was also deliberately passed over by the therapist.)

In summarizing the structure of this case, the therapist is greatly limited by the fact that, from almost the very beginning, no attempt was made to understand the experiences contributing to this young man's emotional conflicts. It is believed, however, that the boy's earliest relationship to his mother was probably unsound and involved with considerable ambivalence on her part. The mother failed him not just because of her limited intellectual abilities and incapacity to appreciate him on that level, but probably also because of a resentment which he displaced to her lack of intellectual appreciation. Through the treatment relationship, the patient experienced a warmth and lack of ambivalence from the therapist which he had not had in relation to his mother.

It is felt that the oedipal conflict was a later disturbance, stemming from the deeper earlier ambivalent relationship with his mother. The therapist doubts if the dependent yearning characteristic of the dreams told in the beginning of the treatment was wholly regressive. Such speculations, however, must rest until treatment is resumed at a later date.

Adelaide McFadyen Johnson, M.D.

Chapter 6
Child Psychoanalysis and Therapy

Before we discuss Dr. Bornstein's case specifically, it will be useful to make a few general remarks about child psychoanalysis. The theory of therapeutic change in child psychoanalysis is similar to the theory of change in adult psychotherapy. It is hypothesized that developmental stages and issues are not being successfully resolved, and even for the small, weak, dependent child, many of the fears and anxieties are unrealistic. If the child can have more insight into what is bothering him, he will be less anxious, have more freedom, and will be able to progress more adequately in his development. As pointed out in the introduction to this section, the child analyst uses the child's free play-associations (including drawing, painting, etc.) to understand the conflicts, fears, and anxieties besetting the child. At the appropriate time and in language suitable to the child's level of comprehension, the therapist then tries to help him or her be aware of the source of the difficulties.

In addition to working with the child, quite typically child therapists frequently see the parents as well. It is difficult to help a child unless the parents can be made aware of how they are consciously or unconsciously encouraging the child's neurotic behavior. No matter how often the child sees the analyst, she still spends the majority of her time with her parents so they too often need to be aware of the issues involved. In any case, the goal is to remove those developmental inhibitions that have arisen in the child, and to let natural psychological growth and development, which had been blocked in various ways, continue on its course.

The age at which child analysis may begin is in doubt. Melanie Klein once "analyzed" a child just under three years of age! It is natural for all children to have various neurotic symptoms (e.g., phobias, obsessions, compulsions, etc.), but it is only when the problem exceeds the realm of normal childhood difficulties that child analysis or therapy is indicated. It is difficult to decide when this point is reached. On the one hand, if therapy is not really needed, there is the possibility of mis-labelling the child and of causing the child, his parents, and involved others an unnecessary amount of guilt and anxiety. Such a result may cause more problems than the "normal neurosis" from which the child suffered.

As the age of the child increases, there is an increasing shift from reliance upon play to reliance upon verbalization, which, of course, is consonant with our knowledge of cognitive development. Analysis is practiced successfully upon children, but at adolescence it becomes quite difficult. Psychotherapy with adolescents is complex because of the psychic dislocations and shifts which are normal for this developmental period. With the recrudescence of sexual, aggressive, and dependency conflicts at puberty, the formation of a good working alliance with the adolescent is most complicated. Many writers have suggested ways to facilitate the treatment of adolescents, but a generally successful technique still evades therapists. We cannot go into the specifics of dealing with adolescents here, but the reader should be aware that there are difficulties in forming a working alliance with persons of this age.

Child analysis and therapy require special training. In order to become a child psychoanalyst or therapist, the student must first complete the usual training for adult analysis or therapy and only then can further instruction begin. Thus preparation for work with children is long and arduous; and, much like other types of therapy, success in this field is a result of a combination of personality characteristics, an artistic feel for the work, and trained and disciplined skill.

The case described here involves a five-and-a-half-year-old-boy named Frankie whose overt symptoms were a marked school phobia and an inability to have his mother or nurse be out of his sight. Dr. Bornstein used traditional child analytic procedures in working with this boy, and the case report is considered a classic in the child psychoanalytic literature. At first an environmental manipulation had to be attempted so that the child would recognize his own maladaptive behavior. Even a child must suffer some pain in order to be motivated to undergo analysis. It is obvious from this case how close to the surface conflictual and pathogenic material may be in a child, yet how difficult it is to help the child gain insight. Dr. Bornstein did not criticize or console Frankie, but rather she conveyed information to him, a bit at a time, when he was ready for it. The child analyst must be especially careful not to overwhelm the child's fragile and developing ego with premature interpretations or ones that would provoke too much anxiety. At all times Frankie's parents were involved in the treatment, which was enormously helpful.

It is interesting to note that although he was so young, Frankie was able to recognize paradoxes and contradictions in his life. Admittedly he was a child of superior intelligence, but this demonstrated the usefulness of cognitive factors as well as noncognitive factors in therapy with children. Dr. Bornstein was especially prone to make constructions, that is, inferences about the probable events of Frankie's past and how they have influenced his current life and difficulties. The reader might consider how convincing her constructions were and how useful they were in the treatment.

Of special interest is that after quite a time in treatment, and after much success in ameliorating his problem, Frankie began to become unmanageably wild. Dr. Bornstein confronted him very directly at this point, demonstrating to him the unreality of his expectations and the probable consequence (i.e., hospitalization) of his behavior. Such direct confrontation is unusual in child analysis, and this particularly decisive therapeutic incident merits special attention.

As an interesting sidelight, Frankie returned to psychoanalysis as an adult after more than fifteen years. This later treatment was reported by Samuel Ritvo (1966). Frankie needed treatment again because he was having trouble remaining in school during an "intensely competitive phase of career training," a school problem similar to the one that brought him to child analysis. Although his adult presenting problem was more obsessional than phobic, Ritvo notes that the same issues (e.g., passivity) were still dominant in Frankie's life, although expressed differently. Ritvo's note is an unusual follow-up to Dr. Bornstein's closing remarks: "A prognosis in child analysis is not easy. We are by no means sure that we have forestalled a later recurrence of Frankie's neurosis."

Although Frankie did indeed have later difficulties, the reader of this intricate case cannot help but feel that the dynamics of personality are too enormously complex ever to be completely comprehended, and that if it had not been for Dr. Bornstein's intervention, Frankie's childhood and later difficulties would have been considerably more serious.

Finally, in the section on behavior therapy of this book, we have included a case of behavioral treatment of a young child (Ayllon & Skuban, "Accountability in psychotherapy"). Aspects of that case are very similar to those in Frankie's case, and it is fascinating to see how differently similar problems are treated by different types of therapists. Further comparisons are made in the introduction to the Ayllon case, and the interested reader may wish to read that case in conjunction with the case of Frankie.

REFERENCE

Ritvo, Samuel. Correlation of a childhood and adult neurosis—based on the adult analysis of a reported childhood case. *International Journal of Psychoanalysis*, 1966, *47*, 130–131.

The Analysis of a Phobic Child

Some Problems of Theory and Technique in Child Analysis

BERTA BORNSTEIN

This paper attempts to clarify some theoretical and technical aspects of child analysis by correlating the course of treat-

Reprinted from *The Psychoanalytic Study of the Child* (Vols. 3 & 4), 181–226, by Berta Bornstein. By permission of International Universities Press, Inc. Copyright 1949 by Berta Bornstein.

ment, the structure of the neurosis and the technique employed in the case of a phobic boy who was in analysis over a period of three years. The case was chosen for presentation:

1. Because of the discrepancy between the clinical simplicity of the symptom and

the complicated ego structure behind it;

2. because of the unusual clearness with which the patient brought to the fore the variegated patterns of his libidinal demands;

3. because of the patient's attempts at transitory solutions, oscillations between perversions and symptoms, and processes of new symptom formation;

4. because the vicissitudes and stabilization of character traits could be clearly traced;

5. and finally, because of the rare opportunity to witness during treatment the change from grappling with reality by means of pathological mechanisms, to dealing with reality in a relatively conflict-free fashion.

I

Frankie, a 5½-year-old boy of superior intelligence who was eager to learn, was brought into analysis because of a severe school phobia. He liked to play with other children and was friendly and amenable with them, but shy and withdrawn in the presence of any stranger. He became panic-stricken if his mother or nurse were out of sight. Even when left with his father in his own home, he was occasionally overwhelmed by attacks of anxiety. His phobic symptom had existed for more than 2 years.

Frankie was the older of two children of intelligent middle class parents. His father was a kind man with slightly compulsive character traits. His relationship to the child was predominantly protective and had the character of friendly interest. However, he resented the tension which the child's neurotic behavior caused in the family. His reproaches were not openly directed against the boy, but against his wife whom he did not consider affectionate enough to the child. Moreover, he accused her of having surrendered Frankie's care to a nurse.

The mother reported that Frankie was a planned child, that her pregnancy had been uneventful, and that she had felt happy and contented in anticipating her first baby's arrival. The delivery was normal, the child healthy, yet the very first moment she held the baby in her arms, she had felt estranged from him. The little boy's crying had given her an uncanny and uneasy feeling. She felt quite different toward her second child, a girl.

She herself was an only daughter, between an older and a younger brother. Her own mother had not displayed any warmth toward her, but was preoccupied with the older boy. This brother was "selfish, undisciplined, queer, and insisted on obtaining whatever he craved;" she used the same words in describing her son Frankie. Just as she had lived in terror of her brother, she now lived in terror of her son. Yet, in spite of her determination not to repeat her mother's behavior, her own feeling of aloofness toward Frankie was an exact repetition of her mother's attitude toward her. She was completely unaware of the fact that her primary rejection of Frankie was her unconscious revenge on her brother; later, after Frankie's neurosis made her suffer, her identification with her mother made her devote herself exclusively to Frankie.[1] In the end, however, the child's phobic symptoms, which made her and the nurse his prisoners, discouraged her profoundly, and made her realize her defeat as a mother. Thus she became not only eager to seek therapeutic help for the child but was also ready to identify herself with the analyst. Actually, her relationship to her son changed radically during the course of the treatment.

Frankie's first disturbance, his constant screaming and crying as an infant, were incomprehensible to the mother. She was

[1] She gained insight into the motivation of her attitude only during the course of the child's analysis. She then understood that her longing to find a protective substitute mother had resulted in her dependence on her son's nurse.

convinced that the child's reactions were caused by unsatisfactory feeding in the hospital. And it is a fact that as soon as the intervals between feeding periods were decreased, the screaming attacks became less violent and less frequent. He was a bottle-fed baby and was described as a greedy eater. Night feeding was continued for an unusually long time and when, at the age of 5½ months, the 2 A.M. feeding was stopped, the child again evidenced his discontent. For several months he continued to scream at this hour. It could not be ascertained whether the baby's crying and screaming spells were unusually violent or whether they seemed so because the parents were over-sensitive. As a matter of fact, the parents did not dare to fall asleep because of their anticipation of the baby's screaming.

When Frankie was 2, it became especially difficult to put him to bed at night. Regularly, he screamed for an hour before he fell asleep, and also whenever he awoke during the night. A third screaming period occurred at the age of 4½ years and was stopped only after the nurse threatened to punish him. As we shall learn later, it was during this period that the child developed his unusually severe insomnia which subsided only in the last period of the analysis.

We were told that toilet training did not lead to any neurotic reaction. Bowel control was easily established at the age of 1. Bladder control at night was established at the age of 3. However, Frankie refused to use any bathroom outside of the home, but instead retained urine for hours.

His sister Mary was born when Frankie was 3 years and 3 months old. Upon the mother's return from the hospital he displayed marked anxiety. He grew more ill-tempered toward his mother and his coolness toward her increased to such an extent that she became disturbed and made conscious efforts to win the child's affection. Despite her strong urge to devote herself to her little daughter, she left the baby in

the care of a second nurse while she and Frankie's nurse were at the boy's disposal. Thus she hoped to prevent any further cause for the boy's jealousy. Yet her concerned attention did not improve Frankie's relationship to her. He refused to let his mother touch him and reserved all the intimacies of his care for his nurse. His distrust of his mother, especially during illness, became so intense that he accepted neither medicine nor food from her. Nevertheless he insisted tyrannically on her presence at all times and had outbursts of wild aggression if she did not adhere meticulously to his demands. When she occasionally wanted to leave him, he became violent, panic-stricken, and clung to her desperately. But immediately after, when left alone with the nurse, his outburst subsided, and the tyrannical child became curiously submissive.

The mother had suffered considerably from Frankie's rejections. In his clinging attitude she began to see a sign of the child's love, and she was so deeply impressed by his fear and his need of her protection that she succumbed to his phobic arrangements.

The child's anxiety reached its first peak when he was brought to nursery school at the age of 3 years and 9 months. At that time, his sister's nurse had just left the home, and he had to share his own nurse with the baby. He went to school for only 2 days. Each time, he had to be taken home because of his wild attacks of fear and screaming, and nothing could make him return to school. A second attempt to send him to a different school was made when he was 4½. Although the mother not only accompanied him to school, but actually stayed in the classroom with him, his anxiety did not subside. After 2 weeks, this attempt also was given up.

At the time of the third attempt, the teacher noticed that Frankie observed the activities of other children with the greatest interest, that he wanted to join their play, but could not move from his mother's side. Only when he could believe his teacher's promise that his mother would not leave the room without his knowledge, was Frankie able to play with the other children. However, even then he periodically interrupted his play to check on his mother's presence. Because of the intensity and duration of the child's anxiety, analysis was advised by the school.

The analyst suggested that treatment be postponed until after a period of preparation for analysis in which the school was to co-operate with the analyst.[2] This pre-analytic phase was designed to create a conflict in the child between his symptom and reality (8). To be sure, Frankie was already suffering from an internal conflict as shown by his phobia. However, as long as his phobic demands were met, he was insulated against anxiety or its equivalent, and in this state there was no reason for him to want to overcome his phobia. By our pre-analytic scheme we hoped to produce in him insight into his need for help, without which no psychoanalytic treatment can make any progress.[3] Thus, as soon as the child showed signs of a firm positive attachment to the school, his teacher was to inform him that his mother could no longer be permitted to be present. When the child protested that he could not remain alone, he was to be told that there was a person, the analyst, who might be able to help him stay at school, and to withstand the pain of his mother's absence. This pre-analytic scheme worked just as we had planned. Frankie, conscious of his conflict and his desire for help, was brought to the analyst, who now could act as a mediator between him and the school. The analyst "persuaded" the school to extend the trial period, and to agree that his

2 The psychological insight of the school's authorities and teachers was of great help. Such co-operation with the analyst is not frequent and should be commended.

3 For a further discussion of the need for an introductory phase in child analysis, see Anna Freud (16).

mother be permitted in the classroom. We also had to promise that his mother would be present during the analytic sessions. By this arrangement the analyst quickly became an important person for the child and the ground was prepared for a positive transference patterned after the child's relationship to his nurse—a relationship which at that time the analyst did not know in all its complexity.

The first period of Frankie's analysis was characterized by his desire for help. As long as he was in a state of anxiety, his understanding of analysis and his willingness to co-operate were remarkable.

His dramatic play during his first session led straight into his conflicts, just as in adult analysis the first dream often leads into the core of the patient's neurosis. His play revealed at once the experiences that had led to his phobia and thus betrayed the meaning of his symptom.

Frankie started his first session by building a hospital which was separated into a "lady department," a "baby department," and a "men's department." In the lobby, a lonely boy of 4 was seated all by himself, on a chair placed in an elevated position. The child's father was upstairs visiting "a lady" who, he informed us, when questioned, "is sick or maybe she's got a baby, maybe—I don't know, never mind." He made the point that newborn babies and mothers were separated in this hospital. Casting himself in the roles of a doctor and a nurse, he attended to the babies in a loving way, fed and cleaned them. However, toward the end of the play, a fire broke out. All the babies were burnt to death and the boy in the lobby was also in danger. He wanted to run home, but remembered that nobody would be there. Subsequently he joined the fire department, but it was not quite clear as to whether the firemen had started the fire or put it out. Frankie announced: "Ladies, the babies are dead; maybe we can save you!" Actually only those lady patients who had no babies were rescued by him. The one whom he several times—by a slip of the tongue—had addressed as "Mommy," however, was killed in the fire. No particular attention was given to the men's department. Most of the men had died anyway.

This game, which was repeated in the analysis for many weeks, betrayed the intensity of the boy's fury against his mother and sister. He could not forgive his mother for her unfaithfulness. He took her going to the hospital as a desertion of him and a sign of her lack of love. She must suffer the same tortures which he had suffered when she left him. He said, as it were: "I don't love you either; I hate you, I don't need you, you may die in the hospital. If you hadn't had a baby I would love you."

The dramatization of this biographical episode of his relationship with his mother was expressed repeatedly in a later period of his analysis, when in his play he reversed the roles: it was he who did the abandoning. A little boy escaped with his nurse into foreign countries and the mother was unable to find him. She looked for him but was usually killed by an army of enemies while he watched the execution from a hidden place. Sometimes he and his nurse joined the enemy army, sometimes he returned with his nurse to live with his father, who minded the mother's loss as little as did the boy.[4]

Frankie, who so thoroughly punished his mother by the withdrawal of his love, naturally lived in continual fear of retaliation. He could not stay at home or go out without his mother because he needed the presence of just that person against whom his aggressive impulses were directed. The presence of the ambivalently loved person prevents the phobic from being overwhelmed by his forbidden impulses and assures him that his aggressive intentions have not come true. But while the unconscious hatred directed at the protecting

[4] For more about this interesting detail in Frankie's play, which reveals his relationship with his father, see below, p. 15.

person is usually difficult to uncover in the analysis of adults, it was still very close to the surface in this 5½-year-old boy (10).

The following methods of technical approach might have been applied in the subsequent analytic period:

1) We might be tempted to interpret to the boy the various motivations for his aggression against his mother and the newborn baby as: (a) his revenge for her abandonment of him—an aggression which was close to his consciousness; (b) the desire to take his mother's place, which was repressed and indicated only by the loving way in which he took care of the babies when playing doctor and nurse, and by his peacefully living with his father after his mother had been killed; (c) his desire to kill his mother, which we might interpret, as Melanie Klein probably would, in terms of the child's original sadistic intentions to destroy the mother by disembowelment (30). (In the last period of his analysis these fantasies were openly expressed by the child.)

This approach, in which the ego is brusquely forced to face unconscious impulses, would result either in a quick suppression of the phobic symptom or in the strengthening of the phobia and of the resistance. The suppression of the symptom would make the patient temporarily independent of further analysis, but his ego, still in jeopardy from this suppression, would not have won the freedom which is essential for sound development. The strengthening of the phobia might lead to a stage in which the analyst himself would become an object of the phobia, preventing the continuation of the analysis.

2) By our participation in the play, we might refrain from any interpretation and thus, or actively, encourage the child to express his hostility in further play actions. This catharsis might soon lead to a diminishing of his phobia. The cathartic approach would mean, in terms of the id, a temporary discharge of tensions, but would leave the conflict between ego and id un-

touched. This would correspond to the pre-analytic procedure which Freud described in 1895 before he introduced the theory of psychodynamics. A return to such therapeutic procedures is encountered not infrequently at present.

3) We might devaluate the conflict by reassuring the child that such conflicts are frequent, natural, and understandable. This would mean a consolation and encouragement for the ego but would tend to scotomize the conflict instead of analyzing it (25).

4) The therapist might take a criticizing attitude, by appealing to the child's desire to grow up and not to indulge in such infantile phobic mechanisms (4). This approach, also directed to the child's ego, would be an appeal to give in to superego and reality demands, and would amount to an overpowering of his ego.

Any of these four ways might be applied, depending on the therapist's aims and personality. They all might lead to a quick disappearance of the symptom.

In order to bring about an *ego change* we chose for interpretation from the different themes revealed in the child's play that element in which the patient represented his ego. It was evident to us that he himself was the lonely 4-year-old boy in the hospital game, although feelings of sadness and loneliness had not been mentioned by him in his play. On the contrary, in his game he demonstrated only the *defense* against loneliness and sadness.

By placing the little boy's chair in an elevated position he had reversed the reality situation, presenting himself as omnipotent and successful. Thus he became a person who actually knew what went on in the hospital, who directed the events, and who had no reason whatever to feel excluded and unhappy. The omnipotence, as well as the destruction of mother and infant, were used as defenses by which he denied the affect of sadness. But before the defense proper could be dealt with, it was necessary to have the child recognize and experience such affects.

We must remember that at the time of the analysis Frankie himself did not know anything of his sadness. This sadness had been the original response of the child's ego to an external occurrence of traumatic effect. It had existed only temporarily and was not particularly noticed by those about him. The patient had successfully concealed from himself the affect of sadness which evidently had been too painful for him to bear. He had replaced it by his aggressive and tyrannical demands to which he later reacted with his phobic symptoms. Both aggression and anxiety were the end-product of an initial sadness and without recapturing that initial affect so that the patient was aware of it, no real ego change could be brought about.

The warded-off affect is a barrier to a successful interpretation of the conflict and therefore must be made conscious before any further step can be taken, lest the ego be pushed into a course beyond its integrative power (15). Bringing an affect into consciousness furnishes an opportunity for the unravelling of both genetic and dynamic elements. The re-experiencing of the original affects provides the emotional ground for the subsequent interpretation of unconscious material and makes it possible for the child to deal with a conflict consciously (17). Our aim, of course, was to make him conscious of the fact that behind the sadness, aggression and anxiety, there was an intense, unrewarded and repressed longing for the mother.[5]

In order to introduce this emotion into the child's consciousness without arousing undue resistance, the loneliness of the little boy in his game became the subject of our analytic work for several weeks. The analyst expressed sympathy for the lonely child

[5] It may appear that bringing an emotion to consciousness is a scanty result of many weeks of analytic work. However, it is noteworthy that the uncovering of recent emotions is often extremely painful for the child, more painful than the direct interpretation of deep unconscious content, which is frequently easily accepted by children and taken as a permission to obtain instinctual gratification.

who is barred from his mother's sickroom and who is too little to understand why his father is admitted. Frankie responded to the analyst's sympathy with growing sadness, which could be discerned only from his facial expression. The analyst's sympathy made it possible for him to tolerate this affect.

Once he had been able to face his sadness, Frankie showed relatively little resistance when his specific situation was examined. We asked whether by any chance he was a child who had been left alone while his mother was in the hospital. Or had someone taken care of him during that difficult period? He turned to his mother with the question: "Was I alone, Mommy?" and before she could answer, he told about his father and his nurse's presence, adding that his nurse would "never, never leave him alone."

By taking advantage of the variations of the hospital game slowly introduced by the child, we were able to go into the details of his life immediately before his sister's birth and again after the mother's return from the hospital. We learned from him how strong his affection for his nurse had been even before his sister's birth; that she had appeared a far more reliable person than his mother, who frequently went out and left him alone with the nurse. Gradually he remembered periods of separation from his parents before the sister's birth. Once when his parents left for vacation he stayed at his grandparents' home with his nurse.[6] One of his memories referred to his watching the departure of his parents

in a plane,[7] and his subsequent illness. He assured us that the nurse never left his side while the parents were absent.

This ample material referring to abandonment corroborated the appropriateness of selecting his sadness as the first content of our interpretation. To him, being sent to school was an aggravating repetition of former separations: it happened just after his sister's nurse had left and his own nurse and mother had to share in the care of the baby. Thus, he lost not only his mother but also his nurse "who would never, never leave me alone." *This repetition of the traumatic experience of being abandoned* brought about the climax of his anxiety.

In his play, and later, in direct memories, he revealed the specific contents of his fear. He was afraid that he might not be able to stop the school bus which brought the children home, that he might not recognize his own home, that he might never find his way home and, worst of all, even if these obstacles were overcome, the door of the school bus might not open and he would be trapped.

His school phobia and the mother's stay in the hospital were thus linked. His fear of not finding his way home corresponded to his unconscious, revengeful wish that his mother who had abandoned him would never return, an interpretation which was confirmed by many play actions and verbalizations.

The same aggression against the mother underlay his fear that he would not recognize his house. When the mother returned from the hospital, he, of course, recognized her, but behaved as if he could not acknowledge her to be his mother. The fear of being trapped, which later became an important overt factor in his neurosis, referred to his original death wish against the newborn baby. The one who was to be

---

[6] I shall not follow up this episode because analysis did not reveal that any definite trauma occurred during this visit. However, incidental remarks and Frankie's behavior toward his grandfather led me to assume that the patient experienced a castration threat from his grandfather at that time. It would seem that this trauma did not have any immediate pathological effect on the child. The analytic material suggests that subsequent events led retroactively to a revival of that experience—a delayed effect comparable to that which similar occurrences had on "Little Hans."

[7] An interesting relationship seemed to connect this incident of the plane with the later development of the child's neurosis, particularly as manifested in his elevator phobia.

trapped was his little sister. In a later phase of his analysis he said: "If Mommy had not opened her belly, my sister would never have come out." (30)[8]

The feeling of jealousy toward the sister whose birth had caused him such suffering found almost no overt expression. Frankie had learned to spare himself jealousy by denying the baby's existence almost completely during her first two years of life. He ingeniously escaped the pain of jealousy by creating exactly the same feeling of frustration in his mother as that which was gnawing at him. He refused to accept any affection from her, while he encouraged the nurse to cuddle him in his mother's presence.

The contradiction in his attitude toward his mother was the next step in our own interpretation. He was shown the discrepancy between his inability to be without her and the rejecting way in which he treated her. Our interpretation suggested that he had exaggerated his affection to his nurse because he wanted to take revenge for the disappointments he had suffered at the hands of his mother. Throughout the months following this interpretation he told us that his nurse had forced him to obedience by threats. We understood that some of his criticisms against his mother were based on the nurse's deprecating remarks. Moreover, he intimated that there were some secrets between him and the nurse which he was determined not to reveal, and about which we learned only after the nurse had left the home. "Only God knows about my secret," he used to say, "and even God may not know it."

By continually connecting his recent experiences and emotions to their genetic counterparts, his sadness and jealousy, the pathological tie to his nurse was loosened. The analysis of the triangular relation between the mother, the nurse, and himself enabled him to desist from arousing his mother's jealousy. Only now his own jealousy appeared in its proper place, openly directed against his little sister.

Once the hostility toward his mother was diminished, his relationship to her seemed greatly improved, and his repressed love came to the fore. With this resolution the manifest school phobia subsided. He was able both to stay in school and to attend his analytic sessions without his mother's presence. This situation continued even after the nurse left. He took her leaving without an unduly exaggerated reaction, dared to express his sadness, and remained free of fear. In spite of all these encouraging signs, his neurosis was by no means dissolved.

In describing the first phase of Frankie's treatment it appears that we dealt with what might be called the preoedipal constituent of his disorder. Although his hostility as well as the clinical symptom revolved exclusively around female persons, such as his mother and nurse, two circumstances make one hesitate to speak of this phase of Frankie's disorders as preoedipal. There were indications that he had entered the oedipal phase prior to the onset of this phobia, but that this oedipal phase was interrupted by the outbreak of his neurosis. Furthermore, as we shall see later, the nurse was partly a representative of the father.[9] This may be one reason why, in the clinical manifestation of his illness, so little material regarding his father came to the fore at this period.

Although Frankie's conquest of his aggressiveness toward his mother now made it possible for him to re-experience and to express his normal positive oedipal conflicts, he did so only in the analytic session. At home, the child's reaction to the father seemed to be emotionally neutral. He was, for instance, apparently unaffected by his father's frequent arrivals at and departures from home during war-time and even the analyst's reference to this failed to provoke any direct response. Only in his dramatic

8 See also p. 121.

9 See also pp. 124 ff.

play and fantasy material did he reveal his hostility toward men. Innumerable play episodes also betrayed Frankie's interest in procreation and his urge to know "what was going on" between his parents.

In the most frequent of his play dramatizations, a father was absent and a mother was alone. Then an apparently friendly man, a butcher, a policeman, or a vegetable man (each impersonated by Frankie), came to dinner. The "friendly" visit always ended with an attack on the mother who was killed. The ending was always the same: the visitors were taken by the police and sentenced to death by the judge, both of whom were again personified by Frankie.

It was our next task to connect these fantasies with his actual experiences. This was achieved by confronting him with a paradox: his lack of emotion about his own father's coming and going, and the excitement the child showed in his play when visitors arrived. The mother had reported that prior to the outbreak of his neurosis, Frankie had shown signs of irritability toward visitors, especially toward his grandfather. This irritability was markedly increased when his phobic symptom disappeared. Neurotic anxiety was supplanted by the aggression against which the phobia had been mobilized in an earlier period.

It became evident that the image of the father had been split into two groups of substitutes: male relatives of his mother, of whom the most important was his grandfather, and various tradesmen and craftsmen who Frankie asserted were the nurse's intimates.[10]

In the course of discussing his irritation toward visitors, Frankie admitted that there was actually no reason for him to assume that visitors would attack his mother. Nevertheless, he felt that he had to guard her against threatening dangers, especially if she were out of his sight. "She might run away," he said. "She might be

[10] See footnote 6.

run over, or her car might break, or men might kill her in the subway." We finally understood that he was afraid that all of these dangers would lead to a second hospitalization, just as when his mother had had her baby.

The circle was closed. The danger which threatened the mother from relations with men would result in what was the gravest danger to him: the arrival of a new baby. He had to guard against a repetition of this traumatic experience.

It was this concern that was responsible for the insomnia which became acute at this point of his analysis. There had been previous occurrences of insomnia when he was $2\frac{1}{2}$ and again when he was $4\frac{1}{2}$. Now again it took him hours to fall asleep. He listened silently and anxiously to the noises at night. Whenever his parents spent an evening at home, he ran back and forth between the living room and his bedroom. He wanted to know, as he expressed it, what plans they were making. They might eat something special and he wanted to share it. Or someone might come and hurt his Mommy. Ideas about the problem of procreation filled the hours of his severe insomnia.

Our attempts to discover what Frankie thought about birth and procreation met only with resistance. Even with our help, he could not verbalize his sexual theories, but expressed them in further dramatizations. His games presented scenes of attack duplicating those which he undoubtedly assumed were taking place in his parents' bedroom. The role of the attacker soon aroused anxiety, and he shifted in his play to the role of an observer of the attacks.

When he began to present this new content, and for some time thereafter, he became quite excited. It is not easy to describe his complex emotional state at such moments. It was a mixture of rage and triumphant conquest, of irritability and anxiety. These emotions changed rapidly and erratically without any obvious reference to the content of the dramatic play characterized by overactivity. Gradually the character of his dramatizations changed: the wild emotions became pacified, the kinesthetic storm was subdued to meaningful gestures. One element which was already present in his wild performances became the predominant and all-important feature: a strong inclination to gain pleasure by use of his eyes. This voyeuristic element led him to a new impersonation, that of an omniscient God.

In his new role he made the analyst a frightened, sleeping child into whose ears God whispered dreams of wild colliding horses, of violent scenes in which "Daddy throws Mommy out of the window so that she has to go to the hospital for eighteen days." The "sleeping games" revealed his suspicions of something frightful happening between his father and mother during the night—something he would have liked to observe. As God, he had the right to see and watch everything. His new role of God provided him with greater power than he had previously enjoyed as attacker, judge, or policeman—roles in which he had experienced the triumph of the conqueror, but also suffered the pain of the conquered.

The dynamics of these games may be reconstructed as follows: when Frankie made the analyst act the part of a child whose dreams were supplied by God's whispers, he was revealing his reaction to the noises emanating from his parents' room. The child obviously completed visually what had been suggested audibly. He was unable to endure his own conception of what was taking place and tried to overcome this terror by putting himself in control of the events—by becoming God who can create dreams by his whisper.[11]

Later, however, when he realized that God was not only his own creation but a concept shared by others and that he could not rule "his" God to the extent necessary to be protected from anxiety, he replaced his fantasy of an omniscient God by an imaginary television apparatus which belonged exclusively to his fantasy and thus was completely at the disposal of his wishes and plans. ("God sees everything, but the television apparatus sees only if *I* turn it on.") The television apparatus brought the child closer to reality. When he was God, he made the analyst dream about those frightful scenes between his parents, while with the introduction of his imaginary television apparatus, he himself attempted to face those scenes. The analyst was made a co-observer of eating scenes in restaurants, for which Frankie provided the music (another auditory manifestation) while explaining the observed events to the analyst. He reassured the analyst many times that the observations were "make believe" and actually he never again reached the previously described state of excitement and anxiety. By means of his invention of the television apparatus, he removed himself not only from the scenes he imagined, but also from the feelings of desire and concomitant guilt which those scenes aroused.

It was noteworthy that with his exchange of the machine for God, the content of his problems was no longer expressed on the phallic level, but in oral terms. The aggressive element persisted, but apparently the content of his fantasies became more acceptable to his dawning conscience when expressed in the relative innocence of oral gratifications.

The following is one of the scenes observed through the apparatus: Father was in the restaurant and ordered the most delicious food for Mother from the restaurant owner. Then he had a secret talk with the owner. As soon as Mother had eaten, she collapsed and died; the food was poisoned. (In his thoughts, eating was linked with being impregnated, for which Frankie had not yet forgiven his mother, and for which he still punished her by death.) Father and the owner of the res-

---

[11] His role of God might be construed as an identification with the sexual father, but this was only partly true. The identification with the father was, in this instance, a defense against a greater danger, the yielding to passivity. The basic identification was with the mother, whose sexual role Frankie really craved.

taurant were unconcerned by her death; they continued their pleasant talk and play, shoving Mother under the table.[12] Some drawings of this time show God and God's wife feasting at a dinner table, disturbed by "little gnomes" who alternately attack God and his wife.

These games helped the investigation and understanding of a past period of his life: We had reason to assume that when he was 4½, his screaming attacks had reappeared as his reaction to audible primal scene experiences. His father once wrote us that in former times, "in his prankish days," he used to pinch his wife and throw her into the air, "all in fun and for exercise . . . , I can imagine what it must have seemed like to someone who heard it but did not see what actually happened." Frankie's running back and forth between his bedroom and the living room occurred in reaction to auditory stimuli and continued until his nurse quenched his active interest and nightly curiosity by a threatening and punishing attitude.

With the process of internalization of his conflicts the actually threatening nurse was replaced by imaginary objects, mainly wolves, who stood guard under his bed and kept him from getting up and investigating what might be happening in the parental bedroom.

---

[12] This scene is rich in its overdetermined factors; it permits the reconstruction of Frankie's oedipus complex. The element, "Mother is shoved under the table," refers to the child's resentment against his mother, who did not pay any attention to him when he, sitting under the table, tried to disturb his parents' meal. The next element, "Father and restaurant owner confer about the food for Mother (from which she dies)" is an indication of Frankie's wish to participate in his father's sexual activities. Frankie's position as restaurant owner was evident in many daydreams: he possessed "all the restaurants in New York." This detail makes us anticipate that Frankie's hostility toward his mother contained also some envy of her role as father's wife. Owner and father-Frankie and father do together what otherwise mother and father do. We shall see later how strong the child's desire was to take the passive role with the father.

These imaginary wolves under his bed were able, like the God he had played, to see what he did and to surmise his intentions. As soon as he put out hand or foot to go into his parents' bedroom,[13] the wolves would snap at him; "but they would let me go to the bathroom." For a protection from their attacks the boy armed himself with many weapons, preferably with a long stick, in order to beat the wolves down when they raised their heads. He maintained that they observed all his movements, and he in turn countered with an equally watchful attitude. His configuration of the wolves contained as elements the punitive and protective parent figures as well as his own impulses. The wolves punish his intentions and prevent their fulfillment. Their symbolic role as superego was strikingly confirmed in a drawing which Frankie called the WOLVES' STATUE. It showed an oversized wolf (in human form) with outstretched arms, floating above Frankie in his bed, under which a number of smaller-sized wolves (also in human form) were engaged in mysterious activities, obviously of a sexual nature. In his comments on this picture, Frankie said: "It shows what the wolves hope for, what they will look like some day."

The dread of wolves which had haunted the child for weeks finally led to the analysis of his castration fear. In his stories and in his play, the mother's attackers who previously had been punished by death, now were punished by almost undisguised castration. In his pictures he endowed God with monstrously elongated arms and legs, only to cut off these limbs with scissors. Immediately after such operation he tried to undo this symbolic act of castration by drawing innumerable new arms and legs. Frankie derived reassurance from the idea that destruction is not necessarily irrevoc-

---

[13] The element of uncovering the hands and feet is overdetermined and it is obviously a presentation of its opposite, i.e., a reverse of the original warning against touching his genital under the bedcover.

able and consequently dared to express the thoughts of castration without any symbolic disguise. Mother's attackers were imprisoned and he, as a doctor, subjected the prisoners to operations which usually threw him into a state of exaltation. Playing the doctor, he exclaimed: "Those criminals, they have to be operated on. Off with their wee-wees. It has to come off!" In his play he guarded himself against any awareness of his fear by identifying himself with the person performing the act of castration. His fear of anticipated retaliation found expression in his behavior toward his pediatrician. Frankie had always been a difficult patient, but during this period he absolutely refused to be examined, and assaulted the doctor by throwing blocks or potatoes which he carefully had stored under his bed for this purpose.

The emphasis in our interpretation was on Frankie's preoccupation with the mechanisms of undoing, and his identification with the aggressor. After this, we were able to approach the theme of his castration fear by confronting him with a comparison of his impersonation of a cruel doctor and the kind attitude of his own doctor; with the fearlessness of his prisoners in contrast to his own frightened aggressiveness toward his doctor.

In view of the anxiety which was kept in abeyance by his identification with a castrative figure, particular caution was necessary in the interpretation and dissolution of this identification. Abrupt release of such large quantities of anxiety would have produced a traumatic effect. Therefore it seemed indicated to decrease this defense only gradually. In a preparatory period of several weeks, we "amused" ourselves by imagining how frightened the brave prisoners of his fantasy would feel if *they* were suddenly exposed to the reality of a doctor's office. By our bantering his fantasy-prisoners, Frankie was enabled to take a more tolerant view of these frightening thoughts which he had formerly warded off by identification with the aggressor.

Through this playful approach we prepared him for the fact that it was he himself who feared for his genitals, or at least that in the past he had once done so, even if the past were only ten minutes ago. Introducing *humor* (23) as a benign defense, we saved Frankie the full impact of the suffering which accompanies castration fear. He learned to understand that the wolves represented not only the prohibiting nurse and the father, but also himself with his strong voyeuristic and castrative impulses.

Although his masturbation was not yet approachable, the decrease of his castration fear enabled him to bring his sexual curiosity into the open and to ask the questions to which he had tried to find the answers by his compulsive running back and forth to his parents' room.

The material obtained from his play actions, in which men violently attack women, was interpreted to him in terms of his fantasies about intercourse. The treatment made it possible for him to re-enter the oedipal phase, and the father then acquired that emotional importance in the child's reality which was due him in terms of the oedipal relationship. Yet despite this progress, we did not expect his behavior in this new phase to be free of neurotic disturbances. . . .

III

So far, we have given the material in almost chronological sequence, in order to round out the clinical picture and to illustrate the actual course of the treatment. Such further chronological presentation of complex analytic material would leave the reader with a feeling of confusion. Therefore we shall now discuss two of Frankie's symptoms, without regard to the order of their appearance in the analysis: his retention of urine and his elevator phobia.

The retention of urine could be traced back to the age of 3 shortly after bladder control had been established. One of the stories in the first period of Frankie's analysis indicated that the act of urination was connected with threats of castration:

"Two giants once ate up a river, so each river said: 'Get bigger so that the giants won't be able to eat you up.' " A big river equals a big penis "which holds lots of water."

Frankie had confessed with shame that he refused to use strange bathrooms because he thought that they were inhabited by giants who might *bite* off one's penis. However, when the retention of urine became the subject of his analysis, he denied ever having had such a fear, and claimed that the analyst had invented it.

Previously we had learned about a number of his oral impregnation theories, among which the most prominent had been that a woman conceived by swallowing a man's penis or, as revealed in his restaurant games, by taking in poisoned food. Frankie's present impregnation fantasies still contained the element of poison but now poisoning was linked with urination: the drinking of wine led to impregnation. In analysis he squirted the analyst with his water pistol, aiming at her mouth, and shouting: "I'll poison you, I'll poison you. My arrows are poisoned with germs." Many times he slipped, and said "sperms" instead of "germs."

Here the analyst should have become aware that the sense of urgency which he betrayed in his actions indicated an attempt to demonstrate more than a mere theory, namely a past experience which he could not verbalize. Such emotional urgency appears to us as a clinical indication that we are dealing not with a fantasy but with a reality experience—and furthermore, an experience the impact of which probably came before verbalization was possible.

Frankie's play with the water pistol showed his masculine intention toward women. When we pointed out the contradiction in his behavior, namely his excessive retention of urine (at this time from

eight to nine hours) and his pleasure in squirting water, he recalled that in the past he had gaily and wilfully urinated on the floor. His nurse had threatened and shamed him into obedience. He did not recognize that his prolonged retention of urine was his defiant revenge upon the nurse.

The retention of urine exemplified his conflict between active tendencies and passive desires and it was patterned after the conflict between him and the nurse when she was intolerant of his urethral eroticism. At first, Frankie's wilful urination had been the expression of his exhibitionistic masculine tendencies. The nurse grabbed him whenever she saw him prepare to urinate and carried him into the bathroom against his will. He recalled that soon after this the struggle with her became more pleasant than the intended urination. Therefore he often *pretended* to urinate into the corner of the living room in order to be picked up by her and carried to the toilet.

At the time of his analysis, there was no open manifestation of any desire to be carried. On the contrary, we knew from his parents' complaints that, even as a very young child, he had a marked objection to being touched, lifted, or carried about. In view of the fact that the child's later struggle was directed at preventing passive locomotion, we concluded that he had once experienced great pleasure from equilibrium sensations, and that this pleasure must subsequently have had undesirable consequences for him.

We assumed in our reconstruction that he had urinated while being carried by the nurse and that the loss of urine had added to the pleasure of passive locomotion. We further assumed that the nurse must have threatened or punished him for this, and that his retention of urine also was aimed at preventing a repetition of that experience. Her threats or punishment must have contributed to his later anxiety over the loss of urine.

We may then recapitulate the history of his urinary symptom as follows:

At first, acting as if he wanted to urinate in the living room was a means of forcing the nurse to carry him to the toilet and provided him with gratification through passive locomotion. Later, however, the retention of urine became an adequate defense both against losing control during passive locomotion, and against being touched. His panicky fear of being touched pointed to an originally pleasurable tactile experience. He recalled that he often refused to urinate in order to force the nurse to take out his penis.

We assume that the craving to be touched was not satisfied in the way he expected. He must have expected a gentle handling whereas the nurse, annoyed by his provocative behavior, was rough and may even have accompanied her actions with direct castration threats, an assumption supported by the previous story of the giants in the bathroom.

In another of his stories he further confirmed this reconstruction: "A king killed his mother when he was three years old. He wanted her to cut trees in his garden, a hundred thousand trees. And she should do it with her *hands*. But she was fresh, she dared to ask for an axe—therefore she must die."

He told this castration story after an episode at school when he refused to submit to a medical examination by the school physician, a woman. The only fear which he would admit was a dread of the smallness of the consultation room. He denied any fear that the doctor might harm him although he had reported only the day before that his school friends claimed this doctor "is used to cutting off wee-wees." "Anyhow," he continued, "I will not permit a ladydoctor to look at my penis."

We might add here what the child could not express: The smallness of the consultation room revived recollections of the bathroom in which the scenes with the nurse had taken place. It was as if he were saying by his refusal: "I am afraid that women in 'small rooms,' even if only

looking at my penis, might arouse my desires. Women are as fickle as my beloved nurse. When I wanted to have my penis touched she hurt it." Her hands, instead of giving pleasure, might perform castration with an axe as the mother did in the king's story. (The experience in the bathroom with his nurse had contributed to his claustrophobic ideas of being trapped in small rooms.)

His panicky fear of being touched was a defense against the desire to obtain this passive satisfaction. While at the beginning wilfully retaining urine was a means of obtaining the gratification of being touched, subsequently the retention of urine—which by now had become an established symptom—was a means for defense against this danger. Furthermore, his urinary inhibition guarded him against his masturbatory wishes. By not urinating he avoided both the temptation to touch and the act of touching. He had even learned to direct the stream of his urine without touching his penis.

Frankie had already indicated his fear of losing control in his first phobic attack at school when he was afraid that he would not be able to stop the bus and the car would pass his house. He projected onto the school bus his own fear of being overwhelmed by a tidal wave of anxiety, and of being helpless in its grip.

On his second and last schoolday in the first school he was brought home crying and inconsolable. In analysis he described his plight in the following words: "I was crying and crying, because I had no handkerchief." Again his complaint is against being overwhelmed—this time by crying which he could not stop. He rejected our suggestion that he might at that time have feared the loss of bladder control, but then volunteered the statement that he could not bear the smell of the toilet at school, that the cot on which he should have rested smelled of urine, and he insisted that the teacher had threatened to lock up bad children in the bathroom.

Such a stream of recollections is unusual in child analysis. Whenever it occurred in Frankie's case it was a precursor of therapeutic gain. Soon after this, the retention of urine was given up.

While the child's memories were concerned with tears, a more basic fear was concerned with the loss of urine, a striking example of the oft-claimed connection between urination and tears. We should like to note here that the fear of uncontrollable flowing of tears and of urine both correspond to the uncontrollable flow of neurotic anxiety (26).[14] The main complaint of phobic patients is the danger of being overwhelmed by an uncontrollable flow of anxiety.

We shall now present, in some detail, Frankie's elevator phobia, which was one of his most impressive symptoms since it was a compound of all the etiological factors involved in his neurosis. It contained his aggression against and identification with his father on the oedipal level; his aggression against and identification with his mother; his death wish against his sister and his desire to take her place, and finally it included his masturbation conflicts: the fear of erections, the fear of losing control over his own emotions and the fear of being lifted, all of which were components of the danger of castration.

The child summarized the dangers which the ride in the elevator involved as follows: "The elevator might crash down, or the door might not open, and I would be trapped."

We recall that when Frankie was 4½ he spent hours at night trying to get out of bed to observe his parents and his nurse. His nurse curbed this restlessness by threats. She said she would call the elevator man to teach him not to disturb people. The threat was effective, and the boy stayed in bed. Whenever he heard the sound of the elevator, he was terrified, expecting the man to come in and take him away. He wished that the elevator would crash with the operator. Then what he wanted to have happen to the dreaded elevator man, by his familiar mechanism, recoiled against himself, and he feared that the elevator might crash down while he was in it. Here the factors of aggression and retaliation stemming from his oedipus complex are encountered again; the elevator man represented his father, a fact which Frankie himself recognized.

A fear concerning his mother was also involved in his elevator phobia. Here his memories led into a period of life before his sister was born. He was deeply moved when he recalled that his father used to greet his mother by lifting her "high, high up in the air . . . I always thought, he'll suddenly throw her out of the window.[15] Daddy whirled Mommy around. I hate this if someone does it to me. It makes you feel crazy." Beneath the verbalized displeasure was longing and envy of the mother because of the pleasure he suspected she derived from being lifted up by the father. The idea that his father would throw his mother out of the window found its analogy in the fearful expectation that "the crazy elevator man" would lose control over the elevator, so that suddenly Frankie would find himself "deep down in the cellar under the building." He would encounter the same fate that he wished for his mother.

The following dream mirrors his desire for participation in the sexual excitement which he believed his mother experienced when his father playfully lifted her up.

"Some boy came to my house and we wanted to make a fire escape so that cars could go down one side and people could go down the other. The boy that I invited to my house—he fell down, way downstairs. Then the room starts to go down, the whole room, and Mommy tried to hold on and Mommy tried to keep up.

[14] K. R. Eissler has suggested that the biological root of full-fledged phobic attacks is the sensation of the uncontrollable flow of urine.

[15] The same element is present in the sleeping game. See p. 115.

And my sister fell into the business—into the room. *She* started to go down. Mommy did not fall down (Daddy helped to keep up things). I was falling down with the rest. Finally we all landed in the cellar." (Actually, the emphasis on "going down" was a representation of its opposite, being lifted up.)[16]

This dream would seem to be a scarcely distorted representation of some experience of the primal scene, an experience which had been condensed with the frequently observed lifting scenes between his father and mother and both experiences must have impressed him with the idea that a unity existed between father and mother from which he felt excluded. In his dream, he tried to participate in this unity: "I was falling down with the rest. Finally we *all* landed in the cellar."

The elevator phobia revealed another element, one which was contained within the phobia. This was a claustrophobia which was the result of Frankie's desire for being carried in his mother's womb and his defense against it.

Being carried symbolized to the child a means of unification with the mother's body (28). The perfect way to insure himself against his mother's desertion would be to be inside her body. He reflected this fantasy by stressing the great advantages the fetus has in being so closely united with the mother, or, as he expressed it, "in being tied to her." His desire for the womb was accompanied by a great fear of it. It was seen as a castrating organ, and was visualized as a "lion's mouth," and a "trap which can bite or pinch off an arm or a leg." He projected his own aggression upon the womb, especially when he realized with frustration that his little sister had enjoyed the unity with mother at a time he was already separated from her. In one analytic session, he told us that he had actually wished that his sister should be trapped in the mother's womb; in his own words, "If Mommy had not opened her belly, my sister would have never come out."

The wish for his sister's entrapment aroused a fear of retaliation, but this time from all small spaces, such as buses, bathrooms and elevators. Being trapped in the elevator was the punishment for the identical wish against the sister. We find in his claustrophobia a condensation of his identification with his sister, the aggression against her, and the ensuing danger to himself.

When he was confronted with the contradiction between his desire to be a fetus and his fear of being trapped in small places, he explained that the embryo did not mind the restriction in space since it participated passively in the mother's locomotion. These thoughts had found expression in the following questions in which the connection between passive locomotion and the flow of urine was again emphasized. "Does the child feel every little step of the mother or does only the mother feel the child kicking around?" And another time, "What does the mother say if the child wee-wees into her?"

In view of these questions his claustrophobia appears as a fabric in which activity and passivity are interwoven. This

---

[16] It might be of value to summarize what we learned through Frankie's preoccupation with equillibrium sensations and the feeling of being lifted. This preoccupation and the conflicts it aroused were the result of: (1) His pleasure as a young child, when his nurse lifted him, and the fear that her castration threats made him attach to the act of being lifted. This was tied up with his dread of an uncontrollable flow of urine—and of anxiety. (2) His fear and loneliness at the airport when his mother had been "lifted away" from him in the plane. Somehow, the child connected this flight with the later birth of his sister. It is actually a fact that the mother became pregnant during this trip with her husband. In other words, Frankie felt, "If one is lifted, one becomes pregnant. I would like to be lifted. I would like to have a child, as my mother did. But being lifted, and being mother, means losing my penis. I want to be lifted, but I dare not pay the price for it." Naturally, Frankie did not reason out all of these factors in this manner. Our presentation is a reconstruction of the way he *felt*—his emotional, rather than intellectual, reasoning.

appears to us as a possible reflection of an early ego state in which activity and passivity had not yet found separate representation.

The movement of the elevator became for Frankie an important factor through its affinity to kinesthetic sensations. The ride in the elevator was dangerous because it aroused his sexual sensations. He projected his own sexual excitement onto the elevator man and assumed that the operator, aroused by passive locomotion, would lose control over the elevator. He would therefore be unable to stop the elevator which would either continue to move indefinitely up and down, or would crash down in a sudden fall. This explains why Frankie called every elevator man "crazy," and why he drew dozens of pictures of "crazy elevators" which rolled up and down and could not stop, so that "the passengers would become dizzy and crazy like being whirled around."

For Frankie the up and down movement of the elevator had gained another symbolic meaning. It was equal to an erection, an analogy which the child directly communicated, and which at long last made it possible for us to approach his problem of masturbation.

Several times during the course of his analysis he had made allusions to this problem, for instance when he feared the wolves would snap at his fingers and later, when he dramatized the game of "bad children" who spoil pipes and electric appliances, and even more openly, when we discussed his retention of urine. But our previous attempts to interpret to him the connection of this material with his masturbation had been of no avail. The child assured us that masturbation had never occurred in his life. However, he finally admitted that he derived some pleasure from another activity. It consisted in the contraction of the pelvic muscles and Frankie told us that he indulged in it for hours. We consider these manipulations as a masturbatory equivalent.

Frankie could not recall ever having been reprimanded for masturbation or threatened with castration for it. He did remember, however, that the nurse had interfered with his sister's masturbation and that she had warned him that retaining urine might cause a poisoning of the blood. To our questions as to the character of the disease of blood poisoning, he responded without any hesitation: "Blood poisoning? You might lose a finger or a leg!" and the following associations showed that to him, blood poisoning meant bleeding like a woman, being castrated like his sister, losing control over one's own emotions—in short, "going crazy." Frankie's behavior was occasionally called "crazy" when he indulged in his outbreaks of uncontrollable wildness. Since he had occasionally experienced erections during such outbursts, he felt that there was a link between phallic sexuality and craziness. He told us that erections were once a desired experience, especially if they could be brought about indirectly. He admitted that he had sometimes consciously used retention of urine as a means of producing erections. Later he discovered accidentally that by contraction of the pelvic muscles he could likewise produce erections. However, at the height of his elevator phobia he complained he could not produce any erections despite conscious efforts to do so.

The hour long contractions of the pelvic muscles had either led to or were accompanied by painful spasms in the umbilical region. He called these sensations "wee-wee ache," and had always feared that these symptoms were proof that he had the dreaded disease of blood poisoning, especially since he had actually experienced pains when retaining urine for hours. These pains represented the hysterical nucleus which is regularly to be found at the root of an obsessional neurosis(21). When analyzing this symptom, the pains around the navel shifted to the penis where the sensations probably had their origin. By the displacement of the sensation from the penis to the navel, he utilized an existing identity between his sister and himself. The furrow of the navel appeared to him similar to the female genital, and while his castration fear still did not permit him to accept the female genital itself as the point of similarity, he proudly pointed out that he had a navel like his sister's, that in this respect he was like her. By accepting the fantasy of being similar to his sister—by being a girl—he achieved the escape from the dreaded castration by an external force. We remind the reader that Frankie had been convinced that his sister had been deprived of a penis because she, like the "bad children" in the plumber game, had spoiled her genital by touching it.

Frankie's pelvic contractions, his first obsessional symptom, were a defense against the temptation of manual masturbation. In contrast to adult compulsive patients in whom the secondary struggle against anal-sadistic impulses is in the foreground,[17] Frankie's first compulsive symptoms still showed their connection with masturbation in an undistorted way. His prohibition against touching referred directly and consciously to the genital. The curbed impulses for masturbatory satisfaction had produced a state of tension which contributed to his insomnia. He called this state, in which he lay awake for hours, "boredom in bed," and vainly attempted to distract and amuse himself with games. He crowded his bed with a variety of toys in order always to be sure of finding something to play with. Unfatigued, he manipulated his toy vehicles, cards, and toy money for hours. As soon as the analyst explained that his need for toys in bed was a means of assurance against the temptation to masturbate, he strengthened his defense by extending his taboo to the touching of his toys at night.[18] He now substituted thought operations for the handling of the toys, which originally had diverted him from manual masturbation. He learned to play all his card games in his "head only," and was proud of being able to count his money "even without money." The fantasies which accompanied his masturbatory equivalent emphasized likewise the taboo of touching. They were centered around the automatic working of imaginary machines. "I need not even press a button to make trains or my elevator move upward," he explained. He imagined a truck or train or a passenger car going over a bridge, or "up, up, up the hill" and "slowly, slowly, down." To our question as to how his penis behaved during these fantasies, he answered that he tried to direct the descent of vehicles carefully so that the erection would not subside too quickly. "It goes up and down again, just as I want, and I try not to let it drop."

The blocking of sexual satisfaction had resulted in an uncontrollable outbreak of sadism and aggression. While he refrained from using his hands for masturbation he could not refrain from grabbing, in an almost obsessional manner, whatever he could get hold of. He destroyed possessions of his own as well as those of adults. It may well be that the breaking of objects symbolized the destruction of his own genital were he to touch it (11). His obsessional symptoms were transitory, but his pre-occupation with certain thought operations made us aware of a nascent compulsive character. A tendency to brood about problems of life and death and morals emerged while he still indulged in sadistic outbursts. All these uncontrollable sadistic acts were designed to provoke

[17] The conspicuous absence of anal material in this patient can be explained by the fact that a temporary compulsive neurosis *in statu nascendi* subsided quickly under analysis.

[18] The other side of his taboo of touching was expressed in his worry lest other people touch his eating utensils. He developed a preoccupation with contagious diseases which might be contracted through touch.

repercussions, which in their turn served to gratify his passive desires.

Eventually he started to masturbate and his confession of manual masturbation was made through his drawings. Silently he spent many hours drawing hands. At first his hands could not be recognized as such. Later he used the analyst's hands and his own to trace around, but often left out a finger, once more indicating the danger of "blood poisoning," "losing a finger or a leg." Eventually, when interpretation had diminished his anxiety so that he could verbalize his problem, he could draw whole figures with complete limbs without resorting to tracing. This sequence of drawings from shapeless to accurate representations shows how the lifting of anxiety promotes simultaneously both greater sexual freedom and sublimation.

IV

Until now our presentation of Frankie's case may have given the impression that we centered our analysis primarily around symptoms and ignored his actual life experiences. However, we omitted to stress those parts of his treatment which referred to his current life only because we wished not to distract the reader's attention from the formative process of Frankie's neurosis. In presenting these processes we have been forced to schematize and simplify some of them but we hope that the reader will recognize that the forces which are now to be described as a sequence, were often at work simultaneously.

In analyzing two of Frankie's symptoms—the retention of urine and the elevator phobia—we learned about certain behavior patterns. In the past, they had been mainly related to his nurse but now they were centered in his father and reflected his fight against his passive desires. His passivity determined much of the nature and structure of his problem.

His symptoms were the carriers of the past and represented his experiences with his nurse. The dawning character formation could be observed in changes of his behavior, which were related to his contining impressions and experiences pertaining to his father. The progressive analysis of his symptoms freed energy for the development of his character. But the passive drives which he turned toward his father stimulated the ancient memories of past passive gratifications connected with his nurse.

We mentioned that she was partly a representative of the father. It would be more correct to say that for the child, the father was a representative of the nurse. In many respects the status of the nurse in the family, and her behavior, were confusing to the child, because they involved functions usually associated with the father's rôle. To Frankie it was she who laid down the rules and regulations and the mother seemed to be almost as dependent on her guidance as he himself was. This was actually true in periods of the father's absence, and facilitated the fusion of the father's image with that of the nurse.

When the nurse left the house, Frankie tried to re-enact the bed ritual with his mother, who complied with his wishes for a while. After a few weeks, probably disturbed by the importance the patting ritual had acquired for him, his mother gradually dropped it. It was this satisfaction the frustrated child sought to obtain by his aggressive acts against women.

The women's reaction to his sadistic outbursts again made him retreat from them and turn to his father. For a short time his role toward his father was like the one he had toward his nurse after she had frustrated his masculine impulses, and this made him resort to his infantile dependence, which the nurse had been willing to gratify. Frankie had gone through at least three phases of obedience. All of these three phases followed periods during which his active strivings had been frustrated. His obedience was always dictated by his desire to obtain passive gratification and all three phases were abruptly ended when his expectations were disappointed. First he behaved like an obedient child with his nurse, who gladly accepted that pattern since it eased her responsibility for the child's care; she was motherly and kind when he was ready to play the rôle of the dependent little boy, but was intolerant of his active self-assertions. Next he acted as his mother wanted him to. He expressed love for her and suppressed all the signs of anxiety for which she had previously reprimanded him. In the third phase, in his relationship to his father, he indulged in long discussions on philosophical subjects, ranging from the existence of God, to the justification of laws, political and racial problems and, above all, questions about life and death—again behaving in a way satisfying to his father.

This intellectual relationship provided some gratification to his passive desires. His intellectual growth during this period was marked but this desirable sublimation was soon disturbed. The profuse passive gratification which he saw his little sister enjoying became a direct and potent stimulus to his own cravings. The longing for passive physical contact made him keen and alert in his observations and he meticulously noted any passive gratifications his mother and sister received from his father. When he saw his father stroke his sister's hair, he became depressed and longed for similar gratifications.[19] In order to experience the pleasures of a baby, he regressed to a behavior even more infantile than his sister's. He insisted on being

[19] In his analytic sessions at this period, he cut off the hair of all dolls before he could express this longing. We assume that the child displayed here a delayed reaction of jealousy which would have been appropriate when mother and nurse took care of his sister as an infant. The jealousy was focused on the father, since the father was to him at this time the phallic representative of mother and nurse.

washed and dressed like an infant, demanding this "love service" from his father. Once when his family was in a hurry to go out with him, he suddenly undressed completely and insisted that they dress him.

During this passive period he wanted to take the rôle of the woman, which meant, in his terms, to possess everything a woman has, while ignoring the difference in the sex organs. He said that he wanted breasts like his mother's and silky hair like his sister's. He asked his father to rest in bed beside him and he spoke openly about his wish to give birth to children.

His conscious desire for feminine satisfaction and the idea of change of sex was expressed in his attitude toward injections. While formerly even the thought of an injection resulted in unmanagable resistance, he now suddenly craved injections. In one of his uncontrollable outbursts during his analytic sessions he shouted ecstatically while looking at a picture of a boy he had been painting, "Give him an injection, make him a girl, make him a girl!"

His persistent courtship of his father was partly successful. He managed to achieve some anal-passive gratification in various ways, such as having his father throw a ball against his buttocks and rubbing his buttocks against the father's knee. The anal gratification aroused genital sensations (erections had been observed on such occasions) and he then craved to have the genital region treated by his father in the same way that he had wanted the nurse to treat it. He induced his father to button his fly and the coyness he displayed on such occasions made the father recognize the child's attempt at seduction, and caused him to become reserved. Here the patient must have felt a disappointment similar to the one he had experienced at an earlier age when his nurse, and, later, his mother withdrew gratifications. Like the father, they probably did so because his insistence and the intensity of his desires alarmed them.

After Frankie failed to obtain gratification from his father, he concluded that his mother was granted those gratifications which his father denied him, because she had no penis. Therefore, since the fulfillment of his passive desires was not obtainable without the loss of his penis, Frankie's fears forced him away from his father.

Frankie's castration fears compelled him to make an attempt to achieve an independence commensurate with his age. On the one hand, he joined the older boys in their play, and roamed the street far beyond his permitted limits. On the other hand, in his fantasies his desire for the passive rôle still prevailed. His passive cravings had, however, undergone marked changes and now were no longer pleasurable, but aroused anxiety. The passivity, which up to then had been openly and fearlessly expressed, was worked into a fearful fantasy of being kidnapped by strangers. He was preoccupied with this fantasy for months. The image of men lifting him up and carrying him away contained derivatives of earlier observations when he had seen his father lifting his mother. His ambivalent desire to be lifted and carried was condensed into the kidnapper fantasy, similar to that described in the elevator phobia.

The essential feature of these new kidnapping fantasies was that they contained no open reference to genital or anal gratifications and that the *factor of passive locomotion was dominant*. As long as these fantasies were of moderate intensity, carrying two toy revolvers sufficed as a magic gesture to ward off anxiety. But whenever his repressed passive desires increased in intensity, the fantasy of being kidnapped lost its playful features, and he went into attacks of violent panic in which he was unable to distinguish between the world of fantasy and reality.

Such an attack of panic was once observed within the analytic hour. It followed his return from a vacation trip. On the train, he happened to hear that two criminals had broken out of jail, and were hiding somewhere in the country. His first response to the news was to refuse to see the analyst any more. The next day, against his will he was taken to her office by his father. As soon as he saw the analyst, he lost all control, burst into tears, and assaulted her. He made attempts to choke her, and threatened to burn down her country house. (He had frequently referred to this house as a "hideaway," or "witch place," and had jokingly called the analyst a kidnapper, who kept kidnapped children hidden under the house.) His panic subsided when the analyst interpreted that he suspected her of hiding escaped criminals in her "hideaway," in order to give him up to them.[20]

We must assume that the train ride had touched off his conflct about passive locomotion and increased his susceptibility to anxiety.[21] The news of the jailbreak, therefore, stimulated his fantasies about being kidnapped and he repeated in analysis the reactive panic he had experi-

[20] The following elements were involved in the transference: The child reacted to the interruption of the work as if the analyst had abandoned him although it was the child and not the analyst who went on vacation. This separation from the analyst had revived the trauma when his mother had left him and then returned with a baby. The analyst is also accused of having children who live under her house. The child is saying—as it were—the analyst, like the mother, is unfaithful. She had taken advantage of his absence to give birth to another child and will give him up to kidnappers.

[21] Trains always seemed dangerous vehicles to him, for the travelers were at the mercy of the conductor, who could create deadly accidents at will. In his games Frankie dramatized the following scene: children are separated from their mothers during a train ride. German soldiers masked as friends enter the train, shoot the mothers and take the children prisoners. Frequently the father and conductor are killed either by the German army or by burglars, and the children are left to the robbers, who are cannibals and murderers.

enced when his nurse had threatened to give him up to the police or the elevator man.

It would seem therefore that behind his peremptory refusal to see the analyst there was an unconscious challenge to be kidnapped. Indeed he provoked his father to take him forcibly to the analyst, thus succeeding in making the father his kidnapper.

To avoid such states of panic which the intensity of his passive desires repeatedly brought about, Frankie was forced to evolve an entirely new attitude. He began to ignore reality. Signs of passivity were eradicated and were replaced by feelings of omnipotence. He gave his parents nonsensical orders and was greatly annoyed if they were not carried out; he struck his sister and parents for not obeying unspoken orders. His world was divided into two camps: rulers and slaves—and he belonged to the world of rulers and supermen, who were characterized by incredible cruelty. He demanded that his father read him books in the middle of the night, and insisted on being served steak at two o'clock in the morning. In his analytic hour, he threatened that those who did not obey his orders would be sent to jail. When asked whether this could ever happen to him, he assured the analyst that if committed to such an institution, he would always find means of escape. He said: "They couldn't get me in, even if they carried me,"—indicating again his wish for passive locomotion and the resulting fear.

The analyst suggested that he was identifying himself with his tough radio heroes and criminals in order to ward off his passive desires. This interpretation had a negative therapeutic result. He reacted to it by strengthening this particular defense. His demands became even more fantastic, and from time to time his behavior resembled that of a megalo-maniacal patient. He claimed that he was actually a king: "Even if you don't know it and if you

don't believe it." The fantasies of omnipotence were extensive; he called the exalted role he played in the universe, King Boo-Boo.

King Boo-Boo is master over life and death. Anyone who disobeys his orders will die. King Boo-Boo's thoughts are sufficient to cause another person's death. Sometimes some of his victims die, although they do not know of their own death and pretend to be alive.

King Boo-Boo also has power in political matters. "The U.S.A. only thinks she is a democracy, whereas in reality he governs her as a king. His army is stronger that that of the U.S.A. and Russia together. He is more cruel than Hitler, but people are so afraid of him that they don't dare to hate him. His soldiers and slaves love him so much that they finally *want to do* whatever he wishes" (an obvious projection of Frankie's passivity). Once in an outburst of exaltation he screamed:

"All the people, they like me better than anyone else in the world. I am better and I can kill everyone I want. I can even kill President Truman, I'm tired of him. I'm rid of him. I am going to make a new war against America. I am the manager of the world. I see that it goes around quick enough. I'm the executive committee. 'Execute her! execute her!' I said." (This referred to his little sister whose picture he had just drawn and which, at this point, he began to cut up).

A few minutes after this outburst, he tried to be Frankie again, but could not endure this rôle. While he was casting our parts in play, he shouted: "I am the policeman, I am the delivery man, I am the truck man, I am all the men together in the whole world!" Frankie's earlier fantasies about God were the predecessors of his later King Boo-Boo imagery and had contained similar elements of cruelty. His rôle of the all-powerful served two purposes: it was a defense against the fulfillment of the wish for passive gratification, and, at the same time, it was a means of obtaining that very gratification.

His dictatorial behavior at home and his fantastic ignoring of reality took on such proportions that it became questionable whether he could remain in his usual environment. This acute situation threatened the continuation of his treatment and necessitated special measures. As a last resort we had to bring to the child's attention the serious consequences his behavior would entail.

It was necessary that he be told that his behavior had actually one aim: to be sent away. This would be the realization of the one thing he had dreaded most: to be separated from his parents. We should like to amplify on the session which followed, and which brought about the decisive change in Frankie's attitude.

The analyst found him in the waiting room, the paper basket on his head, hilariously throwing books and blocks at his mother. After much maneuvering the analyst got him into the office. When alone with him, she asked him what he *really* thought the effect of his actions would be. She conceded that he acted as if he were a great king and as if he expected complete submission from his environment. But she expressed her doubts that he himself really believed in the truth of these ideas. She called to his attention the fact that his behavior would not have the desired effect and that no matter what he did, nobody would accept him as a superman or as King Boo-Boo. Frankie replied quickly: "Oh, they will find out some day, and they will do what I want!" The analyst then suggested that Frankie might not even know exactly what it was he really wanted and that he would probably achieve just the opposite of what seemed desirable to him.

Referring to several incidents during the analytic sessions in which he had acted out his King Boo-Boo ideas, she told him that even her positive relationship to him was influenced by his "actions." Even be-fore you enter my office, I can't help thinking: 'For goodness sake, what will Frankie try to do today; what is he going to break and to destroy today?" He interrupted quickly: "Oh, you shouldn't care. You get paid for that, even more than it costs."

He was then asked whether he knew what had brought about this change in his behavior; after all, there had been a time when he had cared quite a bit for people, and when he had wanted to be with his mother all the time. Frankie replied triumphantly: "So that's fine; now I am cured of my fears, and I don't want to be with Mommy."

The analyst did not agree with him as to his being cured. She thought that he was still very much afraid, just as scared as he was at the time when he did not want to come to his session because he believed the analyst was a kidnapper. Only now he tried to hide his fear even from himself. He had never let her tell him what she actually thought about his kidnapper fantasies and about King Boo-Boo. But now she was seriously worried about his behavior. Therefore, she must show him that his King Boo-Boo behavior would end in something of which she had always thought he was terribly afraid. She had understood only recently that he really wanted to be carried off by someone, to be lifted and taken away. Didn't he himself see that he was behaving now just as he had when he used to attack people and then scream with fear, "Don't grab me! I surrender, I surrender!" Perhaps he was again looking for the old excitement, always waiting to see whether people would not eventually do the very thing which he dreaded.

The analyst told him she was compelled to assume that he wanted to create a situation where his being sent away was the only possible outcome. She was reminded of his nurse's threats to have elevator men and policemen come up and take him away. Perhaps these thoughts had always been somewhat pleasurable to him, although he had been aware of *only his fears.*

The child listened calmly, although this was quite unusual in this period of unmanagable wildness. Eventually he asked seriously: "Where can you send me? My parents promised they would never send me to a camp or to a boarding school if I didn't want to go there. And you yourself told me that children cannot go to jail. And a reform school wouldn't even take me because I'm very good at school."

Thereupon the analyst told him about hospitals which specialized in treating children whose sickness led them to behave in unacceptable ways.[22] He interrupted: "But I'm not sick; I have no temperature." The analyst stated that people who seriously believed that the world was divided into two camps "of an almighty king and the rest slaves" are seriously ill, even without a temperature and belong into special hospitals. He replied: "But Hitler could do whatever he wanted. Only, if I had been Hitler, *I would not have killed myself. I would have waited until they come and do something to me.*" Suddenly realizing that the analyst referred to mental illness, he became quite frightened and asked, "Do you think I'm crazy? Do you think I belong in a crazy house?"

Without waiting for an answer, he wanted to know in detail how those hospitals were run, how children were kept there, whether they were visited by their parents, what kind of toys they had, whether they were permitted to have knives and blocks and whether they were analyzed there. Our answers obviously disappointed him; they did not fit into his picture of exciting fights between attendants and patients and between kidnappers and the kidnapped.

The psychodynamics of this analytic

session brought about a decisive therapeutic gain which may be explained as follows:

1) The beginning of the analytic session permitted Frankie to re-experience and to act out the full grandeur of his world of fantasy. He had an opportunity to demonstrate his narcissistic omnipotence, his disdain for reality and his belief in the inferiority and weakness of the analyst.

2) The next analytic step was a thrust into his unconscious, and a demonstration that his unconscious aim was to enforce a separation from home. This was a contradiction of his omnipotence which even the almighty King Boo-Boo could not overlook.

3) He readily picked up the suggestion about enforcing a separation and revealed his unconscious desire by the great interest he showed in the place to which he would be sent. By asking one question after another, he began to consider the reality of what would happen if his unconscious desires were really fulfilled. This process then effected a valuation of what might have appeared in brilliant colors if left in terms of the unconscious. The ego discovered that fulfillment of these unconscious desires was drab and monotonous if carried out in reality. Thus, step by step, he gratified his wishes in his imagination and simultaneously learned that the price he would have to pay was not in proportion to the pleasures to be obtained.[23] The analyst succeeded in proving that this defense was not perfect but

---

[22] The particular technique used in this session was an emergency measure in a very crucial situation, and should not be viewed as a typical or terminal procedure.

[23] Two other factors may have contributed to the child's willingness to accept the interpretations of this decisive hour: The analyst had discussed with his parents the possible necessity of removing him from the family. The parents were depressed by the prospect and the patient had probably sensed their depression and the seriousness of the situation. The analyst, through her active interference, had again contributed to his identification of her with his image of the nurse who, like the analyst, had threatened him, but on the other hand, had also acted as his protector.

would lead finally to the victory of his passive desires by commitment to an institution. Only then did Frankie start to doubt the wisdom of carrying his King Boo-Boo fantasies into reality. It is of interest to note why our earlier interpretations of his feelings of omnipotence as a defense against passivity did not have the desired effect. As long as the analyst merely discussed his megalomaniacal behavior as a defense without interpreting in detail his unconscious desire, she was doing nothing to impede the use of this mechanism. If anything, her remarks only helped him to consolidate this defense.

The threat which the child felt in our discussion of "craziness" had contributed to the deflation of his kidnapper fantasy. The final devaluation of the kidnapper fantasy and of the defense of being King Boo-Boo came about after we succeeded in showing him how the warded-off desire for passive gratification was contained even in this very defense. In addition, it was designed to result in satisfaction which he might have missed as an infant. After all, we said, acting as an almighty King was indeed a repetition of infantile behavior. We referred in particular to those scenes in which he demanded food in the middle of the night and we compared his behavior to that of a hungry infant whose screaming usually brings the desired food.

Nothing in our interpretation caused Frankie more despair than the analogy between his temper tantrums when his wishes were not fulfilled and the attacks of screaming and fury which an infant shows when its hunger is not immediately satisfied. Here we touched on what we probably might consider his "primal trauma" in a period in which he, hungry for milk and affection, screamed for hours. This, as the reader will recall, had happened when night feeding was stopped at the age of 5 months.

In brief, in the following months we were able to discuss with Frankie's active participation his feeling of omnipotence

and his belief in the omnipotence of his thoughts. In so doing we followed Ferenczi's conception, presented in his paper, *Stages in the Development of the Sense of Reality* (13).

After our frequent interpretations of his feelings of omnipotence as derivatives of infantile behavior Frankie announced that he had something to tell us. He had a "remembering machine," a "projecting machine"—which he could turn backwards as far as he liked. In it he saw that the analyst's mother had killed the analyst at the command of King Boo-Boo, because she, the analyst—when a baby—had screamed so violently that she had disturbed the whole world. When our discussion led to the motives for his projecting his feelings of frustration and fear onto the analyst he gave way to a fit of rage and ran away from his analytic session. Pale and disturbed, he hid in the family car, and requested his mother to "throw the analyst out," or else he would smash the car. It took several hours to calm him. We had to discuss with him the fact that though he might not remember his infancy, he must have heard many comparisons of his own baby behavior with that of his sister, and he must have received the impression that his parents had never forgiven him his screaming at night. His sister had always been praised as a good, quiet baby which must have made him even more angry at her. Perhaps it was not only the analyst who should have been killed as a baby by her mother—maybe he had often wished the same would happen to his sister, so that his family could not rave about her. Finally we had to enlist his mother's help in reassuring him that in spite of her despair about his early screaming attacks, she now felt no resentment whatsoever toward him. Since her relationship to him had become genuinely warm, this reassurance was of therapeutic help.

The following months during which the child was able to work through the conflict about his passivity were a period of consolidation during which he was preparing himself for the termination of his analysis.

The prospect of ending the analysis revived for him the pain of separation from his mother at the time his sister was born. This prompted us to use these last months for further working through his relationship to his mother. During the weeks of our analytic interpretation of his early oral frustrations, his anger against her was reactivated and he demonstrated an unusually strong oral envy and aggression. Whenever he suspected that his mother preferred his sister to him, whenever she did anything for the little girl, he either gave vent to his fury against his mother and sister, as in earlier periods, or became depressed. The investigation of these moods produced a flood of material referring to early orality. We could witness the changes which his oral impulses underwent and how the freed energy was diverted for reaction formation and sublimation.[24]

[24] When Frankie came into analysis he was a greedy child who devoured huge bags of "animal crackers" during his analytic hour and frequently asked for more food from the analyst. His orality was characterized by possessiveness and cruelty. God was drawn as a creature with a huge mouth, and he frequently described God's teeth in detail. Devouring was a frequent element in his dramatizations, and impregnation was linked with oral incorporation. Punishment was seen in oral terms. During his analytic hour, he often had fantasies of cutting his sister into pieces, cooking her and preparing "totem" meals. In the period of working through his oral aggressive fantasies an expression of oral sharing appeared. He bought candies with his own allowance and offered them generously to the analyst, her secretary and the patient whose session followed his. He made plans to give a present to his sister before his analysis was ended and in an especially generous mood wanted to invite her to share an analytic session with him.

His desire to devour huge quantities of food was sublimated into his interest in the origin and preparation of food. Food, the object of incorporation, became the subject of investigation and learning. At school he wrote a long paper about the food of Indian tribes in which there was no reference to taste or to the act of eating as such; his report was exclusively devoted to the technique of food preparation and the use of eating

Even when he was on the verge of giving up most of his megalomaniacal fantasies, he still used King Boo-Boo's "remembering machine" to deny his own past experiences of frustration, aggression and fear of retaliation. He first claimed that this machine did not remember what had happened in his own life but knew exactly the analyst's misdeeds and *her* mother's rage. Under the cover of the remembering machine, and through the voice of King Boo-Boo he expressed his aggressive fantasies regarding his intrauterine existence.

For example, King Boo-Boo—in contrast to all other people—could remember when he, the King, was still an embryo "and ate up his mother from the inside and also any other children she wanted to have." Only gradually could King Boo-Boo's "remembering and projecting machine" be focused on Frankie's own childhood and on more than the intrauterine period. Presently we could ask him to focus it on the transference situation and on events which had recently occurred in his analysis.

He wanted to know exactly who would take his particular hour after he had finished his analysis, and it seemed to us an important step when Frankie could say laughingly, "I hope that you won't take a child younger than me." And only in those last months of analysis was it possible for Frankie to realize the twofold nature of his transference to the analyst. On the one hand, he repeated the dependence which originally he had developed toward his

utensils. His oral possessiveness was not only sublimated into the sharing of food and theoretical food interests, but he discovered the institution of keepsakes. Keepsakes, not only for the child, but also for the adult, mean, "I do not devour you as a whole, but I take a little piece of you and let you live." Frankie's tendency to start a collection of keepsakes, such as the little toys and vases which he asked the analyst to give him, impressed her as a definite sign that his oral greediness had developed into a socially acceptable though still narcissistically colored attachment.

nurse, and, on the other, the aggression with which he reacted to any frustration caused by his mother.

Only now could he be shown, for instance, that his rage and his fear at the thought that the analyst would give him up to kidnappers was also based on his fear of abandonment. He feared that the analyst would turn away from him as he had withdrawn from his mother when she came home from the hospital.

An important and new therapeutic gain was achieved when Frankie realized that his megalomaniacal behavior and fantasies were a defense not only against his passive strivings (kidnapper fantasy) but also a protection against suffering and death. Though he had rejected God and life-after-death at an early age, he had felt in need of some substitute consolation. He had tried to gain this consolation by making himself believe that at least a creation of fantasy, King Boo-Boo, was endowed with immortality. And when he was faced with the demand that he gave up even this buttressing fantasy he once more had resorted to phobic mechanisms, albeit this time only in his thoughts.

The following incident which occurred at a time when he was eager to attend a day camp during the summer will illustrate this: Having injured his leg, Frankie was worried that this injury might prevent him from starting on time. So he mentally rehearsed his phobic mechanisms, all the ways of avoiding a repetition of such accidents. He told his sister that he would not leave the house so as not to hurt himself before going to camp. To her response that she had once hurt herself in their own house, he replied: "That's right, but I could just sit in my room and I would not move at all." She, however, showed him that there still could be dangers, since he might fall off his chair and hurt himself that way. To this he retorted: "Well, I could stay in bed. I wouldn't even dress, and then certainly nothing could happen to me." He was somewhat ashamed when reporting this plan to the analyst, adding: "That's very stupid, I know. For instance, it would be dumb not to use the subway because you might catch a cold from germs. I know that germs are all over the world and I might get a cold anywhere." Then he said triumphantly: "But it would not be stupid to stay away from school, or from camp if the Mayor tells you to, because there is an epidemic of infantile paralysis." Here for the first time Frankie took a reasonable stand toward real dangers, which mirrored a significant and far-reaching change in his superego formation. It may be worth while to review the long road which had led to this achievement.

When Frankie entered his analysis, he was completely enslaved by his symptoms. His preoccupation with his mother and with the need for assurance that he could obtain gratification without endangering his existence, resulted in a constriction of his ego. He had not accepted any external ideals and there were hardly any indications of internal prohibitions. These are the signs of a severe lag in the formation of a superego.

During his oedipal phase, his fears were displaced from real objects such as his mother, his nurse, and his father, to imaginary objects and situations. The fears referring to his mother were shifted to "uncanny places" in which there was danger of being trapped, such as bathrooms, elevators and small consultation rooms. His fears referring to his father were projected to imaginary objects like wolves from which he expected retaliation for his aggressive impulses. As the reader will remember, the resolving of those fears temporarily resulted in an eruption of instinctual impulses as, for instance, when he rejected his father's authority with the words, "I'm no longer afraid of my wolves, I can do whatever I want."

Considering what had caused the lag in superego formation, we must refer to two factors. One is that his environment did not provide him with a clear-cut frame of reference as to objects of identification. For example, his mother acted like a child in relation to the nurse, and it was the nurse who exercised authority. Yet he sensed that the nurse took a secondary position whenever his father made his sporadic and brief appearances during wartime and that she was paid to take care of him. The second and more important factor was that this nurse combined her prohibitions with libidinal gratifications. Normally, as the oedipal phase ends, the prohibitions of the environment are internalized and accepted. The sexual demands are renounced and these prohibitions and the growing demands of reality are consolidated to form the core of the superego. In Frankie's case, however, his nurse's prohibitions were sexualized as soon as they were expressed and therefore instead of forming the basis of a superego, these sexualized prohibitions laid the foundation for a masochistic perversion.[25]

[25] Throughout Frankie's analysis we pursued the vicissitudes of his passive drives, hoping that our observations would permit us some general assertions with regard to the origin of passive homosexuality in boys, as well as of masochism. We must admit that his analysis did not offer sufficient material to draw final conclusions about either. Whether the activation of Frankie's brief perversion was accelerated by some prohibition by the patient's nurse or even caused by it, is not the point of our discussion in this context. Whatever the biological roots of Frankie's passivity, his turning toward his father as a love object was preceded by the traumatic rejection of his phallic activity by nurse and mother, the two most important feminine figures in his life. We have reason to believe that the rejection itself had been preceded by manipulation of the child's genitalia by the nurse. Whatever his biological readiness for this passive satisfaction, it is still important that he had been habitually passively gratified by his nurse. By tradition, by training, and because of convenience, it is certainly a temptation to settle the question of genesis by recourse to the biological explanation. However, the ascription to constitutional factors as an explanation serves to block rather than to help our understanding. It is permissible only after we have exhausted all other possibilities. We should rather focus on those environmental elements which seem to be unique in each case, elements which

It was only after the nurse's departure that we could observe the first brief and unsuccessful attempts at building a superego. We refer to Frankie's interest in laws and regulations. At about that time he suggested to his family the founding of a "Club for Democracy and Being Good." He invented rules and punishments, but they were so exaggerated that no one could abide by them. The slightest infringement was punished by complete annihilation, such as being "stamped to death by an elephant" "or being tied to a lion's mouth."

Once he drew a diagram for his father, explaining to him the battles which it represented. It showed a head and in it two "control towers" of good and bad Frankies. The "control towers" were responsible for the outcome of those battles. He himself could not control these battles, since "there is no bone connecting my mouth with my head or the control tower." He added, however, that there might be a chance that his good part and the good control tower would win the battle if his father were ready to do exactly what Frankie wanted him to do. Here he showed again the pattern of libidinizing the fulfillment of a duty. But this fantasy also shows the dawning of internal demands, expressed in his wish that the forces of good

although apparently accidental, may contain the common factors in the development of passive homosexuality and masochism.

The present disagreement among analysts on this topic will yield to constructive discussion after more analytic material on children will have been collected and scrutinized. Although child analysis will not solve the problem of the biological components of passivity and masochism, it may help to clarify it by bringing to light in greater detail the environmental influences. Especially if the parents' personalities are well-known to the analyst, he may be able to make a fair appraisal of the extent to which the environment may have been conducive to favoring or blocking the behavior which the child shows. It will probably be easier to observe fine gradations and to weigh the relative influence of external and biological forces in the analysis of children than in that of adults.

should win, although this internal prohibiting agent is still feeble and impotent.

We must draw the reader's attention to one more factor of this child's superego pathology. It is most significant in the development of his psychic structure that his earlier internalized superego configuration —King Boo-Boo—was not felt as something separate from his ego. Most children who have created such a primary and tyrannical superego, let it modify their behavior. Their ego accepts the superego as a prohibitory influence. When Frankie first invented King Boo-Boo, his ego, on the contrary, sided with this figure, and derived from it, in so doing, the strength and permission to act out an unrestrained omnipotence. This omnipotence served as an aggrandizement of his ego which had been tortured, humiliated, and frightened throughout the years of his neurosis.

Once he could give up acting out his King Boo-Boo fantasies, he could transfer his omnipotence to others who represented his ego-ideals. He could accept his father as a strong and enviable figure without becoming passively dependent on him. He had given up his wish for physical gratifications and therefore his anxiety had vanished. He could now compete in healthy and constructive ways with people of his environment, such as his athletics teacher, whom he admired for his strength and his justice, and the camp director, whom he praised for his ability and experience. In short, he had accepted the fact that there were people from whom he, a little boy, could learn.

The material produced in the next to the last hour of his analysis illustrates his new-found capacities.

The first topic related to the termination of his analysis. He had difficulty in bringing up his impending separation from the analyst, although he was now able to speak about his past separation from his mother. Frankie's acknowledgment that he did not really want to part from his analyst for good came indirectly. He suggested that

the present which was to be given to him at the end of his analysis should be postponed until Christmas, rationalizing that "by that time, those particular trains will be of a better make." The analyst admitted that she herself did not consider the analysis completely finished, but that she trusted his ability to get along without her and to come back whenever he might need help. Thereupon Frankie showed his readiness to depend on people in the outside world for protection by announcing with a solemn expression his decision to let King Boo-Boo die. "Do you know that King Boo-Boo will not live always? I've made up my mind. Tomorrow is the day he is going to be 100 years old, and before that, he is going to commit suicide. First, all other people will die; his soldiers have killed all the other people; and then all his soldiers will commit suicide because they know King Boo-Boo will die and they do not want to live without him."

We hinted that though his King Boo-Boo was to die, Frankie was still not willing to admit that death was something he could not control; otherwise, he would have allowed King Boo-Boo to die a natural death. Frankie understood. He laughed wholeheartedly.

During this conversation he was toasting a biscuit over a gas flame. The biscuit suddenly caught fire and flared up. Frankie let it drop to the floor. For a second his clothes were in danger of catching fire. He showed no panic, but did what he was told. Only his sudden pallor betrayed his justifiable fright. Suddenly he went to the window and asked the analyst: "Would you let me jump out of the window? I mean just jump to the next roof [a distance of about twelve yards]?" He tried to convince her that he could hold on to the telephone wire, and when told that the analyst would not let him jump, he asked: "Why not? Would you jump?" "No," was the reply, "I would be afraid of being killed." Frankie asked: "What would you like better—to die jumping down, or to be trapped here?" When the analyst answered that she would neither like to jump nor to be trapped, but that if there were a fire, she would obey the instructions of the fire department, and even jump if told to, he replied: "I think I would too, if I were told; but I would not do it gladly."

What Frankie needed in order to let King Boo-Boo die was the reassurance that not only he, a little boy, but every person is exposed to injuries, sickness and death, and that mastering reality is a difficult task for all of us.

In this significant hour we see recapitulated all the elements which we encountered in his first analytic session when he dramatized the lonely boy and the fire in the hospital. We could observe that the derivatives of his initial fears were firmly embedded in an adequate relationship to reality without eliciting fear, although the contents of his past conflicts were present to his mind.

A prognosis in child analysis is not easy. We are by no means sure that we have forestalled a later recurrence of Frankie's neurosis. But when he stood at the window, gauging the distance to the next roof, when at last fear, fantasy of omnipotence, and reality had become synthesized in one constructive act, when he was able to ask how we guard ourselves from danger,—when he could face danger without resorting to pathological anxiety or belief in magic and omnipotence,—then we knew that the secondary process had won a victory over the primary process. And this we thought, was the utmost a boy of 8½ can achieve—even with the help of child analysis.

BIBLIOGRAPHY

1. Abraham, K. "A Constitutional Basis of Locomotor Anxiety," *Selected Papers*, Hogarth, 1942.
2. Abraham, K. "Zur Psychogenese der Strassenangst im Kindesalter," *Klein. Beiträge z. Psa. Internat. Psa.* Verlag, Wien, 1921.
3. Alexander, F. and French, T. M. *Psychoanalytic Therapy*, Ronald Press, 1946.
4. Allen, F. *Psychotherapy with Children*, Norton, 1942.
5. Bonaparte, M. "Passivity, Masochism, and Frigidity," *Intern. J. Psa.*, XVI, 1935.
6. Bornstein, B. "Clinical Notes on Child Analysis," *this Annual*, I, 1945.
7. Brunswick, R. M. "The Preoedipal Phase of Libido Development," *Psa. Quar.*, IX, 1940.
8. Burlingham, D. T. "Probleme des psychoanalytischen Erziehers," *Zeit. f. psa. Paed.*, XI, 1937.
9. Daly, C. D. "The Role of Menstruation in Human Phylogenesis and Ontogenesis," *Internat. J. Psa.*, XXIV, 1944.
10. Deutsch, H. "The Genesis of Agoraphobia," *Internat. J. Psa.*, X, 1929.
11. Federn, P. "Beiträge zur Analyse des Sadismus and Masochismus," *Internat. Zeit. f. Psa.*, I, 1913, and II, 1914.
12. Fenichel, O. "Remarks on the Common Phobias," *Psa. Quar.*, XIII, 1944.
13. Ferenczi, S. "Stages in the Development of the Sense of Reality," *Contrib. to Psa.*, Badger, Boston, 1916.
14. French, T. M. "Some Psychoanalytic Applications of the Psychological Field Concept," *Psa. Quar.*, XI, 1942.
15. French, T. M. "Integration of Social Behavior," *ibid.*, XIV, 1945.
16. Freud, A. *The Psychoanalytical Treatment of Children*, Imago, 1946.
17. Freud, A. *The Ego and the Mechanisms of Defence*, Internat. Univ. Press, 1946.

18. Freud, S. "The Economic Problem in Masochism," *Coll. Papers*, II.
19. Freud, S. "Analysis of a Phobia in a Five-Year-Old Boy," *Coll. Papers*, II.
20. Freud, S. "Notes Upon a Case of Obsessional Neurosis," *ibid.*, III.
21. Freud, S. "From the History of an Infantile Neurosis," *ibid.*, III.
22. Freud, S. *The Problem of Anxiety*, Norton, 1936.
23. Freud, S. "Der Humor," *Ges. Schriften*, XI.
24. Fromm, E. *Escape from Freedom*, Farrar & Rinehart, 1941.
25. Gerard, M. W. "Alleviation of Rigid Standards," in Alexander, F. and French, T. M. *Psychoanalytic Therapy*, Ronald Press, 1946.
26. Greenacre, P. "The Predisposition to Anxiety," *Psa. Quar.*, X. 1941.
27. Greenacre, P. "Pathological Weeping," *ibid.*, XIV, 1945.
28. Hartmann, H. "Ich-Psychologie und Anpassungsproblem," *Internat. Ztschr. f. Psa.*, XXIV, 1939.
29. Hermann, I. "Sich Anglammern-Auf Suche gehen," *ibid.*, XXII, 1936.
30. Klein, Melanie, *Psychoanalysis of Children*. Hogarth, 1948.
31. Lampl-De Groot, J. "The Pre-oedipal Phase in the Development of the Male Child," *this Annual*, II, 1946.
32. Lewin, B. D. "Claustrophobia," *Psa. Quar.*, IV, 1935.
33. Loewenstein, R. "Phallic Passivity in Man," *Internat. J. Psa.*, XVI, 1935.
34. Menninger, K. A. *Man Against Himself*, Harcourt, 1938.
35. Rado, Sandor. Review of Anna Freud's *Einführung in die Technik der Kinderanalyse*, in *Zschr. f. Psa.*, XIV, 4, 1928.
36. Schilder, P. "The Relations between Clinging and Equilibrium," *Internat. J. Psa.*, XX, 1939.

Chapter 7
Neo-Freudian Analysis and Therapy

Unlike the previous case selections, in which therapists describe entire treatments, Erikson recounts only one hour in the treatment of a fairly disturbed, hospitalized young man. In this therapeutic session, a dream is reported to Erikson by a patient who was undergoing what Erikson has felicitously termed an "identity crisis." One should note that this particular session was a period of crisis, but Erikson sees the crisis as having much positive as well as negative potential for the patient. When the "pieces are coming apart," so to speak, it is a time when they may perhaps break up irreversibly, or they may be "put back together" in new and more constructive ways. Erikson intuited that the latter possibility was the case with this young man, and he proceeded upon that assumption. This attitude toward crisis exemplifies Erikson's view of development, which sees psychological growth as a sequence of weathering and working through the crises inherent in the developmental stages of life. Also noteworthy is that although Erikson proceeds with therapy in an orthodox manner by noting transference implications of the dream, and so on, the substantive focus of understanding the dream is centered on psychosocial, interpersonal, cultural, and historical issues. Erikson focuses mainly on ego psychology, not on "id psychology." While indicating that, indeed, this particular dream may be interpreted psychosexually, Erikson points out that it is the interpersonal and psychosocial aspects of it that were important at this time in the treatment. This case fragment gives the reader an unusual opportunity to follow the thought processes of a great psychotherapist as he puzzles out with his patient the meaning of a brief but vastly important dream.

The Nature of Clinical Evidence

ERIK H. ERIKSON

We must follow the tracks of clinical evidence. No wonder that often the only clinical material which impresses some as being at all "scientific" is the more concrete evidence of the auxiliary methods of psychotherapy—neurological examination, chemical analysis, sociological study, psychological experiment, etc.—all of which, strictly speaking, put the patient into nontherapeutic conditions of observation. Each of these methods may "objectify" *some* matters immensely, provide inestimable supportive evidence for *some* theories, and lead to independent methods of cure in *some* classes of patients. But it is not of the nature of the evidence provided in the psychotherapeutic encounter itself.

To introduce such evidence, I need a specimen. This will consist of my reporting to you what a patient *said* to me, how he *behaved* in doing so and what I, in turn, *thought* and *did*—a highly suspect method. And, indeed, we may well stand at the beginning of a period when consultation rooms (already airier and lighter than Freud's) will have, as it were, many more doors open in the direction of an enlightened community's resources, even as they now have research windows in the form of one-way screens, cameras, and recording equipment. For the kind of evidence to be highlighted here, however, it is still essential that, for longer periods or for shorter ones, these doors be closed, soundproof, and impenetrable.

By emphasizing this I am not trying to ward off legitimate study of the setting from which our examples come. I know only too well that many of our interpretations seem to be of the variety of that given by one Jew to another in a Polish railroad

Reprinted from *Insight and Responsibility*, 56–75, 79, by Erik H. Erikson. By permission of W. W. Norton & Company, Inc. Copyright © 1964 by Erik H. Erikson.

station. "Where are you going?" asked the first. "To Minsk," said the other. "To Minsk!" exclaimed the first, "you say you go to Minsk so that I should believe you go to Pinsk! You are going to Minsk anyway—so why do you lie?" There is a widespread prejudice that the psychotherapist, point for point, uncovers what he claims the patient "really," and often unconsciously, had in mind, and that he has sufficient Pinsk-Minsk reversals in his technical arsenal to come out with the flat assertion that the evidence is on the side of his claim. It is for this very reason that I will try to demonstrate what method there may be in clinical judgment. I will select as my specimen the most subjective of all data, a dream-report.

A young man in his early twenties comes to his therapeutic hour about midway during his first year of treatment in a psychiatric hospital and reports that he has had the most disturbing dream of his life. The dream, he says, vividly recalls his state of panic at the time of the "mental breakdown" which had caused him to interrupt his studies for missionary work abroad and enter treatment. He cannot let go of the dream; it seemed painfully real on awakening; and even in the hour of reporting, the dream-state seems still vivid enough to threaten the patient's sense of reality. He is afraid that this is the end of his sanity.

THE DREAM: "There was a big face sitting in a buggy of the horse-and-buggy days. The face was completely empty, and there was horrible, slimy, snaky hair all around it. I am not sure it wasn't my mother." The dream report itself, given with wordy plaintiveness, is as usual followed by a variety of seemingly incidental reports of the events of the previous day which, however, eventually give way to a rather coherent account of the patient's relationship with his deceased grandfather, a country parson. In fact, he sees himself as a small boy with his grandfather crossing a bridge over a brook, his tiny hand in the old man's reassuring fist. Here the patient's mood changes to a deeply moved and moving admission of desperate nostalgia for the rural setting in which the values of his Nordic immigrant forebears were clear and strong.

How did the patient get from the dream to the grandfather? Here I should point out that we consider a patient's "associations" our best leads to the meaning of an as yet obscure item brought up in a clinical encounter, whether it is a strong affect, a stubborn memory, an intensive or recurring dream, or a transitory symptom. By associated evidence we mean everything which comes to the patient's mind during and after the report of that item. Except in cases of stark disorganization of thought, we can assume that what we call the synthesizing function of the ego will tend to associate what "belongs together," be the associated items ever so remote in history, separate in space, and contradictory in logical terms. Once the therapist has convinced himself of a certain combination in the patient of character, intelligence, and a wish to get well, he can rely on the patient's capacity to produce during a series of therapeutic encounters a sequence of themes, thoughts, and affects which seek their own concordance and provide their own cross-references. It is, of course, this basic synthesizing trend in clinical material itself which permits the clinician to observe with "free-floating attention," to refrain from undue interference, and to expect sooner or later a confluence of the patient's search for curative clarification and his own endeavor to recognize and to name what is most relevant, that is, to give an *interpretation*.

At the same time, everything said in an hour is linked with the material of previous appointments. It must be understood that whatever insight can result from one episode will owe its meaning to the fact that it clarifies previous questions and complements previous half-truths. Such *evidential continuity* can be only roughly sketched here; even to account for this one hour would take many hours. Let me only mention, then, the seemingly paradoxical fact that during his previous hour the patient had spoken of an increased well-being in his work and in his life, and had expressed trust in and even something akin to affection for me.

As to the rest of the hour of the dream-report I listened to the patient, who faced me in an easy chair, with only occasional interruptions for the clarification of facts or feelings. Only at the conclusion of the appointment did I give him a résumé of what sense his dream had made to me. It so happened that this interpretation proved convincing to us both and, in the long run, strategic for the whole treatment. (These are the hours we like to report.)

As I turn to the task of indicating what inferences helped me to formulate one of the most probable of the many possible meanings of this dream-report, I must ask you to join me in what Freud has called "free-floating attention," which—as I must now add—turns inward to the observer's ruminations even as it attends the patient's "free associations" and which, far from focusing on any one item too intentionally, rather waits to be impressed by recurring themes. These themes will, first faintly but ever more insistently, signal the nature of the patient's message and its meaning. It is, in fact, the gradual establishment of strategic intersections on a number of tangents that eventually makes it possible to locate in the observed phenomena that central core which comprises the "evidence."

I will now try to report what kinds of considerations will pass through a psychotherapist's mind, some fleetingly, others with persistent urgency, some hardly conscious in so many words, others nearly ready for verbalization and communication.

Our patient's behavior and report confront me with a therapeutic crisis, and it is my first task to perceive where the patient stands as a client, and what I must do next. What a clinician must do first and last depends, of course, on the setting of his work. Mine is an open residential institution, working with severe neuroses, some on the borderline of psychosis or psychopathy. In such a setting, the patients may display, in their most regressed moments, the milder forms of a disturbance in the sense of reality; in their daily behavior, they usually try to entertain, educate, and employ themselves in rational and useful ways; and in their best moments, they can be expected to be insightful and to do proficient and at times creative work. The hospital thus can be said to take a number of calculated risks, and to provide, on the other hand, special opportunities for the patient's abilities to work, to be active, and to share in social responsibilities. That a patient will fit into this setting has been established in advance during the "evaluation period." The patient's history has been taken in psychiatric interviews with him and perhaps with members of his family; he has been given a physical examination by a physician and has been confronted with standardized tests by psychologists who perform their work "blindly," that is, without knowledge of the patient's history; and finally, the results have been presented to the whole staff at a meeting, at the conclusion of which the patient himself was presented by the medical director, questioned by him and by other staff members, and assigned to "his therapist." Such preliminary screening has provided the therapist with an over-all diagnosis which defines a certain range of *expectable mental states,* indicating the patient's special danger points and his special prospects for improvement. Needless to say, not even the best preparation can quite predict what depths and heights may be reached once the therapeutic process gets under way.

The original test report had put the liability of our patient's state into these words: "The tests indicate border-line psychotic features in an inhibited, obsessive-compulsive character. However, the patient seems to be able to take spontaneously adequate distance from these border-line tendencies. He seems, at present, to be struggling to strengthen a rather precarious control over aggressive impulses, and probably feels a good deal of anxiety." The course of the treatment confirmed this and other test results. Thus, a dream-report of the kind just mentioned, in a setting of this kind, will first of all impress the clinical observer as a diagnostic sign. This is an "anxiety dream." Such a dream may happen to anybody, and a mild perseverance of the dream state into the day is not pathological as such. But this patient's dream appears to be only the visual center of a severe affective disturbance: no doubt if such a state were to persist, it could precipitate him into a generalized panic such as brought him to our clinic in the first place. The report of this horrible dream which intrudes itself on the patient's waking life now takes its place beside the data of the tests and the range and spectrum of the patient's moods and states as observed in the treatment, and shows him on the lowest level attained since admission, i.e., relatively closest to an *inability* "to take adequate distance from his borderline tendencies."

The first "prediction" to be made is whether this dream is the sign of an impending collapse, or, on the contrary, a potentially beneficial clinical crisis. The first would mean that the patient is slipping away from me and that I must think, as it were, of the emergency net; the second, that he is reaching out for me with an important message which I must try to understand and answer. I decided on the latter alternative. Although the patient acted as if he were close to a breakdown, I had the impression that, in fact, there was a challenge in all this, and a rather angry one. This impression was, to some extent, based on a comparison of the present hour and the previous one when the patient had seemed so markedly improved. Could it be that his unconscious had not been able to tolerate this very improvement? The paradox resolves itself if we consider that cure means the loss of the right to rely on therapy; for the cured patient, to speak with Saint Francis, would not so much seek to be loved as to love, and not so much to be consoled as to console, to the limit of his capacity. Does the dream-report communicate, protesting somewhat too loudly, that the patient is still sick? Is his dream sicker than the patient is? I can explain this tentative diagnostic conclusion only by presenting a number of inferences of a kind made very rapidly in a clinician's mind, and demonstrable only through an analysis of the patient's verbal and behavioral communications and of my own intellectual and affective reactions.

The experienced dream interpreter often finds himself "reading" a dream report as a practitioner of medicine scans an X-ray. Especially in the cases of wordy or reticent patients or of lengthy case reports, a dream often lays bare the stark inner facts.

Let us first pay attention to the dream images. The main item is a large face without identifying features. There are no spoken words, and there is no motion. There are no people in the dream. Very apparent, then, are omissions. An experienced interpreter can state this on the basis of an implicit inventory of dream configurations against which he checks the individual dream production for present and absent dream configurations. This implicit inventory can be made explicit as I have myself tried to do in a publication reviewing Freud's classic first analysis of a "dream specimen."[1] The dream being discussed, then, is characterized by a significant omission of important items present

[1] Erik H. Erikson, "The Dream Specimen of Psychoanalysis," *Journal of the American Psychoanalytic Association*, 2:5–56, 1954.

in most dreams: motion, action, people, spoken words. All we have instead is a motionless image of a faceless face, which may or may not represent the patient's mother.

But in trying to understand what this image "stands for," the interpreter must abandon the classic scientific urge (leading to parsimonious explanation in some contexts but to "wild" interpretation in this one) to look for the one most plausible explanation. He must let his "free-floating" clinical attention and judgment lead him to all the *possible* faces which may be condensed in this one dream face and then decide what *probable meaning* may explain their combined presence. I will, then, proceed to relate the face in the dream to all the faces in my patient's hierarchy of significant persons, to my face as well as those of his mother and grandfather, to God's countenance as well as to the Medusa's grimace. Thus, the probable meaning of an empty and horrible face may gradually emerge.

First myself, then. The patient's facial and tonal expression reminded me of a series of critical moments during his treatment when he was obviously not quite sure that I was "all there" and apprehensive that I might disapprove of him and disappear in anger. This focused my attention on a question which the clinician must consider when faced with any of his patient's productions, namely, his own place in them.

While the psychotherapist should not force his way into the meanings of his patient's dream images, he does well to raise discreetly the masks of the various dream persons to see whether he can find his own face or person or role represented. Here the mask is an empty face, with plenty of horrible hair. My often unruly white hair surrounding a reddish face easily enters my patients' imaginative productions, either in the form of a benevolent Santa Claus or that of a threatening ogre. At that particular time, I had to consider another autobiographic item. In the third month of therapy, I had "abandoned" the patient to have an emergency operation which he, to use clinical shorthand, had ascribed to his evil eye. At the time of this dream-report I still was on occasion mildly uncomfortable—a matter which can never be hidden from such patients. A sensitive patient will, of course, be in conflict between his sympathy, which makes him want to take care of me, and his rightful claim that I should take care of him—for he feels that only the therapist's total presence can provide him with sufficient identity to weather his crises. I concluded that the empty face had something to do with a certain tenuousness in our relationship, and that one message of the dream might be something like this: "If I never know whether and when you think of yourself rather than attending to me, or when you will absent yourself, maybe die, *how can I have or gain what I need most—a coherent personality, an identity, a face?*"

Such an indirect message, however, even if understood as referring to the immediate present and to the therapeutic situation itself, always proves to be "overdetermined," that is, to consist of a *condensed code* transmitting a number of other messages, from other life situations, seemingly removed from the therapy. This we call *"transference."* Because the inference of a "mother transference" is by now an almost stereotyped requirement, and thus is apt to lead to faulty views concerning the relationship of past and present, I have postponed, but not discarded, a discussion of the connection between the patient's implied fear of "losing a face" with his remark that he was not sure the face was not his mother's. Instead, I put first his fear that he may yet lose himself by losing me too suddenly or too early. . . .

The young man in question was one among a small group of our patients who came from theological seminaries. He had developed his symptoms when attending a Protestant seminary in the Middle West where he was training for missionary work

in Asia. He had not found the expected transformation in prayer, a matter which both for reasons of honesty and of inner need, he had taken more seriously than many successful believers. To him the wish to gaze through the glass darkly and to come "face to face" was a desperate need not easily satisfied in some modern seminaries. I need not remind you of the many references in the Bible to God's "making his face to shine upon" man, or God's face being turned away or being distant. The therapeutic theme inferred from the patient's report of an anxiety dream in which a face was horribly unrecognizable thus also seemed to echo relevantly this patient's religious scruples at the time of the appearance of psychiatric symptoms—the common denominator being a *wish to break through to a provider of identity.*

This trend of thought, then, leads us from the immediate clinical situation (and a recognition of my face in the dream face) to the developmental crisis typical for the patient's age (and the possible meaning of facelessness as "identity-confusion"), to the vocational and spiritual crisis immediately preceding the patient's breakdown (and the need for a divine face, an existential recognition). The "buggy" in the dream will lead us a step further back into an earlier identity crisis —and yet another significant face.

The horse and buggy, is of course, an historical symbol of culture change. Depending on one's ideology, it is a derisive term connoting hopelessly old-fashioned ways, or it is a symbol of nostalgia for the good old days. Here we come to a trend in the family's history most decisive for the patient's identity crisis. The family came from Minnesota, where the mother's father had been a rural clergyman of character, strength, and communal esteem. Such grandfathers represent to many today a world of homogeneity in feudal values, "masterly and cruel with a good conscience, self-restrained and pious without loss of self-esteem." When the patient's parents had moved from the north country to then still smog-covered Pittsburgh, his mother especially had found it impossible to overcome an intense nostalgia for the rural ways of her youth. She had, in fact, imbued the boy with this nostalgia for a rural existence and had demonstrated marked disappointment when the patient, at the beginning of his identity crisis (maybe in order to cut through the family's cultural conflict), had temporarily threatened to become somewhat delinquent. The horse and buggy obviously is in greatest ideological as well as technological contrast to the modern means of locomotor acceleration, and, thus, all at once a symbol of changing times, of identity-confusion, and of cultural regression. Here the horrible motionlessness of the dream may reveal itself as an important configurational item, meaning something like being stuck in the middle of a world of competitive change and motion. And even as I inferred in my thoughts that the face sitting in the buggy must *also* represent the deceased grandfather's, also framed by white hair, the patient spontaneously embarked (as reported above) on a series of memories concerning the past when his grandfather had taken him by the hand to acquaint him with the technology of an old farm in Minnesota. Here the patient's vocabulary had become poetic, his description vivid, and he had seemed to be breaking through to a genuinely positive emotional experience. Yet as a reckless youngster he had defied this grandfather shortly before his death. Knowing this, I sympathized with his tearfulness which, nevertheless, remained strangely perverse, and sounded strangled by anger, as though he might be saying: "One must not promise a child such certainty, and then leave him."

Here it must be remembered that all "graduations" in human development mean the abandonment of a familiar position, and that all growth—that is, the kind of growth endangered in our patients—must come to terms with this fact.

We add to our previous inferences the assumption that the face in the dream (in a *condensation* typical for dream images) also "meant" the face of the grandfather who is now dead and whom as a rebellious youth the patient had defied. The immediate clinical situation, then, the history of the patient's breakdown and a certain period in his adolescence are all found to have a common denominator in the idea that the patient wishes to *base his future sanity on a countenance of wisdom and firm identity* while, in all instances, he seems to fear that his anger may have destroyed, or may yet destroy, such resources. The patient's desperate insistence on finding security in prayer and, in fact, in missionary work, and yet his failure to find peace in these endeavors belongs in this context.

It may be necessary to assure you at this point that it is the failure of religious endeavor, not religiosity or the need for reverence and service, which is thereby explained. In fact, there is every reason to assume that the development of a sense of fidelity and the capacity to give and to receive it in a significant setting is a condition for a young adult's health, and of a young patient's recovery.

The theme of the horse and buggy as a rural symbol served to establish a possible connection between the nostalgic mother and her dead father; and we now finally turn our attention to the fact that the patient, half-denying what he was half-suggesting, said, "I am not sure it wasn't my mother." Here the most repetitious complaint of the whole course of therapy must be reviewed. While the grandfather's had been, all in all, the most consistently reassuring countenance in the patient's life, the mother's pretty, soft, and loving face had since earliest childhood been marred in the patient's memory and imagination by moments when she seemed absorbed and distorted by strong and painful emotions. The tests, given before any history-taking, had picked out the following theme: "The mother-figure appears in the Thematic Apperception Tests as one who seeks to control her son by her protectiveness of him, and by 'self-pity' and demonstrations of her frailty at any aggressive act on his part. She is, in the stories, 'frightened' at any show of rebelliousness, and content only when the son is passive and compliant. There appears to be considerable aggression, probably partly conscious, toward this figure." And indeed, it was with anger as well as with horror that the patient would repeatedly describe the mother of his memory as utterly exasperated, and this at those times when he had been too rough, too careless, too stubborn, or too persistent.

We are not concerned here with accusing this actual mother of having behaved this way; we can only be sure that she appeared this way in certain retrospective moods of the patient. Such memories are typical for a certain class of patients, and the question whether this is so because they have in common a certain type of mother or share a typical reaction to their mothers, or both, occupies the thinking of clinicians. At any rate many of these patients are deeply, if often unconsciously, convinced that they have caused a basic disturbance in their mothers. Often, in our time, when corporal punishment and severe scolding have become less fashionable, parents resort to the seemingly less cruel means of presenting themselves as deeply hurt by the child's willfulness. The "violated" mother thus tends to appear more prominently in images of guilt. In some cases this becomes an obstacle in the resolution of adolescence—as if a fundamental and yet quite impossible restitution were a condition for adulthood. It is in keeping with this trend that the patients under discussion here, young people who in late adolescence face a breakdown on the borderline of psychosis, all prove to be partially regressed to

the earliest task in life, namely, the acquisition of a sense of basic trust strong enough to balance that sense of basic mistrust to which newborn man (most dependent of all young animals and yet endowed with fewer inborn instinctive regulations) is subject in his infancy. We all relive earlier and earliest stages of our existence in dreams, in artistic experience, and in religious devotion, only to emerge refreshed and invigorated. These patients, however, experience such partial regression in a lonely, sudden, and intense fashion, and most of all with a sense of irreversible doom. This, too, is in this dream.

The mother's veiled presence in the dream points to a complete omission in all this material: there is no father either in the dream or in the associated themes. The patient's father images became dominant in a later period of the treatment and proved most important for the patient's eventual solution of his spiritual and vocational problems. From this we can dimly surmise that in the present hour the grandfather "stands for" the father.

On the other hand, the recognition of the mother's countenance in the empty dream face and its surrounding slimy hair suggests the discussion of a significant symbol. Did not Freud explain the Medusa, the angry face with snake-hair and an open mouth, as a *symbol of the feminine void,* and an expression of the masculine horror of femininity? It is true that some of the patient's memories and associations (reported in other sessions in connection with the mother's emotions) could be easily traced to infantile observations and ruminations concerning "female trouble," pregnancy, and post-partum upsets. Facelessness, in this sense, can also mean inner void, and (from a male point of view) "castration." Does it, then, or does it not contradict Freudian symbolism if I emphasize in this equally horrifying but entirely empty face a representation of facelessness, of loss of face, of lack of identity? In the context of the "classical" interpretation, the dream image would be primarily symbolic of a sexual idea which is to be warded off, in ours a representation of a danger to the continuous existence of individual identity. Theoretical considerations would show that these interpretations do not exclude each other. In this case a possible controversy is superseded by the clinical consideration that a symbol to be interpreted must first be shown to be immediately relevant. It would be futile to use sexual symbolism dogmatically when acute interpersonal needs can be discerned as dominant in strongly concordant material. The sexual symbolism of this dream was taken up in due time, when it reappeared in another context, namely that of manhood and sexuality, and revealed the bisexual confusion inherent in all identity conflict.

Tracing one main theme of the dream retrospectively, we have recognized it in four periods of the patient's life all four premature graduations which left him with anger and fear over what he was to abandon rather than with the anticipation of greater freedom and more genuine identity: the present treatment—and the patient's fear that by some act of horrible anger (on his part or on mine or both) he might lose me and thus his chance to regain his identity through trust in me; his immediately preceding religious education —and his abortive attempt at finding through prayer that "presence" which would cure his inner void; his earlier youth—and his hope to gain strength, peace, and identity by identifying himself with his grandfather; and, finally, early childhood—and his desperate wish to keep alive in himself the charitable face of his mother in order to overcome fear, guilt, and anger over her emotions. Such redundancy points to a central theme which, once found, gives added meaning to all the associated material. The theme is: "Whenever I begin to have faith in some-

body's strength and love, some angry and sickly emotions pervade the relationship, and I end up mistrusting, empty, and a victim of anger and despair."

You may be getting a bit tired of the clinician's habit of speaking for the patient, of putting into his mouth inferences which, so it would seem, he could get out of him for the asking. The clinician, however, has no right to test his reconstructions until his trial formulations have combined into a comprehensive interpretation which feels right to him, and which promises, when appropriately verbalized, to feel right to the patient. When this point is reached, the clinician usually finds himself compelled to speak, in order to help the patient in verbalizing his affects and images in a more communicative manner, and to communicate his own impressions.

If according to Freud a successful dream is an attempt at representing a wish as fulfilled, the attempted and miscarried fulfillment in this dream is that of finding a face with a lasting identity. If an anxiety dream startling the dreamer out of his sleep is a symptom of a derailed wish-fulfillment, the central theme just formulated indicates at least one inner disturbance which caused the miscarriage of basic trust in infancy.

It seemed important to me that my communication should include an explicit statement of my emotional response to the dream-report. Patients of the type of our young man, still smarting in his twenties under what he considered his mother's strange emotions in his infancy, can learn to delineate social reality and to tolerate emotional tension only if the therapist can juxtapose his own emotional reactions to the patient's emotions. Therefore, as I reviewed with the patient some of what I have put before you, I also told him without rancor, but not without some honest indignation, that my response to his account had included a feeling of being attacked. I explained that he had worried me, had made me feel pity, had touched me with his memories, and had challenged me to prove, all at once, the goodness of mothers, the immortality of grandfathers, my own perfection, and God's grace.

The words used in an interpretation, however, are hard to remember and when reproduced or recorded often sound as arbitrary as any private language developed by two people in the course of an intimate association. But whatever is said, a therapeutic interpretation, while brief and simple in form, should encompass a *unitary theme* such as I have put before you, a theme common at the same time to a dominant trend in the patient's relation to the therapist, to a significant portion of his symptomatology, to an important conflict of his childhood, and to corresponding facets of his work and love life. This sounds more complicated than it is. Often, a very short and casual remark proves to have encompassed all this; and the trends *are* (as I must repeat in conclusion) very closely related to each other in the patient's own struggling mind, for which the traumatic past is of course a present frontier, perceived as acute conflict. Such an interpretation, therefore, joins the patient's and the therapist's modes of problem-solving.

Therapists of different temperament and of various persuasions differ as to what constitutes an interpretation: an impersonal and authoritative explanation, a warm and parental suggestion, an expansive sermon or a sparse encouragement to go on and see what comes up next. The intervention in this case, however, highlights one methodological point truly unique to clinical work, namely, the disposition of the clinician's "mixed" feelings, his emotions and opinions. The evidence is not "all in" if he does not succeed in using his own emotional responses during a clinical encounter as an evidential source and as a guide in intervention, instead of putting them aside with a spurious claim to unassailable objectivity. It is here that the prerequisite of the therapist's own psychoanalytic treatment as a didactic experience proves itself essential, for the personal equation in the observer's emotional response is as important in psychotherapy as that of the senses in the laboratory. Repressed emotions easily hide themselves in the therapist's most stubborn blind spots.

I do not wish to make too much of this, but I would suggest in passing that some of us have, to our detriment, embraced an objectivity which can only be maintained with self-deception. If "psychoanalyzed" man learns to recognize the fact that even his previously repudiated or denied impulses may be "right" in their refusal to be submerged without a trace (the traces being symptoms), so he may also learn that his strongest ethical judgments are right in being persistent even if modern life may not consider it intelligent or advantageous to feel strongly about such matters. Any psychotherapist, then, who throws out his ethical sentiments with his irrational moral anger, deprives himself of a principal tool of his clinical perception. For even as our sensuality sharpens our awareness of the orders of nature, so our indignation, admitted and scrutinized for flaws of sulkiness and self-indulgence, is, in fact, an important tool both of therapy and of theory. It adds to the investigation of what, indeed, has happened to sick individuals a suggestion of where to look for those epidemiological factors that should and need not happen to anybody. But this means that we somehow harbor a model of man which could serve as a scientific basis for the postulation of an ethical relation of the generations to each other; and that we are committed to this whether or not we abrogate our partisanship in particular systems of morality.

A certain combination of available emotion and responsive thought, then, marks a therapist's style and is expressed in minute variations of facial expression, posture, and tone of voice. The core of a therapeutic intervention at its most decisive thus defies any attempt at a definitive account. This difficulty is not overcome by the now widespread habit of advocating a "human," rather than a "technical" encounter. Even humanness can be a glib "posture," and the time may come when we need an injunction against the use in vain of this word "human," too.

What do we expect the patient to contribute to the closure of our evidence? What tells us that our interpretation was "right," and, therefore, proves the evidence to be as conclusive as it can be in our kind of work? The simplest answer is that this particular patient was amused, delighted, and encouraged when I told him of my thoughts and my feelings over his unnecessary attempts to burden me with a future which he could well learn to manage—a statement which was not meant to be a therapeutic "suggestion" or a clinical slap on the back, but was based on what I knew of his inner resources as well as of the use he made of the opportunities offered in our clinical community. The patient left the hour—to which he had come with a sense of dire disaster—with a broad smile and obvious encouragement. Otherwise, only the future would show whether the process of recovery had been advanced by this hour.

But then, one must grant that the dream experience itself was a step in the right direction. I would not want to leave you with the impression that I accused the patient of pretending illness, or that I belittled his dream as representing sham despair. On the contrary, I acknowledged that he had taken a real chance with himself and with me. Under my protection and the hospital's he had hit bottom by chancing a repetition of his original breakdown. He had gone to the very border of unreality and had gleaned from it a highly condensed and seemingly anarchic image. Yet that image, while experienced as a symp-

tom, was in fact a kind of creation, or at any rate a condensed and highly meaningful communication and challenge, to which my particular clinical theory had made me receptive. A sense of mutuality and reality was thus restored, reinforced by the fact that while accepting his transferences as meaningful, I had refused to become drawn into them. I had played neither mother, grandfather, nor God (this is the hardest), but had offered him my help as defined by my professional status in attempting to understand what was behind his helplessness. By relating the fact that his underlying anger aroused mine, and that I could say so without endangering either myself or him, I could show him that in his dream he had also confronted anger in the image of a Medusa—a Gorgon which, neither of us being a hero, we could yet slay together.

The proof of the correctness of our inference does, of course, not always lie in the patient's immediate assent. I have, in fact, indicated how this very dream experience followed an hour in which the patient had assented too much. Rather, the proof lies in the way in which the communication between therapist and patient "keeps moving," leading to new and surprising insights and to the patient's greater assumption of responsibility for himself. . . .

I have given you an example which ends on a convincing note, leaving both the patient and the practitioner with the feeling that they are a pretty clever pair. If it were always required to clinch a piece of clinical evidence in this manner, we should have few convincing examples. To tell the truth, I think that we often learn more from our failures—if indeed we can manage to review them in the manner here indicated. But I hope to have demonstrated that there is enough method in our work to force favorite assumptions to become probable inferences by cross-checking the patient's diagnosis and what we know of his type of illness and state of physical health; his stage of development and what we know of the "normative" crisis of his age-group; the co-ordinates of his social position and what we know of the chances of a man of his type, intelligence, and education in the social actuality of our time. This may be hard to believe unless one has heard an account of a *series of such encounters* as I have outlined here, the series being characterized by a progressive or regressive shift in all the areas mentioned: such is the evidence used in our clinical conferences and seminars.

Chapter 8
Jungian Analysis and Therapy

It will be helpful to begin the discussion of Dr. Jacobi's case with a few general remarks about Jungian analysis. Jolande Jacobi, one of Jung's foremost adherents, has described (1968) the fourfold aspect of the Jungian analytic situation. First, the analysand describes his or her conscious situation in words. Second, the therapist gains access to the unconscious by using the dreams and fantasies of the analysand (including, we may add, artistic productions of the patient). Third, the relationship between therapist and patient adds an "objective" side to the first two subjective ones. Last, the first three aspects are amplified and elaborated by the therapist (including active and intrusive relation of the *analyst's* free associations to the patient's material).

Like Freud, Jung believed that insight into the unconscious is the agent of therapeutic change, but he added new techniques to those developed by Freud. Importantly, he shifted the temporal perspective of the therapy. Although Jung recognized the importance of past causal events, he based many more interpretations on the present meanings and significance of conflicts and on the future goals of the patient. Every age level requires a *different* solution to even identical problems. In Jungian analysis, the patient proceeds through defined stages, finally learning to understand and to come to terms with both his personal unconscious and the archetypes in his collective unconscious. Jungian therapy emphasizes not only insight but also self-realization. Jung considered adulthood a period of possible great growth toward spirituality and maturity, and one task of therapy was to help the patient achieve these goals. Symbols and dreams are far more extensively interpreted by Jungian than by Freudian or neo-Freudian therapists, and often they are related to the archetypes in the unconscious. Finally, Jungian analysts are consistently more active than psychoanalysts. They rarely use a couch and see patients less frequently and for a shorter duration of time.

Dr. Jacobi presents the case of Werner, a twenty-four-year-old man who sought her help because he was troubled by strong homosexual desires and an inability to develop satisfactory relationships with women. The analysis lasted for many years with gaps between phases when Werner stopped treatment. In her work with Werner, Dr. Jacobi focussed on his dreams and his paintings, productions which she heartily encouraged him to bring to her. Attention should be paid to the heavy emphasis on symbolic interpretation of these dreams and paintings and to the way the dreams and paintings were used to help Werner express and understand his affects and conflicts. Much of Werner's material seems equally explicable by psycho-analytic principles, and one might ask oneself how some of the other therapists in this section might have understood Werner and how they would have dealt with him. Because the treatment was successful, it raises the interesting question noted in the General Introduction to this volume of whether the particular substance of thera-peutic or psychological theory is the crucial factor, or whether it is simply having a "therapeutic" relationship with someone that helps, be that someone a Jungian, Freudian, or whomever.

Without preaching or criticizing, Dr. Jacobi was willing to guide Werner, make suggestions, and give advice. Clearly, she sees her therapeutic role as flexible, and even during the times when she was not treating Werner, they maintained contact through telephone calls and letters. She also used correspondence and telephone calls during treatment, because he only saw her once a week. Because Freudians would rarely indulge in these activities, the reader should consider whether they were helpful, and why or why not. Despite Dr. Jacobi's nonjudgmental attitude toward Werner, some modern readers might find her attitudes toward homosexuality and homosexuals somewhat disturbing. In response, we must point out that Dr. Jacobi's attitude was rather liberal given her traditional training, the locale of the treatment (conservative Switzerland), and the time during which it occurred (from the late 1940s until the middle 1950s).

Finally, as in the other cases in this section, the goal was insight and under-standing. Werner never became heterosexual, but he was less anxious, worked and loved better, and generally was in much better control over his life.

REFERENCE

Jacobi, Jolande. *The psychology of C. G. Jung.* New Haven, Conn.: Yale University Press, 1968.

A Case of Homosexuality

JOLANDE JACOBI

Jung (in personal communications) held that homosexuality had to do with a shadow problem; that is, with a repressed, undifferentiated element of masculinity in the man and of femininity in the woman which, instead of being developed on a psychological level from the depths of the individual's own psyche, is sought on a biological plane through "fusion" with another man or another woman, as the case may be. This takes place either through identification with the mother in order to be loved by the father, or by seeking fusion, or identification, with the father in order to gain greater strength to possess a woman. In the case of most homosexuals, both forms occur alternately, according to whether the feminine or masculine role is assumed in homosexual relations. It is known that the integration of the shadow, and thus the masculinity which is lacking, gives a feeling of security and strength, and results in the courage necessary to approach the other sex. . . .

CASE STUDY

I should now like to present a case. Readers may judge for themselves whether it may be considered successful therapeutically or not.

Werner, a timid, soft and pale young man, was 24 years old when he first came to see me in 1948. He was a government clerk in another city and could come to Zurich only on Saturdays. His treatment took place in several phases over a period of time. The first lasted for three years;

From *Journal of Analytical Psychology*, 1969, *14*, 48–64. Extracts from "A case of homosexuality" are reproduced by permission of *The Journal of Analytical Psychology.* Copyright Andreas & Ernst Jacobi, Zurich, Switzerland.

the second for about six months after a gap of over a year; and the third for about three months, a year and a half later. Altogether, we had a total of 180 sessions, each lasting one and a half hours. Later, he also came to see me from time to time whenever something rather special disturbed him; at first, three or four times a year, then later, every Christmas.

Werner came from a Protestant family and was the second youngest of five children. There were two elder sisters, an elder brother and one brother who was three years young than Werner. His maternal grandmother was very poor but he loved her "more than anyone in the world." His father's mother, on the other hand, he considered an ugly old witch, who was always complaining about something. She died while Werner was still young.

Both sides of the family had histories of severe psychological disturbance. On his mother's side, there were members of the family showing evidence of religious fanaticism, schizophrenic episodes, hospitalizations. Those who were not so grossly disturbed were "difficult." On his father's side, there were alcoholism, crime, depression, violent tempers. In the immediate family, Werner's mother had asthma and was often hysterical; his father, a farmer, was uncouth and infantile. Among his sisters, one was paranoid and another was depressive. His elder brother had no children. In fact there was no member of the family that did not show some abnormality.

The discovery that his mother was an illegitimate child and that her father was unknown struck Werner like "a bolt out of the blue." This knowledge reduced him to a state of panic and personal distress. He was 15 years old at the time. Even as a child, however, he had already become convinced in his fantasy life that his parents were not really his true ones and that he was a "foundling," so out of place did he feel in his surroundings. Only his sisters and brothers were the real children of his parents, thought Werner, while he was "so completely different."

On completing his high school studies, he took a commercial apprenticeship, since he lacked the money to continue with his studies. He reported that it had been his greatest wish to become a minister or psychiatrist—as so many do who would like to cure their own infirmities through other people. After hearing a lecture of mine, he came to me because he wanted "to assist in the moral betterment of man through self-sacrifice and unflagging work and research." He loved to philosophize and was enamoured with music and religious problems.

Werner was an idealist and a dreamer—as are so many homosexuals. Up until his 16th year he had been, he said, "normal," although often ill and spoiled by his mother. Then, during a holiday in the French part of Switzerland, he was seduced by his room-mate, taught to masturbate and, as he himself expressed it, to obtain sexual gratification in an abnormal fashion. This sexual "derailment," as he called it, had a great bearing on his life from that time on. He thought himself sinful and depraved, but could not offer any resistance. Inwardly, he thus became increasingly unstable and despondent.

Success with his final school-leaving examination again gave Werner some support for a short time, but there soon followed a "nervous breakdown," which was accompanied by feelings of anxiety and guilt, trembling and insomnia. These symptoms resulted in a short period of treatment with a psychiatrist. Shortly after this he was also hurt in a serious accident caused by a defective electrical system. It was in this state of upset that he came to me. He often tried to make friends with girls, but these efforts were constantly rewarded with disappointments, so that finally he came to hate women. Since his experience in Lausanne, he had lived out his homosexuality only in fantasy, but not in concrete physical form. He felt immensely attracted to strong young men, especially if they were in uniform—for example, bus conductors, whose strength he marvelled at. Nevertheless, at the beginning of treatment he did not give up hope of eventually becoming "normal" and of being able to fall in love with a woman.

Werner plunged into his treatment with great zeal. Since we could see each other only once a week, he poured out all that he had to say to me in long letters, confessions and diary-like "meditations," which grew into volumes. Much emotion was involved. In a very short time he developed a strong positive transference and became full of hope. He reported only a few dreams, but these were meaningful to him.

The first dream, which came after the fourth hour, illustrates his sense of persecution by his mother's shadow. He found himself standing on a sloping alpine meadow which dropped off sharply (he stood on an "inclined plane"). Cows with pointed horns approached him from the rear (that is, from the unguarded background). Then his mother also appeared and standing beside her there was a single cow. In Jungian terms, this would be her other side, her shadow side, a symbol of her archetypal great mother. This cow ran towards him with its tail raised, threatening him with impalement on its horns. (Here, behind the real mother, we see *the existence* of her shadow side and how it menaced Werner with its sharp, penetrating, phallic aspect, the horns.) He sprang to the left (he sought refuge in the unconscious) behind a wooden partition, which strangely was transparent as glass (this represents a defence mechanism). He was thus able to see what threatened him and his mother problem became clear to him.

But this terrified him to such a degree that he awoke bathed in perspiration, his heart pounding.

During this first phase of treatment he wrote of his mother (in his diary): "Her look, her love, her warmth are becoming much too oppressive; they close in on me, and it is as if I were trying to break through an invisible shell that encloses me. I have strong resistance in me. She would like me to be neat, well-behaved and strong. Is it so pious and Christian to spend the entire Sunday in church listening to a sermon and then act like the devil the rest of the week?"

His fourth dream illustrated his second problem. In it he re-experienced how his neighbour, Fred, showed him his naked posterior in the attic and how he got ready to begin sexual relations with him. At that moment, however, when Werner was about to insert his penis into the anus of Fred, he awoke, confused and frightened. Fred often appeared in his dreams, and it was clear that even when he was a small boy, homosexual tendencies were present.

Some time later he dreamt of a male monkey with whom he had sexual relations, as he had earlier performed with his friend. In the dream he was younger than in reality. "The monkey stood against the wall and I with my back to him," reported Werner. "He then put his penis into my anus, whereupon I felt mild pain. Somehow I was convinced that it was a monkey, and yet it seemed to me that I recognized in him Fred, my neighbour, with whom my first sex play had taken place. I couldn't forget this dream."

On another occasion he recalled that he had experimented sexually with his brother when he was about seven years old. Such childhood play among brothers is often encountered in homosexuals.

The first months of treatment were occupied with the discussion of childhood memories, his relationship with his parents, with his brothers and sisters, and, above all, the ambivalence towards the mother and hate for his father. Werner always had the notion that he must make the conquest of a girl. He would be successful some day—he *had* to be, so he thought. He made several attempts, but they all ended in defeat. He went to bed with the wife of one of the men with whom he worked, but he was impotent. He then wrote to me: "The top part of me wanted to, but the lower part didn't"—a characteristic remark in respect of the efforts of a homosexual. Then he told me that since his childhood he had had a phimosis, and it was probably because of that "that it didn't work out!" He then decided to have an operation, which was accompanied by pain and a long period of bleeding, legitimately preventing him from having any longings for women or men for some time.

A change set in after the phimosis operation. Formerly, when he went swimming, he feared going into the water, and he did so, if his genitals stood out in his tight bathing suit, only to show that he was a man and also with the urge to observe in fascination the genitals of the other men. Afterwards, he felt less ashamed and "more moral," he said. However, he continued to write: "I would like to live, to develop. It's all the same who one takes in one's arms, whether it's a man or a woman. Whatever God might offer would be all right. I took no stand and let him—though with heavy heart—continue to fight his battle, anxious as to what the outcome would be. I reflected that he needed to feel free, uncriticized and accepted by me as he was and that I should not interfere.

After his convalescence, he wavered constantly between each sex; once he became fascinated with a man and ran after him, but only out of longing to have platonic discussions. However, he also wanted to be together with him all the time. He still hoped to be able to have sexual relations with a woman, and he worked himself up into such a nervous state over this that he consulted a doctor who prescribed treatment consisting of injections of vitamins.

But such an approach was of no avail. He became increasingly restless and found it more difficult to sleep. After 31 hours of treatment he had the following dream, which disturbed him deeply because it so crudely depicted the "animal" aspect of his homosexual relations with his brother Paul and his friend Fred.

"I am in a gravel pit, probably the one belonging to my father where my first homosexual activities took place. On my right there is a wall constructed of piled-up stones. Surrounding me is a rather shallow pond. I am standing on some rocks which project into it. My brother Paul is near me. Large and small lizards are crawling around all over the place: the ground and the water is teeming with them. In a crack in the wall, which is right next to me, I see a large, colourful snake, which moves as if it had become stuck between the stones and is now trying to free itself. Finally, it slips out of the crack and jumps into the water. I see very clearly how it swims around in the water close to me. Although the water is not deep at all, and I am very near the shore, I cannot move forwards or backwards. It seems as if the snake wants to bite me on the foot if I dare to leave the place."

On the basis of this dream a number of pictures developed at my instigation. I will describe a number of the most significant of these pictures. They fall into well-defined phases. At first, in 1949, they were meagre in content and weak in colour: they showed his inner situation graphically. He drew the gravel pit of the dream I have recounted; the eyes of God, which illustrated his bad conscience; a three-headed dragon, who was the animus-mother; and a death-bringing combination of a Buddha and a mother.

Early in 1950, Werner began painting in water colours and in poster paints. The next picture showed, in intense colours, a mandala; then there followed, the black scythe of death, on a background of red, which was suffering. Werner was sleeping very badly. "Every little noise," he wrote to me, "upsets me; the slightest effort, climbing stairs and so on, makes me dizzy; my heart pounds and makes me anxious. Everything and everybody arouses my disgust. I would like to sleep, to sleep. I would like to poison myself, and yet I abhor the idea; I would like to run away, yet I want to stay where I am. Sleeping pills don't help me any more; all they do is make me groggy. Perhaps you know of a solution, otherwise I must put an end to my life."

I then advised him to paint his insomnia. This was a stroke of luck, since it set the dammed-up instincts flowing and brought the emotions into play. The picture he did was called "Insomnia" and the dark wall it showed was keeping him from masturbation and from his longing for a man.

Now the ice was broken. A series of richly coloured pictures followed, full of feeling for life. 1950 was the year of pictures, through which he was able to give vent to his feelings. They brought calmness and joy to his heart. He painted about 25. The most important of them were of music; they showed a musical mandala, the rhythmic, revolving world of music. But his attempts at portraits of women were pallid, uninspiring. He could not be stirred by a woman, although he still set his hopes in that direction.

Next, in May of that year, he painted a colourful picture, which he entitled *"Lebensfreude"* (Joy of Life). In connection with it, he wrote: 'I worked on this water colour for several evenings. Originally it consisted only of the vertical loops in the middle of the picture, in the four basic colours. But this didn't satisfy me; it was too trite and lifeless, so I started to work on it again. It's too bad that I don't have more time; I would like the colours to flow into each other more (in contrast to the sharp outlines of the others) and to get rid of the spotty places.

"I call this picture 'Joy of Life.' I don't really know why, myself. I feel a great happiness with life as the picture stands before me and I observe it. Everything in my soul seems to vibrate in unison, and I am pleasantly touched by this play of colours. I feel so unburdened, aside from the inevitable difficulties, so carefree, confident and full of hope.

"When I look at the picture, such a broad range of colours and forms emerge in me. I would like to sit right down and continue. The forms remain very clear before me, and my inner eye beholds them very sharply for a long time after they have risen up. I will continue to paint and create; what will come of it, I will know only after I have begun.

"I am happy each time something comes out that provides deep inward satisfaction to me, and I bring such things to Zurich full of expectation, and if 'she' likes it, then the well-spring in me begins to overflow!"

Later that month, and during that summer, Werner painted several pictures which showed how his feelings were developing. There was "The revolving swastika"; there was "Birth," in which a butterfly, a symbol of the psyche, was finally fledged; there was a colourful spiral which represented the birth of the sun; there was an egg, in which picture rather darker colours began to appear; and there was one in which there were labyrinthine convolutions coiling back on themselves.

This movement towards introversion, perceptible already in the egg picture, became more pronounced with a picture of a brown cross, made of earth, on which he suffered, suspended between his hope of becoming "different" sometime and the rapidly growing insight that this was not to be. At the time of the butterfly picture he had written me a letter about it in which he said: "Seeing this most extraor-dinary event in nature once, even though only a film and within very limited out-lines, had an uncanny effect on me inwardly. (I would never have thought earlier that I could observe this act completely free of sensation and curiosity, free also of resistance and aversion. But it was so; an unfathomable miracle revealed itself to me, it jolted my innermost being.) An irresistible force drove me then to find some way to put this tremendous inner fullness on to paper. I wanted to go out this evening for relaxation, but I cannot. I must sit down and paint in order to wear myself out. This powerful drive must be able to flow."

By the time of the brown earth cross picture his fear of women was becoming more certain and he wrote me the description of a dream which shows this clearly: "I saw two girls in a wood; one ran after me. She had almost caught up with me, and so I ran faster. In my right hand I had a little switch, which I used in defence, hitting backwards with it. Then I turned around so that I was facing her. Wide-eyed, she rushed at me. It was amazing how quickly I could run backwards; I glided, or better, I floated. Nevertheless, she was already quite near, and then I stumbled. I ducked in the hope that she would rush over me with her legs apart. But my head got caught in her skirt, and she fell on me." The women were actually his brown cross of earth.

He met a governess and hoped to gain a closer contact with her. At the same time, however, he had a deep platonic friendship with a young chemist, who interested him more. He dropped the girl because he could not stand the fact that she smoked. Then he had a disturbing experience with a married woman, the wife of one of his friends. She had made eyes at him and constantly extended invitations to him. One evening she unexpectedly appeared in his room and seduced him. After a quick and premature ejaculation, he became deeply disgusted by such an act and resolved to never see the woman again.

Then in December he received a severe blow: he was not accepted into the pension scheme of his office, which meant that he could not become an established regular employee. It turned out that he had pretended to be mentally ill when recruited for military service in order to be released, and this was entered in his records. His pretence had been taken seriously, and it was not possible to get the authorities to delete this erroneous entry. I sent him to the psychiatrist who had made the diagnosis and to another one too for a re-examination. Yet despite the sympathetic treatment of the matter by these two doctors, the government physician would not alter the original entry. So Werner remained only an auxiliary employee. In spite of everything, he did not lose heart. He applied for a job as a tour guide and conducted an interesting trip to Italy. He learned to swim, which was quite a test of his courage, but he stood up to it.

Without criticizing or preaching, I accompanied him on the right paths as well as on what I took to be the wrong ones which he followed. I pointed out the advantages and disadvantages of all that confronted him and tried, with genuine sympathy, to stress the final, prospective aspects of all his sufferings and experiences. He felt that I believed in him and in his chances. Slowly, he became aware that he did not have a place in the outer world, but in his own inner world "between being a man and a woman," that basically he was a homosexual. His relationship to men was examined closely and he perceived that when he loved he pursued his partner constantly with jealousy, nagging, curiosity and romantic ideas, but that at the same time he made a victim of himself, in purely masochistic terms, since he singled out sadistic men as his best friends. With these he had no sexual

relations, only with those he did not love and desired solely on a physical basis. In this case, he became active and sadistic himself. He wanted completely to possess the others spiritually as well as make them feel small physically. He could not have both forms of feeling for the same man. Two important episodes of this type occurred simultaneously and troubled him deeply. Since he not only described them in detail in his diary, but we also discussed them, he then began an earnest struggle with his shadow. This was early in 1951.

He painted a frightening picture of his shadow, an alarming head of a deranged man. He reported that he had to observe it without retreating and set it on a chair in front of him in a desperate effort to understand himself. Then a demonic urge from within prompted him to look *behind* the picture in order to grasp what might lie in the background.

Then he produced a second picture, in which it became clear how rich, and even in a certain way how ordered, this background was. But since he saw it in its chaotic aspect, he called it "Insanity." Although there were in the upper part two devil masks and in the middle a red cross of passion, in the lower right there was a symbol of wholeness, a circle, which united the two opposing colours, red and blue. And to the left, above the glowing fire, there were three notes and a green, hopeful, masculine triangle. In the middle, however, there was again a colourful butterfly, the soul. The insanity, of which he was secretly afraid and which was firmly established in his family, was simply a notion, since the picture did not indicate this, but rather—despite the devil masks—showed an inner richness, containing in itself the possibility of further formation and development. The interpretation I gave to the picture, not to mention Werner's inner knowledge of its meaning, gave him new drive. At this time, he rather resignedly declared that he suspected that it would be his fate to go through life alone, but that now he could do this happily.

I commented on the many musical themes which his pictures contained and I thought that he should perhaps learn to sing. Singing occurred to me because with this the whole body acts as an instrument. He threw himself keenly into studying singing. After three years of treatment with me, he wanted to pause, so we stopped. He continued, however, to send me weekly reports, which I answered in detail, either in writing or by telephone conversations. In the meantime he moved out of his room, took his own apartment and rented a piano, which gave him great delight. During the summer he again served as a tour guide and also the following Christmas. In the early spring he wrote to me: "I have become much stronger inwardly and take things in my stride. I have also been calmer and again sleep very well."

After a year's interval, Werner wanted to resume his therapy. He had just come back from an automobile trip with a diplomat, a tour which had come about from his answering an advertisement. He had become disgusted with the man's promiscuity. Werner had always had a longing for a single friend who could satisfy all the aspects of his being, but he had not found such a person yet. He did not associate with just anyone that he happened to meet on the street, or spend the night with such acquaintances in anonymity, only to change partners each day.

He felt extremely lonely, but his concentration on his music kept his courage up. Music took the place of his painting and gave him great satisfaction as his voice improved. During this second period of our work together, we gave special attention to discussing the relationship to his parents. "How I would like to show my parents that I love them," he wrote; "but I simply can't do it. I can't stand the way they look at me; I'm at a loss for words with them, as if I were sealed up, and, unfortunately, constantly irritated." He could not forgive them for being as they were; he could not consider them without thinking they should be ideal parents.

The family history, the various deep disturbances among the relatives and their possible consequences were all unsparingly laid bare. Werner had to see that psychological dangers would also threaten him if he did not stand up to what he was, if he repressed his psychic material instead of courageously learning to understand and accept it. Slowly he was able to disentangle himself from the oppressive family circumstances and to gain insight into the fact that he himself was an individual who needed to build his life according to his own potentialities. His singing teacher, a wise woman, told him that perhaps God had intended him for some other purpose rather than that of raising a family. Suddenly, he began to deal seriously with religious questions, in which I eagerly supported him. For once, he had to examine carefully all that he had learned at home and at school, to question openly and to revitalize his outlook. He gradually began to sense that humility was demanded of him in order to find peace through prayer. With this feeling of new faith he again decided to stop his therapy.

The diary and the reports to me were continued. And after two more years, during which we never lost contact (he sometimes visited me nonprofessionally), he again found himself in trouble. He came to me one day in mid-March. He had again become involved with a sadistic friend with whom he shared a two-room apartment. His "friend" brought a girl to stay overnight in the apartment in order to upset Werner. However, with a resolute spirit, he gave the man notice and, though left behind with a broken heart, he was strengthened by his decision. He thought of this as a test of his mettle, which reinforced his feeling of self-confidence tremendously.

During the last few years two things have changed his life immensely: first, he achieved a financial stability such as he had never before known. "My debts have been paid, and I have understood how to handle my affairs, in contrast to how things were for so long—I was always in financial difficulties. As my character has grown stronger, my relationship to money has also improved," he said. Secondly, as he explained to me, "I am generally regarded now—also in contrast to earlier days—as an open, happy and sociable person. Only if someone tries to get too close to me do I become abrupt and disdainful. I have learned not to mix the inner and the outer." Indeed, he needed to extravert, and he learned to make the right use of it.

This last period of our work together lasted only three months. We concentrated, above all, on dreams and incidents which related to Werner's underlying tendency to fall for sadistic men. His unconscious efforts to manoeuvre himself into the role of the victim and his proclivity to derive pleasure from a masochistic situation slowly became clearer to him. I only hoped that the trick he was playing on himself would occur to him when he was about to become a victim of one of these men.

Our relationship continued, although on a somewhat looser basis. In 1956 I saw him four times, and in 1957 he reported a dream to me that gave me the hope that he would finally discover where his masculinity lay hidden. In this dream he sought a close friend throughout a large house, until he found him in the cellar. He wanted to embrace him in delight, but the friend resisted. When he finally gave in to Werner's wish, Werner saw that it was not the friend he had hoped to find, but a complete stranger. Nevertheless, he still felt happy because he then became

aware that this person was the one he felt so deeply attached to. This image would not leave him in peace. He wrote to me: "I believe that I am not wrong in thinking that in the cellar of my unconscious I have found my "brother," my repressed side, which I have sought for such a long time in a living person. This dream has had a lasting effect on me." He then decided to begin a serious search for the inner friend.

With this our work together came to a close. Werner knew enough now to explore his inner world alone. He had become stable, discerning, humble and unafraid. He had developed an ego that could no longer be so easily overrun. Two years later he wrote to me that he had been offered a position in a large concert hall, where the chances for advancement were very good. He had long become bored with his government job and had been trying to find a way to change his work. He asked me whether I thought he should accept the offer. I heartily affirmed that he should; it was exactly what he needed—a place where he could prove himself and a place where he belonged with his love of music. He began soon after, and with this his life found its proper course, and he derived a great sense of purpose from his daily work. His friendships with men therefore diminished in their urgency, although he could never quite renounce them altogether. However, sexuality began to play an evermore limited role in his life.

I saw Werner again at Christmas a few years ago. He had changed greatly; he was more serious and solid, a person who had something to expect from life. Even his boyish appearance was no longer so striking. It was a happy reunion. Since then, however, I have heard nothing from him, which I take as a good sign. As I was preparing this paper I telephoned him to see how he was getting along. He said: "Things are going marvellously; I'm very satisfied and would never have imagined that I could have worked as I now have to. But it's wonderful to be able to do it. My private life has also settled down. For two years now I have had a very dear friend, a Spaniard, with whom I have much in common artistically. With him I have been able to reconcile both sides of my life. I love him physically, it is true, but that is secondary. The important thing is our spiritual contact."

CONCLUSION

I did not lead Werner to heterosexual relations. But I consider his case a relative success. He ceased to pursue hopeless contacts with women, which would only have resulted unfavourably for them and for himself. He found complete satisfaction in his work and also a friend to whom he could be faithful and with whom he could sublimate his sexuality to a certain degree.

When one has treated as many homosexuals as I have, one becomes modest.

Therefore, if I speak of relative success, it is because I have not even been able to rescue many of them from the self-deception and despondency in which they were entangled, not to mention being able to change their way of life, although in each case I have poured my whole heart into the attempt. These individuals require, in particular, a great deal of love, understanding and protection, perhaps much more than others. They are unfortunate individuals, but in most cases are highly gifted. If this latter aspect of their personality can be awakened, the chances for recovery are better; if this awakening does not occur, such individuals become subject to depression and neurosis. I was deeply grateful that Werner was able to free himself from this threat. Could I wish for anything more than his statement that he was happy and content in his work? Great progress had been made and considerable maturity achieved. However, whether Werner ever finds his way to a woman lies in the hands of fate.

REFERENCES

Adler, A. (1918). *The neurotic constitution*, trans. B. Glueck and J. E. Lind. London, Kegan Paul.
———— (1930). *Das Problem der Homosexualität*. Leipzig, Hirzel.
Augustine. *Confessions*.
Aquinas, Thomas. *Summa theologia*, Secunda Pars 2, Quaestio 154, Art. 11–12.
Bailey, D. S. (1955). *Homosexuality and the western Christian tradition*. London/New York/Toronto, Longmans Green.
Boss, M. (1966). *Sinn and Gehalt der sexuellen Perversionen*. Bern, Huber.
Cory, D. W. (1951). *The homosexual in America*. New York, Greenberg.
Ford, C. W. and Beach, F. A. (1952). *Patterns of sexual behaviour*. London, Eyre and Spottiswoode.
Freud, S. (1948). *Standard Edition*, 12 and 13. London, Imago.
Gillespie, W. H. (1964). "Symposium on homosexuality (I)." *Int. J. Psycho-Anal.*, 45, 2–3.
Hirschfeld, M. (1952). *Sexual anomalies and perversions*. London, Encyclopaedic Press.
Jung, C. G. Personal communications.
Kerényi, K. (1951). *Mythologie der Griechen*. Zürich, Rhein.
———— (1951a). *The gods of the Greeks*. London/New York, Thames & Hudson.

Kimball-Jones, H. (1967). *Towards a Christian understanding of the homosexual.* London, S.C.M. Press.

Kinsey, A. C., Pomeroy, W. B. and Martin, C. E. (1948). *Sexual behaviour in the human male.* Philadelphia/London, Saunders.

Mead, Margaret (1935). *Sex and temperament in three primitive societies.* London, Routledge.

Plato. *The Symposium,* ed. R. G. Bury. Cambridge, Heffer, 1932.

Rees, J. T. and Usill, H. V. (eds.) (1955). *They stand apart: a critical survey of the problems of homosexuality.* London, Heinemann.

Schreber, D. P. (1955). *Memoirs of my nervous illness.* Trans. & eds. I. Macalpine and R. A. Hunter. London, Dawson.

Terman, L. M. and Miles, C. C. (1936). *Sex and personality: studies in masculinity and femininity.* London, McGraw-Hill.

Section Two
HUMANISTIC PSYCHOTHERAPY

Chapter 9

An Introduction to Humanistic Psychotherapy

ROBERT I. WATSON, JR.

In the first section of this book we have attempted to present a number of forms of therapy based primarily on psychoanalytic techniques and a dynamic model of man. This section will deal with what we have chosen to call humanistic therapies, which include existential analysis, client-centered therapy, Gestalt therapy, transactional analysis, and rational therapy. Based on a different view of people but influenced to some degree by the dynamic therapies, humanistic therapies are sometimes described as "third-force therapies." While this term indicates that they are different from both the dynamic and the behavior modification therapies (which will be presented in the final section of this book), it should not be taken to mean that they are little used. In fact, client-centered/nondirective therapy has a very large following, especially in the United States, and existential therapy has a strong following in Western Europe. Yet these therapies are not so well-known to the general public and are, to a degree, still being developed.

The humanistic psychotherapies are not bound by common techniques nor are they a unified school of psychotherapy. Rather they represent a general approach to understanding human beings. All are outgrowths of similar philosophical views of the nature of man. Thus, certain similar threads, interwoven in different ways, continue throughout the fabric of these different humanistic therapies.

What can be termed a "humanistic creed" is adhered to by and influences all humanistic therapies. The creed rests on two basic beliefs. First, the therapist must have a fundamental respect for the patients with whom he or she works and must see them as active agents capable of change. Second, the therapist must perceive each patient as an *individual* with whom one must have an interpersonal relationship for the therapy to be effective. This relationship must be visualized in terms of the individual patient, and not on the basis of preconceived ideas about the present condition or past life of the patient. The prevailing view that the therapist is only a guide for the patient is related to these beliefs. The therapist can give aid and some direction, but it is the patient primarily who holds the key to success in the therapy. Therapists' activities do vary among the different therapies; for example, the role of the therapist is much more passive in nondirective therapy than in rational therapy.

Furthermore, in all these forms of therapy the emphasis is placed on the patient's feelings or affects. The therapist should understand and be "in touch" with the patient's feelings, since it is primarily these feelings that he works to redirect. These therapies are based on an optimistic view of people and the assumption that patients inherently improve through their own effort with some guidance from the therapist. In contrast to dynamic therapies, it is perhaps best to think of the process of humanistic psychotherapies as principally a freeing process rather than a rebuilding one.

Apart from these common underlying elements in all of the humanistic therapies, there are significant differences in the aspects emphasized and techniques employed by the practitioners of each. Existential psychotherapy places great emphasis on viewing the patient as a unique individual, and working with him or her as a partner in the therapeutic interaction. Nondirective therapy believes the key issues are to allow the patient to direct the therapy and to work with the patient's affects. Gestalt therapy specializes in the patient's perceptions of the world, himself, and their interaction. Transactional analysis sees change coming about through basic understanding of one's feelings followed by insightful interactions. Rational therapy places its emphasis on the patient being convinced of the irrationality of her acts and thoughts, which in turn should lead to changes in her behavior. Thus, these therapies diverge in practice while maintaining the basic optimistic position of the inherent improvability of man. A review of the history and specific techniques of the humanistic therapies will now be presented.

EXISTENTIAL ANALYSIS

An example of existential analysis was chosen to begin the humanistic section because of the intimate relationship of existential therapy with the dynamic therapies of the preceding section. Many of the leading proponents of existential analysis were originally trained in psychoanalysis, and existential therapy borrows many of its techniques from dynamic therapies. Also, existential analysis, like the dynamic therapies, is basically a European movement, though it is now receiving more acceptance in the United States. Chronologically, it was the first of the humanistic therapies to follow the dynamic therapy movement.

The Philosophical Basis

As its name implies, existential therapy is based on the existential philosophical view of man. Before attempting to understand the therapy, it is important to understand at least some of its philosophical basis. The term *existence*, from the root *ex-sistere*, literally means "to emerge, to stand out," and this is exactly the existentialist's primary concern—how to describe man as emerging and becoming in his entirety, not as a collection of mechanisms or dynamics. If one sees man only as such a collection, one has then lost sight of the basic fact of that individual's existence. Overall, existential therapy is an attempt to do away with the division of subject and object so dominant in Western thought. This concern with the ontology of the individual, the being of a person, is its major departure from earlier philosophical thought. It is probably best expressed as emphasizing the difference between the "existence" of anything and the "essence." Since the Renaissance, Western thought has concentrated on the essence or basic principles and laws of various problems such as human behavior. To understand reality it has attempted to separate it into discrete parts. Existence was often ignored. This concentration on essence was most clearly brought forth in the work of Georg Hegel, who identified reality with abstract thought. Søren Kierkegaard revolted against this view and began the existential movement. However, neither Kierkegaard nor Friedrich Nietzsche rejected the concept and meaning of essence. Existentialism is in no way an antirational or anti-intellectual movement. They believed that both views of the individual, as subject or as object, do not clarify the existence of the individual and the reality of his or her experience. Both the person and the experience must be studied.

Since Kierkegaard, a number of important philosophers have continued the development of existentialism. The works of Martin Heidegger are considered seminal in existential literature. Among others influential in the existential movement are Jean-Paul Sartre, Gabriel Marcel, Karl Jaspers, and Martin Buber.

The Therapy

Therapy based on existentialism does not have one clear-cut leader or originator, because much of it was developed by a number of therapists concurrently in the 1930s and 1940s; however, if the therapeutic movement does have a major spokesman whose name is synonymous with existential analysis, it is Ludwig Binswanger. We will now turn to a brief discussion of this man and his work, hoping to gain better insight into existential analysis.[1]

Binswanger was born in 1881 in Switzerland into a family already deeply involved in psychiatry, his grandfather having founded Bellevue Sanatorium. He went through the usual medical course of studies, taking his internship

[1] For a much more detailed view of the history of existentialism and phenomenology in psychology, one should turn to Spiegelberg (1972).

under Eugen Bleuler, famous for his studies of schizophrenia. Binswanger also worked with Bleuler's assistant, C. G. Jung, who brought about a meeting between Sigmund Freud and Binswanger in 1912. Binswanger had taken over the directorship of the Bellevue Sanatorium and had turned it into a unique meeting place for many of the intellectual leaders of the time. Freud deeply influenced much of Binswanger's work. Although they remained personal friends, Binswanger found Freud's concentration on "naturalism" and the natural sciences constraining. He wished to find a better foundation for psychotherapy in some form of philosophical psychology, but it must be remembered that he never rejected Freud. He simply went beyond Freud's ideas to look for more adequate answers than he thought possible within Freud's framework. What Binswanger especially wanted was a better methodology, for which he turned to the work of the phenomenologist, Edmund Husserl. For a more complete and comprehensive anthropology or study of man, he consulted the works of Martin Heidegger. The phenomenology of Husserl especially aided him in overcoming his "naturalistic cataract," while through Heidegger and his *Daseinsanalytik,* he came to see the importance of human existence as "being-in-the-world," and thus of overcoming the split of subject-object.

Dasein is a difficult concept to translate into English. Literally it means "to be there" and is usually translated as "existence." It was an extremely important concept for Binswanger since it allowed for understanding both consciousness and the unconscious in terms of the particular individual and his "being-in-the-world" (1963). This "being" is in relation to the entire surrounding world, not just one or two aspects or specific objects of it. The concept of an individual surrounded in a world became very important in Binswanger's understanding of his patients, and he began to use it in his treatment of them. Using the concept of being-in-the-world, he showed that there were characteristic ways of living and moving within one's space, which became important in his method of dream analysis. It is also implied by the concept of *Dasein* that one is aware of this existence and because of this awareness is able to make choices and decisions about one's life. Because of the ability to make choices one is also held responsible for one's own actions. Binswanger delineated three different modes of the world for each person, which aided the therapist in his understanding of the individual. These are the *Umwelt*, the "world around" or nonpersonal biological environment; the *Mitwelt*, the world of fellow beings and social relationships; and the *Eigenwelt*, the private world or one's relationship with oneself, one's self-identity.[2] *Dasein* was a concept that Binswanger felt could be applied to the full continuum of human behavior whether it be normal, neurotic, or psychotic. He was especially interested in the problem of schizophrenia and did a great deal of his work with schizophrenic and

---

[2] It is recognized that much of the conceptualization and terminology of existential philosophy is unfamiliar to students of psychotherapy, but only by letting the concepts speak for themselves can the student appreciate their unique quality.

manic-depressive patients, attempting to use his *Daseinanalyses* to understand their problems.

What form of therapy came out of concentration on the existential nature of man? Many existential analysts use primarily the same techniques as the dynamic therapists. There are, however, great differences in the theoretical and methodological treatment of the material and of the patient due to the existential viewpoint. The first important difference is that the life history of the patient is seen as her way of being-in-the-world. No preconceived theory is used to understand the patient's past life. Each individual patient is seen as a completely unique individual with a unique background that plays an important role in his or her present being. No assumptions are made about the meaning of past incidents. For example, for one individual a homosexual encounter with another sibling might be seen as a traumatic incident involving rage and shame, while for another it might be an instance of affection and tenderness that might have been lacking in other interaction within the family. The meaning can only be discovered by working with the patient. It is also very important that the therapist should not direct the patient, but rather should be an existential partner to the patient, helping him reestablish communication with others and with himself, which has been lost in some way. Therapy should be understood as an encounter between two individuals who optimally treat each other mutually as subjects and not as objects. Both individuals must feel they are participating in this encounter, and most of the work of the therapy is accomplished in the encounter. What dynamic therapists describe as transference is one aspect of this encounter.

In existential therapy dreams are treated quite differently than in dynamic therapy. They are not interpreted, but instead are seen as one manifestation of the individual's being-in-the-world. The various modes of the patient's world, the *Mitwelt, Umwelt,* and *Eigenwelt,* and the patient's characteristic movement through his world are also used to allow the patient to see his own being-in-the-world. All of these techniques are based on the concept of the patient coming to see and understand his own being, and then to return from his neurotic or psychotic existence to a normal form of being for him. Even though Binswanger observed that this form of therapy could achieve great gains for both neurotic and psychotic patients, he recognized that there were limits to its therapeutic possibilities.

There are a host of other well-known existential analysts, including Eugene Minkowski, Viktor Frankl, and Rollo May, who have made important contributions to existential analysis. We will now deal with the life and work of still another noted existential analyst, Medard Boss, the author of the case study presented in this book.

Boss has a background much like Binswanger's. He, too, is Swiss, has a medical degree, and worked primarily in sanatoriums, though he now holds a chair in psychotherapy at the University of Zurich. He was deeply influenced in his early career by the works of both Freud and Jung. He was a friend of Jung's and was considered a Jungian analyst for many years, but he became dissatisfied with Jung's emphasis on symbols and archetypes. Boss felt a more direct interpretation of phenomena was needed to understand a patient's problems. Naturally, his next step was toward the work of the already well-known Binswanger. It was through Binswanger that Boss became interested in the work of Heidegger. Boss is now considered one of the major interpreters of Heidegger's philosophy and has worked closely with him since the end of World War II.

Boss admired the work of Binswanger, especially his use of being-in-the-world as a fundamental property of any subject. However, he felt an extended study of *Dasein* in relation to being, not necessarily being-in-the-world, was necessary (1963). [He especially felt that Binswanger had not seen the important property of *Dasein* as a means of clearing within being, and this insight could lead to a greater understanding of one's being and the eventual improvement of the patient.] Boss also emphasized the idea of restraining the use of symbolic or theoretical interpretations of any of the experiences of a patient. He felt it was especially important not to attempt symbolic interpretations of dream material but rather to treat it as one aspect of an individual's existence and allow the dream to speak for itself. For example, if a patient was to report a dream in which he or she felt trapped and confined, the therapist would relate this to feelings in the patient's everyday life. Similarly, Boss believed that a patient's symptoms should not be interpreted as strivings or ideas from the unconscious, but should be viewed in terms of their specific reality, and be understood in terms of the way they were exhibited by the patient. He was especially interested in applying an existential analysis to the problems of sexual perversions and psychosomatic symptoms.

Boss believed that the procedures developed by Freud and employed by psychoanalysts are the best techniques available for therapy. In fact, he believed that *Dasein* analysts often adhere more strictly to Freud's techniques than many psychoanalysts. The difference again lies in the way the therapist views her relationship with the patient and the interpretations she makes. Perhaps the most important difference is in Boss's existential view of what Freud described as transference. The patient's feelings about the analyst are accepted simply as feelings about the analyst and not necessarily as emotions connected to important figures from the patient's past. By viewing the relationship between analyst and patient as simply one between two individuals, Boss has redirected the emphasis of therapy from discovering causation in the past to exploring feelings and relationships in the present. Gaining insight is part of the process, but insight into the present situation.

Even though many existential analysts do follow the same classical techniques used by Boss or Binswanger, Rollo May (1958) has pointed out that in existential therapy the techniques follow understanding in importance. The task is to understand the patient and have him experience his existence as real by whatever method is best for that patient. The therapist must be flexible in his or her use of techniques. May has also made the important point that removal of a symptom is only a by-product of the patient coming to experience her existence as real. The aim of the therapy is not to alleviate a symptom or to help the patient "adjust" to society, but rather to have the patient discover her own being. If the therapy is successful, the patients experience their existence as real and become fully aware of this existence so that options and potentials become evident and change is therefore seen as possible. The therapy is seen as helping the patient carry out these options in life; it influences decision making and helps the patient achieve an attitude of commitment in his or her life. This effect of the treatment is especially appropriate given the concept of an existential neurosis in which emotional problems are not the result of repression of drives or pathological object relations but rather the result of an inability to see life as meaningful. Overall, it is still impossible to delineate specific techniques of therapy that are existential; existential therapy is more an orientation toward others or as May has put it, an "attitude" that the therapist adopts toward others and that guides his work with patients but does not dictate specific techniques for therapy.

CLIENT-CENTERED THERAPY

We now turn from a therapy that originated from a different philosophy but borrowed the techniques of dynamic therapy, to a form of therapy that grew out of specific and contrasting techniques from dynamic therapy and then developed a philosophy akin to existential analysis. This is the therapy developed primarily by Carl Rogers (1942, 1951), known as nondirective or client-centered therapy. Both terms are apt descriptions of the therapy. It is nondirective, because the therapist does not have any preconceived ideas concerning the patient's problems and does not attempt to direct the patient toward any one resolution of the problems. The "client," which is the term used instead of "patient," also has control of the direction of each session. The therapist does not try to lead him in any way. It is client-centered, the preferred term, because the therapist holds the attitude that a client has the capacity to deal with his or her life in a constructive fashion. It is also centered on the client because the therapist should attempt to perceive the world as her client sees it and to communicate her empathic understanding to her client. The focus is on the private world of the client, which is very similar to the relationship in existential analysis.

All of these techniques demonstrate a basic phenomenological view of man. In client-centered therapy, the phenomenal field of the individual is all important. It is through perception of oneself that problems arise, and it is through facilitating the change in this perception that the therapist helps the client. The therapist aids the client in gaining "self-acceptance" and in differentiating the perception of his field so that the client can better understand, recognize, and resolve his problems. The client is able to do this difficult task of restructuring his field because of the special conditions brought about by the therapeutic relationship, which give the client freedom to explore his perceptual field to the fullest, and freedom from any threat to his self-concept. The basic motivating force of an individual, the need to preserve and enhance the self, is also seen in terms of the phenomenal self. Experiences which do not fit with the individual's self-concept can be perceived as threats to the self. Some of these are "disowned" by the individual, while others cause the self to become rigid in attempting to protect itself. One other important point is that the client is considered the only valid source of information about his own phenomenal field. The therapist must believe the client and use the information the client gives him, not any preconceived ideas that the therapist might hold.

The relationship that evolves from the client-centered approach is the most important factor in the process of change. As Rogers (1959) has delineated the process, it follows a pattern of gradual change for the client brought about by the relationship with the therapist. The client begins to express feelings freely, refers more to the real self, and begins to differentiate and discriminate the objects of these feelings. Second, the client begins to see inconsistencies between experiences and the concept of self as well as feelings that were denied or distorted so that the client was not truly aware of them. Third, the concept of self begins to be reorganized, assimilating the previously distorted and denied experiences and feelings, and the self-concept itself begins to change, becoming more congruent with these experiences. The client also begins to experience more and more the unconditional positive regard of the therapist and the positive self-regard as well as seeing the self as the locus of evaluations.

Perhaps a brief description of Carl Rogers's background is in order so that one can better understand his theory and his therapy. Rogers was born in 1902 in a suburb of Chicago. He was the son of a minister and attended the liberal Union Theological Seminary before transferring to Columbia University. He went on to Teachers College of Columbia in clinical psychology and learned the usual dynamic view, but he was also further exposed to the humanistic philosophy of John Dewey.

At his first full-time job as a counselor and director of the Rochester Guidance Center he became much more disenchanted with what he considered the authoritarian position in dynamic therapy. He began to formulate his own views on counseling, aided somewhat by the work of Otto Rank, who took a much more permissive attitude toward his patients than was usual in classical psychoanalysis. Rogers left Rochester in 1940 to take up both teaching and research, as well as clinical work at Ohio State. From there he went to the University of Chicago, then to the University of Wisconsin, and he is now teaching and doing theoretical work at the Western Behavioral Sciences Institute in California. Besides developing a theory of personality, formulating his ideas on the techniques of client-centered therapy, and training many students in its use, he has been especially interested in research dealing with many aspects of therapy and particularly outcomes of therapy.

The Basic Themes of the Therapeutic Relationship

Another way of understanding the therapeutic interaction is through the five basic themes of the therapeutic relationship that Rogers has outlined (1956). All actually take place concurrently within the process of therapy but can be seen as separate elements. First, the client *explores incongruences* in his experience, why he feels one way at one time and then changes, or why he attempts actions which displease him. The process of differentiation mentioned earlier is important in aiding the client to understand his or her experiences. It is especially important for the client to discover feelings that she has distorted or denied from awareness. Second, the client *experiences feelings.* The client comes to feel a deep emotional experience that until then was blocked in some way. She can experience the emotions within the therapeutic situation, even though it may be very disorganizing, because she feels the acceptance of the therapist. Third, the client experiences the *unconditional positive regard* of the therapist. She feels safe in presenting even her weakest points to the therapist, because all of what she exposes is met with the same positive regard. She takes in the experience of being loved in a completely undemanding way. She relaxes defenses and also begins to value herself. Fourth, the client discovers a *changed concept of herself* in her experience. She has been able to restructure her self-concept and accept feelings that she could not in the past. The client experiences some disorganization of her self-concept, which then goes through a process of reorganization resulting in a new and more complete self-concept. This new self-concept is built upon the client's own experiences and not the ideas which others have believed about him or her. Fifth, the client experiences this *new self in action.* Like the dynamic therapy patient, he has been held responsible for his actions throughout the therapy, and after a period of time, he begins to see his actions are changing along with his new self-concept. The client's final responsible act within the therapy is to decide to leave it. As indicated by these five themes, the outcome of client-centered therapy is considered in terms of the growth of the individual, and not in terms of the removal of specific symptoms or the social acceptability of the client after therapy. How the client perceives himself or herself in the end is the most important factor in judging the result of this therapy.

The Techniques, Actions, and Attitudes

After this brief overview of the themes of this therapeutic process, let us turn to the specific techniques, actions, and attitudes employed by the client-centered therapist. One attitude is quite different from most other therapies. Diagnosis is considered not only unnecessary but possibly harmful to the therapeutic interaction, because it may create an image of the therapist as an expert, encouraging the client to form a dependent relationship. It also may give the therapist preconceived ideas about the problems of the client, which must be avoided. A client-centered therapist must also hold an attitude of acceptance and positive regard toward his or her client, if the therapy is to aid the client. The therapist should also have a continuous desire to understand the private world of his or her client. She should attempt to understand the world through the eyes of her client, and she must communicate her empathic understanding to her client. However, in more recent years the genuine feelings of the therapist have also been emphasized. For example, if she feels bored in the relationship, she is able to tell her client that there is something pertaining to herself that is making her feel bored in the situation.

There are a number of specific techniques that aid the therapist in his interaction with the client. You will see some of these techniques demonstrated by Rogers in the case described in this section. One technique is *clarification of the client's feelings*, where the therapist reflects the feelings of the client. The clarification can be a short statement like, "I get worried about my mother. I can never be sure what she's going to do," which could be clarified by the therapist as, "You often feel anxious about your mother." A clarification can also involve a much longer statement, only part of which might deal with feelings. It places the focus on the feeling the client is trying to present. It communicates to the client the empathic understanding of the therapist. Other techniques are simple acceptance, restatement of content, and nondirective leads. *Simple acceptance*, in which the therapist lets the client know his statement is accepted, adds to the communication of empathetic understanding and unconditional positive regard. It can be done both verbally and nonverbally. *Restatement of content* is meant to aid the client's understanding of issues that may be confusing. *Nondirective leads* are especially evident in the beginning of therapy. They help the client to develop topics and to direct the discussion in the therapy situation.

There is also some cautious use of approval and interpretation in the therapy, but only at times when the therapist is sure of the material he or she is interpreting or positive the client has gained insight.

Rogers at first felt that client-centered therapy should be limited to certain types of clients. However, he and other therapists have had a good deal of success with a wide range of psychopathologies, even at times working with schizophrenic clients. By the late 1940s nondirective techniques were also being used in conjunction with play therapy. Virginia Axline was one of the innovators of client-centered therapy with children. As we saw in Section I, play therapy had already been used in conjunction with various forms of analytic therapy. Axline's contribution was to use play within the context of the principles that were set forth for client-centered therapy. Ray H. Bixler, who was a student of Roger's at Ohio State, was also among the first to apply nondirective techniques to cases with children. The case reported in this section demonstrates the advances which can be made with children using play therapy. It employs basically the same techniques as client-centered therapy with adults but changes the context of their application to play since children can more easily express themselves in a play situation.

GESTALT THERAPY

The third form of therapy to be presented in the humanistic section is Gestalt therapy. As the name implies, it is a form of therapy that has used many of the concepts of Gestalt psychology. This therapy has also been greatly influenced by the psychoanalytic movement and by the work of Otto Rank and Wilhelm Reich. Gestalt psychology is primarily a theory of perception developed by Max Wertheimer and Wolfgang Kohler in part as a reaction to earlier atomistic theories. It emphasizes the whole of any perception and not individual elements. The term *Gestalt* is, again, not entirely translatable but is perhaps best described as a meaningful organized whole or as a configuration. The "figure" and the "ground" are the two primary concepts delineated in the theory. Whatever is the present focus of one's attenion is the figure, while all other elements of the environment at that moment make up the ground. This conception of an individual's perception of his or her world becomes important in Gestalt therapy for understanding a patient's problems as well as his or her basic auditory or visual perception. The Gestalten (plural of Gestalt) of an individual can be strong or firm, meaning that he is capable of differentiating clearly figure and ground, can use selective perception to focus on specific elements, can use motor activity directed at satisfaction of a specific need, and then can shift to a new Gestalt and new activity. Gestalt therapy emphasizes the integrating qualities of the individual within his own world. Any situation, including a person, must be understood as a whole, and the whole is always more than the sum of its parts. Gestalt psychology emphasizes other elements of perception such as the concept of closure—in which figures organized in certain ways seem as though they are complete even if they are not—or the idea of the perceiver being an active part of the perception, but it is the concentration on integration and the whole that was especially helpful as an analogy to the Gestalt therapists. Essentially, Gestalt therapists have used some of the basic concepts of Gestalt psychology and applied them to an individual's perceptions of emotions and bodily sensations.

Among the many contributors to Gestalt therapy, it was primarily Frederick S. Perls who combined these concepts of perceptual psychology with concepts of motivation. After Perls received his medical degree in Berlin in 1921, he became interested in psychoanalysis and received training in the institutes of Vienna, Frankfurt, and Berlin. In addition to being influenced by the Gestalt approach Perls was also affected by a number of intellectual traditions present in Germany in the 1920s such as the writings of Martin

Buber and Paul Tillich. Forced to flee Germany in the early 1930s because of the Nazi oppression of Jews, he first began private practice in Amsterdam, and then he immigrated to Johannesburg, South Africa, where he became a training analyst. He was accompanied by his wife Laura, who was also a trained psychoanalyst, and who aided him in his work on his new approach to therapy. She is also the author of the two case reports included in this section. Frederick Perls's first major work on Gestalt therapy came out in 1944, and after World War II he immigrated to the United States. In collaboration with Ralph F. Hefferline and Paul Goodman (1951), he published the seminal work on Gestalt therapy. He helped establish institutes for Gestalt therapy in a number of cities in the United States and remained active in private practice until his death in 1970. In the 1960s he carried out a number of workshops and seminars on Gestalt therapy at the Esalen Institute in Big Sur, California.

The Techniques

As mentioned earlier, the focus of Gestalt therapy is on the figure-ground relationship. The normal individual is well able to differentiate these two factors and the movement of them, but in a person having psychological difficulties there can be a lack of figure formation or a rigidity of a figure-ground relationship. The interplay of this figure-ground relationship is all important, and it is through understanding the problems of this relationship that the individual can come to live with less difficulty. In his or her encounter with the patient, the Gestalt therapist tries to help the individual's understanding by focusing on overlooked psychological mechanisms. She shows the patient how he is contradictory in his actions. Many therapists use the nonverbal behavior of the patient—movements, breathing, expressions—to aid the patient in achieving better self-understanding and in completing his or her Gestalt. The therapist is attempting to remove blocks in the patient's awareness of self and others, which create difficulty. She also attempts to show the patient that he must be responsible for his own actions, no matter how trivial they may seem; the therapist does this by having all statements made in terms of "I did" rather than "it happened." Everything is part of the Gestalt and therefore is important.

The Gestalt therapist has many ways of helping patients reach their goals of awareness and wholeness. One technique is to have the patient play out roles in what is termed "hot-seat" "two-chair" work; the individual interacts not with another real person but with an empty chair, at times taking the other chair and playing the other person he is imagining in the interaction. This assures that no other individual will influence the patient's experience at that moment (Perls, 1969). The person can also play out fragmented aspects of the self and by doing this become aware of and develop a better integration of opposing aspects. Role playing can also help individuals to understand their dreams. Gestalt therapists believe that all the elements of our dreams, (other people and even objects) are representations of the self.

Therefore, they have the patients play the different roles from their dreams to come to a better understanding of these parts of themselves and to integrate the fragmented aspects both intellectually and emotionally. If, for example, a person dreams of an empty house, the therapist would ask him or her to play that empty house, experience the feelings of emptiness, and by doing this capture some of his or her feelings about being empty, deserted, and left behind.

Joen Fagan (1970) has outlined a number of tasks that must be carried out by a Gestalt therapist. First, the therapist must come to a decision on the behavior patterns of the patient who has come to him—he must understand the problems of the patient and decide how to correct them. Second, the therapist must have control in the therapy—he must be able to induce the patient to follow his suggestions and procedures. However, the patient also has control in the situation because she has sought therapy by choice, and because *she* must specify the changes which she desires in herself. Third, the therapist's techniques must be potent in order to bring about the change in the patient. Fourth, the therapist must be willing to meet the patient in a full and open human interaction. He must care for the patient and not hold back. Fifth, the therapist must be committed to his individual patients and to his work as a therapist. These tasks may be the sine qua non of any successful psychotherapeutic interaction, but the emphasis on these humanistic goals is noteworthy among third-force therapists.

Perls and other Gestalt therapists felt that the therapeutic situation must be as undogmatic as possible. Explicit demands should not be made of the patient, but "experimental" situations should be set up so that she can better understand and cope with her problems. Some experimental situations for the patient should be designed to help her be in contact with the environment and her awareness of it. Techniques to help the patient feel the actual or to show the patient opposed forces in her environment are used so that the individual can become aware of the variety of processes which result in integrated psychological functioning. There are a number of experimental situations that are designed to aid an individual when she is not functioning properly in her environment. These are experiments involving *retroflection*, where the patient should learn to understand misdirected activities and energies; *projection*, where the patient understands that certain feelings really originate in her and not in others to whom she had attributed them; and *introjection*, where the patient sees that she has been forced to accept certain aspects about herself that are really not genuine parts of herself. These experimental explorations are done gradually, one experience building on another.

There are many differences in the techniques employed by the Gestalt therapist compared to other therapists, and perhaps one of the most striking is his emphasis on the here and now. He is interested in the awareness of the patient at the particular instant, not how he or she felt ten years before. As they do in other areas of his living, the problems of the patient's

Gestalt formation will take place in the therapy session, so the therapist can use the material immediately before him to show the patient his problems. The therapist may also ask the patient to retain a certain feeling so that it can be fully experienced and therefore better understood by the patient. Similarly, the patient might be asked to exaggerate a symptom to explore both the feelings and intellectual associations that are involved in it. Calling attention to awareness of bodily sensations and emotions, and all the other various experimental techniques have as their goal the breaking up of the badly organized field of the patient, and allowing him to make a creative adjustment with a new, well-interpreted Gestalt that is his own.[3]

TRANSACTIONAL ANALYSIS

The fourth form of therapy to be dealt with in this section is transactional analysis (TA). Eric Berne was the primary creator of transactional analysis. He was born in Montreal in 1910 and received his medical degree from McGill University in 1935. He was then a resident at the Yale clinic and studied at the New York Psychoanalytic Institute. During World War II he served as a psychiatrist and neurologist for the United States Army, and later, he was appointed as a consultant to the Surgeon General. Most of Berne's work as an innovative therapist was done in the San Francisco area. Besides his private practice, he did much of his teaching and therapy at Mt. Zion Hospital, the Langley Porter Neuropsychiatric Institute, and the McAuley Clinic. He has also been chairman of the San Francisco Social Psychiatry Seminars, and he was editor of the *Transactional Analysis Bulletin* until his recent death in 1970. Berne was deeply influenced by the works of Freud and other psychoanalysts and was especially impressed by the ideas of Paul Federn on ego states, which again stressed a much more phenomenological approach to a patient and his problems.

The Techniques

Before a patient goes into transactional analysis proper, he participates in structural analysis, in which he learns to differentiate the different states of his ego and is aided in his reality testing of them. The structural analysis segment of the therapy examines in detail the ego states of the patient. In Berne's terms an ego state of an individual simply means a state of mind and all behaviors relative to that state of mind. The basic concept for structural analysis is that these ego states can be classified and clarified, and through an understanding of them a patient can understand his or her own behavior and improve it. Throughout his writings and therapeutic work, Berne has attempted to use clear, concise English and to avoid "jargon" as

---

[3] It is often unclear, except in the most general way, how Gestalt therapy is based on the principles of Gestalt psychology. Although we cannot resolve this issue here, the reader should constantly consider this issue. It becomes more crucial, as we shall see, in the behavior therapies.

much as possible. Therefore, he has termed the three basic ego states, *Parent*, *Adult*, and *Child*, all of which have a common-sense connotation. The Parent is the ego state derived from the person's parental figures, and in it the individual acts just as one of his parents did when he was small. The Adult is the objective ego state dealing with the reality of the world. The Child is just that—the ego state of the remainder of the individual responding in its own childlike fashion. It is especially important for the therapist to help the patient differentiate between the Child and the Adult in his actions.

In therapy the patient comes to observe these three individual ego states within himself and learns to recognize them in the behavior of others. The therapist wants the patient also to recognize how these ego states interact with each other and may use a structure diagram to illustrate this. The diagram can be drawn to show the influence of the different ego states on each other and also the way one individual's states interact with another's. Besides demonstrating to the patient the different ego states, the therapist must be very sensitive in diagnosing ego states, and in understanding symptoms in terms of the ego states to which they belong. The primary purpose of transactional analysis is the gaining of social control by having the individual's Adult retain the executive control of all social situations. Other ego states would be allowed to come into interaction by the Adult, but it should remain in control. There is, however, a technique called "regression analysis." Berne uses this to highlight the Child in the patient—he or she will reexperience phenomonologically the feelings of the Child. At this time it is not the individual's Adult talking about the Child, but instead the Child itself talking and experiencing. Berne believed that such an experience can be greatly enriched if the therapist takes over the role of the Child in him or her and interacts with the patient from this position. The therapist begins the regression analysis by stating "I am five years old and I have not yet been to school. You are whatever age you choose, but under eight. Now go ahead (Berne, 1969, 227)." The interaction then proceeds with the patient experiencing his or her own Child to a much greater extent than if it was only spoken about. Both the therapist and patient learn about issues that affect the Child ego state as well as the person's Adult and Parent.

Even though the transactional therapist works with a wide range of psychopathologies, he or she must believe in the Adult of all patients. The therapist must also keep his patients aware of the progress they have made and where they are going. There should be a very complete understanding between the therapist and patient on the therapeutic situation, which stage the patient has reached, and where he or she is going.

After the patient has gained as much as he can through the work in structural analysis, the therapist has three possibilities open to him or her. She can terminate the therapy either permanently or for a trial period; she can follow it with psychoanalysis; or she can place the patient in transactional analysis. While structural analysis is usually done in an individual setting, transactional analysis usually takes place within the context of a group. It may seem that this form of therapy is outside the context of this volume since it does deal with group therapy, but transactional analysis does have an individual element to it, and it demonstrates that individual and group therapy work can be done with the same patient without undue stress. There is a good reason, as well, for transactional analysis to take place within a group. Its basic aim is control of the self in a social interaction, and the patient can best learn this control within a group situation. The transactional therapist is flexible so that he or she can also explore problems with a patient in individual sessions at any time during the therapy if the patient requests a private meeting. Following transactional analysis proper, game analysis and script analysis can be employed along with a continued use of transactional. Game analysis is useful in attaining social control, while script analysis is designed for long-term or "life-plan" control. There are numerous psychological games that an individual plays, many of them destructive to that person and the others involved in the transaction. Games appear to be like other interactions on the surface but have hidden ulterior transactions within them and involve payoffs often not evident to those involved. The basic problem with all games is that they do not allow intimate and honest relationships to result from the interactions. Berne (1961, 1964) has given a number of distinctive descriptive names to the games he saw many of his patients playing. For instance, many couples play "Uproar" in which any minor incident leads to a fight, the outcome being withdrawal on one or both member's part. The ulterior motive of the game is the avoidance of sexuality and intimacy between the couple, which is successfully accomplished by the game. A few other games are: "Wooden Leg" in which a person cannot possibly do what is expected because of some defect; "Rapo" in which a person is first seductive and then completely unwilling, blaming the other for making advances; "Kick Me" where one player gets another to put him or her down in some way. All of these games have different levels of intensity and most become repetitive and therefore even more destructive for those involved. Scripts are more than the repetition of games. They are the overall way one plays out one's life. They are usually laid down early in childhood and are greatly influenced by our culture, family, and especially our parents (Berne, 1972). The problem with scripts, just as with games, is that they are limiting. Scripts restrict the aspirations and the potential of each individual. Script analysis should aid patients in seeing how and why they are playing a role throughout their lives. For example, if an individual always snatches defeat from the jaws of victory, getting right to the point of being successful in a career and then managing to undo all of his or her hard work, this would be the script of "Sisyphus, or There I Go Again" (Berne, 1972, 216). The individual must learn to see this pattern in his life and understand how it relates to parental demands placed on him many years before. He or she then has the possibility of changing the script.

Besides the use of structural analysis, game analysis, and script analysis Berne (1961) has suggested a number of helpful technical points. First, the therapist should always have a number of examples from the experience of the patient to explain a diagnostic point. Second, historical material, actual behavior, confirming a diagnostic point should be found; if not, then a diagnosis should be held in abeyance. Third, terms such as "childlike" or "immature" should never be used to describe actions. Fourth, intellectual insight on the part of the patient is useful, but it is necessary for her to experience the ego state of the phenomenological Child, to really feel as she once did, for the best results in the therapy. Just as in the dynamic therapies, insight is not enough. After the patients are made aware of their selves, seeing as clearly as possible their transactions, games, and scripts, the therapist and patient will often attempt to set up a bilateral contract focusing on the changes the patient wishes to make, outlining possible changes and methods of change. Once again, it is up to the patient and not the therapist to decide what is to be changed. The patient may decide to work on a specific symptom such as laughing inappropriately or overeating, or may work on more general issues such as gaining better control of his life or better understanding of childhood experiences that still affect him. The patient works on these problems with the therapist and with group members, gaining both intellectual and emotional insights. The eventual goal is to be able to use both emotions and intellect fully in dealing with these specific issues and everyday problems.

RATIONAL PSYCHOTHERAPY

The final form of therapy in this section is rational psychotherapy, a technique developed by Albert Ellis, which, as the name implies, emphasizes the rational nature of man and the control of emotion through the thought process. It is based on the theory that thought and emotion are closely interrelated, and that for any emotion to be sustained it must be reinforced by the thought process. Therefore, to control emotion in a patient one should explore his thought processes and show him how certain thoughts are illogical and unrealistic and then how they can become less so.

Even before developing this form of therapy in the mid 1950s, Albert Ellis was a well-established psychotherapist and marriage counselor, who was best known to the general public for his work on sex. He had graduated from Columbia University with a doctorate in clinical psychology in 1947. He has a private practice in New York City and has founded the Institute for Rational Living there (now the institute for Advanced Study in Rational Psychotherapy). He was influenced in his work by the psychoanalytic school, but he was also greatly impressed by Charles Cobb's ideas on emotion. Emotion, to Cobb (1950) was not to be considered a simple state but rather a holistic integration of a number of closely related phenomena. In his therapy, Ellis emphasized the thought process and its relation to this experience of emotion.

The Techniques

The basic purpose of the therapist is to aid his or her patients in their rational thought processes so that they can better control their emotions and avoid neurotic and self-defeating thoughts and actions. To do this the therapist must demonstrate to the patient how his self-verbalizations can control his emotional problems. The therapist must also believe and show to the patient that self-defeating thoughts can be controlled by using more rational self-verbalizations. Concentrating primarily on the specific illogical thoughts disturbing the patient, the therapist must teach him or her to rethink these internalized sentences. He must also work on a number of general irrational ideas which many people hold, to be sure the patient does not substitute one of these other problems for his original one. There are a number of these general illogical ideas which Ellis believed should be worked through with any client (1958). A few of these ideas are: Certain acts are completely wrong and wicked, and one must be punished for them; an adult must be loved and approved by everyone for everything he or she does; it is easier to avoid life's difficulties and responsibilities than to face them. The therapist must act as a "counterpropagandist," contradicting these self-defeating thoughts as much as possible. In whatever way he can, the rational therapist should direct the patient to act in a manner contradictory to his or her illogical thoughts. If the patient is afraid to speak to women, the therapist must direct him to speak to some women and thus show him that the terrible thoughts he has had about what would happen did not come true.

Ellis certainly did not reject the use of other techniques, especially if the patient was particularly upset when he first came to therapy. Expressive techniques such as role playing and free association can aid greatly. He did warn, however, that these other techniques are not doing the real work of therapy, which is dissuading the patient from her illogical thoughts, and aiding her to think in a more rational fashion. Ellis also made the point that this form of therapy is limited in the type of patient that it can aid. Some people are not intelligent enough to understand the rational thought process, others are too emotionally upset to follow logical procedures, while still others are too rigid in their illogical thought processes to gain anything from this therapy. However, there are many serious and difficult problems that this form of therapy can help solve, such as Ellis's case of a psychopath presented in this section.

CONCLUSION

Now that the review of humanistic techniques is complete, a few concluding remarks are in order. Unlike both the dynamic and behavior therapies, in general humanistic therapies disavow a deterministic view of man, and therefore they are often considered "unscientific." Furthermore, they are the therapies most often associated with broad concerns, self-actualization, growth of potential, and so on—goals that seem to some observers to be overly optimistic. The humanistic psychotherapist's answer to these criticisms is that while science and technology (the ultimate purveyors of the subject–object split) may have increased man's power over the physical world, they have not made men substantially happier, nor have they made interpersonal existence more satisfying. The goal of understanding man needs a methodology unto itself, an empathic methodology that the humanists seek to provide. Even if the method proves less effective than we hoped, it is still valuable to treat others with caring and respect as fellow subjects. Understanding one's fellow man should no longer depend upon a "cool" detached therapist-observer, but upon a therapist willing to allow himself to reach out toward, and to be at one with, his patient.

REFERENCES

Berne, Eric. *Transactional analysis in psychotherapy*. New York: Grove, 1961.

Berne, Eric. *Games people play*. New York: Grove, 1964.

Berne, Eric. *What do you say after you say hello? The psychology of human destiny*. New York: Grove, 1972.

Binswanger, Ludwig. *Being-in-the-world*. (J. Needleman, trans.). New York: Basic Books, 1963.

Boss, Medard. *Psychoanalysis and daseinsanalysis*. New York: Basic Books, 1963.

Cobb, S. *Emotions and clinical medicine*. New York: Norton, 1950.

Ellis, Albert. *Rational psychotherapy*. Journal of General Psychology, 1958, 59, 35–49.

Fagan, Joen. The task of the therapist. In J. Fagan & I. L. Shepard (Eds.), *Gestalt therapy now: Theory, techniques, applications*. New York: Science and Behavior Books, 1970.

May, Rollo. Contributions of existential psychotherapy. In R. May, E. Angel, & H. F. Ellenberger (Eds.), *Existence: A new dimension in psychiatry and psychology*. New York: Basic Books, 1958.

Perls, Frederick S. *Ego, hunger and aggression: A revision of Freud's theory and method*. Durban, South Africa: The Knox Publishing Company, 1944. Also London: Allen & Unwin, 1947.

Perls, Frederick S. *Gestalt therapy verbatim*. Lafayette, California: Real People Press, 1969.

Perls, Frederick, Hefferline, Ralph F., & Goodman, Paul. *Gestalt therapy*. New York: Julian Press, Inc., 1951.

Rogers, Carl R. *Counseling and psychotherapy*. Boston: Houghton Mifflin, 1942.

Rogers, Carl R. *Client-centered therapy*. Boston: Houghton Mifflin, 1951.

Rogers, Carl R. Client-centered therapy: A current view. In F. Fromm-Reichmann & J. L. Moreno (Eds.), *Progress in psychotherapy, 1956.* New York: Grune & Stratton, 1956.

Rogers, Carl R. A theory of therapy, personality and interpersonal relationships, as developed in the client-centered framework. In S. Koch (Ed.), *Psychology: A study of science.* New York: McGraw-Hill, 1959.

Spiegelberg, Herbert. *Phenomenology in psychology and psychiatry.* Evanston, Ill.: Northwestern University Press, 1972.

Chapter 10
Existential
Analysis

The first case in this section deals with F. F., who was diagnosed as a sadistic pervert. There are, of course, many problems in treating this type of patient, and these were exacerbated in this case because the patient was confined to an asylum by the court.

The techniques of existential analysis closely parallel those of the dynamic therapies but do differ in the forms the interpretations take and the way the material is used. Note particularly how the therapist handles the dream material. Few symbolic interpretations are made; instead, the dreams are used as guides to the present experiences of the patient. Common psychoanalytic concepts such as transference or the oedipal situation are also not utilized in the work with F. F., though the material for such interpretation was present. The incidents that could be interpreted are seen by the existential therapist as reflecting the being of the patient and not necessarily as having any specific connection with past experience. Throughout the therapy the safety of the relationship between the patient and therapist is emphasized, and Boss attributes the insights and emotional understanding of the patient to this relationship. F. F. was allowed to experience a new way of adjusting to the world through this relationship. The work with dreams and other techniques are not so important as the affinity between the patient and therapist. It is through the caring of the therapist that the patient begins to experience himself and the world in a new way.

The Case History of a Sadistic Pervert

MEDARD BOSS

Freud contrasted sexual perversions with the transference neuroses, but he distinguished these in a different way than he had done in the case of the psychoses. He saw sexual perversions as the negative versions of transference neuroses. It seemed to him that the different sexual instincts and partial instincts which are repressed in the transference neuroses break through in the sexual perversions. Later, however, he discovered that this breaking through of some partial instincts in perversions is also based on repression, though of other instincts.

Daseinsanalysis cannot regard man's instincts as the basis of human love. For this reason, it cannot regard sexual perversions as originating from instincts either. Daseinsanalysis regards sexual perversions as results of specific concealments and restrictions of possibilities for loving. Since we have dealt with this subject in detail in another context,[1] we shall restrict our present discussion to the case history that follows.

On July 15, 1950, F. F., a commercial clerk twenty-six years of age, requested admission to the psychiatric clinic of the medical school of Zurich. Previous to this he had consulted a doctor in private practice and told him that he had been on the brink of committing a crime. A few days earlier he had asked a girl he hardly knew to go for a walk with him to discuss some business matters. When, late that evening, they were walking along the dark and lonely road by the River Limmat, he was

Chapter 11 of *Psychoanalysis and Daseinsanalysis,* by Medard Boss, M. D., translated by Ludwig B. LeFebre, © 1963 by Basic Books, Inc., Publishers, New York.

[1] M. Boss, *Meaning and Content of Sexual Perversions,* New York: Grune & Stratton, 1949.

seized by an overpowering impulse to strangle the girl with his two hands. Having once begun he was powerless to stop, and he would have murdered the girl if she had not somehow managed to extricate herself. He had thereupon regained his self-control and apologized to her, saying that he had not known what he was doing. He then fled, leaving her standing there. Since he could not conceal from the doctor that he still felt within him "an irresistible urge to kill someone," the doctor advised him to enter our clinic voluntarily for observation. F. F. did so because he actually no longer felt sure of himself.

According to the statements of our patient and of a large number of other people, there had been in his family numerous cases of insanity and of endocrine disturbances such as obesity and slight acromegaly. A maternal aunt had suffered for years from severe chronic schizophrenia. Another maternal aunt had died of extreme obesity. A maternal uncle had suffered from depressions and had committed suicide at the age of forty-five. The maternal grandmother had died in an asylum. On the other hand there were neither physical nor mental abnormalities to note in the patient's parents or his four brothers and a sister. The father, a bookbinder, gave the impression of coolness, severity, and self-control. In a personal interrogation the mother seemed to be the more yielding, affectionate, and communicative of the two.

F. F. was the second child of six. One brother is two years older; another brother, a sister, and the two youngest brothers are respectively two, three, six, and seven years younger than he. The patient attended primary school for six years and secondary for three, showing throughout a better than average intelligence and making quick and uninterrupted progress in all subjects. At the age of twelve he had expressed a great desire to take holy orders, and the parents consented to his entering a Catholic seminary. Not more than two years later, however, he suddenly ran away, having heard of the practice of mutual masturbation among some of his fellow seminarians. He was so revolted and terrified by the discovery that he returned to his parents there and then. He began his apprenticeship as a clerk, and obtained his diploma, with very good marks, in two and a half instead of the usual three years.

However smoothly his intellect functioned, his emotional peculiarities had stood in his way since childhood. Even when he was a little boy, the rest of the family had noticed his lack of feeling for them and for everybody about him. Further, he showed a marked tendency to solitude and irritability. For his part, the patient thought that his family did not understand him. He felt that his mother had betrayed him and cast him out by telling his father of his first love relationship at the age of eleven with a little girl of the same age. His father, whom he regarded as unfeeling and distant, had promptly and brutally "stamped out" the affair. To the patient, his parents' marriage seemed neither harmonious nor happy, and so he withdrew inwardly from his family, sharing less and less in their daily life. Even for meals he preferred to be alone, and would often come in at quite odd times, since he scorned punctuality as narrow-minded. He would not take Christmas presents from his family and gave them none. Christmas, he declared, was a purely inward, religious festival. On the other hand, he was deeply hurt by having to pay something toward his keep even during his apprenticeship. He was still more indignant over his parents' charges that he earned too little because he did not work hard enough, and yet long after obtaining his

diploma he got himself into debt through his own fault and for reasons to be explained. In the end he was involved in an automobile accident which was his fault and which made him liable for considerable damages. As he could see no lawful means of getting the money, he took it from the safe at his office. Legal proceedings were avoided only because in the end his father had guaranteed the money.

The same affective abnormality also made its appearance in the development of our patient's sexuality. From the time his first, childish love relationship was destroyed by his parents, he was incapable of any deep feeling for girls of his own age. He had certainly had relations with a number of girls soon after puberty and, on the purely physical side, had shown perfectly normal potency, but these connections were all short-lived, and in his sexual intercourse with these girls he remained emotionally cold and aloof. According to his own statement, these affairs had always seemed to him a mere game, and had never given him any deep satisfaction. This was the case even in the early stages of his relations with his present mistress, an unhappily married and childless woman sixteen years older than he, whom he had met when he was about twenty. Even with her, sexual intercourse at first had meant nothing to him, but gradually it took on increasingly marked sado-masochistic characteristics. He began to bite, beat, and strangle her. Then he would make her do the same to him. At the same time, however, for the first time in his adult life, he felt stirrings of feeling for a woman, and the more markedly perverse his sexual habits became, the deeper his emotional attachment to her grew. Soon his sadistic bent developed into an obscure urge to strangle her to death. At first these murderous impulses had arisen in him only in the form of sinister premonitions, but in time they moved into the light of clear and conscious knowledge, the more so because the woman, burdened with her own conflicting situation, was making repeated attempts to break with him. Meanwhile, he felt more and more lonely, since he had finally quarreled with his parents, who had refused to condone his relations with a married woman so much older than he, and he had gone off to live by himself.

The more severe and frequent his murderous impulses became, the harder and more exhausting was the struggle to master them. He was reduced to complete despair when the woman, under the pressure of a situation which was growing intolerable to her, actually broke with him and forbade him to see her. This break had taken place a few weeks before his criminal attack on the girl, which had led him to seek the protection of a mental asylum. In the weeks preceding the attack he had suffered from continual and severe headaches, and had repeatedly expressed the wish to be put in an asylum. On the other hand, he had planned to go abroad in order to forget his mistress; since she had broken with him, the impulse to murder her had grown stronger, to the point that his work deteriorated and he was reduced to earning commission as a commercial traveler without a fixed salary. Especially in the evening, between 9 and 11 P.M., the urge came over him with increasing force, and it drew him with such overwhelming power to murder some woman or other that he would lock himself in his room, hide the key from himself, and try to regain his self-control by perpetual smoking. In spite of this desperate struggle, the impulse to murder overcame the patient in the criminal attack on the girl of twenty. When he had asked her to go for a walk, he certainly had had no evil intentions toward her; according to his statement the impulse to strangle her had arisen quite unexpectedly and swept him irresistibly into action. He described very vividly how, in the act of strangling, he was split into two. He had felt himself a double being; the one, perfectly normal,

cool and collected, had no power to stop the other from strangling the girl. As he committed the act he had stood beside himself like a "scientist at a dissection," looking on helplessly while the other strangled. According to the victim's account, the second personality, the stranger, had distorted the patient's face into a "devilish" expression. The patient could not recall having felt any specific sexual satisfaction as he strangled her; he felt only considerable general relief and relaxation afterward. Here, however, it must be pointed out that his memory of the attempted murder was very sketchy compared with the excellence of his memory in general. With the best will in the world he could not remember details. He could not recall what he and the girl talked about at the beginning of their walk, nor did he remember having tried to kiss the girl before strangling her, which we subsequently learned from the girl herself. He could not remember how long and how violent the attack was or how she managed to escape at the very last moment when she was on the point of losing consciousness.

CLINICAL FINDINGS

The physical examination of the patient yielded no markedly pathological findings. All the internal organs functioned normally. The Wassermann test for syphilis was negative. The only noteworthy finding was that his physical constitution as a whole showed signs of slight endocrine disturbances, in the form of acromegaloid and tetanoid tendencies, and there was some oversensitiveness of the neuro-vegetative system.

Mentally, the patient's sense of time and place was unimpaired. He could reflect, think connectedly, and answer questions clearly and comprehensively. During his whole time in the clinic he gave no signs whatever of schizophrenic delusions or hallucinations or any symptoms of an organic psycho-syndrome. Intelligence tests gave, at the very least, average results. On the other hand, even in the clinic the abnormality of his affective behavior was striking. During the first few days he still suffered from his evening attacks. He felt an extreme inward discomfort and agitation and was tormented by impulses to murder various women who came into his mind. These attacks soon subsided when he came to feel properly protected from himself in the mental hospital and realized that he had something to rely on. Yet even after his evening attacks had disappeared, his behavior in the clinic gave an impression of extreme abnormality. When telling his life story he displayed almost total indifference toward his family. He dismissed his parents contemptuously as *petit bourgeois*. Even when telling the story of his attack on the girl, which had nearly made a murderer of him, he remained cool and unmoved. Nothing that had ever happened in his life seemed to concern him personally at all, nor did he feel the least repentance or pity for his victim. On the contrary, he declared that the death of a human being did not matter much; it took only a moment to die, and it was of no consequence whether a human being departed this life sooner rather than later. His frequent flippant remarks of this kind, together with his utter indifference to everybody and his unyielding affective rigidity, made him look like a case of severe schizoid psychopathy. There were moments when the doctors in charge actually suspected hebephrenia. The diagnosis now in the records of the clinic, based on the case history and clinical findings, runs "Sexual perversion (sadism) with compulsive states and succeeding impairment of memory arising from schizoid psychopathy."

THE ANALYSIS

Circumstances at the beginning of the patient's analysis could not have been more unfavorable. He had asked for admission to the mental hospital of his own free will, but since he constituted a serious public danger, the director of the clinic had no choice but to have him certified by the proper authorities and confined to the asylum for a considerable time. Although we had saved him from possible arrest by testifying to his lack of responsibility for his actions during his compulsive states, he could not but regard his certification by the authorities as a breach of faith, for as soon as those states had subsided after a few days in the clinic, he felt quite normal and actually regarded further detainment as quite unnecessary. We ventured on an analysis in spite of these difficulties because we realized that this was probably the only way the young man could be saved from being committed to the asylum for an indefinite time. The analysis took about eight months.[2] For practical reasons no more than two sessions weekly could be devoted to it, yet even at the end of six months, such a radical transformation of the whole structure of the patient's personality had been achieved that we were able to discharge him from the clinic without risk and from then on treat him as an outpatient.

In the introductory stage of the analysis the patient pleased us as much by his exemplary endeavors to keep to the fundamental analytical rules of free association as by his willingness to keep to the general regulations of the establishment for the remainder of the day. He had already consented to our suggestion of analysis with surprising insight and without misgivings, and repeatedly thanked us for all the time we were spending on him. No trace could be seen of open resentment, defiance, or even rebellion against his continued detention although he had long since regarded it as superfluous. But however carefully he might ob-

[2] The treatment was conducted by G. Benedetti, M.D., while the author supervised and directed it weekly as the training analyst.

serve the rule of free associations, it left him inwardly quite indifferent, and his polite gratitude to us was obviously sham; thus even at this early stage we were able to interpret his behavior as a pose carefully calculated to obtain his discharge from the institution as soon as possible. His dreams at this time also led us to suspect that his confinement had become the essential or even the sole problem of his life. He once dreamed that he was being kept prisoner in a hotel; everybody else had been released; only he was unjustly detained. In another dream he tried to escape from the asylum in secret, but met his analyst outside. Moreover, the road by which he was trying to escape was blocked. He was separated from his mistress by a barrier. Thus no other course was open to him but to return to the asylum. We did well not to regard his outward, artificial docility as mere calculated deception or as a reaction called forth only by his current situation. We might easily have succumbed to the temptation of breaking off the analysis as useless. We were saved from that false step by the results of our clinical observations and the preliminary interrogation. We had seen that the patient's present attitude toward his analyst was by no means invented for the occasion, derived from his present and to him completely open desire to be discharged. It was, rather, a slightly cruder version of the schizoid relationship to his environment which had always been characteristic of him. It was not only now, and not only toward the analyst, but for years, and toward everybody, he had displayed the same smooth mask, concealing all his genuine attitudes behind it.

Wherever he happened to be he would indulge freely in the wildest and most abstruse speculations. For instance, he would proclaim to those about him that all schemes of value were "mere paltry checks on divine being and living, creative power." Of his real existence behind these high-faluting phrases nothing could be divined. If the patient for a long time ran true to form in the analysis by interpreting away at his dreams and ideas in a completely aloof and purely rational way, his sole aim was to appear as clever and obedient as possible; the questions and problems he touched on in so doing had not the remotest effect on him. Was it that he *would not* show any feeling or that he was *incapable* of effective participation in life and of getting out of himself? Could it be that he had become his own jailer behind this huge intellectual façade?

From the outset we had adapted our therapy to the changing aspects of the patient's character, so we carefully avoided any interpretation of his dreams and ideas, since that would simply have offered him a welcome opportunity for setting out again on his purely rationalistic interpretations and intellectual speculations. Above all, however, we avoided interpreting his inordinate amiability and obsequious attitude toward his analyst as a transference phenomenon, i.e., as a shift to his analyst of a behavior or even an isolated, abstracted "affect" which actually implicated his father or mother. By speaking of such a "transference" to this patient we would not only have provoked from him endless intellectualized speculations about this theoretical conception, but—much worse —we would have degraded his authentic, though still restricted, relation with his analyst to an unreal, falsely derived, ghostly something. The error, then, would have been on our side. There was little doubt in our mind that the *restriction* of this patient's existence to the one attitude of aloofness and intellectual speculation about his fellow men and the things which came his way was brought about by the experiences of his childhood. From this it follows that in regard to his analyst, too, no other kind of relationship was available and open to him. But in this analysand-analyst relationship it was the analyst, and not his father or mother, who disclosed himself to the patient, notwith-

standing the fact that this disclosure of
the analyst could happen only within the
early deformed and narrowed-in world-
openness of the patient's existence. The
theoretical destruction inherent in the concept of transference is the more dangerous, the more aloof the patient is and the
more precarious and fragile his relationships to his world in general are. Much
evidence is available to indicate that patients, particularly severely sick ones like
our sadist, experience the usual transference interpretations as a misunderstanding and a cruel rebuff on the part of the
analyst. The reaction of those patients
tends to be further withdrawal from everybody and everything.

Instead, for the time being, we only
tried to bring home to this patient the contrast between his conventional pose of
considerateness, his perfect playing of a
part, in his waking life, and the hatred and
aggressiveness which were beginning to
appear in his dreams, which were all directed to his imprisoning environment. The
patient's reaction was paradoxical. His
amiability increased till it became grotesque. For instance, with an anxious expression, he began to ask the analyst if
he had done anything to offend him. Only
after persistent and repeated questioning
on our part as to whether this exaggerated,
aloof politeness was really the only approach he dared to use in dealing with his
fellow beings in his waking life in general,
and with his analyst in particular, did
serious fits of rage and truculence begin to
break through. Then his passionate protest
against his continued detainment and his
fierce charges against all the doctors in
the asylum at last found vent. Once, for
instance, he wrote:

Moral ideals—conventions with rats
and mice, revolting, stinking vermin,
gnawing and nesting in their dusty in-
terior through ages and worlds. Marriage is nothing but a prison, the imprisonment of life. Men—a litter of

otters. Can these be men and women?
Or are they mass creatures, herd animals, living only for the law and by
each separate letter of the law? Man
does not live for others; he lives first
and foremost for himself; therefore let
every man live as he likes.

It would have been an easy matter for
the analyst to convince a young man of
his intelligence of the factual groundless-
ness of most of his charges. In all probability he would then have promptly re-
tired behind his façade again and once
more cut himself off from fuller experience of his life possibilities. For this reason we assured him that his candor would
in no way prejudice his future release, as
perhaps he feared. The decisive factors for
his discharge would be solely the maturity
it was to be hoped he would achieve in
the course of the analysis and the knowledge of himself which he could attain only
by ruthless frankness. Thanks to our benevolent tolerance of his truculence, the
patient soon began to believe us. With
that, an atmosphere of sincerity and mutual confidence was established which
made possible the rapid progress of the
analysis in spite of his internment. For
weeks on end, our work in the analytic
sessions consisted in simply allowing the
patient to revile the analyst, the entire
staff of the asylum, and the world in general. Every time we suspected that he was
hesitating before some especially crass in-
sult to ourselves, we encouraged him to
still greater bluntness by asking him why
he would not speak out. Thus for a long
period he was allowed for the first time in
his life, and within the safe realm of the
analyst-analysand relationship, to learn to
know his possibilities of hating the world
openly and to appropriate this way of relating to people as belonging to his existence, too.

On one occasion when the patient,
again without hindrance from us, had
blasphemed against God and the world,

cursed his compulsory confinement, and abused all the staff of the asylum including the analyst, he told us a dream in which, quite in accordance with the reality of his waking life, he was interned in the relatively free wing of the asylum where the quietest patients were kept. However, in the dream the patient wished to be transferred to the back wing where internment was in cells and much stricter. This dream made us realize that the time had come to bring home to the patient, first and foremost, the crass contradiction between his waking rebellion against his internment and his dreaming desire to be still more strictly interned. Since he could find nothing to object to in this, we ventured a step further. We asked him if, in asking for still stricter confinement in his last night's dream, he was really rebelling only against being kept in the asylum? After all, we added, even in his waking life his own voluntary application for admission had preceded his internment, and weeks before that he had repeatedly felt the wish to put himself behind the protecting walls of an asylum. Furthermore, the withdrawal of his whole affective being behind the thick walls of his impenetrably cool and rationalistic façade dated from much earlier times. After the eruption of his violent hatred of the whole world, he had himself realized that the hermetically sealed armor of his character was internment in its most inward form.

Then the patient's eyes were opened. He began to realize that the schizoid blockage of all emotional relationships, his waking wish and sleeping dream of strict voluntary confinement, his application for admission to our clinic recommended by his doctor, and finally the unavoidable certification by the authorities, could scarcely be an unrelated series of events. As time went on he came to see this whole range of variations on the imprisonment theme as phenomena corresponding to the extreme restriction of his world-openness and therefore as the only

phenomena which in fact could appear and come forth in his life. From then on it did not take long for him to realize that in the furious rebellion against his enforced detainment, which had come out in the analysis, he was actually avoiding the real work of salvation and self-liberation by concentrating his whole strength upon fighting only the most peripheral and external restriction of his existence, and thus evading his true and full duty to his destiny as a human being. Once that bitter pill was swallowed, he gladly accepted our consolation that there could be no question about his eventual discharge from the asylum, and that it would come about of itself as a result of the liberation of his own, genuine self, just as his former emotional petrifaction had inevitably led to his confinement behind actual stone walls.

The realization of the total closure of his nature and his world gave rise to a further question. What was he hiding behind his former façade of utter indifference, of rationalistic speculations and empty phrases, and why did he have to hide it? We admitted that a considerable quantity of hatred and aggression had found vent in the analysis, but after all, who would not be seething with rage and resentment if he had lived the wretched life of a lonely prisoner since early youth? For that matter, we added, his recent dream about his dead confessor seemed to offer some help here; it hinted that behind the hard, cold, psychopathic crust of his character and the hatred it engendered, utterly different ways of living stood waiting to be revealed which might even be the original, soft, warm, love-seeking, and child-like core of his being. In that dream he had gone to see his former confessor but had found him dead. In the dream he felt deep sorrow. Long after the patient's confidence in his parents had been totally destroyed by their ruthless intervention in his first love relationship, this confessor had been the only human being to whom he had dared bring his deepest feelings, the only one he had come to when most in distress. The fact that in the dream the confessor was removed from him by death reveals to what depth the breach in his communication with his fellow men had struck and the extreme isolation to which he had been brought. At the same time the confessor was a signpost to the patient's genuine love of a boy toward a fatherly man, which at one time he had been able to bring to the priest without reserve. Thus if those warm, child-like, love-seeking relationships had not been part of the patient's existence *in posse*, even in the form of a kind of *rigor mortis*, he could not possibly have dreamed of the beloved dead confessor. For the very appearance of such a person who belongs to a world of fatherly love presupposes the corresponding openness of the dreamer's existence, i.e., presupposes his possibility to love as a son, however deeply this potentiality of loving may still be buried in his waking and dreaming life.

In fact, after weeks of relentless questioning as to what he was hiding behind the coldness of his façade and the noise of his truculence, the patient slowly ventured to confess that he did not trust his own warm feelings. Indeed he had at all times warded off with all his might emotional relationships of any kind because he regarded them as silly and senseless sentimentalities and irrational fuss. From childhood on he had striven "to replace all unpredictable feelings by clear, rational ideas, which were always at hand and which guaranteed continuity of thought." Soon the shame he felt for his feelings turned out to be a very essential motive for warding them off, yet in its turn that very shame was based on the (to him) shameful infantilism of the impulses he had till then warded off. With their gradual appearance in the analysis, a completely new stage began in our therapeutic work, which was eventually to reveal the root of his sadism. The beginning of a new phase in an analysis never, of course,

appears as a sharp line of demarcation. Old patterns of behavior persist, now stronger, now weaker, but they no longer govern the entire bearing of a patient as they did at the beginning of the analysis.

The next thing in the analysis of F. F. was his confession of his terrors as a child. He recalled how panic-stricken he had been every time he had to go through the woods at night. Then he was bitterly ashamed when he remembered how soft-hearted he had really been as a child. This sadist and near murderer was incapable of looking on while other boys killed small animals. Tears would always come into his eyes, just as they did when he so much as heard or read touching stories. His family often teased him about it. He was also ashamed because he was sorry for a man who had lost his life in the mountains and because he once took a little lost girl affectionately under his wing. It still happens today that intense feeling of pity of this kind are interpreted as repressions of still deeper aggressions. If we interpreted them this way, we should have been guilty of a quite unjustifiable underestimation of them. We should have willfully blinded ourselves to their overt content, replacing the actual phenomena by mere hypotheses not susceptible of proof. Therefore, each time he confessed to his shame of these gentler feelings, we confined ourselves to asking him whether there was any need actually to feel so ashamed of them. Through this relentless probing of his stereotyped shame reactions to everything that had to do with feeling, the patient came gradually to see that this was not, as he had assumed without question, the obvious, the only possible and right attitude to his own self. He then realized that he had unwittingly adopted this attitude from his stern, unfatherly, and cold father, who set no store by feelings but was prone to outbursts of brutal anger. On the other hand he had never been able to find an outlet for his affections for his mother, who was more warmhearted by nature but who had succumbed completely to the father's mentality. At this point the patient complained once more of his mother's betrayal of his first love secret to his father. It took weeks for him to realize, under the consistently kindly and reassuring guidance of the analyst, that the dislike of and contempt for feeling which dominated his parents' world was not universally valid.

To allow him to turn this realization into experience, the analyst had to be very careful not to raise the slighest objection to his existing love relationship to the woman who was sixteen years older than he. On the contrary, he had to impress on the patient that he took the matter very seriously; otherwise he would have been promptly relegated to the forbidding and heartless parent-world, while the patient's own world would have completely closed again. For the patient was only too prone to regard all persons in authority, even the analyst, in the humanly atrophied form in which he had experienced his father. In order to undermine this narrowed-in perception we had to ask him again and again why we should wish to separate him from his mistress as his parents did. Meanwhile, having heard of his being committed to the asylum, the mistress had approached him again and would not admit that there had been any breach between them. We assured him that we respected his judgment and could therefore leave the decision to him. Only then did he reveal the really paranoid ideas he had held back until then. In all seriousness the patient dreaded that the analyst was conniving with his father behind his back to have him put away for years in order to stop his love affair for good and all. He imagined that the analyst would also have him expelled from the country by the authorities.

The totally different attitude of the analyst—steady, calm, reassuring, and adapted to the patient's essential nature—finally succeeded in breaking the spell of the narrow and frozen father-world so that the patient's deep and positive emotional capacities ventured to show themselves. At this time all the long-forgotten memories of his childhood came back to him spontaneously—rather, they overwhelmed him. This phenomenon of "recalling" can throw a peculiar light on the so-called human memory. Psychologists and psychiatrists usually think of the memory as being a special function of the psyche, capable of picking up memory traces which had been left somewhere in the brain by earlier impressions and of bringing them back into consciousness again. However, nothing of the kind has ever been observable. When our patient suddenly recalled so many events which had happened in his childhood, they simply became present again in his *Dasein*'s light in the form of memories because the patient had allowed himself to get attuned once more to the same soft mood which had opened him up to their occurrence at that earlier stage of his life. At any rate, our patient remembered now, for instance, trying to protect his helplessly weeping mother from his father's harshness, but along with it came the memory of the punishment to be expected from the bullying rage of his father. Again we were careful not to take the father's part in all these accusations, although we realized that his picture of his father might be completely distorted. What was real for the patient in our work was the experience derived from the whole relationship between the actual father and this particularly sensitive and affectionate child. As regards the mother, the patient remembered having said often, when he was six or seven, that he instead of his father should be married to her, always with the idea that he could make her much happier than his father could. He had often suffered agonies of fear that she would not come back when she had gone out.

As these events of his childhood presented themselves to him again he came straight and without transition to the realization of the continued child-mother quality of his relationship to his present mistress, a woman so much older and of a truly motherly nature. With this woman, he was often overwhelmed by the dread of her returning to her husband and leaving him for good. He told us that she often complained of his lack of respect toward her; he would importune her and run after her. On the other hand, girls of his own age seemed to him immature and childish. He could not get on with them at all as his existence was not yet open to an adult partnership between man and woman, but only for a son-mother relation.

The dreams which now began brought out very clearly the child-like pattern of his actual relationship to his motherly friend. He dreamed once that he was falling into an abyss and that she saved him at the last moment by catching hold of his collar. In another dream he was having a dispute with an innkeeper because he could not pay his bill and she helped him out of her own purse. Again, he was nearly run over by a truck; she came and scolded him and taught him how to behave on the road. In yet another dream, after a boat trip on the lake, he could not find the boat's moorings. He stood helpless, fearing that the waves would carry the boat away, but his friend came and showed him how to bring the boat to land. In a last dream, he was lying in bed in one of the busiest squares in the town. She came, shielded him from the jeers of the people, and took him home. In the end the patient saw that in his waking life he was treating his friend's husband with disgraceful rudeness, like some hated father he wished in hell.

The last point for the patient to realize, and the one he was most unwilling to admit, was that his rivalry with the husband was an essential factor in this whole love relationship. Even here his dreams spoke with the utmost candor. Thus in one dream he met the husband, who threatened him,

but the patient took not the slightest notice of him, to his own extreme satisfaction. Finally he confessed, both to himself and to us, that the very fact that his friend had never been able to make a final breach with her husband, but had always left open the possibility of a reconciliation, had been the permanent fascination of the whole affair. If his friend had run after him, he went on, to use his own words, "it would all have become uninteresting, banal, and commonplace."

In this way we were able to bring the patient to grasp his so-called Oedipus complex by actual experience, simply by never so much as mentioning the word. Indeed, we carefully avoided belittling his relations with his mother-mistress by labeling them as infantile. Only too often this word "infantile"—so commonly used by psychoanalysts—gives the patient the impression that the behavior so designated is something rather shameful which one should long ago have outgrown. Actually though, in the case of such patients it is a hitherto unexperienced way of relating to the world, which they should be allowed to accept and to venture into for the first time in their lives in their relation with the analyst. They must go through this experience, because this child-like behavior constitutes a normal phase of every man's development, which cannot possibly be omitted without all subsequent growth being jeopardized. Therefore, if such a patient eventually dares in analysis to allow himself, for once, to be cared for like a child, we have good reason to encourage him and praise his courage, rather than to urge him to overcome this "infantile" attitude as soon as possible. Consequently, in the case of our patient, we led him to see that in the relevant dreams and ideas his obvious need of love and protection by an older, mature woman was entirely justified and legitimate. It was only by proceeding in this way that we were able to avoid blocking the way to his own experience of his still child-like emotional condition, which he had to take upon himself if it was ever to become the source of a new and real maturity. We had, indeed, been put on the alert by learning from the patient that a doctor had once told him point blank that he was suffering from an Oedipus complex. He had been deeply hurt by this reduction of his love to a mere technical term, and had clung to his friend all the more defiantly. It was due to our caution in this respect that in the end he admitted, of his own free will, that he would never have been so much in love with the woman if his parents had not objected so strongly and if he had not been stimulated by the rivalry with her husband.

But the tactless doctor's explanation of the patient's love for his much older mistress and of his hatred of her husband as "actually" meaning, respectively, his own concrete mother and father was a mistake not merely of timing but of content. For his former experiences with his parents had so hampered the unfolding of his existence that, emotionally, he had been open only to a distorted child–parent relationship. His mistress fitted admirably into this existential world-openness as the actual motherly woman she was, without any other "meaning" or "symbolizing." In the facts themselves, at any rate, there is not the slightest hint to be found to justify such a derivative interpretation. Even a dream of an "unveiled" sexual intercourse with his own mother, which he might well have dreamed at this time of his life, would not in the least alter the truth of this statement. Such a dream would merely have been an event in his dreaming state which could be paralleled in waking life by his love for his mistress, both occurrences being nothing other than that which they showed themselves to be, both equally authentic and corresponding equally well with the patient's reduced world-openness.

The most important question still remains, however—the appearance of sadistically perverted behavior in this life history. The clearest and promptest answer

to that question is given by the remarkable change in the character of the patient's dreams in the course of his last twenty years. As far back as he could remember, from the age of six to that of pre-puberty, nearly all his dreams were extremely terrifying. He dreamed mostly of fires which burned down his parents' home, wreaked havoc through the whole village, or attacked great forests, without rain ever falling or the fire brigade ever appearing in time. These fire dreams appeared at a time when, in his waking life, he was still capable of intensely warm relations with his environment, when he suffered agonies of pity at the sight of another boy torturing an animal and still greater agonies when he met the little girl lost in the road. From his twelfth or thirteenth year on, these scenes were replaced by one in which the patient was buried under an avalanche or a landslide. In these dreams he felt little or nothing and coolly allowed everything to happen to him. Finally, in a dream he had only a few days before the criminal attack on the girl which had led him to apply for admission to the mental hospital, he was wandering about on an arid steppe. There was not a human being, not a refuge in sight. Then he caught sight of a burning farmhouse in the distance; suddenly he was in front of the burning house, where he met his mistress and told her that he was going to kill her.

The fires in the dreams of the early part of the patient's life had been called into his dreaming world by his hot, impetuous, and as yet uncontrolled temperament. The fire of his sensual attachment to most of the people of his world was terrifyingly wild and untamed, burning up all the social institutions and structures of his home and village. In his child-like instability and weakness he stood in need of adequate help from his parents, from the grownups, the "fire brigade," or the soothing rain from heaven to bring order to his existence. But the father, himself deeply inhibited, failed him. That is why the patient, from his twelfth or thirteenth year on, dreamed only of avalanches and landslides, which buried him. There is no further trace of his emotional participation in what was going on around him. In and around him was merely an arid void, and it was an arid steppe which surrounded him in the dream that immediately preceded the most serious and dangerous of his sadistic acts. His existence and (because man's existence is nothing else but his luminating world-openness) his whole world had closed down and dried up. Now, through the arid, desert crust of this land, the old, unruly flame of his vitality shot up again. They burn down the peaceful farmhouse, and at that precise moment there erupts in the dreamer the sadistic decision to kill his mistress. Thus the impulse to acts of sadism here, too, proved to be an outbreak of fire, the fire of his attachment to a motherly woman, which, although warded off, had been burning behind the rigid crust of his outwardly detached pose. The harder and thicker the crusts appear in the light of such a narrowed-in existence, the more violence is needed to break through them with sadistic practices. It was exactly the same blow-up of a character armor as happened in the case of Erich Klotz, described elsewhere.[3] The spontaneous remarks made by these two sadists about their sexual relations agree almost word for word. Thus F. F., in his sadistic practices with his partner, also felt as if "a wall between us had blown up," and as if it was only by his brutal biting, beating, and strangling in the sexual act that "the two bodies could melt in a single fire of love and a feeling arise of union unknown till then." This patient also felt the impulse to commit a sexual murder "because only then would the woman belong to him and him alone; then he would be one with her." Thus the sadists remind us more than any other patients of the profound sentence which Freud wrote about the "most horrible per-

versions": "The omnipotence of love is perhaps never more strongly proved than in such of its aberrations as these."[4]

We learned in the course of the analysis that, in addition to his sadistic sexual impulses, the patient had at times been overcome by an irresistible urge to travel far away. He would get up in the middle of the night, take a train leaving for some distant destination, and not return home until the following day. During the journey he always felt relief and relaxation. The changing scenery in the moonlight and dawn gave him a feeling of inward freedom. He felt the pressure in his head and the tension in his chest yielding, and his insomnia left him. The stars drew him as a "magically fascinating picture," a "distant realm of joy, of freely flowing life outside the rigid walls of narrow-mindedness and philistinism." Even when not under the influence of such moods, the patient would indulge in daydreams, planning to go to Africa, "to the tropical south, where [he] could start out on a great adventure and build up an entirely new life." Thus these imagined excursions in space and his poriomania were merely another and less brutal form of bursting through the intolerably cramped state of his existence to discover all the wealth of living there was in him and in his world.

RECAPITULATION OF THE PSYCHOTHERAPEUTIC PROCESS

Just as the dreams occurring before the analysis showed clearly and logically the development of the patient's sadistic behavior, a small series of dreams during the analysis showed his way to recovery. In a quite early stage of treatment he had dreamed as follows:

> I am in a wood with my father and my elder and younger brothers. I am still a boy. My mother and sisters are not

[3] M. Boss, *op. cit.*, p. 96*ff.*

[4] S. Freud, *Three Essays on the Theory of Sexuality*, in SE, Vol. VII, p. 161.

there. The path leads deep into the wood where dense bushes and trees have grown. Suddenly I realize that all the trees look as if they were made of cement or are actually encased in a hard, impenetrable crust of cement from root to top. It is, in fact, rigid, lifeless, and impenetrable—as if life itself were frozen behind a mask. We four walk on to a house which stands at the top of a high stairway. There my father and brothers have to stop; I am to go in alone. In the dream I have been told that a young and loving woman will receive and welcome me there and that a child will call me father. But before I can really enter the house, everything vanishes and I am suddenly quite alone on the edge of the town.

Only a few details of the extremely rich content of this dream need be dealt with here. Even as a boy the patient lacked the female members of the family, who might have let him share in their gentler, softer, more affective way of life. In his father and brothers he has only the male, reserved, and cold aspect of relating to the world around him. Rich vegetable life, however, is met in the middle of the wood, yet this natural growth at once freezes behind a mask of cement. The possibility of meeting with the warmhearted, feminine way of being in the later part of the dream can appear only in the form of a promise which is not fulfilled. Finally, this way of being human vanishes entirely and he is driven to the periphery of the human community, "on the edge of the town."

About halfway through the analysis, however, one of his dreams showed a somewhat different state of affairs. The patient is sailing down a river in a boat. At one point the river narrows a little and a bridge connects the two banks. He decides to land here and climbs onto the bridge which connects the two parts of the town on the right and left banks. There he meets a watchman, a kind of policeman,

who asks him where he is going. The dreamer replies that he wants to have a look at the town, whereupon the policeman warns him that both sides are extremely dangerous. There is plague on the left bank, cholera on the right. After a little reflection, however, the patient disregards the warning and ventures first into one part of the town, then into the other. He is surprised to find, in both parts, a calm picture of perfect health. The people are going about their business in perfectly normal fashion and they assure him that there is no sickness. Therefore, the dreamer thinks, the watchman must have been mad.

The dreamer already has the wish and the desire to put an end to his lonely voyage. He enters the living community of the town, but he meets a watchman who assures him that it would be a most dangerous venture, leading to sickness and death. The policeman tells us of a world of precaution, of barriers, dangers, and sickness against which one must be warned. Such a world is disclosed only in the light of a *Dasein* which is attuned to an attitude of mistrust against all human community. The early acquired attunement to a fundamental distrust, however, is no longer the only possible way of world-openness. The patient is already capable of an attitude of some venturing and some trusting. He dares to disregard the policeman's warning and to enter the human communities of the cities. He discovers that this friendly and trustful mixing with people is the normal and healthy way of existing, whereas the distrusting and all too precautious attitude toward people amounts to madness.

Not long before the end of the analysis the patient had a third dream. He is out in the country, in a pretty landscape with a lake in the middle. The scene makes him think of a novel by Herman Hesse, in which the lake is the place of contemplation and an Indian fakir meditates on the sunny lake shore by the edge of the wood. The patient, with five friends, is sailing on the lake in a boat. There is also an older man in the boat, a skipper. The skipper proposes a contest to the young men. At a sign from him all six are to dive from the boat and pick water lilies at the bottom of the lake; the one who brings up the most will get first prize. The dreamer is a little nervous, afraid of losing the race. In telling the dream, the patient's childhood came back to him at once. At home there were six children, and the others had always teased him for being the weakest. Later the dream takes an unexpectedly favorable turn. All six friends reach the surface at the same moment. Each has exactly the same number of water lilies, twelve, in his hand. None has outstripped the others. All are glad and feel united in mutual respect.

To stress only the most essential point: the beginning of the dream is still colored by a feeling of nervousness and insecurity and by the suspense of rivalry. The fact—at least in his dreaming state—that the patient had already appropriated quite different ways of existing by the psychoanalytic plunge into his own depths is shown by the concluding incident in the dream. The full dozen of delicate water lilies in the hand of each man bears impressive witness to the blossoming out into the fullness of his life, as well as a reconciling balance of male and female. The man who has achieved this is beyond egocentric greed and fear and has found himself as a member of an ordered human community.

This dream might well have tempted many a psychoanalyst to interpretations of a symbolic manifestation of the patient's "transference." The older man would have been thought of as "meaning" the analyst, especially if his appearance had shown some similarity to the analyst. The next step after this interpretation would have been to undo the "wrong connection" of the "transference" and to interpret the old boatman-analyst as ultimately signifying the patient's father.

We, however, took great care not to make any such an allusion, since the phenomenon itself does not offer the slightest justification for such a speculation. True, the "transference" interpretation might even have proved to be therapeutically helpful to some extent. It would nevertheless have been a completely arbitrary action, in no way warranted by any demonstrable fact. We have no proof whatever for the supposition that the boatman actually signifies or symbolizes anything else. He is and remains the boatman, as whom he shows himself in this dream world. The most we can say is that the analyst enters the picture only in that the patient, through his experience of the analyst's constant benevolence and care, has been able to open his existence to a more trusting relationship with his fellow men in general. This more friendly world-openness of his existence can now also call into its luminating realm correspondingly more friendly appearances, such as the clever leader, the kind boatman. Thus it can also be said that this boatman's entering into the dream world of our patient gives evidence of the newly acquired possibility of a trustful attunement of his *Dasein.*

What had made this opening up of his existence possible was not any of the unwarranted interpretations of psychoanalytic theory but, above all, the analyst's unshakable caring for the patient. Just because this attitude of the analyst contrasted so completely to the patient's former experiences with his parents, the analyst-analysand relationship had been able to offer him the necessary existential abode which his parents had failed to give him. A parent-child relationship, though, whose openness is sufficiently in accord with all of the child's genuine nature is the only realm into which his possibilities of existing can come forth in a healthy way.

The second reason was that whenever the patient's behavior, in either the waking or the dreaming state, showed the slightest evidence of his former attitude, the analyst tirelessly emphasized the "narrowed-inness" of this existence, which left him only open to distrustful, distant ways of relating to his fellow beings. With this went the repeated question, What was it that still made him afraid to exchange this way for a more open kind of relationship to his world?

Meanwhile, profound and striking changes could be seen in the patient's waking behavior. There could be no further suspicion of schizoid psychopathology, much less a schizophrenic psychosis. He had become much freer, more accessible and communicative. Even his relations with his parents, at one time so strained, had become friendly, and his attachment to his motherly friend lost its morbid fascination. His convulsive clinging to her yielded to much steadier judgment; he abandoned his original plan of persuading her to get a divorce so that he could marry her, since the difference in age was, after all, too great. His attitude toward her was much more independent and he would not let her mother him. *Above all, his sadism had completely disappeared.* In his sexual relations with her he experienced a satisfying orgasm with complete mental and physical relaxation and no urge to sadistic practices. He could hardly believe that he had once taken pleasure in them; they now seemed subhuman. Nor did any of his compulsive states return. His work also showed considerable improvement.

In the spring of 1951, after eight months of analysis, the patient fell ill with slight exudative pleurisy, which made a stay of several weeks in the mountains advisable. It would be as irrelevant to the main problem to discuss the psychosomatic aspects of this illness here as it would have been to trace the psychosomatic connections in the auto accident preceding the analysis. However, it is noteworthy that the patient recovered quickly and entirely from this illness and was able to assume his work in town. He also felt so far recovered mentally that after his return from the mountains a continuation of the analysis seemed unnecessary, both to him and his doctors.

SUBSEQUENT HISTORY

We learned not long ago that the patient had not only been able to part without difficulty from his older woman friend but that ten years ago he had married a girl some years younger than himself and is living happily in a normal love relationship with his young wife and is already the father of a child.

Chapter 11
Client-centered Therapy

AN ADULT CASE

Consistent with the theoretical practice of this type of therapy, no attempt was made to diagnose or categorize the client, Mary Jane Tilden, at the outset of her treatment. Again this is not an ideal case in that the desire for the therapy is not, at first, self-directed. Instead, the client was brought to the first few sessions by her mother, however, this soon changed.

Notice that from the very beginning the therapist, Dr. Rogers, attempts to have the client direct the session. He asks her in a nondirective fashion why she is coming to him and what she believes her problems to be. The therapist begins immediately to use the basic techniques of client-centered therapy such as giving clarification of feelings or direct leads to the client. (Note that these techniques are referred to in footnotes throughout the case, and in the third interview the techniques are noted above the statements.) In the first interview the therapist also attempts to explain the goals of the treatment and the basic methods used to try to attain them.

At the end of this first interview the client is very tentative in her appraisal and desire to continue. By the third interview she is becoming more active and positive during the therapy session. As the treatment continues, the patient begins to take actions with people outside of the therapist's office. Throughout the interviews Dr. Rogers attempts to remain in empathetic contact with the feelings of the patient and demonstrate to her that he understands and is in touch with these feelings. There is one major shift in the concerns of Mary as the therapy continues. At first she is most distressed about anxiety, but this eventually changes to the area of sex and sexuality. In concluding the treatment the therapist allows the patient to decide when it is time to terminate, which Mary does after she feels significant change has taken place and she no longer needs the relationship with the therapist. Many cases take longer than this case did. Also in more recent years attempts have been made to use a time-limiting technique—at the inception of the therapy the client and therapist agree on a set number of treatment sessions.

The Case of Mary Jane Tilden

CARL R. ROGERS

The first contact with the case of Miss Tilden was a telephone call from her mother, who desired help for her daughter. She raised a number of questions about the counseling services, which had been described to her by a friend. She described her daughter as "needing to be set straight on some matters," as "staying in too much," and as "acting strange." She was sure Miss Tilden could not come in alone, and finally made an appointment to come in with her, with the plan of talking to a counselor herself, although she was ambivalent about this.

The mother and Miss Tilden arrived for their appointment a few minutes late. Miss Tilden was attractive in appearance, a twenty-year-old young woman, who came willingly with the counselor for the first interview, cited below. The mother talked with a second counselor, and during the first interview enlarged on the difficulties which the family was having with Miss Tilden. Some statements from her conversation will give the picture. "She sleeps all the time. If I wake her she just broods and introspects and is harder to get on with." "Should I let her sleep until twelve o'clock? I don't know. She can't just do that, then not get dressed. She just sits by the radio or goes back to bed. Then sometimes I force her to get dressed and take a walk. Then she meets someone and they ask why she isn't working, she gets so ashamed—she's afraid of people's opinions of her." "Oftentimes she says she's fearing insanity." The mother confessed that she also worries about this because a relative who exhibited similar behavior became psychotic. She explained that Miss Tilden gave up her job some time ago, and has also given up her social life.

The mother came for two interviews, but then she felt she did not wish to return for more. She brought Miss Tilden for the third interview, but simply waited during the interview. From the fourth interview on, Miss Tilden came by herself.

FIRST INTERVIEW

October Seventh

C1. [1]I really know very little as to why you came in. Would you like to tell me something about it?

S1. It is a long story. I can't find myself. Everything I do seems to be wrong. I can't get on with people. If there is any criticism or anyone says anything about me I just can't take it. When I had a job, if anyone said anything critical, it just crumpled me.

C2. You feel things are all going wrong and that you're just crushed by criticism.

S2. Well, it doesn't even need to be meant as criticism. It goes way back. In grammar school I never felt I belonged. Oh, sometimes I would try to feel superior, but then I'd be way down. I used to be the teacher's pet, but that didn't help with the other girls.

C3. You feel the roots go back a long way but that you have never really belonged, even in grammar school.

S3. Lately it's been worse. I even feel I ought to be in a sanitarium. There must be something awfully wrong with me.

C4. Things have been so bad you feel perhaps you're really abnormal.

[1] C1. This is a good opening lead which allows full freedom for the client to develop the material in his own way, and also places the responsibility for doing so with him.

S4. Yes. Of course, in school I used to get high grades, but I think I sort of memorized things.

C5.[2] Excuse me. You speak pretty rapidly and I can't get it all down in my notes. Would it bother you if I set up a microphone and recorded the interview on this machine?

S5. No—that would be all right. (*From this point on the interview is recorded.*)

C6. Now just forget that's there and you'll be all right. You used to get high grades and you used to——

S6. I got them, but I think I just must have memorized books. I know I just studied all the time. I didn't go out with anybody. I sorta shut myself away because I was hurt so much. So I——

C7.[3] You said that you were hurt so much?

S7. Yes, because when I was with people I just didn't feel comfortable. I felt so left out of social things and things of that sort. And well, I guess I just sorta— when I studied it was sort of an escape for me and I tried to forget. But I didn't study—I guess I didn't study with the right attitude to learn so I could get out of my dilemma. I sort of made it like it was a different world, my studying. I sort of secluded myself. You know what I mean? So that my studying wasn't something that could lead me to normality and to being with other people, and to having something in common with them.

C8. Your studying and your good grades and all you felt was just something sort of separate from the rest of your life and didn't help you very much.

S8. M-hm. That's right. And I—and that wasn't the right attitude, I know it wasn't. Because it was supposed to inte-grate you with life but it didn't—I guess I just made it an escape.

C9. You feel your studying and work was a way of getting away from things?

S9. That's right. And everybody else wondered why I liked to do homework and I just enjoyed it—I seemed to enjoy it—and, well it gave me something—it sort of stood me up a little but I don't seem to have learned very much from it—because well—my memory doesn't seem to be good at all now. It's all so mixed up. I mean, I've been mulling it over and over in my mind and trying to get at the bottom of it. (*Pause.*) But I just don't seem to be able to. And then when I think that it's such an effort for me to just go around living and just thinking these things I would think that something would have to be done. It isn't right and it isn't normal. It's an effort for me to walk down the street sometimes. It's a crazy thing, really.

C10.[4] Even just little things—just ordinary things, give you a lot of trouble.

S10. M-hm, that's right. And I don't seem to be able to conquer it. I mean it just—every day seems to be over and over again the same little things that shouldn't matter.

C11. So, instead of making progress, things don't really get any better at all.

S11. That's right. And I just seem to have lost faith in everything—I don't know, I can see good for other people, but I can't—I can't believe it's true when it happens to me. It's such a terrible thing. (*Laughs.*) It's nice to be—to be able to believe in good but I think it's sort of a— I sort of persecute myself in a sort of a way—sort of self-condemnation all the way through. And it's been growing for a long time.

---

[2] C5. This unusual technique for recording the counseling situation appears to be readily accepted.

[3] C7. Here we find a direct lead which the counselor uses to follow up an expression of feeling the client has made. This allows the client to go further in her discussion of her unhappy childhood.

[4] C10. This response recognizes the feeling of despair about the difficulties the client is having with her life-experiences. It might well have gone even farther in catching and reflecting the hopelessness and personal inadequacy she feels.

C12. So that you—condemn yourself and don't think much of yourself and that's gradually getting worse.

S12. That's right. M-hm. (*Pause.*) I don't even like to attempt things—I mean —when I go on a job or something—I just—well—I feel like I am going to fail. It's a terrible thing, but——

C13. You feel that you're whipped before you start in.

S13. M-hm. It's when I come in contact with other people. I did hold a job selling because I thought I should get out and be with people. And as soon as I started to think of myself in relation to it, instead of being able to face it, you know, and get over the fear, as soon as I think of myself in it—why, it just scares me—and then I can't do anything, and, well, it just seems that other people, they react to things and seeing how they take them it makes me feel that I know that I am not reacting to things right. And it makes me feel that I am inferior and that I am not normal. That's what always gets me.

C14. Other people do things you just feel that you can't measure up to. You just don't stack up to the other girls.

S14.[5] M-hm. It's sort of a comparison. It is. It's just when I compare myself to the other girls it seems—I don't feel at all up to it. And just lately I've sort of gotten concerned about it. My girl friends—well —I guess it's funny for me to say, but they are all getting married—and—well,

[5] S14. This is a real self-evaluation that is both problem-stating and insightful. It is perhaps the only real indication that this girl gives during the first interview that she has any motivation to work through the problem. There appears to be here some indication of a force for positive growth, very tentative in character, in the implied regret she feels in not being able to go onto the richer aspect of living that she witnesses in the situation of her girl friends. This may be an example of the "positive drive for growth" that Rogers postulates for the basis on which therapy takes place, i.e., the force within the individual which leads him to change himself.

it wasn't that I was jealous, it was the fact that they were ready for it—and they seem to be so normal in everything they did and they were unfolding the way everybody should unfold in this world. And when I thought about myself, I thought, "Well, my gosh! I'm not even coming *near* it." And it was just such a blow that—I just started to realize that I wasn't coming along the way I should— I mean I just wasn't progressing.

C15. It wasn't that you were jealous, but that you gradually realized that here they were ready for a new part of their life and you just weren't ready for it.

S15. M-hm. It's a terrible feeling. It's just that I should have been because everybody else was, so naturally I guess I should have been, too. I just don't.

C16. That made you feel more than ever that somehow you weren't progressing as you ought to. . . .

S32. There must be something somewhere to counteract all this. I mean, other people must be going through part of the things I've gone through or they all feel they could. I don't know how they do it. I realize I am feeling something everybody must feel. Because I didn't just make them, they were here before I came, I suppose. But I don't know, I just don't seem to find a way out.

C33. You feel that other people must feel some of the same things you feel and that some way they handle them, but for you, you don't see the way it can be done.

S33.[6] That's right. Because I know that I'm not smart enough to invent all these things. It's not something that I invented.

[6] S33. At this point, the client says in effect: "The problem is beyond me; it's up to you to tell me what to do next." The counselor, in C34, explains what can be expected of the therapy situation. This is structuring. More important, the counselor also indicates that if a solution is achieved it is likely to come through the positive efforts which the client herself is willing to make. He also carefully disclaims any ability to guarantee that results are certain to occur.

It must be something everyone goes through to a certain extent. I read about it. That's all I know about it. People don't usually talk about it. So I just wonder what the next step should be. (*Pause— ten seconds.*)

C34. Well, I might say just a word about the kind of thing that we do here, and the kind of thing that you are starting to try, I suppose, today, and that is if you come in to try to talk through these things that do bother you and concern you—there's a chance at least that you may be able to discover for yourself some of the things that you can do about the situation, and I think it's up to you whether or not you think it's worth trying—and all I can say is that a number of people have tried that sort of thing and have found that it helped, but you can't be guaranteed anything. It might help or it might not. I think you're wondering whether anything might help.

S34.[7] M-hm. I suppose I want to know just what to do, but then maybe nobody could give me that.

C35. You realize that you are probably looking for immediate answers that nobody could give you.

S35. I just don't know. I don't know what I'm looking for. It's just that I wonder if I'm insane sometimes. I think I'm nuts.

C36.[8] It just gives you concern that you're as far from the normal as you feel you are.

S36. That's right. It's silly to tell me

not to worry because I do worry. It's my life. What is the theory behind this sort of thing? Do you sort of find things for yourself? I don't know. I guess nobody can really help you, can they?

C37.[9] We can help you go about working on your own problems, but a lot of what happens will be up to you.

S37. Is it just the talking about things? I mean, is that the whole thing? You don't say a word? (*Laughs.*) I mean you try to understand, but I mean you don't guide people in any way, do you?

C38. I won't be giving you a lot of answers, except to help you work through some of the answers that you would be satisfied with. It's just like you say—someone may say, "You're nuts" and some people may say, "No, you're normal." Well, I could tell you you're normal, somebody else could, somebody else could tell you you're nuts. There's no—the thing that really matters is how you really feel about yourself.

S38. Well, I don't know how I can change my concept of myself—because that's the way I feel.

C39. You feel very different from others and you don't see how you can fix that.

S39.[10] I realize, of course, that it all began a long time ago—because everything begins somewhere. I wasn't just— somehow or other something failed somewhere along the line. And I guess we sort of have to get at it, a sort of re-

[7] *S*34. The client recognizes that there is no short answer to her problem, although how deeply she is convinced of this question remains a problem through several succeeding interviews.

[8] *C*36. As in *C*26, the counselor attempts to recognize and clarify the client's concern about her sanity, but does not attempt to reassure her on the point, feeling that the reassurance would only direct her farther away from understanding her problem and doing something to alleviate it. In *S*36 the client admits that the reassurance would not help her much, and goes on to face the problem of whether she can do anything to help herself.

[9] *C*37, *C*38. The counselor clarifies the counseling situation, showing the part that both he and the client must play. In *S*37 and *S*38 the client states clearly the quandary that many clients feel when faced with this new experience. The explanation in *C*38 is a very clear statement of the reasons for avoiding the giving of "guidance." Later evidence suggests that there has probably been no lack of "guidance" in this client's life, but, on the contrary, probably a great deal too much.

[10] *S*39. Nothing could be more clearly stated than the client's grave doubts as to whether she has within herself the power to find a solution to this problem.

education. But I don't feel as though I can do it myself.

*C*40. You realize that the roots must go a long way back, and that at some point you will have to start in reworking it, but you're not sure whether you can do it.

*S*40. That's right. (*Pause.*) It's just the idea that I can see myself going through life this way, fifty, sixty, and seventy years old—still thinking these horrible thoughts. And it just doesn't seem worth while—I mean, it's so ridiculous. While everybody else is going their way and living life, I'm sort of at the edge, and looking on. It just isn't right.

*C*41. The future doesn't look very bright when you look at it that way.

*S*41. No. (*Long pause.*) I know I'm lacking in courage, that's the big thing I'm lacking. That must be it, 'cause other people aren't swayed so easily. It's a funny thing, though—when I think of those—those qualities, I always think of them, I don't know, not as realities, but as something that's far off somewhere. It's a hard thing to explain these things. It's just as though—it's—it's true but I laugh at it in a way. Sort of a feeling that I am sort of sneering at it—but I know it must be true 'cause other people go around expressing those things. It's a very confused feeling.

*C*42.[11] Logically, you realize that courage is one of your deficiencies, but inside yourself you find yourself laughing at that notion and feeling that it doesn't really have anything to do with you. Is that it?

*S*42. That's right. I always sort of make myself different. That's it.

*C*43. M-hm. You sort of say that might apply to other people but it's not for you because you're different.

*S*43. I don't know whether that's exactly right or not. I can't put my finger on it. Sometimes I feel lonely and some-

times I feel another way. Do you have cases this bad?

*C*44. You really wonder whether anybody else could be——

*S*44.[12] I think I'm worse than anybody that I know. That's just it. I feel as though I am terribly, terribly low. It just does not seem worth—bothing with it, it doesn't seem worth while, that I can't get up there to first base.

*C*45. You think about making the struggle, but it doesn't seem possible.

*S*45. That's right. I just wonder what other people do when they find problems and stuff. I just wonder whether they see it through or try to find out something else.

*C*46. You feel that you'd like to know how somebody else would handle it.

*S*46. That's right. And yet I—I go through situations and put myself there, and then (*few words lost*). For instance, if I went to a dance or something—and then if I wasn't asked to dance, it would hurt me terribly, and immediately I would feel that I was just no good, and that that proved it. But then there were others there who went through the same thing, and they carry on. I mean—and then—I can think of other times when I was asked to dance and then other people weren't and yet it didn't do anything for me. I mean it didn't make me feel any more different about myself. I just accepted that sort of thing and it didn't add anything. The best you can say is that it wasn't bad.

*C*47.[13] The highest peak you ever

---

[11] *C*42, *C*43. These are excellent reflections of the client's feeling.

[12] *S*44. Here, and again in *S*48, the client expresses the full depth of her hopelessness. It simply is not worth the struggle to try to find a way out. Rogers believes that in such situations the counselor relies upon one element only—the basic drive of the individual toward growth. Note that in *C*45 the counselor simply endeavors to show a deep and empathic understanding of the client's hopelessness.

[13] *C*47, *C*48. The counselor makes it quite clear that the client's coming must be because of a desire to do so, and not because the counselor is persuading her to.

reach is just not to feel bad. And, on the other hand, if any little thing happens of a negative sort *that* throws you clear down—well, I see our time is up for today. Want to come back next week?

*S*47. (*Laughs.*) I guess so.

*C*48. You're really puzzled, aren't you, whether or not to come back?

*S*48. I don't know whether this would help me any. I mean I don't know whether anything would help me. (*Pause*). Have you ever had cases that were this bad? (*Laughs.*) Or anywhere near this bad?

*C*49.[14] You're coming back to that question again, aren't you—wondering—well, I could answer that question—yes.

*S*49. Do they eventually go to the insane asylum? (*Laughs, and C laughs.*) Sounds crazy, doesn't it? I know it does, but that's just how I feel.

*C*50. Well, you say the word on whether or not you'd like to come back next week. (*Long pause.*)

*S*50.[15] All right, I'll come back. (*Very softly spoken.*)

*C*51. O.K. (*Time is set.*)

Significant Feelings Expressed in the First Interview

1. Everything is wrong with me. I feel I'm abnormal.
2. I feel my studies were just an escape for me.

[14] *C*49. The question asked by the client in *S*48 is not unusual in rather difficult cases. The counselor points up the client's need to know whether she is the worst case he has seen, but he does give her a certain amount of reassurance in stating that he has seen other cases just as bad.

[15] *S*50. Although this statement is made in a whisper, and only after a long hesitation, it is the one indication, throughout the whole interview, of a positive or purposeful attitude. It represents the first positive step this client makes. She has come in because of her mother's urging, she sees her own situation as definitely hopeless, but, when given an opportunity to act, she *acts* as though there were some hope. Rogers believes that this constructive force is present in every client.

3. I can't do even the ordinary things of life.
4. I have lost faith in everything, especially myself.
5. I'm sure I will fail on anything I undertake. I'm inferior.
6. I'm realizing that other girls are growing normally into marriage, and I'm not even coming near this readiness.
7. I have absolutely no self-confidence.
8. I can't act natural because I don't like myself.
9. I think about suicide, because I can see no justification for living.
10. I'm childish, but people expect me to be adult.
11. I am abnormal.
12. Successes do not buoy me up; failures, even small ones, floor me.
13. I should be more mature than my sister, but I'm not.
14. I can't take my normal place in society.
15. I have a real flaw in my character.
16. I do not dare to be unselfish or outgoing for fear I will be hurt.
17. When I try to imitate successful people, I'm only acting.
18. I feel others can cope with the kind of problems I have, but I cannot.
19. I realize the roots of the problem go back a long way, and I do not feel that I can change the situation myself.
20. I can't go on like this.
21. I'm lacking in courage, but somehow I sneer at the idea.
22. I feel I'm worse than anyone I know.
23. I wonder if you can help me. I doubt it.
24. I guess I will come back.

SUMMARY OF THE SECOND INTERVIEW

October Fourteenth

Miss Tilden starts the interview by exploring her relationships with people. She feels she is not capable of any depth in such relationships, and has never really "belonged." She has no interests, because she would be afraid she could not carry them through properly, so will not attempt anything. She fears others will find out how "dumb" she is, especially men. "I wonder if there is any answer. What can you do with a person who doesn't have any faith in the idea that he will arrive at an answer? You really can't do anything with that kind of person, can you?" She feels that she does not even measure up to a little child, but feels that she should be beyond these things. "Is there any solution for me?" The counselor structures the relationship in a fashion similar to that given in the first interview. Miss Tilden replies that she has gone out and done things that were suggested in psychological books, but it has not helped. The interview ends as follows:

*S*51.[16] The point is—I mean—I know that nobody can really help me—I mean —I guess they can point out the way partly—but they can't do my thinking for me.

*C*52. You feel that other people can be of some help but you realize, too, that the essence of it has somehow got to be in you.

*S*52. That's right. (*Pause.*) I—I'm really so mixed up that I don't know what I hope to accomplish, actually.

*C*53. You really aren't sure what— what you're aiming toward.

*S*53. That's right.

*C*54. Well, I see our time is about up. Want to come back next week?

*S*54. (*Laughs.*) Do you really think you could help me in any way? I mean, do you feel as though you can?

[16]*S*51. Here the client is giving a very clear statement of the concept on which the non-directive technique is based. It is still apparent, however, that she doubts whether she can be helped at all. In *S*54 she raises the same question. In *C*55 the counselor skillfully restates his position, and this is accepted by the client in *S*55. When the clear-cut choice is before her, either to give up and to continue in her maladjustment or to struggle to find the answers within herself, she chooses the latter.

*C*55. I think I would have to leave it that—a—it comes back to the question— do you feel you want to work on it? If you do, we'll save time next week. If you feel that it is so hopeless that nothing can be done——

*S*55. It's really all in my own attitude, isn't it? (*Pause.*) O.K. Let's make it next week, then.

THIRD INTERVIEW

October Twenty-First

Non-directive-lead

*C*56.[17] Well—how do you want to use the time today?

Answer   *Insight*

*S*56.[18] Well—I don't quite know. A——. (*Long pause.*) I was just wondering, I was reading a book the other day. It was called, uh—*Your Life as a Woman*, and in this book—and the subtitle was "How to make the most of it." In this book it showed different types of people and their work, and it didn't go into the causes of it or anything—but—uh—it showed how that person is not living a full life, and it sort of shows why—I mean, uh—it shows why there are different responses to people and it defines for you the reasons why people didn't like them— I mean, uh—it went into how, uh—they thought too much of themselves when they were in a group. They didn't give anything and it explains very carefully that that person was just lazy—and didn't make the effort to do those things. Well, I thought the book was very good, and it said that the person who doesn't grasp those things isn't necessarily crazy, he just hasn't made the effort to do those things,

[17] *C*56. This is a very good beginning for an interview. It emphasizes the idea that the client is free to make use of the time as she sees fit, and that it is not the counselor who will direct the interview.

[18] *S*56. The client has been making an effort to learn something about behavior; although she is unsure about what she has learned, the sign of positive effort on her part is a good one.

and it's a constant effort to improve—to change. Well, when I read it, it gave me a sort of clear insight into the thing.

Problem
But still—I didn't know where to start. When I read it I realized that people do

Miscellaneous
go through those things—I don't even know why I brought that up—it just seemed to be sort of a good start.

Simple Acceptance
Clarification of Feeling
C57.[19] M-hm. You felt that you gained something from reading that book that indicated that not getting along with a group wasn't necessarily abnormal, but that it might be a constant effort to keep building an association with a group. Is that it? But it still leaves you feeling "where do I start?" Is that right?

Agreement
S57.[20] That's right. (*Long pause.*)

Problem—Negative Attitude toward Self
Well, in the first place, if I *were* to take a job right now I don't think that it would be fair to the employer, I mean, I really don't think that it would be—when I'm in

Insight—Ambivalent Attitude
a rut like this. The point is, am I just

toward Self
raising that as a defense mechanism for not getting out? Or am I really thinking that it just wouldn't be fair? That's an important question to me.

[19] C57. The counselor avoids evaluating the material read, responding instead to the feelings that the client has about what it has done for her. If he had criticized the book, as he might justifiably have done, an intellectual discussion of the book and probably a defense of it by the client would have ensued. Such a discussion would not have been very profitable in helping the client to a better understanding of her own feelings.

[20] S57. The client has shown some sophistication regarding psychological concepts; her question about whether her thinking is a defense mechanism gives some estimate of her fairly high level of intelligence, and her sophistication regarding behavioral mechanisms.

Clarification of Feeling
C58. You feel that it wouldn't be fair, and at the same time there rises in your mind a question, are you just putting that up to keep from undertaking what would be a hard thing to do.

Agreement
S58.[21] That's right. (*Pause. Laughs.*)

Asking for Information
You shake your head. Is that all?

Clarification of Feeling
C59. You feel perhaps *I* should know the answers, then.

Agreement   *Asking for Information*
S59. That's right. Is it fair to an employer to go out and take a job that you feel, well, it may help you but it may not do very much for him? (*Pause.*) Is it justifiable?

Clarification of Feeling
C60. You feel you might really be cheating the employer by doing that.

Agreement
S60. That's right. I've said that before. I know we've covered that once before.

Asking for Information—Negative
Uhuh. (*Long pause. Laughs.*) Well,
Attitude toward Counselor
what's the answer? Am I supposed to get the answers?

Clarification of Feeling
C61. You are wondering that, too, aren't you, whether maybe the answer is in you?

Insight
S61. In other words, I'd have to make a radical change before I—— I'm sup-

[21] S58, S59, S60. The client attempts here to force the counselor to give her an answer to her questions. First, she asks, can she work this thing out by herself, and secondly, why can't the counselor give her some suggestions such as telling her whether she is justified in not going to work. She alternates between a feeling that such a solution is not feasible and one that the counselor may be niggardly about the help he offers.

posed to change in attitude, and change in everything.

Clarification of Feeling
C62. You realize that it would mean a pretty radical shift if—uh—if you tried some of those things.

Agreement
                    Insight—Ambivalent Attitude
S62.[22] That's right. (*Long pause.*) I

toward Self
suppose it would be better for me, I mean, I probably wouldn't like it at first, but then maybe it would help me, wouldn't it? It would sort of force me to do the things I don't want to do, I guess——

Clarification of Feeling
C63. You think that maybe it would be a tough proposition, but maybe it would really have a lot in it for you.

Agreement   *Insight*
S63. Yes, it would probably force me

Asking for Information
to do something. (*Pause.*) But then where do you go from there? What's next?

Clarification of Feeling
C64. You realize that, even if you did that, there'd still be plenty of unanswered questions and plenty of difficulty still ahead. . . .

Clarification of Feeling
C82. That is, you're wondering if you —picked some goal like a job or something that you could definitely work on, would that really change any of your basic thinking or would it just be a temporary distraction, kind of?

Agreement   *Insight*
S82. That's right. In other words, if I ever stopped thinking about—the things

Problem—Negative Attitude toward Self
that are bothering me—somehow or other I still don't think that just by not thinking

about those things for a month or two months and trying to think about other things—still I don't feel as though it would have changed me much, basically.

Clarification of Feeling
C83. You feel that just putting it to one side or shoving it out of mind for a little bit, that isn't quite the thing you are looking for or what would really help.

Agreement   *Insight*
S83. That's right. (*Pause.*) Well, actually I don't see how it could help if I was just going back to think the same things over again. (*Pause.*) So I suppose you just have to change your ideas—for better, I guess—I mean if something tells you one thing and then you say "no" you've got to think about it this way.

Asking for Information
Does that actually help, attacking each idea as it comes to you, I mean each thought about something?

Clarification of Feeling
C84. At least you are wondering whether you could really tackle what you feel is wrong with your ideas as well as what you do.

Miscellaneous
S84. (*Statement unintelligible.*)

Clarification of Feeling
C85. You feel it must really be a petty way of thinking about the whole situation that distorts your thinking about others and their attitudes toward you.

Agreement   *Asking for Information*
S85. That's right. (*Long pause.*) And then the next step is (*laughs*) what am I going to do about all this?

Clarification of Feeling
C86. You feel that that might be another forward march, hmmm?

Agreement
                    Problem—Negative Attitude toward Others
S86. Yes. But the funny thing is that when we—when you do that then somebody will do you a dirty trick—you lose

---

[22] S62. Left to her own thinking, she is able to evaluate clearly the advantages a job would have.

faith all over again—I mean it just doesn't seem to jibe, you think it a—well, most things seem right and then they'll do you a dirty trick—and a—and you don't seem as though you're justified in thinking of them that way.

Clarification of Feeling

C87. If you try to put some trust in other people—and—be—to feel they're broadminded and tolerant—then you're pretty sure they'll "do you dirt" and disillusion you.

Agreement

S87. Well, it's happened quite often.

Problem

(*Pause.*) Oh, I used to take things—you

Insight

just take them. (*Pause.*) I guess you have to figure that you do them, too, sometimes.

Clarification of Feeling

C88. You feel you have to figure that no one is perfect all the time, that you make some slips and they make some slips. . . .

Agreement   Asking for Information

S97. Yeah. (*Very long pause.*) Does anybody actually feel as though he's—he's reached his ideal of himself? I mean, certain goals that he's set in his mind. Does anybody actually feel as though he's sort of satisfied with himself? I mean—a sort of an assured feeling, about himself?

Clarification of Feeling

C98.[23] You are puzzled to know whether anybody ever really gets up to the point of their ideals or the place where they have set their goals. Is that——

Disagreement   Problem

S98. Well, not exactly. I mean just in

---

[23] *C*98 to *C*103. These are very good reflections of the client's feelings. The response in *C*102 carefully skirts a religious question that might stimulate a time-consuming and profitless discussion.

their own eyes—the way they've handled things or done things.

Clarification of Feeling

C99. Does anybody really *feel* satisfied that they have reached their own goals—satisfied with themselves.

Problem—Ambivalent Attitude toward Self

S99. (*Pause.*) See, that's just it, I—I—can do something, or I can go through an experience, and I feel, well, I haven't done so badly, and then the next minute, "Oh, no." Immediately something inside attacks me and tears me down. And it discourages me, discourages me to the point where I don't want to repeat it.

Clarification of Feeling

C100. In other words, your own evaluation of yourself fluctuates so that it's very discouraging.

Agreement

S100. That's right. You just fluctuate—that's a good word for it.

Clarification of Feeling

C101. One minute you feel pretty good, and the next you'd sell yourself for a dime a dozen.

Asking for Information

S101. What causes that? I mean, I wonder if there is any—if anyone knows what causes it. Is that the devil? (*Both C and S laugh.*)

Interpretation

C102. You feel as though maybe it's your devil anyway.

Agreement   Problem

S102. Yes. The trouble is, why can't I answer it back and say, "Well, I have done all right." There's always that doubt, that I haven't. And why it should matter so much, I don't know, but it does.

Clarification of Feeling

C103. You just feel that gnaws away at you.

Agreement   Insight

S103. That's right. (*Pause.*) It really

seems ridiculous when you bring it out in the open, but I must think those things, because I am saying I do and I guess I

Problem

do. (*Pause.*) The point is, is it really important or is it just something I think is important. Is it just something that I'm building up because I'm egotistical, I'm always thinking about myself, or is it something that really counts. (*Pause.*)

Asking for Information

Yes—(*laughs*)—go on—(*trying to get answer from counselor*).

Miscellaneous

C104. (*Seriously.*) I—I'm just trying

Clarification of Feeling

to understand that. In other words you're feeling that it is possibly because you are egotistical that this whole business matters so much, and causes so much difficulty.

Problem   *Insight*

S104. It's a funny thing when you can't—I've heard of people who've had inferiority complexes, but they've used it to overcome things and they've harnessed it. In other words, instead of making them go backwards they make themselves go forward with it. That's a very good thing.

Asking for Information

The point is, how do you get it—to keep it from destroying you.

Clarification of Feeling

C105. You feel that the same motive power that drives some people who've had inferiority complexes might really destroy somebody else because it wasn't turned in the right channel.

Agreement   *Insight*

S105. That's right, m-hm. I mean instead of it getting you down, I suppose it should make me go forward instead of—thinking, well, I just botched that up.

Problem—Negative Attitude toward Self

(*Very long pause.*) The funny thing is that at times I can be so terribly depressed that I just don't want to attempt anything.

And then when I get there—I just—it's so unstable, it's so funny that my ideas change—and well—I think that I'm too good for the job. It just turns that way on me—sometimes I—I just don't feel as though I can do it—and then at other times if I do something well—it's just something within me that—well—it's a terrible thing, really. It makes me feel as though—I shouldn't be satisfied with it—but it's a sort of smug feeling—and it isn't a—it's a funny feeling—I—I mean it's—it really doesn't make very much sense, actually.

Clarification of Feeling

C106. You feel that either you have that very depressed feeling of inadequacy, or you go clear to the other extreme which you don't like either—of a very smug feeling that this is beneath me—I'm too good for this activity.

Agreement   *Problem*

S106. Yes, but somebody else—my neighbor or something might be going through the same thing and won't take it in that way—I mean—they won't feel—a—well it isn't exactly that I would be too good for it. It's just a sort of a feeling that—well—I can't explain it. (*Pause.*) Sort of like—if I were like somebody else I wouldn't have to do that—or that somebody else might not have to take it—that they are too good to take it, or something like that. It's a little bit difficult to explain.

Simple Acceptance

C107. M-hm.

Problem

S107. And yet I know that somebody else will be going through it, but their attitude—their attitude is so different toward it. I mean—they accept it as a matter of course. And I might want to and yet there's something that—some little devil that rears its head and says—something like that, and it's really so—it just seems to be so much a part of me.

Clarification of Feeling

C108. You feel that it's some little devil right in your own attitudes.

Agreement   *Problem*

S108. That's right. (*Pause.*) And then if I try to change my attitudes—I think, "Oh you're just being a sap—you're just feeling foolish." It's really very funny.

Insight

I guess it's just a matter of conquering those suggestions that sort of come. I guess the more you get into them the stronger they grow. I think that's just it—that's what I've always felt, I have known that other people go through certain things and yet when I say I wanted to be like them I won't accept them in a way. (*Pause.*) I just sort of think that I've just thought life was meant to be a bed of roses—and that if I don't have it that way it just isn't right or something——

Clarification of Feeling

C109. You feel that maybe way down deep you've sort of felt that things should be easy and perfect for you or else—you won't take them at all.

Agreement   *Insight*

S109. Yeah, I guess that's it. (*Long pause.*) I hadn't thought about that in that way before, but that's just the way it is. I guess I've always felt that it's sort of a shame—or sort of something to be ashamed of not to have things perfect or to be struggling with something. I don't know, I guess it's a snobbery in a way.

Clarification of Feeling

C110. You have felt that it wasn't quite, mm—proper to be in a situation where it was a real struggle to make——

Agreement   *Insight*

S110. That's right. (*Pause.*) That's just a big laziness! (*Both laugh.*) That's what it is really. I've sort of—I think that's the way I've always been but I didn't really know it. (*Long pause.*) Isn't that a silly attitude to take? That's just something that a—that's just one of those things that

I've always had and not really known. That's really a prejudice, isn't it?

Clarification of Feeling

C111. You feel that's just something in yourself that you've always had but that you're not very proud of.

Agreement   *Insight*

S111. That's right. And when I change it—I mean when I've tried to change it, I've always had a smug feeling about it, when it shouldn't be that way. And that

Problem

I resent, too. (*Laughs.*) I mean things that other people would just do because they take for granted, because that's the way it is. It's just the extremes all over again. It's just jumping from one place to another.

Clarification of Feeling

C112. You feel it's the kind of struggling in between that you have never quite been willing to face or to take.

Agreement   *Insight*

S112. M-hm, yeah. (*Long pause.*) I can just see it as an opera or something. It's a funny thing, but when I was in grammar school—that's where it all started—my sense of values—got off to a very funny start. I was a sort of—I was the teachers' pet—and a—I was also a lawyer's daughter and everybody sort of made me feel—or something made me feel—as though I was too good—or I couldn't—was better than somebody else —or that I wouldn't make the effort to be nice to somebody because I was—I didn't have to, because I was better. And that just grew and grew and grew, and then when I wanted to make an impression, I really did not know how to.

Clarification of Feeling

C113. You feel you can see those roots of it going—back into some of those experiences.

Agreement   *Insight*

S113. That's right. It was a childish—

it was a sort of a funny world I lived in. It wasn't a world of reality, really. And I think I really enjoyed it—I enjoyed that kind of a world. The point is—why didn't

Asking for Information

I do something about it? Why didn't something awaken me?

Clarification of Feeling

C114. You wonder why you accepted that kind of a world.

Agreement

S114. That's right. (*Pause.*)

Clarification of Feeling

C115.²⁴ The sleeping princess just wasn't awakened.

Agreement   Insight

S115. No. Not at all. I really always expected—I expected to be getting things without working for them. That was just it.

Clarification of Feeling

C116. You expected to reach the goal without the work or struggle that went in between.

Agreement   Insight

S116. That's right. Oh, I worked hard for my marks as far as that went, but I mean socially and other things that determined my attitudes. I expected things to be a certain way. And I guess I just thought they were because I wanted to think it. I mean—a—if they did make a pet out of me, I enjoyed it, I mean I liked the idea. But yet it wasn't really right. It wasn't being like the rest.

Clarification of Feeling

C117.²⁵ You enjoyed it, but I take it you felt that even then that wasn't quite what you wanted.

Agreement

S117. That's right.

²⁴ C115. This is another use of a figure of speech as a means of expressing in clearer form the feeling of the client.

²⁵ C117. The ambivalence of the client's feeling is recognized.

Miscellaneous

C118.²⁶ Well, I see our time's up—

Miscellaneous

S118. M-hm. I guess it is.

Miscellaneous

C119. Next Monday?

Miscellaneous—Ambivalent Attitude toward Counseling

S119.²⁷ Well, I don't know whether the time is so good. (*Pause.*) What other time could you suggest? What's the very latest that your office hours ever are?

Miscellaneous

C120. Well, till five.

Miscellaneous

S120. Well, is it possible to call up?

Miscellaneous

C121. Yes.

Miscellaneous—Negative Attitude toward Counseling

S121. I mean, how far in advance would I have to call up?

Miscellaneous

C122. Well, I—it's hard to say, it all depends on how my schedule fills up. But if you want to, you could take one of those times and I would save it if you wanted to use it. Would you like to leave it that way, or would you rather call me and let me know when you want to come in?

²⁶ C118. As is usually the case, the counselor takes the responsibility of terminating the session.

²⁷ S119. In view of later developments, the most likely interpretation of these questions is that Mary Jane was contemplating the possibility of getting herself a job, which would make usual office hour appointments impossible. Actually, she did not have the courage to get a job until after the seventh interview.

It is quite possible that the insight achieved in the latter part of this interview, and the impulse toward getting a job (if this interpretation is correct) proved to be rather discouraging to Mary Jane when she got away from the interview. The realization that she was undertaking a difficult and painful process of self-understanding and action may well account for her "illness" of the following week.

Miscellaneous—Negative Attitudes toward Counseling

S122. Well, let's put it this way, you save a certain time and then I'll call you and let you know for sure. How soon would I have to call you?

Miscellaneous

C123. Well, try and call me by Thursday or Friday if you can. O.K.?

Miscellaneous

S123. M-hm.

DEVELOPMENTS BETWEEN THE THIRD AND FOURTH INTERVIEWS

On the day before Miss Tilden's next appointment her mother telephoned to say that she was ill, and the appointment was postponed one week. On this later date, the mother telephoned shortly before the hour to say that Miss Tilden was "reluctant to come. I've been urging her to come, but she's reluctant. I don't believe this is doing her much good. She feels better after an interview, but then she gets depressed, and goes to bed. I wonder if counseling is enough in a situation as bad as hers. Could you suggest a psychiatrist that she could go to?" The counselor replied that he would wish to think over that possibility and would make suggestions if Miss Tilden felt she was not getting help. He thought, however, that he would first write a note to Miss Tilden. The mother offered to have her come to the telephone but the counselor said this was not necessary.[28]

28 Several significant factors stand out regarding the technique used here. The counselor avoided allowing this relationship to become one between himself and the mother, but placed the decision with the girl herself. He also implied the question, "Is it you, the mother, or the client herself who is ready to admit defeat in the attempt to use this method?" The interpretation is inferred that, if the girl herself wants to change, the method still offers an answer. It is significant that this mother, who is later shown to be largely responsible for the overdependence that represents her daughter's maladjustment, is fulfilling her role here in a manner that could be predicted.

The letter was carefully written to give an expression of warmth and interest but to be as non-directive as possible. It was written as follows:[29]

Dear Miss Tilden:

Your mother gave me your message about feeling reluctant to come in. I can understand that reluctance, and realize that you feel somewhat discouraged about your situation. I do not wish to urge you in any way, and if you prefer not to come in again, that will be perfectly all right.

However, I am going to take the liberty of holding an appointment next Tuesday at the usual time, until Friday of this week. I would appreciate it if you would please phone me to let me know whether or not you wish to keep it. If I do not hear from you on or before Friday I will know you do not wish to return. In any event you have my sincere best wishes.

Yours truly,

Miss Tilden telephoned Friday afternoon saying she would keep the appointment.

SUMMARY OF THE FOURTH INTERVIEW

November Eleventh

Miss Tilden found it rather difficult to get started talking about her feelings and

29 The careful thinking which went into the preparation of this letter may not be apparent to the reader who is not too familiar with the non-directive technique. Every word in this letter is deliberately planned so as to imply one of the following ideas:

a. The decision of whether to return must be your own.

b. The counselor can understand the difficulty involved in making the decision.

c. If you decide not to come in, I will not be critical of you, but I am making it possible for you to continue coming.

d. You do not have to explain if you do not wish to come, or you do not need to feel too guilty if you do not explain.

It is significant that the next telephone call is from the girl herself, and not from her mother.

remarked on this fact. She told of a social gathering at her home, and said she felt that she had entered into it—had really forgotten to think so much about herself. She had done better. She had particularly learned from one of the girls present. In a rather intimate conversation with this girl she had realized that this young woman accepted herself as she was, did not feel jealous of her sister who was prettier, or of fellows who were brighter. "That's remarkable," was Miss Tilden's comment.

Miss Tilden recounted her experiences in various fields, showing how similar the pattern had been. In music, in sculpture, in dancing, she can do entirely satisfactory work as long as the teacher is directing and coaching her. Then when she is supposed to be at a level where she can go on for herself, she simply cannot go forward. "I was always afraid that I wouldn't just do it quite right or something—I was just afraid to take a chance."

Miss Tilden was somewhat disgusted at the picture she had been painting of herself. "The point is, does just seeing it as ridiculous, does that change it? I mean —I guess it should, really." She realized that she believes that other people can be helped, but she cannot accept that fact for herself. She concluded that there are two forces in herself, and one of them is a very "arrogant force" which just doesn't want to accept things or be helped.

She talked about the problem of trying to be natural, but "I don't know when I'm natural." She discussed problems of marriage and the manner in which she thinks about all the ways it might fail. "You see, it's that old pattern, that same thing repeats itself, I mean that I want to be sure that I'm going to be perfect. It's that fear that just keeps repeating itself." She wants especially to feel that she is not too different from others.

At no time during the interview did she mention her failure to come in the previous week, or refer to the letter. The counselor made no mention of this aspect. She wished to return, but wondered about a late afternoon or evening hour. She did not say why she wished to change the time.

FIFTH INTERVIEW

November Seventeenth

*S*124. Hello again.

*C*124. What's what today?

*S*125. I don't know what. Every time I come I think I don't know what to talk about. I just come. (*Pause.*) The point is that I come and I talk but it doesn't seem to make too much of an impression on me, I mean, while I'm here I feel better. Then when I go away I just don't seem to be able to hold on to it.

*C*125. You feel you make certain progress in an interview but after that it kind of slips.

*S*126. Yes, what I mean is, I can see things clearly for the moment while I'm here but then I go home—I don't think any differently about things. That's what the funny part is, I'm sure of it—I don't.

*C*126. You feel that it doesn't quite carry over to life in between times.

*S*127. That's right. Well, I've gone out a little bit more than I had been going out—that is—visiting more—and I've been with people more, but I still basically feel the same. I mean, it doesn't seem to make too much difference whether I am with them or I am not. Well, maybe I sort of shrink back from being with them and then I stay off and I sort of feel guilty about that. And then when I do go out and mix with them, I guess I don't have the feeling that I'm lost somewhere by myself. But it still doesn't seem to help too much.

*C*127.[30] As I get that, you've done

[30] *C*127, *C*128. The counselor recognizes the first tentative steps in the direction of the client's planning and taking action directed toward improving her situation, but also accepts her ambivalence about that progress.

some things about it, I mean like trying to mingle a little bit more with people, but it still leaves something to be desired.

*S*128. Yes, m-hm. (*Pause*). I enjoy listening to people, I mean, I—uh—it really is wonderful. I was over to my sister's house and they had some people over, and they talked about some very interesting things. And it was stimulating while I listened to it, it was lovely. I tried to see that they saw things from an impersonal viewpoint. They were perfectly normal people and yet it didn't help me —I tried to get it to help me—and yet it didn't really.

*C*128. You've enjoyed getting more of an understanding of other people, and even tried to apply some of that understanding to you, but without much effect.

*S*129. That's right. I can appreciate that there were different people there that I thought were really very charming, and I could appreciate them all right. But somehow it didn't add anything—to things the way I thought of them. When I went home I told Mother that it was very nice and that I enjoyed it, but I didn't feel as though I contributed very much. And she told me that it was all right just to be there and just to be a good listener. There have to be people to listen and people to talk, too, so here's a good listener. But that, uh—that isn't satisfactory because I see what's behind it. Maybe *they* can't, but *I* know what's behind it.

*C*129. Your mother tries to assure you that you are doing all right, but I take it that you feel that if you were really just being a good listener that would be one thing but actually the motivation behind listening is a little bit different.

*S*130. That's it exactly. M-hm. Because I didn't feel as though I was contributing. (*Pause*) In other words, I don't want to just feel what people think about me is all right, I want to know that it's justified and I don't seem to be able to find a justification. Do you see what I mean?

*C*130.[31] I'm not sure, let me see if I do. That you want to really deserve inside some of the approval, etc., you might get from other people. Is that, uh——

*S*131. That's right. (*Pause*.) But I constantly have that feeling that I don't. That's just it. And yet it isn't just the feeling—it's almost a certainty—more or less, I mean. It's just a dead certainty, that's all.

*C*131. There's plenty of proof that you don't deserve approval. Is that it?

*S*132. That's right. (*Long pause*.) Sometimes I wonder whether this is quite the right track. I don't know. I mean I realize that this has been going on a long time and that I can't expect to effect a change right away, because it has been such a long time. But I just wonder whether—I mean—my reactions don't seem to be very much better—on the face of it. I can't really tell, I guess, maybe you can tell a little better. But, uh——

*C*132. At any rate, you can't help but feel a little bit disappointed, perhaps, in the lack of obvious change in you, even though, on the other hand, you realize that it probably is somewhat likely to be a slow process since the problem has been present for a long time.

*S*133.[32] Yes, that's true. The only thing is that I can't help but feel that I work against myself. I mean it's just so obvious to me that I *do* work against myself. And it seems rather silly to be one minute trying to do something about it, and then it seems so certain that there's something present that doesn't want to do

---

[31] *C*130. The counselor's gesture of tentativeness of response is probably a useful technique, at times, when the client may be expressing a feeling which may be somewhat hard for her to face too rapidly.

[32] *S*133. The client begins to recognize the elemental conflict within herself between the urge to change and the "neurotic" urge which attempts to defeat the more healthy desire. The unhealthy goal has its own values which have caused the patient to cling to it in the past. The counselor effectively recognizes the conflict in *C*133.

anything about it. (*Pause.*) It's such a contrary thing—the whole problem is just——

*C*133. So that the very time that one part of you is perhaps really taking hold of this whole situation, another part of you is just sabotaging the whole business.

*S*134. That's right. (*Pause.*) The whole thing is that somehow or other along the trail I lost fortitude—I know I did, because I just—I don't feel it. If somebody else might say, "Oh, well, cheer up, just look at it from another angle"—I just—it's just like a big balloon that's just deflated. . . .

*C*142. In other words, in a sense, even when an experience does prove something about yourself, still you can't accept the proof. That is, you might do something well and you would have reason to say, "Well, I did a good job on that," but you couldn't even feel that way.

*S*143. Well, I—maybe I felt it on top, but then there would be doubts about it, and then I would really begin to wonder.

*C*143. Any acceptance of it would be just a surface acceptance.

*S*144. M-hm. Yeah. I guess that's about it. (*Pause.*) I guess I was behind the door when all those nice little gifts were handed out. (*Both S and C laugh.*) That's the way I feel about it though. . . .

NINTH INTERVIEW

January Thirteenth

Miss Tilden begins with her feeling that she is making no progress. "I keep coming in here and I don't seem to be getting anywhere, and I think that isn't right." She quickly adds, however, "Well, actually I guess I have gotten somewhere because I see things a little clearer. But I still have the same feelings about things." She voices the attitude that she is not too well connected with reality. She discusses this and realizes that many of her past problems lie within herself. "I guess I wasn't

so willing to change. It never occurred to me that all this trouble was my own, I mean the way I looked at things."

"The actuality of it is that I never really knew what the real 'me' was—it was all covered over really, and I got to thinking it was me. And then when that 'me' didn't strike the bell anywhere, it was pretty hard." She goes on in regard to the struggle to discover her real self and adds, "I'm looking for what everybody's always looking for, and that's probably finding yourself."

She realizes that she is always dissatisfied with anything she does—her job or any other undertaking. Part of the reason for this is that she feels she never achieves more than a mediocre standard, and this she cannot accept, but "I've got to face it, it just was." She is convinced that whatever she might do, it just would not work out well. She is convinced she is a moron because she can follow a teacher, but can do nothing on her own initiative. She continues:

*S*154. I've either been afraid to trust my own ability and afraid to go out on my own or something. That's just a habit, that was just sort of a habit that I formed. I mean, relying on my teachers, really, just groping at meanings.

*C*154. As long as someone else was in charge, why, it was O.K., you got along, but when it came to a question of doing something on your own ability, in your own direction, to choose and manage, why you don't have any luck.

*S*155. That's right.

*C*155. It boils down again to what's come up in some other ways, doesn't it, that you just trust others (*she cries*) and believe in them, but belief in yourself, that's just impossible.

*S*156. Yes, that's just the idea. Don't you think that somewhere along the line something would happen—something might turn up that—it's a very funny situation.

*C*156. You feel that something should

have turned up to give you that confidence in yourself.

S157.[33] Yes. It should. I should have thought of it or something. (*Crying.*) When you watch a little child he seems to—well, he seems to want to get out on his own, he seems to be happy when he can get out.

C157. You feel very deeply about it, that even a little child feels so much pleasure in standing on his own two feet.

S158. Well, possibly being—oh, dear, here comes the rainstorm. (*Cries.*)

C158.[34] They say the rain makes things grow.

S159.[35] Very aptly put. (*Long pause, crying.*) Well, perhaps being at home has something to do with it—I mean my mother has always been very good to me. She had a very miserable childhood, her parents never paid any attention to her, then she tried to make up for it, and that way it didn't affect the others because they didn't accept it, but I accepted what she did for me and I just took it for granted, and it made me more reliant on her, really.

C159. You feel that because of some of her very real needs that—she did a great deal for you and you accepted it and depended on her.

S160. That's right.

C160.[36] You stood on her two feet.

---

[33] S157. As the client approaches a problem very painful to her, i.e., her lack of initiative and independence, she breaks into tears. This is frequently a measure of the depth of feeling associated with ideas the client is expressing.

[34] C158. By this slightly interpretive analogy the counselor gives reassurance and encouragement when the client is feeling especially pained at facing her less acceptable characteristics of personality. The client seems to accept this interpretation when she remarks, "Very aptly put."

[35] S159. The client expresses some positive feelings toward her mother along with the negative ones in recognizing the reason for her mother's overprotecting attitude.

[36] C160. The simplicity of this recognition of feeling makes it almost epigrammatic in character; this clarity of recognition of feeling combined with originality and style of expression is acquired only through a rich clinical experience.

S161. That's right. Now my little sister, she isn't that way, she's in the adolescent stage right now; she is branching out for herself, I mean she just doesn't like it. She wants to be consulted about everything that she does, and everything like that. Well, my sister isn't letting it affect her. I know she feels in her own heart that it's right, and I used to wonder about that, I mean every time that I did something I used to think, well, maybe she is right, maybe I should do the way she does, and then I switched over, and I wouldn't stand up on my own two feet.

C161. You watched your sister stand out against some of your mother's thinking, and some of your mother's requests, but when you were in that stage you couldn't—you didn't feel it was quite right to stand up against her on any of those issues. . . .

C164.[37] That's a very deep question you keep facing me with—whether a person who for twenty years has been guided by the thinking and standards of others could possibly feel that they could take the reins into their own hands.

S165. That's right. The trouble with my answer is that the answer's always no. When I ask myself that question, the answer is always no.

She decided that from this time on she will come in every two weeks instead of every week.

TENTH INTERVIEW

January Twenty-Eighth

At the beginning of the interview Miss Tilden's statements show that more progress is being made, though her initial sentences still sound negative. . . .

She continues with a discussion of the fact that when she is feeling good she feels much more adventurous, and is

---

[37] C164. The counselor gives some reassurance when he implies that the question is a "very deep" one. It is as if he were saying, "I know it's difficult work facing these things."

now thinking of taking a very different and interesting job during the coming summer, with a girl with whom she has become friendly at work. She is sure her family would disapprove of the work, would think it beneath her, and this tends to make her waver. However, she looks back on the decisions they have made for her, and does not have much confidence in them. Of course, she does not have much confidence in herself either, but she begins to think better of her own choices. She indicates that she can understand her parents, but that now she knows she differs from their attitudes and standards. In expressing some of this feeling about her mother, she says:

S173. I realize lately that when my mother wants me to go out with her, I find that I'm not too happy to go with her, it's just her personality that I don't like. Now I realize that mine isn't what it should be but then I don't enjoy hers either, and it's sort of a guilty feeling, too.

C174.[38] You feel that in some very real ways—you just don't like your mother particularly well, and it bothers you that you should feel that way.

S174.[39] That's right, because I know it's wrong, because I know she has done so much for me, and yet—I think, well, maybe she hasn't done so much for me— she was trying to merge herself in her children—actually she did it too much, though. She was just escaping, I guess. She didn't want to face things. And then she complains that now it's all gone—I mean there's nothing left practically. Instead of developing her own interests. And yet she has a certain amount of happiness. It may be just a little but she's getting something. . . .

C179. All right.

---

38 C174. The counselor responds to the ambivalence of the client's feeling.

39 S174. Real insight is shown here in the client's being able to recognize the mother's weakness in assuming the attitude she has toward her children.

She asks for a book that she might read, and the title of Travis and Baruch, *Personal Problems of Everyday Life*, is given to her with the remark that she may find it helpful, and she may not.

She tells of a friend she has made, a very interesting girl, whom she rejected at first, but has now come to like. Her sister thinks this girl is inferior, and discourages the friendship. Miss Tilden feels, however, that her sister has her crowd, a group which is suitable for her, but that she will make her own friends. She continues to discuss the family situation. Her sister reacted to the family situation by getting away from it, but "me, well, it completely sunk me."

ELEVENTH INTERVIEW

February Tenth

(This interview is given in full from verbatim notes.)

S180.[40] Well, I have been doing some very serious thinking this week. I got the book you suggested and I have been reading that. I've enjoyed it a lot. I've gotten a good many things from it.

C180. You found that you have gained something from reading it.

S181.[41] Yes, I have, and I also started the millinery course. I find it isn't a course in millinery design but more of a course in making hats, but I have been having a good time. You know I find myself

---

40 S180. The use of the technique of suggesting reading when the client requests it is commented on. . . . In the present case, it seems to be of some real help, as indicated in this interview. It is interesting that in her previous reading of books the client did not make very satisfactory use of the material she had read. Perhaps the reason she is able to now is that she is now prepared to assimilate the reading after having passed some of her emotional blockings. Of course, it must be admitted that the material read is different, too.

41 S181. In this and numerous subsequent statements, the insights and discussion of plans occur with amazing rapidity, showing that as the client begins to make progress in understanding herself the process picks up in speed, each forward step apparently making the next one easier.

holding myself back a little this time. I'm beginning to show real signs of benefit. I used to throw myself into any new thing and then tire of it very quickly. This time I'm going in it more naturally and calmly. I'm really changing.

C181. You feel that you've really noticed that you're becoming a different kind of person.

S182. Yes, I haven't felt so up until recently, but now I begin to realize that's true. A girl I've been going with, a girl I've gotten to know—she's helped me a lot. You know my idea of what I should be is changing. I always had ideas that were too high. I've always had a definite feeling of the kind of person I should be and now some of those thoughts are changing.

C182. You feel that where you used to be trying for something way up high now it is different. . . .

S190. Yes. (*Pause.*)

C190. You find that you can even feel hatred toward somebody and not be bothered about it.

S191. Yes. I just don't care. You know it's suddenly as though a big cloud has been lifted off. I feel so much more content. Up to now I haven't been willing to admit that I have changed much, but I begin to feel that I have.

C191.[42] You feel that all this has made a great deal of difference in your own comfort. I've noticed the changes, too, and have wondered when you would break through and realize that they have occurred.

S192.[43] Well, the friendship with this

girl has helped me a lot too. She and her husband have really accepted me. They tell me I'm as bright as other people. Oh, of course, that is flattery, but it has helped me, and then just the fact that they really seem to like me, that has made a lot of difference.

C192. You have felt that you have built up a real relationship there and it has helped to have them like you.

S193. The thing is that I've always been striving to be what other people have wanted me to be—my family mostly. I couldn't be satisfied with what I might really be. I've always tried to live up to what others have wanted.

C193. The standards you have been trying to reach have always been out in other people, not something you have really believed in yourself.

S194. Part of the trouble is my parents. They have never really sat down to talk with me. I don't think they understand me. Of course, my father has always been proud of things I have done and when I would bring home a good mark he would praise me. Well, that's it. I've always just lived for his praise and that is why I've felt it awful if I fail to come up to what they expect. I guess that is the kind of relationship it has been with them.

C194. You feel that rather than any relationship of understanding, you've just lived for a pat on the back from your dad.

S195. Yes. I think that is what has been the matter. Of course, until I was seven I was the youngest and they made a lot of me, and then, of course, when my younger sister came along and I suppose I sort of lost out and they—well, I suppose that is why it meant so much to me to have them praise me. You know that

---

[42] C191. This statement is frankly approving in character. The counselor's indication that he has seen the changes coming might not be too helpful to the client, however, who might be inclined to wonder, then, whether the counselor could not have said something to encourage her a little earlier.

[43] S192. It should be recognized that outside situations can contribute to the client's adjustment process; in this case, the friendship with the married couple seems to have done so. Perhaps the

more significant fact, however, is that the client reached the point of being able to make the effort to cultivate this friendship, and then to gain help from it. It is doubtful if this would have been possible before the treatment started.

you read about things like that in books but——(*pause*).

C195. Now you've come to understand that sort of situation in your own experience.

S196. Yes, that's it. (*Pause.*) The thing is I've always had a feeling of looking down upon someone who is dumb. I've never wanted to be that kind and I never would look at anything in myself that contradicted the notion of being superior.

C196. It made you afraid of looking clearly at yourself.

S197.[44] Yes. Now I have begun to think if there is one other person like me in the world then I can get along. Other people get along without lots of ability. I have the right to exist, too.

C197. You've come to believe that you can get along like others.

S198. Well, take like my sister—she is willing to admit that she is dumb. I talked to her about that. I said, "How can you go with somebody you know is brighter than you are and not feel badly about it?" And she said, "Well, in some ways I always think that I'm better than they are."

C198. You feel that she has come to accept the fact that, although the other person might be brighter, still she thinks, "I've got some good qualities, too."

S199. Yes. Well, she's comfortable and content so she gets along well with other people. . . .

S215. Well, right now I feel I'm using instinct more than I ever did before. Re-

[44] S197. The client has decided to accept herself, rather than try to be someone different. The theoretical question might here be raised as to whether the client is as "dumb" as she thinks she is. Many of her responses in this treatment suggest that she has a fairly good mentality. The philosophy which motivates the non-directive method holds that it makes little difference regarding the real situation. The aspect that is important is the client's attitude toward her intelligence. Even very bright people frequently cannot be convinced of their superiority if they have emotionally satisfying reasons for believing themselves inferior.

member what I said at first about how some people could go by their natural feelings and I always had to think what I did? Now I find that I can just act natural.

C215. You feel that you're being guided more by the real feelings within yourself than you used to be.

S216. Yes. I'm much more comfortable, too, with the people I'm working with. I think that it is partly because I have been there now for awhile. It takes me awhile to build up any feeling of confidence. You know I'm finding that by taking an interest in the customers, everything goes much better. Instead of thinking about myself or making a sale, I just get interested in them and really try to help them. It takes longer to deal with a customer that way, but I like it better.

C216. You're putting out more of your interest in them.

S217. Yes, and the customers thank me for it. That helps me build up my confidence. You know, I really help them think through what they really like. (*She tells of an incident in which she felt particularly good about a sale.*) I guess it is even more profitable that way, because the customers come back to me.

C217. You're finding that forgetting yourself and forgetting sales is really good business in the long run.

S218. Yes. That's right, so—actually, if I failed I'd be down in the dumps, failed in my job I mean, but I've been told that I'm doing nicely and that I'm getting along well. So being more interested in them has helped me.

C218. You're really getting a feeling of success out of that job.

S219. Well, I find people more responsive to me now. They think better of me and they talk to me more easily. I'm more friendly and I guess they sense it.

C219. You feel that being more natural yourself has made people respond to you.

S220. Yes. (*Pause.*) Though even as I

say this, I have a fear that it may not be permanent. I want to be honest about it, and I just don't know if this can really last.

*C*220. You're sure that these things have happened, but still it seems to you that it might be too good to be true, that you might slump again.

*S*221. Yes, I've had times before when I've been up.

*C*221. You feel this might be just another temporary wave of encouragement.

*S*222.[45] Well, I doubt it. I think I know now if there is a down or slump, it is because I'm impatient with myself. You know, that is always a part of my trouble. I just can't wait to get there and if I should get discouraged it would be because of that.

*C*222. You feel if you do get discouraged it will be primarily because you're impatient about getting somewhere in too much of a hurry.

*S*223. That's right. And then I wonder —I get afraid that maybe I'll get tired of myself this way. That's what always happened to me before. You know I told you I would try to be a different kind of person but then I'd get tired of it.

*C*223. You think that you have a new self now, but that you might not like it in time.

*S*224. Well, I see other people and some of them seem to be quite boring people, and they don't seem to get tired of themselves. Maybe I won't either. The point is I feel I've made a real start. I no longer want to be superior. I just want to feel equal to people. In fact, if I'm like the least person it is O.K.

*C*224. You feel that that is very important, that you no longer desire to be above everybody but if you can even be equal to *some* of them you can then live

with yourself and feel it will be all right.

*S*225. Well, I've made myself realize that I can't be a certain type of person. If I didn't accept that idea, I would be very unhappy. You know I've always felt that —well, you know bright girls can go to college, they can make a name for themselves and all, and I've always tried so hard to be that kind of girl but I can't. I've just got to realize that I'm not that sort of person. And then the fact that most of my relaives are that kind of people, it has made it hard, do you see what I mean?

*C*225. You've always respected and looked up to that intellectual group and now it comes kind of hard to accept the fact that perhaps you don't belong there but in another group.

*S*226. Yes, that's just it.

*C*226. I see our time is up. Will you be wanting to come back or not?

*S*227. Well, I think I would like to leave it this way—I'll call you and let you know. You know, I felt this wouldn't do any good, but it has. But I don't want to get out of touch with you. I don't feel quite steady yet. I think that probably I would like to come in in three weeks, but I'll call you.

*C*227. All right. You call the office and they'll give you an appointment even if I'm not in. You really have come a long way in your thinking, haven't you?

*S*228. Good-bye—and thanks.

*C*228. Good-bye.

Significant Feelings Expressed in the Eleventh Interview

1. I am taking a new course of my own choosing.
2. I am really changing.
3. I have had too high ideals for myself, but those are changing.
4. I have always tried to live up to a false front which wasn't genuine.
5. I realize I am actually like other people.
6. I wonder if I should be what I am

---

[45] *S*222. Although the client herself wonders whether her new feelings are going to remain with her permanently, she herself seems to believe that there is not too much question about their doing so.

instead of what others think I should be.

7. I believe that is what I want to do.
8. I have changed a great deal.
9. I am no longer afraid or guilty about my feelings.
10. I feel more free.
11. I feel more content.
12. I haven't been willing to admit that I have changed, but I have.
13. I have been helped by these talks, by books, by a friendship I have made.
14. I understand how my family relationships made me what was.
15. I've come to realize that I'm not so bright, but I can get along anyway.
16. I can accept marriage, if it comes, or accept the lack of it.
17. I've been out much more with friends and enjoy it.
18. I find it easier to make social adjustments with another girl who has had similar difficulties.
19. I still feel that I'm not good at anything specific.
20. I admire people who can accept their limitations.
21. I wonder if a husband could accept a wife who lacked ability.
22. I guess I could balance that lack with other positive qualities.
23. I no longer think so much about myself.
24. I talk more freely than I used to.
25. I find I can just act natural, be guided by my real feelings.
26. I'm much more comfortable with people.
27. I'm getting a feeling of success out of my job.
28. I'm fearful this may not last, but I think it will.
29. I'm afraid I may tire of my new self, but I don't think I will.
30. It's really hard for me to accept abilities as not being superior, but I am doing it.
31. I feel this has really helped.
32. I don't feel quite steady yet, and

would like to feel that I can come for more help if I need it.

FOLLOW-UP INFORMATION

Following the conclusion of the counseling interviews Miss Tilden continued to hold her position. She engaged more actively in social life. Also, she went with her family on a trip and here, too, was much more socially active. In general her improvement seemed to be beyond question in the ten months following the conclusion of the counseling interviews.

Shortly after a year had elapsed Miss Tilden was invited to come in for a follow-up interview. At that time she reported that until recently things had been going much better for her but that within the past two months many of the old feelings of worthlessness, doubt of her own ability, and feelings of futility had returned. She reported that she had recently given up her job. Some of her conversation in talking about herself sounded very much like a repetition of the first interviews. She also raised the question of whether perhaps something "stronger" was needed to help her. She wondered if she ought to go to a psychiatrist. The counselor expressed willingness to help her find such a resource or to have her return for further counseling, but left the decision up to her. She stated she would telephone for an appointment or information if she desired it. She did not call. The only intimation she gave for the cause of her slump was that a boy friend with whom she had been going had seemed to her to look down upon her as a person of little ability. She felt this had tended to destroy her confidence.

Some weeks later a telephone conversation with her mother indicated that Miss Tilden was getting along more satisfactorily. She had another job with a relative and seemed again more cheerful and better adjusted.

It will be seen that the evaluation of

final outcome in this case remains somewhat in doubt. There can be no question that the eleven counseling hours were followed by a period of improved adjustment. Whether the recent regression is temporary remains to be seen.

A CHILD CASE

The therapist in this nondirective form of play therapy, as in the previous case, does not attempt any direct diagnosis of the client's problems. The techniques used in this case are, of course, based on client-centered therapy with adults. Therefore, we will again find many incidents of the therapist using clarification of feeling and simple restatements of the material presented by the client, but these are carried out within the context of the child's play. Especially note the way the child, William, tests the tolerance of the therapist and the importance to the child of the change of therapist. Carefully read Bixler's notes on each session, especially those comments which in retrospect, he would change. It would also be of use to the reader to contrast the verbalizations of both the child and therapist in this case with what was said in the dynamic case with a child (see the Bornstein article).

Bixler has recently written a comment that follows the case material and gives good insights into what he considers to be the important elements in this case and what has changed in nondirective therapy over the years.

Treatment of a Reading Problem through Nondirective Play Therapy

RAY H. BIXLER

The series of interviews presented here is unique in that it provides more psychological elements than are usually found in a single play-therapy case. However, the procedure itself is typical of the nondirective technique described by Carl Rogers

and his students who have used the method at the verbal level.[1,2]

The therapist knew very little about William at the time of their first contact, primarily because the former feels that a

From *Journal of Consulting Psychology*, 1945, 9, 105–118. Ray H. Bixler, Department of Psychology, University of Louisville. Copyright 1945 by the American Psychological Association. Reprinted by permission.

[1] Carl R. Rogers. *Counseling and Psychotherapy.* Boston: Houghton Mifflin Co., 1942.

[2] William U. Snyder. "A Short Term Nondirective Treatment of an Adult," *Clinical Supplement to the Journal of Abnormal and Social Psychology,* 1943, 38 (2): 87–137.

great deal of diagnostic knowledge can sometimes impede treatment in a nondirective situation. The therapist knew that the psychiatric social worker felt William's difficulty to be psychogenic at the time of the intake interview. He also knew that William was ten years old and that a month had passed since he was last seen by another therapist with whom he had formed a deep relationship. Although the therapist himself did not have any additional information at the time of his first contact, it is felt that more diagnostic material should be made available to the reader who may be disturbed by this practice.

The principal referred William to the center because he was failing in the third grade. His major problem was reading. William's Stanford-Binet I.Q. was 101 but the results of his Progressive Achievement Test showed him to be working at a level a year or more below his actual grade placement. The older of his two brothers is eleven years old and in the sixth grade and the younger is three and a half. The social worker described William's mother as, "a very deprived woman," who, "was not rejecting William." However, his behavior at home was of considerable concern to her. She is in her early thirties. The father is five years older. Both are employed in war industries.

There were twenty interviews with William prior to his transfer to the new therapist. These will be covered briefly. He was very willing to talk about his school problems and referred to his school as, "one of the rottenest." He explained that he hated his teacher and wished that he could read better. In the eighth contact he expressed concern about other children coming to the clinic and mentioned that his baby brother had broken his (William's) sailboat. In the ninth contact he mentioned both of his brothers. The therapist concludes, "In general, William expresses quite a bit of feeling towards this older brother."

Appointments were frequently broken by the parent (and child). There were five weeks between the tenth and eleventh contacts, three between the twelfth and thirteenth and four of the next eleven were broken. During this period the content concerned the school problem and in the last two or three interviews, the trauma of breaking relations with the therapist. William threatened to lock the counselor up so that he'd be there when he came back and later he decided that he would bring a "bean shooter" and "shoot pins at the new person."

The remainder of this paper is concerned with the last nine contacts, some of which are reported in detail. During this period there were two broken appointments and one cancellation by the center. There are numerous errors in counseling which the writer attempts to point out, following each interview.

8/16. William's attitude as he left the waiting room was one of utter disappointment.

1. C. "It's sorta hard to come up here with a new person."
   W. "Yeah." (Sniffs a few times and then with delight.) "It smells like you've been smokin' the same tobacco that Dr. S. did!"
   C. "That surprises you and makes you sorta happy."
2. W. "Umhuh." (Reserved.)

During the first part of the hour he mentions Dr. S. with nearly every incident. A few moments later:

   W. (Finds children's overalls in closet.) "Who wears these?"
   C. "You wonder if the other children who come up here play with those on."
   W. "Yes; Do they?"
3. C. "No."
   W. (Returns to play table and picks

up tongue depressors.) "These are funny sticks."

C. "There are lots of funny things since Dr. S. left."

4. W. (Nods.) "Did you know Dr. S.?"

C. "I met him a couple of times. You miss him pretty much."

W. "Yes." (Goes on to explain at length about Dr. S., how well he liked him and that they were going to write to each other.)

5. C. "You were very unhappy to see him go and wish he were back."

W. (Nods.) "I imagine you know how it is to come to the same room and see a different person."

6. C. "You would much rather have him here than me."

W. "Yes, but I'll probably get used to you. Dr. S. was such a nice man."

7. C. "You liked him very much—you know he is a nice man but you are still wondering about me."

W. "Oh, I imagine I'll get used to you."

8. C. "You'd like to like me but you think it's gonna be pretty hard."

W. "Are you married?"

9. C. "Yes."

W. (Referring to Dr. S.) "He said some one would take his place but I wish he did himself."

10. C. "You liked him better than me."

W. "Yes, but I might like you when I get used to you."

11. C. "I'm pretty new to you—you don't know me well enough to know whether you like me or not."

W. (Smiles.)

A few moments later:

W. (Has baby bottle and begins to squirt water on table, laughing—stops suddenly and looks at C.)

C. "That's a lot of fun but you are afraid it might make me mad."

12. W. (Nods yes.) "How do you act when you get mad?"

C. "You want to be sure and know when I get mad."

W. (Smiles.) "I don't think you are now."

He spent most of the remaining time mixing various paints in a basin. He mentioned that they might turn out to be explosives and if asked by the government who made them he would say, "I did," and then after a pause added, "with his help" pointing to C.

C. "You think I ought to be included."

W. (Nods and discusses invention in detail.)

C. "It's sorta fun to imagine that you can make wonderful things."

W. (Smiles.)

At end of period:

13. W. (Looks in waste basket, sees tobacco can and grabs it quickly and holds it in air.) "You even smoke the same kind of tobacco!"

14. C. "There are a lotta ways in which you think I'm like Dr. S."

W. "Yes." (Smiles.)

C. "Time's up, William." (W. makes no move to leave but has returned to play bench.) "I know you'd like to stay but your forty-five minutes are up and it is time to stop." (W. leaves reluctantly.)

COMMENTS CONCERNING FIRST INTERVIEW[3]

1. This is a response obviously dependent to some degree upon the counselor's diagnostic information. Detailed diagnostic material in the hands of the counselor may cause him to carry recognition of attitudes beyond the point that the child has gone and it has been the experience of those

[3] [The number of the comment identifies the response to which it refers.—Editor.]

who utilize a nondirective approach that such "pushing" is a hindrance to therapy. Here it has done no harm nor has it hastened his expression in any way.

2. Had the counselor been sensitive to this, he might have replied, "You're not sure that you're happy."

3. C. closes a pertinent discussion here before W. has actually exhausted it, by answering a question colored with feeling. "You wonder about what other children do when they come here," would have touched the area of feeling W. was expressing and also would have permitted him to carry it further, had he wished.

4. It is likely that W. was expressing a desire to know more about C. at this point. Here diagnostic material may have interferred to some degree.

5. This is a good response and plays a strong part in the development of the following statements by W. Statements (6), (7) and (8), are adequate responses. Certainly a permissive stage is being set and anxiety is being relieved.

9. Here again C. squelches expression by answering a question. He might have said, "You wonder how much I'm like Dr. S." W. has been struggling with this point, finally bringing it out indirectly.

10. C. digresses here and shifts emphasis to self. Considerable resistance might have ensued had this same attitude that C. erroneously "recognizes," not already been expressed. "You miss him a great deal and it makes you very unhappy because he didn't come back," would have been appropriate.

11. Excellent response to the deepest of W.'s present anxieties. It is interesting to note that he makes only one more remark about Dr. S. in the remainder of the interview and that is a positive one concerning C.

12. W. is more interested in what kind of a person C. is than in how he acts when he is mad. Thus C. misses a chance to develop gains previously made.

13. This was very vividly executed and handled in good fashion by C. (14).

8/23. Canceled by center.

8/30. W. and mother arrived half an hour early. Miss J., who sees the mother, was in conference until shortly after the hour began and C. was waiting for her to finish. Exactly on the hour, however, W. appeared at the door of C.'s office, evidently having quietly slipped upstairs.

1. **C.** "Come in, William."

W. (Goes to play table, picks up cannon and runs rough shod over several small dolls and finally pushed the cannon into a toy house at a point very near a window.) "What would you do if I broke the window?"

2. **C.** "You wonder if it would make me mad."

W. "Yeah, so I'd know what would happen if I break it."

3. **C.** "You'd like to break it, but are afraid you'd get into trouble if you did."

4. **W.** (Smiles and nods.)

The telephone rang at this point. (W. had gone without his mother's knowledge, and Miss J. wondered if he was upstairs.) W. asked what the telephone call was about, and C. told him. W. was pleased.

C. "It's fun to fool people."

W. "Yeah, nobody knows me, I'm the second Red Skelton."

5. **C.** "You mean you're bad like Red?"

W. "Yeah." — (Has overalls.) — "Whose are they?"

C. "You wonder if they belong to one of the kids who come here. They don't belong to anyone."

W. "Can I have them?"

C. "You may play with them here as much as you wish, but they must be left here when you leave."

W. (Puts overalls on and speaks of being a great chemist or doctor and then names a number of other professions as if he belonged to them.)

C. "It would be fun to be great at something."

W. "Yeah. Who left the overalls, maybe Doctor-Doctor, Mr. S. did."

6. C. "You sorta miss him."

7. W. (Slight pause.) "Yeah, he was a nice man." (Pause. W. takes off overalls and goes to dresser, picking up a number of small dolls and putting them in the dresser.)

W. "It's time to go to sleep—you have to go to sleep now." (Commanding tone.)

8. C. "It's fun to make people do what you want them to do."

W. "I'll even put a soldier to bed."

C. "It'd be fun to make everybody do what you want them to do."

W. "Yes." (Nods.)

A few minutes later W.'s play became quite aggressive and finally he turned to C. with a gun in his hand.

W. "What am I?"

C. "I don't know, what are you?"

W. "I'm a crook, but I'd rather be a cop."

9. C. "You're bad, but you'd rather be good."

W. "I'd be a cop if my cousin'd be a crook," (shoots realistically.)

C. "It'd be fun to shoot your cousin."

Notes are incomplete at this point but W. accepts this recognition and goes on to express positive feelings toward cousin. His play becomes more aggressive. He pushes things around roughly and shoots frequently.

C. "You feel like being rough and when you are, you feel better."

W. "Would you get mad if I broke the dresser by throwing at it?"

10. C. "You may do what you want to with the toys."

W. (Throws and breaks drawer.) "Is there something else that I can throw at?" (Upset.)

11. C. "One of the dolls?"

W. (Picks up breakable doll, puts it down and takes rubber one.)

12. C. "It's fun to knock things around, but you don't want to break them."

W. "Yeah." (Starts throwing at doll.)

The rest of the hour was spent in this fashion. Two attitudes were brought out during this play by W., and recognized by C. They were (1) "I get pretty sore when things don't go the way I want them to," (2) "I'm surprised whenever I do anything well in athletics."

COMMENTS ON SECOND INTERVIEW

1. Weak. W. would have entered without invitation. "You just couldn't wait for me and slipped up here," would approach the real feeling.

2. C. jumps a little too fast. "You wonder what I would do," fits the puzzlement of the child regarding this new person whom he knows little about. This does not turn out to be a serious error as evidenced by (3) and (4).

5. O.K., but "You don't want people to know much about you," is recognition of a more important feeling.

6. Should have been, "You hope that he left them." C.'s orientation has thrown him into error. Statement (7) was not said with deep feeling.

8. Adequate response to a commanding tone of voice. Recognition of this attitude leads to fuller expression although the attitude is not very significant in itself.

9. Most pertinent attitude expressed so far. It is well verbalized by C.

10. Bad mistake, although client does not capitalize on it, as he does in third interview, (15). Permissiveness is not developed by verbalizing. C. loses a toy and

guilt feelings arise because he attempted to structure the relationship at this point. The feeling expressed is, "What kind of a fellow are you and what things can I do when I'm with you?"

11. C. stays on an intellectual plane. "You'd rather throw at something that doesn't break," or, "It made you unhappy to break the dresser."

12. C. finally corrects error.

9/6. Broken.

9/13. W.'s younger brother was with him today and W. wanted to bring him upstairs.

1. **C.** "I'm sorry he can't come upstairs, he can play down here if he wishes." (W.'s face falls.) "That makes you unhappy." (W. makes no move to come upstairs.) "I'll be upstairs, you can come when you are ready, W."

    W. (Tells brother what he can play with and comes up immediately. Quite aggressively shoves things around.) "Do many girls come up here?"

2. **C.** "Several. You wonder what other children come up here and what they do when they are here."

    W. (No answer. Looks at C. and his notes.) "Why are you doing that?"

3. **C.** (Explains briefly.) "You wonder who I might be giving them to, to read."

4. **W.** "Yes." (Play is rough. Toys are being thrown on floor. Picks up nursing bottle and begins to drink. Stops.) "Why didn't you let my brother come up here?"

    C. "You're pretty angry because I didn't let him come up. This is an hour for you and me to be up here alone."

    W. "What would happen if I threw the bottle?"

5. **C.** "Maybe you are trying to make me mad."

6. **W.** (Nods yes. Talks about being a great doctor and measuring the amount of milk a baby should have.)

7. **C.** "Sometimes you'd like to be a little baby and sometimes you'd like to be a grown up person."

    W. (Smiles).

Later:

   W. "What would happen if my brother came up here?"

   C. "You wonder if I would let him come in."

   W. "Dr. S. let him come up here."

   C. "You wonder why I won't let him come up when Dr. S. did, and you think I oughta let him come."

   W. "Yeah, he did." (Begins tearing up doll house and throwing things on floor.)

8. **C.** "You're mad and you want to make me mad."

   W. "There are ways—an operation!" (Immediately he goes to the buzzer and starts to ring it.)

9. **C.** "That's one of the things you can't do. Perhaps you are trying to find things I won't let you do."

   W. "I've been here long enough."

10. **C.** "It is puzzling to have a new person that has different ideas about what you should and shouldn't do."

   W. "Dr. S. hasn't written me a letter yet."

11. **C.** "You're sorta mad at him." His play becomes wilder. He threatens to break a bottle.

   C. "You're still trying to make me mad."

   W. (Throws at doll, and it bounces back and knocks bottle onto floor. Quite disturbed because it breaks. Looks at C.)

   C. "You're worried about the bottle and wonder what I'm going to do about it."

12. **W.** (No overt reaction. Starts to throw at doll which is in line with windows. C. limits.) "You sound like you're a little mad too."

13. **C.** "You hope that I'm mad but

you're a little afraid that I might be too."

W. (Smiles. Goes outside, returns and goes out again by another door. Wants to play with a fire extinguisher.)

C. (Limits.) "You don't like it very well in here today."

W. (Returns immediately.) "That used to be my room."

14. C. "In some ways you like the old room and Dr. S. better."

W. (Smiles broadly. Play takes on a more constructive quality.)

15. C. "Sometimes you like to be good."

W. (Cleaning up glass, stops, picks up largest piece and drops, grabs nursing bottle and squeezes water on floor.)

C. "It's fun to make messes when you're mad at me." (Begins to squirt water very close to C. C. limits and W. starts to squirt water on chair cushion.) "You can't do that."

16. W. "Oh, I can't eh, I'll show you."

C. "I made a mistake when I said can't, didn't I? You caught me up on it. I should have said you aren't supposed to squirt water on the chair."

W. (Stops.)

A few moments later:

W. "What time is it?"

C. "We have three minutes left."

W. "Time to clean up." (Starts to clean up glass and water.)

17. C. "Sometimes you fell like being good and sometimes you feel like being bad."

W. "I've been taught."

C. "You aren't doing this because you wanta be good but because you've been taught to clean up your messes."

Later:

W. (Picks up doll, shakes and scolds it. Refers to it as "baby.")

C. "You don't like babies."

W. "No!" (Twists doll and almost tears it apart, then drops it quickly and returns to sweeping.)

As W. prepared to leave his brother appeared outside of door. W. brought him in "to show him the toys." W. grabbed nursing bottle and squirted water on his brother.

C. "It's fun to be mean to your brother."

W. "Yeah."

C. "I know you want to stay longer but time is up now."

18. W. (Preparing to leave.) "What would happen if I came late next time?"

C. "You don't particularly want to come next time."

W. "Naw, just what would happen?"

C. "Maybe you're still mad at me and wonder if that'll make me mad at you. It is all right for you to come late if you want to."

COMMENTS ON INTERVIEW

1. C. handles this situation well and W. comes upstairs immediately as a result.

2. No doubt this is at the basis of W.'s question but C. should have stayed at, "You wonder what kind of kids I see."

3. C. continues to build up antagonism. "You wonder what I'm going to do with them," is the feeling. W.'s behavior is indicative of C.'s work in (2) and (3).

5. This is good, but, "Some of the things I say make you mad," should have preceded this.

7. This is a response to the behavior of (4) as well as (6) and provides considerable relief.

8. Good response which leads to expression of deeper feeling in W.'s next bit of behavior which is excellently handled (9).

10. This points up one of W.'s major difficulties and is in keeping with the feeling expressed.

11. Pretty poor. W. was disappointed, not mad. "You miss him and it has made you unhappy because he hasn't written." This error leads to the aggression that follows.

12. C. is under strain and W. in true fashion picks it up. This is typical of W.'s ability to put C. on the spot time after time. C. (13) handles a very difficult situation well. Perhaps this is in part due to W.'s recognition of C.'s feeling.

14. Good response to behavior of last few moments.

15. Recognition of positive feelings without including negative which has preceded it, inevitably leads to the type of thing W. does next. "Sometimes you like to be good and sometimes you like to be bad," would have avoided trouble.

16. C. has rightly deserved the difficult position he is now in. "You're trying to find things I won't let you do because you're mad at me and want to make me mad. That is one of the things you're not supposed to do." C.'s following response to another trying situation is good and leads to another attempt by W. to be constructive.

17. C. has learned his lesson.

18. Resistance, which has accrued out of frequent mishandling during period, is treated in good style.

9/20. W. (Walks in, sits in chair.) "Now what can we do to start things off wrong?"
1. C. "You're still a little mad."
   W. (Shakes head no.) "I wanta have some fun today."

Later:

2. W. (Painting an airplane). "This is all I used to do with Dr. S."
   C. "You do a lot more things now."
   W. "Yes."

Later:

   W. (Looks at C. taking notes. Shows concern.)
   C. "It bothers you because I take notes on what you do."
   W. "If my mother wanted to look at that record she could."
   C. "You think we let other people know what you're doing while you are in here."
   W. "Well, I think she could if she wanted to."
3. C. "You don't think she'd be that much interested in it."
   W. (Emphatically.) "No."

COMMENTS ON INTERVIEW

1. Weak and interpretive. "You want to get started right away," would have led to fuller expression. This is anticipation, not anger, although anger is in the background.

2. Here is ambivalence in a very important area and C. fails flatly to pick it up. C. should have added, "In some ways you like it better now and in other ways you don't like it nearly as much as when Dr. S. was here."

3. Excellent recognition. The expression of this pertinent attitude has resulted from recognition of simple material in the preceding statements by W.

9/27. This period started wildly. W. talked about his poor painting, nature, and new pennies. Then he made a remark which seemed to show concern regarding other children the therapist saw.

1. C. "You wonder what other kids do when they come up here."
   W. "No." (Takes rubber doll and begins to hit it.)
   C. "You feel better when you beat up the baby."
   W. "Yes." (Continues.)
   C. "You feel like being mean to it."
   W. "Yes, (feeds didy doll,) don't talk back to your elders."
   C. "You don't like the baby when he won't do what you want him to do."
   W. "One thing I don't like is babies!"
2. C. "You don't like live ones or play ones."
   W. "Oh, I like real ones." (Takes doll over and begins to throw at it.)
   C. "It's a lot of fun to knock the baby around."

W. (Picks up doll.) "This is one thing I don't like!"

C. "You don't like babies at all."

(W. throws at doll much harder than before.) "You want very badly to knock the baby down."

W. (Hits finally and sighs in relief.)

C. "It makes you feel much better when you knock it down."

W. "Yah." (Begins to pound doll with hand. Hits it so hard that head flies off. Is so angry that he fails to look for C.'s reaction.) "Tell me if you come out alive, Henry!"

3. C. (Pointing carefully at doll,) "You're pretty mad at Henry."

W. "Who says so! He's my brother. I like him."

4. C. "I meant the doll—you called him Henry."

W. (Changes subject·entirely.)

Later:

W. "How many children do you have?"

5. C. "You'd like to know more about me."

W. (Concentrates, then) "I'll bet you have one child."

C. "You think it'd be best to have only one child."

W. "Yes." (Begins to beat on doll with mallet and billy club singing at same time.)

6. C. "It's fun to sing."

W. "What song don't you like?"

7. C. "You'd like to sing a song I don't like because you're mad at me because of some of the things I've said today."

W. (Tries to sing *Pistol Packin' Mama*, then returns to dolls and begins to hit one of them.)

8. C. "You hate them. Sometimes you don't even like Henry."

W. "Who says so!"

C. (Weakly) "I just thought so."

9. W. "Well—you're right! (Short pause.) It's sorta hard to play with you—if you

just looked a little like Dr. S. or if you just talked like him."

10. C. "You liked Dr. S. very much and miss him since a new person is here."

W. (Begins to throw things around. Is very unhappy.)

C. "You're very unhappy."

W. (Stops and comes over to sit by C.)

Later:

W. (Gets doll and begins to hit it.)

C. "You still feel like you want to hurt the baby."

W. "You oughta take all these dolls and turn 'em in for defense."

C. "You'd like to get rid of all the babies."

W. (Emphatically.) "Yah!" (Picks up big breakable doll.) "Can I break this dolly's head?" (Hits head on crib fairly hard.)

11. C. "You're so mad at babies that you'd just like to break this baby's head all to pieces."

W. (Bangs head but much easier. Stops. Gets bottle and begins to feed. Time is up.)

C. "Our time is up, W."

W. "You can't talk, it's against the law."

C. "You don't want to leave yet and don't want me to tell you when time is up."

W. (Continues to feed dolly and then beats it with his hand.)

12. C. "In some ways you like the dolly and in some ways you hate it. Time is up. (No reaction.) You still feel like doing a lot of things and don't want to go, but time is up and you're supposed to leave now."

W. (Leaves readily.)

COMMENTS CONCERNING INTERVIEW

1. C. probably has not hit the true feeling but this is impossible to determine because of the incompleteness of his notes.

2. C. is in a hurry, W. is not. "They *really* make you mad," would have been in keeping with the feeling.

3. Perhaps if C. had felt on safe ground this would not have happened. He spoke and acted quite cautiously at this point.

4. W.'s rebuke was sharp and it overwhelmed C. "It made you mad for me to say that," might have kept the movement in the same direction. As it was, C.'s very weak and yet challenging response forces W. into another field.

5. Finally.

6. Poor. "You would like it if there were only one child in your family," should have followed W.'s yes.

7. Excellent.

8. There is very little excuse for this and W. again places C. in a very difficult position.

9. W. accepts this deep feeling in spite of C.'s bungling. He immediately strikes out with a most pertinent attitude which C. again mishandles (10). "I'm quite different. Some of the things I say make you very uneasy."

11. This is an example of how adequate recognition avoids destruction of toys. Frequently, recognition is sufficient when limits are on the verge of being broken.

12. Excellent handling.

10/3. Broken. Mother called to ask for change in time of appointment.

10/13. W. began his play in a very belligerent fashion. He pounded on a porcelain pan for a few moments with a billy club.

1. W. "You told me I couldn't break these (lights) and I couldn't break them (windows), but there's *one* thing you haven't told me I couldn't do."

   C. "But you don't think I'd let you do it."

   W. "No. You haven't told me that I couldn't hit you over the head. I'm pretty sure you wouldn't let me do that."

   C. "You're pretty mad at me."

W.'s play became more aggressive. He verbalized his antagonism towards C., threw toys on the floor, and jumped from the table as hard as he could. He returned to the play table and pounded the porcelain pan until it was badly chipped. The noise was deafening. C. mentioned that W. was angry and trying to make C. angry but to no avail.

W. (Takes large tin truck and begins to pound on it. Looks at C.)

2. C. "Maybe you're trying to find something I won't let you do."

   W. (Stops. Draws for a period at blackboard. After few moments he stops, steps to C.'s desk and prepares to push the buzzer. C. limits and W. accepts, he sits down at the table). "I can't touch this, I can't play with this or this (pointing to various objects on desk).

3. C. "You're finding a lot of things I won't let you play with."

   W. (Changes activity.)

Later:

   W. (Limited when he wishes to go through drawers of desk.) "Dr. S. let me go through his drawers."

4. C. "Dr. S. let you and you can't see why I don't."

   W. (Sings, "You're in my power," gleaming at C. as if in anticipation.)

   C. "You'd like to have me in your power."

   W. "Boy, what I wouldn't do."

   C. "You'd really give me the works."

   W. "Yeah. Mother thinks you're nicer than Dr. S." (Sadly.)

5. C. "That puzzles you because it is a little harder for you to play with me than it was Dr. S."

   W. (Smiles.)

Time was almost up at this point and the remainder of the period was spent in constructive play.

COMMENTS

1. Extreme aggression such as that exhibited in this interview is due to fault of handling by the counselor. Here it is due to interpretative responses in the previous interview and failure to respond adequately in the period in which the aggression is expressed. This is further complicated, however, because the mother has expressed a desire to withdraw from counseling since "things are getting along much better." Such a move is threatening to the child.

2. Responding to the feeling expressed in a child's play, is often quite difficult. Here C. has recognized that W. is angry and wants to make C. angry. Undoubtedly this is part of the feeling but W. continues his aggressiveness. The response (2) which results in cessation of this behavior could be used only when it seemed quite obvious that he was attempting to break limits. The first indication of this is (1) but not until he had tested C.'s reaction to destructive acts, could one feel safe that this is the feeling expressed. The next response (3) is good and results in change of activity.

4. When W. has so frequently expressed amazement, disappointment, pleasure, and antagonism, concerning the differences between counselors, a much more adequate response could have been made. This response would have been adequate in the earlier interviews, when W. had expressed only one or two of his feelings regarding the counselors. C.'s continual failure to cope with this is an indication that he should survey his own attitudes.

5. Much better.

10/20. This period was equal in aggression to the previous periods. He brought up material which indicated that he was thinking of closing but when C.

mentioned this he was sharply rebuked. W. got out the Snellen chart and read all lines correctly at approximately fifteen feet. Later he spelled "Mississippi." He threatened to break a doll and did because C.'s attempted recognitions were inaccurate.

> **W.** (Half of doll's face held in front of his.) "I'm only three and a half years old." (Whiny voice. Pounds on the face.)
> **C.** You don't like the three-and-a-half-year-old."
> **W.** "No, my brother is three and a half years old."

There was no further aggression.

10/25. Mother called. W. passed all of his school work. (Several D's, however, mother reported that there was no longer any need for help as far as W.'s behavior in the home was concerned.)

10/27. Shortly after W. arrived he spelled Halloween with considerable pride.

> **1. C.** "You feel you are getting along better."
> **W.** "Yah." (Gets mallet and begins to pound on remains of doll which he destroyed in last interview.)
> **2. C.** "When you break toys others can't play with them."
> **W.** "Yah. Isn't that a good reason?"
> **3. C.** "Maybe that's the reason that you break them."
> **W.** "Yah."
> **4. C.** "You don't want other children to play with the toys."
> **W.** "No." (Completes destruction of doll and gives the legs to C.)

Later:

> **C.** "You won't be coming to see me much longer."
> **W.** "Who says?"
> **C.** "Your mother feels it's about time to quit."
> **W.** (Angry.) "Why, why does she feel that way?"

C. "You want to come and it makes you pretty unhappy that you won't be coming and makes you a little mad at your mother."

W. (Smiles and goes on with play. Play is constructive for quite a period.)

C. "Sometimes you like to be good and sometimes you like to be bad."

W. (Smiles and nods.) "Give me a single reason why my Mom doesn't want me to come here any more."

C. "What reason do you think she had?"

W. (Mad and hurt.) "To have my brother come."

5. C. "You don't think that's very fair."

W. "No." (Some material omitted.) "How many more weeks will I be coming?"

6. C. "That is up to you and your mother to decide."

W. (Leaves his play and immediately begins to break a cannon.)

C. "You want to break that up too."

W. "I want to break everything."

7. C. "So your brother can't play. You think if you break everything up your brother won't want to come and you can still come."

8. W. "No, I want to get my share of play in—my money's worth." (Stops pounding immediately.) W. was mad at C. and threw a piece of clay on the floor several times mentioning that he wished it were C. His anger was recognized and it soon began to fluctuate between C. and Hitler.

COMMENTS

1. C.'s own needs gain expression.

2. This simple statement helps W. to express his feelings which are well responded to in (3) and (4).

5. Weak, but in no way harmful.

6. The only realistic response which can be made to a question of this type.

7. Based upon what had previously transpired, but still quite interpretive. W.

is not able to accept this in full, and aggression results.

(Mother reported W.'s teachers says he is getting along well in his reading. She added that she doesn't see why he's coming.)

11/3. W. asks C. to pronounce his spelling words. He is aware that his mother has decided this is to be the last interview. He misspells every word. He expressed concern about this.

Later:

W. "I'm gonna study hard and get a hundred."

C. "You want to do better in school."

W. "Yeah. Who cleaned this all up?" (Meaning the room.)

C. "You think it's a lot different than it was last time."

W. "Yeah, I'm gonna mess it up. Have you got any old toys?"

C. "Why?"

W. "Well, if you've got any old broken toys I'd like to have 'em."

C. "I know you'd like to have them very much, W., but they have to stay here when you leave."

W. "I've heard that piece, I've heard that piece." (Disgust.)

C. "You heard that before and you don't think there's any sense in hearing it again."

W. "What was the last person's name who was up here and why was he up here?" (Angry and disappointed.)

1. C. "You don't like anyone else to come."

W. "No, not if I can't come."

2. C. "You see no reason why you shouldn't come."

W. "Well, who is he? I just want his name. I'll let him feel my fist."

C. "You're awfully mad at him."

Later:

3. W. "Who put grease on my wall paper?"

4. C. "You wish it were your wall paper."

W. "No."

5. C. "Someways you want to come badly and in some ways you don't want to come any more."

W. (No answer. Plays constructively.)

C. "It's fun to be good and sometimes it's fun to be bad."

W. tried to protest near the end of the period that he had fifteen minutes more than he actually had.

C. "You hate to leave today."

6. W. "This is my last day."

7.   When C. tells W. it is time to clean up, he spills water on the floor.

C. "Time is up."

W. (Continues play.)

C. "You aren't ready to leave yet. It's especially hard to leave today. Our time's up."

W. (Leaves immediately and plays downstairs quite aggressively until mother arrives from her interview.)

COMMENTS

1. Seems to be interpretive but is only mildly so.

2. "And if you have to stop, you want others to stop also," could have been added quite profitably to this statement.

4. Interpretive. "It makes you mad for people to do things like that."

5. This is a response to such items as (3), W.'s anxiety about closing and his expressed antagonism. However, it does seem to be misplaced.

6. This is the first time C. has known that this is to be the last contact.

7. Seldom does aggressive behavior occur in the closing contact of nondirective therapy. Perhaps it occurs here because the mother is withdrawing from therapy one or two contacts before the child is ready.

CONCLUSIONS

Before drawing this paper to a close, several conclusions should be emphasized. They are:

1. *Every feeling which is apparent* to the counselor *should be recognized* because it may lead to very pertinent material despite its seeming unimportance.

2. Merely answering a question laden with feeling, can squelch expression. Care should be taken, however, to answer simple questions as well as to respond to feeling in order to avoid taking issue with the client.

3. Children in a thoroughly nondirective setting, can find the core of their problems and work out the solutions, apparently in a shorter period than under a more directive procedure. The writer has treated children as young as five years of age and has found them equally able to cope with their own problems.

4. Diagnostic data are not essential to the nondirective therapist but whether or not they interfere with therapy would be difficult to determine. Certainly, the possibility of misinterpreting the feeling expressed by the child is greater when the therapist has a definite orientation. This may seem odd to counselors who have leaned heavily upon diagnosis in treatment. However, in a nondirective setting, it is important that the orientation of the interview be that of the client. For example, if the therapist feels that the basis for the client's difficulty is sibling rivalry, there will be a tendency on his part to interpret feelings in the light of this knowledge rather than holding strictly to what the child is expressing. The writer does not mean to imply that a diagnosis should not be undertaken, however. It is essential. The clinic must know whether institutionalization, foster home placement, or some other type of environmental manipulation is superior to psychotherapy.

5. Questioning is not essential to therapy. Response to feeling leads to further expression and insight equally as well, if not better.

6. Intellectual capacities, such as reading, arithmetic and general intelligence, are frequently impaired by emotional dif-

ficulties. The I. Q. score may rise as much as 20 to 30 points during therapy.[4] Just what the psychological dynamics are is not clear, although numerous hypotheses have been offered, most of them so intangible, however, that scientific verification is impossible. Nevertheless, it can be safely stated that in any behavioral distortion or adaptation, the total organism is involved. There is little likelihood that

[4] *See* Phyllis Blanchard, "The Interpretation of Psychological Tests In Clinical Work With Children." *Mental Hygiene*, 1941, 25 (1): 58–75.

W.'s reading would have cleared up through tutoring alone. If it had, the neurotic symptom would probably appear in some other form, such as enuresis or finger nail biting, for the problem was not one of reading, but of sibling rivalry.

7. It is hoped that the contribution of full notes to the counseling situation is made apparent in the discussion of these interviews. Errors, such as failure to respond to feelings expressed or the use of interpretative statements, can be detected. Without full notes the counselor is usually unaware of these errors.

ADDENDUM[1]   Ray H. Bixler

This article was written during one of the most exhilarating, but brief, movements in the history of applied psychology. Before Carl Rogers arrived at Ohio State University, few psychologists had been trained in psychotherapy and far fewer had received this training while graduate students. Furthermore, at a time when the psychologist's right to practice psychotherapy was seriously challenged by psychiatrists, we Rogerians were being trained in a new therapy developed by a psychologist and, obviously, for psychologists.

In less than a decade after this article was published, the battle against psychiatrists had been won, graduate students were being trained in psychotherapy in almost every major university, and the first evidence challenging the efficacy of the dynamic psychotherapies had shattered our bliss!

But the early and middle 1940s belonged to us. We knew with the passion that transcends the need for verification that we were in the forefront of a vital new movement. Absolute conviction is stuff from which powerful placebos are made. Our therapy was unparalleled. During this period, very few interviews were required for successful treatment, and the apparent success rate was very high.

The therapy became characterized as "client-centered," while Rogers was at the University of Chicago. The novelty was wearing off, and the number of interviews required for successful therapy soared. This increase in interviews per case was seen at the time as progress—progress toward a deeper, more meaningful relationship.

There was a corresponding change in theory. Insight, which had been the central therapeutic force in nondirective therapy, became less important and the warm, permissive, allegedly neutral relationship itself became the principal therapeutic element.[2]

Rogerian therapy has undergone more or less continuous revision, but later developments are not relevant to the clarification of the climate at the time my article was written.

[1] Prepared by the author for inclusion in this volume.

[2] For Rogers, therapy had come full circle. He had earlier been most receptive to the relationship therapy of Jessie Taft and Frederick Allen. The short-lived emphasis upon insight appears to have evolved at Ohio State.

The most important elements in the article are:

1. The intuitive, prescientific analysis characteristic of almost all classical psychotherapies.
2. The firm conviction, typical of the period, that any problem in the therapy encounter arose from the failure of the therapist to use the nondirective method properly. Such mental gymnastics served our needs if not those of science, but placing the blame on the therapist was certainly a refreshing departure from the psychoanalytic practice of holding the patient responsible for failure!
3. My idiosyncratic emphasis upon diagnosis to determine whether or not psychotherapy was the most appropriate treatment method for the child in question (item 4, p. 234).[3]
4. The first draft of the article was returned with a firm request that I drop the reference to changes in IQ scores (item 6, p. 234) or offer documentation for such an unusual statement. I was delighted to find Blanchard's article (see footnote 4 in reading), which reported changes greater than I had estimated in the original draft. The fixed IQ was still in vogue, and we were among its early critics.

In retrospect I am relatively certain that a convinced, God-fearing faith healer would have obtained similar results had he told William that if he would but study hard and love his brother, God would be pleased.

My harsh comments are directed at our smugness and the prescientific nature of the dynamic therapies. However, Rogers's respect for democratic principles and his firm belief that man has a right to determine his own fate probably played a role in stimulating the great humanitarian and egalitarian movements of the fifties, sixties, and seventies.

REFERENCES

Rogers, Carl R. The clinical treatment of the problem child. New York: Houghton Mifflin, 1939.

[3] *The Clinical Treatment of the Problem Child* written by Rogers (1939) was a truly remarkable effort to develop objective diagnostic criteria for the selection of the appropriate method of treatment. It is unfortunate that prevailing winds blew in the wrong direction. Rogerians, almost to a man, rejected diagnosis as unnecessary if not harmful.

Chapter 12
Gestalt
Analysis

Two classic cases analyzed by Laura Perls are presented as representative of Gestalt analysis. These are cases from the early years, and some changes have been made in the therapy. Yet, these two cases do capture most of the important elements of the Gestalt form of therapy.

Claudia, the first case, begins her first session with Dr. Perls by challenging her as a therapist. Claudia has set the therapy in a competitive context. Notice how the therapist handles this challenge. Most of the therapeutic experiences for Claudia centered on the here and now and not on past experiences. Perls called special attention to Claudia's body movements, and she slowly began to realize her own self-sabotage. Series of experiments were run to let her see her problems in concentration. Her voice was especially worked on in terms of this "half-experience."

The second case, that of Walter, also involved quite a bit of therapeutic work with the voice. It was used to get Walter in touch with his feelings by helping him realize what the different tones in his voice meant. The therapist also worked on Walter's motor experience. Walter became aware that his movements contained no outgoing motions—he was literally turned in on himself. Walter's therapy differed from Claudia's in that he successfully went into a group where Gestalt therapy was also practiced.

Two Instances of Gestalt Therapy

LAURA PERLS

The two cases selected for presentation represent "typical" examples of a well-known clinical picture. Both patients come to therapy with similar complaints, namely, they have difficulties in contact and concentration. They are intelligent and gifted but second best. They cannot make adequate use of opportunities but think afterward of what they could or should have said or done. They find it nearly impossible to start anything new and waste a lot of time and energy on repetitive "dummy". activities. Both are self-conscious, feel awkward and ridiculous, think that most people don't care for them. Their concept of what they should be like amounts essentially to the ideal image of a near-Victorian lady or gentleman. Their main support is their pride in the ability to do without. Nevertheless, there is in both an all-pervading feeling of frustration and dissatisfaction. In short, the diagnostic emphasis in both cases would be on the obsessional and more or less paranoid character features.

However, the similarity in diagnosis does not necessarily indicate a similarity in therapeutic procedure. I have chosen two cases for this discussion rather than a single one in order to demonstrate in greater detail the difference in therapeutic techniques which is necessary and possible by taking into account the uniqueness of the patient's contact (or avoidance) techniques and the availability (or lack) of support functions.

The assumption of contact and support

From P. D. Pursglove (Ed.). *Recognition in Gestalt Therapy*, 42–63. New York: Funk & Wagnalls, 1968. Copyright 1956, Department of Psychology, Kings County Hospital, Brooklyn, 11203.

functions does not, as it may appear at first glance, reintroduce a dichotomy into the holistic concept of the functioning of the organism but is a differentiation according to the figure-ground principle. Contact—the recognition of "otherness," the awareness of difference, the boundary experience of "I and the other"—is more or less alert, specific, concernful awareness and activity. It is so much "figure" in the organismic functioning that neurosis has been defined as *avoidance of contact*, and the different types of neurosis as different *stages of withdrawal* from or limitation of contact.

But "who is all eyes does not see." The contact functions—by way of a specific organ or a specifically structured activity—take place against a background of organismic functions that are normally unaware and taken for granted; yet these latter provide the indispensable support for the foreground function of contact. They comprise hereditary and constitutional factors (primary physiology, etc.); acquired habits that have become automatic and thus equivalent to primary physiology (posture, language, manners, techniques, etc.); and fully assimilated experience of any sort. Only what is completely assimilated and integrated into the total functioning of the organism can become support.

Thus, contact and support are not identical with Conscious and Unconscious. The Unconscious, as far as it is repressed and introjected, is not support but the very lack of it. It is interference with and blockage of successful contact.

If we redefine neurosis as a state of malcoordination of contact and support functions, and the different neuroses as different types of malcoordination, we may define the goal of therapy as the achievement of optimal coordination of contact and support functions. We also may in time, with further research, arrive at the realization of a functional typology of neurosis.

At this point I find the contact/support concept a useful tool in the therapeutic situation. It immediately takes into account the patient's total behavior, not only his history and his verbalizations. The patient learns to work with material that is immediately available to him in the actual situation, without speculation or interpretation, by taking stock of all the aspects of his actual behavior, by bringing into the foreground and making figure out of what usually remains unrealized in the background. The questions "How?" or "What?" or "Where?" or "What does this do for you right now?" take preference over "Why?" or "What for?"; description prevails over explanation, experience and experiment over interpretation. Working strictly from the surface, e.g., from the actual awareness at any given moment, we avoid the mistake of contacting depth material prematurely that in the first place was and had to be "repressed" because at a certain point in the patient's history it was unsupportable. Making it available by interpretation of dreams or symbolic actions does not mean making it more usable but often causes a strenghtening of the defense mechanisms, waste of time or, worse, loss of the material by projection. The "negative therapeutic reaction," like the negative reaction to any other experience, is the result of unsupported contact.

On the other hand, the strengthening and expansion of the support functions mobilizes the alienated emotions and potentialities for contact, and makes formerly repressed depth material easily accessible. The process could be compared with the creation of a work of art (the highest form of integrated and integrating

human experience) in which the conflict between a multitude of incompatible and unmanageable experiences is realized only at the point where the means for its interpretation and transformation become available (Perls, 1950).

How the concepts of contact and support are applied in therapy will become more evident in the actual case discussions.

THE CASE OF CLAUDIA

Claudia, a twenty-five-year-old Negro, comes from a lower-middle-class West Indian background. The family is socially ambitious in a Victorian way; they try to emulate white society and to segregate themselves from "black trash" by strictness of morals and manners which in actual white society do not apply anymore. They are religious in an obsessional-conventional way.

Her father was domineering and rather brutal; he left the family when Claudia was about twelve to follow Father Divine. She has no contact with him now. Once terrified of him, she now feels only contempt. Her mother is meek and submissive, self-sacrificing, religiously moralizing. Her younger sister is pretty, feminine, soft, motherly-protective. A younger brother committed suicide while in jail for an alleged and likely homosexual involvement.

The patient regards herself as emancipated. She is very intelligent, has a degree in social science, is a caseworker with a city agency. She is coffee-colored, tall and slim, quite attractive but indifferently dressed and made up. She is well-behaved, uses "refined" language, is principled as to "what a young lady can or cannot do." Motorically, she is rather jerky; her voice has a hard edge to it. She is bony and rather flat-chested, her head thrown aggressively forward, the muscles in her broad, boyish neck tense. She lives at home with mother, sister, and aunts, whom she scares and bullies, and a righte-

...s, religious uncle, whom she despises and is afraid of.

She comes for therapy because she is "just not good enough at anything." She is not interested enough in her work; she is afraid of and feels contempt for her clients. She gets behind in her casework. She cannot concentrate on her studies and had to repeat several exams. Socially, she is awkard and unhappy. People don't like her; they seem to be scared of her. She cannot get hold of the "right" people; she cannot be alone, either. She diagnoses herself as paranoid and is afraid of insanity. Occasional suicidal fantasies are reported which she herself does not take very seriously. More serious are headaches, which bother her at times for a period of several days. She complains that she cannot wear feminine clothes and that she dreads going to dances and parties looking silly in frilly dresses. Nevertheless she goes, suffering agonies. The patient has no manifest sex life, feels vaguely excited by and vaguely attracted to both sexes. She condemns both inclinations, feeling wanton and sinful with the one, weird and perverted with the other.

She is also subject to numbers of obsessional rituals and habits, among them a severe hand-washing compulsion, which she does not even mention. As these habits are her safety devices, her support attitudes, they are automatic and taken for granted. In spite of the emphasis on how sick, weak, and confused she feels, and how she suffers, the patient gives the impression of competence, articulateness, and great strength.

The patient was seen once a week for three separate periods of seven to eight months since 1949. The interruptions were due partially to time and money reasons but more because of her inability to restart after long vacations or even after a week's interval. From 1952 to 1953, after she had achieved a certain level of functioning, I did not see her until she returned, voluntarily, at the end of 1953 to work through some difficulties that she had become aware of in the meantime. Since then, she has been working steadily, more and more concentrated and successfully, and is rapidly approaching the end of her treatment.

But we shall go back to the beginning. Her first sentence, after she had plunked herself down on the couch was, "I am in a bad way, doctor. You'll have to do something for me. I doubt if you can. You won't be any better than Dr. X. [a psychiatrist with whom she had worked for a short period and who had sent her to me]. She couldn't do anything with me," etc., etc.

It was obvious that the patient was challenging and taunting me. She was making demands, telling me how to handle her, trying to dominate and control the situation. Of course, from her family history it became quite evident that she identified with the bullying father and tried to manipulate me into the role of the submissive, hardworking, despised mother. But during the first few minutes of the first interview I did not have this information and I did not need it. I had only to consult my own reactions to the patient's behavior, my awareness of being belittled and imposed upon, the feeling of hostility that she provoked in me, to realize the specific pattern that the patient was acting out in this meeting as well as in any other contact situation. For her it was a contest in which she had to get the better, a question of victory or defeat, nearly of life or death. When she is unable to control the situation, she gets confused and anxious and has to withdraw.

If I had allowed her to ramble on in the same vein, she would have felt only that she was getting away with it again, that is, it would have increased and fortified her contempt for the feminine sex and with it her own basic inferiority feeling. If I had pointed out that she was telling me my business, but that I was the doctor and conducting the therapy, I would only have provoked a sharpened contest, as she would have been quite unable to cope with the ensuing confusion. In fact, whenever she felt that I was in some way getting the better of her, she ran back to her former analyst and usually succeeded in manipulating her either into accepting her for a visit or at least an hour-long telephone conversation to gain reassurance of her own superiority. Thus in the first few weeks of working with me, she went back frequently and without telling me about it. At later stages she went sporadically and told me in the next session, at first brazenly, "I went to see Dr. X. . . . So what do you have to say to that!" and later on, more and more embarrassed, "[*smile*] you know, [*wiggle*] *I called Dr. X.* [*blush*]!"

In the first session, neither withdrawing from nor entering into the contest pattern that the patient tried to impose on the situation, I asked her if she really wanted help. "Yes, of course, that's what I am coming for." I pointed out that she was asking for help in a rather peculiar fashion, not really asking for something that under the circumstances she might reasonably expect but demanding it as if I were trying to withhold something from her and she had to assert her right to get it—"you better, or else!" She did not really know me, yet she tried to pigeonhole me, put a label on me from her store of past experience and to fantasy what I was or was not going to do in the future. The only thing that she did not do was to consider me here and now (face to face), to look at and listen to me, to make contact with me and find out about me in this present actual situation. For a moment the wind was taken out of her sails; she was deprived of her habitual support. She got a little confused and embarrassed but quickly collected herself, threw her head forward, and barked, "I don't know anything about your qualifications. Do you have any? For all I know you may be a quack!" I satisfied her curiosity in this respect, but then pointed out that again

she had looked for reassurance from the past (this time *my* previous experience and training) rather than through an evaluation of whatever she could experience of me and through me in the present.

The following weeks and months were spent mainly in concentrating on the here-and-now experiences. The patient was discouraged from dwelling too much on her history and family background. It soon became more and more evident to her that she used the past as a convenient excuse and justification, and that she burdened the family with the whole responsibility for whatever she was now, so that she need not make any effort toward any relevant change now, in the present. The questions "What effort?" or "Effort against what?" mobilized intensive work on her so-called laziness and lack of concentration and contact. It was pointed out that contact can be made easily and adequately only when support is adequate and continuous. The obvious *discontinuities* in her behavior, her jerky motions, the break in her voice, her shallow arhythmical breathing, her separation of head (mind) and body (animal), her double moral standards, her masculine superiority fantasy against the reality of her femininity, to name only a few, were all in turn brought into the foreground to that degree of awareness at which, if not an immediate change, at least an experimental approach, a fantasy, or homeopathic play with different modes of behavior became possible.

The inability to concentrate for any length of time provided the first opportunity to make her aware in more and more detail of her techniques of self-sabotage. She came to therapy apparently with great interest in helping herself, but very soon in every session got either bored and somewhat foggy, erratic and distracted by incidentals. She said, "I can make some sort of a start [her head pushed forward, her voice raised, her eyes piercing], but then . . ." (the head drooped, she looked squashed, the voice fizzled out, the sentence remained unfinished). A whole series of experiments was conducted around every detail of this "half-experience." She learned to pay attention to the sound of her voice and how she produced it. The voice did not carry through, as she gave herself no chance to re-inhale during the act of speaking. The rhythm of breathing became arrested, the diaphragm got fixed at the bottom of the exhalation, and the voice had to be pushed out from the throat with great tension in neck, face, and throat muscles. She found that her speech was not really an expression, it did not come from the center (that is, from balanced posture and a continuity of rhythmical breathing, the indispensable support for optimal functioning), but it was a "pre-tense" in the literal sense of the word (coming from head and neck only). Listening to her voice, she recognized spontaneously, with a shock, "I sound like my father—raucous, bullying." Then, without pushing from the top, "And I shut up like my mother—confused, stupid." Her breathing became deeper, more rhythmical, she felt her "stomach getting warm. Now it is fluttering and twitching." And she started to cry. Thus, from the increasing self-awareness in the actual therapeutic situation, without digging into memories and without interpretation, the patient realized the double identification with both parents and the resulting inner conflict together with the means of resolving it.

Her motoric awkwardness and jerkiness also were revealed as part and parcel of the masculine pretense. Just as in conversation and argument only the head and voice came forward, so in actual motion in any direction or toward any object only the extremities moved, or rather jerked, while the torso remained rigid and the center of gravity (the pelvic region) was retracted. The joints were tight; there was no spring action and no swing in her movements. Since she is tall and lanky,

she looked and felt not just awkward but grotesque. With increasing awareness and with the help of detailed exercises she acquired gradually more and more mobility, more continuity in breathing, more fluidity in motion. She felt "more energy, more confidence, more swing, more stride, more excitement." She started to play tennis and soon became quite proficient. She worked more easily and with greater interest, and she made new social contacts.

At this stage she went through an intense homosexual phase. She still maintained a predominantly negative concept of femininity, together with a comparative rigidity and insensitiveness of the pelvic region. During the last few months—after we had worked through her initial disgust barrier (which in turn led to some work on her eating and learning habits, her indiscriminate stuffing and gobbling and swallowing of food as well as of information and principles and her feeling "fed up")—she has developed more and more sensitiveness and flexibility in her middle region and with it a greater acceptance of herself and her possibilities as a woman. She has become interested in and excited by men and has lately had some intimate heterosexual experiences. She does not feel too confident yet, and it will take her some time to develop more positive feminine "techniques."

Her former brazenness, the pretense of strength that is not centrally supported, has given way to genuine embarrassment, the awareness of a temporary malcoordination of contact and support functions, which means uncertainty, curiosity mixed with reluctance, a little anxiety, and a lot of excitement. The patient's physical appearance has changed considerably, quite apart from the changes in posture and coordination. Her bone structure, of course, is the same, but her bust is more developed, her thighs are heavier, her face is more relaxed and looks rounder. Her menstrual period, which was usually early (twenty-three days), had become at first retarded (thirty-three to thirty-five days) and now more normal (twenty-eight to thirty days). She has found her own style in clothes which is feminine in a sporty way, without frills, quite smart. She has, at least for the time being, given up her job as a social worker and taken up library work. She feels that it gives her more support in the process of learning to handle herself with her own problems than did her previous effort to manipulate other people with their difficulties. She has left her family's home and moved into a boarding house near the place where she is working. She is now considering sharing an apartment with a friend. Claudia has become in fact what formerly she only imagined, but in some way always wanted to be, an emancipated female.

THE CASE OF WALTER

Walter, forty-seven years old, is a Central European Jewish refugee. He comes from an impoverished middle class family, which nevertheless provided him with a university education. He became a lawyer, but with his degrees invalid in the successive countries of his emigration, he had to enter business life.

His father was an unsuccessful businessman, colorless, meek, and mild, with no initiative. His mother was ambitious and domineering, bitter about the father's failure. She was irritable, inconsistent in her demands, more amiable when the son finally achieved some professional and social status. She died in an asylum following a complete paranoiac breakdown in the emigration. A younger brother is happy-go-lucky, apparently unaffected by the family situation.

The patient is married to an intelligent, subtly manipulating woman. They have two children, one of whom is slightly spastic. Walter is fond of the children, but feels he does not handle them well; he is too anxious, too constraining. The originally quietly companionable marriage has

lately become somewhat precarious. His wife, interested in psychology by way of the child's handicap and therapy, is undergoing therapy herself and becoming increasingly dissatisfied with their relationship, mainly with his indifference to her interests.

The patient looks tired, resigned, and old. He walks with a slight stoop, elbows tight to his body, feet shuffling. His expression is intelligent, but worried. The eyes dart furtively around looking for an "out," the mouth is set in an apologetic smile. His speech is hesitant, he talks only "when he is spoken to." The voice is monotonous, has a wailing quality.

He is dissatisfied and in a dull way unhappy with nearly everything in his life. He is not so much complaining as berating himself for being such a failure in business, in social contacts, in family life. He postpones everything that is not strictly routine, minor business phone calls as well as major decisions. He dreads meeting people, has to break his head for something to say, feels awkward and self-conscious. He is afraid of losing old business connections and convinced of his inability to make new ones. In spite of all these obvious limitations and self-recriminations, the patient is not unsuccessful in business, makes a comfortable living as an agent for some foreign business concerns, has kept the same accounts for many years, and is appreciated for his reliability and foresight. His children love him. He also has a small number of good friends. He gets great enjoyment from being out in the open, in contact with nature. But this more positive information was not available at the beginning of his therapy.

The patient was seen twice weekly for about four months (March through June, 1953), then once weekly, with an additional weekly group session, for ten months. Group therapy proved particularly effective in this case, and the patient is still a member of a therapy group, while his individual treatment has been terminated.

In his first interview the patient stumbled into the room not looking right or left, as if he were wearing blinkers. He sat down at the edge of a chair, literally "on edge," squirming, saying nothing for several minutes. To my question, "What brings you here?" he clasped his arms tightly, shrugged his shoulders, finally mumbled diffidently, with a faint undertone of irritation and nagging, "I don't know what I am coming for. . . . My wife thinks I should. . . . I don't think it is of any use. . . . I don't know what to say. . . . My wife says. . . ," etc., etc. (*shrug, collapse*).

I felt somewhat squashed, too, and a little bored. The patient had, at least for the moment, achieved his neurotic aim, he put me off, he bored me with his monotonous wail and his repetitiousness; in fact, he did his best to discourage me from becoming interested. Obviously he regarded the whole situation as a nuisance and wanted to be left alone. But in presenting this entirely negative front, he also exposed in detail the techniques that supported his withdrawal pattern and thus, quite unintentionally, provided me with exactly what he so desperately tried to withhold, the very "handle" by which he could be reached.

As in the case of Claudia, it was pointed out to the patient that his way of asking for assistance was not too well designed for actually obtaining it, and that if anything, it watered down whatever interest one might develop in doing anything for him. "Yes," his voice sounded much stronger now, nearly defiant, "I know I am boring. I never know what to say. I don't like asking people for anything. I always worry what they expect of me, I have to figure out what I should say; it takes too much time and I know only afterward what I should have said."

Considering the question of how all this applied in the actual therapy situation, the patient discovered that he was always so busy anticipating other people's needs and demands or berating himself for having missed out on something in the past that he had no chance to realize his own needs and interests and actions in any present situation, even when it was specially designed for no other purpose but his own self-realization.

It took a number of months to make him realize that what he felt was not, as he maintained, "nothing," but was rather discomfort, tension, impatience, irritability, distrust, apprehension; that what he did also was not "nothing," but was rather pulling himself together, suspending animation, waiting for something to be over, whether it be a business meeting, an argument with his wife, or a therapy session.

Listening to his voice, the patient found to his surprise not only that he sounded like his father (a fact that he had always known) but also, particularly when he was berating and belittling himself, that he sounded like his mother having an argument with his father. The suspended animation attitude was thus revealed as a most adequate support for the child to keep out of an unmanageable and unsolvable conflict. The ensuing desensitization led to the introjection of and identification with that very conflict, and in turn to an externalization, which transformed every contact situation into a potential threat.

Even when he succeeded in mobilizing his voice on his own behalf, it was mainly in the service of keeping out of reach, of escaping from some imposition or responsibility that might possibly be put on him. He was most emphatic in saying, "I can't!" "I am not able to. . . ," "I don't know!" The tone of his voice left no doubt that what he was really expressing was "I won't!" But he had found a technique by which he did not have to realize, and therefore did not have to feel guilty about, his own spitefulness.

It was comparatively easy to make the patient sensorially and intellectually aware of *what* he was doing, *what* he was doing it *for*, that his techniques provided support for *withdrawal* from undesirable and unmanageable experiences in the *past*, that they *now* constituted a blockage and *interference with the desired contact*. It was very laborious and took many months of concentration and a great number of experiments and exercises around every detail of his withdrawal techniques to get the patient to that degree of *motoric* awareness at which he became able to make a relevant change.

In Claudia we found a certain mobility of the extremities unsupported by the more central coordination of posture and breathing; in Walter we find hardly any mobility at all. He was all in one piece, literally pulled together. Claudia had the possibility of comparing the rigidity of her back, chest, and pelvis with the jerkiness of the extremities, and consequently she could experiment with the extension of both modes of moving in either direction, until she had achieved some continuity of coordination and flexibility. But Walter had nothing to compare—that is, there was not enough difference in his motoric experience to make any particular movement or tension foreground figure, nothing except the shrug of the shoulders. From the awareness of the shoulder shrug, the stock-taking expanded. The patient experienced the comparative mobility of the shoulders as against the rigidity of the adjoining regions—neck, arms, chest. He spontaneously recognized the shrugging not just as a symbolic gesture but as an actual motoric expression of "I can't!' or "I don't know!"—the onset of a movement without reach, without direction, without continuity. Experimenting with reach, continuity, and direction, the patient realized that he did not make any outgoing movements at all, that he was completely pulled together in the vertical, and had no expansion whatsoever in the horizontal direction, no flexibility of the neck, no swing or lift in his arms, no buoyancy, no stance, no stride.

When, after several months of awareness experiments and exercises, he had partially succeeded in loosening up, his dutiful schoolboy attitude ("My wife thinks . . . ," "My analyst says . . . ," "I know I should . . .") changed to real interest and curiosity. He became easier with people and much friendlier. At this stage he went through a period of intense embarrassment. He was encouraged to admit and express the embarrassment rather than to withdraw from the embarrassing situations or, worse, to stick them out with grim determination. It was pointed out that embarrassment is the inevitable awareness of lack of support that accompanies the initial exciting contact with any new experience. Thus, it is the emotional state applying to all stages of rapid growth and development. It is typical for the small child at a certain stage as well as for the adolescent. It is due to a lack or an unawareness of adequate techniques to cope with the new experience. If one can stay with the situation in spite of or, better, *with* the embarrassment, he has a chance, by discovering and developing new support attitudes, to make more successful contact with the new experience and thus to overcome the embarrassment. If, on the other hand, one avoids the embarrassment either by withdrawing from possibly embarrassing situations (like Walter) or by brazening them out with a pretended courage (like Claudia), he will never acquire new valid support techniques— that is, he will have to confine his contact experiences either in fact (like Walter) or in sensitivity and consequence (like Claudia).

For several weeks Walter felt and behaved like an adolescent; he blushed and giggled and his voice changed. In a few instances, when the discrepancy between his new involvement and the lack of support, mainly the rigidity in his diaphragm and his upper arms, became too overwhelming, he became quite hysterical, laughing and crying and wildly gesticulating. He was able to recognize the attack afterward as the spontaneous mobilization of these most inflexible and insensitive parts of his organism (the hysterical attack is probably a motoric emergency reaction of the total organism, just as yawning is in the case of oxygen deficiency). Consequently, he could extend this awareness into more and more coordinate mobility.

At this stage group therapy became the most effective agent in the patient's development. At first he balked at even remotely considering the possibility of taking part in a group. But gradually he agreed, at least intellectually, that it might be a desirable step. Finally, he joined, at first very shyly sitting on the fringe, a silent observer. He refused even to take the most minor part in any psychodramatic experiment. But soon, encouraged by his observation of other group members, he began to admit and express his own uneasiness and embarrassment.[1] It was in the group situation that Walter became fully aware of how vigorously and emphatically he insisted on being ignorant

and incapable. He recognized it as a rather clever and, in its own way, competent avoidance technique. From here on it was only a few steps—via some experiments with direct mutual criticism among the group members and an exciting psychodramatic experience where he acted his mother shouting, scolding, and slapping a little boy—to a greater realization of his own present-day contact with people, his own interests, opinions, criticisms, needs, demands.

With increasing self-awareness he simultaneously became more genuinely aware of others, too. He no longer has to figure out what is expected of him, he responds immediately to the situation, and resists vigorously when he feels imposed upon. He is intelligently helpful to anyone in need; to everybody's great surprise, he was the only one who, when one of the group members stormed out of the room in a fit of anger and tears, went the next day to visit her to find out if she was all right.

Today he is the "father" of the group, benevolent, a little reserved but not shy, dignified without being stuffy, critical without nagging, quite gay with a keen sense of humor. His family relationships have improved; he enjoys the children (the child's therapist is delighted with his patience and understanding); he shares more interests and experiences with his wife. His business contacts are much easier; he feels more confident and less apprehensive; his income during the last year has substantially increased. At present he is abroad, an honored house guest of someone whom formerly he was afraid of as his boss, but now appreciates as his client. He acts his age and he looks ten years younger.

---

[1] This is also in contrast to Claudia, who had to control and dominate the proceedings from the very beginning. When her brazenness and phoniness were attacked, she had no support at all and could not face her embarrassment. She attended only very few meetings and dropped out of her group (1952) after one of the members had pointed out the senselessness of her handwashing compulsion by showing her the dirt on her hands through a magnifying glass. A few weeks ago she returned to the group of her own accord, more interested, more observant, more cooperative.

REFERENCE

Perls, Laura, "The Psychoanalyst and the Critic," *Complex 2*, 1950.

Chapter 13
Transactional
Analysis

As in most examples of transactional analysis, this case begins with the structural analysis of the patient. The patient, Mrs. Enatosky, demonstrates a feeling for structural analysis in her second session and soon begins to use the categories of Child, Parent, and Adult in the therapy and sees many connections with actions in her life. Regression analysis is also utilized to put her more in touch with her Child elements. After a number of individual sessions, she is introduced into a therapy group and transactional analysis in its complete form. In the group context the patient begins to see the games she played with other people and realizes she was doing this outside the group as well. Note that structural analysis is used in the group sessions to better understand what is taking place in the interactions between the members. Although script analysis is not used to any extent in this particular case, it is now being employed in an increasing number of cases.

A Terminated Case with Follow-up

ERIC BERNE

The following case illustrates the procedure and outcome in a completed course of structural and transactional analysis. Because the systematic use of this approach from beginning to termination has only recently become possible with the full flowering of its theoretical development, the follow-up is relatively short. Nevertheless, this is not an isolated instance, and whether by good luck or because the therapy accomplishes its purpose, there now exists a small group of cases whose ultimate outcome will be observed with special interest through the years. This consists of patients who made unexpectedly rapid (by former standards) symptomatic and social improvement under controlled therapeutic conditions.

Before taking up in more detail the case of Mrs. Enatosky, the case of Mrs. Hendrix, a 30-year-old housewife, is worth considering briefly. Mrs. Hendrix was first seen ten years ago, when she was suffering from an agitated depression. She was treated by conventional supportive methods ("offering oral supplies," as it is colloquially called) for one year, in the course of which she recovered.

When she returned a decade later, she was, if anything, worse than she had been during her previous episode, with more active suicidal fantasies. This time she was treated by structural and transactional analysis, and within six weeks she improved more than she had during the whole year of therapy in her former episode; this in the opinion not only of herself and the therapist, but also of her

From *Transactional Analysis in Psychotherapy*, 247–262. New York: Grove, 1961. Reprinted by permission of Grove Press, Inc. Copyright © 1961 by Eric Berne.

family and intimates; and this improvement was brought about by a procedure decidedly different from "supportive" offering of "supplies." After another six weeks, she was coping better than she had ever done in her life, having relinquished some of her long-standing autistic ambitions in favor of living in the world. She had also given up an unhealthy tendency to postulate her position on her unfortunate childhood; instead of playing "Wooden Leg" and "If It Weren't For Them," she was beginning to find her identity within the framework of new possibilities which unfolded in her family life. This case is mentioned because it offers about as well-controlled a situation as it is possible to hope for in clinical practice: the same patient with two similar well defined episodes separated by a distinct interval, treated by the same therapist with two distinct approaches.

To return now to Mrs. Enatosky, . . . this woman complained initially of "depressions" of sudden onset. It may be recalled that she had three previous forms of treatment: Alcoholics Anonymous, hypnosis, and psychotherapy combined with Zen and Yoga. She showed a special aptitude for structural and transactional analysis, and soon began to exert social control over the games which went on between herself and her husband, and herself and her son. The formal diagnosis is best stated as schizo-hysteria. The case will now be reviewed session by session with significant extracts.

1. APRIL 1

The patient arrived on time for her initial interview. She stated she had been going to other therapists but had become dissatisfied and had called a municipal clinic, and after some discussion with a social worker had been referred to Dr. Q. She was encouraged to proceed and at relevant points appropriate questions were asked in order to elicit the psychiatric history. She stated that she had been an alcoholic for ten years and had been cured by Alcoholics Anonymous. She dated the onset of her drinking from her mother's psychosis when she was 19. She said that her depressions began at the same time. The nature of her previous psychiatric treatment was discussed. The preliminary demographic information was obtained so that she could be placed as a native born 34-year-old once-married Protestant housewife, a high school graduate, whose husband was a mechanic. Her father's occupation, the length of her marriage, her sibling position in years and months, and the ages of her children were noted. A preliminary search for traumatic events elicited that her father drank heavily and that her parents separated when she was seven years old.

The medical history revealed headaches, and numbness of one arm and leg, but no convulsions, allergies, skin afflictions, or other physical disorders with common psychiatric implications. Her age at the time of all operations, injuries, and serious illnesses was noted. Her childhood was explored for gross psychopathology such as sleep walking, nail-biting, night terrors, stammering, stuttering, bed wetting, thumb sucking and other preschool problems. Her school history was reviewed briefly. Chemical influences such as medications and exposure to noxious substances were also noted. A cautious exploration of her mental status was undertaken, and finally she was asked to relate any dream that she could remember. Recently she dreamed: "They were rescuing my husband from the water. His head was hurt and I started to scream." She mentioned that she often heard inner

voices exhorting her to health, and once, two years ago, an "outer" voice. This satisfied the requirements for preliminary history-taking, and the patient was then allowed to wander as she pleased.

DISCUSSION: The history-taking was carefully planned so that at all times the patient seemed to have the initiative and the therapist at most was curious rather than formal or openly systematic in gathering information. This means that the patient was allowed to structure the interview in her own way as far as possible and was not required to play a game of psychiatric history-taking. Because of her complaint of numbness she was referred to a neurologist for examination.

2. APRIL 8

The neurologist suspected cervical arthritis, but did not recommend any specific treatment. The patient conducted this interview as a kind of psychological survey. She spontaneously mentioned wanting approval and rebelling "like a little girl," as some "grown-up part" of her judged it. She said the "little girl" seemed "childish." It was suggested that she let the "little girl" out, rather than try to clamp down on her. She replied that that seemed brazen. "I like children, though. I know I can't live up to my father's expectations, and I get tired of trying to." This also includes her husband's "expectations." Such expectations were generalized for her as "parental expectations," since she had practically said as much herself. She sees the two most important "parents" in her life as her husband and her father. She is seductive toward her husband and recognizes that she was the same with her father. When her father and mother separated she thought (age 7): "I could have kept him." Thus she has not only a conflict about compliance, but also an attitude of seductiveness, toward parental figures.

DISCUSSION: The patient's special aptitude for structural analysis is already evident. She herself makes the separation between "the little girl" and "a grown-up part" and recognizes the compliance of "the little girl" toward certain people whom she relates to her parents. It was only necessary, therefore, to reinforce this trichotomy in a nondirective way. With many other patients this might not have been undertaken until the third or fourth session, perhaps even later.

3. APRIL 15

She resents people who tell her what to do, especially women. This is another reaction to "parents." She mentions a feeling of "walking high." It is pointed out that this is the way a very small girl must feel, that this is again the Child. She replied: "Oh, for heaven's sake, that's true! As you said that I could see a little child . . . it's hard to believe, but that makes sense to me. As you say that, I feel I didn't want to walk: a little girl in rompers. . . . I feel funny now. They pull you up by your right shoulder and you're outraged . . . yet I do the same to my own son. I disapprove while I'm thinking 'I don't disapprove, I know just how he feels.' It's really my mother disapproving. Is *that* the Parent part you mentioned? I'm frightened a little by all this."

It was at this point that it was emphasized that there was no mysterious or metaphysical aspect to these diagnostic judgments.

DISCUSSION: The patient has now experienced some of the phenomenological reality of the Child and has added to the behavioral, social, and historical reality she established in the previous interviews. The indications, therefore, are favorable for treatment with transactional analysis.

4. APRIL 22

"This week I've been happy for the first time in fifteen years. I don't have to look

far to find the Child, I can see it in my husband and in others too. I have trouble with my son." The game with her son was clarified in an inexact but timely and illustrative way in terms of Parent (her disapproval and determination), Child (her seductiveness and her sulkiness at his recalcitrance), and Adult (her gratification when he finally did his work). It was hinted that an Adult approach (good reason) rather than a Parental approach (sweet reason) might be worth a try.

DISCUSSION: The patient is now involved in transactional analysis proper and the idea of social control has been suggested.

5. APRIL 28

She reports that things work better with her son. Regression analysis is attempted to find out more about the Child. She relates: "The cat soils the rug and they accuse me and make me wipe it up. I deny that I did it and stammer." In the ensuing discussion she remarks that both Alcoholics Anonymous and the Anglican Church require confession to "messes." For this reason she gave them both up. As the session ends she asks: "Is it all right to be aggressive?" Answer: "You want me to tell you?" She understands the implication that she should decide such things on Adult grounds rather than asking Parental permission, and replies: "No, I don't."

DISCUSSION: During this session some of the elements of her script are elicited. It can be anticipated that she will try to repeat with the therapist in some well-adapted form the cat situation. Her question "Is it all right to be aggressive?" is perhaps the first move in this adaptation. This gives the therapist an opportunity to decline to play and to reinforce her Adult. The patient has made such good progress in understanding structural and transactional analysis that she is already considered adequately prepared for fairly advanced group therapy. The group she is to enter consists largely of women.

6. MAY 4

A dream. "I look at myself and say: 'That's not so bad.' " She liked the group but it made her uncomfortable during the rest of the week. She relates some memories, including homosexual play during childhood. "Oh! That's why I didn't like AA. There were two homosexual women there and one of them called me sexy." She complains of vaginal itching. "My mother and I slept together and she bothered me."

DISCUSSION: The manifest content of her dream is taken to be Adult and indicates the possibility of a good prognosis. The experience in the group has activated sexual conflicts, and this is the first indication of their nature.

7. MAY 11

She felt highly excited on leaving the group meeting. "Things are moving quickly. Why did they make me laugh and blush? Things are better at home. I can kiss my son now and my daughter for the first time came and sat on my lap. I can't be a good lover when things are monotonous."

DISCUSSION: The analysis of her family games . . . has resulted in the establishment of some Adult social control. It is evident that this improved control has been perceived by her children and for the first time in a long while they have the feeling that she can maintain her position and they react accordingly. Her excitement in the group and her statement that she can't be a good lover when things are monotonous indicate that she is involved in a sexual game with her husband.

An experience in the group later this week rather clearly showed her need for parental figures in some of her games.

There was a new patient in the group, a male social worker, and she was very much impressed by his occupation. She asked him what they were supposed to do there. It was pointed out that she knew more than he did, since it was his first meeting and her third. She says she resents it when people tell her what to do, yet peasant-like, in spite of her superior experience, she asks a novice for instructions because she appears to be impressed by his education: evidently an attempt to set up a game. This interpretation strikes home. She recognizes how she "cons" a likely candidate into being parental and then complains about it.

8. MAY 18

She was upset by regression analysis in the group. It made her think of her fear of insanity, and of her mother in the state hospital. Her own production was of some elegant gates leading into a beautiful garden. This is a derivative of a Garden of Eden fantasy from before the age of five. The material indicates that the garden has become adapted to the gates of the state hospital where she visited her mother many years ago. This experience in the group offered a timely opportunity to mention to her that she might want to be hospitalized and so relieved of responsibility.

She has visited her mother only once in the past five or six years and it was suggested that it might be advisable for her to do that again. This suggestion was very carefully worded so as to be Adult rather than Parental. Any implication that she was a bad girl for not visiting her mother had to be avoided. She was able to understand the value of such a visit as an exercise for her Adult and as a means of preventing future difficulties between her Parent and her Child if her mother should die. The good reception of this suggestion was manifested by her bringing up new information. Her husband never washes his hair and always has a good excuse, which she accepts. He has not washed it for many months. She says it doesn't bother her too much. The therapist said she must have known that when she married him. She denied it.

9. MAY 25

She said she has always been more afraid of sick animals than of sick people. This week her cat was sick, and for the first time she was not afraid of him. Once when she was little her father hit her and her dog jumped on him, whereupon he gave the dog away. She told her children that her mother was dead. Whenever she would think of her mother she would start to drink. One time she was told that when her mother was eight months pregnant, her father tried to poison her. They saved the patient and thought her mother was a goner, but then she was revived. The aunt who told her this story says: "Your life has been a mess since birth."

DISCUSSION: The import of this is not clear. It is evident, however, that she is working through some rather complex conflicts concerning her mother. Her maintenance of social control with the sick cat is evidence that a visit to her mother may be possible in the near future.

10. JUNE 1

"Frankly, the reason I'm afraid to visit my mother is that I might want to stay there myself." She wonders: "Why do I exist? Sometimes I doubted my existence." Her parents' marriage was a shotgun wedding and she has always felt that she was unwanted. The therapist suggested that she get a copy of her birth certificate.

DISCUSSION: The patient is now involved with existential problems. Her Adult has evidently always been shaky because her Child has implanted doubts about her existence, her right to exist,

and the form in which she exists. Her birth certificate will be written evidence that she does exist, and should be particularly impressive to her Child. As social control is established and she learns that it is possible for her to exist in a form which she herself chooses, her desire to retreat to the state hospital should diminish.

11. JUNE 8

She describes her husband's alcoholic game. At AA she was told that she should bless him and comfort him, and that made her sick. She tried something different. "One day I said I would call the ambulance for the hospital, since he didn't appear to be able to take care of himself, so he got up and didn't drink again." He said he was only trying to help her stay sober by drinking himself. This comes up because he was drinking heavily last week and she had pain in her shoulders and wanted to hit him, but told him off instead.

It appears from this that their secret marriage contract is based partly on the assumption that he will drink and she will function as a rescuer. This game was reinforced by AA to her benefit. When she refused to continue as a rescuer and became a persecutor instead, the game was thrown off and he stopped drinking. (Evidently it was reinstituted due to her insecurity of the past week.)

This outline was presented to her. She first said: "It couldn't have been part of our marriage contract, because neither of us drank when we met." A little later in the interview she suddenly said: "You know, now I remember I did know when we were married that he didn't wash his hair, but I didn't know that he drank." The therapist said that the unkempt hair was also part of the secret marriage contract. She looked skeptical. Then she thought a minute and said: "By golly, yes, I did know he drank. When we were in high school we used to drink together all the time."

It now appears that in the early years of their marriage, they played a switchable game of alcoholic. If she drank, her husband didn't; and if he drank, she stayed sober. Their relationship was originally based on this game, which they later interrupted, and must have exerted considerable effort to forget about.

DISCUSSION: This session helped to clarify for the patient the structure of her marriage, and also emphasized the amount of time and effort which is required to keep marital games going, and equally, the amount of energy involved in their repression without conscious control.

12. JULY 6

There has been an interval of a month for summer vacation. The patient returns with a sore shoulder. She has been to the state hospital, and her mother sent her away. This made her feel hopeless. She has some olfactory illusions. She thinks she smells gas in the office, but decides it is clean soap. This leads into a discussion of her mental activity. During her recent Yoga training, she developed imagery which was almost eidetic. She would see gardens and wingless angels with sparkling clarity of color and detail. She recalled that she had had the same kind of imagery as a child. She also had images of Christ and her son. Their complexions were clear and lively. She sees animals and flowers. As a matter of fact, when she walks through parks she likes to talk secretly but aloud to trees and flowers. The longings expressed in these activities are discussed with her. The artistic and poetic aspects are pointed out, and she is encouraged therefore to write and to try finger painting. She has seen her birth certificate and her existential doubts are less disturbing.

DISCUSSION: These phenomena and the auditory manifestations she had previously mentioned, are not necessarily alarming. They point to childhood restitutive tendencies related to a deeply disturbed relationship between her and her parents. The conventional approach would be to give her "supportive" treatment and help her repress this psychopathology and live on top of it. Structural analysis offers another possibility which requires some boldness: to allow this disturbed Child to express herself and profit from the resulting constructive experiences.

13. JULY 13

She went to her internist and he gave her Rauwolfia because her blood pressure was high. She told her husband she was going to finger-paint and he got angry and said: "Use pastels!" When she refused, he started to drink. She recognizes what happened here as a game of "Uproar" and feels some despair at having been drawn into this. She says, however, that if she does not play "Uproar" with him then *he* will feel despair, and it is a hard choice to make. She also mentions that the gate on the beautiful garden is very similar to the gate on the day nursery where her mother used to send her when she was very small. A new problem now arises: how to distinguish the effect of psychotherapy from the effect of Rauwolfia. She is eager to help with this.

14. JULY 20

She is losing interest and feels tired. She agrees it is possible that this is an effect of the medication. She reveals some family scandals she has never mentioned to anyone before, and states now that her drinking did not begin after her mother became psychotic, but after these scandals.

At this session a decisive move was made. During her therapeutic sessions, the patient habitually sits with her legs in an ungainly exposed position. Now she complains again about the homosexual women at AA. She complains that the men also made passes at her. She doesn't understand why, since she did nothing to bring this on. She was informed of her exposed position and expressed considerable surprise. It was then pointed out to her that she must have been sitting in a similar provocative way for many years, and what she attributes to the aggressiveness of others is probably the result of her own rather crudely seductive posture. At the subsequent group meeting she was silent most of the time, and when questioned she mentioned what the doctor had said and how this had upset her.

DISCUSSION: This is a crucial session. At the price of sacrificing the possibilities of a normal family life, the patient has obtained a multitude of gains, primary and secondary, by playing games with her husband and other men and women. The primary external gain is the avoidance of pleasurable sexual intercourse. If she can relinquish these gains, she may be ready to undertake a normal marital relationship whose satisfactions should more than repay her for her abdication. The schizoid elements in her Child are clear from her symptomatology. The hysterical elements are most clearly manifested in her socially acceptable game of "Rapo." Hence the diagnosis of schizo-hysteria.

In her case, the naming of the game is avoided since she is still too soft-boiled to tolerate such bluntness. It is simply described to her without giving it a name. In very sophisticated groups, however, it is known technically as "First-degree Rapo." It is the classical game of hysterics: crude, "inadvertent," seductive exhibitionism, followed by protestations of surprise and injured innocence when a response is forthcoming. (As previously noted, "Third-degree Rapo," the most vicious form, ends in the court-room or the morgue.) The therapeutic problem at the moment is whether her preparation has been adequate and the relationship between her Child and the therapist sufficiently well understood to make this confrontation effective. In a sense, her life and those of her children hinge on the therapist's judgment in these matters. If she should decide to become angry and withdraw from treatment, psychiatry might be lost to her for a long time afterward, perhaps permanently. If she accepts it, the effect could be decisive, since this particular game is her chief barrier to marital happiness. The therapist, naturally, has not ventured to bring the matter up without considerable confidence of success.

15. AUGUST 10

The therapist returns after a two-week vacation. The confrontation has been successful. The patient now describes an assault by her father in early puberty while her stepmother pretended to be asleep. He also molested other children, but her stepmother used to defend him. She relates this "assault" to her own seductiveness. This situation she discusses at some length, eliciting her feeling that sex is dirty or vulgar. She says she has always been very careful sexually with her husband because of this feeling and has tried to avoid sex with him for this reason. She understands that the games she plays with him are an attempt to avoid sex, as she feels she cannot let go enough to enjoy it and it is merely a burden to her.

DISCUSSION: The patient is evidently shocked at the therapist's directness, but is gratified because it lays bare still further the structure of her marriage and indicates what could be done about it.

16. AUGUST 17

(Terminal Interview)

The patient announces that this is her last session. She no longer fears that her husband will think she is dirty or vulgar if she acts lusty. She never asked him if he thought so but just assumed that he did. During the week, she approached him differently and he responded with gratified surprise. For the last few days he has come home whistling for the first time in years.

She also realizes something else. She has always felt sorry for herself and tried to elicit sympathy and admiration because she is a recovered alcoholic. She recognizes this now as a game of "Wooden Leg." She feels ready at this point to try it on her own. She also feels different about her father. Maybe she contributed even more than she thought to the seduction. The remark about her skirts being too short shocked her but helped her. "I would never admit I wanted sex. I always thought I wanted 'attention.' Now I can admit I want sex." During the week she visited her father who was ill in another city in a hospital. She was able to observe her visit with considerable objectivity. Now she feels that she has divorced him and doesn't want him any more. That is why she was able to proceed sexually with her husband. She feels the transfer was accomplished through the intermediary of the therapist, who took her father's place for a while at first; but now she doesn't need him any more. She can talk freely to her husband about sexual repression causing her symptoms, and about her sexual feelings for him. He said he agreed with her and reciprocated her feelings. After she thought all this out, following the last visit, she had a dream that night in which there was a beautiful, feminine, peaceful woman, and it made her feel really good inside. The children are different too; they are happy, relaxed, and helpful.

Her blood pressure is down and her itching is gone. The therapist thought the improvement might be due to the medicine. She replied: "No, I don' think so, I would know the difference, I've taken it before. The medicine makes me feel tired

and nervous when it's taking hold, but this is an entirely new feeling."

She reports that she is drawing instead of finger-painting, doing what she wants; she feels this isn't wrong, it's like learning to live. "I don't feel sorry for people any more, I feel they ought to be able to do this too if they went about it right. I no longer feel I'm below everyone although that feeling isn't completely gone. I don't want to come to the group any more, I'd rather spend the time with my husband. It's like we're starting to go with each other again when he comes home whistling, it's wonderful. I'll try it for three months and if I feel bad I'll call you. I don't feel so 'neurotic,' either: I mean having psychosomatic symptoms and guilt feelings and my fear of talking about sex, and like that. It's a miracle, is all I can say. I can't explain my feeling of being happy, but I feel we [you and I] worked together on it. There's more closeness and harmony with my husband and he's even taking over the children like he's becoming the man of the house. I even feel a little guilty about AA because I used them in my game of 'Wooden Leg'."

She was asked directly whether structural analysis helped and whether game analysis helped, and in each case replied: "Oh, yes!" She added: "Also the script. For example, I said my husband had no sense of humor and you said 'Wait a minute, you don't know him and he doesn't know you because you've been playing games and acting out your scripts, you don't know what either of you is really like.' You were right because now I've discovered that he really has a sense of humor and that not having it was part of the game. I'm interested in my home and I'm grateful for that. I can write poetry again and express my love for my husband. I used to keep it in." At this point the hour was drawing to a close. The therapist asked: "Would you like a cup of coffee?" She replied: "No thanks,

I've just had some. I've told you now how I feel, that's it, that's all, it's been a great pleasure to come here and I enjoyed it."

GENERAL DISCUSSION: There is no need to regard this gratifying improvement with either skepticism, alarm, or pursed lips, in spite of the apparent raggedness of the above extracts. The patient herself has already answered many of the questions which might occur to an experienced reader.

For example, she herself perceived the substitution of the therapist for her father and the subsequent substitution of her husband for the therapist, so that this cannot be labeled a classical blind cure. The most impressive items are the changed attitudes of her children and, particularly, of her husband. Such indirect criteria are usually more convincing than the opinions of either the therapist or the patient. There is evidence that the original therapeutic aim has been systematically accomplished. She has given up playing many of her games and has replaced them with more satisfying direct relationships and intimacies. Her dress and behavior are more modest, and at the same time she looks more sexually attractive and sexually satisfied. A concise interpretation of what happened at the archaic level can be offered. She came to the therapist with a provisional fantasy of being dominated and hypnotized, as had happened with her other male therapists. She had slowly to give up this fantasy as she was confronted with her games, and the remark about her seductive posture made it clear to her that he was not going to be seduced. With her strengthened Adult she was then able to make the decision to relinquish her child-like ambitions and go about her grown-up business.

Although in some current thinking the course of this case may not indicate that the improvement is stable, it requires only one assumption to take a more optimistic view, and that assumption is borne out

by experience; namely, that playing games and playing through one's script are optional, and that a strong Adult can renounce these in favor of gratifying reality experiences. This is the actionistic aspect of transactional analysis.

A few days short of the three-month trial period she had suggested, the patient wrote the therapist as follows: "I feel fine. I don't have to take any pills and have been off those blood pressure pills for a month now. Last week we celebrated my thirty-fifth birthday. My husband and myself went away without the children. The water was beautiful, and the trees. Gosh, if only I could paint them. We saw a huge porpoise, the first time I have ever seen one, and it was beautiful to watch, so graceful in movements. . . . My husband and I are getting along so nicely. Night and day such a difference. We have become closer, more attentive, and I can be me. That's what seemed to stump me most of the time. I always had to be polite, etc. He still comes whistling up the stairs. That does more good for me than anything. I am so glad you suggested drawing. You have no idea what that alone has done for me. I am getting better and I might try paints soon. The children think they are very good and have suggested that I exhibit some of them. Next month I am going to take swimming lessons, no fooling, something I would never have been able to do. As the time gets closer I am a little afraid but I have made up my mind I am going to learn. If I can learn to put my head under water, that alone will be a great thrill for me. My garden looks so nice. That's another thing you helped me with. By golly, I go out there at least twice a week now for several hours and no one objects. You know I think they like me better this way.

"I didn't intend to ramble on this way but it seemed I had so much to tell you. I'll write and let you know how my swimming progresses. Love from all of us in Salinas."

This letter reassured the therapist of two things:

1. That the patient's improvement persisted even after the medication for her blood pressure was discontinued.

2. That the improvement in the patient's husband and children persisted even after psychotherapy was discontinued.

It should be added that the husband now washes his hair. The most pessimistic thing which can be said about this case so far is that it represents a flight into a healthy family life. The only clinical demand that can legitimately be placed on transactional analysis is that it should produce results which are as good as or better than those produced by any other psychotherapeutic approach, for a given investment of time and effort. In the case of Mrs. Enatosky, there were 16 individual interviews and 12 group sessions.[1]

[1] The improvement was still maintained on a one-year follow-up.

In this connection, and for purposes of comparison, the words of a thoughtful psychoanalyst of wide experienece should be borne in mind: "What we conquer are only parts of psychogenesis: expressions of conflict, developmental failures. We do not eliminate the original source of neurosis; we only help to achieve better ability to change neurotic frustrations into valid compensations. The dependence of psychic harmony on certain conditions makes immunity unattainable. Freud's 'Analysis Terminable and Interminable' brought for those of us who nourished unlimited therapeutic ambitions both disappointment and relief."[2]

[2] Deutsch, H. "Psychoanalytic Therapy in the Light of Follow-up." *J. Amer. Psychoanal. Assoc.* VII: 445–458, 1959.

Chapter 14
Rational
Therapy

The case demonstrating the techniques of rational psychotherapy once again deals with a difficult individual. Psychopaths are especially noted for their resistance to change in therapy. Dr. Albert Ellis believes that rational therapy is especially suited for the psychopathic personality as he states in his addendum to this case.

Ellis initiates therapy by allying himself with the patient. Once Jim, the patient, has begun to feel safe in the relationship with the therapist, Ellis starts the key work of convincing him that he is not helping himself with his behavior and in fact he is really being self-defeating in his antisocial acts. The therapist then begins to turn Jim's attention to the idea of change for his own sake. They then both concentrate on the self-sabotaging beliefs and internalized sentences, working together until Jim can finally question and analyze the beliefs himself. As these thoughts slowly change Jim's feelings, his actions also begin to change. In the follow-up Dr. Ellis indicates that he visualizes a relatively stable life for this young man.

The Treatment of a Psychopath with Rational Psychotherapy

ALBERT ELLIS

So-called psychopaths, or individuals suffering with a severe character disorder whose behavior is distinctly antisocial, are exceptionally difficult to treat with psychotherapy. They only rarely come for treatment on a voluntary basis; and when they are treated involuntarily, they tend to be resistant, surly, and in search of a "cure" that will involve no real effort on their part. Even when they come for private treatment, they are usually looking for magical, effortless "cures," and they tend to stay in treatment only for a short period of time and to make relatively little improvement.

Psychoanalytic techniques of approaching psychopaths are particularly ineffective for several reasons: These individuals are frequently non-introspective and non-verbal; they tend to be not overly-bright or well-educated; they are impatient of long-winded procedures; and they are highly sceptical or afraid of involved psychological analysis or interpretation. It is therefore only the exceptional psychopath who can be helped with analytic methods such as those employed by Lindner (1944) in his *Rebel Without a Cause.* Considerably modified techniques of interpretation, such as advocated by Cleckley (1950) and Schmideberg (1956) are often recommended instead.

Before attempting to treat any young delinquents or older criminals in my present private practice of psychotherapy, I had considerable experience in examining and treating them when I was Chief Psychologist at the New Jersey State Diag-

From *Journal of Psychology,* 1961, *51,* 141–150, and Chapter 16 of *Reason and emotion in psychotherapy.* New York: Lyle Stuart, Inc., 1962. Copyright 1961 by The Journal Press.

nostic Center and later Chief Psychologist of the New Jersey Department of Institutions and Agencies. At that time I became impressed with the fact that whether the offender was a thief, a sex deviate, a dope addict, or a murderer, about the very worst way to try to help him rehabilitate himself was to give him a moral lecture, appeal to his superego, or in any way blame him for his misdeeds. For I began to see at that time that, in their own peculiar ways, virtually all these offenders really were anxious and guilty underneath their façade of psychopathic bravado; and that, in fact, their criminal acts were frequently committed as a defensive attempt to protect them against their own feelings of low self-esteem. In other words, many of them were already being compulsively driven to psychopathic behavior by underlying guilt and anxiety; and to endeavor to make them more guilty and anxious, as is often at first attempted in psychoanalytic technique, would hardly help them lose their need for their compulsive defenses.

Instead, I found that if I temporarily showed the offender that I was *not* critical of his behavior, and if I at first allied myself with him (if necessary) against the authorities of the institution in which he was incarcerated (and whom he almost invariably saw as being persecutory), a notable degree of rapport could be established between us. Then, once the prisoner felt that I was really on his side, it was often possible to show him that his pattern of criminal behavior was not merely immoral and antisocial (which he of course knew without my telling him so) but that, more importantly, it was *self-defeating.* If I could convince him, which

I often could, that however much society might be (from his standpoint, justifiably and revengefully) harmed by his crimes, he *himself* was invariably even more self-sabotaged by these acts and their usual consequences, then I had a fairly good chance of getting him to change his behavior in the future.

My many investigatory and therapeutic relationships with criminals taught me, then, that so-called hardened psychopaths, like other disturbed human beings, act in an irrational and self-defeating manner because they believe, quite falsely, that they are helping themselves thereby; and when they are calmly, unblamefully, and yet vigorously disabused of this belief, they are often capable of radically changing their philosophic orientation and their antisocial behavior which springs from that orientation. Because many or most of the classic psychopaths are, as Cleckley points out, basically psychotic, they are often most difficult to treat; and one must usually be contented with reasonably limited gains. Nonetheless, remarkable improvements in their general living patterns, and particularly in the reduction of their antisocial behavior, may result from proper treatment.

Partly as a result of my experience in treating youthful and older offenders, as well as considerable experience in working with run-of-the-mill neurotics and psychotics, I have in recent years developed a technique of psychotherapy, called rational therapy, which is particularly applicable to the treatment of severely neurotic and borderline psychotic individuals with whom psychoanalytic and other treatment methods have had poor success. Rational therapy, as I have explained in several previous publications (Ellis, 1957a, 1957b; 1958a, 1958b, 1958c), is based on the assumption that human beings normally become emotionally disturbed through acquiring irrational and illogical thoughts, philosophies, or attitudes. Emotion itself is conceived of as largely being a certain kind—a biased, prejudiced kind —of thought; and it is held that people can be taught to change their negative and disturbed feelings by changing the thoughts that invariably underlie these feelings.

The rational therapist believes, in other words, that patients (and other people) literally talk themselves into their neurotic or psychotic states by telling themselves illogical and irrational sentences, or ideas, which they have previously learned from their parents and their culture, and have internalized and keep ceaselessly—and senselessly—repeating. The main emphasis of the therapist who employs rational technique is on analyzing the patient's current problems—especially his feelings of anger, depression, anxiety, and guilt—and concretely showing him that these emotions arise not from past events or external situations but from his present irrational attitudes toward or illogical fears about these events and situations.

Thus, the patient is shown that he has one or more basic philosophic assumptions underlying his behavior and that if this behavior is self-defeating these assumptions must necessarily be ill-grounded. The main illogical assumptions which most patients have at the base of their disturbances include the following: (*a*) that it is a dire necessity for an adult human being to be approved or loved by almost everyone for almost everything he does; (*b*) that an individual should or must be perfectly competent, adequate, talented, and intelligent in all possible respects and is utterly worthless if he is incompetent in any way; (*c*) that one should severely blame oneself and others for mistakes and wrongdoings; (*d*) that it is terrible, horrible, and catastrophic when things are not the way one would like them to be; and (*e*) that most human unhappiness is externally caused or forced on one by outside people and events and that one has virtually no control over one's emotions and cannot help feeling badly on many occasions. These misleading assumptions are continually revealed and attacked by the rational therapist.

Where, in psychoanalytic techniques, considerable time is spent on showing the patient how he originally *became* disturbed, in rational analysis much more emphasis is placed on how he is *sustaining* his disturbance by *still* believing the nonsense, or illogical ideas, which first led him to feel and act in an aberrated fashion. Rational therapy differs from psychoanalytic procedures in that (*a*) not merely the facts and psychodynamics of the client's behavior are revealed but, more to the point, his underlying philosophies or ideas which lead to and flow from these historical facts; (*b*) a concerted *attack* is made on the irrational beliefs that are disclosed in the course of the therapeutic process; (*c*) emphasis is placed far less on the disclosure of the individual's unconscious drives or feelings than on revealing his unconscious and irrational *attitudes* which underlie these drives or feelings; (*d*) the therapist literally *teaches* the patient how to observe his (unconscious) illogical thinking and how, instead, to think straight; and (*e*) the patient is usually encouraged, urged, or commanded into emotionally reeducating *activity*.

A case involving the rational therapeutic treatment of a psychopath will now be described. The patient was a 25-year-old son of a well-to-do family and had been engaging in antisocial behavior, including lying, stealing, sexual irresponsibility, and physical assaults on others since the age of 14. He had been in trouble with the law on five different occasions, but had only been convicted once and spent one year in a reformatory. He displayed no guilt about his offenses and seemed not at all concerned about the fact that he had once helped cripple an old man whose candy store he and his youthful comrades had held up. He had

two illegitimate children by different girls, but made no effort to see them or contribute to their financial support. He came for psychotherapy only at the insistence of his lawyer, who told him that his one chance of being put on probation, instead of being sent to prison, for his latest offense (rifling several vending machines) was for him to plead emotional disturbance and convince the court that he was really trying to do something to help himself in regard to this disturbance.

For the first few sessions the patient was only moderately cooperative, kept postponing appointments without good cause, and came 10 or 15 minutes late to almost every interview. He would listen fairly attentively and take an active part in the sessions; but as soon as he left the therapist's office he would, in his own words, "forget almost everything we said," and come in for the next session without giving any thought to his problems or their possible alleviation. It was not that he resentfully was resisting therapy; but he quite frankly was doing little or nothing to "get with it."

During the first several sessions, little attempt was made by the therapist to get the full details of the patient's history. It was merely determined that he was the only son of a doting mother, who had always given him his way, and of a merchant father who had ostensibly been friendly and permissive, but who actually had held up to him almost impossibly high standards of achievement and who was severely disappointed whenever he fell below these standards. The patient—whom we shall call Jim—had been a spoiled brat with other children, over whom he was always trying to lord it; had never lived up to his potentialities in school; had started to gain attention from his peers and his teachers at an early age by nasty, show-off behavior; and had only been able to get along reasonably well with girls, one or more of whom he usually managed to have serve him while he sadistically exploited her masochistic tendencies.

Although the patient was quite intelligent, and could easily understand psycodynamic explanations of his behavior—such as the possible connection between his failing to satisfy his father's high standards of excellence and his trying to prove to others, by quite opposite antisocial actions, how "great" he was—no attempt to interpret or clarify such connections was made. For one thing, he stoutly opposed such "psychoanalytic crap" whenever the psychodynamics of his situation were even hinted at; for another thing, the rational therapist frequently makes relatively little use of this kind of historical clarification, since he deems it highly interesting but not necessarily conducive of basic personality change.

Instead, the patient's current circumstances were first focused upon, and he was quickly and intensively shown that he kept defeating himself in the present—as well as in the past. Thus, he kept discussing with the therapist the possibility of his violating the terms of his bail and "skipping out of town." The therapist, without being in the least moralistic about this notion or taking any offense at the implied concept that therapy was not going to help the patient and that therefore he might as well go on living the kind of life he had always lived, calmly and ruthlessly showed Jim that (a) he had very little likelihood of being able to skip town without being caught in short order; (b) he would only lead a life of desperate evasion during the time he would remain free; and (c) he would most certainly know no mercy from the court if and when he was recaptured. Although, at first, the patient was most loathe to accept these grim facts, the therapist patiently persisted in forcing him to do so.

At the same time, the therapist kept showing Jim the silly and totally unrealistic philosophies behind his self-defeating notions of trying to skip bail. He was shown that he was grandiosely and idiotically telling himself that he *should* be able to do what he wanted just because he wanted to do so; that it was totally unfair and unethical for others, including the law, to stand in his way; and that it was utterly catastrophic when he was frustrated in his one-sided demands. And these assumptions, the therapist kept insisting, were thoroughly groundless and irrational.

"But why," asked Jim at one point in the fourth session, "shouldn't I want things to go my way? Why *shouldn't* I try to get what I want?"

THERAPIST: No reason at all. To want what you want when you want it is perfectly legitimate. But you, unfortunately, are doing one additional thing—and that's perfectly illegitimate.

PATIENT: What's that? what's the illegitimate thing?

THERAPIST: You're not only *wanting* what you want, but *demanding* it. You're taking a perfectly sane desire —to be able to avoid standing trial for your crimes, in this instance—and asininely turning it into an absolute *necessity*.

PATIENT: Why is that so crazy?

THERAPIST: For the simple reason that, first of all, *any* demand or necessity is crazy. Wanting a thing, wanting any damned thing you happen to crave, is fine—as long as you admit the possibility of your not being able to get it. But as soon as you demand something, turn it into a necessity, you simply won't be able to *stand* your not getting it. In that event, either you'll do something desperate to get it—as you usually have done in your long history of antisocial behavior—or else you'll keep making yourself angry, exceptionally frustrated, or anxious about not getting it. Either way, *you* lose.

PATIENT: But suppose I *can* get what I want?

THERAPIST: Fine—as long as you don't subsequently defeat your own ends by getting it. As in this case. Even assuming that you could skip bail successfully—which is very doubtful, except for a short while—would you *eventually* gain by having to live in terror of arrest for the remainder of your life or by having to give up everything and everyone you love here to run, let us say, to South America?

PATIENT: Perhaps not.

THERAPIST: Perhaps? Besides, let's assume, for a moment, that you really could get away with it—you really could skip bail and that you wouldn't get caught and wouldn't live in perpetual fear. Even then, would you be doing yourself such a great favor?

PATIENT: It seems to me I would! What more could I ask?

THERAPIST: A lot more. And it is just your *not* asking for a lot more that proves, to me at least, that you are a pretty sick guy.

PATIENT: In what way? What kind of crap are you giving me? Bullshit!

THERAPIST: Well, I could get highly "ethical" and say that if you get away with things like that, with rifling vending machines, jumping bail, and such things, that you are then helping to create the kind of a world that you yourself would not want to live in, or certainly wouldn't want your friends or relatives to live in. For if you can get away with such acts of course, others can too; and in such a pilfering, bail-jumping world, who would want to live?

PATIENT: But suppose I said that I didn't mind living in that kind of world—kind of liked it, in fact?

THERAPIST: Right. You might very well say that. And even mean it—though I wonder whether, if you really gave the matter careful thought, you would. But let us suppose you would. So I won't use that "ethical" argument

with a presumably "unethical" and guiltless person like you. But there is still another, and better argument, and one that you and people like you, generally overlook.

PATIENT: And that is?

THERAPIST: That is—your own skin.

PATIENT: My own skin?

THERAPIST: Yes, your own thick and impenetrable skin. Your guiltless, ever so guiltless skin.

PATIENT: I don't get it. What the hell are you talking about?

THERAPIST: Simply this. Suppose, as we have been saying, you are truly guiltless. Suppose you, like Lucky Luciano and a few other guys who really seem to have got away scot-free with a life of crime, really do have a thick skin, and don't give a good goddamn what happens to others who may suffer from your deeds, don't care what kind of a world you are helping to create. How, may I ask, can you—you personally, that is—manufacture and maintain that lovely, rugged, impenetrable skin?

PATIENT: What difference does it make how I got it, as long as it's there?

THERAPIST: Ah, but it does!—it does make a difference.

PATIENT: How the hell does it?

THERAPIST: Simply like this. The only practical way that you can get guiltless, can maintain an impenetrable skin under conditions such as we are describing, where you keep getting away with doing in others and reaping criminal rewards, is by hostility—by resenting, hating, loathing the world against which you are criminally behaving.

PATIENT: Can't I get away with these things without hating others? Why can't I?

THERAPIST: Not very likely. For why would a person do in others without hating them in some manner? And how could he not be at least *somewhat* concerned about the kind of dog-eat-dog social order he was creating unless he downed his potential concern with defensive resentment against others?

PATIENT: I don't know——. Why couldn't he?

THERAPIST: Have *you*?

PATIENT: Have I, you mean, managed not to——?

THERAPIST: Exactly! With your long history of lying to others. Leading them on to do all kinds of things they didn't want to do, really, by your misleading them as to your feelings for them. The girls you got pregnant and deserted, for instance. The partners in crime you double-crossed. The parents whose help you've always run back for after breaking promise after promise to them? Would you call that *love* you felt for these people? Affection? Kindliness?

PATIENT: Well—uh—no, not exactly.

THERAPIST: And the hostility, the resentment, the bitterness you felt for these people—and must keep perpetually feeling, mind you, as you keep "getting away" with crime after crime —did these emotions make you feel good, feel happy?

PATIENT: Well—at times, I must admit, they did.

THERAPIST: Yes, at times. But really, deep down, in your inmost heart, *does* it make you feel good, happy, buoyant, joyous to do people in, to hate them, to think that they are no damned good, to plot and scheme against them?

PATIENT: No, I guess not. Not always.

THERAPIST: Even most of the time?

PATIENT: No—uh—no. Very rarely, I must admit.

THERAPIST: Well, there's your answer.

PATIENT: You mean to the thick skin business? You mean that I thicken my skin by hating others—and only really hurt myself in the process.

THERAPIST: Isn't that the way it is? *really* is? Isn't your thick skin—like the lamps made of human skin by the Nazis, incidentally—built of, nourished on little but your own corrosive hatred for others? And doesn't that hatred mainly, in the long run, corrode you?

PATIENT: Hm. I——. You've given me something to think about there.

THERAPIST: By all means think about it. Give it some real, hard thought.

In a similar manner, the therapist, in session after session with this intelligent psychopath, kept directly bringing up, ruthlessly examining, and forthrightly attacking some of his basic philosophies of living, and showing him that these philosophies underlay his antisocial thoughts and behavior. No criticism of or attack on the patient *himself* was made; but merely on his ideas, his thoughts, his assumptions which (consciously and unconsciously) served as the foundation stones for his disordered feelings and actions.

After 22 sessions of this type of rational therapy, the patient finally was able to admit that for quite a long time he had vaguely sensed the self-defeatism and wrongness of his criminal behavior, but that he had been unable to make any concerted attack on it largely because he was afraid that he *couldn't* change it—that (*a*) he had no ability to control his antisocial tendencies; and (*b*) he felt that he would not be able to get along satisfactorily in life if he attempted to live more honestly. The therapist then started to make a frontal assault on the philosophies behind these defeatist feelings of the patient. He showed Jim that an individual's inability to control his behavior mainly stems from the *idea* that he cannot do so—that long-standing feelings are innate and unmanageable and that one simply *has* to be ruled by them. Instead, the therapist insisted, human feelings *are* invariably controllable—if one seeks out the self-propagandizing sentences (e.g., "I must do this," "I have no power to stop myself from doing this," etc.) which one unconsciously uses to create and maintain these "feelings."

Jim's severe feelings of inadequacy—his original feelings that he never could gain the attention of others unless he was a problem child and his later feelings that he could not compete in a civilized economy unless he resorted to lying or thieving behavior—were also traced to the self-propagated beliefs behind them (to the sentences, "I am utterly worthless unless I am always the center of attention, even though I gain this attention by unsocial behavior"; "If I competed with others in an honest manner, I would fall on my face, and that would be utterly disgraceful and unforgiveable"; etc.). These self-sabotaging beliefs, and the internalized sentences continually maintaining them, were then not merely traced to their source (in Jim's early relations with his parents, teachers, and peers) but were logically analyzed, questioned, challenged, and counter-attacked by the therapist, until Jim learned to do a similar kind of self-analyzing, questioning, and challenging for himself.

After 31 sessions (mainly on a once-a-week basis) of this type of highly active rational psychotherapy, Jim (who by that time had been placed on probation) voluntarily gave up the fairly easy, well-paying, and unchallenging job which his family, because of their financial standing, had been able to secure for him, and decided to return to college to study to be an accountant. "All my life," he said during the closing session of therapy, "I have tried to avoid doing things the hard way—for fear, of course, of failing and thereby 'proving' to myself and others that I was no damned good. No more of that crap any more! I'm going to make a darned good try at the hard way, from now on; and if I fail, I fail. Better I fail that way than 'succeed' the stupid way

I was 'succeeding' before. Not that I think I *will* fail now. But in case I do—so what?"

Jim is now (two years later) finishing up college and doing quite well at his school work. There is every reason to believe that he will continue to do so at his chosen field of endeavor. A self-defeating psychopath has finally turned into a forward-looking citizen. In this case, the patient's high intelligence and good family background unquestionably contributed to making him a more suitable prospect for psychotherapy than the average psychopath would usually be. The same technique of rational psychotherapy, however, has recently been used with several other individuals with severe character disorders and symptoms of acute antisocial behavior and it appears to work far better than the classical psychoanalytic and psychoanalytically oriented methods which I formerly employed with these same kind of patients. While rational therapy is no quick panacea for all human ills, it can be a remarkably effective technique when adequately and forcefully used with a wide variety of severely and moderately disturbed patients.

SUMMARY

A summary is given of the main aspects of the technique of rational psychotherapy; and a case illustration is presented showing how this technique has been applied to a 25-year-old male with a long history of psychopathic behavior. It is held that individuals with severe character disorders, including symptoms of extreme antisocial behavior, can often be successfully treated if the therapist is not moralistic but he directly and actively institutes a rational-persuasive attack on the basic illogical beliefs and unrealistic ideologies which invariably underlie psychopathy.

REFERENCES

Cleckley, H. The Mask of Sanity. St. Louis: Mosby, 1950.

Ellis, A. Rational psychotherapy and individual psychology. *J. Individ. Psychol.*, 1957, 13, 38–44. (a)

————. Outcome of employing three techniques of psychotherapy. *J. Clin. Psychol.*, 1957, 13, 344–350. (b)

————. Neurotic interaction between marital partners. *J. Counsel. Psychol.*, 1958, 5, 24–28. (a)

————. Rational psychotherapy. *J. Gen. Psychol.*, 1958, 59, 35–49. (b)

————. Hypnotherapy with borderline schizophrenics. *J. Gen. Psychol.*, 1958, 59, 245–253. (c)

Lindner, R. Rebel Without a Cause. New York: Grune & Stratton, 1944.

ADDENDUM[1]   Albert Ellis

Since this article was first published in 1961, rational psychotherapy has been developed into a more comprehensive system of therapy that stresses a good many emotive-evocative and behavioral techniques. It is consequently often referred to as rational-emotive or rational behavior therapy and is perhaps the most widely practiced form of cognitive-behavior therapy. RET is employed in many correctional setups and is often the therapy of choice of probation officers, who are able to use it because of its directness, simplicity, and relative brevity. Case histories and verbatim transcripts of cases where RET has been used successfully with so-called psychopaths, sex offenders, alcoholics, and psychotics have been published in many books and articles, especially in some of my own books (1962, 1965, 1971, 1973).

As I pointed out (1962), RET hardly works wonders with all psychopaths or sociopaths. It (or any other type of psychotherapy) does not. Even moderately neurotic individuals can be and usually are difficult to reorient in their disordered thinking and emoting, since almost all humans find it easy to behave idiotically about themselves and in regard to others. Psychopaths and psychotics (who, to my way of thinking, significantly overlap) find it still more difficult to change their own self-defeating ways. Even when they are not organically predisposed to act aberrantly (which many of them probably are), their disordered and delusive thinking is so deeply ingrained that only with the greatest effort on their and their therapists' part are effective inroads against their slippery thinking likely to be made.

To make matters even worse, most individuals with persistent psychopathic behavior tend to be "goofers": that is, consistent offenders against society's moral codes who *want* to get away with "murder" and who do not *wish* to work very hard at almost anything, including their own characterological functioning. They consequently will rarely *do* much to understand and reconstruct their cognitive-behavioral processes. Though they can sometimes, as shown in my article, be reached on a hard-headed, practical level, they infrequently will think their way through to an elegant therapeutic solution. This means that they will resist giving up their basic grandiosity and (the other side of the same egoistic coin) their pervasive underlying shithood. The rational-emotive concept that humans do not have to rate their *selves*, their *essences*, their *beings* at all but had better merely rate

[1] Prepared by the author for inclusion in this volume.

their *acts, deeds,* and *performances,* is a rough one for them to understand, and they rarely comprehend it fully.

Therefore, the therapist who treats individuals with psychopathic behavior should preferably be unusually persistent and unblaming and also be able to maintain vigorously a challenging, circuit-breaking attitude, so that by his determination to tackle the slipshod cognitions of his antisocial clients he makes up for their tendency to goof and shirk. Left to their own devices, psychopathic individuals can brilliantly avoid facing basic issues and evade accepting a long-range view of life. If the therapist stubbornly refuses to let them get away with this kind of cognitive shoddiness, but at the same time refrains from scorning them for being addicted to it, he has some chance—not, to be honest, a very good, but still a fair chance—to interrupt and help break up the rigid rationalizing patterns that sociopaths keep inventing and sustaining.

Directness, forcefulness, and freedom from absolutistic moralizing are among the most effective methods in the armamentarium of the therapist who would assail the citadels of psychopathy. These attitudes are heavily emphasized in rational-emotive therapy; and that is probably why this comprehensive technique is one of the most effective means of treating individuals with severe character disorders.

REFERENCES

Ellis, Albert. *Reason and emotion in psychotherapy.* New York: Lyle Stuart, Inc., 1962.

————. *Homosexuality.* New York: Lyle Stuart, Inc., 1965.

————. *Growth through reason.* Palo Alto, Ca.: Science and Behavior Books, 1971.

————. *Humanistic psychotherapy: The rational-emotive approach.* New York: Julian Press, Inc., 1973.

Section Three

BEHAVIOR THERAPY

Chapter 15

An Introduction to Behavior Therapy

STEPHEN J. MORSE and ROBERT I. WATSON, JR.

Behavior therapies were developed from the discoveries made in experimental psychology and physiology laboratories. Unlike the dynamic and humanistic therapies, which evolved from the clinical efforts of therapists seeking to help clients, behavior therapies evolved from basic, nonclinical research often done on infrahuman species. Behavior therapies rely largely upon experimentally derived principles of psychology, especially learning principles, to help change maladaptive behavior. Although we have defined the psychotherapeutic process in all therapies as a learning process, the behavior therapists primarily have attempted to base techniques on systematic experimental studies of the psychology of learning. In fact, behavior therapists would claim that psychotherapeutic change occurs in the dynamic and humanistic therapies because of unrecognized and unsystematic applications of the same learning principles applied in behavior therapy.[1]

The fundamental tenet of behavior therapy is that behavior disorders are learned behaviors that are maladaptive in the life of the individual; they are not caused by unconscious conflict, lack of insight, lack of positive regard, or any other such concept. In other words, a maladaptive behavior (e.g., a symptom) is itself the disorder, and it is not a manifestation of a more basic, underlying disturbance.[2] All behavior is lawful, and unadaptive behavior is learned and unlearned according to the same principles as adaptive behav-

[1] The terms *behavior therapy* and *behavior modification* are often equated in scientific and popular literature. More precisely, behavior therapy is usually associated with non-operant methods, whereas behavior modification is associated with operant methods (Rimm & Masters, 1974). In this section we shall use the terms interchangeably to refer to the total range of methods based on experimentally derived psychological principles, especially the principles of learning.

ior. Thus behavior therapists attempt to help the client unlearn unadaptive behaviors and, more often than not, to replace them with newly learned and more adaptive behaviors. Choice, rational understanding, insight, and so on are not seen as ameliorative except as they actually function according to usual learning principles.

HISTORICAL OVERVIEW

Human beings have been concerned with behavior and behavior change since Homo sapiens appeared on earth. The earliest persons must have recognized that rewarding an action was likely to cause it to occur again, and that punishing an action was likely to cause it not to occur again. Understanding of the principles of learning, however, was a matter of conventional wisdom and quite unsystematic until the latter part of the nineteenth century.

In the latter part of the nineteenth century and the early decades of the twentieth century, concomitant with the growth of scientific psychology, there was an increasing dissatisfaction with "mentalistic" psychologies such as introspectionism and an increasing emphasis on both physiology and overt behavior. Scientists such as Ivan Pavlov, E. L. Thorndike, John B. Watson, Edward Tolman, George Guthrie, Clark Hull, and B. F. Skinner began to do systematic experiments to elucidate the laws of learning. Because the focus was on the organism as an overtly responding biological animal, and because mental states were considered largely irrelevant, it was considered justifiable to carry out the experiments on easily manipulable lower-order species.

The history of behavior therapy and its relation to behavioral psychology in the United States begin, in large measure, with John B. Watson (1879–1958), the "father" of the behaviorist movement, who coined the term *behaviorism*.[3] While performing certain animal experiments as a doctoral student at the University of Chicago, Watson noted that some data could be verified reliably by other psychologists (e.g., overt acts), whereas other data could not be so verified (e.g., the supposed mental state of the animal). Watson theorized that introspection was a faulty method per se, and he urged that scientific psychological research be limited to observing overt acts. Because he focused on observable behavior, he called himself a "behaviorist." Watson wrote, "The rule or measuring rod which the behaviorist puts in front of him always is: Can I describe this bit of behavior in terms of 'stimulus and response'? (1924, 6)." Confining himself to overt acts, Watson was most instrumental in abolishing the distinction between

---

[2] Although most behaviorists do not deny that biological abnormalities may be implicated in the causation of some maladaptive behavior, until biological etiology is demonstrated, behavior therapists prefer to conceptualize maladaptive behavior psychologically.

[3] This thumbnail historical sketch of John B. Watson is adapted from Rychlak (1973, 285–286).

different species for psychological theorizing. Finally, Watson was responsible for the following noteworthy evangelical statement.

> I should like to go one step further now and say, "Give me a dozen healthy infants, well-formed, and my own specified world to bring them up in and I'll guarantee to take anyone at random and train him to become any type of specialist I might select—doctor, lawyer, artist, merchant-chief and, yes, even beggar-man and thief, regardless of his talents, penchants, tendencies, abilities, vocations, and the race of his ancestors." (104)

Persons were seen as infinitely malleable if only they would learn the proper stimulus–response sequences. The psychotherapeutic ramifications of such a view are self-evident.

The period before World War II was marked by the flowering of behavioral psychology and the study of learning among American academic psychologists. At the same time, dynamic psychology, especially psychoanalysis, was gaining influence among American psychiatrists. Behavioral psychology became predominant in academic psychology, but it remained mostly restricted to the laboratory and had little influence on therapeutic practice. There had been reports in the literature of the therapeutic use of behavioral principles (e.g., Jones, 1924), and certainly principles of learning were recognized to have ramifications for therapy, but the growth of behavior therapy was quite limited until after World War II.

Despite the accumulating data in the laboratory there were many institutional reasons for the limitation of the premeditated use of behavioral principles in therapeutic settings. Mental disorders were predominantly conceptualized as diseases, and were seen as the province of medical specialists, especially psychiatrists. Psychiatrists rarely had training in the techniques or theories of behavioral psychology, and it is probably fair to surmise that they rarely read psychological journals. Because medical therapists had little acquaintance with scientific psychology, it is not difficult to understand why they did not experiment with behavior therapy techniques. Behavior psychologists believe that disordered behavior, although maladaptive, is learned like all other behavior. The disease concept of mental illness was therefore largely rejected by most behavior psychologists; this viewpoint probably further contributed to their exclusion from the treatment of mental disorder.

After World War II, however, there was an explosive increase in demand for mental health services. The clinical psychologist on a treatment team, formerly relegated to the role of diagnostic testing, was now given the opportunity to do psychotherapy. Although many clinical psychologists had a psychodynamic and disease approach to mental disorders that was similar to the approach of their medical colleagues, a number of factors probably contributed to the growth of behavior therapy. First, clinical psychologists had been trained as scientific psychologists, and thus the experimental method and the substance of learning theory were a fundamental part of their background. Second, it was clear that the dynamic and humanistic therapies were costly, time consuming, too often ineffective, and seemed to have little empirical scientific rationale behind them. Third, the discovery of effective physical treatment methods, especially chemotherapy, did not lead to the wholesale eradication of psychological disorders. Fourth, the unique contribution that the psychologist could make as a mental health professional was in the application of his or her laboratory-developed techniques to the problems of mental disorders. For all these reasons and others, psychologists turned increasingly to the psychological laboratory as a source for new psychotherapeutic techniques.

The first use of the term *behavior therapy* evidently is found in a mimeographed report of operant-conditioning research done with psychotic patients by B. F. Skinner and others in 1953 (Lazarus, 1971). Lazarus noted that he himself was the first person to use the terms *behavior therapy* and *behavior therapist* in a scientific journal article published in 1958 that sought to "point out the need for adding objective, laboratory-derived therapeutic tools to more orthodox psychotherapeutic techniques (1971, 2)." Also Joseph Wolpe (1958) published his epochal book *Psychotherapy by Reciprocal Inhibition*, which may fairly be said to be the most influential work espousing behavioral techniques (although he did not use the term *behavior therapy*) that had yet appeared. Following the work of these early pioneers and others such as H. J. Eysenck, interest in, research on, and publication about behavior therapy techniques has increased geometrically. Behavior therapy is now a leading therapeutic tool used by psychologists, especially younger psychologists, and it is used increasingly by psychiatrists (*cf.* Marks, 1976).

Because of their background in experimental learning psychology, early behavior therapists were determinedly antimentalistic. They felt that neither theory nor practice (allegedly) should properly focus on inferred, internal events such as thoughts and feelings. Only observable actions that could be reliably operationalized and measured were the proper focus of theory and practice. Furthermore, many early behaviorists hypothesized that behavior was totally determined by environmental stimuli. Current behavior therapists, however, increasingly rely on all relevant aspects of experimental psychology, not only on learning psychology (Franks & Wilson, 1975). They eschew mentalism but recognize the importance of cognition, feelings, and social interaction in the control of human behavior. As behavioral scientists, current therapists do insist that "mental" phenomena be capable of operationalization and reliable measurement. Finally, in addition to placing emphasis on changing and controlling behavior by changing and managing the environment, current practitioners are stressing the importance of self-control and self-direction in altering behavior (Thoreson & Mahoney, 1974).

An example may help clarify the shift. Suppose that a client's presenting problem is that he or she seems to drink too much. How many ounces of alcohol a person consumes in a given period is quite measurable. A strict antimentalist might then try to extinguish directly the drinking behavior by any number of possible techniques. A more sophisticated analysis, however, might demonstrate that the client's drinking behavior is causally related to his thoughts and feelings about his boss and his interaction with him.

Clearly, the therapist cannot change the boss. But she might attempt to change those aspects of the client's psychology that interfere with his ability to deal effectively with his boss. For instance, the client might be taught to be assertive with the boss, or he might be counterconditioned so that he would no longer be anxious in the presence of the boss, or he might even learn techniques for increasing his sense of self-esteem so that he would no longer feel so weak and helpless in the boss's presence. Although the techniques used for ameliorating the client's relationship with the boss may be based on learning principles, focussing on the relationship rather than on the drinking per se clearly reflects a more mentalistic and complex approach to problem drinking than strict learning principles would admit.

Today there is a wide disparity among those who consider themselves behavior therapists concerning theoretical and practical issues. There is disagreement about how behavioristic behavior therapy really is, or about how much consideration mental states would be given. Despite the disagreements, however, among all behavior therapists there is a commitment to a scientific approach to therapy that ideally includes a careful evaluation of operationalizable behavior and a choice of techniques based on experimentally tested principles.

We can best end this general overview by quoting a tentative definition of behavior therapy adopted by the Association for the Advancement of Behavior Therapy. Although this definition would not be accepted by all behavior therapists, it does represent an attempt to reflect the broad scope of present behavior therapy.

> *Behavior therapy involves primarily the application of principles derived from research in experimental and social psychology for the alleviation of human suffering and the enhancement of human functioning. Behavior therapy emphasizes a systematic evaluation of the effectiveness of these applications. Behavior therapy involves environmental change and social interaction rather than the direct alteration of bodily processes by biological procedures. The aim is primarily educational. The techniques facilitate improved self-control. In the conduct of behavior therapy, a contractual agreement is usually negotiated, in which mutually agreeable goals and procedures are specified. Responsible practitioners using behavioral approaches are guided by generally accepted ethical principles (Franks & Wilson, 1975, 1–2).*

Before we examine behavior therapy in detail, however, we shall first review its scientific background.

THE SCIENTIFIC BACKGROUND
OF BEHAVIOR THERAPY[4]

Classical Conditioning

The scientific background of behavior therapy[5] stems from the laboratory of the great Russian physiologist, Ivan P. Pavlov (1849–1936). After winning the Nobel Prize in 1904 for his discovery of the secretory nerves of the pancreas, Pavlov turned to the study of digestive functions which led to his discovery of the principles of *classical* or *respondent conditioning*, one of the two fundamental types of learning. Using dogs as experimental animals, Pavlov had originally set out to study the physiology of the secretion of digestive fluids in the mouth and stomach. He was interested in such questions as: what was the mechanism that linked ingestion of food to the secretion of digestive juices?

Classical conditioning was discovered through an artifact in his research: After the dogs became familiar with his procedures, they would secrete juices as soon as Pavlov walked into the room, well before food was presented to them. He called these secretions "psychic," believing that they resulted from the dogs' mental activity. Instead of dismissing this finding as a nuisance, however, Pavlov was sufficiently intrigued to study this phenomenon in its own right, and he noticed its similarity to physiological reflexes.[6] In classic terminology, Pavlov's arrival in the laboratory had become a conditioned stimulus, because it was paired with the unconditioned stimulus, the food, and it would now lead to the conditioned response, saliva secretion, before the presentation of food.

In a series of ingenious experiments, Pavlov demonstrated that natural behavioral responses could be conditioned to appear upon the occurrence of another stimulus not usually associated with the appearance of the response. The first element necessary, however, is a previously established reflex that consists of a stimulus and response, whereby the stimulus reliably elicits the response.

For instance, if food (*unconditioned stimulus*-US) is placed in a dog's mouth, the dog will salivate (*unconditioned response*-UR). This is an established reflex. However, if an arbitrary unnatural stimulus such as a bell (*conditioned stimulus*-CS) is presented to the dog either with or slightly before the food is given, after several such pairings the conditioned stimulus alone will produce the salivation. When the conditioned stimulus alone

---

[4] The reader wishing a full treatment of the history and theory of behavioral psychology is referred to Boring (1950) and Hilgard & Bower (4th ed., 1975).

[5] The following discussion of classical and instrumental conditioning is based upon Rachlin's excellent exposition (1970).

[6] It may be remembered that Freud was able to formulate the all-important concept of resistance and to discover its role in psychoanalytic therapy, because he was willing to study the occurrence of a patient breaking the fundamental rule of free association, rather than judging it or dismissing it as an inconvenience.

reliably produces the previously natural response, the response is now called a *conditioned response* (CR). This whole procedure of conditioning a response to a conditioned stimulus is known as *classical conditioning*.

Success in classical conditioning may be measured by two methods, the magnitude of the response (e.g., amount of saliva excreted) and/or by the size of the latency period, the time between the presentation of the conditioned stimulus and the appearance of the conditioned response (e.g., how soon salivation follows the sound of the bell). During conditioning, the magnitude of the response may approach, but never equals, the size of the UR—the established biological reflex. As conditioning proceeds successfully, the length of the latency period ought to decrease. Furthermore, classical conditioning is considered a biological process because the US, the agent that could produce the association (e.g., food), termed a *reinforcement*, is hypothesized to be reinforcing because it satisfies basic physiochemical needs.

Pavlov observed that after conditioning was achieved, if the presentation of the CS was not paired with presentation of the US, the magnitude of the response would decrease until eventually the response would not appear. This process is called *extinction*. Pavlov hypothesized that extinction did not simply eradicate conditioning, but that it seemed to inculcate a "force" counter to the conditioning, a force Pavlov termed an *inhibitory force*. Another principle of classical conditioning is that as new behaviors are learned, some *generalization* is certain to accompany the learning. This means that not only the CS will produce the CR; stimuli very similar to the CS will also produce the CR. As the stimulus becomes less similar to the CS, the magnitude of response decreases. Finally, organisms may learn to differentiate stimuli and learn not to respond to another stimulus as if it were the CS. This capacity is known as *discrimination*. It has been observed that the capacity to discriminate is limited, and if the organism is asked to make distinctions that are too fine, maladaptive behavior will usually result.

Pavlov, an M.D., and physiologist, attempted to explain classical conditioning neurophysiologically. His work is replete with neurophysiological speculation and theorizing. Although it is now recognized (Franks, 1969) that much of Pavlov's physiology was unsophisticated and incorrect, this should not detract from the weight of his psychological observations of learning. Other behavior theorists, notably Wolpe (1958), have also felt the need to theorize about the neurophysiological foundations of observed behavior. But again, even if neurophysiological "explanations" of the therapeutic process may be incorrect, this does not detract from the *observation* that the behavior in question has been changed through learning, and that the client now behaves more adaptively.

Instrumental Conditioning

The second fundamental type of learning that has been identified and studied by psychologists is known as *instrumental conditioning* or *instru-*

mental learning or *operant conditioning*. Although some psychologists would distinguish among the three, the similarities are far more important than the differences, and we shall treat them as one for our purposes. Instrumental conditioning occurs when a connection is established between a behavior and the reinforcement or punishment that *follows it*. Behavior is thus viewed as a function of the *consequences* of the behavior, and behavior change is a function of a change in the consequences.

The history of the study of instrumental conditioning properly begins with the American, E. L. Thorndike (1874–1949) and his discovery of the "law of effect." The law of effect holds that if a behavior is followed by rewarding consequences, then it becomes more probable that under similar circumstances the behavior will occur again. In Thorndike's experiments, hungry cats were confined in boxes with food in view outside the box. To escape and obtain the food, the cat had to learn to perform some mechanical operation. At some point in its behavior within the box, the animal would perform randomly the correct operation to permit escape, and thus would be able to obtain the food. If the animal was repeatedly put back in the box, it took a decreasing time under similar conditions of hunger for the animal to escape from the box. After many trials, the animal would have learned to escape almost immediately. The food, a reinforcement or *reward* because positively valued by the animal, is a rewarding consequence of the behavior or response (escape), and thus the response is more likely to occur in the same circumstances (hungry animal in box).

The original principle was expanded in later types of experiments. For instance, a pigeon may be placed in a box that contains a lever that may be pecked. Among its random movements, the pigeon may peck the lever, and a food pellet will then be immediately delivered to it. If food is delivered whenever the lever is pecked, soon the pigeon will begin to peck the lever far more frequently. At this point, it should be noted that instrumental conditioning can only work by *strengthening behaviors that already occur*. For more complex behaviors the conditioning process may be quite slow, because the organism is unlikely to emit at random and with any degree of frequency, the complex responses for which it can be rewarded. Thus, the method of "successive approximations" or "shaping" is used. The organism is rewarded when it behaves in any way approaching or similar to the final goal set by the experimenter. Thereby, the probability is increased that the desired behavior will itself finally be emitted so that it can be reinforced. Note well that behavior is conditioned by the enviromental consequences of behavior originally emitted by the organism.

According to Rachlin (1970), there are four basic principles of instrumental conditioning: reward, punishment, escape (negative reinforcement), and omission. A reward, or positive reinforcement, tends to increase the probability that the behavior it follows will recur because the reward is pleasant for the organism (Thorndike's "law of effect"). Punishment decreases the probability that the response will recur because the response is followed by painful or aversive stimuli. Negative reinforcement or escape increases the probability that the response will recur because the response is followed by the removal of, or escape from, an aversive stimulus. Omission decreases the probability that the response will recur because a reward, usually present in the environment, is absent after the response.

Although Thorndike pioneered the study of instrumental conditioning, and although some of Pavlov's students studied this form of conditioning as well as classical conditioning, it is B. F. Skinner (1904–   ) and his students who have made the greatest advances in the study of instrumental conditioning. He termed instrumental conditioning *operant conditioning*, because the responses that seem to have a common effect on the environment are called *operants*. Skinner was interested in the ways the animal "operates" on the environment to cause the environment to reinforce or punish the animal, and thus to increase or decrease the rate of the response. Skinner is an avowedly atheoretical psychologist who claims that he is interested only in the empirical relation between the rate of the response and the stimuli that follow the response. He is not concerned with why a particular stimulus is reinforcing or punishing—he answers this question purely operationally by noting whether the rate of a response is increased or decreased. Unlike Pavlov or Wolpe, he is not interested in neurophysiological variables or other variables internal to the organism. He is interested only in how environmental consequences shape the behavior of the organism.

One of Skinner's main contributions has been his elucidation of the *contingencies of reinforcement*. He and his students have studied the differential effects on learning produced by following responses (operants) with different types of stimuli (reinforcers) according to different *schedules of reinforcement*. Thus, the stimuli might follow the response every time or every "nth" time (fixed ratio schedule), or the stimuli might be presented at set intervals of time (fixed interval), or one could vary the presentation of the reinforcement from every "nth" to every "xth" and then back to every "nth" time the response is emitted (variable ratio schedule), and so on. Different schedules strengthen or weaken learning differentially. For instance, it is found that behavior reinforced according to a variable ratio is very hard to extinguish. These are not matters of theory for the Skinnerian; they are questions to be investigated empirically.

The relationship between classical and instrumental conditioning is complex, but we may make a few observations. In classical conditioning the reinforcement (US) is always presented by the experimenter, and its presentation is unrelated to the behavior of the subject. The precondition for classical conditioning is that the response should always follow the presentation of the US, and that the US and CS are paired in a trial. In instrumental conditioning, on the other hand, reinforcement is presented *only* if the desired behavior is *emitted* by the subject. Thus, the precondition for instrumental conditioning is the environmentally determined relationship between response and reinforcement. In sum, in classical conditioning the subject need not do anything to be reinforced, and the desired response is elicited by the stimulus. In instrumental conditioning, the subject must *do* something and only then, after the desired response is emitted, does the reinforcement follow. Extinction is similar in both types of conditioning; reinforcement is not presented to the subject and the rate of response decreases.

In terms of classifying behaviors to be measured, there are again differences. In classical conditioning the US is always presented and invariably evokes a similar response. In classical conditioning, then, responses are categorized together if they are elicited by a particular stimulus. In instrumental conditioning, we may measure any behavior emitted by the organism, not simply the responses to particular stimuli. It is only necessary that a behavior be capable of measurement, so that we may reward or punish the organism when it is emitted. Behaviors are categorized together if they have a common effect on the environment, and as noted, are then known as operants.

Observational Learning Theory

Although classical and operant conditioning are still the two major paradigms in learning theory, an increasingly influential group of behavioral psychologists believe that denying the relevance of cognition and feeling to learning is unrealistic. The leading theory that attempts systematically to integrate cognitive psychology with traditional learning principles is known as *observational learning theory* or *social learning theory*, a new paradigm being developed by American psychologists, especially Albert Bandura, Walter Mischel, and Julian Rotter. In their influential textbook, Hilgard and Bower (1975) claimed that "social learning theory provides the best integrative summary of what modern learning theory has to contribute to solutions of practical problems," and that "social learning theory would appear to be the 'consensus' theoretical framework within which much of learning research (especially that on humans) will evolve in the next decade (605)." Let us therefore turn to a brief examination of the background and principles of this newer and influential third paradigm of learning.

Traditional learning theories are theories of action; the subject learns, because he performs an action that has consequences for him. Social learning theory accepts traditional learning theory, but it also considers the common-sense observation that persons learn not only by doing, but also by observing behavior of *models* (either in the real world, or through various media). It is beyond doubt that completely novel responses can be learned by observation. For instance, it is easier to teach a beginner the forehand stroke in tennis by having her watch a film of a skilled tennis player, rather than by rewarding her after each discrete portion of the stroke is performed. Furthermore, emotional as well as physical responses may be learned through observation. Such common-sense observations, which are not explained by traditional learning theory, are the base of social learning experimentation and theory.

In an important, much cited, and typical experiment, Bandura (1965) demonstrated many of the principles of social learning theory. In this experiment, nursery-school children were assigned to three groups; each group watched a film in which a model attacked an adult-sized "Bobo doll" in various specific ways. Children in the first group only saw the model attack the doll; the second group also saw an extra scene in which an adult copiously rewarded the model for attacking the doll; the third group saw an extra scene in which the adult punished the model for attacking the doll. After seeing the film, each child was placed in a room which contained a Bobo doll and various other toys. There were sufficiently varied toys so that the child could behave like or unlike the model in the film. The child's aggressive behavior in this situation, which was recorded through a one-way mirror, is known as a *performance* measure. The results demonstrated that children who saw the model in the film receive either a reward or no punishment for attacking the doll now responded more aggressively (i.e., imitatively) than did the children who had seen the model punished. The process by which an observer's behavior is modified by seeing the environmental consequences of the model's behavior is known as *vicarious* learning.

To determine if the children had acquired the ability to imitate the response, whether or not they had performed imitative behavior when alone, the experimenter returned after a brief isolation period to inform the child that for every imitative response he or she could perform, a reward would be given. The results were that in every group the children produced more imitative aggressive behavior than they had when alone. Thus a person may acquire a new response through observation and learning, known as *acquisition*, even if he or she does not perform that response immediately. Vicarious reward and punishment might thus affect a person's *performance* of the observed response, but it need not affect his *acquisition* of the responses. In sum, real-life and experimental observation clearly confirm that learning occurs through observation of the behavior of models.

Observational learning is affected by numerous variables, many of which have been empirically investigated. Hilgard and Bower (1975, 601) summarized well a sampling of variables studied by Bandura.

A. Stimulus properties of the model
   1. The model's age, sex, and status relative to that of the subject are varied. High-status models are more imitated.
   2. The model's similarity to the subject: the model may be either another child in the same room, or a child in a movie, or an animal character in a movie cartoon, etc. Imitation induced in the subject decreases as the model is made more dissimilar to a real person.
B. Type of behavior exemplified by the model
   1. Novel skills are compared to novel sequences of known responses. The more complex the skills, the poorer the degree of imitation after one observation trial.

2. Hostile or aggressive responses. These are imitated to a high degree.
3. Standards of self-reward for good versus bad performances. The subject will adopt self-reward standards similar to those of the model. Also, the subject will imitate the type of moral standards exhibited by an adult model. Techniques of self-control can be transmitted in this manner.

C. Consequences of model's behavior
   1. Whether the model's behavior is rewarded, punished, or "ignored" (neither reinforced nor punished) by other agents in the drama is varied. Rewarded behaviors of the model are more likely to be imitated.

D. Motivational set given to the subject
   1. Instructions given to the subject before he observes the model provide him with high or low motivation to pay attention to and learn the model's behavior. High motivation might be produced by telling the subject that he will be rewarded commensurate with how much of the model's behavior he can reproduce on a later test. Under minimal instructions, learning is classified mainly as "incidental."
   2. Motivating instructions may be given after the subject views the model and before he is tested. This aids in distinguishing learning from performance of imitative responses.

Naturally, a subject can only learn through observation if she pays attention to the model's behavior. It should be noted that many of the variables listed above, such as subject–model similarity, have an effect on whether or not a subject will pay attention to a model.

Bandura suggested that there are three main effects of exposure to modeling stimuli (1969, 120). First, an observer may acquire new response patterns. Second, observation of a model receiving reward or punishment will respectively *disinhibit* or *inhibit* the observer's responses. If the observer believes that he too will be rewarded for an observed response, the probability increases that he will perform the (vicariously learned) response (and vice versa for a punished response). Third, observation of the behavior of others may serve to facilitate the occurrence of previously learned responses. Liebert has also suggested that observational learning can be described fruitfully as a three-stage process: *exposure*, *acquisition*, and subsequent *acceptance* of modeled responses. According to Liebert, acceptance occurs if after being exposed to and acquiring modeled responses, "the observer now employs them or accepts them as a guide for his own action (in Liebert & Spiegler, 1974, 389–390)."

It should be obvious that observational learning might be quite effective in teaching a person not to perform maladaptive behaviors or to learn new adaptive behavior (either per se or as a substitute for maladaptive behavior).

To conclude our section on the scientific background of behavior therapy, we may note that learning theory has a substructure of comparatively few principles. It is claimed that learning operates according to the principles of classical or instrumental conditioning, with the addition of a few principles of association (Franks, 1969), and that all the techniques of behavior therapy are based on these same few principles. As London (1972) argued, it really all boils down to one-and-one-half principles: "namely that learning depends on the connections in time, space and attention between what you do and what happens subsequently (913)." As the reader studies the cases in this section of the book, she should constantly ask herself: which principles of learning seem to be employed by each therapeutic technique, and how have these principles been adapted from the laboratory situation to use in clinical practice?

THE PRACTICE OF BEHAVIOR THERAPY

Although all behavior therapists attempt to base their therapies on empirically investigated psychological principles, especially learning principles, and on an operational approach to human behavior, there are fewer commonalities of technique among behavior therapy schools than among dynamic or humanistic schools. As Goldfried and Davison noted, "[t]o define behavior therapy in terms of certain techniques . . . is illusory (1976, 16)."

Behavior therapists approach their work with a pragmatic and even technological viewpoint that leads to free tinkering with therapeutic technique in order to achieve successful behavior change. Rather than present a cataloguing of the many behavior therapy techniques, in this part of our introduction we shall confine ourselves to a few brief remarks that apply to all behavior therapies. Then we shall give a brief example of how a particular behavior problem might be treated by various techniques. The broad range of discrete behavior therapy techniques will be examined in the various case studies.

The Techniques

Behavior therapy of all types basically proceeds in four steps: analysis of the maladaptive behavior, choice of technique, preparation of the client for the treatment, and the application of the treatment technique chosen.

A careful systematic analysis of the client's behavior is crucial to the success of behavior therapy. Clients often come to therapy unclear about exactly what is troubling them; it is rare that a client can articulate a highly specific, focused problem. The behavior therapist, therefore, must help the client pinpoint exactly which behavior needs changing and which variables in his or her life seems to be causing the maladaptive behavior. Put in experimental language, the therapist helps the client identify the independent variables, the causes, that produce the dependent variable, the maladaptive behavior. Goldfried and Davison (1976, 24–26) have identified four types of variables that need to be considered: *stimulus antecedents* (the environmental determinants), *organismic variables* (the intrapersonal variables, such as client expectations and client physiological states such as fatigue), *response variables* (the situation-specific maladaptive behavioral response, "including information on duration, frequency, persuasiveness, and intensity") and *consequent variables* (the environmental response to an emitted behavior).

Although there is no substitute for direct observation in performing a careful behavioral analysis, in clinical practice (unlike the laboratory) such observation is impractical and the behavior therapist must rely mainly on the clinical interview. It is necessary, therefore, that behavior therapists, as well as dynamic and humanistic therapists, be skilled interviewers. In addition to the interview, behavior therapists may also use other methods such as questionnaires and outside informants to gather information. When the behavioral assessment is complete, the therapist should have identified clearly the maladaptive behavior to be changed and the variables that cause it.

Having identified the target of the therapy, the behavior therapist is then ready to choose the most appropriate technique to change the behavior. Unlike most other types of therapists, behavior therapists have a wide range of techniques from which to choose their treatment program, but "[a]t present, we have relatively little empirical data on specific variables associated with the effective implementation of the various behavior therapy procedures (Goldfried & Davison, 1976, 26)." Goldfried and Davison claim that the choice of technique is based on the intrinsic nature of the problem itself (e.g., in the treatment of certain sex problems, the availability of a caring partner has relevance to the technique used) and on clinical experience (1976, 26–28). Aspects of the client, such as the ability to report life events specifically or to imagine scenes easily, are also important in the choice of technique. Preferences for certain techniques will certainly influence the therapist's choice. Finally, the therapist selects a group of techniques that would probably be effective and tries them in turn until success is achieved (Goldfried & Davison, 1976, 28; Wolpe, 1969, 12).

The third step in behavior therapy is to prepare the client for the treatment. Often, the rationale of a technique must be explained, or preparatory "homework assignments" must be given, or the ground rules for a technique must be explained. Whatever preparation is required, including insuring that the client's expectations are realistic, must be carried out. Fourth, the actual technique is applied.

All four steps are clearly part of the same therapeutic program and all may overlap. Behavioral assessment, choice or modification of technique, and preparation are all ongoing processes that do not cease once a treatment begins. Furthermore, preparation and treatment may be blended into one process. Part of the technique application may involve homework assignments and self-observation on the client's part. At all times, the behavior therapist is alert to new behavioral data that might indicate a need for modification or change in technique.

An issue facing all therapists, including behavior therapists, is the role in effecting change played by the relationship between therapist and client. Jerome Frank (1973, chap. 6) has shown persuasively that the client's expectation of help from the expert therapist exerts a strong therapeutic effect. This expectation is as strong in behavior therapy as in any other form of therapy. Furthermore, behavior therapy, like all other psychotherapies is a human interaction. Although behavior therapists strive for rigorous scientific objectivity in assessing the client and the treatment, the therapist's attitude toward the client should be warmly caring and nonjudgmental. The strongest possible type of "fireside induction" (Meehl, 1971) or intuition indicates that a relationship can be psychologically healing. It would be totally counterintuitive to hold that such a relationship per se cannot be curative in an unspecific way, even in behavior therapy.

Rigorous behaviorists might claim that the effect of even these unspecific relational factors could be explained in learning theory terms. But as Goldfried and Davison forthrightly reply from the vantage point of great clinical experience, "[a]ny behavior therapist who maintains that principles of learning and social influence are all one needs to know in order to bring about behavior change is out of contact with clinical reality (1976, 55)." Although behavior therapists do not depend so heavily on the therapeutic effects of the therapist–client relationship as do other therapists, the relationship does have profound influence and it must be carefully attended to and managed. As we stated above, behavior therapy is a human interaction.

Wolpe (1969) claimed that there are three reasons for failure in behavior therapy: a faulty behavioral analysis of the case, improper choice or application of technique, and lack of proper technique for the case in the therapeutic armamentarium. This list of reasons logically follows from the sensible step-by-step process of behavior therapy described above, and to it we may add another reason—the improper management of the therapeutic relationship.

Behavior therapy is a new and evolving field, and lack of complete success is not surprising. Because the behavior therapist is trained to be pragmatic and innovative and to take responsibility for the treatment, however, she will be more willing to modify her techniques than a therapist unconditionally wedded to a given technique for theoretical reasons. So long as behavior therapists remain committed to an empirically evaluative approach to their work, we may expect behavior therapy to become increasingly sophisticated and effective.

The Treatment of a Problem

We shall now give an example of how a behavior therapist might approach a specific problem. Earlier in this chapter (see page 273) we gave the example of a person who consults a behavior therapist because he drinks too much. Let us return to that problem.

As always, the treatment would begin with behavioral analysis through a careful interview, including the taking of a detailed history of the client. Systematic inquiry should disclose that the drinking behavior is related to the client's relationship with his boss. There might be other problems discovered as this time, but we shall confine ourselves to the work-related difficulties.

After the first interview the therapist might ask the client to observe carefully his relationship with his boss and his drinking behavior in order to determine exactly what types of interaction produce the problem drinking. The client might be asked to keep a log to increase the precision of the analysis. Let us assume that together the client and therapist discover that in addition to experiencing generalized anxiety in the presence of the boss, the client is especially anxious unless the boss specifically praises him, and that the client tends to "cave in" when the boss criticizes him or opposes his suggestions. Of course, if the client then ingests alcohol, a central nervous system depressant, his anxiety is inhibited and the drinking behavior may be reinforced, possibly increasing the likelihood of its recurrence.

A behavior therapist might choose any one of a number of techniques to help the client. First, she might try various methods to *countercondition* the client so that he is no longer anxious in the presence of his boss. (Note that the focus of therapy is on the present problematic relationship to the boss, and not on an hypothesized underlying source of the problem such as the client's relationship to his father.) For instance, it has been found that if clients are taught to express directly appropriate feelings that they have been suppressing in given situations, such assertiveness seems to inhibit anxiety in these situations. Our client is fearful of showing resistance or anger to his boss because he is too anxious to do so. Yet resistance or anger are quite appropriate under certain conditions. The therapist might therefore rehearse with the client the expression of anger or resistance to the boss. Such training is known as *behavioral rehearsal*, a type of *assertive training*, and it prepares the client to attempt the new and appropriate behavior in the real world.

Now suppose the client does appropriately express his feelings to the boss. More likely than not, the boss will respond favorably and will reward the new behavior. Not only will general anxiety be inhibited, but also, in operant-conditioning terms, the real-world consequences will reinforce the new behavior (taught largely without operant conditioning), and thus the behavior is more likely to be emitted again in the same and similar circumstances. Cringing and passive behavior in the face of the boss will begin to be extinguished.

In addition to training the client to be assertive, the behavior therapist might also countercondition the anxiety through a very widely used procedure known as *systematic desensitization,* another therapeutic technique that inhibits anxiety. In the initial stage of planning of this procedure the therapist constructs an *anxiety hierarchy*, "a list of stimuli on a common theme ranked in descending order according to the amount of anxiety they evoke (Wolpe, 1969, 107)." In our case, the hierarchy might consist of a group of imagined scenes involving contact with the boss; the *least* anxiety-provoking one might be, "seeing the boss at a party at the end of four weeks vacation," or even simply the word "boss," while the *most* anxiety-provoking one might be, "being severely criticized by the boss for inept performance." The client is also prepared by teaching him a technique that inhibits anxiety, *deep-muscle relaxation*.

The way in which this treatment begins is by asking the client to imagine the least anxiety-provoking scene. If the client feels anxious, he communicates this to the therapist who commands the client to begin deep-muscle relaxation, which inhibits the anxiety. This process is repeated until the pairing of relaxation with the scene has counterconditioned the client so that he no longer feels any anxiety when imagining the scene. Then the process begins anew with the client imagining the next most anxiety-provoking scene,.and so on, until finally the client can imagine the most anxiety-provoking scene in the hierarchy without feeling anxious. This training should generalize to the real-world situation.

Some modeling procedures, such as covert modeling, might also be used to train the client to be more assertive with his boss. The client may be trained to imagine scenes with his boss where the client acts assertively and is rewarded. This training may indeed generalize to the real world, facilitating assertive behavior with the boss and reducing the client's anxiety.

The nonoperant techniques suggested so far might be attempted in conjunction with some related operant techniques. For example, a type of *token economy* (cf. Ayllon & Azrin, 1968) might be instituted whereby the client earns points for behaving appropriately with the boss. When he accumulates a number of points previously agreed upon, he might then engage in a specially rewarding activity such as a meal at a favorite restaurant. Of course, it would probably be more effective if the client could be rewarded immediately after behaving properly with the boss, but the constraints of the real world make such rewards difficult. The client's thought that he has accumulated a point, however, is a *covert reinforcer* that should be efficacious. In addition to resembling a classical token economy, such a procedure resembles a technique known as *covert control*, because it asks the client to control his or her own behavior through reward by covert (thought) processes.

We have stated that the cause of the client's difficulty is his relationship with his boss, but we have also noted that it was problem drinking that brought the client to therapy. The drinking increases the probability that the maladaptive behavior with the boss will recur, because it inhibits the boss-related anxiety that might motivate the client to change or seek help. Furthermore, the drinking is rewarding per se and thus increases the probability that the client will continue to drink. In addition to treating the relationship to the boss, therefore, the behavior therapist might also attempt to change the drinking behavior itself.

To treat the drinking the therapist might employ some form of aversive behavior techniques based on operant principles. In the treatment situation, positive responses to alcohol expressed by the client might be followed by shock. Or, the client might be trained to administer the shock to himself, using a small portable machine, every time he begins a chain of thought responses favorable to alcohol. Or, when such thought chains begin, the client may be taught to interpose thoughts of extremely averse consequences following alcohol ingestion, for example, nausea and vomiting. This is another example of covert behavioral self-control. Finally, the therapist might even suggest the use of a drug such as Antabuse (disulfiram) which is antagonistic to alcohol. A person who has taken Antabuse becomes violently ill if she ingests any alcohol, even the trace amounts present in sauces and pastries. Thus, the ingestion of alcohol is followed by extremely punishing consequences for the Antabuse user. Finally, the probability of drinking should decrease even without the Antabuse.

The techniques we have briefly described do not begin to exhaust the possibilities available to the behavior therapist. They do, however, demonstrate a wide range of techniques that all attempt to change specific, present maladaptive behaviors that are currently creating difficulties. A competent behavior therapist would be willing to use any and all of these, and others, in an attempt to extinguish the maladaptive behavior and to replace it with new, adaptive behavior. A preview here of our cases would be prohibitively long, but our selection of behavior therapy cases includes representative examples of most of the important techniques.

ISSUES IN BEHAVIOR THERAPY

Learning psychologists have been split for decades over the understanding of the process of learning although, as we have seen, learning theory is dominated by two schools of thought. As behaviorism has evolved during the course of this century, there has been decreasing emphasis on discovering a unifying theory that will account for learning. The behaviorist has instead emphasized the empirical investigation of limited behavior situations in an attempt to discover the conditions that govern behavior in specific circumstances. The approach has been pragmatic and technological. For instance, there are many theories about why a stimulus reinforces, ranging from drive reduction to brain stimulation. But attempts to answer this question definitively or even to classify reinforcers have failed because the evidence is often contradictory and inconclusive.

Theories may help us to predict which reinforcer may work best in a given situation, but the only method to know for sure is empirically to test the proposition by learning trials. Thus the emphasis has been on devising such studies and less on theorizing. The evolution of behavior therapy has followed a similar course. Theory is still important, but empirical clinical experimentation is considered more fruitful in changing specific behavior during the course of therapy.

A major issue in behavior therapy, which is related to the shift toward pragmatic clinical practice, is: To what extent have practitioners of clinical behavior therapy actually followed the principles and empirical relations discovered in the psychologist's laboratory (Mahoney et al., 1974)? There are two opposing views on this question among behavior therapists: namely, that practice does follow theory and should do so (e.g., Franks, 1969), and that practice does not follow theory and does not necessarily need to do so (e.g., Lazarus, 1971; London, 1972).

London argued persuasively that learning principles do not have a systematic application to behavior disorders, and in any case, even the most basic principles are open to dispute. He claimed that learning theory was originally used as a base of ideological commitment by behavior therapists in an environment that was basically hostile to them. Although the study of learning by behavior therapists was more for "metaphor, paradigm and analogy than for strict guidance (London, 1972, 914)," behavior therapists rallied to the cause of learning theory to give themselves a supposedly firm scientific base. Now, it is argued, behavior therapy has shown that it is effective and can abandon its mechanical obeisance to learning theory. In fact, what truly links behavior therapists is a commitment to the careful, operational analysis of problems and to the systematic search for techniques that lead to observable changes. Behavior therapy is really a technological system that needs few theoretical underpinnings.

Conversely, Franks (1969) argued that the behavior therapist ought to be a scientist and that to function as a scientist it is necessary to have some theoretical framework. It is certainly arguable, however, that science involves no more than systematic, careful observation. The pragmatic therapist who empirically chooses techniques appropriate for the behavior to be modified, and who carefully distinguishes techniques that succeed from those that do not on the basis of observation, is behaving scientifically even though the therapeutic endeavor is largely atheoretical. As the reader goes through the cases, he or she should consider how strong the links are between the treatment of individual humans with disorders and the laboratory studies that were mostly based on the learning of infrahumans or on extremely restricted behaviors of human beings.

According to London (1972, 917) for example, the link between classical conditioning or counterconditioning studies and systematic desensitization (developed by Wolpe) is weak for a variety of reasons. First, it involves the use of language which is uninvolved in classical conditioning. Second, it includes a mechanism of sequential imagination that has not been studied in conditioning studies. Third, it is subject to successful variations that were not predictable from studies that led to the technique in the first place.

Despite these seemingly alarming factors, the study of learning did lead Wolpe to devise new techniques based on observable behavior, and the technique and its variants have proved very successful in the treatment of a wide variety of neurotic disorders. Like a good dynamic or humanistic therapist, the behavior therapist should not allow theory to limit him or her. He uses theory as a guide and is willing to experiment with different techniques until success is achieved.

Learning principles have, however, been a scientifically reputable base from which to launch the use of behavior therapy. The student of behavior therapy techniques is bound to be astounded by how innovative and eclectic behavior therapists are. Of course, there are some therapists who prefer one method and probably use it in too broad a variety of situations. In the complexity of day-to-day practice with human beings, however, where the goal is the alleviation of suffering, most behavior therapists have expanded their range of techniques to encompass anything that works and that does not violate the dignity of the client.

The theoretical purity of the laboratory, itself a myth, is impossible to maintain in the world of clinical practice. As we have seen, despite the antimentalism of many behaviorists and of much learning theory, many behavior therapists use fantasy and other subjective cognitive processes to help change behavior and alleviate suffering (e.g., overt and covert desensitization). But, as always, the emphasis is on changing specifiable maladaptive behaviors by techniques explicitly aimed at changing the particular behavior in precise and measurable ways.

Another major issue in behavior therapy is the extent to which the therapist dehumanizes his client by mechanically controlling the therapeutic interaction, and, to some extent, the client's life. Because behavior therapists are often criticized for not respecting the autonomy of their clients, it is useful to explore this issue. Among all the psychological therapies used to treat behavior disorders, behavior therapy has received the most intense criticism. Behavior therapy (and by extension, its therapists) has been accused by critics of being antihumanistic, because it treats persons as "machines," and because it does not treat whole persons but only restricted parts of them—"symptoms." To note, however, that the behavior of persons is subject to certain governing principles is not to dehumanize, but simply to be realistic. The behavior therapist attempts to change the client's maladaptive behavior in order to achieve the humanitarian goal of alleviating suffering. Because the new learning program simply treats specific behavior does not prevent the behavior therapist from conveying to the client her compassion, sympathy, and respect for the client as a whole person.

The goal of the behavior therapist is to change particular behavior efficiently and specifically, and the theoretical underpinning of the endeavor is the determinism of scientific psychology. Consequently, the behavior therapist assumes much greater control than dynamic or humanistic therapists over the detailed ongoing process of the treatment sessions and often over the outside life of the client. And the behavior therapist takes responsibility for the outcome of the treatment (London, 1964). The behavior therapist believes that he or she is being consulted as an expert on how to change behavior; not telling or showing the client how to do so is thus an abdication of therapeutic responsibility. Because he is an expert, it is the behavior therapist's responsibility not only to guide the treatment overtly and directly, but also to take responsibility for its outcome.

Because behavior therapists take responsibility for and guide the treatment very directly, they have been accused of having pretensions of omnipotence and of infantilizing their clients. But if the behavior therapist is an expert who has a service to offer, it makes sense that the therapist should control the service and take responsibility for its success or failure. We do not expect a client with legal problems to try his own case, nor do we blame the cooperative client if the case is lost. With the information given him, we expect the lawyer to manage the case and to take responsibility for its outcome (including being flexible enough to switch tactics if those being used prove unsuccessful). The behavior therapist is willing to assume the responsibilities of presenting herself as an expert professional.

Another important issue raised in recent years is whether and to what extent behavior therapists should attempt to integrate the theory and practices of the dynamic therapists within one holistic therapeutic framework (Franks & Wilson, 1974; Wolpe, 1976). Some thinkers feel that dynamic theory has much to offer, but that behavior therapy offers more effective techniques for behavior change. For instance, in the example given above of our problem drinker who could not deal effectively with his boss, a dynamic theorist might hypothesize that it is the client's relationship to his father that is at the root of the difficulties with the boss. Those calling for "integrated" behavior therapy might thus suggest that desensitization directed toward the relationship with the father is the treatment of choice.

Although it is too early to predict how successful the movement toward integrating dynamic and behavioral approaches will be, our impression is that this movement has more adherents among those therapists whose orientation is largely dynamic. This is probably so because dynamic theory does not mutually exclude behavior theory, whereas behavior theory largely does mutually exclude the extremely mentalistic, inferred variables that form the core of dynamic explanations. Most prominent behavior therapists probably reject an integrated approach, because they feel that dynamic theory is incorrect, or because they feel that behavior therapy will evolve more quickly if it is not diluted with the concepts and practice of the dynamic school.

Another very crucial issue facing all behavior therapists is the current concern that powerful behavioral techniques, especially operant techniques and aversive conditioning, will be used for improper purposes such as changing supposedly undesirable political or social behavior that the subject does not wish changed. The concern is that behavior therapy can be used to overbear the "will" and thus the dignity of the individual. Of course, if an uncoerced client chooses to change his or her behavior and gives informed consent to the procedure to be employed, then few ethical, moral, or political problems are raised.

It is true, however, that behavior therapies can be *imposed* on clients more easily than can traditional therapies. Techniques such as aversive conditioning can be applied without either consent or cooperation. This is not a fault with the therapy, however, but with the social or political use of the therapy. Like any other technological innovation, behavior therapy can be used for good or ill. Behavior therapists must be open-mindedly and actively concerned with the social and ethical concerns engendered by the use of behavior therapy. In conclusion, it should be pointed out that in the long run the extent to which involuntary behavior therapy may be employed is a question that must and should be left to social decision makers such as courts and legislatures that represent society and that express its values.

CONCLUSION

Today behavior therapy has achieved increasing acceptance (in some quarters it may even be considered quite modish). Papers dealing with behavior therapy appear in prestigious psychiatric as well as psychological journals, and all mental health professionals should be acquainted with behavior therapy. Even if a particular professional does not practice behavior therapy himself, he or she ought to know for which cases it is more appropriate than other techniques, and why. With an emphasis on empirical observation, measurable variables, and innovative techniques, the behavior therapist will make significant contributions to meeting the demands for effective treatment of the complex maladaptive behaviors called mental disorders.

REFERENCES

Ayllon, T. & Azrin, N. *The token economy.* Englewood Cliffs, New Jersey: Prentice-Hall, 1968.

Bandura, A. Influence of models' reinforcement contingencies on the acquisition of imitative responses. *Journal of Personality and Social Psychology*, 1965, *1*, 589–595.

Bandura, A. *Principles of behavior modification*, New York: Holt, Rinehart and Winston, 1969.

Boring, E. *The history of experimental psychology.* New York: Appleton-Century-Crofts, 1950.

Frank, J. *Persuasion and healing: A comparative study of psychotherapy,* rev. ed. Baltimore: Johns Hopkins University Press, 1973.

Franks, C. Behavior and its Pavlovian origins: Review and perspectives. In

C. Franks (Ed.), *Behavior therapy: Appraisal and status.* New York: McGraw-Hill, 1969.

Franks, C. & Wilson, G. T. The nature of behavior therapy: Recurring problems and issues. In C. Franks & G. T. Wilson (Eds.), *Annual review of behavior therapy,* Vol. 2. New York: Brunner/Mazel, 1974.

Franks, C. & Wilson, G. T. Ethical and related issues in behavior therapy. In C. Franks & G. T. Wilson (Eds.), *Annual review of behavior therapy,* Vol. 3. New York: Brunner/Mazel, 1975.

Goldfried, M. & Davison, G. *Clinical behavior therapy.* New York: Holt, Rinehart and Winston, 1976.

Hilgard, E. & Bower, J. *Theories of learning,* 4th ed. Englewood Cliffs, New Jersey: Prentice-Hall, 1975.

Jones, M. C. Elimination of children's fears. *Journal of Experimental Psychology,* 1924, *7,* 383–390.

Lazarus, A. A. *Behavior therapy and beyond.* New York: McGraw-Hill, 1971.

Liebert, R. & Spiegler, M. *Personality: Strategies for the study of man,* rev. ed. Homewood, Illinois: Dorsey, 1974.

London, P. *The modes and morals of psychotherapy.* New York: Holt, Rinehart and Winston, 1964.

London, P. The end of ideology in behavior modification. *American Psychologist,* 1972, *27,* 913–920.

Mahoney, M. *et al.* Behavior modification: Delusion or deliverance? In C. Franks & G. T. Wilson (Eds.), *Annual review of behavior therapy,* Vol. 2. New York: Brunner/Mazel, 1974.

Marks, I. The current status of behavioral psychotherapy: Theory and practice. *American Journal of Psychiatry,* 1976, *133,* 253–261.

Meehl, P. Law and the fireside inductions: Some reflections of a clinical psychologist. *Journal of Social Issues,* 1971, 27, 65–100.

Rachlin, H. *Introduction to modern behaviorism.* San Francisco: W. H. Freeman, 1970.

Rimm, D. C. & Masters, J. C. *Behavior therapy: Techniques and empirical findings.* New York: Academic Press, 1974.

Rychlak, J. F. *Introduction to personality and psychotherapy: A theory-construction approach.* Boston: Houghton-Mifflin, 1973.

Thoreson, C. & Mahoney, M. *Behavioral self-control.* New York: Holt, Rinehart and Winston, 1974.

Watson, J. B. *Behaviorism.* New York: W. W. Norton, 1924. (Norton ed. 1970)

Wolpe, J. *Psychotherapy by reciprocal inhibition.* Stanford, California: Stanford University Press, 1958.

Wolpe, J. *The practice of behavior therapy.* Elmsford, N.Y.: Pergamon, 1969.

Wolpe, J. Behavior therapy and its malcontents. I: Denial of its bases and psychodynamic fusionism. *Journal of Behavior Therapy and Experimental Psychiatry,* 1976, *7,* 1–5.

Chapter 16
Systematic
Desensitization

The selections in this chapter illustrate the use of desensitization. As we previously indicated, this is a behavior therapy technique that inhibits anxiety through a form of counterconditioning. Behavior therapists who rely more heavily on classical conditioning principles to explain maladaptive behavior often view anxiety as the primary etiological factor in maladaptive behavior. That is, anxiety has somehow been inappropriately paired with an otherwise neutral stimulus situation, and now the patient's response to the situation is maladaptive because of the anxiety.

For instance, in the child therapy case of "Little Hans" that Freud reported, Hans was afraid to go out in the street because he feared that a horse would bite him or that a horsecart would fall and frighten him. Indeed, he had been subjected to both circumstances or the threat of them. Freud hypothesized that what Hans really feared was either castration by his father, or the birth ("falling") of his sister, and that the frightening events stood for these fears. A behavior therapist, on the other hand, would theorize that a formerly neutral stimulus (e.g., horse or horsecart) had become paired with anxiety and now produced fright and flight (or a maladaptive fear of going out), when it was presented to Hans.[1] Whereas the Freudian treats such a situation by facilitating insight into the symbolic connections between the neutral stimulus and the patient's unconscious wishes and fears, the behaviorist reasons that the patient must be taught to inhibit anxiety when presented with the neutral stimulus and to learn new responses. In other words, the behavior therapist seeks to break the learned pairing between the neutral stimulus and the anxiety and to substitute new constructive responses for the maladaptive response habit.

The behavior therapist uses systematic desensitization to help the patient gradually unlearn the maladaptive response habits. A physical state (usually deep-muscle relaxation) antagonistic to anxiety is paired with increasingly powerful anxiety-provoking stimuli in an attempt to break the pairing between anxiety and the stimuli. The

[1] Wolpe and Rachman (1960) make this comparison in great detail.

anxiety-provoking stimuli may either be imagined, or at times may be presented in vivo. In either case, as the patient breaks the pairing between anxiety and a stimulus, the training proceeds to an even more powerful anxiety-producing stimulus, and so on. Naturally it is all important that the therapist determine the true anxiety-producing stimuli lest he decondition anxiety to the wrong stimuli.

In the first selection, Joseph Wolpe describes how he trains his patients in deep-muscle relaxation.

In the second selection, Dr. Wolpe describes the way systematic desensitization works, including a description of the way the hierarchies of anxiety-producing stimuli are constructed. Although Wolpe suggests the routine use of hypnosis in desensitization procedures, today he uses it in only a small percentage of cases; most behavior therapists do not use hypnosis in such cases. Then he presents a case where impotence was treated by desensitizing the patient to fear of injury and suffering, which were hypothesized to be the true anxiety-producing stimuli that led to the impotence. It is noteworthy in this case that it was not sex itself, or the vagina that was primarily anxiety producing, but the fact that sex meant suffering and injury to this patient. Freud noted that children often understand sexuality as an attack or trauma, and such insight might be applicable here if explained in terms of the patient's learning history and capacity to symbolize. As always, however, the goal is the breakup of an anxiety–response habit; here, the anxiety response to sex.

The final case involves the treatment of a homosexual pedophiliac who was afraid to have sexual contact with adults of either sex. Like Jolande Jacobi, in the case presented in Section I with which this case should be compared, Robert Kohlenberg did not attempt to change the patient's sexual orientation; he only tried to desensitize this man's fear of adult males. To do this he employed an actual adult male rather than simply using imagery. This is known as in vivo desensitization, and it is extensively used by William Masters and Virginia Johnson. Some behavior therapists are willing to use partners who are strangers, as well as lovers and friends, for in vivo desensitization. Dr. Kohlenberg's case also demonstrates the behavior therapist's flexibility; he uses two quite different techniques in the treatment, each aimed at a different goal of the therapy. This case is followed by a comment upon it by Hans H. Strupp. Dr. Strupp deals with the value questions involved in the treatment, some of which were briefly alluded to in the general introduction to this section.

REFERENCE

Wolpe, Joseph, & Rachman, Stanley, Psychoanalytic evidence: A critique based on Freud's case of "Little Hans." *Journal of Nervous and Mental Disease*, 1960, *130*, 135–148.

Training in Relaxation

JOSEPH WOLPE

The method of relaxation taught is essentially that of Jacobson (1938), but instruction is completed in the course of about six interviews, in marked contrast to Jacobson's very prolonged training schedules. The patient is asked to practice at home for two fifteen-minute periods a day.

In introducing the subject of relaxation, I tell the patient (who has usually already gained a general idea of the nature of conditioning therapy) that relaxation is just one of the methods in our armamentarium for combating anxiety. I continue as follows:

Even the ordinary relaxing that occurs when one lies down often produces quite a noticeable calming effect. It has been found that there is a definite relationship between the extent of muscle relaxation and the production of emotional changes opposite to anxiety. I am going to teach you how to relax far beyond the usual point, and with practice you will be able to "switch on" at will very considerable emotional effects of an "anti-anxiety" kind.

There is no established sequence for training the various muscle groups in relaxation, but whatever sequence is adopted should be systematic. My own practice is to start with the arms because they are convenient for purposes of demonstration and easy to check on. The head region is next because the most marked anxiety-inhibiting effects are usually obtained by relaxations there.

The patient is asked to grip the arm of his chair with one hand to see whether he can distinguish any qualitative differ-

From *The Practice of Behavior Therapy*, 100–107. Elmsford, New York: Pergamon, 1969. Copyright © 1969 by Pergamon Press, Inc.

ence between the sensations produced in his forearm and those in his hand. He is told to take special note of the quality of the forearm sensation because it is caused by muscle tension in contrast to the touch and pressure sensations in the hand. He is also enjoined to note the exact location of the forearm tensions in the flexor and extensor areas. Next, the therapist grips the patient's wrist and asks him to bend his arm against this resistance, thus making him aware of the tension in his biceps. Then by instructing him to straighten his bent elbow against resistance, he calls his attention to the extensor muscles of the arm. The therapist goes on to say:

I am now going to show you the essential activity that is involved in obtaining deep relaxation. I shall again ask you to resist my pull at your wrist so as to tighten your biceps. I want you to notice very carefully the sensations in that muscle. Then I shall ask you to let go gradually as I diminish the amount of force exerted against you. Notice, as your forearm descends, that there is decreasing sensation in the biceps muscle. Notice also that the letting go is an activity, but of a negative kind —it is an "uncontracting" of the muscle. In due course, your forearm will come to rest on the arm of the chair, and you may then think that you have gone as far as possible—that relaxation is complete. But although the biceps will indeed be partly and perhaps largely relaxed, a certain number of its fibers will still, in fact, be contracted. I shall therefore say to you, "Go on letting go. Try to extend the activity that went on in the biceps while your forearm was coming down." It is the act of relaxing these additional fibers that will bring

295

about the emotional effects we want. Let's try it and see what happens.

The therapist then grips the patient's wrist a second and asks him to tense and then gradually to relax the biceps. When the forearm is close to the arm of the chair the therapist releases the wrist, allowing the patient to complete the movement on his own. He then exhorts him to "go on letting go," to "keep trying to go further and further in the negative direction," to "try to go beyond what seems to you to be the furthest point."

When the patient has indicated that he fully understands what is required, he is asked to put both hands comfortably on his lap and try to relax all the muscles of both arms for a few minutes. He is to report any new sensations that he may feel. The usual ones are tingling, numbness, or warmth, mainly in the hands. After a few minutes the therapist palpates the relaxing muscles. With practice he learns to judge between various grosser degrees of muscle tension.

Most patients have rather limited success when they first attempt to relax, but they are assured that good relaxation is a matter of practice, and whereas initially twenty minutes of relaxation may achieve no more than partial relaxation of an arm it will eventually be possible to relax the whole body in a matter of a minute or two. However, there are some fortunate individuals who from the first attempt experience a deepening and extending relaxation, radiating, as it were, from the arms, and accompanied by general effects, like calmness, sleepiness or warmth.

I customarily begin the second lesson in relaxation by telling the patient that from the emotional point of view, the most important muscles in the body are situated in and around the head, and that we shall therefore deal with this area next. We begin with the muscles of the face, demonstrating the tensions produced

by contracting the muscles of the forehead. These muscles lend themselves to a demonstration of the characteristic "steplike" character of increasing relaxation. The therapist simultaneously raises the frowning groups of muscles in his own forehead very intensely, pointing out incidentally that an anxious expression has thus been produced. He then says: "I am going to relax these muscles in a controlled way to give you the feeling of the step-like way in which decrements of tension occur during attempts at deep relaxation, although in actual relaxing, the steps are usually much less rapid than in my demonstration." The muscles are then relaxed as stated, making an obvious step-down about every five seconds until, after about half-a-dozen steps, no further change is evident; nevertheless, it is emphasized to the patient that relaxation is continuing and that this relaxation "beneath the surface" is the part that matters for producing the desired emotional effects. The patient is then told to contract his own forehead muscles and is given about ten minutes to relax them as far as possible. Patients frequently report spontaneously the occurrence of "relaxation feedback" in their foreheads, which they may feel as tingling, or "a feeling of thickness, as though my skin were made of leather." These sensations are as a rule indicative of a degree of relaxation beyond the normal level of muscle tone.

This lesson usually concludes by drawing attention to the muscles in the region of the nose by getting the patient to wrinkle his nose, and to the muscles around the mouth by making him purse his lips and then smile. All these muscles are now relaxed.

At the third lesson the patient is asked to bite on his teeth, thus tensing his masseters and temporales. The position of the lips is an important indicator of relaxation of the muscles of mastication. When these are relaxed, the lips are parted by a few millimeters. The masseters cannot be re-laxed if the mouth is kept resolutely closed. Of course, it does not follow that an open mouth is proof of relaxation.

At the same lesson, I usually also introduce the muscles of the tongue. These may be felt contracting in the floor of the mouth, when the patient presses the tip of his tongue firmly against the back of his lower incisor teeth. Relaxing the tongue muscles may produce such local sensations as tingling or a feeling of enlargement of that organ.

Patients who have special tensions in the neck region are now shown how to relax the pharyngeal muscles—which can be felt beforehand by the act of preparing to clear one's throat. Other muscle groups that receive attention only for special purposes, are those of the eyeball (which are first individually contracted by having the eyes turned in succession left, right, up and down), and the infrahyoid group (which the patient can be made to feel by trying to open his jaws against resistance).

The fourth lesson deals with the neck and shoulders. The main target in the neck is the posterior muscles that normally maintain the head's erect posture. Most people become aware of them merely by concentrating on sensations in the back of the neck. When they relax these muscles the head falls forward, but because in the unpracticed individual the relaxation is incomplete, stress is imposed on muscle fibres that are still contracted, and dis-comfort, and even pain, is frequently felt. As Jacobson has pointed out, persist-ent practice, while ignoring the discomfort leads to a progressive yielding of these muscles, and usually in a week or so the patient finds his neck is comfortable though his chin will press against his sternum. Those who find the discomfort of the forward leaning head too great, are instructed to practice relaxing against a high-backed chair.

Shoulder muscle tensions are demon-strated by the following routine. The deltoid is contracted by abducting the arm to the horizontal, the lateral neck muscles by continuing this movement up to the ear, the posthumeral and scapulo-spinal groups by moving the horizontal arm backward, and the pectorals by swinging it forward across the chest. In relaxing these muscles the patient is directed to observe their functional unity with those of the arm.

The fifth relaxation lesson deals with the muscles of the back, abdomen and thorax. The procedure in respect to the first two areas follows the usual pattern. The back muscles are contracted by back-ward arching of the spine. The abdominal muscles are tensed as if in anticipation of a punch in the belly; and after contracting them the patient lets them go as far as he can. The thoracic muscles, or, more ac-curately, the muscles of respiration, are necessarily in a different category—for total inhibition of breathing is not an achievement to try to promote! But the respiratory rhythm can often be used to augment relaxation. Attention to the musculature during a few fairly deep breaths soon reveals that while some effort is involved during inhalation, ex-piration is essentially a "letting-go." Some patients find it very helpful to coordinate relaxation of various other muscles with the automatic relaxation of the respiratory muscles that takes place with the exhala-tion during *normal* breathing.

In making patients aware of the mus-cles to be relaxed in the lower limbs it has been my custom to start with the feet, and work upwards. The flexor digitorium brevis is felt by bending the toes within the shoe; the calf muscles by placing some weight on the toe; the peroneal and anterior tibial muscles by dorsiflexing the foot; the quadriceps femoris by straighten-ing the knee; the hamstrings by trying to bend the knee against resistance; the ad-ductors of the thigh by adduction against hand pressure on the inner aspect of the knee; and the abductors (which include some of the gluteal muscles) by abduction against pressure.

All these muscles are the subject of the sixth lesson, and the patient should be allowed enough time for relaxing them.

REFERENCE

Jacobson, E. *Progressive relaxation.* Chicago: University of Chicago Press, 1938.

Systematic Desensitization Based on Relaxation

JOSEPH WOLPE

Of the methods of therapy considered in this book the present parallels most closely the experimental procedure of feeding cats in the presence of increasing "doses" of anxiety-evoking stimuli. . . .

An anxiety hierarchy is a list of stimulus situations to which a patient reacts with graded amounts of anxiety. The most disturbing item is placed at the top of the list, the least disturbing at the bottom. These hierarchies provide a convenient framework for systematic desensitization, through relaxation, to increasing amounts of anxiety-evoking stimuli.[1]

The theory may be summarized like this: If a stimulus constellation made up of five equipotent elements $A_1A_2A_3A_4A_5$ evokes 50 units of anxiety response in an

From *Psychotherapy by Reciprocal Inhibition*, 139–142, 152–160 by Joseph Wolpe, M.D., with the permission of the publishers, Stanford University Press. © 1958 by the Board of Trustees of the Leland Stanford Junior University.

[1] A basic assumption underlying this procedure is that the response to the imagined situation resembles that to the real situation. Experience bears this out. People are anxious when they imagine stimuli that are fearful in reality. This is in keeping with Stone's observations (1955) in another context.

organism, proportionately less anxiety will be evoked by constellations made up of fewer elements. Relaxation that is insufficient to counter the 50 units of anxiety that $A_1A_2A_3A_4A_5$ evokes may be well able to inhibit the 10 units evoked by A_1 alone. Then if the anxiety evoked by A_1 is repeatedly inhibited through being opposed by relaxation, its magnitude will drop, eventually to zero. In consequence, a presentation of A_1A_2 will now evoke only 10 units of anxiety, instead of 20, and this will similarly undergo conditioned inhibition when opposed by relaxation. Through further steps along these lines the whole combination $A_1A_2A_3A_4A_5$ will lose its power to arouse any anxiety.

The raw data for a hierarchy are obtained in several ways. The patient's history frequently reveals a variety of situations to which he reacts with undue disturbance. Further areas of disturbance may be revealed by perusal of his answers to the Willoughby questionnaire. Then he is given the "homework" task of making up a list of everything he can think of that is capable of frightening, disturbing, distressing, or embarrassing him in any way, excepting, of course, situations that would frighten anybody, such as meeting a hungry lion. Some patients bring back extensive inventories, others very scanty ones; and with the latter a good deal of time may have to be spent during interviews eliciting further items.

Confronted at last with anything between about 10 and 100 heterogeneous items, the therapist peruses them to see whether they belong to one or more thematic categories. If there is more than one theme the items of each are grouped together. For example, one patient had a subdivision into enclosure, death and bodily-lesion themes; another into social disapproval, disease, and aloneness; a third into trauma, death, and being in the limelight; a fourth into rejection and scenes of violence.

The subdivided list is now handed to the patient, who is asked to rank the items of each sublist in descending order according to the measure of disturbance he would have upon exposure to each. The rearranged list constitutes the hierarchical series that will be used in treatment. Modifications or additions may of course be made later.

At the first desensitization session the patient, already trained in relaxation, is hypnotized and in the trance is made to relax as deeply as possible. He is then told that he will be required to imagine a number of scenes which will appear to him very vividly. If he feels disturbed by any scene, he is to raise his hand as a signal. The weakest scenes from the hierarchical series are now presented in turn, usually for between two and three seconds each in the beginning. The raising of the left hand or any manifestation of increased bodily tension leads to the immediate curtailment of the ongoing scene. When it is judged that enough scenes have been given, the patient is roused from the trance and asked how clear the scenes were and whether any of them were disturbing. Even if he has not raised his hand during the trance, he may report having been very slightly to very considerably disturbed by one or more of the scenes. (Patients almost never raise their hands to a disturbance that is only slight.)

At the second desensitization session, a day or more later, the procedure is largely determined by what happened at the first. A scene that produced no disturbance at all is omitted and the next higher item in the hierarchy presented in its place. A scene that was slightly disturbing is presented again, unchanged. If there was a considerable disturbance to the weakest scene from any hierarchy, a still weaker stimulus must now be substituted. Suppose for example, that the disturbing item was seeing a funeral procession. Typical weaker substitutions would be the word "funeral," seeing the procession from a distance of 200 yards, seeing an isolated and presumably empty hearse, or a *very brief* presentation of the original scene. The verbal substitution would usually be the weakest of these and would therefore be preferred. No harm is ever done by presenting a stimulus that is too weak. A stimulus that is too strong may actually increase sensitivity, and, especially during early experiments with the method, I have occasionally produced major setbacks in patients by premature presentation to them of stimuli with a high anxiety-evoking potential.[2]

In most patients, when the same scene is presented several times during a session there is a weaker reaction to each successive presentation. When this occurs, it accelerates therapy.[3] In other patients there is perseveration of anxiety re-

---

[2] When sensitivity is increased as a result of an error of this kind, no scenes must be presented at the next session or two, and during these the hypnotic trance should be utilized merely to relax the patient as deeply as possible. At subsequent sessions scenes are introduced very cautiously from far down in the hierarchy whose subject matter produced the setback.

[3] I frequently inquire whether the reaction is weakening or not by saying after, say, the third presentation of a scene, "If your reaction has been decreasing, do nothing; if not, raise your hand." If it has been decreasing, I present the same scene two or three times more.

sponses, so that the anxiety produced by a second presentation summates with that from the first, the repetition tending thus to have a sensitizing effect rather than a therapeutic one.

With suitably cautious handling some headway will be made in the hierarchies at each session, and *pari passu* with this the patient will report a progressive decrease of sensitivity to the relevant kinds of stimulus situations encountered in the normal course of his life. The total number of sessions required varies greatly but is usually between 10 and 25.

The introspections of a clinical psychologist who was treated by this method are of interest:

> Most typically the emotion associated with a situation tended to diminish or disappear between one session and another. On three or four occasions, however, the desensitization seemed to occur quite suddenly in the course of a session. On these occasions the change was subjectively a dramatic one: I would feel, all at once, a sense of separation, or apartness, or independence of the situation; a feeling that "I am *here*, it is *there*." To say simply that I attained greater objectivity, or more simply that the emotional component of the image disappeared, would be accurate but not quite as descriptive of my subjective experience as the preceding sentence.
>
> The change, even when sudden, never seemed to constitute an "insight." My insight into my difficulties was perhaps fairly good initially, and was not altered one way or the other by the desensitization process *per se*. It might be said, however, that my "perception" of situations changed.

Patients who cannot relax will not make progress with this method. Those who cannot or will not be hypnotized but who can relax will make progress, although apparently more slowly than when hypnosis is used. The method necessarily fails with a small minority who are unable to imagine the suggested scenes. A few, perhaps about 5 per cent, do not make progress because although they can visualize clearly, they do not have the disturbed reaction to the imagined scene that they would have to the reality. Experience has shown that most of these can arouse the relevant emotions by *verbalizing* the scenes, and they then progress in the same way as other patients.

Occasionally, one comes across a patient who, having been desensitized to a hierarchy list, reveals a range of further, previously unrecognized sensitivities on a related but distinct theme. After desensitization to the latter, a third theme may become evident, and so on. It is surmised that this profusion of variations is due to unusually numerous and severe past stresses having brought about a conditioning of anxiety responses to an extraordinarily large number of aspects of certain situations. In these cases, abreaction is sometimes a valuable adjuvant because it involves the whole of the original conditioning situation. . . .

CURE OF IMPOTENCE FOLLOWING DESENSITIZATION TO SITUATIONS INVOLVING INJURY AND SUFFERING

FIRST AND SECOND INTERVIEWS. (The content of these two interviews has been rearranged to make a more or less consecutive story.) Mr. L., a tall, thin man of 22, consulted me for the first time on August 23, 1953. He had suffered from impotence for three years without seeking treatment, but was now very anxious to overcome his disability because he had recently fallen in love with a very attractive girl (Irene) who reciprocated his feelings.

His sexual history was as follows. He had first become aware of sexual impulses at the age of 13 when he started noticing girls and occasionally managed to kiss them. At 15 he began to masturbate in accompaniment with sexual fantasies— about once a week, without any feelings of guilt. He began to meet girls in the course of various social activities, and at 16 he became interested in Eve, a pretty, intelligent, and lively girl with whom he "went steady" for the next two years, though they quarreled a good deal because she was moody. They frequently petted, but he never went further than to fondle her breasts through her clothes.

While he was still friendly with Eve, he met Nina, who pursued him with great determination, although he neither felt nor displayed any particular interest in her. Nina was quite easygoing sexually and one day when he visited her in her parents' absence they had coitus. He ejaculated prematurely on the first occasion but later performed very successfully. This was the beginning of a sexual relationship which went on very satisfactorily for a year, in the course of which Mr. L. also had a few casual experiences with other girls.

Then in 1950 when he was 19 years old he found himself strongly attracted to Alice in the same pharmacy class. After a platonic phase of a month or so, they began mild petting which gradually grew warmer until by the fourth month they had begun to lie in bed together. Mr. L.'s sexual responses to Alice were extremely powerful and he invariably had strong erections even if they were only flirting in the mildest way. On the third occasion on which they lay in bed together, Mr. L. suggested intercourse but Alice, a virgin, was afraid. But she yielded at last to his insistent pressure, and then he found that his erection had vanished and could not be reinstated, even though they spent the night together. From that time onward, although he had innumerable opportunities to make love to Alice, he never had another erection with her. At no time since then had he had anything like a full erection with anyone. However, his *general* responsiveness to sexual objects was only slightly reduced.

Mr. L's association with Alice continued for nine months after this incident, when it was ended by a trifling argument. He had a severe reaction and kept away from people as much as possible for about three months. Then he began casual associations with women, avoiding physical contact. One day late in 1952 when an easy opportunity to make love to an attractive girl arose, Mr. L. made the necessary advances but failed to get an erection. He was very upset at this but went on seeing the girl until February 1953 when she went to live in a distant city. From April to July he went out with another girl whom he found quite attractive, but he never had the slightest semblance of an erection.

Early in July he met and became strongly attracted to Irene, who bore some physical resemblance to Alice but was better looking and shared more of Mr. L.'s important interests and attitudes. He was finding it pleasant to fondle her and was noticing a trace of an erection. Caressing her also increased the rate of his breathing and made him perspire to some extent, and sometimes after very prolonged lovemaking he had orgasms despite the virtual absence of an erection. A pleasurable feeling accompanied the orgasm but much less so than when he had been able to experience it in a normal way.

Other details of Mr. L.'s life were as follows. He was the eldest of three boys. Both parents were living. His father, pleasant, sociable, and unpractical, had always treated him kindly and rarely punished him. He described his mother as "nervous, often depressed, somewhat vicious, and very belligerent." She displayed a certain amount of affection and throughout Mr. L.'s childhood was constantly asking him to tell her how much he loved her. She did not often give beatings but kept shouting and nagging so that from the age of six onward, Mr. L. felt an increasing dislike of her. He became so sensitive to her bullying that once when he was eight years old and his ear was cut by a stone he delayed returning home as long as possible because he feared her tongue. She quarreled endlessly with her husband mainly over trifles, so that the atmosphere in the house was one of perpetual discord.

Mr. L. recalled two occasions on which he could overhear his parents having intercourse in the next room when he was about seven years old. On each occasion he heard his mother shout, "No, stop" and then weep. He was greatly upset by this, felt his father was being brutal, and hated him for it. Until he was 12 years old, he thought that sexual intercourse was painful, and this idea had recurred when he was trying to seduce Alice.

He had been happy at school and a good deal above the average as a scholar. He was a good sportsman, representing his school at cricket and rugby football. Making friends was easy for him and there were always one or two who were especially close. He had done well in his pharmacy studies and was happy in his present job.

Until the age of 12 he had felt extremely unhappy and insecure but had become increasingly confident in relation to most aspects of life—and this confidence had continued to develop even in the past three years despite the onset of sexual impotence.

THIRD INTERVIEW (SEPTEMBER 12, 1953). At this interview I gave him the Willoughby questionnaire to answer. His relatively low score of 26 confirmed his statement of relative confidence in most social situations. However, he gave the maximum positive answer of 4 to question 23—"If you see an accident, does something keep you from giving help?" When, as usual, I went into the reasons for this, it turned out that he had very strong disturbed

reactions to pain or suffering or evidence of tissue damage to other people. These reactions were sometimes so marked that it became very difficult for him to concentrate on his work for a day or two afterward. He said that he had been aware of the traumatization that would have occurred if he had deflorated Alice.

He then stated that on the evening of September 9, lying in bed with Irene, he had had a partial erection and had attempted intercourse. She, being a virgin, told him that it was beginning to be painful. At this, his erection subsided completely. On the evening of the 10th, they made another attempt at intercourse, but this time Mr. L. had no vestige of an erection. Both of them were greatly depressed at this.

Pointing out that his experience of September 9 had increased his sexual inhibition, I advised him to desist for the time being from further attempts at coitus.

FOURTH INTERVIEW (SEPTEMBER 13, 1953). Mr. L. stated that he had been giving a good deal of thought to his sensitivity to pain and tissue damage in other people, and had been surprised to realize how many of his experiences in the shop were colored by it. He recalled also that he had had such a strong reaction at the age of five when a gang of boys attacked a slightly older friend of his; he had remained upset for days after and for years had avoided the street in which this had happened. When he was seven years old he had become involved in a fight with a bigger boy. Hitting the latter in the solar plexus and seeing the reaction, he had run home in terror. He was not disturbed by injuries to his own person. Watching a boxing match was intolerable to him. He found quarrels a shade less disturbing, but if he was one of the participants, they disturbed him scarcely at all.

I discussed muscle relaxation with him and instructed him in relaxation of the muscles of his arm and forehead. Before he left I asked him to bring me next time a list of everything he could think of that could possibly disturb him.

FIFTH INTERVIEW (SEPTEMBER 14, 1953). The earlier part of this interview was devoted to training Mr. L. to relax the muscles of his face and jaws. After this, taking the list of disturbing items he brought me and adding to it items from his history and others that arose during discussion, we constructed the following three hierarchical lists of anxieties (in descending order).

HIERARCHIES

A. Injury and suffering
1. Idea of uterus being scraped
2. An untreated fractured limb (what is most disturbing is the idea of the broken ends scraping together)
3. A raw wound bleeding (worse if large; worse on face than on trunk and not so bad on a limb)
4. A person being injected (would be worse if Mr. L. had to give the injection himself)
5. A very small facial wound with much bleeding
6. Dissecting an animal
7. Injecting a drug into an animal
8. The sight of a dead human body
9. Watching someone else dissect an animal
10. Seeing a patient propped up in bed short of breath
11. An old unhealed wound: the worse the larger
12. Seeing an animal that has just been killed by a car
13. Seeing an animal that has died evidently of disease
14. A small facial wound with slight bleeding
15. Traumatic epistaxis
16. A schoolboy being caned

B. Vocalizing of suffering
1. An unseen hospital patient groaning

2. His father groaning
3. A child crying
4. A customer comes in groaning and says he has abdominal cramps
5. A kicked dog howling

C. Vocal violence
1. A quarrel in his family
2. A quarrel anywhere else
3. A child being shouted at

SIXTH INTERVIEW (SEPTEMBER 16, 1953). Mr. L. said that there was no significant change in his reaction to Irene, but perhaps his sexual arousal was slightly quicker. He had observed in himself numerous examples of reacting unpleasantly to trauma associated stimuli. For example, he had been upset for many minutes after hearing somebody in his shop mention a uterus being scraped.

He was instructed in relaxation of the muscles of the tongue, eyes, pharynx, and neck.

SEVENTH INTERVIEW (SEPTEMBER 19, 1953). Mr. L. reported that on the evening of the 16th while petting with Irene he had had a rather better erection than before.

He recalled that at school he had had a private game with a friend in which they used to twist other boys' arms. One night Mr. L., then aged eight, had had an overwhelming sense of guilt about this and the next day had apologized to all the victims. He had always been somewhat unhappy about this game.

He was shown relaxation of the shoulder muscles and then a hypnotic trance was induced by the light fixation method. He was made to relax all the muscles he had learned to relax, and then the following scenes were presented: a neutral scene of standing at a busy street corner; C-3 (see list)—a mother shouts at her child because he is dirty. On waking, Mr. L. reported the scene to have been very clear and that C-3 was slightly disturbing initially only.

EIGHTH INTERVIEW (SEPTEMBER 20, 1953). The previous evening Mr. L. had seen a film about a man wrongly committed to a mental institution, being depressed but not insane. In the past he would have been considerably disturbed by such a film but this one did not affect him at all.

After instruction in relaxation of the muscles of the back and abdomen a hypnotic trance was again induced by the light fixation method and the patient was made to relax as deeply as possible. The following scenes were presented: C-3 (see above); A-16—standing outside the door of the headmaster's office at his old school, Mr. L. hears the sound of caning; A-15— a customer comes in with a slightly bleeding nose. On waking, Mr. L. reported a slight initial disturbance to A-16 but none to the other scenes.

NINTH INTERVIEW (SEPTEMBER 23, 1953). Mr. L. reported that when making love on the 21st he had again had no erection at all.

On the 22d he had seen a doctor treat a collapsed patient for three-quarters of an hour in his pharmacy. He had been aware of occasional muscle twitches but had not been really badly disturbed on the whole. He also had a feeling of interest in the procedures that the doctor had used and thought that he would like to see more now.

After training in relaxation of the inferior extremity a hypnotic trance was induced as on previous occasions. The well-relaxed patient was made to visualize scene A-16 twice; A-14—a customer comes in with a small facial wound slightly bleeding, twice; A-13—dead laboratory rat. Mr. L. reported afterward that none of the presented scenes disturbed him at all, but after the last of them he had a spontaneous image of a mangled rat and this disturbed him considerably. He still felt rather shaky.

TENTH INTERVIEW (SEPTEMBER 27, 1953).

Mr. L. reported that he had had a row with Irene the previous evening, and that in the past week or so they had had several arguments over trivialities. On questioning it turned out that the reason for the previous evening's argument was that Mr. L. had refused to go to a party because he knew that one of Irene's old boy friends was there and he feared the competition—as he was so inadequate sexually.

He was also depressed because his mother had seen a psychiatrist who had said that he could do nothing to remove her highly emotional behavior, her nagging, and her tantrums. This meant that the unpleasantness at home would persist. He always had a feeling of anxious anticipation when going home.

Under hypnosis the scenes presented were A-3—a man comes into the shop with a half-inch bleeding cut on his hand; A-12—a dog killed in an accident seen from a distance of 50 yards; A-11—a man in his shop removes a bandage to reveal an old unhealed wound on his forearm about one inch long. None of these scenes disturbed him.

11TH INTERVIEW (SEPTEMBER 30, 1953). Mr. L. had overcome his differences with Irene and the relationship was sailing smoothly, but he was seeing little of her as she was studying for an examination. He had had no real anxiety in the past two weeks despite some arguments at home. Even the arguments with Irene had not provoked him as much as he would have expected. The scenes presented under hypnosis were A-3, modified—a one-inch bleeding wound on a man's forearm; A-12, modified—a dog killed in an accident seen from a distance of about 20 yards; A-10—an old man ill in bed and slightly short of breath; C-2—while waiting for a bus, he sees two men quarreling across the road; A-7—he sees a dog being injected against distemper. A-7 alone was slightly disturbing.

12TH INTERVIEW (OCTOBER 3, 1953). Mr. L. was getting on better with Irene but still having small arguments at times. On September 30 they made love and he "came near to full erection." He had been upset the previous day by hearing a puppy's prolonged howling.

The scenes presented under hypnosis were: A-7, twice; A-16, modified—a boy receives three strokes with a cane in Mr. L.'s presence; A-11, modified—a man has an old three-inch wound on his forearm; B-5—a kicked dog yelps, thrice. Mr. L. reported slight disturbances to the first presentations of A-7 and B-5 only.

13TH INTERVIEW (OCTOBER 7, 1953). As Mr. L. came very late, there was just time for a hypnotic session. The scenes presented were A-7, four times; B-5; A-11, second modification—the old wound is five inches long; B-4—a customer comes in groaning with abdominal pain. None of these scenes disturbed the patient.

14TH INTERVIEW (OCTOBER 11, 1953). Mr. L. reported having felt unusually contented. He had been getting on well with Irene and had had no arguments with her at all. He was aware that her parents disapproved of him but didn't mind this in the least. During the weekend there had been a violent quarrel at home between his mother and one of his brothers but for the first time this had not worried him.

Under hypnosis the scenes presented were B-3—walking past a house and hearing a child crying within; A-3, modification 2—a man comes into his shop with a three-inch bleeding wound on his forehead; A-9—seeing a frog with its abdominal organs exposed by dissection, twice. He was slightly disturbed by the first presentation of A-9 only.

15TH INTERVIEW (OCTOBER 14, 1953). On October 12, Mr. L. had engaged in prolonged petting with Irene. He had been quite excited and experienced some erection but had rightly abstained from intercourse. I now told him not to abstain if his erection should become really strong as part of a powerful general sexual excitation.

The scenes presented under hypnosis were A-9, twice; B-2—the sound of his father groaning at night in the next bedroom; C-1—overhearing his parents quarreling in another room; A-9, modified—watching the incision made in the animal. There was a very slight disturbance to A-9, modified, only.

16TH INTERVIEW (OCTOBER 17, 1953). Mr. L. had nothing to report. During hypnosis, he was presented with A-9, modified, three times; and B-1—standing in a hospital corridor and hearing the groaning of an unseen patient. There was moderate disturbance to the first presentation of A-9, modified, decreasing with repetition, but none to the other scenes.

17TH INTERVIEW (OCTOBER 20, 1953). On October 18 Mr. L., finding that he had quite a good erection while making love to Irene, attempted coitus and succeeded in deflorating her. He ejaculated after about half a minute with normal feeling. On the 19th Irene began to menstruate and, having severe dysmenorrhoea, groaned in his presence persistently. In a few minutes Mr. L. found himself growing tense and this increased until he left her about an hour later.

The scenes presented under hypnosis were B-1, modified—the patient groans with every exhalation (Mr. L. was made to imagine this continuously for about a minute, and then after a pause it was presented to him again for another minute); A-9, modified, three times. There was no disturbance.

18TH INTERVIEW (OCTOBER 22, 1953). Mr. L. reported that as he lay in bed the previous night a dog outside howled for a very long time. He had felt slightly disturbed initially but then relaxed, becoming only dimly aware of the still-continuing sound.

Scenes presented under hypnosis were B-1, modified; A-7—making a prick on the skin of an animal, twice. There was no disturbance.

19TH INTERVIEW (OCTOBER 28, 1953). Mr. L. said that he had had entirely satisfactory sexual intercourse on the 22d. Irene had had her first coital climax—simultaneously with his. In the past week he had noticed a great increase in the general level of his sexual reactivity. He perceived all women in a more sexual way. Kissing Irene was sufficient to produce an erection.

The scenes presented were A-7, modification 1—scratching the animal's skin; A-3, modification 3—a customer comes into the shop with a profusely bleeding cut on his forearm; A-3, modification 4—profusely bleeding wound on his forehead. There was no disturbance.

20TH INTERVIEW (NOVEMBER 15, 1953). Mr. L. had had intercourse on four occasions, each perfectly satisfactory.

He had felt slightly uncomfortable when a student who had failed an examination broke down weeping in the shop. He had also been deeply affected at a film in which a deaf and blind person gave evidence in the witness box, and particularly at sequences of him as a child groping around and being roughly treated by his harsh and impatient mother. However, this was not an anxious feeling, but a "lump in the throat" affair.

The scenes under hypnosis were A-3, modification 4; A-7, modification 2—he gives an animal an injection, the syringe entering easily. There was slight dis-

turbance to the last of these scenes only.

Mr. L. had always loathed doing dissections and giving injections during his training as a pharmacist. He had kept away from such tasks as much as possible and had always tried to get his friends to do them for him when they were impossible to avoid entirely.

21ST INTERVIEW (NOVEMBER 18, 1953). Mr. L. was well pleased with life. The scenes presented under hypnosis were A-7, modification 3—he pricks the animal's skin so as to draw blood; A-6—he moves aside with forceps a frog's liver so as to expose the kidney. There were no disturbances.

22D INTERVIEW (NOVEMBER 21, 1953). The scenes presented were A-7, modification 4—he pricks the skin of a friend so as to draw blood; A-2—a customer comes in with a fracture of his wrist. Mr. L. reported a considerable disturbance to the first presentation of A-2 and somewhat less to the second. There was no disturbance to the other scene.

23D INTERVIEW (NOVEMBER 29, 1953). Under hypnosis the scenes presented were A-2, thrice; A-1—a young man comes in with an abrasion of the knee and says that he fell and scraped it on concrete, twice. There was some disturbance to the first presentation of A-2, but this decreased to very slight by the third presentation. The first presentation of A-1 produced a very slight disturbance, the second none at all.

This patient was encountered from time to time and on each occasion stated that his sexual performance was excellent. He was last seen in July 1956.

REFERENCE

Stone, D. R. Responses to imagined auditory stimuli as compared to recorded sounds. *Journal of Consulting Psychology*, 1955, *19*, 254.

Treatment of a Homosexual Pedophiliac Using In Vivo Desensitization

A Case Study

ROBERT J. KOHLENBERG

Behavior therapists have used two principal approaches in the treatment of sexual problems associated with the choice of sexual objects. The first approach involves building in an avoidance response to the inappropriate sexual stimulus. The second approach is based on the notion that appropriate sexual stimuli are aversive to the patient and are hence avoided. The second approach thus involves increasing approach behavior to the appropriate stimulus by using desensitization (Wolpe, 1958). Masters and Johnson (1970) have developed an extensive sexual counseling program which corresponds to the desensitization approach. The Masters and Johnson program is oriented toward increasing approach behavior and hence reducing the aversive properties of the sexual interaction. The essential components of this treatment plan include (*a*) a history-taking and feedback session in which the patient is given an explanation for his or her current sexual behavior, (*b*) a graded sequence or hierarchy of instructed sexual interactions that range from touching to intercourse (This sequence of directed interactions is prescribed by the therapist, and the couple practices these assignments at home), and (*c*) a progression through the sequence of directed interactions at a rate that results in minimal anxiety and discomfort. An important feature of the Masters and Johnson program is that the

hierarchy is presented in vivo, that is, the patient actually engages in the behavior specified in the hierarchy. This in vivo approach necessitates the involvement of a sexual partner, and hence the Masters and Johnson treatment always involves a couple.

The sexual treatment program described above has been used with a wide variety of male and female sexual problems such as orgasmic dysfunction, premature ejaculation, impotency, etc. Although Masters and Johnson limit their program to male–female couples, it would seem that certain homosexual problems could be treated in a similar manner. That is, from a learning viewpoint, the nature of the sexual response is the same for all people and techniques that apply to the treatment of heterosexual problems would also apply to homosexual problems.

The present paper is about a male homosexual who stated he was unable to become sexually aroused with adult males or females but was sexually attracted to male children. At the patient's request, a therapy program was instituted to bring about increased sexual responsiveness to adult males. Adult males were chosen as the positive goal sex object because the patient's social contacts were homosexual, and heterosexual sex was not one of the therapeutic goals requested by the patient.

METHOD AND PROCEDURE

Subject

The patient, Mr. M., was 34 years old and had been arrested twice for child molest-

From *Journal of Abnormal Psychology*, 1974, *83*(2), 192–195. Copyright 1974 by the American Psychological Association. Reprinted by permission.

ing. The first arrest occurred eight years ago, and the second occurred three years ago. The patient considered his sexual orientation to be homosexual, but he became aroused only with young males of about 6–12 years of age. He claimed that he "prowled" or actively looked for sexual contacts with male children about twice each week by going to the playground or swimming pool where he would be likely to see children. Mr. M. reported that this "prowling" or active looking did not currently result in sexual contacts but did result in both sexual arousal and subsequent discomfort and stress. Another troublesome behavior for Mr. M. was what he referred to as "thinking about children," which occurred about two times per day. These "thoughts" were centered on male children who were sexually attractive to him. Fantasies during masturbation were also centered on male children and masturbation occurred several times a week.

The patient's social life centered on the homosexual community which resulted in many opportunities for sexual contacts with adults. Several times each year he would have a sexual contact with an adult, but these never ended in an orgasm for himself, although he would occasionally become aroused and obtain an erection for brief periods when he was passive during the sexual encounter. He became apprehensive and tense whenever a sexual encounter with an adult was imminent, and as a result he would tend to form relationships with men who were "married" or committed in some other way that would preclude sexual involvement. Mr. M. stated that the problem was that he did not find adults sexually attractive, whereas children were highly arousing. Mr. M's. first sexual contacts occured when he was about 8 and involved his 12-year-old brother. This involvement with his brother lasted several years and then included his younger brother who was three years younger than Mr. M. Mr. M. cannot recall ever being attracted to adult females and claims his only self-satisfying contacts have been with male children.

Mr. M. stated that his desire for children was immoral and had ruined his life. He had sought treatment twice before and received three years of individual and one year of group therapy. Mr. M. felt this therapy had given him some understanding of his behavior but had not led to any changes in his desire for young males.

Data Collection

There were three dependent variables in this study. The first variable was the number of thoughts that were centered on young males. The second variable was the number of prowling incidents, and the third was the number of sexual encounters with adults who were sexually arousing. Mr. M. was instructed to keep a daily record of the occurrences and circumstances of these events. These daily records were to be turned in at the weekly therapy sessions, or if no session was scheduled the records were to be mailed in each week. The return and keeping of these records was required as a condition or treatment and for rebate of approximately one half of the fees charged. The patient paid a $20 fee for each treatment session and received a $5 rebate for each weekly report turned in. The total amount of rebated monies was to be paid at the completion of the six-month follow-up period.

Therapy Plan

Since Mr. M's attraction to children was a problem that could lead to harm and trauma to another person and serious legal consequences for Mr. M., the initial phase of treatment was directed at reducing the sexual arousal value of children by pairing imagined stimuli with electric shock.

The second phase of treatment was to be directed at increasing the arousal elicited by male adults and reducing apprehension and tension associated with sexual contacts involving adults. The second phase was to be accomplished by using a treatment plan modeled after Masters and Johnson.

Baseline Period

The first four weeks involved weekly interview sessions during which Mr. M's history was obtained and a treatment plan was developed. This phase also provided an opportunity to obtain pretreatment measures of sexual activities as discussed above. The rates of "thoughts," "prowling," and "adult" events are given in Figure 1. The first two weeks resulted in the lowest rate of prowling for this phase; the rate then increased during the last two weeks. Mr. M. indicated that the rate of prowling events during the last two weeks was more typical of his behavior. There were no sexual contacts with an adult male during this phase.

Phase 1: Aversive Conditioning

Weeks five through eight involved the pairing of arousing stimuli with electric shock. The shock source was a Lehigh Valley 551-12 finger shocker. Shock in-

tensity was set at a level judged to be painful by Mr. M. Shock duration was less than a second and consisted of a momentary depression of the operate button.

The first session of this phase involved pairing the shock with imagined scenes of prowling and thoughts of children. The sequence was as follows: instructions were given by the therapist to imagine a scene; Mr. M. then signaled when the image was vivid; shock was delivered. Eleven such pairings occured during the first session of aversive conditioning.

The second session involved six more pairings of imagined scenes and shock. Mr. M. reported that the previous week's pairings seemed to be effective, and the number of events during the week following the first aversive conditioning session was lower than previous values.

The procedures for the third and fourth aversive conditioning sessions were similar to the previous sessions. As shown in Figure 1, the shock did not, however, appear to have an effect on the number of incidents. The apparent failure of the aversive conditioning could have been due to both an insufficient number of pairings

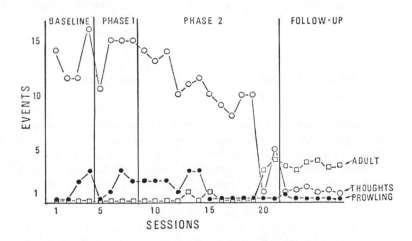

Figure 1. The number of "thoughts" and "prowling" incidents concerning children and "adult contacts" for the three treatment phases and follow-up. The follow-up data are means for each of the six months following treatment.

between the shock and imagined stimuli and inadequate shock intensity. Thus, at this point in the treatment program, continuation of the aversive conditioning phase would have necessitated increased shock levels. Rather than continue aversive procedure, it was decided to proceed with the in vivo desensitization approach described below.

Phase 2: Masters and Johnson Type Therapy

The basic goal of this phase was to produce sexual arousal and orgasms for Mr. M. with an adult male partner. Since the therapy was to involve a series of sessions attended by Mr. M. and a sexual partner, the first task involved finding a suitable partner. The requirements for the sexual partner were as follows: (a) he was to be at least 30 years old; (b) he was willing to commit himself to attending at least 10 weeks of therapy sessions and at least two encounters with Mr. M. during the week; and (c) he was willing to follow the therapeutic regimen which included sexual encounters that did not lead to orgasm. Mr. M. contacted a 32-year-old man, Mr. C., who met the above requirements. Mr. C. had been an acquaintance of Mr. M. for several years and was willing to participate out of friendship for Mr. M.

The therapy sessions were conducted on a once a week basis with both Mr. M. and Mr. C. present. The therapist was the author. The first session of this phase included a discussion of learning principles, as related to choice of sexual object. Instructions were given for Mr. M. and Mr. C. to engage in at least two encounters during the week. These first encounters were to take place with both men in bed without clothes. As described in Masters and Johnson for heterosexual couples, they were instructed to take turns giving each other sensate pleasure. Touching, caressing, etc., of any kind was permissible, but there was to be no touching of

the genital or anal area and sexual arousal was not a goal.

During the second treatment session of this phase, Mr. M. reported that he was very tense and perspired profusely during the previous week's encounters with Mr. C. Mr. C. found the encounters pleasant and arousing.

According to Masters and Johnson a primary source of inhibition to sexual arousal is that of performance anxiety wherein the patient acts as an "observer" of his own sexual behavior. In the present case, Mr. M. seemed to have been concerned about his performance during the previous week's encounters and was also concerned about Mr. C's negative evaluation of his own (Mr. M.'s) lack of sexual arousal. The importance of eliminating the observer role and its inhibitory effects was emphasized to Mr. M. and Mr. C. Mr. C. reassured Mr. M. that it was okay with him if Mr. M. did not become sexually aroused. A restatement of the goals for the coming week's encounter was made. The goal was to become relaxed and have pleasant feelings: sexual arousal was not a goal.

The second week of encounters was reported to be relaxing and pleasant by Mr. M. Mr. M., incidentally, reported that he also became sexually aroused.

The following steps were taken during the remainder of the program. Instructions to proceed to the next step were given only after the patient was completely relaxed at the preceding item: (a) touching for sensate pleasure, no genital involvement; (b) touching for sensate pleasure, some exploratory touching of genital area; (c) simultaneous genital touching, orgasm not permitted; (d) simultaneous genital touching and belly rubbing with genital contact, orgasm not permitted; (e) no restrictions, orgasm permitted.

The last step of treatment was reached during the thirteenth week of Phase 2. Mr. M. was seen six months later for a follow-up interview, at which time he turned in daily reports covering some of the previous six months behavior.

RESULTS

The primary result of treatment was that Mr. M. became sexually aroused with Mr. C. as a partner. Reports of fantasy during masturbation also indicated that Mr. M.'s sexual object was becoming older. Mr. M. also reported that he found other adult men attractive and had sexual contacts with adults (other than Mr. C.) that were sexually arousing. Figure 1 also shows that the number of incidents involving children decreased as Mr. M. progressed through treatment and for the six-month period following termination.

Mr. M. reported that he had become less preoccupied and attracted to children. He ceased "prowling" for children after the sixth week of Phase 2 treatment, and at the six-month follow-up he reported that he had not actively sought any sexual contact with children since the termination of treatment.

DISCUSSION

This case seems to indicate that the acquisition of new, appropriate sexual behavior was effective in reducing child-related sexual behavior. The lack of effect of the aversive stimulus may have been due to several different factors including a lack of generalization, insufficient shock intensity, and an insufficient number of aversive conditioning trials. The difficulty of generalization is that the office situation with finger electrodes applied and imagined stimuli is no doubt highly discriminable from actually seeing a child at a playground in the natural environment.

It is not completely clear as to why the increase in attraction to adults would reduce attraction to children. Increasing the amount of appropriate sexual behavior toward adult males probably resulted in a repertoire of behavior that was incompatible with "prowling" for children. That is, those periods of times that normally would have been spent seeking contacts with children were now spent making contacts with adult males. The number of "thoughts" concerning children decreased as the amount of experience increased with the adult males. This could be accounted for by the respondent conditioning model in which successful sexual experience with adults produced pairings between adult males and sexual arousal (including orgasm). After a number of such pairings, adult males served as conditioned stimuli for sexual arousal, and thoughts that elicited sexual arousal were similarly changed.

It would also seem reasonable to suggest that in addition to the sexual attractiveness of children, there was also some aversive properties associated with children. In fact, Mr. M. sought treatment because of the aversiveness associated with his sexual desire for children. The effect of treatment then, could have provided Mr. M. with the choice between children associated with approach-avoidance characteristics and adults associated primarily with approach properties. The reduced rate of child-related sexual activities would thus reflect that Mr. M. selected the least aversive of the two types of sexual objects.

The results of this case also indicate that an in vivo treatment similar to Masters and Johnson type of treatment for heterosexual dysfunction can be used for homosexual dysfunction problems and holds promise as an effective means of changing sex object choice.

REFERENCES

Masters, W., & Johnson, V. *Human sexual inadequacy.* Boston: Little, Brown, 1970.

Wolpe, J. *Psychotherapy by reciprocal inhibition.* Stanford, Calif.: Stanford University Press, 1953.

Some Observations on the Fallacy of Value-free Psychotherapy and the Empty Organism

Comments on a Case Study

HANS H. STRUPP

Because Kohlenberg's (1974) article goes to the heart of what psychotherapy and behavior modification are about, I was challenged by the Editor's invitation to discuss some relevant issues.

Let me begin with the patient's "motivation" for therapy. It is generally conceded (Meltzoff & Kornreich, 1970) that a patient's motivation to seek change augurs well for success, whereas lack of motivation tends to be associated with failure. For example, a patient *decides* to consult a psychotherapist because he *wants* to be cured of claustrophobia. (The italics in the preceding sentence serve to emphasize the patient's volition, intention, and status as an independent agent.) Regardless of whether the matter is openly discussed, the patient and the therapist agree that (*a*) the treatment of claustrophobia (by whatever means) is a desirable goal for the patient; (*b*) the problem principally relates to the patient's personal happiness and competence; and (*c*) society at large has no particular stake in the matter (except perhaps in the sense that if the patient loses his job as a result of his difficulty he might become a public burden). The patient may also have a domineering wife who derives certain

From *Journal of Abnormal Psychology*, 1974, 83(2), 199–201. Copyright 1974 by the American Psychological Association. Reprinted by permission.

gains from her husband's incapacity and dependence on her. In general, however, most therapists would agree that other things being equal, the foregoing constellation is "ideal" for successful psychotherapy.

What makes the situation ideal is that by and large the therapist can count on the patient's cooperation throughout therapy. I can only mention in passing that from a technical standpoint this "therapeutic alliance" provides the therapist with enormous leverage and that it always remains the ultimate appeal when the going gets rough and the patient becomes "resistant." The latter term suggests that the patient may on some level oppose the therapist and the treatment but in the final analysis both remain committed to a more or less identical goal. While I cannot develop the argument here, I believe that the term *psychotherapy* should be restricted to those situations in which therapist and patient share a set of common goals and at least in a broad sense agree to work collaboratively on their realization. Contrariwise, when such an agreement does not exist or when the nature of the contract is not fully understood by the two parties, for example if the therapist imposes goals of his own or attempts to "shape" the patient's behavior in conformance with external standards, the enterprise should be designated differently.

It seems indefensible for a therapist to pretend that he is working under the first set of assumptions when in reality there is a hidden agenda.

It is certainly true that the patient becomes at times a reluctant or unreliable collaborator. Therapy proceeds to the extent that these roadblocks can be removed through collaborative efforts and it fails if this becomes impossible. Again, I consider it objectionable and unprofessional for the therapist to pursue ulterior goals.

But what about a situation in which the patient is a child who is brought to "therapy" by his parents and who has no intrinsic interest in change? What about the adult patient who suddenly begins to contemplate suicide or a criminal act? What should be the therapist's stance? To be sure, these are difficult dilemmas that cannot be answered in one sentence. In general, however, I agree with Szasz (1965) that these vicissitudes may compromise the therapeutic contract and therefore call for renegotiation when they occur. A major reason for this insistence is the continuing confusion concerning the role and function of the psychotherapist which is still so fuzzy and poorly defined that almost any activity designed to change another person's feelings, attitudes, or behavior can be termed therapeutic.

Does it not seem reasonable to expect that patient and therapist should be clear about the general goals of their work; how at least in a general way, these goals are to be achieved; what reservations (if any) the therapist might have about the worthwhileness, legality, or ethicality of these goals; the nature of the patient's and the therapist's obligations as long as the contract is in effect; and the consequences of breaches in the contract? There can be no doubt that the therapist's moral and ethical values are always "in the picture." While, in my opinion, the psychotherapist is primarily the patient's agent, not the agent of society, the family, the school system, or whatever, he cannot really espouse a "value-free" position. Ideally, he should encourage the patient to work out his own destiny and find his own solutions. However, it is also true that the therapist, whether he acknowledges it or not, does influence the patient's moral and ethical values.

While this position seems, in principle, unassailable, it does not begin to answer many difficult problems. The profession of psychotherapy is often attacked these days on the ground of being an instrument of the establishment, and it is alleged that therapists train their patients to conform to the values of society which in many respects are oppressive. This is a strange turn of events from the beginnings of psychoanalysis when Freud's work was regarded as threatening because it undermined the repressive atmosphere of a Victorian society. Again, I can only call attention to an important problem: however, I do wish to add a strong personal conviction that the therapist should keep uppermost in his mind the goal of his client's autonomy, independence, self-determination, and personal freedom.

How do these observations apply to Kohlenberg's (1974) patient, Mr. M.? From the patient's standpoint, "the problem was that he did not find adults sexually attractive whereas children were highly arousing [p. 308]." We also learn that

At the patient's request, a therapy program was instituted to bring about increased sexual responsiveness to adult males. Adult males were chosen as the positive goal sex object because the patient's social contacts were homosexual and heterosexual sex was not one of the therapeutic goals requested by the patient [p. 307].

In other words, the patient defined the goal of treatment in a particular way, and the therapist agreed to work with him toward this objective.

Kohlenberg, adopting the stance of a

value-free agent, never stated what *he* thought about the worthwhileness of Mr. M.'s goal, but we can infer that he fully approved of it. Had it been otherwise, he would not have agreed to work with Mr. M. (see below). I am not suggesting that he should have disapproved—after all, whose business is the sexual activity of freely consenting adults as long as it is conducted in the privacy of their bedrooms—but I am asserting that he took a definite stand on the issue. It may be true that "from a learning viewpoint, the nature of the sexual response is the same for all people . . . [p. 307]" and that, in mechanical terms, "attraction to adults would reduce attraction to children," but Kohlenberg was in fact doing a great deal more than treating a "sexual response."

Suppose Mr. M. had stated as his problem the relative ineffectiveness of his "prowling" behavior with respect to children to whom he felt sexually attracted? Would a value-free behavior therapist then have instituted a program of assertive training to improve Mr. M.'s "performance"? Since I doubt this, I must conclude that the therapist made a judgment that (*a*) homosexual behavior between consenting adults was in keeping with his own moral position; (*b*) Mr. M.'s sexual attraction to children was undesirable because of adverse social, moral, and legal consequences; and (*c*) it seemed reasonable *and in keeping with his own, as well as society's values*, to institute a treatment designed to change Mr. M.'s sexual interests in a particular direction (especially one in keeping with the patient's wishes).

Kohlenberg chose to describe the nature of his treatment as "in vivo desensitization" and he invoked "learning principles" to account for the successful outcome. If it is true, as I have asserted above, that more was involved than "shaping" a sexual response, perhaps a different description of the treatment may not be entirely fanciful.

Mr. M. enlisted the help of a professional therapist because "his desire for children was immoral and had ruined his life." Previous therapy "had given him some understanding of his behavior, but had not led to any changes in his desire for young males [p. 308]." Note that Mr. M. was in a state of *conflict* (an intrapsychic problem): On the one hand, he felt an inner urge to make sexual approaches to children but he was also mindful of the serious social consequences of acting on these impulses. This was not like a situation in which a judge might suspend a sentence on condition that the defendant seek psychiatric help but in which the latter is not motivated to "work" on his problem except to avert imprisonment. Instead, Mr. M. seemed genuinely interested in arriving at a solution to his problem, such that he would have a measure of sexual gratification *and* avoid adverse social consequences. In short, he had made up his mind that he wanted to change and that he was willing to collaborate with someone who was committed to helping him. As stated earlier, he was *motivated* to seek change but he was also *conflicted* about it. Something needed to be done to help him resolve his conflict.

While Kohlenberg reported very little concerning his interview sessions with Mr. M., it does not seem farfetched to assume that over the course of their meetings a number of exceedingly important messages were communicated by the therapist. I shall try to compress these into a few terse statements:

I understand, Mr. M., that you are experiencing an intense conflict. I am genuinely interested in helping you, and I will work with you if you are really serious about effecting a change. I firmly believe that I can help you. I understand your predicament, and I will at no time criticize you. That is not my job. But you must follow my instructions.

While I am not interested in blaming you, it is clear that your sexual interest in young children has gotten you into serious trouble. We both agree that something must be done to help you stop it. Since you feel that a good solution would be to have a more pleasurable relationship with an adult male, let me try to concentrate our efforts in this direction. Please understand that homosexual relationships among adults are fine as far as I am concerned.

To start with, I am going to ask you to keep a record of your "prowling" behavior, the frequency of your sexual contacts, and your fantasies. I have already made it clear which of these activities I approve and disapprove of. [Later] To underscore my position, we will give you electric shock whenever you imagine "prowling" and "thoughts" of children. [Later] The results indicate that you have not yet become convinced on a deep level that homosexual activity is really much preferable to pedophilia. Since I really want you to channel your sexual interests along the former lines, I have made arrangements with Mr. C., who has agreed to meet with us once a week. . . . [Later] I really think this is working out very well and I strongly encourage you to continue.

My purpose in the foregoing is not to parody the therapy but rather to indicate that the treatment can be readily described as an effort to *persuade* Mr. M. to choose one course of action rather than another, to enlist his cooperation in bringing it about, to use the therapist's high status position and the patient's positive emotional response to the therapist as a means of influencing him. Just as children refrain from behavior proscribed by the parents if their love for them is stronger than the temptation to go against their wishes, it may be said that Mr. M. became "desensitized" to males not because he went to bed with Mr. C. or because the therapist discussed "learning principles as related to the choice of sexual object" but because he became convinced of the therapist's interest, sincerity, and good will. He came to accept the idea that by following the program advocated by the therapist, he would be better off in the long run than by going against it. Consequently he chose to comply.

This version of what produced change may not be very "scientific," but it may be quite accurate. It also serves to make the point that the therapist is a powerful moral force and that value-free therapy is a fiction. By the same token, the patient is always a thinking and decision-making human being, never a passive organism that merely emits responses. Like it or not, the issues are with us and cannot be ignored.

REFERENCES

Kohlenberg, R. J. Treatment of a homosexual pedophiliac using in vivo desensitization. *Journal of Abnormal Psychology*, 1974, *83*, 192–195.

Meltzoff, J., & Kornreich, M. *Research in psychotherapy*. New York: Atherton Press, 1970.

Szasz, T. *The ethics of psychoanalysis*. New York: Basic Books, 1965.

Chapter 17
Assertive Training and Behavioral Rehearsal

For patients whose neurotic anxiety in interpersonal situations prevents them from expressing feelings that might appropriately be expressed, behavioral rehearsal or assertive training is indicated. In fact, some rehearsal training is probably useful for all neurotically anxious persons. It is thought that inhibiting the expression of powerful feelings leads to inner upset and even psychosomatic reactions. The therapist attempts to teach the patient to express these previously inhibited feelings (often by assertive or active behavior) because it is hypothesized that expressing them will reciprocally inhibit anxiety. Role playing with the patient is often engaged in by the therapist in order to teach the individual to assert the previously inhibited behaviors. The new behavior reciprocally inhibits anxiety because it is antagonistic to anxiety and, as a result, the maladaptive, learned anxiety-response habit is weakened. In *The Practice of Behavior Therapy* (1969), Wolpe notes that acting out new behavior augments the newly-expressed emotion and further inhibits anxiety. At the same time, the new and more appropriate behavior is itself rewarded because other persons respond favorably, the patient feels more in control, and so on. We might note that assertive training is a favored form of treatment with women whose culturally conditioned inhibitions cause them to behave maladaptively submissive or passive.

In the selection Arnold Lazarus eschews the term *assertive training* because he considers it only a subset of *emotional freedom* training. He feels the latter term expresses more suitably the "recognition and appropriate expression of each and every affective state." In this case, he uses behavioral rehearsal with a "nervous, confused, and unfulfilled" twenty-eight-year-old man in order to teach the man how to be emotionally free. Note that this is the type of case with which dynamic and humanistic therapists are very familiar. But unlike these therapists, Lazarus's goal is not, for example, insight into oedipal difficulties or the provision of a particular type of relationship. Instead, Lazarus wishes to teach Sam new ways of behaving through role-playing rehearsal. He teaches Sam to tell his father how he really feels when the father is treating Sam like a small boy. Lazarus ends his selection by noting that this type of training makes some patients more anxious, and that at times it must be combined with systematic desensitization.

The focus of this case is on feelings, but the reader should note that the therapy appears to be very cognitive. Also note that Lazarus is quite directive and quite confident about what ought to be the appropriate content and mode of expression of the client's feelings in various situations. After reading this case, the reader may wish to reconsider Strupp's comments (in Chapter 16) on the values and persuasive powers of the therapist.

REFERENCE

Wolpe, J. *The practice of behavior therapy.* New York: Pergamon, 1969.

Acquiring Habits of Emotional Freedom

ARNOLD A. LAZARUS

People who derive benefit from therapy, regardless of the type of treatment they undergo, often state that they have become more outspoken, less inhibited, and able to stand up for their rights. For example, Storrow and Spanner (1962) reported that after short-term insight therapy, patients who described themselves as more dominant after therapy than before, (i.e., "able to give orders," "manage others") also tended to describe themselves as improved.

When stressing the need for dominance, it is necessary to emphasize that the goal is not to become domineering. Similarly, the difference between assertion and aggression should also be noted, since outbursts of hostility, rage, or resentment

usually denote pent-up or accumulated anger rather than the spontaneous expression of healthy emotion. Habits of emotional freedom imply the ability to give honest feedback (i.e., to show one's true feelings, and to do so in a frank and open manner). Emotional freedom opposes hypocrisy, phoniness, and deception. Contrary to popular belief, the result of emotional freedom is not alienation or increased vulnerability, but decreased anxiety, close and meaningful relationships, self-respect, and social adaptivity.

The virtues of emotional freedom were eloquently documented by Salter (1949) under the term *excitation* (as distinct from *inhibition*). Since Salter's Pavlovian underpinnings seem tenuous, and since many people confuse excitation with excitability (which it is not intended to connote) I prefer to avoid this term. Wolpe (1958) proposed the term *assertiveness* in place of *excitation*, but many people associate "assertive training" with one-upmanship and other deceptive games and ploys which Wolpe includes under this heading and which have no place in the forthright and honest expression of one's basic feelings. Besides, the word *assertive* cannot (unless stretched beyond its lexical boundaries) convey all the nuances of "emotional freedom" which would include the subtleties of love and affection, empathy and compassion, admiration and appreciation, curiosity and interest, as well as anger, pain, remorse, skepticism, fear, and sadness. Training in *emotional freedom* implies the recognition and appropriate expression. of each and every affective state. Throughout this book, the term *assertive behavior* will denote only that aspect of emotional freedom that concerns standing up for one's rights.

Many conventional psychotherapists are extremely skilled at bringing people in touch with their affective states. This is often insufficient, for patients, in addition to recognizing their emotions, also need to learn how to express their feelings in a mature and honest fashion. Specific techniques are often necessary to teach people to express feelings appropriately. One of the best ways of achieving this end is by means of role playing or behavioral rehearsal (Lazarus, 1966; Friedman, 1969; Piaget & Lazarus, 1969). Instead of describing the process in generalities, a slightly edited interview protocol will be presented.

CASE BACKGROUND

Sam, a bright twenty-eight-year-old tax lawyer, complained that he felt "nervous, confused, and unfulfilled." He was divorced, had no children, and viewed himself as "a failure and a loser." His father, a surgeon, and his mother, a teacher, were deeply religious and raised Sam and his sister to "mind our P's and Q's." Sam had always excelled in school, although he had no close friends and usually felt uncomfortable around people. His ostensible reason for seeking therapy was to overcome his claustrophobia.

Toward the middle of the second interview, the following dialogue ensued:

THERAPIST: I sense a lot of anger in you.

SAM: Anger? I don't see how you arrived at that. I'm not aware of any special anger as such. I'll admit I was pretty peeved at my ex-wife, but even then, I showed no violence or undue harshness toward her.

THERAPIST: Yes, but how did you *feel?*

SAM: Well, I thought she was extremely immature.

THERAPIST: Never mind what you thought. How did you feel?

SAM: I was going to say that I resented her, but I think that would be considered normal under the circumstances.

THERAPIST: Anger is a normal and basic emotion. You don't have to apologize for it.

SAM: But you seem to be implying that I have more than my normal share of anger. You said that I struck you as being extremely angry, or words to that effect. Obviously I get irritable at times and perhaps minor things annoy me more than they should, but I don't walk around with a chip on my shoulder as far as I can see. Or are you saying that I do?

THERAPIST: Well let me ask you how much resentment you feel toward your parents. You mentioned that they were very strict, and I gathered that they often withheld privileges to which you were entitled. . . .

SAM: If you are asking whether I felt mad at them when I was a kid, obviously I did. But in retrospect I realize that they meant well and did the best they could. But when I was a kid, I did get awful mad.

THERAPIST: And when you were a kid and felt mad at them, how did you show your anger?

SAM: What do you mean? I guess kids wail or gripe. I don't know.

THERAPIST: Whenever I zero in on your anger, past or present, you start intellectualizing. Never mind what kids in general do when angry. For instance, did you ever have a temper tantrum and really blow your stack?

SAM: I guess I must have. Which kid hasn't? I really don't remember.

THERAPIST: When you were a child and threw a real tantrum, such as screaming, cursing, kicking, biting, maybe smashing things, and so on, what did your parents do? How did they handle it?

SAM: I don't know. I mean I can't remember anything of that sort. I know I sometimes cried and my dad would tell me to be a man or something to that effect. I don't know.

THERAPIST: In other words, be a man and don't show your emotions, hide your feelings, keep a stiff upper lip, etc., etc.

SAM: Yeah, that about sizes it up.

THERAPIST: So with that background let's just suppose that little Sam had a temper tantrum. How would mom and dad react?

SAM: Well, they certainly wouldn't like it.

THERAPIST: Would they beat little Sam, lock him up, verbally reprimand him, or what?

SAM: Oh, I would say they'd do all of it. My dad used to hit first and my mother was called "crab" because she would pinch my sister and me when she was riled.

THERAPIST: And all of this gives you no cause for anger or resentment?

SAM: Are you deliberately trying to create a feeling of antagonism in me? Do you want to hear that I hate my parents?

THERAPIST: Only if it's true. I feel that you deny your own emotions and that you find anger especially threatening. I'm trying to put you in touch with your anger so that you can learn to express it in a socially acceptable way. With your background, I would find myself hating and resenting certain things above my parents while, at the same time, loving other qualities and attributes. But I wouldn't deny the negatives, and while focusing on them, I would feel aggressive if not rather murderous.

SAM: Maybe you should have some treatment yourself. (Laughs) I'm only kidding.

THERAPIST: That, in the profession, is what we call a passive-aggressive reaction.

SAM: Oh come now. I was only kidding.

THERAPIST: But let's look at it seriously. I am advocating responses that are quite foreign to you. I am saying the very opposite of the things you were raised to believe in, such as don't hide your feelings, do express your true emotions, let people into your real thoughts and attitudes, say what's on your mind.

SAM: I'm all confused. When we spoke on the phone last Monday and I asked what you thought of the rational approach used by Ellis you said that you were all for it. Now you are telling me to blow my top which seems to go against what Ellis advocates. A rational person wouldn't be bugged by things. As I understand it, he would reason them away.

THERAPIST: Let me try and clarify my position. Your point is an excellent one. When a person recognizes his self-worth and acquires a fitting indifference to the stupid or inconsiderate reactions of certain people, he will indeed be governed by rational and logical perceptions. But, hopefully, he will always be capable of emoting and feeling. When something annoys him, he won't catastrophize. He will be annoyed and express his proportionate anger, and do so toward the source of his irritation. He won't rationalize and kid himself that he is not angry. Being rational is not the same as rationalizing. The irrational person compounds the situation and works himself up into a disproportionate rage, or he may deny that he is angry. The rational person says, "I found Tom's behavior very annoying, and I will tell him so the very next time I see him. I didn't get a chance to do so when it was happening, because I didn't want to embarrass him in front of his employer." Observe that he is showing consideration despite his anger.

SAM: But why give someone the satisfaction of letting him know that he can bug you or hurt you?

THERAPIST: Meaning that you should pretend that Tom isn't capable of bugging you?

SAM: Exactly. Why play right into his hands? If he knows what hurts you or bothers you, he has a weapon to use against you whenever he feels like it.

THERAPIST: Many people make the same error that you are making. Rationally speaking, you can only be hurt by someone in a physical or economic sense. If our hypothetical friend Tom beats you up or causes the loss of your job, you have indeed been injured by him. But we are not talking about that. If you tell Tom that it bothers you when he keeps on making wisecracks, or if you tell him that it hurts you when he makes nasty remarks about your brother, you are being truthful and not placing yourself at his mercy. If Tom is even slightly reasonable, he can apologize and change his behavior, or he can discuss it more fully and inquire why you feel so strongly about the matter and ask you to examine whether you are needlessly supersensitive.

SAM: But what if he decides to needle me still further?

THERAPIST: Then you inform him that you find him a real pain in the ass and that you intend severing all connections.

SAM: But what if Tom happens to be your boss or if you need him for other reasons?

THERAPIST: In that case, you have to decide whether the price is right. I once worked for an outfit where I could have made a mint if I was prepared to pander to a vicious millionaire who headed up the board of directors. All it needed was some double talk and duplicity. But I hated this sort of thing, and so I cut out leaving others to do the brown-nosing which they didn't mind doing.

SAM: I can see how you can cut relations with friends, acquaintances, or even employers, but how can you escape from parents? Look, you know I think you're right. I do resent a hell of a lot of things about my parents. My dad has the typical surgeon's sense of humor. As a kid he used to threaten to cut off my toes and fingers unless I behaved. The Freudians would enjoy that one, hey? And my mom has always been a goddamn teacher. All she does is lecture. "Sam, I told you not to marry so young. I knew you weren't ready for it." And so on ad infinitum. So tell me, how the hell do I get them off my back?

THERAPIST: So how do you handle matters that arise with your parents?

SAM: I've tried everything. If I talk back my mother gets hurt and says, "Don't talk to your parents like that!" My dad chips in and says, "Have you no respect?" They have an incredible knack for putting me on the defensive and for making me feel guilty.

THERAPIST: Do you think the four of us could meet together? If I could have you and your folks interacting with me being present. . . .

SAM: We went through that act once when we saw a family therapist. He also had my sister in on it. My folks succeeded in twisting everything to their own advantage. It was a disaster.

THERAPIST: When was all this?

SAM: Just before I got married. I was very unsure and went to a psychiatrist. He said he practiced family therapy and he had us all in together for three or four visits. Then I quit because it was leading nowhere. So what I'm saying is that I don't want to go through all that again.

THERAPIST: Can you be specific about the sorts of binds you get into with your parents?

SAM: Oh man, these can vary from my mother telling me to have a haircut, or to keep my apartment more tidy, or to visit them more frequently, or to shave off my mustache. And my dad keeps on about the fact that I don't visit my grandmother, and that I am too much of a pleasure seeker. Here's his favorite line: "I'll never understand how any son of mine can have fast cars, fast women, and wear those garments you pass off as clothes." And another favorite line whenever I try to get my point of view across is: "Sam, I'm not *asking* you to show us some respect. I'm *telling* you to."

THERAPIST: So how do you handle these situations?

SAM: Pretty poorly, I guess. Look, I know they mean well.

THERAPIST: The intention may be good but the effect of it all seems to keep you a boy instead of a man. It's the usual conflict of wanting to be a part of mommy and daddy versus the desire to become an autonomous adult. This seems to be a good opportunity to do some role playing or what I call "behavior rehearsal." Let me play the role of your father and let's see how well you can handle his onslaughts in a rehearsal situation.

SAM: You mean you want me to pretend that you are my father?

THERAPIST: Right. I'll say the sorts of things he says to you and let's see how well you can handle them in this situation.

SAM: But I know it's phony and we're just acting. What good will that do?

THERAPIST: I'll explain the theory behind role playing another time. Let's just see how you make out. Okay, now I'm your father. (role playing) Sam, I agree with your mother. You shouldn't have married so young, and you should have more respect for us. Shave off your mustache and start wearing some decent clothes.

SAM: Go to hell!

THERAPIST: (role playing) How dare you speak to me like that! You little, ungrateful upstart. You apologize this instant or I'll disown you completely.

SAM: (role playing) Drop dead!

THERAPIST: Is that the way you'd really like to handle it?

SAM: Well, that's what I say under my breath. No, I realize that's no way to set things right but I feel kind of foolish doing this sort of thing.

THERAPIST: Just try to pretend that you really are talking to your father and try to be as realistic as possible. (role playing) Sam, when are you going to grow up, listen to your mother, have a haircut, wear some decent clothes, and be a man?

SAM: (role playing) I am a man.

THERAPIST: (role playing) Men don't go in for fast cars, flashy clothes, and cheap women.

SAM: (role playing) That's your opinion.

THERAPIST: (role playing) Are you questioning my judgment?

SAM: (role playing) No, I'm not questioning your judgment but I'm also entitled to an opinion.

THERAPIST: Hold it! You are in fact questioning his judgment. Why deny it?

SAM: Yes, yes I know what you mean. But if I said, "Listen, you old goat, your judgment's way behind the times" nothing except maybe hysteria and a real ugly scene is likely to follow.

THERAPIST: Now that's the aggression or the anger to which I was referring earlier. There's a vast difference between an *assertive* and an *aggressive* response. I think that your anger is legitimate. In fantasy, you can picture yourself going even further than merely hurling verbal insults. You can fantasize punching him and really letting rip. In fantasy, you can imagine yourself committing murder, but in your real confrontations you don't have to be either submissive or aggressive. Here we should aim for a balanced and rational response.

SAM: Okay, so even if I just told him, "Yes, I am questioning your judgment" there'd be a big row.

THERAPIST: Right. So what I want you to learn is how to express your feelings. For instance, instead of saying, "Yes, I am questioning your judgment," what would happen if you said, "Dad, you're making me feel like a little kid"?

SAM: He'd snap right back with. "Well, you are nothing but a kid."

THERAPIST: Let's reverse roles. Let me be you and you act as your father. Why don't we take it from the part where your father comes on all critically?

SAM: You want me to act as my dad? Okay (hesitates) here goes. (role playing) Mother and I deserve better treatment, more respect, and a bit of consideration. Are we any worse than Aunt Hilda and Uncle Mike? And you know how nicely your cousin Herb treats them.

THERAPIST: (role playing) Dad, I wish you wouldn't make comparisons; it makes me feel like a kid. Besides, since Herb is someone I do not particularly admire. . . .

SAM: (role playing) Well you are a kid. You think that being divorced adds up

to being a man. And you're always criticizing other people. Believe me, you can learn a lot from Herb.

THERAPIST: (role playing) Dad, I don't wish to get into an argument. I get the message that I am a disappointment to you, that you wish Herb was your son, and that you look upon me as a child who should make no independent decisions but. . . .

SAM: (role playing) Don't get smart with me, young man!

THERAPIST: (role playing) Dad, will you please stop talking to me like a ten-year-old child.

SAM: (role playing) Well, you don't act much different.

THERAPIST: (role playing) Look, Dad. By the time a person reaches my age he has gone beyond the stage where he is open to parental guidance. You and Mother have done the best for me, and if I am a failure and a disgrace in your eyes try to look upon it as my bad luck instead of worrying about the way it reflects on you.

SAM: Actually, I'd like to go further than that and point out to him that ever since I can remember he's never had anything positive to say about me. Whenever he opens his mouth to speak to me he invariably puts me down or finds fault with me.

THERAPIST: Excellent. You should certainly make that point. But why is it, in fact, so important to you to win your father's approval? Let's say you heeded all his advice and lived your entire life according to his specifications, would he approve of you then?

SAM: I see what you're getting at. I think I've been avoiding an inevitable showdown. It's like you said. There is a certain amount of security in knowing that you can turn to your parents if necessary. Actually, I don't have to put up with their carping criticisms. I'm financially independent for one thing. But before I can become, what's the word . . . fully emancipated, we'll have to work on my feeling of guilt. Also, back of it all I guess, there's a sneaky feeling that daddy really knows best and I really am some kind of louse.

THERAPIST: Yes, we can try to change all that. Let me make one important suggestion. Instead of waiting for your father to attack you or to criticize you, why don't you approach him at a time when he is not on the attack? For instance, when all's quiet and all's going well, why not go up to him and say, "Dad I'd like to talk to you," and then tell him how you feel about the fact that he seems to think so negatively about you.

SAM: Um . . . yes. I suppose there may be an advantage in tackling it cold like that.

THERAPIST: Before going ahead with Plan A, I'd like to rehearse it with you to be sure that your overall tone is assertive but conciliatory.

SAM: I think I can handle it.

Sam was an apt pupil, verbally facile, intelligent, personable, and ready to implement the various therapeutic suggestions. He seemed to need explicit approval from an objective outsider to accept his own anger and to give vent to his feelings. At the next interview he reported that the actual confrontation with his father had proceeded extremely well. He reported that his father was eminently more reasonable than he had anticipated ". . . and for the first time that I can ever remember, he said some really positive things about me . . . like he thinks I'm a good lawyer, and that I'm honest, and some other things of that sort." After four sessions, Sam was no longer troubled by nervousness or claustrophobia.

In more, disturbed patients, assertive training and role-playing techniques may augment their anxiety and render them evasive or overdefensive. It is often necessary to apply behavior rehearsal within a desensitization framework so that the patient receives the simultaneous advantages of both processes. This method, termed *rehearsal desensitization* (Piaget & Lazarus, 1969) follows a fairly typical sequence:

1. Nonthreatening role-playing situations are employed until the patient enjoys the procedure per se.

2. Very mildly threatening encounters, arranged on a hierarchy, are enacted. The items on the hierarchy must consist of specific anxiety-producing situations which can be enacted in the consulting room.

3. The therapist models the way in which he thinks the patient should respond to each item (i.e., the initial presentation of each item calls for role reversal).

4. The patient attempts to enact the role only when the therapist's modeling leads him to feel that he can do so quite adequately.

5. New items are attempted only when patient and therapist are satisfied with each performance.

The therapist makes sure that his patient understands that he has graduated to a more difficult item because he has succeeded at a task which earlier would have been difficult for him to perform. Results are often rapid and quite dramatic. The expressive behavior seems to intensify counteranxiety responses. At the same time, if the new expressive behavior is followed by positive consequences of various kinds (e.g., the achievement of respect or control in situations that were previously out of hand) they become an integral part of the person's repertoire.

REFERENCES

Friedman, P. H. The effects of modeling and roleplaying on assertive behavior. Unpublished doctoral thesis, University of Wisconsin, 1968.

Lazarus, A. A. Broad spectrum behavior therapy and the treatment of agoraphobia. *Behaviour Research and Therapy*, 1966, *4*, 95–97.

Piaget, G. W., & Lazarus, A. A. The use of rehearsal-desensitization. *Psychotherapy: Theory, Research* and *Practice*, 1969, *6*, 264–266.

Salter, A. *Conditioned reflex therapy*. New York: Farrar, Strauss, 1949.

Storrow, H. A., & Spanner, M. Does psychotherapy change patients' attitudes? *Journal of Nervous and Mental Disease*, 1962, *134*, 440–444.

Wolpe, J. *Psychotherapy by reciprocal inhibition*. Stanford, Ca.: Stanford University Press, 1958.

Chapter 18

Implosive
and
Flooding
Techniques

Dr. Frankel, in this case, uses a variation of the implosive therapy techniques of Stampfl and Levis (1967). The basic technique of implosive therapy is to increase the anxiety of the client to a maximal level and hold it at this level until the cues for the anxiety spontaneously lose some of their anxiety-causing characteristics. These cues are imagined by the client, usually with the aid of the therapist. Producing these imagery sequences and holding them past the point of extreme anxiety are thought to reinforce anxiety control and to extinguish the fear response. The therapist aids the client during the description of the images by describing the contents of the sequences. In this case Dr. Frankel had the client self-administer the implosive sessions both on a set-time framework and whenever the anxiety occurred, while he himself never took an active role in the imagery sequences. The particular problems of this client were manifold so that all three of her basic fears were worked on during the same time period, though no connection was found in the reduction of one leading to reductions in the others. The follow-up demonstrates the promise of this form of implosive therapy, since the three basic fears of the client were reduced greatly and no other symptoms appeared to be substituted for them. Note especially the interesting comment on experiencing "insight" after the behavior change; this experience appears to be quite a different type than one undergoes with the dynamic therapies.

REFERENCE

Stampfl, T., and Levis, D. Essentials of implosive therapy: A learning theory-based psychodynamic behavioral therapy. *Journal of Abnormal Psychology*, 1967, *72*, 496–503.

Treatment of a Multisymptomatic Phobic by a Self-directed, Self-reinforced Imagery Technique

A Case Study

A. STEVEN FRANKEL

This paper presents the treatment of a series of disabling fears in an individual by a variation of the Stampfl and Levis (1967) implosive therapy technique. As Rardin (1969) has so aptly stated:

> The purpose of this report is not to add to the list of exotic fears treated by implosive therapy, but rather, to illustrate a variation in technique which to the author's knowledge has not appeared in the literature [p. 125].

HISTORY AND CLINICAL DATA

The client, a 24-yr.-old Caucasian married female, was referred by a public marriage counseling agency to the university clinic at which the author was a member of the clinic faculty. Upon referral, the client reported her major difficulty as an inability to have sexual relations with her husband, a 26-yr.-old Mexican-American blue-collar worker. She also reported two other fears which were interfering with her daily functioning.

The Sexual Fear

The client reported that she had been able to have sexual relations with her husband approximately 10 times in the 3 yr. of their

From *Journal of Abnormal Psychology*, 1970, 76(3), 496–499. Copyright 1970 by the American Psychological Association. Reprinted by permission.

marriage. A son was conceived during the third month of marriage, and sexual relations occurred but twice in the time between the birth of the son and the client's referral to the author. The client gave the following account of her social and sexual history:

1. She was "molested" (her body was manipulated by an older male who then exposed himself to her) at age five.
2. During her early adolescent years, she developed a severe skin disorder, resulting in her being ridiculed and scorned by her peers.
3. At age 15, she was taken to a party by one of the "hoods and juvenile delinquents I hung around with," became intoxicated, was gang-raped, and was left unconscious on the lawn of her home the next morning.
4. Her mother, a divorcee, frequently was visited by males who were intoxicated and who would "paw" the client.
5. She had sexual relations with three men before meeting her husband. Each of these men told her that he loved her, but none saw her again after sexual contact.
6. In her late teens, she took a job as a "go-go dancer" in a bar in which she later met her husband.
7. She had premarital sexual relations several times with her husband in an effort "to hold him," but she always felt

"a cold feeling, like I'm going to suffocate—like I can't breathe" during sex.

8. As abstinence from sexual relations continued throughout her married years, her husband increased his consumption of alcoholic beverages, which made her remember her mother's visitors and served to increase her anxiety.

The Earthquake Fear

The client reported that her thoughts were often occupied by the fear of being in an earthquake. She stated that her thoughts about the earthquake were uncontrollable, and that she had them at various times during the day, but that they were especially prominent when she tried to sleep. She reported a consistent sequence of thoughts, involving the ground shaking, the house trembling, her rushing to pick up her baby and standing in a doorway as the house began to collapse around her. At this point in the imagery sequence, she found her anxiety "unbearable," and said, "I do anything I can to put the thoughts out of my mind." She had never actually been in an earthquake and did not personally know anyone who had.

The recurrent thoughts of being in an earthquake interfered with her sleep, such that she appeared physically tired and worn. She was often anxious and irritable during the day. A physician had prescribed tranquilizers for her, but she claimed that these did not help. On at least three occasions, she became so afraid of being in an earthquake that she got up during the night, picked up her son, and ran to a doorway. At no time was there actually an earthquake.

The Fear of Enclosed Places

The client reported that she had always been afraid of enclosed places, such as elevators, very small rooms, and even being surrounded by a large group of people. She did not remember ever being locked or shut up in a small enclosure, nor did she know anyone who had such an experience. She avoided using elevators, preferring to climb many sets of stairs if necessary. On one occasion just prior to her referral to the author, she was accidentally caught up in a large crowd of people who had gathered to greet a visiting dignitary. She felt anxiety and panic and feared that she would suffocate. She screamed and pushed the people around her until she successfully fled the scene.

While the author and client both agreed that the sexual fear seemed to be crucial to the client's marriage, it was also agreed that the most disabling fear at the time was the fear of earthquakes, since the client's daily functioning was so grossly impaired by the latter. It was therefore decided to treat the fear of earthquakes first, followed by the sexual fear, and finally the fear of enclosed places.

TREATMENT PROCEDURES

While it is not necessary to present a detailed account of Stampfl's implosive therapy technique, it is important to note that the technique involves the attainment of a maximal level of anxiety on the part of the client. "When a high level of anxiety is achieved, the patient is held on this level until some sign of spontaneous reduction in the anxiety-inducing value of the cues appears (extinction) [Stampfl & Levis, 1967, p. 500]." The description given by the client of the manner in which her thoughts about the earthquake moved uncontrollably through a stereotyped sequence which inevitably terminated in a high degree of anxiety may be seen as a situation in which an escape response is made in a fear-arousing situation such that the fear response can never be extinguished (Kimble, 1961).

The implosive technique raises the client's anxiety level and maintains it until it passes a peak and begins to decline. This reduction in anxiety is seen as the beginning of extinction of the fear response, but it also may be seen as providing the occasion for reinforcement for the toleration of a high degree of anxiety. That is, the ability to proceed through an imagery sequence which elicits high anxiety is itself reinforced first by success in sustaining anxiety and then by the mastery implied by its reduction. The feared experience may, in fact, become more desirable (as well as less fearful) as a function of experiencing positive reinforcement as the patient demonstrates his capacity to deal with the feared (and hitherto avoided) situation.

Another aspect of the implosive technique is that the therapist helps to direct the client's imagery sequence by describing the contents of the images he wishes the client to experience. As Stampfl (1967) noted,

> once the cues associated with the anxiety-evoking situation are deduced, the therapist can attempt to extinguish their anxiety-eliciting properties by verbally describing in detail to the patient the sequence in which the cues occur [p. 500].

Since the client was unable to come to the author's office more than once a week, it was felt that a version of the implosive treatment which could be self-administered would be important to develop.

Using the assumptions of the necessity for the client to go beyond the peak of anxiety in an imagery sequence and the necessity for a self-administered treatment approach, the following general technique was used: The client was instructed to imagine sequences involving her fears and to concentrate on and report the content of the imagery as well as the concomitant feelings. Each time she reached a point in the sequence at which she found herself "too upset to go on" (at which point she had previously made escape responses by putting the imagery "out of her mind"), she was encouraged to continue the imagery se-

quence. The author at no time provided content for the imagery, but urged the client to "go on. Keep going. What happens next?" These comments, along with reflections of the client's description of her imagery sequences and her feelings, were the only responses made by the author.

Imagery sequences ranged in duration from 15 to 30 min., and the rest of the 50-min. session was devoted to a discussion of the vividness of the imagery sequences and the client's feelings during the sequences.

The Earthquake Fear

The client was instructed to close her eyes and begin the imagery sequence associated with the fear of earthquakes. She was instructed to concentrate on and report as precisely as possible what she pictured and what she felt. When she reached the point in the sequence at which she had always terminated the thoughts (the house beginning to collapse around her as she stood in a doorway with her son), she was instructed to "go on. What's happening now? What's happening next?"

The content produced by the client involved the house collapsing on her, her son trapped under her as large beams fell on her, the earthquake finally ending, her being pinned under beams and being unable to move, screaming for help for several hours with no one coming to her aid, and finally being able to move a beam, stand up, walk away from the rubble, and breathe a sigh of relief at being alive and unharmed. She was instructed to force herself to proceed along the entire imagery sequence on her own whenever her thoughts turned toward the fear of earthquakes. Under no circumstances was she to put the thoughts "out of her mind." This treatment was continued until she was no longer troubled by the fear of earthquakes, as measured in terms of her rating of the fear (see below).

The Sexual Fear

The client was instructed to begin an imagery sequence which involved her sexual fear. She had difficulty imagining beyond the point at which penetration occurred, but with encouragement, was able to go on. The mode of encouragement was the same as discussed above. She finally was able to imagine the entire sexual act occurring, with strongly expressed feelings of being cold, frightened, and suffocating. The sequence, as she described it, ended with her husband's withdrawal and a sigh of relief from her. She was instructed to proceed through the entire sequence three times per day. She was thus instructed because she rarely thought about sex, as opposed to the earthquake fear which was often in her thoughts.

The client's husband cooperated in the treatment of the sexual fear by not making any sexual demands until the client stated that she believed she could complete the sexual act. She was able to begin having sexual relations during the ninth week of treatment (the fifth week of the treatment of the sexual fear—see Table 1).

Fear of Enclosed Places

Since the client had had a recent experience with being trapped in a crowd of people, it was decided to use her experience in the treatment procedure. She was instructed to proceed through an imagery sequence involving being trapped in a large crowd. She was able to proceed through the sequence with little encouragement and was instructed to practice the sequence three times per day.

RESULTS AND DISCUSSION

The client was asked to make a weekly rating of "how strong each fear is," and "how much each fear interferes with your life." The entire treatment procedure

TABLE 1
Weekly Subjective Ratings of "How Strong Each Fear Is" and "How Much Each Fear Interferes with Your Life"

Week	Earthquake		Sex		Enclosed places	
	St	I	St	I	St	I
1	10	10	10	8	8	7
2	6	6	10	8	8	7
3	2	1	10	8	8	7
4[a]	0	0	10	8	8	7
8[b]	0	0	6	5	8	7
12	0	0	3	3	4	1
16	0	0	3	3	0	0
20	0	0	2	2	0	0
6 mo.	0	0	1	0	0	0

Note.—St = strength; I = interference.
[a] Beginning of the treatment of the sexual fear.
[b] Beginning of the treatment of the fear of enclosed places.

took 5 mo., and the ratings made by the client appear in Table 1.

It should be noted that while significant fear reduction occurred as treatment progressed, the fears seemed to be independent of each other. That is, diminution of the earthquake fear did not seem to have any generalized effect on the other fears.

The Earthquake Fear

The earthquake fear was reduced from the highest possible ratings (10 on each scale) to the lowest possible ratings in four sessions. She reported that she thought less and less of earthquakes, and that she no longer had difficulty sleeping. *The ultimate criterion was that a mild earthquake did, in fact, occur about 6 wk. after treatment began, and the client reported that she was "not bothered in the slightest by its occurrence."* A 6-mo. follow-up found no recurrence, of the fear, even though several earthquakes occurred during that period.

The Sexual Fear

As reflected in Table 1, the sexual fear decreased to a point such that the client was again able to have sexual relations with her husband. At first she still did not enjoy the sexual act, but, with time, her fear diminished such that she was able to experience some degree of pleasure. She had not, at 6-mo. follow-up, been able to achieve orgasm, but she reported increasing pleasure and confidence. Her ability to enjoy sex also helped change her husband's drinking pattern, such that they believe their relationship to be "better than it has ever been before." (At 1-yr. follow-up, the client reported that she was able to achieve orgasm approximately once in every three or four sexual experiences. She stated that she was able to experience a great deal of pleasure in sex, and that her sexual fear was no longer a problem for her or her marriage.)

Fear of Enclosed Places

The fear of enclosed places diminished from a fairly high rating to zero after seven sessions (see Table 1). At 6-mo. follow-up, the fear had not recurred. It is interesting to note in the light of Stampfl and Levis' (1967) statement that "after a few sessions, patients frequently recall various memories which previously had evaded them [p. 500]," that the client recalled being accidentally trapped in an air-tight cabinet at approximately age six, and that her mother discovered her in time to prevent suffocation. This experience was reported during the fifth treatment session involving the fear of enclosed places. The client reported that she experienced the memory just after successfully riding down three floors of a building in an elevator. In other words, the memory of a "traumatic event" relating to the fear of enclosed places occurred after her behavior had changed. Thus, further evidence exists for the view that behavior change can be followed by "insight."

There is little doubt that the present case history lends itself readily to dynamic interpretation. However, such an interpretation, which could have led to years in treatment, seemed unnecessary to deal with the patient's most distressing symptoms. While a more traditional therapeutic approach might have achieved the same goal, it is unlikely that such a goal would have been achieved so fast.

In general, the treatment of the fears of the client by a variation of Stampfl's implosive therapy technique was effective through a 6-mo. follow-up. There were no recurrences of the fears, and no discernible "symptom substitution" occurred. It is clear that the client could provide her own imagery sequences, given initial instructions to this effect. Part of the explanation for a positive outcome may be self-reinforcement as one sucessfully proceeds through frightening images. This allows for a largely self-administered treatment, a marked advantage over the more usual approach.

REFERENCES

Kimble, G. A. *Hilgard and Marquis' conditioning and learning.* New York: Appleton-Century-Crofts, 1961.

Rardin, M. Treatment of a phobia by partial self-desensitization: A case study. *Journal of Consulting and Clinical Psychology,* 1969, 33, 125–126.

Stampfl, T., & Levis, D. Essentials of implosive therapy: A learning theory-based psychodynamic behavioral therapy. *Journal of Abnormal Psychology,* 1967, 72, 496–503.

FOLLOW-UP

A. Steven Frankel[1]

After having dealt with a considerable number of people who present themselves as having phobias, it has become clear that one very important dimension along which to view such individuals is whether they tend to be the more "obsessive type" or the more "hysteric type."

The former do not often respond to imagery techniques well, unless, as in the case presented here, the obsessive thoughts are not easily controlled by the client. This is because obsessive types seem to make what might be called covert escape responses; they do not maintain the threatening image for a long enough period of time to allow symptom reduction to occur. The client discussed here was virtually unable to stop the obsessive thoughts whenever she wanted to once the sequence began (only when they were unbearable), and this may have significantly aided the treatment.

The hysteric type of client may be characterized as one who is suggestible and cooperative enough to maintain exposure to the imagery for a considerable amount of time, thus allowing the ameliorative effects of such exposure to occur.

Thus, any decision to utilize imagery techniques such as that presented here should be made with careful consideration of the client's ability and willingness to maintain the experience of aversive imagery for some duration.

[1] Prepared by the author for inclusion in this volume.

Chapter 19

Covert Desensitization and Self-control Procedures

In this case, Dr. Wisocki primarily uses covert sensitization methods to treat a young man who wished to give up his addiction to heroin, a problem particularly difficult to treat. Covert sensitization procedures involve the use of scenes imagined by the client that are both rewarding and punishing; these scenes are used as reinforcements and punishments for emitting adaptive and unadaptive responses respectively. Using his own imagination as the tool, the client becomes his own behavior modifier under the guidance of the therapist. This case is especially interesting, moreover, because the client also presented broader problems in living such as a negative attitude toward himself and society with which Dr. Wisocki also attempts to deal. Furthermore, Dr. Wisocki demonstrates flexibility and ingenuity in her attempt to treat the range of problems presented by the client.

Dr. Wisocki has added an honest and sensitive comment to her case in the form of "Afterthoughts," in which she discusses the alternative ways her therapeutic success with this refractory problem might be explained, especially focussing on the nature of her relationship with the client. Once again we face the question of whether the curative agent is really the relationship with the therapist. Dr. Wisocki thinks not, but the reader must make a private judgment.

Finally, Dr. Wisocki emphasizes that the client was able to perform therapy on himself and to be in control of his own treatment to some extent. This point should be compared with Dr. Boyer's emphasis on the same behavior in his case presented in Section One.

The Successful Treatment of a Heroin Addict by Covert Conditioning Techniques

An Updated Report

PATRICIA A. WISOCKI

INTRODUCTION

In the spring of 1971 a 26 year old man with a three year history of heroin addiction presented himself to me for behavior therapy. At this first meeting the patient disclosed that he often became despondent, experienced frequent feelings of self-debasement, and refused all social contact with former friends, as well as any possibility of new friends. He spent hours writing poetry and reading literature of all kinds. His attitude toward society and toward himself was extremely negative. His chief desire, after completing therapy, was to buy a van and travel to South America to live "somewhere" for an indefinite period. At this time he was living with his parents who were frequent sources of tension and anger.

According to his statement, he began taking opium in 1968 in reaction to a "split" with his girlfriend. Two months later he was mainlining heroin and soon developed a habit requiring at least twenty "bags" a day. He was active as both a pusher and a user of heroin and an accomplished thief and cheat. Before using these drugs he had frequently ingested barbiturates, amphetamines, and mescaline. His previous attempts at therapy included three years of private psychiatric

Most of this material was first published in *Journal of Behavior Therapy and Experimental Psychiatry*, 1973, *4*, 55–62. Copyright 1973 by Pergamon Press Ltd. Reprinted by permission.

treatment, a three month membership in a Synanon group and two methadone maintenance programs. The longest period of time he reported abstinence from drugs was six weeks. At the time he saw me the patient had just completed a 15 day methadone withdrawal program, but was not under any other treatment.

Due to three important reasons, I was reluctant to accept this young man as a patient. For one thing, I believed that constant surveillance, rigid control, and medical facilities were essential to insure a stable treatment program. I worked in an office setting and could see the patient not more than two hours a week. Secondly, in a private practice one relies heavily on self-report for verification of progress. Without available toxicological reports of the fact, degree, and course of addiction, and influenced by reports of the "cunning" and deceit of addicts, I felt I could not depend on the patient's word as a reliable monitor. Thirdly, since the patient had attempted several forms of drug therapy without success, a negative prognosis was indicated.

I conveyed my doubts to the patient and recommended a hospital program. He refused to be dismissed and indicated his eagerness to cooperate fully with any suggestion I made. This to me was the only favorable point in his presentation, although he reported that he had been enthusiastic over other forms of therapy previously undertaken. But I agreed to see him.

TREATMENT PROGRAM

The patient and I determined that the goals to be achieved during the course of treatment were these: he must stop "shooting up" with heroin; he needed a more positive attitude toward himself; and he must re-align himself with society, at least to a level where he could feel comfortable. This order of priorities was observed in therapy.

I. The Addictive Behavior

The majority of studies dealing with the behavioral treatment of drug addiction are directed exclusively at eliminating the drug-taking habit. Generally an aversive conditioning procedure, either physical or imagerial, is employed for this purpose. Thus we have the reports of Anant (1968), Lesser (1967), Liberman (1968), O'Brien, Raynes, and Patch (1972), Raymond (1964), Steinfeld (1970), Thompson and Rathod (1968), and Wolpe (1964) indicating the value of aversive conditioning for decreasing the frequency of drug usage.

Also concerned exclusively with the addictive behavior, but employing an extinction technique, Gotestam, et al. (1972), reported favorable pilot work with amphetamine addicts.

Relying on much of this evidence for the accomplishment of our first goal, I constructed a program involving three methods of treatment: the reinforcement of thoughts and behaviors antagonistic to the use of heroin, the elimination of positive thoughts and urges for heroin, and the creation of an aversion for all aspects of heroin usage.

Concerned over insuring the return of the patient to the second therapy session, (a problem that occasionally occurs with the use of aversive conditioning methods) I decided not to risk the initial introduction of an aversion technique. Instead, after taking a brief behavioral history, the first session was spent in teaching the pa-

tient to reinforce himself for refusing drugs. The technique employed for this purpose was covert reinforcement (Cautela, 1970).

After determining which items were regarded as sufficiently pleasurable by this patient for use as reinforcers (e.g., living peacefully in South America; getting a Master's degree; having good people around to care for him; and having a manuscript accepted for publication), covert reinforcement "scenes" were constructed on two levels: (1) those involving some elaboration of situations in which he might be tempted to "cop," as from contact with a friend, seeing a known pusher on the street, seeing road signs indicating the cities where it was possible to obtain heroin easily, etc.; and (2) those consisting of brief thoughts which we wanted to increase, as: "I'm really glad I'm straight"; "It's good to be clean"; "When I do heroin everything goes against me"; "I'm not going to let drugs win over me", etc.

I described these scenes in sequences with pauses for specific segments which contained the target behaviors we desired increased. When the appropriate response was imagined, the patient signaled by raising his finger and I immediately pronounced the word "reinforcement." This word was the cue for the patient to imagine one of the pre-selected pleasurable scenes. Thus, imagining the appropriate behavior was paired with a reinforcing stimulus.

A typical covert reinforcement scene for this patient was as follows:

Relax and try to imagine that you're driving your car through the city. You're tired, anxious to get home and take a shower. Try to feel the situation as much as possible. Try to imagine the streets you're passing through; try to feel the steering wheel in your hands; try to hear the noises of the city. The only thing on your mind is that shower and how good it'll feel. You suddenly see a familiar scene. You see a friend of yours, _____, in the process of making contact for a fix. The thought immediately passes through your mind: "What a fool that guy is. Heroin is just no good. It's too bad he doesn't see it." But you feel glad you're not involved with it any longer.

At the signal from the patient for clear imagery, I responded with the word "reinforcement" and the patient imagined his pleasurable scene of getting a manuscript accepted.

This was one of several different scenes presented each week in therapy. Each scene was developed around actual "temptations" the patient described during each session and was practiced approximately 20 times in alternating sequences. I described it once and then the patient imagined it by himself, etc. Each scene practiced in the office was assigned for "homework."

Gradually, after some practice with the covert reinforcement technique, the patient began constructing his own individual scenes, incorporating the problems he actually experienced in avoiding heroin each day. It was assumed that teaching him to adapt the technique to on-the-spot feelings and situations would strengthen his drug-avoidance behavior and demonstrate to him his own abilities to control his behavior.

The technique of thought stopping (Wolpe, 1958) was used to reduce the frequency of thoughts dealing with the positive aspects of heroin usage, as: "How easy it would be to get some smack"; "It would really feel good to trip out"; "I wonder what it would be like now to get high." The patient and I alternated trials with this technique and practice of it was assigned for homework.

After a week of using thought stopping and covert reinforcement regularly on his own, the patient reported feeling that he had finally acquired practical tools with which he could control his own addiction.

At this point I decided to introduce the aversive conditioning technique (Cautela, 1967) to condition a negative response to the use of heroin. While ordinarily in the application of this technique, the stimulus to an aversive response is a sensation of nausea, for this particular patient, and apparently for many heroin addicts (e.g., Steinfeld, 1970), the idea of vomiting was positively associated with a good grade of heroin. Consequently, it was necessary to obtain a suitable list of other aversive stimuli.

Scenes were constructed in which the patient visualized himself in the acts of thinking about "copping" heroin, driving to places where he often obtained a supply of the drug, making the contact with the pusher, and the "shooting up" procedure. At each point in the scenes where he made a positive approach response to the drug, he was instructed to imagine himself suddenly and immediately assailed by a swarm of flying insects, attacked by spiders, contacting an instant case of leprosy, or being immersed in sewage. These stimuli were varied among the scenes to avoid the problem of satiation. Fortunately, the patient could readily visualize the descriptions. (In cases where a person is not easily able to depict the scenes to himself, the therapist may initiate training sessions in imagery. Such training consists of detailing descriptions of images, the use of audio and visual supplements, and the incorporation of other sensory modalities.)

A typical covert sensitization scene used with this patient was the following:

Imagine that you're in the car, on your way to _____ to get some junk. You see a road sign indicating the distance to that city. You're thinking about how easy it will be to get drugs there. As you have that thought a wasp flies into the car. You can hear it buzzing. You can see it flying in front of your eyes. It's all brown and ugly. A fear starts to rise in you, but you shake it off and think about how you'll feel when you have the fix. Then suddenly that wasp is joined by a horde of wasps . . . all buzzing and flying around your eyes. You keep driving to _____, thinking about your pusher and making the contact. And then you see him —the guy who will sell you the heroin. Suddenly the wasps attack—swarms of them come crashing down on your head. They land on your hands; the steering wheel is covered with them. You can't see in front of you. The sounds are terrible. You can feel a hundred stings all over your body. They're in your clothes, on your face— all over everything. You decide it's not worth it. You decide to turn back. You think how nice it would be to be home and away from this whole scene of copping heroin, people on the street, and everything connected with heroin. And, as you turn your car away, the wasps begin to leave. The further away you get, the fewer wasps around you. Everything is quiet, peaceful, and calm. The radio is playing your favorite song. You begin to feel happy that you resisted the urge.

This scene, along with several others concerning various behaviors connected with obtaining and using heroin, was described to the patient about ten times during the course of a therapy hour. After each description by the therapist, the patient was told to imagine the scene by himself, trying to achieve as much clarity and vividness of imagery as possible. At the end of the session the scene was assigned for homework practice ten times three times a day. The patient was further instructed to think of the aversive images any time he considered obtaining or using heroin.

Results of Phase I

The patient began behavior therapy for his addictive behavior at the conclusion of a 15 day methadone maintenance program. At that point he had been off heroin for two weeks. He remained "clean" for a total of three weeks and three days (this included two behavior therapy sessions). On the fourth day of the fourth week he obtained half a spoon of heroin and, upon injection, felt immediately depressed.

During the next six weeks of therapy the patient practiced his homework faithfully and frequently. He reported that the thoughts of the aversive images were with him constantly. Whenever he had an urge to try heroin he would think about how terrible his life had been with it and that now he was content. His dreams of huge dope-filled rooms steadily decreased. Every time he saw an insect he reminded himself to resist the urge to "cop" heroin. Occasional offers of the drug from other addicts and pushers were rejected after several trials of thought stopping and relaxation.

During the third week into therapy, I began to add techniques directed at improving the patient's self-concept and reducing his social anxieties on the assumption that the development of new, more positive behaviors would aid in strengthening his desire to avoid heroin.

II. The Self-Concept

A behavioral definition of "self-concept" for this patient consisted of particular negative thoughts and verbal statements concerning his supposed "ugly and nasty" physical appearance, the idea that no one could like him and that his life had been completely wasted. (In other cases, the therapist might also consider the type of clothing worn by the patient, his level of neatness, etc. as indicative of his level of self-concept.)

To improve his self-image the techniques of thought stopping and covert reinforcement were combined. I instructed the patient to begin to imagine specific situational stimuli which occasioned the negative ruminations (i.e., sitting alone in his room, looking in a mirror, and seeing other men involved in worthwhile activities) and to shout "stop" to himself before the thought progressed. Additionally, the patient was given a list of positive self-statements to reinforce. Therefore, at each point when he stopped his negative statements, he called to mind a positive statement and rewarded himself for it with a pleasurable scene.

For example, a sequence went as follows: he imagined looking in the mirror, beginning to think about his worthlessness, shouted "stop" to himself, imagined the statement, "Just because I made one mistake my life isn't over" and reinforced it with a scene of sitting by a quiet stream in South America.

Results of Phase II

These techniques were rehearsed continually in the therapy hour until, after four weeks, the thoughts were no longer troublesome. The patient spontaneously made positive comments about himself and began thinking that a girl might find him attractive after all.

He also began wearing short sleeve shirts and shorts into the therapy sessions, proudly displaying his arms minus the telltale needle marks. His appetite had improved; his weight increased; and he took on a tanned and healthy appearance from hours spent on the beach.

III. Attitudes toward Society

Assuming that the patient's addiction to heroin was at least in part maintained by the ability of the drug to remove him from the aversive elements of his social environment (as suggested also by Cahoon and Crosby, 1972), I felt it crucial to teach the patient more adaptive ways of dealing with "The Establishment," as he referred to society in general. Since many of his early drug binges were precipitated by break-ups with girlfriends, it was also necessary for him to learn ways of interacting comfortably with females. (Some support for this position has been presented by Kraft, 1969a; 1969b; 1970a; 1970b and Polakow and Doctor, 1973 in which the successful treatment of drug addicts has been accomplished by the reduction of social anxieties and the reinforcement of drug-antagonistic behaviors.)

Consequently, the target goals to bring about a re-alignment with the social structure were: (1) the performance of specific initiating behaviors in the direction of long-term future goals, as looking for a job, attending social functions, and seeking out people for social relationships; (2) the elimination of anxiety responses attached to such situational stimuli as fears of rejection, loneliness, and criticism; (3) the reduction of negative thoughts about society.

Because the patient was intensely fearful of projecting himself back into the original stimulus situation which he saw as provoking his use of heroin, treatment in this area required a more subtle approach. For the reduction of such initial fears, I have found the technique of covert reinforcement sampling (Wisocki, 1971) especially useful.

Covert reinforcement sampling, suggested directly by the work of Ayllon and Azrin (1968) for the establishment of reinforcers for hospitalized persons, consists of instructing the patient simply to imagine without any positive or negative connotations, various events which he was reluctant to perform. For this patient these events included approaching a girl, asking her for a date, going to the beach, playing tennis, seeing a movie alone, and taking guitar lessons.

Once his anxieties lessened over dealing with these problems and he began to think positively about performing the behaviors sampled in imagination, other techniques were employed to continue therapy.

Covert reinforcement was used to encourage his performance of the sampled behaviors and to teach him to shrug off potential slights and injuries from people he would contact (e.g., females and persons in authority over him).

A typical scene depicted the patient inviting a girl out to the beach and receiving an unceremonious rejection. Continuing the scene, he calmly shrugged and commented philosophically on the uncertainties of life and the preferences of women and refused to consider the situation serious. Immediately upon taking that positive attitude, he was reinforced with a pleasant image.

Other scenes, similar to this one, were detailed around various fears he experienced about social customs and were practiced daily by the patient.

The thought stopping technique was used to eliminate his ideas that society was a wilderness, a place where he would be destroyed, and was populated with hateful and hurtful persons. An alternative list of positive thoughts about coping with society and the valuable aspects of social ization was composed and each one was reinforced on a formal practice basis.

Results of Phase III

This aspect of treatment began very early and required the longest amount of time. In fact, even upon termination, I felt that the patient had reached only a fledgling level of social performance.

After about eight weeks of therapy he began looking for a job; two weeks later he was dating. These new situations produced new problems, however. The father of the girl he was dating strenuously objected to him. His supervisor at work was overly aggressive and insulting. After months of free time, he felt the job was too confining. His parents, seeing improvement, exerted more pressure to "shape up" by getting a haircut and a better job.

From this point, the therapy hour was spent discussing methods of handling these complex events. On his own initiative, the patient was adapting his previously learned techniques to the new difficulties and actually reported enjoying what he considered "healthy problems."

Often during these final sessions, without prompting, the patient verbally stated his determination to avoid drugs, and reported a sense of happiness, contentment and confidence in himself for dealing with his problems. I verbally reinforced these statements with much enthusiasm.

At an eighteen month follow-up meeting the patient reported that he had not used heroin during that period and no longer felt a desire to revert to his old patterns of behavior. He had taken a job as a counselor for emotionally disturbed children and delighted in it. He had married, despite much adversity from the girl's family, and was experiencing an active social life.

DISCUSSION

This patient may be considered atypical in that he was educated, highly motivated (i.e., he attended all the scheduled therapy sessions and reported that he practiced assignments), presented himself for therapy voluntarily (and on a paying basis), and was able to imagine the depicted scenes. These factors undoubtedly influenced the treatment outcome.

Also, as is usual in clinical cases, it is impossible to conclude which, if any, of the therapeutic techniques employed produced the behavioral changes. In this case, these points are notable, however. Other forms of drug therapy attempted by this patient were unsuccessful for him. The expectancy factor for success on the therapist's part was small. The entire course of therapy was conducted in a non-institutional setting on a once-a-week basis. The dependency on heroin, according to the patient's statement, was eliminated in a relatively short time, and in fact did not require as much effort to treat as did the establishment of the pro-social behaviors. After twelve sessions of therapy a person exhibiting one of the most difficult forms of maladaptive behaviors had become a worthwhile and productive member of society.

The "withdrawal" symptoms of this patient were unpleasant, expressed in backaches and severe nausea for a two week period, but by no means difficult for him to cope with. Since there is some evidence supporting the notion that withdrawal symptoms are to some extent at least a function of expectation (Barber, 1972; Ullmann & Krasner, 1969), I was careful to simply make a record of complaints without paying undue attention to them.

"Homework" assignments, which are written out for each patient on an individual form (Wisocki, 1970), were apparently a valuable adjunct to the entire therapy program. From the therapist's viewpoint, such assignments provided the patient with many more conditioning trials than were possible to give once a week in the office. According to the patient's report, however, they also enabled him to acquire readily accessible "tools of control" and a resulting sense of self-mastery which helped him continue in therapy despite occasional setbacks. The lack of emphasis on self-control in other forms of drug therapy attempted by this patient was to him the reason for their ineffectiveness.

The description of this case is presented to indicate the promise held by behavioral methods in the treatment of drug users and to encourage other therapists to attempt such treatment even when success appears improbable. The positive results of this case point certainly toward further experimentation and application.

REFERENCES

Anant, S. (1968) Treatment of alcoholics and drug addicts by verbal aversion technique. *Int. J. Addictions*, 3, 2.

Ayllon, T. and Azrin, N. (1968) *The Token Economy*, Appleton-Century-Crofts, New York.

Barber, T. (1972) Personal communication. Medfield State Hospital, Harding, Massachusetts.

Cahoon, D. and Crosby, C. (1972) A learning approach to chronic drug use: Sources of reinforcement. *Behav. Therapy*, 3, 64–71.

Cautela, J. (1967) Covert sensitization. *Psychol. Rep.* 20, 549–568.

Cautela, J. (1970) Covert reinforcement. *Behav. Therapy*, 1, 33–50.

Gotestam, K. G., Melin, G. L., and Dockens, W. S. (1972) A behavioral program for intravenous amphetamine addicts. Paper presented at the International Symposium on Behavior Modification, Minneapolis, Minnesota.

Kraft, T. (1969a) Successful treatment of a case of chronic barbiturate addiction. *Brit. J. Addictions*, 64, 115–120.

Kraft, T. (1969b) Treatment of drinamyl addiction. *Int. J. Addictions*, 4, 59–64.

Kraft, T. (1970a) Successful treatment of "drinamyl" addicts and associated personality changes. *Canad. Psychiat. Assoc. J.*, 15, 223–227.

Kraft, T. (1970b) Treatment of drinamyl addiction. *J. Nerv. Ment. Dis.*, 150, 138–144.

Lesser, E. (1967) Behavior therapy with a narcotic user: A case report. *Behav. Res. & Therapy*, 5, 251–252.

Liberman, R. (1968) Aversive conditioning of a drug addict. A pilot study. *Behav. Res. & Therapy*, 6, 229–231.

O'Brien, J., Raynes, A., and Patch, V. (1972) Treatment of heroin addiction with aversion therapy, relaxation training and systematic desensitization. *Behav. Res. & Therapy*, 10, 77–80.

Polakow, R. and Doctor, R. (1973) Treatment of marijuana barbiturate dependency by contingency contracting. Unpublished manuscript, Los Angeles County Probation Department, Reseda, California.

Raymond, M. (1964) The treatment of addiction by aversion conditioning with apomorphine. *Behav. Res. & Therapy*, 1, 287–291.

Steinfeld, G. (1970) The use of covert sensitization with institutionalized narcotic addicts. *Int. J. Addictions*, 5, 225–232.

Thompson, I. G. and Rathod, N. H. (1968) Aversion therapy for heroin dependence. *Lancet*, 2, 382–384.

Ullmann, L. and Krasner, L. (1969) *A Psychological Approach to Abnormal Behavior*, Prentice-Hall, Englewood Cliffs, New Jersey, p. 506.

Wisocki, P. A. (1970) Homework assignment form. Unpublished material, University of Massachusetts, Amherst.

Wisocki, P. A. (1971) Covert reinforcement sampling. Unpublished manuscript, University of Massachusetts, Amherst.

Wolpe, J. (1964) Conditioned inhibition of craving in drug addiction. *Behav. Res. & Therapy*, 2, 285–287.

Wolpe, J. (1958) *Psychotherapy by Reciprocal Inhibition*, Stanford University Press, Stanford.

AFTERTHOUGHTS   Patricia A. Wisocki

When this case was first presented, credit for the success was variously attributed to the client's high motivation; his educational background; his ability to imagine; my "warm and winning personality"; and our "relationship" (I refuse to detail other Freudian concepts that were raised). Only the client was convinced that the *techniques* were responsible for the resolution of his problem.

I certainly do not deny the value of nontechnical aspects of therapy. In fact, when performing behavior therapy I deliberately try to operationalize warmth, interest, motivation, and so on to enhance the efficacy of the procedures themselves. For instance, twice I took the client out for a beer after the therapy hour to encourage him to sample the life style of his peers. Once I gave him a puppy ("someone who would always love him" in his words). I expressed personal disappointment in him when he failed to practice his assignments and was elated when he did. I was available by phone whenever he wished and did not confine the discussion of his problems to the office.

Other critics questioned the truthfulness of essential facts concerning the actual amount of heroin used, the habit strength of the addiction, and the presence of "track marks." I had trouble believing it myself, considering the information I had on heroin addiction. I chided myself for neglecting to ask for a medical report and for taking the patient's word on the quality of his addiction and about his progress during therapy.

But these were afterthoughts once the case was completed. During the time of therapy my main concern was to change the behavior (although I doubted it was possible under the circumstances). Afterwards, however, I could not determine what rewards would accrue for the patient if he had prevaricated. He had entered therapy voluntarily and had even taken a menial job to pay for it. I wrote no letters for him nor did I obtain any medication for him. (And, in my humility, I cannot believe that anyone would subject himself to twelve hours of my detailed descriptions of wasps and sewage simply to enjoy my presence.)

To this day, two years after the therapy was terminated, I cannot verify the fact and extent of his addiction; neither can I say with certainty what the reasons were for the successful outcome. I can say, however, that the patient reports he is still abstinent and enjoying his job and home life.

In this brief case study, William Reavley demonstrates how biofeedback techniques—the monitoring of biological processes and subsequent giving of feedback to the patient—can be used to treat a problem associated with general anxiety. Often biofeedback involves making the patient aware of not only the biological indications themselves but also the indirect changes in them. In this case, the indication was used to make the patient more aware of his own anxiety rather than to change any specific biological processes. The patient did not realize the effect of anxiety on his handwriting, and the biofeedback equipment served just this purpose. While the writing problem may seem at first glance to be rather minor, for some individuals it can be very debilitating.

Once again, the technique could be followed by the patient at home, and this added greatly to the efficacy of the treatment. GSR equipment was used to monitor his general anxiety while EMG equipment gave feedback on the arm's muscular activity by indicating the muscular tension encountered during writing. In addition to monitoring, the EMG equipment was also used to find the most relaxed position for his arm and hand as he wrote. All of this feedback was instrumental in changing his writing style, especially during the periodic transitional stages of retraining writing; most beneficial was the fact that he could receive immediate feedback on his anxiety and tension. The reader should also note that the training generalized to another behavior, that of competitive shooting in which the patient also improved following this training procedure.

The Use of Biofeedback in the Treatment of Writer's Cramp

WILLIAM REAVLEY

Writer's cramp is a rarely occurring but highly distressing condition. It is generally agreed that writer's cramp often has three main components: spasms, tremors and paralysis, and can present in a number of ways. It has been seen as a neurological disturbance (Wilson, 1963), as an indication of a more broadly based pathology (Cameron, 1947) and as a learned maladaptive habit (Beech, 1960; Sylvester and Liversedge, 1960). This last view has been the most productive in terms of treatment.

CASE HISTORY

The patient was a professional man in his early thirties. In terms of personality, like cases reported by other workers (Crisp and Moldofsky, 1965), he seemed a constrained, conscientious and precise man. He dated his problems from schooldays. He had missed writing lessons due to moving school frequently and had developed his own untidy style. . . "In an effort to please different teachers who complained about the lack of neatness, I merely changed the formation of a letter here and there and experimented with writing especially large and small". On joining the Army the patient decided to improve the legibility of his writing and taught himself italic script. He then found he was unable to write quickly or under any sort of

From *Journal of Behavior Therapy and Experimental Psychiatry*, 1975, 6, 335–338. Copyright 1975 by Pergamon Press Ltd. Reprinted by permission.

pressure. Gradually his handwriting deteriorated to an illegible scribble.

In the investigation particular attention was given to physical presentation of the problem. The patient gripped the pen tightly, bent his wrist inwards and seemed to attempt to write each word in one movement. This resulted in a very spikey scrawl which tended to be written with long pauses between words and after several false starts.

It was possible to establish a hierarchy of situations which regularly provoked writing difficulties. There were two major elements in this hierarchy. One was concerned with constriction of space, necessity for precision and the need for speed; and the other involved the presence of others, particularly superiors.

TREATMENT

As stated by Gibson (1972), writer's cramp may be secondary to general states of high anxiety, or due to concern in an obsessional manner with the nature of the handwriting. The implications for treatment are in the first case that a lowering of general anxiety will lead to improvement and in the second that the patient will benefit from retraining in writing under conditions of low anxiety. The presentation of the problem suggested a treatment approach involving the retraining of writing under conditions of low anxiety. The following techniques were used, singly and in combination; relaxation training, E.M.G. feedback, G.S.R. feedback, writing retraining. There were seventeen treatment sessions spread over seven months. Much of the treatment was carried out at home by the patient, the technique first having been demonstrated and discussed.

Relaxation

Although the patient acknowledged the role of anxiety in his writing difficulties he reported feeling anxious only under extreme conditions. He was unable to detect more subtle gradations in emotional arousal. His awareness of these changes was developed by using a G.S.R. feedback instrument. Within one session he evinced awareness of emotional change in relation to initially picking up a pen and a number of other behaviours associated with writing of which he had been previously unaware. He was readily able to accept the instrument's reporting of emotional change, and began to learn a new self awareness from it.

E.M.G. Feedback

With people suffering from writer's cramp Von Reis (1954) found excessive muscle activity in the whole arm, not only in these muscles directly concerned with writing. The patient was aware of the peculiar contortions of his hand, wrist and forearm but was unaware of the extreme levels of muscle tension in the rest of his arm. Lader and Matthews (1971) identify the primary pathological state in writer's cramp as excessive uncontrolled muscle activity and suggest that methods of lessening or controlling such muscle activity might be of direct therapeutic benefit. Green *et al.* (1969) were able to demonstrate that a single session of E.M.G. feedback was usually sufficient to reduce forearm muscle activity to such a level as to permit the detection and control of single motor unit firing.

Thus the sites chosen for E.M.G. feedback were, in order, upper arm, forearm, hand/wrist, but the precise location of electrodes was arrived at on a "feedback" basis. With the patient adopting a writing posture several electrode sites were tried. For use in treatment we chose the electrode sites which gave the greatest response with the E.M.G. at a constant level. These sites were: outer aspect of the upper arm, the upper insertion of brachialis and the outer aspect of the mid forearm and in the first web space overlying the first interossius muscle and one inch proximal to that point. With continuous E.M.G. feedback[1] the patient was able to experiment with different postures of the whole arm, changing pen grip, modifying writing angle to arrive at a posture which was more "relaxed" in musclar terms than the postures he had previously used. The procedure within each session was for the patient to arrive at a setting of the instrument which reflected a suitable level, operationally defined, of muscle activity. He was instructed to maintain the E.M.G. level while progressing through writing exercises, gradually shaping towards quick, effective, and legible handwriting.

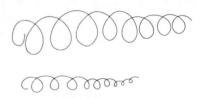

Figure 1.

Writing Training

The patient reported and demonstrated that he was able to write well with chalk on a blackboard. A systematic examination of the possible sources of the differences in handwriting between pen and chalk revealed that the critical variable was the writing movement. Using paper

[1] With the E.M.G. machine used it is possible to give visual or aural feedback. In this case aural was used at the patient's request.

and pencil the patient used to complete the word in one movement. With this style he found it almost impossible to execute a rounded shape.

The first writing exercise was to practice writing continuous lines of large rounded characters while experiencing E.M.G. feedback. While maintaining muscle relaxation he was encouraged to make these characters gradually smaller but keep the rounded shape (Fig. 1). He then proceeded to writing on lined paper using four guide lines as in Fig. 2. Between lines two and three he was instructed to place the body of the letter using the space above and below for the extensions. The instructions were to write so as to fill the space and to use rounded characters while monitoring himself with the E.M.G. and occasionally with the G.S.R. The G.S.R. was used particularly at change points on the treatment gradients. As far as the writing · exercises were concerned one of the two gradients along which the patient shaped his own behaviour concerned the progression from soft pencil to fountain pen. The other gradient concerned a gradual narrowing of the space available for writing. The patient progressively prepared narrower lines as he became more adept at writing in his new style.

Figure 2.

The use of the four guide lines was of importance not only in bringing about change in the patient's handwriting but in maintaining that change. Outside of treatment sessions, and following the learning of new handwriting skills, situations would occur that provoked particularly high levels of anxiety and a return to illegible spikey handwriting. The patient found that writing between the lines for a very few minutes was sufficient to restore good writing.

DISCUSSION

Relaxation and handwriting training have been included in previous treatment programmes for writer's cramp (Crisp and Moldofsky, 1965). This treatment programme differed in its use of biofeedback technology. How critical the biofeedback was in producing change cannot be evaluated in a case study, but it certainly enabled the patient to monitor himself while learning new writing skills. With a treatment programme making use of several techniques singly and in combination it is not possible to demonstrate which of the components of treatment were the most useful.

Follow-up

The improvement in writing has been maintained over the eight months since the last formal treatment session. Whenever the subject has felt his new-found skill threatened by a novel situation, particularly provocative of anxiety, a few minutes' practice writing between the four guide lines has prevented a reversion to his earlier spikey scrawl.

A "spin off" benefit has been that the subject's competition shooting has also improved. Before treatment of the writer's cramp his shooting, good in practice, deteriorated markedly in competition.

Acknowledgement—The author wishes to thank Dr. P. Sainsbury, Director of the Medical Research Council Clinical Psychiatry Unit, Graylingwell Hospital, for referring the patient.

REFERENCES

Beech, H. R. (1960) Symptomatic treatment of writer's cramp, *Behaviour Therapy and the Neuroses* (Edited by Eysenck, H. J.), Pergamon Press, Oxford.

Cameron, J. (1947) *The Psychology of Behaviour Disorders*, Houghton Mifflin, Boston.

Crisp, A. H., and Moldofsky, H. (1965) A psychosomatic study of writer's cramp, *Brit. J. Psychiat. 111*, 841–858.

Gibson, H. B. (1972) Writer's cramp: A behavioural approach, *Behav. Res. and Ther. 10*, 371–380.

Green, E. E., Walters, E. D., Green, A. M., and Murphy, G. (1969) Feedback technique for deep relaxation, *Psychophysiology 6*, 371.

Lader, M. H., and Matthews, A. M. (1971) Electromyographic studies of tension, *J. Psychosom. Res. 15*, 479–486.

Moldofsky, H. (1971) Occupational cramps, *J. Psychosom. Res. 15*, 439–444.

Sylvester, J. D., and Liversedge, L. A. (1960) A follow-up of patients treated for writer's cramp by conditioning techniques, *Behaviour Therapy and the Neuroses* (Edited by Eysenck, H. J.), Pergamon Press, Oxford.

Reis, G. Von (1954) Electromyographical studies in writer's cramp, *Acta Med. Scand. 149*, 253.

Wilson, S. A. K. (1940) *Neurology*, Arnold, London.

Chapter 20
Modeling

During the last few years modeling as a therapeutic technique has become increasingly prominent. Originally, it had been used primarily for changing the behavior of children, but it has now been extended into work with adult populations with severe disturbances. In the case presented, Barry Edelstein and Richard Eisler compare modeling versus modeling combined with instructions and feedback in an attempt to determine which technique is more successful.

As with most behavioral techniques an assessment of the behavior to be modified was first made by the research team. No behavior was selected to be eliminated; rather the focus was only on increasing those social behaviors in which the client was lacking. The therapist sought to involve the client by having him choose a situation which might be encountered after discharge. The client seems to have been very cooperative throughout the sessions and it would appear that he was being maintained on phenothiazines during the modeling.

Although this case report is in the form of an experiment, it nevertheless allows the reader to get an idea of how modeling techniques can be used with a pathological population. In this case, after the baselines for the specific behaviors were established, the modeling videotape was introduced, followed by probe tests to see if the behavior improved in situations with individuals other than those in the modeling sessions. The therapist then added instructions and feedback much as a drama coach might speak to a student attempting to do a difficult scene. As the case report demonstrated, there was improvement in all the behaviors assessed; however, the major question of generalization to a real-life setting outside the hospital was not determined. The reader should compare this case with that presented by Ayllon, who used operant conditioning techniques to treat a more severely disturbed schizophrenic patient.

346

Effects of Modeling and Modeling with Instructions and Feedback on the Behavioral Components of Social Skills

BARRY A. EDELSTEIN and RICHARD M. EISLER

Increasing attention to the social skills of psychiatric patients has become quite evident in recent years. Most of the studies have focused on relatively molar aspects of social skills (e.g., Bennett & Maley, 1973; Kale, 1968; King, Armitage, & Tilton, 1960; Milby, 1970). Few studies have dealt with specific behavioral components, such as eye contact, speech characteristics, head and arm gestures, and affect (e.g., Eisler, Miller & Hersen, 1973; Hersen, Turner, Edelstein & Pinkston, 1975; Eisler, Hersen, Miller & Blanchard, 1975; Foy & Eisler, 1975). Although several studies of social skills of psychiatric patients and college students have used modeling with a variety of other techniques (e.g., Goldstein, Martens, Hubben, Van Bellen, Schaaf, Wiersma, & Goldhart, 1973; Hersen, Eisler, & Miller, 1974; Hersen, Eisler, Miller Johnson & Pinkston, 1973; McFall & Twentyman, 1973; McFall & Marston, 1970; McFall & Lillesand, 1971), there is no concensus on the contribution of modeling to treatment. Generalization of social skills across social settings and individuals also has been neglected until only recently (cf. Goldsmith & McFall, 1975; Hersen, Eisler, & Miller, 1974) when working with psy-

chiatric patients, in spite of the repeated concern expressed for its assessment with nonpsychiatric populations (e.g., McFall & Lillesand, 1971; McFall & Marston, 1970; McFall & Twentyman, 1973).

The present study compared the relative effectiveness of modeling to modeling with instructions and feedback on the social skills of a hospitalized male schizophrenic patient. In addition, generalization to novel social situations and to a variety of individuals was assessed.

METHOD

Subject

The subject, a 32-yr-old, Caucasian, single male, had been admitted to the Psychiatry Service of the Veterans Administration Center on two occasions with the diagnosis of schizophrenia, paranoid type. He had attended a state university for 3 yr, was active in a social fraternity while attending the university, and, upon leaving the university, worked at various jobs with his work performance varying markedly from excellent to poor.

The patient's first admission for psychiatric treatment was at the age of 31, after which he reportedly became quite suspicious, evidenced poor social functioning, and began carrying and sleeping with a knife and gun. The patient was admitted with the diagnosis of schizophrenia and treated with phenothiazines, individual and

From Barry A. Edelstein and Richard M. Eisler, *Behavior Therapy*, 1976, 7, 382–389. New York: Academic Press, Inc. Copyright © 1976 by Association for Advancement of Behavior Therapy. All rights of reproduction in any form reserved.

group psychotherapy. He was discharged following improvement and returned home to live with his parents. Over several months, the patient's behavior markedly deteriorated. He was readmitted to the hospital and stabilized on phenothiazines. Although psychotic behaviors remissed, the patient continued to be unkempt and experienced difficulties in relating to other individuals on the ward. Essentially he avoided social interactions and responded only to direct inquiries.

Design and Procedure

The patient's social interactions were assessed by having the patient interact with several staff members and noting what were conspicuous behavioral excesses and deficits. The following behavioral deficits were then selected as most salient by the authors and two research assistants: (1) low frequency and duration of eye contact: (2) low frequency of head and arm gestures: (3) "flat" affect (overall rating); (4) low frequency of assertive behaviors.

Social skills training was conducted in a television studio in which the patient's verbal and nonverbal responses to a series of verbally presented social situations (scenes) were recorded on videotape. The patient sat next to a male or female stimulus person who served as a prompt (e.g., friend, employer, fellow student, neighbor, secretary). The social scenes were described over an intercom from the adjoining control room by an experimenter, and the patient was asked to respond in a socially appropriate fashion.

The experimental design during training consisted of a modified multiple baseline across behaviors, with the following sequence of conditions: (1) baseline, (2) modeling alone, and (3) modeling with instructions and feedback. The modification of the multiple-baseline design involved the implementation of the modeling condition across all behaviors simultaneously following the baseline, in which the patient viewed a modeling videotape where the model engaged in the behaviors to be accelerated. This was followed by the sequential introduction of the next condition across the target behaviors. In addition, generalization probe tests were conducted prior to modeling and prior to modeling and feedback and instructions.

The target behaviors were defined as follows: (1) eye contact—duration of eye contact with the stimulus person during each 2-min interaction; (2) gestures—number of times the patient made head and/or hand gestures. Head gestures were defined as any nodding of the patient's head in agreement, shaking of the head from side to side in disagreement, and moving of the head to indicate direction. Hand and arm gestures were defined as pointing with finger(s), moving the hand away from the body to emphasize a statement, or moving of the shoulders in an inward direction (shrugging); (3) affect—rated on a scale from one to five (1 = a flat, unemotional tone of voice, 5 = a full and lively intonation). Smiling was also considered as a component of affect, which was defined as any upturning of the lips at the corners, without regard to the appearance of the patient's teeth; (4) overall assertiveness—several components were considered in rating assertiveness. This was also rated on a five-point scale (1 = absence of most components, 5 = their presence). The components included the following: amount of time patient looked at the stimulus person; loudness of voice; ease of conversation (smooth or halting word flow; presence or absence of stutters and hesitations); presence or absence of information seeking; remarks in defense of his position.

The eight social training and generalization scenes were based on situations which the patient considered relevant to those which he would encounter upon discharge from the hospital, i.e., interactions with male employer and women. Half of the scenes involved a female stimulus person and half involved a male stimulus person. One male and one female stimulus person remained as a training person throughout the entire training series and two additional female stimulus persons were used for the generalization probe tests. Only one stimulus person was present at each scene presentation. An example of the scenes is as follows:

> *Narrator:* ("Patient's name), I want you to get to know (female's name) better. (Patient's name), you are at a big party and there are lots of people there that you do not know at all. Finally you recognize (female's name) whom you have seen in your classes. You go over and introduce yourself to her. (Patient's name), you begin talking to her."

Baseline

The patient was seated next to either a male or female stimulus person. The four training and four generalization scenes were presented in random order. Two minutes of interaction between the patient and the stimulus person were recorded on videotape for each of the eight scenes and sessions were conducted daily for three days.

Generalization Probe Tests

This probe test condition differed from the baseline condition in that two novel female stimulus persons were each present, one at a time, during each training and generalization scene. All four female scenes were presented with each of the two female stimulus persons, each stimulus person being free to respond, as was the training person. This probe test was also conducted before (probe) and after (post) the modeling plus instructions plus feedback condition.

Modeling

Training scenes were presented to a male model. At the beginning of each modeling session, the patient viewed the videotape of the model behaving appropriately for the four training scenes. Following presentation of the modeled scenes, the four generalization scenes were again presented to the patient, in random fashion, with instructions for the patient to practice what he had learned from observing the model. The modeling condition lasted six sessions for eye contact, 10 sessions for gestures, and 18 sessions for affect.

Modeling with Instructions and Feedback

This condition actually began at the end of the last modeling session. The training sessions were similar to the modeling condition, however, at the end of each training session the patient viewed videotape presentations of his own performance during the day's session, and comments were made by the experimenter regarding the appropriateness of the patient's behavior during each taped social scene. In keeping with the multiple-baseline design, feedback instructed the patient to maintain eye contact for longer periods of time, then to exhibit more affect, and finally to utilize his hands, arms, and head for gesturing as he had observed the model doing during presentation of the modeling tapes. Feedback was provided on the frequency and duration of eye contact, frequency of components of affect, and frequency of gesturing for that day's session as each set of behaviors was sequentially trained.

RESULTS

Ratings were made independently by two research assistants who each rated all of the videotaped sessions in a random order. Pearson product moment correlations were obtained for eye contact ($r = .98$), affect ($r=.85$), and gestures ($r=.90$), calculated across all scenes for each observer.

The ratings of performance with male and female stimulus persons are presented separately (Figs. 1 and 2). Ratings of training and generalization performance are presented within each of the figures for male and female stimulus persons. Mean duration of eye contact and frequency of gestures remained quite stable during the baseline condition for both male and female stimulus persons, and for the male stimulus person across the modeling condition. Eye contact showed a positively accelerated function for the female stimulus person during modeling. Mean rated affect increased from a value of 1 during baseline to values of 2 and 3 during the modeling condition. These data suggest that the modeling increased rat-

ings of affect with both male and female stimulus persons.

During the modeling with instructions and feedback conditions, the patient increased in mean eye contact, mean gestures, and mean affect ratings. Although ratings of affect did not increase dramatically during this condition, they did stabilize at a value considerably above that obtained during baseline. Eye contact, gestures and affect during generalization scenes closely approximated ratings of these behaviors made during training scenes (Figs. 1 and 2).

Results from the generalization probe-tests prior to training (pre-), following modeling (probe), and following modeling plus instructions plus feedback (post) are in Fig. 3. Ratings of overall assertive-

MALE

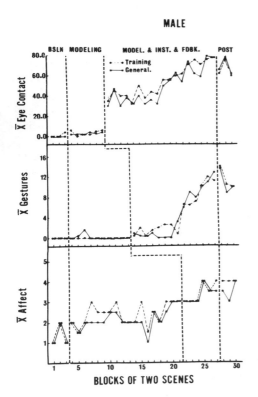

Figure 1. Mean duration of eye contact, mean frequency of gestures, and mean ratings of affect for male stimulus person.

FEMALE

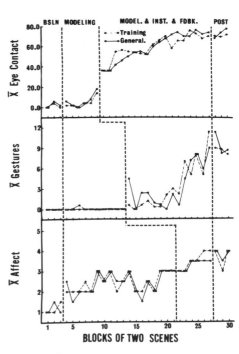

Figure 2. Mean duration of eye contact, mean frequency of gestures, and mean ratings of affect for female stimulus person.

ness were also made during the generalization probe tests, although these ratings included components of eye contact and gestures which were rated independently. Ratings of eye contact, gestures, affect, and overall assertiveness are represented for Female 1 (training stimulus female) and Females 2 and 3 (the generalization testing stimulus females). Though ratings of eye contact and gestures in the pre-training probe condition are essentially of zero values, ratings of affect and overall assertiveness varied to some extent as an apparent function of the female stimulus person present during testing. Ratings of affect for Female 1 and 3 yielded a value of 1 on the four-point scale, however, mean ratings of affect for Female 2 yielded a value of 1.5. Mean ratings for overall assertiveness during the pretraining probe–test were 1.0 for Female 1, 2.0 for Female 2, and 2.5 for Female 3.

Following modeling, duration of eye contact increased slightly for all female stimulus persons. Mean gestures did not differ across first and second probe–tests. Mean affect during the second probe–test markedly increased over the first probe–test for all three stimulus persons. Mean assertiveness increased across stimulus persons, although the increases were not systematic. Following modeling plus instructions and feedback, mean ratings of eye contact, gestures, affect, and assertiveness increased markedly across all stimulus persons. These results clearly demonstrate generalization across stimulus persons and significant increases in all behavioral components of social skills measure.

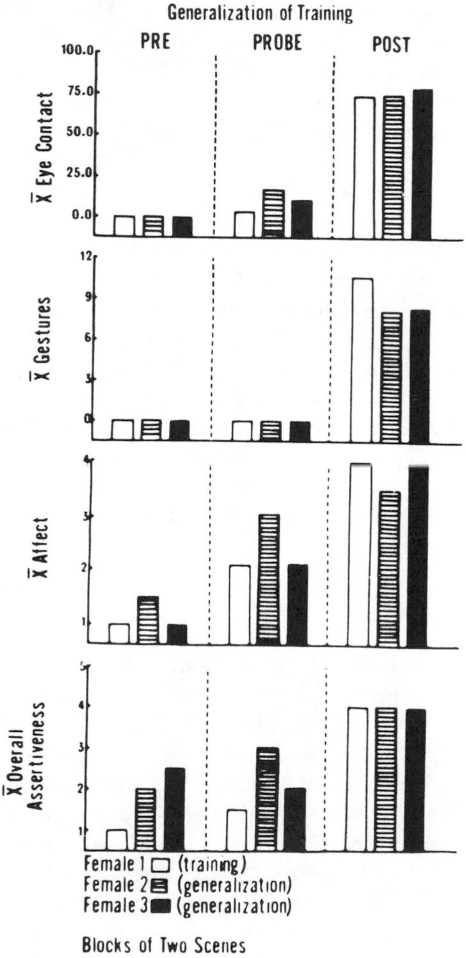

DISCUSSION

The results demonstrated the effectiveness of modeling, instructions, and feedback on the behavioral components of social skills. Unfortunately, modeling could not have been introduced sequentially, because it was impossible to permit the patient to view individually only selective com-

CASE REPORTS AND STUDIES

Figure 3. Mean duration of eye contact, mean frequency of gestures, mean ratings of affect, and mean ratings of overall assertiveness for generalization probe tests.

ponents of the model's behavior. Yet, the data suggest that modeling increased overall ratings of affect but exerted no apparent influence on duration of eye contact and frequency of gestures. Although providing a patient with a model may have helped to develop certain behavioral components of social skills, combining modeling, instructions, and feedback was more effective. These additive effects of conditions are consistent with data obtained by some investigators (Hersen et al., 1973, 1974) but not others (Goldstein et al., 1973; McFall & Twentyman, 1973). This apparent disparity may be a function of the subject's inattention to the specific behaviors studied. Thus, once feedback and instructions conveyed the appropriate behavioral dimensions, those behaviors emitted by the model may have become more salient and served to control appropriate behaviors. Continued feedback may have further decreased the discrepancy between the behavior of the model and patient. Because modeling appeared to increase ratings of affect but not eye contact and gestures in the present study, one can only conclude that some components of social skills may be trained via modeling, whereas others may require more extensive training.

Assessing generalization across social scenes demonstrated performance almost equal to that obtained to training scenes, suggesting that the subject was controlled by classes of stimuli characteristic of all social scenes. Thus, the components of social skills did not appear limited by environmental and interpersonal settings for which no training was specifically provided. Generalization effects are consistent with studies by Hersen et al. (1973) and Goldsmith and McFall (1975). Whether or not the behaviors trained would generalize to "real-life" situations remains to be determined and should be examined in future studies.

REFERENCES

Bennett, P. S., & Maley, R. F. Modification of interactive behaviors in chronic mental patients. *Journal of Applied Behavior Analysis*, 1973, *6*, 609–620.

Eisler, R. M., Miller, P. M., & Hersen, M. Components of assertive behavior. *Journal of Clinical Psychology*, 1973, *29*, 3, 295–299.

Eisler, R. M., Hersen, M., Miller, P. M., & Blanchard, E. B. Situational determinants of assertive behaviors. *Journal of Consulting and Clinical Psychology*, in press.

Foy, D. W., & Eisler, R. M. Modeled assertion in a case of explosive rages. *Journal of Behavior Therapy and Experimental Psychiatry*, in press.

Goldstein, A. P., Marten, J., Hubben, J., van Belle, H. A., Schaff, W., Wiersma, H., & Goldhart, A. The use of modeling to increase independent behavior. *Behaviour Research and Therapy*, 1973, *11*, 31–42.

Goldsmith, J. B., & McFall, R. M. Development and evaluation of an interpersonal skill-training program for psychiatric inpatients. *Journal of Abnormal Psychology*, 1975, *84*, 51–58.

Hersen, M., Eisler, R. M., Miller, P. M., Johnson, M. B., & Pinkston, S. G. Effects of practice, instructions, and modeling on components of assertive behavior. *Behaviour Research and Therapy*, 1973, *11*, 443–453.

Hersen, M., Eisler, R. M., & Miller, P. M. An experimental analysis of generalization in assertive training. *Behaviour Research and Therapy*, 1974, *12*, 295–310.

Hersen, M., Turner, S., Edelstein, B. A., & Pinkston, S. G. Effects of phenothiazines and social skills training in a withdrawn schizophrenic. *Journal of Clinical Psychology*, in press.

Kale, R. J., Kaye, J. H. Whelan, P. A., & Hopkins, B. L. The effects of reinforcement on the modification, maintenance, and generalization of social responses of mental patients. *Journal of Applied Behavior Analysis*, 1968, *1*, 307–314.

King, G. F., Armitage, S. G., & Tilton, J. R. A therapeutic approach to schizophrenics of extreme pathology; an operant–interpersonal method. *Journal of Abnormal and Social Psychology*, 1960, *61*, 276–286.

McFall, R. M., & Marston, A. R. An experimental investigation of behavior rehearsal in assertive training. *Journal of Abnormal Psychology*, 1970, *76*, 295–303.

McFall, R. M., & Lillesand, D. B. Behavior rehearsal with modeling and coaching in assertion training. *Journal of Abnormal Psychology*, 1971, *77*, 313–323.

McFall, R. M., & Twentyman, C. T. Four experiments on the relative contributions of rehearsal, modeling, and coaching to assertion training. *Journal of Abnormal Psychology*, 1973, *81*, 199–218.

Milby, J. B. Modification of extreme social isolation by contingent social reinforcement. *Journal of Applied Behavior Analysis*, 1970, *3*, 149–152.

Chapter 21
Operant Conditioning

The first case presented in this section on operant conditioning techniques is one of behavior therapy's classic cases. In it Dr. Teodoro Ayllon and his co-workers used operant techniques to manage the behavior of a hospitalized chronic schizophrenic. Three major behaviors of this woman patient were treated. First, stealing food, which had resulted in her not losing weight, was eliminated as a behavior by the withdrawal of positive reinforcement (meals) when the stealing occurred. Second, a hoarding behavior (collecting towels) was dealt with by stimulus satiation— giving the patient a great number of towels over a period of time until she herself began to remove them. Third, the wearing of an excessive amount of clothing was reduced through the denial of reinforcement (food) and by verbal shaping. At no time during the use of these techniques was the purpose of the staff's behavior explained to the patient since this might have prejudiced the outcome of this therapy and since it was, of course, not necessary within the operant learning model. It is interesting to note that none of these behavior changes were necessarily desired by the patient nor did they necessarily make her any less "psychotic." But, as Dr. Ayllon correctly points out, patients are often admitted to or placed in mental hospitals not because of general mental disturbance but because of specific behavioral actions that cause difficulty or embarrassment for others. If these specific behaviors (e.g., the overdressing) can be controlled, then the individual may be accepted by society and at least have the possibility of making an adjustment outside the hospital.

354

Intensive Treatment of Psychotic Behaviour by Stimulus Satiation and Food Reinforcement*

T. AYLLON

INTRODUCTION

Until recently, the effective control of behaviour was limited to the animal laboratory. The extension of this control to human behaviour was made when Lindsley successfully adapted the methodology of operant conditioning to the study of psychotic behaviour (Lindsley, 1956). Following Lindsley's point of departure other investigators have shown that, in its essentials, the behaviour of mental defective individuals (Orlando and Bijou, 1960), stutterers (Flanagan, Goldiamond and Azrin, 1958), mental patients (Hutchinson and Azrin, 1961), autistic (Ferster and DeMyer, 1961), and normal children (Bijou, 1961; Azrin and Lindsley, 1956) is subject to the same controls.

Despite the obvious implications of this research for applied settings there has been a conspicuous lag between the research findings and their application. The greatest limitation to the direct application of laboratory principles has been the absence of control over the subjects' envi-

From *Behaviour Research and Therapy*, 1963, *1*, 53–61. Copyright 1963 by Pergamon Press Ltd. Reprinted by permission.

* This report is based in part, on a two-year research project (1959–1961), conducted by the author at the Saskatchewan Hospital, Weyburn, Saskatchewan, Canada, and supported by a grant from the Commonwealth Fund. Grateful acknowledgment is due to H. Osmond and I. Clancey of the Saskatchewan Hospital. The author also thanks E. Haughton who assisted in the conduct of this investigation, and N. Azrin and W. Holtz for their critical reading of the manuscript.

ronment. Recently, however, a series of applications in a regulated psychiatric setting has clearly demonstrated the possibilities of behavioural modification (Ayllon and Michael, 1959; and Haughton, 1962). Some of the behaviour studied has included repetitive and highly stereotyped responses such as complaining, pacing, refusal to eat, hoarding and many others.

What follows is a demonstration of behaviour techniques for the intensive individual treatment of psychotic behaviour. Specific pathological behaviour patterns of a single patient were treated by manipulating the patient's environment.

The Experimental Ward and Control over the Reinforcement

This investigation was conducted in a mental hospital ward, the characteristics of which have been described elsewhere (Ayllon and Haughton, 1962). Briefly, this was a female ward to which only authorized personnel were allowed access. The ward staff was made up of psychiatric nurses and untrained aides who carried out the environmental manipulations under the direction of the experimenter. Using a time-sample technique, patients were observed daily every 30 minutes from 7:00 AM to 11:00 PM.

The dining room was the only place where food was available and entrance to the dining room could be regulated. Water was freely available at a drinking fountain on the ward. None of the patients had ground passes or jobs outside the ward.

Subject

The patient was a 47-year-old female patient diagnosed as a chronic schizophrenic. The patient had been hospitalized for 9 years. Upon studying the patient's behaviour on the ward, it became apparent that the nursing staff[1] spent considerable time caring for her. In particular, there were three aspects of her behaviour which seemed to defy solution. The first was stealing food. The second was the hoarding of the ward's towels in her room. The third undesirable aspect of her behaviour consisted in her wearing excessive clothing, e.g. a half-dozen dresses, several pairs of stockings, sweaters, and so on.

In order to modify the patient's behaviour systematically, each of these three types of behaviour (stealing food, hoarding, and excessive dressing) was treated separately.

EXPERIMENT I

Control of Stealing Food by Food Withdrawal

The patient had weighed over 250 pounds for many years. She ate the usual tray of food served to all patients, but, in addition, she stole food from the food counter and from other patients. Because the medical staff regarded her excessive weight as detrimental to her health, a special diet had been prescribed for her. However, the patient refused to diet and continued stealing food. In an effort to discourage the patient from stealing, the ward nurses had spent considerable time trying to persuade her to stop stealing food. As a last resort, the nurses would force her to return the stolen food.

To determine the extent of food stealing, nurses were instructed to record all behaviour associated with eating in the

[1] As used in this paper, "nurse" is a generic term including all those who actually work on the ward (attendants, aides, psychiatric and registered nurses).

dining room. This record, taken for nearly a month, showed that the patient stole food during two thirds of all meals.

Procedure

The traditional methods previously used to stop the patient from stealing food were discontinued. No longer were persuasion, coaxing, or coercion used.

The patient was assigned to a table in the dining room, and no other patients were allowed to sit with her. Nurses removed the patient from the dining room when she approached a table other than her own, or when she picked up unauthorized food from the dining room counter. In effect, this procedure resulted in the patient missing a meal whenever she attempted to steal food.

Results

Figure 1 shows that when withdrawal of positive reinforcement (i.e. meal) was made dependent upon the patient's "stealing," this response was eliminated in two weeks. Because the patient no longer stole food, she ate only the diet prescribed for her. The effective control of the stealing response is also indicated by the gradual reduction in the patient's body weight. At no time during the patient's 9 years of hospitalization had she weighed less than 230 pounds. Figure 2 shows that at the conclusion of this treatment her weight stabilized at 180 pounds or 17 per cent loss from her original weight. At this time, the patient's physical condition was regarded as excellent.

Discussion

A principle used in the laboratory shows that the strength of a response may be weakened by the removal of positive reinforcement following the response (Ferster, 1958). In this case, the response was food-stealing and the reinforcer was access to meals. When the patient stole food she was removed from the dining room and missed her meal.

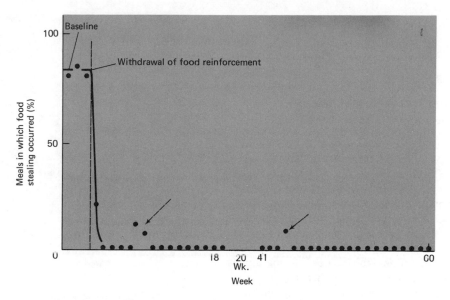

Figure 1. A response, food stealing, is eliminated when it results in the withdrawal of food reinforcement. The dotted arrows indicate the rare occasions when food stealing occurred. For purposes of presentation a segment comprising 20 weeks during which no stealing occurred is not included. (Figure redrawn.)

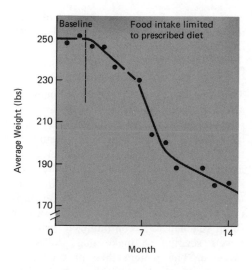

Figure 2. The effective control of food stealing results in a notable reduction in body weight. As the patient's food intake is limited to the prescribed diet her weight decreases gradually. (Figure redrawn.)

After one year of this treatment, two occasions of food stealing occurred. The first occasion, occurring after one year of not stealing food, took the nurses by surprise and, therefore the patient "got away" with it. The second occasion occurred shortly thereafter. This time, however, the controlling consequences were in force. The patient missed that meal and did not steal again to the conclusion of this investigation.

Because the patient was not informed or warned of the consequences that followed stealing, the nurses regarded the procedure as unlikely to have much effect on the patient's behaviour. The implicit belief that verbal instructions are indispensable for learning is part of present day psychiatric lore. In keeping with this notion, prior to this behaviour treatment, the nurses had tried to persuade the patient to co-operate in dieting. Because there were strong medical reasons for her losing weight, the patient's refusal to follow a prescribed diet was regarded as further evidence of her mental illness.

EXPERIMENT II

Control of One Form of Hoarding Behaviour through Stimulus Satiation

During the 9 years of hospitalization, the patient collected large numbers of towels and stored them in her room. Although many efforts had been made to discourage hoarding, this behaviour continued unaltered. The only recourse for the nursing staff was to take away the patient's towels about twice a week.

To determine the degree of hoarding behaviour, the towels in her room were counted three times a week, when the patient was not in her room. This count showed that the number of towels kept in her room ranged from 19 to 29 despite the fact that during this time the nurses continued recovering their towel supply from the patient's room.

Procedure

The routine removal of the towels from the patient's room was discontinued. Instead, a programme of stimulus satiation was carried out by the nurses. Intermittently, throughout the day, the nurses took a towel to the patient when she was in her room and simply handed it to her without any comment. The first week she was given an average of 7 towels daily, and by the third week this number was increased to 60.

Results

The technique of satiation eliminated the towel hoarding. Figure 3 shows the mean number of towels per count found in the patient's room. When the number of towels kept in her room reached the 625 mark, she started taking a few of them out. Thereafter, no more towels were

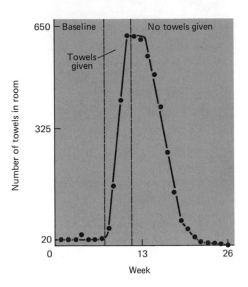

Figure 3. A response, towel hoarding, is eliminated when the patient is given towels in excess. When the number of towels reaches 625 the patient starts to discard them. She continues to do so until the number found in her room averages 1.5 compared to the previous 20 towels per week. (Figure redrawn.)

given to her. During the next 12 months the mean number of towels found in her room was 1.5 per week. . . .

Discussion

The procedure used to reduce the amount of towel hoarding bears resemblance to satiation of a reinforcer. A reinforcer loses its effect when an excessive amount of that reinforcer is made available. Accordingly, the response maintained by that reinforcer is weakened. In this application, the towels constituted the reinforcing stimuli. When the number of towels in her room reached 625, continuing to give her towels seemed to make their collection aversive. The patient then proceeded to rid herself of the towels until she had virtually none.

During the first few weeks of satiation, the patient was observed patting her cheeks with a few towels, apparently enjoying them. Later, the patient was observed spending much of her time folding and stacking the approximately 600 towels in her room. A variety of remarks were made by the patient regarding receipt of towels. All verbal statements made by the patient were recorded by the nurse. The following represent typical remarks made during this experiment. First week: As the nurse entered the patient's room carrying a towel, the patient would smile and say, "Oh, you found it for me, thank you." Second week: When the number of towels given to patient increased rapidly, she told the nurses, "Don't give me no more towels. I've got enough." Third week: "Take them towels away. . . . I can't sit here all night and fold towels." Fourth and fifth weeks: "Get these dirty towels out of here." Sixth week: After she had started taking the towels out of her room, she remarked to the nurse, "I can't drag any more of these towels, I just can't do it."

The quality of these remarks suggests that the initial effect of giving towels to the patient was reinforcing. However as the towels increased they ceased to be reinforcing, and presumably became aversive.

The ward nurses, who had undergone a three year training in psychiatric nursing, found it difficult to reconcile the procedure in this experiment with their psychiatric orientation. Most nurses subscribed to the popular psychiatric view which regards hoarding behaviour as a reflection of a deep "need" for love and security. Presumably, no "real" behavioural change was possible without meeting the patient's "needs" first. Even after the patient discontinued hoarding towels in her room, some nurses predicted that the change would not last and that worse behaviour would replace it. Using a time-sampling technique the patient was under continuous observation for over a year

after the termination of the satiation programme. Not once during this period did the patient return to hoarding towels. Furthermore, no other behaviour problem replaced hoarding.

EXPERIMENT III

Control of an Additional Form of Hoarding through Food Reinforcement

Shortly after the patient had been admitted to the hospital she wore an excessive amount of clothing which included several sweaters, shawls, dresses, undergarments and stockings. The clothing also included sheets and towels wrapped around her body, and a turban-like head-dress made up of several towels. In addition, the patient carried two to three cups on one hand while holding a bundle of miscellaneous clothing, and a large purse on the other.

To determine the amount of clothing worn by the patient, she was weighed before each meal over a period of two weeks. By subtracting her actual body weight from that recorded when she was dressed, the weight of her clothing was obtained.

Procedure

The response required for reinforcement was stepping on a scale and meeting a predetermined weight. The requirement for reinforcement consisted of meeting a single weight (i.e. her body weight plus a specified number of pounds of clothing). Initially she was given an allowance of 23 pounds over her current body weight. This allowance represented a 2 pound reduction from her usual clothing weight. When the patient exceeded the weight requirement, the nurse stated in a matter-of-fact manner, "Sorry, you weigh too much, you'll have to weigh less." Failure to meet the required weight resulted in the patient missing the meal at which she was being weighed. Sometimes, in an effort to meet the requirement, the patient discarded more clothing than she was required. When this occurred the requirement was adjusted at the next weighing-time to correspond to the limit set by the patient on the preceding occasion.

Results

When food reinforcement is made dependent upon the removal of superfluous clothing the response increases in frequency. Figure 4 shows that the patient gradually shed her clothing to meet the more demanding weight requirement until she dressed normally. At the conclusion of this experiment her clothes weighed 3 pounds compared to the 25 pounds she wore before this treatment.

Some verbal shaping was done in order to encourage the patient to leave the cups and bundles she carried with her. Nurses stopped her at the dining room and said, "Sorry, no things are allowed in the dining room." No mention of cloth-

ing or specific items was made to avoid focusing undue attention upon them. Within a week, the patient typically stepped on the scale without her bundle and assorted objects. When her weight was over the limit, the patient was informed that she weighed "too much." She then proceeded to take off a few clothes, stepped on the scale again, and upon meeting the weight requirement, gained access to the dining room. . . .

Discussion

According to the principle of reinforcement a class of responses is strengthened when it is followed by reinforcement. A reinforcer is such when it results in a response increase. In this application the removal of excessive clothing constituted the response and the reinforcer was food (i.e. access to meals). When the patient met the weight requirement she was reinforced by being given access to meals.

At the start of this experiment, the patient missed a few meals because she failed to meet the weight requirement, but soon thereafter she gradually discarded her superfluous clothing. First, she left behind odd items she had carried in her arms, such as bundles, cups and handbags. Next she took off the elaborate headgear and assorted "capes" or shawls she had worn over her shoulders. Although she had worn 18 pairs of stockings at one time, she eventually shed these also.

During the initial part of this experiment, the patient showed some emotional behaviour, e.g. crying, shouting and throwing chairs around. Because nurses were instructed to "ignore" this emotional behaviour, the patient obtained no sympathy or attention from them. The withholding of social reinforcement for emotional behaviour quickly led to its elimination.

At the conclusion of this behaviour treatment, the patient typically stepped on the scale wearing a dress, undergarments,

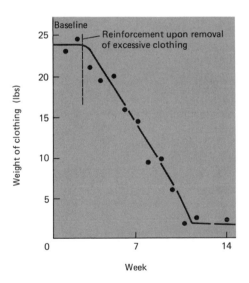

Figure 4. A response, excessive dressing, is eliminated when food reinforcement is made dependent upon removal of superfluous clothing. Once the weight of the clothing worn by the patient drops to 3 pounds it remains stable. (Figure redrawn.)

a pair of stockings and a pair of light shoes. One of the behavioural changes concomitant with the current environmental manipulation was that as the patient began dressing normally she started to participate in small social events in the hospital. This was particularly new to the patient as she had previously remained seclusive spending most of the time in her room.

About this time the patient's parents came to visit her and insisted on taking her home for a visit. This was the first time during the patient's 9 years of hospitalization that her parents had asked to take her out. They remarked that previously they had not been interested in taking her out because the patient's excessive dressing in addition to her weight made her look like a "circus freak."

CONCLUSIONS

The research presented here was conducted under nearly ideal conditions. The variables manipulated (i.e. towels and food) were under full experimental control. Using a time-sample technique the patient was observed daily every 30 minutes from 7.00 A.M. to 11.00 P.M. Nurses and aides carried out these observations which were later analysed in terms of gross behaviour categories. These observations were in force for over a year during which time these three experiments were conducted. The results of these observations indicate that none of the three pathological behaviour patterns (i.e. food stealing, hoarding and excessive dressing) exhibited by the patient were replaced by any undesirable behaviour.

The patient displayed some emotional behaviour in each experiment, but each time it subsided when social reinforcement (i.e. attention) was not forthcoming. The patient did not become violent or seclusive as a consequence of these experiments. Instead, she became socially more accessible to patients and staff. She did not achieve a great deal of social success but she did begin to participate actively in social functions.

A frequent problem encountered in mental hospitals is overeating. In general this problem is solved by prescribing a reduction diet. Many patients, however, refuse to take a reduction diet and continue overeating. When confronted with this behaviour, psychiatric workers generally resort to two types of explanations.

One explanation of overeating points out that only with the active and sincere co-operation of the patient can weight reduction be accomplished. When the patient refuses to co-operate he is regarded as showing more signs of mental illness and all hopes of eliminating overeating come to an end.

Another type of explanation holds that overeating is not the behaviour to be concerned with. Instead, attention is focused on the psychological "needs" of the patient. These "needs" are said to be the cause of the observable behaviour, overeating. Therefore the emphasis is on the removal of the cause and not on the symptom or behaviour itself. Whatever theoretical merit these explanations may have, it is unfortunate that they fail to suggest practical ways of treating the behaviour itself. As a consequence, the patient continues to overeat often to the detriment of his health.

The current psychiatric emphasis on the resolution of the mental conflict that is presumably at the basis of the symptoms, is perhaps misplaced. What seems to have been forgotten is that behaviour problems such as those reported here, prevent the patient from being considered for discharge not only by the hospital personnel but also by the patient's relatives. Indeed, as far as the patient's relatives are concerned, the index of improvement or deterioration is the readily observable behaviour and not a detailed account of the mechanics of the mental apparatus.

Many individuals are admitted to mental hospitals because of one or more specific behaviour difficulties and not always because of a generalized "mental" disturbance. For example, an individual may go into a mental hospital because he has refused to eat for several days, or because he talks to himself incessantly. If the goal of therapy were behavioural rehabilitation, these problems would be treated and normal eating and normal talking reinstated. However, the current emphasis in psychotherapy is on "mental-conflict resolution" and little or no attention is given to dealing directly with the behavioural problems which prevent the patient from returning to the community.

REFERENCES

Ayllon, T. and Michael, J. (1959) The psychiatric nurse as a behavioural engineer. *J. Exp. Anal. Behav.* 2, 323–334.

Ayllon, T. and Haughton, E. (1962) Control of the behaviour of schizophrenic patients by food. *J. Exp. Anal. Behav.* 5, 343–352.

Azrin, N. and Lindsley, O. (1956) The reinforcement of cooperation between children. *J. Abnorm. (soc.) Psychol.* 52, 100–102.

Bijou, S. (1961) Discrimination performance as a baseline for individual analysis of young children. *Child Develpm.* 32, 163–170.

Ferster, C. B. (1958) Control of behaviour in chimpanzees and pigeons by time out from positive reinforcement. *Psychol. Monogr.* 72, 1–38.

Ferster, C. and DeMyer, M. (1961) The development of performances in autistic children in an automatically controlled environment. *J. Chron. Dis.* 13, 312–345.

Flanagan, B., Goldiamond, I. and Azrin, N. (1958) Operant stuttering: The control of stuttering behaviour through response-contingent consequences. *J. Exp. Anal. Behav.* 15, 49–56.

Hutchinson, R. R. and Azrin, N. H. (1961) Conditioning of mental hospital patients to fixed-ratio schedules of reinforcement. *J. Exp. Anal. Behav.* 4, 87–95.

Lindsley, O. R. (1956) Operant conditioning methods applied to research in chronic schizophrenia. *Psychiat. Res. Rep.* 5, 118–139.

Orlando, R. and Bijou, S. (1960) Single and multiple schedules of reinforcement in developmentally retarded children. *J. Exp. Anal. Behav.* 3, 339–348.

In this case operant-conditioning techniques are used in a life-or-death situation involving a woman diagnosed as anorexia nervosa on the basis of an inability to eat and a drop in body weight from 120 to 47 pounds. The major goal of the therapy was to restore her eating behavior. This was accomplished with a good deal of success by using operant-conditioning techniques involving verbal reinforcement of eating behavior and postprandial reinforcement by enjoyable activities following the completion of meals. Again the purpose of these behaviors by the staff was not explained to the patient. The authors, however, were very careful to involve the staff of the hospital and have them fully understand the reason the patient was being treated in such a different fashion. They also enlisted the aid of the patient's family so that the reinforcement techniques could be used at home and the eating behavior would be generalized to nonhospital settings. Note especially the careful discussion of the learning principles involved in this case.

The Control of Eating Behavior in an Anorexic by Operant Conditioning Techniques

ARTHUR J. BACHRACH, WILLIAM J. ERWIN, and JAY P. MOHR[1]

INTRODUCTION

The case to be reported in this paper is that of a patient diagnosed as anorexia nervosa on the basis of a disruption of normal eating behavior and a drop in weight over a period of several years from a customary approximate 120 pounds to a weight of 47 pounds.

Even though it is apparently rare for anorexia patients to perish (Nemiah, 1963, suggests only about 10 percent of the cases), the patient reported herein was definitely in danger of death and, for this reason, the most effective methods for restoring the eating behavior seemed critical. Thus, the basic questions were

From L. Ullmann and L. Krasner (Eds.), *Case studies in behavior modification,* 153–163. New York: Holt, Rinehart and Winston, Inc., 1965. Copyright © 1965 by Holt, Rinehart and Winston, Inc. Reprinted by permission of Holt, Rinehart and Winston.

[1] When this case was worked with at the University of Virginia Hospital, Dr. Bachrach was Director of the Division of Behavioral Science at the University of Virginia School of Medicine, Dr. Erwin was a Resident on Neurology and Psychiatry at the Medical School, and Dr. Mohr was a medical student and research extern.

two: How do we get this patient to eat? and, to effect this, under what conditions will eating occur? The latter question was the basic methodological one, covering such basic data as those events that would be likely to increase the rate of eating behavior, and those events that would be likely to maintain increased eating rate. It might be noted that we talk of *restoring* eating behavior, a term based on the assumption that eating was once a part of the subject's behavioral repertoire, and not, therefore, a new response class to be shaped.

The material will be presented in the following general manner: first, the medical history and clinical course of the patient; then, a narrative account of the behavioral methodologies used to restore and maintain increased eating rate; followed by a restatement of these behavioral methodologies in terms of an operant paradigm formulated as an experimental design before the experiment and modified during its course. Finally, there will be a general discussion, including the latest available data about the patient and some comments about these.

MEDICAL HISTORY AND CLINICAL COURSE

The patient, a divorced, childless, white female was admitted to the University of Virginia Hospital Medical Service on December 14, 1960 at the age of thirty-seven. Her chief complaint was "Why do I have this block about food?" The history of the present illness at the time of admission revealed that this woman's weight had been fairly stable at about 118 pounds between menarche at the age of eleven and marriage seven years later at eighteen. A photograph of her at eighteen is reproduced as Figure 1.

During the first six months of marriage her weight remained stable at 118 pounds. She began to lose weight in September of 1943 and by January 1944 she weighed 110 pounds. Her last menstrual period occurred in November 1944 and has not recurred to date (December 1963). By January 1945 she weighed approximately 95 pounds. Three years later her weight had dropped to 75 pounds. Food intake and body weight continued to diminish to such an extent that by the summer of 1949 she weighed 65 pounds. Between 1949 and the time of admission to the University of Virginia Hospital in December 1960, she had lost an additional 18 pounds. At that time she could stand only with assistance, was 5 feet 4 inches tall, and weighed 47 pounds. Photographs of her on admission are reproduced as Figures 2 and 3.

The physical examination revealed a creature so cachectic and shrunken about her skeleton as to give the appearance of a poorly preserved mummy suddenly struck with the breath of life. Her pasty white skin was mottled a purple hue over her feet and stretched like so much heavy spider webbing about the bony prominences of her face. Edematous ankles and feet ballooned out grotesquely from the margins of her slippers. Cavernous ulcers opened up over the right buttocks, pubis and back of the skull while smaller ulcers stood out over the knees, elbows and ankles. Delicate silky threads of hair hung lifelessly from her skull. Broken, gray teeth peered out between thin, white lips through which there weakly issued forth a high pitched distant voice, remarkable

Figure 1. Age 18; weight 120 lbs.

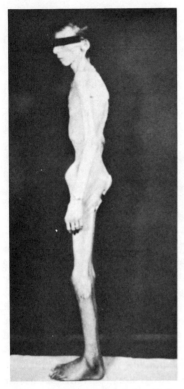

FIGURE 2   12/16/60; weight 47 lbs.

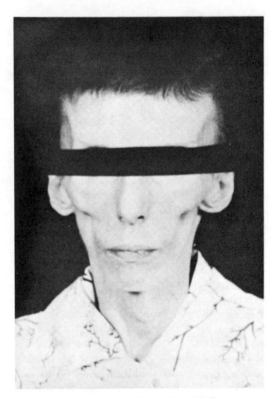

FIGURE 3   12/16/60; weight 47 lbs.

for its lack of pressing concern and alarm, which to the passing observer might have seemed a bit incongruous. Her blood pressure was 100/65. The liver and spleen were not palpable.

The pertinent past medical history probably dates back to 1935, when at 11 years of age she entered menarche with the not unusual problems of menorrhagia and metrorrhagia. At this time she described herself as "real chubby" weighing approximately 120 pounds. The family physician was consulted and advised the patient and her family that she had "glandular trouble," that she said plagued the maternal side of the family, and was the cause of heavy uterine bleeding and the tendency to be somewhat obese. For this reason she was admonished by the physician to never let her weight get out-

of-hand. He prescribed for her one grain of crude thyroid extract daily. Her menstrual periods continued to be heavy and frequent, occurring at approximately two week intervals at the time of her marriage in 1943, but ceasing entirely in 1944. This patient experienced dyspareunia throughout her marriage although she denied fear of sexual relations until after the initial painful experience. Prior to her marriage, the family physician had warned her that she was underdeveloped and that marriage would "make this worse or make it better." The only serious illness from which she has suffered is the present one. As a result of failure to eat, she has sustained numerous pathological fractures. In the past, she had been treated with general supportive measures, vitamins, injections that were said to be pituitary extract,

Nilevar and tranquilizers, all to no avail. Prior to 1960 she had had a total of eight hospital admissions elsewhere with the primary diagnosis being either malnutrition or more commonly, anorexia nervosa. Such secondary diagnoses as hypoglycemic shock, osteoporosis, fractures, and anemia were frequently included. There was no history of prior formal psychiatric treatment.

The review of systems indicated a history of severe headaches, insomnia, pedal edema, decubitious ulcers, nausea, watery diarrhea, nocturia, dysuria, and amenorrhea, as well as episodes of crying and screaming.

It should be emphasized that no specific attempt was made to obtain a psychiatric history from the patient, nor was any psychotherapy engaged in. The reasons for this, as will be discussed later on, were simply that the authors considered the major goal to be that of restoring eating behavior, a critical goal in view of the very poor prognosis and the risk of death. Believing it possible that conditioning techniques might be successful in restoring eating behavior, the interaction was viewed as an experimental situation in which past history was relevant but beyond knowing with any degree of certainty, and that a more effective technique would be a current evaluation of those conditions under which eating could be brought under control.[2] During the course of the experiment, however, she spontaneously divulged certain aspects of her past life without reinforcement by the experimenter. She had always maintained a very close attachment to her mother, and during her marriage, was reported by the family to have been quite homesick, as evidenced by several cross-continent trips

[2] In keeping with this experimental control, no tranquilizers or other psychopharmacological agents were given the patient. The only drugs she received were in the form of daily multi-vitamins and an occasional hypnotic for sleep as needed at night.

to Virginia, while living with her husband stationed in the military service in California. Her life in California was described as a lonely and unhappy one. Meals were taken in war-crowded, cheap restaurants because there were no facilities for cooking in their small apartment. With no attempt to elicit the information, the patient tearfully stated that her food intake while in California had been further reduced when a military physician whom she consulted suggested that she return home if she lost more weight.

A review of the family history indicates that there were two male siblings, both successful and well adjusted to their environment. The mother is an obese, pleasant woman with a history of cholecystitis and pancreatitis. At the time of the patient's admission in 1960, the mother was near complete exhaustion over her daughter's illness. The father, who might be described as a remarkably stoic man, had suffered a fairly recent myocardial infarction which left him without residual symptoms. No history of familial disease suggesting anorexia or cachexia could be elicited.

Following initial evaluation on the medical service, the differential diagnosis was felt to lie between anorexia nervosa and Simmond's disease or panhypopituitarism. Extensive laboratory tests were carried out in an attempt to further illuminate the problem, including ACTH stimulation of the adrenals with concomitant plasma corticoid measurements, urinary gonadatrophins, urinary 17 ketosteroids and urinary ketogenic steroids. Radioactive iodine uptake was carried out and a stool examination and dxylose absorption studies were made. The results of all these tests were found to be within normal limits. The routine laboratory examinations only revealed abnormalities which reflected the secondary results of decreased food intake.

During the time she was being evaluated on the medical service, the patient was offered a diet which fitted her own specifications as well as three interval feedings of fruit ice and ginger ale. Six days after admission she was consuming an average of 1,451 calories daily and had gained 1.6 pounds in weight. Seventeen days after admission, on December 31, 1960, she was begun on 20 units of ACTH daily as a therapeutic and diagnostic trial. On January 10, 1961, this was increased to 20 units twice per day. It was then gradually reduced and finally discontinued on January 24, 1961. Her weight had stabilized at around 52.5 pounds and she was reported to be eating a high percentage of the food offered her. She denied regurgitation of ingested food at this time and throughout her hospital stay. By the end of January 1961, it had become apparent that much of the patient's weight gain was due to the fluid and electrolyte retention secondary to the administered ACTH.

An exhaustive medical and endocrinological evaluation had failed to reveal any specific lesion or disease process which could account for the patient's reduced food intake and state of severe malnutrition bordering on death. With the discontinuation of the ACTH and subsequent water diuresis, the patient weighed 50 pounds. At this time, just prior to her transfer to the psychiatry service on January 3, 1961, she was consuming between 1100 and 1400 calories each day.

TABLE 1

	Date	Wt.
1.	12/16/1960	47 lb.
2.	1/3/1961	50 lb.
3.	2/1/1961	53 lb.
4.	2/10/1961	59 lb.
5.	2/20/1961	61 lb.
6.	3/1/1961	60 lb.
7.	3/10/1961	63 lb.
8.	3/20/1961	64 lb.
9.	3/30/1961	64¼ lb.
10.	4/14/1961	63 lb.
11.	4/18/1961	64 lb.
12.	4/22/1961	65½ lb.
13.	5/6/1961	66 lb.
14.	5/10/1961	68½ lb.
15.	5/13/1961	67 lb.
16.	5/17/1961	70 lb.
17.	7/8/1961	70 lb.
18.	7/15/1961	71 lb.
19.	7/29/1961	72 lb.
20.	8/12/1961	71 lb.
21.	9/30/1961	72 lb.
22.	10/14/1961	75½ lb.
23.	11/11/1961	75¼ lb.
24.	11/25/1961	76½ lb.
25.	12/2/1961	76 lb.
26.	12/9/1961	77¼ lb.
27.	1/18/1962	74½ lb.
28.	1/27/1962	77 lb.
29.	2/3/1962	77½ lb.
30.	2/10/1962	77½ lb.
31.	3/31/1962	88 lb.
32.	4/21/1962	84 lb.
33.	5/14/1962	85 lb.
34.	5/21/1962	86½ lb.
35.	6/16/1962	85 lb.

BEHAVIORAL METHODOLOGIES: THE EXPERIMENTAL PLAN AND ITS EXECUTION

Inpatient Course

When the patient was transferred from the Internal Medicine service to Psychiatry, she was assigned to one of the authors (WJE), then a Resident on Neurology and Psychiatry who got into contact with the other authors to formulate a plan for working with the patient. It was arranged for the junior author (JPM), then a medical student to be assigned to her on the wards. The three experimenters decided to approach the case from a standpoint of experimental manipulation of the relevant variables in order most effectively to restore eating behavior, as noted a critical problem of the moment. Assuming that behavior is largely under the control of its consequences and that it can be maintained and modified by manipulating consequences (among other variables) an analysis of the patient's immediate situation was the first task accomplished.

The patient was in an attractive hospital room, with pictures on the wall, flowers available and usually present, a lovely view of verdant grounds visible through the window. She had free access to visitors; a radio, books, records and a record player, television, and magazines were present, although she had considerable difficulty in reading because of her generalized debility (See Fig. 2). People would visit her and read to her as well as provide television control and record play. In discussion with her it was found that she enjoyed these activities and seemed to enjoy visitors as well. Because these activities apparently provided enjoyment for her and could thus be considered positively reinforcing to her behavior, she was removed from her pleasant hospital room and transferred to the psychiatric ward, to a private room from which all attractive accoutrements had been removed. The room was barren, furnished only with a bed, nightstand and chair. A sink was available at one end of the room. The view was of a hospital courtyard.

At this point, it must be emphasized that the full cooperation of the patient's family and the hospital administration was elicited and received. The family was told that the patient would be treated in an unusual fashion—she would not receive psychotherapy as it is usually conceived of but rather she would be placed on an experimental regimen in which her pleasures would essentially be denied her unless she ate. The procedure and goals were made quite clear and permission was received to try the design out in practice. She was then transferred to the barren experimental "box." At that stage, the cooperation of the nursing staff was solicited because all three experimenters believed that without the aid of the nurses, with whom patients have most contact, the plan would fail. The nurses, graduate and student staff, were consulted and a

series of discussions took place in which the experimenters explained in detail the principles of behavioral modification to be applied and specifically what role the nurse would play in their implementation. The first reaction of "inhuman treatment" of the patient, a natural feeling on the part of the nursing staff viewing the removal of those objects designed to make a patient more comfortable and happier, was avoided by a discussion of the realities of the patient's danger and the lack of success achieved so far in effecting meaningful change. The experimenters felt it would be infinitely more inhuman to allow her to return home with a possible prognosis of death than to subject her to some methods which had proved successful in other situations and which might also be effective in her case. This feeling was transmitted to the others involved and a promise of cooperation was granted by the nurses and the psychiatric staff as well. No drugs were to be given (except, as noted above, multivitamins and occasional hypnotics for sleep); no psychotherapy was attempted by residents or attending staff; medical students were not permitted to see her and no teaching sessions (usual with patients on the ward for didactic purposes with the third-year medical students) were scheduled. The patient was so debilitated at that stage she could not move by herself, so the injunction against visitors and personal contact was easy to effect with the cooperation of the ward personnel. The nurses, of course, had to go into her room to change linen and bring her water and meals, but they were careful not to reply to the patient's verbal inquiries or conversational initiations with any response, other than a simple "good morning" uttered upon entering the room.

The patient was not told anything of the plan. She was told that she was to be transferred to another ward, on the psychiatric service and that there would be three people working with her, the authors of the current paper. It was made clear who these people were, her resident, a medical school staff research psychologist supervising, and a medical student. She was told that each of these would eat one meal with her during the day, the resident (WJE) had breakfast with her, the staff psychologist (AJB) had lunch with her and the medical student (JPM) had dinner with her. All of the meals were brought to her by a nurse and were consumed in her room. The experimenters set up a reinforcement schedule, somewhat gross in its characteristics and difficult to achieve with exactness but nevertheless attempted; this involved verbal reinforcement of movements associated with eating. When the patient lifted her fork to move toward spearing a piece of food the experimenter would talk to her about something in which she might have an interest. The required response was then successively raised to lifting the food toward her mouth, chewing, and so forth.

The same scheduled increase in required response was applied to the amount of food consumed. At first, any portion of the meal that was consumed would be a basis for a postprandial reinforcement (a radio, TV set, or phonograph would be brought in by the nurse at a signal from the experimenter); if she did not touch any of the food before her, nothing would be done by way of reinforcement and she would be left until the next meal.[3] More and more of the meal had to be consumed in order to be reinforced until she eventually was required to eat everything on the plate. The meals were slowly increased in caloric value, with the valued help and cooperation of the dieticians. Initially, she was presented with 2500 calories a day in increments ranging from 50 to 75 calories. Several attempts were made to adjust the

caloric intake with the choice of menu left to the experimenters and dieticians. Later she was placed on a standard hospital menu of 2000 to 2500 calories a day with the menu her own choice from several alternative menus, as was true of all other patients on the ward. This self-choice of menu was provided later on as a reinforcement for eating behavior, in generalizing reinforcements.

As her weight began to rise somewhat, there was a beginning of generalizing reinforcers from the social reinforcement of the experimenters eating with her (which we, at least, assumed to be reinforcing!) to a broader class of reinforcing events, such as having a patient of her own choice eat with her in her room or eating in the solarium with other patients, after her mobility improved. Later on, she was taken for walks around the university grounds by a student nurse or a patient of her choice. Her family and other visitors were also provided in increasing frequency as her eating and weight rose. All such reinforcements—visitors, walks, mail, hair care (such as setting and shampoos)—were postponed until after meal time so as to constitute a reinforcement for eating behavior. Later in her hospital stay she was permitted to go out to eat with family, friends or nurses, as she wished, in keeping with the goal of generalizing eating behavior to nonhospital situations.

At one point during her hospital stay she hit a plateau in which she did not gain any weight; from about March 10 to April 18 she ranged around the same weight, 63 pounds. Internists consulted said that this was understandable to a degree because she was laying down body constituents damaged in her previous noneating behavior. After a while, however, the weight gain could be expected to rise once again. When it did not, it was suggested that she might be vomiting the food she did take in because her caloric intake continued to be sufficient to produce weight gain. The

[3] A consistent reinforcement available to her at all times, incidentally, was knitting, provided to ease some of the potentially aversive qualities of very long waits without directly interfering with the control of eating behavior.

suggestion was made that she was using the sink in her room to dispose of vomited food and someone cut off the water in the sink. The experimenters decided that control of her eating was not to be achieved through cutting off the sink water and so it was turned on again and the requirement for reinforcement was changed to weight gain and not simply eating. After this, any gain in weight, no matter how slight, was required for the walks, TV, and other reinforcements. Eating alone was no longer sufficient. She was weighed every day at the same time, around 3:00 P.M. and the major class of reinforcements, walks and so forth, were made contingent upon her scale reading at 3:00 P.M.

Another question arose early in the experiment with regard to extra caloric intake to be provided by snacks and by such specific caloric light meals as Metrecal. The possibility of giving her between meal snacks was considered and rejected for the simple reason that the experimenters wished to have a clear stimulus situation delineated—mealtimes were for eating. We wished to avoid the problem of having her receive a snack at 4:00 P.M. and then excusing a lowered intake at dinner by claiming to be less hungry because of the snack. To keep the mealtimes as a temporal discriminative stimulus was critical in the initial stages; later on bedtime snacks were permitted.

Again, conversations were always about pleasant topics, never about her problems. Even when she spontaneously began to talk about some of her past history, as noted in the preceding section on medical history and clinical course, the experimenter present would not react but would politely allow her to talk without reinforcing the content, then go back to what the topic had been before-hand. This restraint on therapeutic intervention and interpretation was consistent with the experimental design.

Outpatient Course

She was, as noted, admitted to the hospital December 14, 1960, and transferred to Psychiatry on January 3, 1961. The experiment was begun on February 1, 1961. She was discharged as an outpatient on March 25, 1961 weighing fourteen pounds more than she had when she had been transferred. The question now was one faced by every therapist—how to generalize the methods established under controlled conditions to the outside where such controls are lacking. The aid of the patient's family was enlisted in this regard; they were asked specifically:

1. to avoid any reinforcement of invalid behavior or complaints;
2. not to make an issue of eating (something that had been generally true of family and friends during her losing period before hospitalization);
3. to reinforce maintenance of her weight by verbal reinforcement, for example, as she began to fill out her clothes this was to be reinforced clearly but without overreacting;
4. not to prepare any special diet for her;
5. to refrain from weighing her at home, inasmuch as weight was to be recorded only when she made periodic visits to see the resident (who was to be the only one of the experimenters to continue a direct personal relationship with her);
6. to discuss only pleasant topics at mealtimes;
7. never to allow her to eat alone;
8. to follow a rigid schedule for meals, with an alarm clock to be present for each meal;
9. to use a purple tablecloth initially as a discriminative stimulus for mealtime table behavior, associated with eating, an idea borrowed from Ferster's work with obese patients (Ferster, et al., 1962); and, finally,

10. to encourage her to dine out with other people under enjoyable conditions.

She continued to return at regular intervals to talk to her resident. As an outpatient, she continued to respond favorably to the procedures, as indicated by the graph of weight gain in Table 1. At first, after her discharge, she was seen weekly, then bi-weekly, and finally, intermittently until her readmission to the hospital for further control in February 1962. During the period between March 1961 and February 1962 as an outpatient, the experimenters sought to generalize the reinforcements for maintained eating behavior as much as possible. She was active in church work and social events in the small town in which she lived. The visits to the resident were chats in which she told generally about what she had been doing. Some discussion of the ultimate rewarding and ultimate aversive consequences of her eating behavior took place and she received social verbal reinforcement for weight gain when she stepped on the scales. Her physical activity at that time began to be somewhat tiring as she reported it and she was enjoined against overdoing the social and church functions, if possible, while she was working on weight gain. This hyper-activity, as will be seen in later discussion, proved to be a critical variable.

One report she gave of a social situation in which social reinforcement seemed effective was an incident involving a woman's club of which she was a member. She recounted this experience with some glee. During the refreshment period, coffee and doughnuts were passed to the members and, as was the practice in her pre-hospital membership days, the woman passing the refreshments skipped the patient. She asked if she might have a doughnut and said that everyone turned to stare at her as she devoured a rather

Figure 4. 1/11/62; weight 74.5 lbs.

large doughnut. She reported that it was something like being in the zoo but that she dervied a great deal of pleasure from the event even though it was a little disarming; not the least of the pleasure appeared to stem from the verbal reinforcement by the other members for her eating.

Another reinforcing event was the reappearance of healthy hair. During the severe physical distress caused by not eating, her hair had been brittle and easily cracked when it was touched. As her weight and health improved, her hair returned to a point where she could have it dressed, a reinforcing event. Photographs in later periods (see Figure 4, for example), show this improved hairdressing and a return to care for her hair. She also made her own clothes, as shown in Figures 4 and 5 in the series of photographs and took pleasure in finding attractive clothes to wear.

As noted, she was readmitted on February 18, 1962 to be seen again under controlled conditions. Essentially, the same regimen was applied as had been used on her previous admission and she gained an additional 7 pounds during the month she stayed; she was discharged once again on March 25, 1962 and was last seen on June 16, 1962 when her resident was preparing to leave for service in

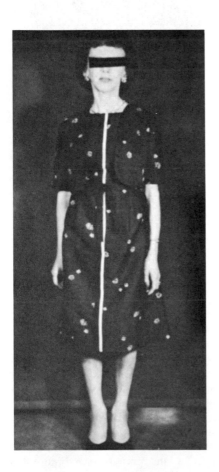

Figure 5. 6/20/62; weight 88 lbs.

the Navy. At that time she weighed 88 pounds.

Behavior Methodologies: The Operant Paradigm

It is apparent that the methodologies used in the restoration of eating behavior in this patient may be subsumed under a general operant conditioning approach. As Barrett (1962) observes, "The basic datum of the free operant method is the frequency of a specific and reliably defined response within a controlled experimental environment. The method is most readily applied, therefore, in cases where changes in the rate of a repeated movement are of primary concern." Certainly, eating as a response class is reliably defined and the desired result of the experiment was an increase in its rate.

Applications of operant conditioning methods to clinical problems have been varied; among the problems approached by the free operant method have been stuttering (Flanagan, Goldiamond, and Azrin, 1958), psychotic behavior (Lindsley, 1960) and autistic children (Ferster and DeMyer, 1961).

The present case was considered to be one in which operant conditioning techniques might be successful because of the specifiability of the response and the possibility of controlled environmental manipulation. The authors essentially used the operant paradigm as described by Goldiamond (1962) as a guide to formulating practices. The paradigm Goldiamond sketches is a summary statement of the general methodology of the free operant. . . . To modify Goldiamond's explanation of this paradigm somewhat, presenting a discriminative stimulus (S^D) in the presence of other constant stimuli (SS^C) will occasion a response (R); whether this response recurs is contingent upon the consequences (S^r) of that response (under these specific conditions) and the state variables (SV) usually referred to as "needs," "motivation," "deprivation," and the like which make the consequence of the response effective in controlling it. Assuming that behavior is governed by its consequences under specified conditions, discriminative behavior can be produced, maintained and altered if the constant stimuli, the discriminative stimuli, the response contingencies and the state variables are specified and controlled.

With respect to the present case, we visualized the variables within this operant paradigm to be as follows:

STATE VARIABLES (SV): essentially unknown; we could not evaluate with any degree of assurance those needs, motives or other inferred conditions that might have occasioned her drop in eating rate. The reinforcement history of any organism first studied is always an unkown; experimentally, the task is to manipulate deprivation states so that the past reinforcement history is less relevant and thereby bring the deprivation variables under experimental control. In the present case, the patient's past reinforcement history was inferred to have occasioned positively reinforcing values for such events as music, reading, social contact and the like and these could then be put on a deprivation schedule.

CONTROLLING STIMULI: The discriminative stimuli to which we wished the patient to respond (S^D_s) were those which eventually were to exercise some measure of control over her behavior, particularly eating behavior. Therefore, two S^D classes were considered, one for the inpatient controlled environment, the other for outpatient control. The Inpatient S^D_s included the experimenters as mealmates, the various utensils (plates, forks, knives, and so forth) and temporal S^D_s such as specific times for eating meals with no in-between eating. The Outpatient S^D_s included the alarm clock for mealtime, the purple tablecloth as an S^D for eating (particularly important if the table is used for other purposes such as sewing) and, again, temporal S^D_s in the form of specific mealtimes.

CONSTANT STIMULI (SS^c): in the hospital it would include the major stimulus class of the room itself and the various objects contained therein; the stimulus change from an attractive hospital room to a barren one is a shift in SS^c classes, limiting the number of S^D_s in the room by removing flowers, pictures, and similar stimuli. The SS^c as an outpatient would be more varied and less controlled but would include major stimulus situations such as the home and church.

RESPONSE (R): clearly, the response to be manipulated was eating. Weight gain, which supplanted eating *per se* as a reinforced event, is obviously contingent upon eating, the major response.

DIFFERENTIAL REINFORCEMENT (S^r— S^o): in the hospital room, the reinforcements included social contact, television, radio, records, reading; the response of eating was reinforced by these events. Not eating (and no weight gain) occasioned lack of reinforcement (S^o) and, later, verbal disapproval, presumed aversive (S^a). As an inpatient, the S^r_s were expanded to include walks around the grounds of the university, eating in restaurants, choosing her own menu and eating with other persons of her choice, as well as verbal approval as social reinforcement.

RECENT DATA REGARDING THE CASE PRESENTED

The data in Table 1 recording the weights over the period of the experiment stop at June 16, 1962. This was the last occasion on which the patient's weight was recorded in the hospital and the last time she had direct experimenter contact. As noted above, her resident left after this date, as did the research psychologist. She was interested in maintaining contact with the resident in particular as he entered the Navy and continued to write. On July 25, 1962 the patient wrote that she was taking a home study course in practical nursing and had passed her exam with a grade of 95, had received her cap and uniform, and was ready for practicum hospital training and her license. She was specialing a private case in her home town, a woman who was invalided by arthritis. The patient wrote that her patient had "an electric organ and I'm enjoying that especially, and play for her as she can not play now because of the arthritic condition in her back and neck. Also a fabulous collection of records. So we have a lot of mutual interests and are getting along fine together!" She also reported that she had hit the 90 mark in weight: "So it's a happy feeling to be out of the 80's!" This was her own self-reported weight. The reinforcements of music and social contact seemed to be available to her, as well as the reinforcing event of caring for someone else which became a major reinforcing class for her. It is also of interest to note that she did all the cooking for herself and her patient and reported good appetites.

At Christmas time, 1962, she wrote that she was working at the university hospital where she had been a patient, as a general practical nurse on a regular 8-hour shift. She had passed the physical required for such employment and reported that she enjoyed the work very much.

A letter dated June 16, 1963 indicated that she had left her nursing work although she enjoyed it: "My hours became more demanding all the time. My schedule was so irregular, as I was relief nurse on all shifts. So often I'd work 3:00-11:30 P.M., then back on at 7:00 A.M. Consequently I was not getting an adequate amount of sleep. But I was so happy and completely wrapped up in my work, and lost weight before I realized. Even then

I had an exceptionally good appetite. . . ." Her reported weight, as she wrote, was 78 pounds at that time, 12 pounds down from what she had indicated she weighed in July 1962 (see Figure 5, June 1962). Figure 6 shows her in January 1963 when she wrote she thought she weighed 76 pounds, as well as she could recall. (It should be noted that she indicates that she weighs herself before breakfast, instead of at the time (3:00 P.M.) at which the majority of the hospital records were made.) Her letter of June 1963 also indicated that she had put herself on a high caloric diet including "egg nog, ice cream, creamed soups, gobs and gobs of mashed potatoes, jello, and so forth, and have not

Figure 6. 11/15/63; weight 76 lbs.

lost 1 lb. through all this." "All this" referred to extensive dental surgery in which her lower jaw teeth had to be extracted on June 15, 1963; her dental problems were residua of the severe physical damage occasioned by the weight loss.

As of this writing, her last letter was dated December 17, 1963 in which she wrote that she was admitted as a student to a rehabilitation center; she was eligible for rehabilitation because of her spinal condition, kyphosis. This support freed her from requiring money from her family to go on with her goal of becoming a medical secretary and working in that role in a hospital situation. Again, she describes a full load:

I entered Business School Sept. 23, and am taking the General Clerical Course with Shorthand Optional. It is a very full course with classes everyday from 8:00 A.M. to 4:00 P.M. With extra activities. Was appointed Dormitory adviser for 25 girls, on my Dorm. So that involves a lot of nightly talks to solve their "petty problems," mostly boy friends, homesickness, etc. But am glad they feel I am capable of helping to solve their problems.

She complains sometimes of pain in her spine, particularly when she overworks and does something to "tax my strength." She wrote that her weight was around 72 pounds although she continues to eat. As she views it, when she works the way she wants to work she loses some weight but that the weight loss is apparently less disturbing than living what she calls a "sedentary life" which she says would be "an unpleasant one, because I've had too many years of idleness."

If it is true, as the patient suggests, that eating is maintained at a high rate and that lack of weight gain or actual weight loss (although nothing close to the dangerous level of before) results from overactivity or even following a routine that might be normal for a person not handi-

capped by the physical residua, the decision might be one of reinforcing a balance between activity and eating, reinforcing a steady rate of eating while reinforcing a lowered activity output, one that would be consonant with her physical capacities and yet also reinforcing her apparent social behavior manifest in counselling and nursing. Ideally, an accurate record of current weights and a direct manipulation of relevant behaviors should be continued. This is now being arranged with a research psychiatrist near her training center. On the positive side, certainly her current level of social interaction, her successful completion of one training program and entry into another, in addition to her ability (despite physical difficulties) to handle a responsible nursing position, both in special private nurse care and hospital nursing, reflect marked change, over and above the increase in weight over her level on admission to the hospital. Irreversible physical damage such as the kyphosis cannot be significantly improved but she did recover from the problems of insomnia, decubitus ulcers, edema and the other physical concomitants of severe weight loss. And, finally, the specific response manipulated—rate of eating behavior—has maintained itself at a high level.

DISCUSSION

The present case has been offered as an example of an operant conditioning approach to a clinical problem. The authors do not wish to suggest that the free operant method is inevitably the treatment of choice in such cases; we merely present this as an experiment in manipulating a specific response in a manner consonant with experimental analysis of behavior. The explanations for the drop in eating rate seen in patients diagnosed as anorexia nervosa have generally centered around symbolic conflicts. Nemiah (1963), for example, suggests that an anorexic may have a "conflict over sexuality," commenting that "Many patients with anorexia nervosa are thus beset by sexual conflicts expressed in an allied disturbance of eating." (p. 237). The fear of oral impregnation as a psychodynamic explanation of the disruption of eating behavior is the most frequent sexual conflict inferred. Nemiah also suggests that there may be a "conflict over aggression," observing that "avoidance of eating is related to the aggressive impulse; it represents a defense against the expression of it." (p. 237). This oral aggressive impulse and the reaction against it is a familiar psychodynamic explanation, also found in dynamic interpretations of speech disorders such as stuttering. It is not our purpose to review the literature on anor-exia; the interested person may consult Nemiah (1950, 1958, 1963), Loeb (1960), and Wall (1959) as standard references.

It is certainly possible that Nemiah's inferences regarding the etiology of anorexia are valid, although they are essentially unproved. Valid or not, it would seem that the most important problem facing the therapist is how to get the patient to increase his rate of eating, to restore eating behavior somehow disrupted. Psychodynamic explanations always remain inferential, no matter how valid or logical they may appear. The specification of the response desired and the analysis of those variables relevant in producing and maintaining that response seem more effective enterprises.

REFERENCES

Bachrach, A. J. Operant conditioning and behavior: some clinical applications. In H. Lief, V. F. Lief, and N. R. Lief (Eds.), *The psychological basis of medical practice*. New York: Hoeber, 1963. Pp. 94–108.

Barrett, B. H. Reduction in rate of multiple tics by free operant conditioning methods. *J. nerv. ment. Dis.*, 1962, 135, 187–195.

Ferster, C. B. and M. K. Demyer. The development of performances in autistic children in an automatically controlled environment. *J. chronic Dis.*, 1961, 13, 312–345.

Ferster, C. B., J. I. Nurnberger, and E. B. Levitt. The control of eating. *J. Mathetics*, 1962, 1, 87–110.

Flanagan, B., I. Goldiamond, and N. H. Azrin. Operant stuttering: the control of stuttering behavior through response-contingent consequences. *J. exp. Anal. Behav.*, 1958, 1, 173–177.

Goldiamond, I. Perception. In A. J. Bachrach (Ed.), *Experimental foundations of clinical psychology*. New York: Basic Books, 1962, 280–340.

Lindsley, O. R. Characteristics of the behavior of chronic psychotics as revealed by free-operant conditioning methods. *Dis. nerv. Sys. Monogr. Suppl.* 1960, 21, 66–78.

Loeb, L. Anorexia nervosa. *J. nerv. ment. Dis.*, 1960, 131, 447.

Nemiah, J. C. Anorexia nervosa. *Medicine*, 1950, 29, 225–268.

Nemiah, J. C. Anorexia nervosa: fact and theory. *Amer. J. Dig. Dis.*, 1958, 3, 249–271.

Nemiah, J. C. Emotions and gastrointestinal disease. In H. Lief, V. F. Lief, and N. R. Lief (Eds.), *The psychological basis of medical practice*. New York: Hoeber, 1963. Pp. 233–244.

Wall, J. H. Diagnosis, treatment and results in anorexia nervosa. *Amer. J. Psychiat.*, 1959, 115, 997.

This case involved the use of operant-conditioning techniques to treat a severely disturbed and often unmanageable eight-year-old boy. The therapy was conducted by the junior author in a therapeutic program directed by the senior author. Noteworthy aspects of the treatment are: First, the treatment was carried out in the real-world settings in which the maladaptive behavior was occurring; second, the treatment was very lengthy, lasting about 210 hours. Although behavior therapy clients are often given homework assignments to carry out in real-life settings, it is unusual for the therapist to carry on the treatment in that manner. In this case, the method was quite successful.

The length of the treatment is interesting, if we compare this case to Dr. Bornstein's treatment of Frankie presented in Section One. Frankie was seen for three years, and if we assume that he was seen twice a week (Dr. Bornstein does not report the frequency of sessions), the number of hours of treatment may be similar. Also, it may be remembered that at about age eight, the same age as the client in this case, Frankie demonstrated similarly unmanageable and manipulative behavior. It is fascinating to compare how differently the unmanageable behavior was treated in the two cases.

This treatment is marked by a concern to operationalize both the behaviors to be modified and the treatment procedures. Reliability checks were constantly carried out. Scientific discipline was thus combined with therapeutic efficacy to produce a most successful outcome. A final word should be said about the unusual *written* treatment contract signed by both the therapist and the client's parents. Such a contract is possible because the behavior therapist emphasizes overt behavioral responses, and he is able to specify exactly what behavior he is attempting to change and what the change ought to be. The change can thus be objectively verified. The seeking of psychotherapy is not a situation of caveat emptor because the prospective client (in this case the client's parents) is able to know what behavior will be changed, and if, in fact, it has been changed.

Accountability in Psychotherapy

A Test Case

TEODORO AYLLON and WILLIAM SKUBAN

In recent years a great deal of concern has been directed toward the quality and cost of medical care (Schorr, 1970;

From the *Journal of Behavior Therapy and Experimental Psychiatry*, 1973, *4*, 19–30. Copyright 1973 by Pergamon Press Ltd. Reprinted by permission.

Page, 1960; Yost, 1969). This attention has focussed on assisting the consumer by means of a critical examination of rising costs and the poor distribution of important medical services. The issues involved in consumer protection have also been found relevant to the drug industry

(Stanford, 1969). Drug companies have been accused of using advertising rhetoric and brand name labeling to inflate prices on some drugs, and in some cases of masking the only marginal effectiveness of others (Consumer Reports, 1969). The time is drawing near when the same public scrutiny and concern for cost-effectiveness will demand accountability in the services provided by the mental health industry. Indeed, criticism has already been registered against the high cost of mental health care and its frequently equivocal results (Mechanic, 1969; Miller, 1966; Stuart, 1970). From within its own ranks, the mental health industry has been accused of being foppish and of utilizing rhetoric to mask its inequities and ineffectiveness (Graziano, 1972). For example, psychotherapy, the traditional treatment of choice, has been the target of criticism from its consumers (Park, 1967; Smith, 1964) as well as from those professionals who have carefully analyzed the effects of therapy (Bergin, 1966; Burstine and Naughton, 1970; Eysenck, 1966; Fiske *et al.*, 1970). It seems likely that as consumers become more aware of the inadequacies in the results and delivery of mental health services, they will demand consistent and clear results from psychotherapy. This changing attitude may explain the growth in popularity of services such as encounters, marathons, and sensitivity groups which at least offer the consumer a fixed price for an agreed upon period of treatment.

Anticipating these problems, Sulzer (1962) made suggestions to reform psychotherapy to meet many of these consumer objections. For example, he suggested that a business-type contract be drawn up between therapist and client before therapy begins. Such a contract would serve as a means of scheduling the exchange of reciprocal benefits between the two parties. Consistent with this view, Stuart (1971) has stressed the desirability of a contract to make explicit the expectations of both client and therapist, and permit the client to examine the benefits offered and the costs involved in a therapeutic relationship. While the notion of a therapy contract may no longer be new, its adoption might well be hastened through empirical research.

The objective of this study was to answer some questions involving the feasibility of a contractual approach to psychotherapy:—what implications contractual agreements present for the therapeutic process; what the relative merits are of different therapeutic strategies in the light of contractual agreements; what kinds of client guarantees are possible regarding outcomes and costs; how to assess outcome most favorably to provide evidence to both therapist and client, of success or failure of therapy. These questions were examined for use in a contractual agreement to treat an emotionally disturbed child.

CASE HISTORY

SUBJECT. Mike, an 8-yr-old white male, was the subject of this study. The child had episodes of severe tantrumming and negativistic behavior both at home and in various other settings including school. Mike had alternately been diagnosed as brain damaged, emotionally disturbed, mentally retarded, and autistic. Efforts by his parents to enter him into a special school had met with failure because of his hyperactivity and general lack of control.

THE FAMILY. Mike had one sibling, a sister (age—2.5 yr) by his mother's second marriage. He was the product of a previous broken marriage. His mother nearly miscarried twice while pregnant with him, and the delivery was premature. The stepfather was employed as a personnel trainer. He had attended college but did not graduate; the mother graduated from high school. The family resided in a middle income apartment complex.

HISTORY OF THE PROBLEM. Mike's mother considered him to be "different" from birth. As a baby he would not sleep at night, would cry or moan, and rock in his crib through most of the evening. However, she herself did not think this unusual until Mike went to school. After a brief period in kindergarten, he was expelled because of his uncontrollable behavior. He was given a psychological evaluation which indicated that he had serious visual-perceptual and motor coordination problems. Then a neurological examination indicated brain damage: EEG patterns, however, showed little signs of irregularity. His mother until then merely thought that Mike was "just bad." At this time she enrolled him in a special school where officials reported that he was "Aphasic," communicating with his hands rather than verbally. Oddly enough, his mother reported, he simply "grew out of" this aphasia. Treatment at the school consisted mainly of physical therapy which did little to change his uncontrollable behavior.

The mother reported a long history of difficulty in controlling Mike, more so in public places. A typical episode involved his being allowed to push the shopping cart in a grocery store, whereupon he promptly banged into displays and people. When his mother tried to control his cart, he emitted high-pitched screams. If he became hungry while shopping, he would again scream, cry, roll on the floor, and throw objects off the shelves if not *immediately* fed. This was highly embarrassing to his mother or anyone else accompanying him. His mother often literally dragged Mike out of the store and locked him in the car.

At home, while the episodes were less embarrassing, they were just as severe. Almost any demand on the child would

occasion non-compliance and tantrumming. His father experienced many similar difficulties, and reported that trying to ignore Mike, though hard on those in earshot, seemed to work for a while.

After consistently failing in their handling of Mike, both parents attempted more direct and drastic methods to control his behavior. These efforts included putting him in the bathroom, withholding privileges, hitting him, calling him names to induce shame, and using a hand inductorium. None of these methods was successful. They found themselves threatening Mike many times and feeling guilty when they finally used the inductorium.

Mike exhibited these behaviors not only with his parents. Tantrums and high-pitched screaming occurred frequently in disagreements over toys with his sister. She would just stare at him or, worse still, mimick him. Relatives encountered similar difficulties with him as soon as they attempted some social control. Subsequently, at the time of the behavioral assessment, his mother stated that life with Mike was "intolerable, hell on earth."

DIAGNOSTIC TEST RESULTS. Before Mike could be admitted to a special school, he was required to have a psychological evaluation. The results of the psychologist's evaluation stated:

Within the first hour he changed from a helpless looking child who seemed unable to speak, to a wild tornado screaming and grabbing all the loose things he could find in the room and throwing them on the floor. . . . Because of his uncontrollable behavior in a demanding test situation, all results indicate that Mike is functioning at a severely retarded level (DAP I.Q. = 57; PPVT 55; Binet 40; KIT 40). There were several instances of echolalic speech patterns and almost constant screaming at a temper tantrum level. The manipulativeness of these outbursts was evident from the first; there were no tears and there was no affect behind the screams.

Since no school would have him, the examiner suggested that the mother join a local group of parents of autistic children to benefit from their program.

BEHAVIORAL ASSESSMENT. As school officials turned down Mike's application for admisison when they received the above report, his family decided to seek help in a therapeutic program for autistic children which was then under the direction of the senior author (T.A.). A co-therapist (W.S.) became acquainted with Mike in an empty classroom. He soon discovered that if he did not do exactly as Mike said, the immediate consequence was loud crying. Furthermore, if he asked Mike to do something, severe tantrumming and throwing of objects resulted. When Mike was asked to sit in a chair at a table, and refused, he was gently prompted. Mike immediately began screaming, crying, and falling on the floor, and tried throwing the chair at the therapist. This behavior continued uninterrupted for approximately 30 min. At this initial meeting, the only stereotypic autistic behaviors observed were when Mike, asked not to climb a sliding board, responsed by screaming, biting his hand, and slapping his head.

A close look at these episodes suggested that Mike had learned how to control adults, rather than let them control him. His failure to follow requests coupled with a loud shriek and tantrumming made many adults give up in despair. If they insisted on his obeying, Mike proceeded to throw a tantrum with such intensity that they immediately withdrew their requests and let him have his own way. Since Mike's characteristic interaction with adults involved frequent antisocial behavior and tantrumming, we decided to record: (1) the frequency of his following instructions and (2) the frequency

and duration of temper tantrums associated with requests.

(1) *Following instructions.* Following the instructions of adults was defined as starting the specified behavior within 10 sec of the request and completing it. This condition had to be fully met before the response was scored as positive. An example might be; "Mike please sit down in this chair." If he walked to the chair, scoring was withheld until he finished the specified behavior. If he made no apparent movements towards complying within 10 sec, this was scored as non-compliance. After a minute, this was again scored as non-compliance. Then an additional procedure was used whereby the therapist physically guided the child to facilitate voluntary compliance (for empirical evidence on the effectiveness of such a procedure see Foxx and Azrin, 1972).

(2) *Tantrumming.* A temper tantrum was defined as crying, loud whining, falling down, foot stomping, screaming, throwing objects, or hitting the therapist. If any of these behaviors took place within 15 sec of a request, they were scored as a tantrum. If the tantrum ceased for more than 15 sec, the episode was considered terminated. Another unit of observation then began whereby the therapist made a request of Mike, which could be the same as the previous one or a new one.

THE THERAPY CONTRACT. After preliminary discussions with the parents the therapists drew up a behavior therapy contract for the parents to read before treatment began. The contract specified the objectives of therapy, its duration, and what constituted criteria of success. The contract stated the overall objective—to equip Mike with significant social and academic behaviors to gain admission to school. More specifically, the behavioral treatment was to reduce the child's high rate of tantrum behavior from 46 per cent to less than 5 per cent of the measured time, and to increase his rate of following adult requests from 59 per cent to above 80 per cent of the measured time.

The contract further specified that therapy would terminate automatically after 35 days of a program of rehabilitation. At this time a test session would be held with the parents present, and if the objectives were met, the therapist would receive his full remuneration; if not, he would receive only two-thirds.

Parents and therapists reviewed all the above points. The parents were then given a copy of the contract (see Table 1), asked to read it over, and decide whether to accept its terms. They signed the contract along with the therapists.

BEHAVIORAL STRATEGY. In a therapeutic relationship two basically different strategies are used to produce psychological changes or new behaviors. The most prevalent is to conduct therapy in a traditional clinical setting anticipating that therapeutic progress will transfer outside the clinic. This popular strategy fundamentally fails to insure this transfer. Indeed, as found by Wahler (1969), Birnbrauer (1968) and Risley (1968) such a transfer is rare. Typically, therapeutic gains are confined to where the actual treatment takes place. This strategy affords convenience to the therapist in the form of clerical assistance, access to phones, privacy, air-conditioned quarters, and so on.

The second strategy, less popular, is to produce behavioral change in those settings where changes are desired. If the therapeutic and post-therapeutic environment were identical, the problem of transfer technically would not exist. In choosing this second therapeutic strategy, efforts were made to teach Mike social skills and self-control in relevant settings. Thus, instead of treating Mike's behavior in a clinic, he was repeatedly exposed to a number of public settings, so that in each he could be taught how to behave.

METHOD

Behavior therapy took place 5 days a week from 5 to 7 hr per day. With the exception of personnel needed for reliability checks on the treatment procedures, the entire therapeutic intervention and the observations were carried out by one person (W.S.). The therapy sequence lasted approximately 210 hr or a total of 35 days. Observations and treatment procedures took place in banks, supermarkets, department stores, restaurants, public parks, a zoo, gas stations, shopping centers, and homes of acquaintances.

Therapeutic procedures were evaluated daily by sampling Mike's responses to sets of 10 adult requests on approximately an hourly basis. Recorded were: (1) the number of requests complied with, (2) the number of requests prompting a tantrum, and (3) the minutes spent tantrumming. Measurement devices included a wrist counter, one hand counter, and two stopwatches.

Two graduate students made reliability checks on the average of once every 3 or 4 days, 10 sessions out of 35. The checks were made on from two to five sets of 10 requests, averaging approximately three checks. Agreement for the scoring of compliance of requests averaged 95 per cent and for the number of tantrums, 90 per cent.

Procedures

The first objective was to develop social skills by increasing Mike's frequency of complying with adults' requests and decreasing his tantrumming. Secondly, these social skills were to be strengthened by increasing the behavioral requirements for reinforcement. Finally, we aimed at a transition to natural consequences for Mike's behavior by fading out all contrived procedures used in therapy. In gen-

TABLE 1.   A Contingency Contract for Therapy

I. *Overview of problem and therapeutic program*

The overall objective of this therapeutic program is to develop and stabilize Mike's behavior patterns so that he may be considered for admission to school this fall. In general, this will involve strengthening some requisite behaviors such as following commands from an adult, and eliminating others, such as the screaming and tantrumming that accompany most of his refusals to follow instructions.

Mike has a discouraging behavior history for most teachers to consider working with. Because his characteristic reaction to requests is to throw tantrums, he is considered "untestable" by standard psychological means. This does not necessarily mean that he cannot do the items on a test, but rather that he has little or no control over his own behavior. His uncooperativeness quickly discourages most people from making much of an effort to work with him. What is clearly needed is an intensive rehabilitation program designed to enable Mike to build patterns of self-control which would lead to the elimination or drastic reduction of his disruptive behavior. This, in turn, would open other possibilities for developing Mike's potential, that is, the avenues which are blocked by his unmanageable behavior.

The overall goal of this 8-week program will be the development of self-control with its reciprocal outcome of decreasing or eliminating tantrums and disruptive behaviors. Implementation of this program will require that the child and his trainer engage in such activities as trips to the zoo, museums, parks, movies, swimming pools, shopping centers, supermarkets, and so on as well as having lunch and snacks together. These settings are included to expose Mike to a maximal number of normal situations where expectations of a standard of conduct are imposed by the setting itself.

As much as possible, the techniques used in the day program will be designed with the ultimate objective of utilization in the home. An attempt will be made to see that procedures used in the program are transferred to home management at the termination of treatment. The therapist will give instructions weekly to the parents by phone to insure that efforts both at home and in rehabilitation do not conflict.

II. *Behavioral objectives of therapy*

1. The objective of the therapeutic program is to teach Mike to comply with between 80–100 per cent of the verbal commands given to him by an adult(s). Compliance will be defined as Mike's beginning to perform the behavior specified by the command within 15 sec after it has been stated and then completing the specified task.

2. In addition, we intend to eliminate or drastically reduce Mike's excessive screaming and tantrumming. The goal is not to tantrum more frequently than once out of 30 commands and for no longer than 1 min at a time.

3. Evaluation of treatment outcome: The decision as to the attainment of these specific objectives will rest upon Mike's performance during a 30 min test session to be conducted in a classroom situation. At this session the therapist, the parents, and an additional person will make 10 verbal requests each of Mike, for a total of 30 verbal requests. Mike must comply with 80–100 percent of these requests for the program to be considered a success. In addition, he must have tantrummed not more than once, and for not more than 1 min, during this final evaluation.

III. *Time and place of therapeutic intervention*

1. The therapeutic program will start on _____ and terminate on _____. Evaluation of the effectiveness of treatment will be held on or about the termination date of the therapeutic program.

2. Location: The meeting place will be at the _____.
Session activities, however, will involve time spent elsewhere, for example, having lunch, trips to shopping centers, amusements, and other special events. If the facility is not available, some other place agreeable can be designated as meeting and base center.

3. Days of training: Therapy sessions will be scheduled 5 days per week. The specific days

TABLE 1. (continued)

III. *Time and place of therapeutic intervention (continued)*

may vary from week to week to comply with the objectives of the program. The family will be advised of the therapy schedule 1 week in advance.

4. Hours per day: Therapeutic sessions will be scheduled for 7 hr a day. Session time may be extended when therapeutically necessary as decided by the therapist.

5. Absences: There will be 4 notified absences allowed. The mother is expected to notify the therapist at least 1 hr before the scheduled therapy session. Any additional absences will require an additional fee of $10 per absence.

IV. *Fees*

Achievement of the behavioral objectives is expected to take 7 weeks of training from _____. This training will cost a total of _____. The monies will be disbursed in the following manner.

1. A check for 2/3 of the total amount will be given to the therapist at the beginning of therapy.

2. The balance of 1/3 will be paid to the therapist upon the achievement of the program objectives as specified above on about the date of termination of the program. In the event that the above objectives are not reached by this date, therapy will be discontinued and the balance will be forfeited by the therapist.

3. All expense incurred during training will be defrayed by the therapist. This will include admission to baseball games, the city zoo, swimming pools, and so on, as well as the cost of field trips, lunch, and snacks.

* * * *

By my signature I do hereby attest that I have read the above proposal and agree to the conditions stated therein.

_____
Parent

_____
Supervising Therapist

_____
Co-Therapist

_____
Date

---

eral, and across all three objectives of treatment, positive reinforcement—money —was presented contingent upon compliance with a request, while tantrumming resulted in time out from positive reinforcement.

A stopwatch was used to time Mike's compliance response. If he met the 10 sec limit for the response, he received as reinforcement, coins (pennies and nickels) which were strictly controlled by the therapist who searched the child each morning for change. The coins served two functions as conditioned reinforcers. The child could use them directly to operate pinball machines, as well as coke and candy machines. Secondly, he could pre-

sent the coins to the therapist to purchase items for him or grant him privileges, e.g. lunch, access to playground equipment for a set time, playing with toys, swimming privileges, pushing buttons on an elevator, playing catch with and being tickled by the therapist. Selection of backup reinforcers was based upon Premack's Principle (1962) which states that highly probable behaviors can be used to reinforce low probability behaviors. Consideration was also given to items or activities requested by Mike.

Mike's total earnings for a day normally ranged between 30¢ and 60¢. Throughout the training day, pennies were exchanged for various backup reinforcers as mentioned above, whose values fluctuated to some degree. A tickle by the therapist might cost one penny, while purchasing a coke out of a machine would be the machine cost of 10 or 15 pennies. Cost of providing Mike's backup reinforcers was approximately $2 per day or around $75 for the entire treatment program.

DEVELOPING SOCIAL SKILLS. Baseline observations indicated that compliance was generally low and variable while tantrumming was relatively frequent. The first objective of therapy was to develop social control by reducing tantrumming and increasing compliance. Specifically, the procedure for increasing compliance involved reinforcement (coins) paired with praise contingent upon compliance with a request. In addition, a discriminative stimulus—the movement of a stopwatch hanging around the therapist's neck —served to cue Mike on when reinforcement was available. The stopwatch was left running except when it was turned off for tantrumming. This procedure functioned as time-out from reinforcement. When a tantrum occurred, Mike was repimanded with a "no" and was told the stopwatch was off. It was left off for the duration of the tantrum and for 1 min after. When the hold time was over, he was told the watch was on and he could once again earn coins by doing what the therapist told him to do.

During the tantrum the trainer would turn away from Mike, withholding all social interaction. In some instances it was necessary to restrain Mike in order that an entire store would not be reduced to rubble. In these cases a firm gripping of the arm was maintained while social interaction was eliminated. The requests during this therapy sequence were largely those that required motor responses. At the park, this might be to stop swinging on the swing, or, at the zoo, merely to follow the therapist. At the grocery store the

therapist might ask Mike to hand him a jar of peanut butter. From these examples it can be seen that for the most part requests were "tailored" to the particular setting.

Once social behavior was established, academic tasks became the major requirement for earning pennies. These consisted of getting Mike to write his name, count to five, make left-right discriminations, and word identifications (park, swim etc.). After a short while the opportunity to do academic work ("school time") became a discriminative cue for reinforcement and was eagerly sought after by the child.

STRENGTHENING SOCIAL SKILLS. To insure that the gains made in the first therapeutic sequence would remain stable, increased requirements were made on Mike for "stress points."

Beginning with the next 80 hr of therapy, Mike was given only praise for each request followed outside of "school time." When he earned five of these verbal reinforcers, he received a nickel. He could exchange the nickels for a "school time" session. Mike was also given a counter to be worn around his neck, and was told how to count his own "good boys." The therapist wore a wrist counter to check Mike's accuracy. During this phase *only* the pennies (earned through academic tasks) were exchangeable for the backup reinforcers; the nickels served only to gain access to the "school time" schedule.

TRANSITION TO "NATURAL CONSEQUENCES." Including many different settings as therapeutic locales was a strategy adopted to resolve one aspect of the problem of transfer. There is, however, another aspect to the transfer dilemma. The use of measurement devices, while desirable as a scientific tactic, does not transfer readily what has been called the "natural communities" of reinforcement (Baer and Wolf, 1970). Therefore, we tried to discontinue the gadgetry while at the same time simulating the natural contingencies at home. Some of these occur in general when parents praise their children for behaving well and ignore or punish them for behaving badly. Sometimes, parents give their children a weekly money allowance for helping with household chores or for merely being good during the week. Often after receiving much praise or after a certain length of time of good behavior, a child might be given a treat, a toy, or a special privilege. With these examples as guides, the objective of the final therapeutic sequence was to approximate as closely as possible the natural contingencies utilized by parents in the social control of their children. Specifically, instead of coins Mike received only social reinforcement (praise) for being "good" (e.g. following instructions). After receiving much praise through the day, Mike was given a special treat on an intermittent basis. Since the therapist paid for these treats, Mike was in a sense on a daily allowance for following instructions. Mike's "bad" behavior, tantrumming, was ignored. To approximate natural control further, Mike's counter was taken away from him and other scoring and controlling devices were kept from sight, with the exception of the intermittent times when data was collected. The only visible piece of equipment remaining at this time was a wrist counter worn by the therapist, which registered the frequency of praise given to Mike for following requests. A highly variable exchange rate was established between the total amount of praise given and that required for treats. Because of the variability of this exchange rate, Mike was often asked to look at the counter to see if he had accumulated "enough" praise to receive his treat.

RESULTS

The results show that when Mike was reinforced for following instructions and was placed on time out for tantrumming, his social skills increased. . . .

[D]uring the behavioral assessment (baseline), Mike's following instructions given by adults averaged 59 per cent. The use of money as a reinforcer in the first phase of behavior therapy increased this percentage by 24 points. By increasing the requirements for reinforcement in the second phase, Mike's rate of following instructions was further increased to 97 per cent—a gain of 14 percentage points. When treatment devices were removed in an effort to approximate the natural contingencies, Mike's high rate of following requests was maintained.

Much the same results were obtained with respect to Mike's major social deficit: tantrumming. . . . [D]uring baseline Mike tantrummed to 42 per cent of the requests given to him. The first therapeutic intervention dramatically reduced this to 10 per cent. The second procedure brought even further improvement as tantrumming was reduced to 2 per cent or 1/20 of the amount seen during the baseline. The third therapeutic sequence maintained this improvement.

The dramatic changes in Mike's behavior were not limited to the frequency of his tantrumming. . . . [D]uring behavioral assessment (baseline) the tantrums sometimes lasted as long as 33 min. The first treatment period served dramatically to decrease the duration of tantrumming from 33 min to 7 min. This improvement was increased during the second treatment sequence as the duration of tantrumming dropped to 2 min, or 1/5 of its original level. Again, these dramatic improvements were maintained when natural control was approximated in the last therapeutic sequence.

EVALUATION OF THERAPEUTIC PROCEDURES ACROSS THERAPISTS. While the improvement in Mike's social skills was impressive, one might question whether someone other than the therapist could utilize the treatment procedures to gain effective control over the boy's social behavior. To test for generalization of the therapeutic procedures, an evaluation was performed using another person in the role of therapist. The test was conducted over a period of 3 days near the end of the first phase of the therapeutic sequence. A female graduate student, who had never met the child before, was briefed on the recording and treatment procedures. Mike and the new therapist went to a new setting. There Mike was given a series of instructions: first, under baseline conditions of no treatment, then under the treatment procedure, and finally, under *no* treatment conditions. Reliability checks performed by another observer indicated that agreement was above 80 per cent on each of the three response dimensions. . . .

[W]hen the treatment procedures were not in effect, Mike's rate of following instructions fell and became extremely erratic. In some cases he followed all the requests given to him during this baseline condition, in others only 20 per cent. When the treatment procedure was instituted by the new therapist, Mike's rate of following requests increased to a perfect level—100 per cent. As the therapeutic procedure was subsequently withdrawn, the rate of following requests again deteriorated, even more quickly, and once again became extremely variable. . . . During the baseline period of no behavioral therapy, he was occasionally "perfect," but often tantrummed to fully 50 per cent of the requests, and on one occasion to all of the requests given to him. When the new therapist applied the treatment again this aspect of his social behavior was brought under complete control. As the treatment was withdrawn, however, he quickly began to tantrum more frequently. Figure 1 shows that the duration of Mike's tantrumming was zero when the new therapist used the therapeutic procedures.

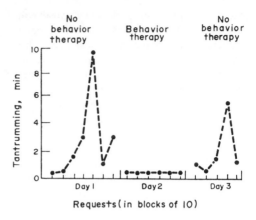

Figure 1. Therapeutic evaluation by another therapist. Duration of tantrumming in the presence and absence of behavior therapy.

When she did not, the duration of his tantrumming increased.

THERAPY CONTRACT: OUTCOME EVALUATION

As the contract had specified, there was an evaluation of the outcome of the therapeutic program. Mike was given 30 requests by adults; 10 by the therapist, 10 by an adult Mike had never seen before, and 10 by his father. Although not specified by the contract, the only instructions given to the other two participants were to smile and act "naturally" whenever Mike did something for them.

The results of this evaluation provide further evidence of the success of the strategy employed and the efficacy of treatment. The therapy contract specified that Mike be able to follow over 80 per cent of the requests given to him by adults. Out of the 30 requests given him in this test session, he successfully followed 28, or 93 per cent, thus exceeding the contract. The contract further stipulated that Mike would not tantrum more than once during the test period and that the duration be less than 1 min. Again, in the actual outcome evaluation Mike did tantrum once but for only 5 sec.

The parents were then asked to re-examine the therapy contract to insure that it had been satisfied and if so to initial it. The father indicated that he was pleased with the results and impressed with the straightforward nature of the contract which prevented him from getting the "run around." With the contract fulfilled, the therapist received his full remuneration, and Mike was admitted into a special classroom of a regular elementary school.

In addition to the measures reported above, there were collateral evidences of Mike's change. For example, near the end of therapy various persons working in the settings where it took place spontaneously commented either on how much better Mike was behaving or that he had "changed a lot." These were the same settings where Mike would often create a scene during the baseline, and the beginning of the therapeutic sequence (e.g. in banks, grocery stores, or the park). His father reported that the neighbors had noticed a definite change in Mike over the 2 months of training. The neighborhood children now seemed to enjoy playing with him and appeared to tease him less. Perhaps Mike's mother, who used many of the reinforcement procedures at home, charaacterized the changes best when she stated, near the end of the program, "Mike is becoming more of an individual. I think he enjoys life much more now."

DISCUSSION

The results of this study demonstrate that clear, objective understanding of the expectations associated with therapeutic success is possible between the patient and the therapist. Contracts are feasible if aims are defined objectively. Only therapeutic aims couched in behavioral terms are likely to pass muster. Aims in terms of hypothetical or internal events (Murray, 1938; Zax and Klein, 1960) may well remain beyond the purview of therapy contracts. It is also obvious that the client will prefer gains in the "real" world to those limited to a clinical setting. He will probably not be impressed with insights or changes that are confined to a clinical setting while he remains the same at home or at school.

It is already apparent that there is increasing use of behavioral intervention in natural settings, e.g. hospitals, schools, home. This behavioral approach has successfully been applied to neurotic problems (Wolpe, 1962), severely retarded children and adults (Hall and Broden, 1967; Zimmerman and Zimmerman, 1962), mental patients (Ayllon and Azrin, 1968) and classroom management (Thomas, Becker and Armstrong, 1968). The Leitmotif in all of these efforts, however, is the clear definition of objectives.

Recently, similar contracts have been written between organizations offering services and buyers in educational settings (Lessinger, 1970; Porter, 1971). With the help of clear-cut objectives and often independent assessment agencies, contracting organizations have successfully carried out large scale intervention programs in education (*Newsweek*, 1971). The important feature of these contracts is that they specify that the agency be given remuneration only upon the successful completion of the objectives within the time period allowed. This report attempts to extend this concept to the delivery of mental health services. Thus, irrespective of the psychotherapist's approach, a therapeutic contract makes him accountable for the effectiveness of his techniques. More important, a therapeutic contract gives the patient or client the confidence that derives from knowing that his expectations will be realized at last.

REFERENCES

Ayllon, T., and Azrin N. (1968) *The Token Economy: A Motivational System for Therapy and Rehabilitation*, Appleton-Century-Crofts, New York.

Baer, D. M., and Wolf, M. M. (1970) The entry into natural communities of reinforcement, *Control of Human Behavior: Volume II* (Edited by Ulrich, R., Stachnik, T., and Mabry, J.), Scott-Foresman, Glenview, Illinois.

Bergin, A. E. (1966) Some implications of psychotherapy research for therapeutic practice, *J. abnorm. Psychol. 71*, 235–246.

Birnbrauer, J. S. (1968) Generalization of punishment effects: A case study, *J. appl. Beh. Anal. 1*, 201–212.

Burstine, D. A., and Naughton, J. (1970) Income and outcome, *J. coun. & clin. Psychol. 35*, 153–156.

Consumer Reports (1969) Once over. *34*, 492–494.

Eysenck, H. J. (1966) *The Effects of Psychotherapy*, International Science. New York.

Fiske, D. W., Luborsky, L., Parloff, M. B., Hunt, H. F., Orne, M. T., Reiser, M. F., and Tuma, A. H. (1970) Planning of research on the effectiveness of psychotherapy, *Am. Psychol. 25*, 727–737.

Foxx, R., and Azrin, N. (1972) Restitution: A method of eliminating aggressive–disruptive behavior of retarded and brain-damaged patients, *Beh. Res. & Ther. 10*, 15–28.

Graziano, A. M. (1972) In the mental health industry illness is our most important product, *Psychol. Today 5*, 12–18.

Hall, R. V., and Broden, M. (1967) Behavior changes in brain injured children through social reinforcement, *J. exp. Child Psychol. 5*, 463–479.

Lessinger, L. M. (1970) *Every Kid a Winner: Accountability in Education*, Simon & Schuster, New York.

Mechanic, D. (1969) *Mental Health and Social Policy*, Prentice-Hall, Englewood Cliffs, New Jersey.

Miller, K. (1966) Mental health treatment services and the lower socio-economic classes, in *Mental Health and the Lower Social Classes* (Edited by Miller, K., and Grigg, C. M.), Florida State University Studies #49; Florida State University.

Murray, H. N. (1938) *Exploration in Personality*, Oxford University Press, New York.

Newsweek (1971) Success in Gary, *78*, 66.

Page, E. (1960) *What Price Medical Care?* Lippincott, Philadelphia, Pennsylvania.

Park, C. C. (1967) *The Siege*, Harcourt Brace & World, New York.

Porter, O. L. (1971) Contracted school—an instrument of educational change, *J. Negro Educ. 40*, 233–239.

Premack, D. (1962) Reversibility of reinforcement relation, *Science 136*, 255–257.

Risley, T. R. (1968) The effects and side effects of punishing the autistic behaviors of a deviant child, *J. appl. Behav. Anal. 1*, 21–34.

Sanford, D. (1969) Giving the consumer class, *New Republic 161*, #4, 15–17.

Schorr, D. (1970) *Don't Get Sick in America*, Aurora, Nashville, Tennessee.

Smith, B. K. (1964) *No Language But a Cry*, Beacon Press, Boston, Massachusetts.

Stuart, R. B. (1970) *Trick or Treatment: How and When Psychotherapy Fails*, Research Press, Champaign, Illinois.

Stuart, R. B. (1971) Behavioral contracting within the families of delinquents, *J. Behav. Ther. & Exp. Psychiat. 2*, 1–11.

Sulzer, E. S. (1962) Reinforcement and the therapeutic contract, *J. counseling Psychol. 9*, 271–276.

Thomas, D. R., Becker, W. C., and Armstrong, M. (1968) Production and elimination of disruptive classroom behavior by systematically varying teacher's behavior, *J. appl. Behav. Anal. 1*, 35–45.

Wahler, R. G. (1969) Setting generality: some specific and general effects of child behavior therapy, *J. appl. Behav. Anal. 2*, 239–246.

Wolpe, J. (1962) Isolation of a conditioning procedure as the crucial therapeutic factor: a case study, *J. nerv. ment. Dis. 134*, 316–329.

Yost, E. (1969) *The U.S. Health Industry*, Praeger, New York.

Zax, M. and Klein, A. (1960) Measurement of personality and behavior changes following psychotherapy, *Psychol. Bull. 57*, 435–448.

Zimmerman, J. and Zimmerman, J. (1962) Alteration of behavior in a special classroom situation, *J. exp. Anal. Behav. 5*, 59–60.

In this case Gerald Davison discusses the use of operant conditioning techniques in modifying the fantasy life of a male client. The basic problem of this young man was that he could respond sexually only to sadistic fantasies, which in turn caused him to feel like an "oddball" who could not establish normal relationships with females. Unlike the client treated by Medard Boss, described earlier in this volume, this client never acted on these sadistic fantasies. Dr. Davison focused the treatment, then, on these fantasies alone, using a counterconditioning technique in which the young man experienced the reward of masturbation while viewing first *Playboy* nudes and then bathing suit photos. During this process the client substituted non-sadistic fantasies for his old ones. One of the most important points of these treatment sessions is that they were entirely client-controlled. The therapist instructed him in this technique and spoke with him at length about relationships with women, but the actual learning procedure was carried out completely by the client. In fact, after relapsing into the sadistic fantasies the young man "treated" himself by using the same technique. In this case Dr. Davison found it necessary to also use aversive counterconditioning to get the client to give up his sadistic fantasies. Notice how he had to search for a proper image so that the client would feel complete disgust.

Elimination of a Sadistic Fantasy by a Client-controlled Counterconditioning Technique

A Case Study [1]

GERALD C. DAVISON

The modification of deviant sexual behavior has been approached largely through the contiguous pairing of a primary aversive stimulus with a stimulus eliciting an undesirable response (the "symptom"), the goal being to endow the inappropriate stimulus with negative properties, or at least to eliminate the unwanted positive attributes. Many such cases have been reviewed by Bandura (1969), Feldman (1966), Grossberg (1964), Kalish (1965), Rachman (1961), and Ullmann and Krasner (1965). Therapy of fetishism, homosexuality, and transvestism has tended to follow this counterconditioning model (e.g., Blakemore, Thorpe, Barker, Conway, & Lavin, 1963; Davies & Morgenstern, 1960; Freund, 1960; Lavin, Thorpe, Barker, Blakemore, & Conway, 1961; Raymond, 1956; Thorpe, Schmidt, Brown, & Castell, 1964). In addition, several workers have introduced complementary procedures in attempts to endow suitable social stimuli with the positive attributes necessary to make less likely a reversion to the inappropriate goal-object. Thus, for example, Freund

From *Journal of Abnormal Psychology*, 1968, 73(1), 84–90. Copyright 1968 by the American Psychological Association. Reprinted by permission.

[1] This paper was written during a postdoctoral traineeship at the Veterans Administration Hospital, Palo Alto, California. For critical comments and helpful suggestions, the author thanks Walter Mischel, Arnold A. Lazarus, David Fisher, and Thomas J. D'Zurilla.

(1960) gave his male homosexuals not only aversion conditioning trials to pictures of men, but also exposures to pictures of nude women after injection of male hormones. Similar procedures have been employed by Thorpe, Schmidt, and Castell (1963) and Feldman and MacCulloch (1965).

Of particular relevance to the present study is the work of Thorpe et al. (1963). These writers report therapeutic benefit following presumably counterconditioning sessions during which efforts were made to pair female pictures with orgasm from masturbation. It was assumed that this intensely pleasurable sexual response counterconditioned the aversion to females which appeared to play a crucial role in the behavior of the homosexuals. These authors recognized the importance of a person's fantasy life to his overt behavioral adjustment, and they assumed that beneficial generalization would occur from pictorial to the real-life situation, similar to the assumptions made for systematic desensitization (Davison, 1968; Wolpe, 1958). Although the therapeutic outcomes reported by Thorpe and his co-workers are equivocal in respect to actual sexual behavior, the procedures did have considerable effect on fantasies.

The possibility of extending this kind of work to an out-patient setting presented itself to the author during the course of his private practice. Various modifications of procedures used by Thorpe et al.

(1963) were employed, apparently to good effect. In addition, other important issues became evident in the course of therapy, which required fewer than 5 consulting-room hours over a span of 10 wk., and it is for these heuristic reasons that the following is reported.

CASE STUDY

The client was a 21-year.-old unmarried white male college senior majoring in history. The university counseling center had received an anxious letter from his parents, requesting help for their son in treating his introversion, procrastination, and "masochism." After working with the student for a few weeks on his tendency to wait until the last minute in his academic work, the psychologist at the center referred him to the author for help with his sexual difficulties.

Mr. M's statement of the problem was: "I'm a sadist." There followed a rather troubled account of a complete absence of "normal" sexual fantasies and activities since age 11. Masturbating about five times a week, the client's fantasies had been exclusively sadistic ones, specifically, inflicting tortures on women. He declared emphatically that he had never been sexually aroused by any other kind of image. Although generally uninterested in dating girls, he felt no aversion to them; on the contrary, he sometimes felt a "warm glow" when near them, but did not describe this at all in sexual terms. Because of his extreme concern over the content of his fantasies, however, he had dated very little and expressed no interest in the co-eds at the college. He recalled having kissed only two girls in his life, with no sexual arousal accompanying these fleeting episodes. He had never engaged in any homosexual activities or fantasies. Although expressing no guilt about his problem, he was very much worried about it inasmuch as he felt it impossible to ever contemplate marriage. This concern had

recently been markedly increased upon reading an account of a Freudian interpretation of "sado-masochism." He was especially perturbed about the poor prognosis for this "illness."

Because his concern over the gravity and implications of his problem seemed at least as disruptive as the problem itself, the therapist spent most of the first session raising arguments against a disease interpretation of unusual behavior. Psychoanalytic notions were critically reviewed, and attention was directed especially to the untestability of many Freudian concepts (Levy, 1963). Instances in the therapist's own clinical work were cited to illustrate the liberating effects observed in many people when they interpret their maladaptive behavior as determined by "normal" psychological processes rather than by insidious disease processes (cf. Davison, 1966; Glasser, 1965; Maher, 1966; Mainord, 1962). Mr. M frequently expressed relief at these ideas, and the therapist, indeed, took full advantage of his prestigious position to reinforce these notions.

At the end of the session, the counterconditioning orientation which would be followed was explained (Davison, 1968;

"Target" and "Back-Up" Sexual Stimuli for Client-Controlled Masturbation Sessions

Week	Target Stimulus	Back-up Stimulus
1	Playboy, real stimulus	Sadistic fantasy
2	Bathing-suit, real stimulus	Playboy, real stimulus
	Playboy, imaginal stimulus	Sadistic fantasy
3	Same as Week 2	Same as Week 2
4	Bathing suit, real stimulus	Playboy, real stimulus
	Playboy, imaginal stimulus	None

Guthrie, 1935; Wolpe, 1958), as well as the specific activities which he was to engage in during the coming week. When assured of privacy in his dormitory room (primarily on the weekend), he was first to obtain an erection by whatever means possible—undoubtedly with a sadistic fantasy, as he indicated. He was then to begin to masturbate while looking at a picture of a sexy, nude woman (the "target" sexual stimulus); *Playboy* magazine was suggested to him as a good source. If he began losing the erection, he was to switch back to his sadistic fantasy until he could begin masturbating effectively again. Concentrating again on the *Playboy* picture, he was to continue masturbating, using the fantasy only to regain erection. As orgasm was approaching, he was at all costs to focus on the *Playboy* picture, even if sadistic fantasies began to intrude. It was impressed on him that gains would ensue only when sexual arousal was associated with the picture, and that he need not worry about indulging in sadistic fantasies at this point. The client appeared enthusiastic and hopeful as he left the office. (Table 1 summarizes the client-controlled masturbation assignments following this and succeeding consulting-room sessions.)

At the second session he reported success with the assignment; he had been able to masturbate effectively and enjoyably three times over the weekend to a particular picture from *Playboy* without once having to use a sadistic fantasy; however, it did take significantly longer to climax with the *Playboy* photograph than with the usual kind of sadistic fantasy. During the rest of the week, when he had not had enough privacy for real-life visual stimulation, he had "broken down" a few times and used his sadistic fantasies.

Much of this session was then spent in talking to him about some of the social-sexual games which most males play in our culture, especially the "mental undressing" of attractive women. The pur-

pose was to engage him in the kind of "stud" conversation which he had never experienced and which, it was felt, would help to change his orientation toward girls. The therapist reassured him that the first direct contacts with girls are sometimes disappointing; he had to admit, however, that his extreme sensitivity about the sadistic fantasies had severely limited his experience.

During the coming week he was, first of all, to ask out on a coffee date any girl whom he felt he *might* find attractive, even for a sadistic fantasy. He was also to spend some time between classes just looking at some of the co-eds and noting some of their more remarkable attributes. Finally, his masturbation sessions were to be structured as follows: The real-life pictorial stimuli were to be girls either in bathing suits or lingerie, used in the same way as the *Playboy* picture the preceding week; this latter stimulus was to be used as "back-up" stimulus, replacing the sadistic fantasies in the event that he was losing his erection. Attention was also to be directed to imaginal sexual stimuli, and when masturbating in this way he was to use the *Playboy* image, with a sadistic fantasy as back-up.

The third session lasted half an hour. He had procrastinated so long in asking for a date that the girls he contacted had already made other plans; the therapist expressed his disappointment quite openly and urged him even more strongly to follow through with this task. He had managed to spend some time looking at girls but did not note significant sexual arousal, except when a sadistic fantasy crept in occasionally. He had masturbated only once to real-life stimuli, using some bathing-suit pictures from a weekly national news magazine; this was successful, though it took longer even than when the *Playboy* material was used previously. When masturbating to imaginal sexual stimuli, he had relied almost exclusively on his sadistic fantasies rather than utilizing the *Playboy* picture in imagination as he had in real life 1 wk. earlier.

His reluctance to give up the sadistic fantasies prompted the use of the following procedure, the idea for which had been obtained from Lazarus (1958). With his eyes closed, he was instructed to imagine a typical sadistic scene, a pretty girl tied to stakes on the ground and struggling tearfully to extricate herself. While looking at the girl, he was told to imagine someone bringing a branding iron toward his eyes, ultimately searing his eyebrows. A second image was attempted when this proved abortive, namely, being kicked in the groin by a ferocious-looking karate expert. When he reported himself indifferent to this image as well, the therapist depicted to him a large bowl of "soup," composed of steaming urine with reeking fecal boli bobbing around on top. His grimaces, contortions, and groans indicated that an effective image had been found, and the following 5 min. were spent portraying his drinking from the bowl, with accompanying nausea, at all times while peering over the floating debris at the struggling girl. After opening his eyes at the end of the imaginal ordeal, he reported spontaneously that he felt quite nauseated, and some time was spent in casual conversation in order to dispel the mood.

His assignments for masturbation during the coming week entailed increasing the frequency of his real-life masturbatory exposures to bathing-suit pictures, along with concerted efforts to use the *Playboy* stimuli in imagination as he had in real life 2 wk. earlier, resorting to sadistic fantasies if necessary.

The fourth session lasted only 15 min. He had managed to arrange a date for the coming weekend and found himself almost looking forward to it. Again, he had masturbated several times to a real-life picture of a bathing beauty. In fantasy he had managed to use the *Playboy* girl exclusively two out of five times,

with no noticeable diminution in enjoyment.

He was to continue using the bathing-suit pictures while masturbating to real-life stimuli, but to avoid sadistic fantasies altogether, the idea being that any frustration engendered by this deprivation would simply add to his general sexual arousal and thereby make it all the easier to use the *Playboy* stimuli in imagination.

The fifth session, also lasting *only* 15 min., opened with Mr. M animatedly praising the efficacy of the therapy. He had masturbated several times, mostly to real-life bathing-suit pictures, with no problems and, most importantly, had found himself *unable* to obtain an erection to a sadistic fantasy. In fact, he even had difficulty conjuring up an image. He had also spent considerable time with two girls, finding himself at one point having to resist an urge to hug one of them—a totally new experience for him. He enthusiastically spoke of how different he felt about "normal dating," and a 1-mo. period without interviews was decided upon to let him follow his new inclinations.

The sixth session, 1 mo. later, revealed that his sadistic fantasies had not reappeared, and that he had been masturbating effectively to both real-life and imaginal appropriate sexual stimuli. He had not, however, been dating, and some time was spent stressing the importance of seeking "normal" sexual outlets. He felt strongly, however, that the sexual problem had been successfully handled and requested that his procrastination problem be taken up. Two sessions were subsequently devoted to following the same general strategy that had been adopted, with some success, by the college counselor, that is, arranging for various rewards to be made contingent upon certain academic task-performances. Mr. M did report doing "an enormous amount of work" during 1 wk.—out of fear of having to admit to the therapist that he had been loafing. Practical considerations, however, made it clear that this handling of the problem, even if it should prove effective, was not as realistic as his facing the reality that there was no "magic pill" to eliminate his procrastination. Therapy, therefore, was terminated, with no sadistic fantasies having occurred for over 1 mo., and with the problem of procrastination left more or less untouched.

A follow-up of 1 mo. was obtained by telephone. Mr. M reported that there was still no sign of sadistic fantasies and that, indeed, he was no longer even thinking about the issue. He had still not "gotten around" to asking any girl out on a date, and the therapist urged him in no uncertain terms to tackle this aspect of his procrastination problem with the vigor that he had shown in regard to his studies (where significant improvement had been made). Extensive and persistent questioning failed to evoke any reported aversion to girls as the basis of his reluctance to ask them out.

DISCUSSION

As with every case study, one must necessarily speculate, to a large extent, on the "active ingredients." Hypotheses are not readily strengthened from such data. As a demonstration of various strategies, however, the present report does seem to be of heuristic value.

1. The first significant event in therapy was the author's general reaction to the client's statement of the problem, "I'm a sadist." After Mr. M had recounted the horror with which he had read about his mysterious "illness" in Freudian terms, the therapist countered with a logical attack that made the hour take on more the characteristics of a graduate seminar than a psychotherapy session, except perhaps for the warmth, support, and acceptance which were deliberately conveyed. A key factor in this initial phase was an

attempt to change the client's general orientation to his problem. As this writer has usually found, the client had been regarding himself as "sick," qualitatively different from so-called "normals." Furthermore, the idea that much of his behavior was determined by forces working in devious ways in his "unconscious" was quite troubling, as was the poor prognosis. As reported in the case material, these issues were dealt with immediately, and significant relief was afforded the young man simply by reconstructing the problem for him in conditioning terms. It would, indeed, have been interesting and valuable to attempt some sort of assessment of improvement at this very point.

2. Inextricably intertwined with the foregoing was the outlining of a therapeutic strategy: his sadistic fantasies were to be attacked by procedures aimed at counterconditioning the maladaptive emotional reactions to specific kinds of stimuli. The client perceived the theoretical rationale as reasonable and was satisfied with the actual techniques which would be employed. Furthermore, being able to buttress the plan with both clinical and experimental data added to its credibility. It must be emphasized that whether the data cited, or the explanation offered, are valid is an irrelevant question in the present situation. The important point is that the client's enthusiastic participation was enlisted in a therapeutic regime which, by all counts, was to be highly unconventional.

3. A third conceivably relevant variable was the "older brother" type of relationship which the therapist established in talking with Mr. M about conventional sex. Clearly the client had missed this part of the average American male's upbringing and, as has been reported, much time was spent in deliberately provocative "locker-room talk," not as an end in itself, but rather as a means of exposing him to the kinds of heterosexual idea-

tions which seemed to the author useful in promoting nonsadistic fantasies about girls.

4. It is likely that the two positive exposures to actual women contributed to therapeutic improvement. Mr. M, having been goaded into direct social contact with girls, was fortunately able to appreciate the enjoyment that can come from a satisfactory relationship with a woman, albeit on nonsexual terms. In addition, having felt a very strong urge to hug one of them, in a nonsadistic fashion, was reported by the client as a highly significant event and must surely have fostered some change in his concept of himself as a sexual misfit. Furthermore, aside from any alleged counterconditioning with respect to appropriate stimuli (see below), it is also suggested that a favorable change in self-concept developed as he saw himself able to respond sexually to imaginal and pictorial stimuli that had previously left him unaroused.

5. It is assumed that the most important variable in therapy was the masturbation sessions which the client carried out privately. As discussed by Thorpe et al. (1963), it was felt that more appropriate social-sexual behavior would probably follow upon a change in sexual fantasies; in the present case a focus on the fantasies seemed all the more reasonable in view of the fact that *they formed the basis of the referral*. According to the client, it was his fantasy life which had retarded his sexual development, and it was this that he was most worried about. It was assumed that generalization to real-life girls would be effected in a fashion similar to the generalization which has been reported for Wolpe's technique of systematic desensitization (Davison, 1968; Lang & Lazovik, 1963; Lang, Lazovik, & Reynolds, 1965; Lazarus, 1961; Paul, 1966; Paul & Shannon, 1966; Rachman, 1966; Schubot, 1966; Wolpin & Raines, 1966; Zeisset, 1966). Of course,

whether Mr. M would actually begin dating regularly, or at all, would seem to depend importantly on factors other than those dealt with in this brief therapy, for example, the client's physical attractiveness, his conversational and sexual techniques, the availability of women attractive to him, and so forth. The generalization spoken of here, then, is best restricted to the thoughts and feelings which he had about women and about the prospects of relating to them nonsadistically; the case-study data contain ample verification for this.

The actual procedure followed was unique in that control of the pairing was vested entirely in the client, as is done in the use of differential relaxation with in vivo exposures to aversive stimuli (Davison, 1965; Wolpe & Lazarus, 1966). The sadistic fantasies were used initially to enable Mr. M to obtain and maintain an erection. During this arousal, he looked at culture-appropriate sexual stimuli (a nude *Playboy* photo) and masturbated. The assumption is made (and must obviously be investigated experimentally) that the pairing of masturbatory arousal with the *Playboy* picture served to replace neutral emotional responses to the picture with intensely pleasurable sexual responses. In succeeding sessions the content of the new sexual stimuli was changed to less openly provocative female pictures (bathing-suit photographs), with the already established *Playboy* picture used as back-up. Then the stimuli were made solely imaginal in similar fashion. Obviously, if this procedure worked for counterconditioning reasons, the client exhibited considerable control over the content of his fantasies, switching back and forth as he had been directed. This control of imagery is a central issue in desensitization research as well (Davison, 1968).

6. Probably very instrumental in changing the content of his fantasies was the intensive "imaginal aversive counter-

conditioning" (or "covert sensitization," viz, Cautela, 1966; Lazarus, 1958) conducted by the therapist, in which extreme feelings of disgust were generated by fantasy and then related to the sadistic image. One can fruitfully compare this technique with the "emotive imagery" procedure described by Lazarus and Abramovitz (1962), in which pleasant images were generated in fearful children and then related by the therapist to conditioned aversive stimuli. The procedure was resorted to in the present case because the client appeared unable to give up the sadistic fantasy solely on the basis of beginning to find the nonsadistic pictures and images effective in maintaining erection and leading to orgasm.

The assessment of therapeutic outcome poses some difficulty here, as indeed it does for any therapy. Explicitly rejected as criteria of "cure" are the client's "self-actualization," "mental health," "ego strength," or other vague notions. While the intention is not simply to beg the question, it does seem more appropriate for the present case report to restrict judgment to the problem as presented by the client, namely, the sadistic fantasies and the attendant worry and doubt about suitability for normal human intercourse.

The clinical data on change in fantasy are self-reports, supplemented by the therapist's inference of the client's credibility. The orderliness of response to therapy, along with the enthusiasm which accompanied the progress reports, serves to bolster the conclusion that Mr. M did, in fact, give up his sadistic fantasies of 10 years' standing in favor of the kinds of fantasies which he felt were a sine qua non for appropriate socio-sexual behavior. Both preceding and accompanying these changes was the radical difference in outlook. Simply stated, Mr. M stopped worrying about himself as an "oddball," doomed to a solitary life, and did make some initial attempts to establish appropriate relationships with girls. That he has not yet

done so (as of this writing) may, indeed, be due to a return of the original problem; however, this alternative seems less likely than that verbalized by the client, namely, that he has always had trouble doing what he knows he ought to do, and that, above all, being a so-called sexual deviate has ceased being an issue for him. Moreover, as mentioned above, variables other than the content of fantasies would seem to bear importantly on the matter of overt sexual behavior. Clearly, if usual dating habits were to be used as a criterion for outcome, the therapy must be considered a failure—although this would qualify many a young adult as "maladjusted" or "abnormal." Be that as it may, a relevant, well-established class of behaviors was modified, setting the stage for a social adjustment from which the client had initially seen himself utterly alienated.

Supplementary Follow-Up Data

A follow-up report was received by mail 16 mo. following termination. The client reported that, since the therapy had so readily eliminated the arousal from sadistic fantasies, and, most importantly, had altered his outlook for "normal" sexual behavior, he allowed himself, "premeditatedly," to return to the use of the sadistic fantasies 6 mo. after termination, ". . . resolving to enjoy my fantasies until June 1, and then to reform once more. This I did. On June 1 [1967], right on schedule, I bought an issue of *Playboy* and proceeded to give myself the treatment again. Once again, it worked like a charm. In two weeks, I was back in my reformed state, where I am now [August 1967]. I have no need for sadistic fantasies. . . . I have [also] been pursuing a vigorous (well, vigorous for *me*) program of dating. In this way, I have gotten to know a lot of girls of whose existence I was previously only peripherally aware. As you probably know, I was very shy with girls before; well, now I am not one-fifth as shy as I used to be. In fact, by my old standards, I have become a regular rake!"

A telephone call was made to obtain more specific information about his return to the sadistic fantasies. He reported that the return was "fairly immediate," with a concomitant withdrawal of interest in conventional sexual stimuli. His self-administered therapy in June 1967 followed the gradual pattern of the original therapy, although progress was much faster. The author advised him not to make any more "premeditated" returns, rather to consolidate his gains in dating and other conventional heterosexual activities and interests. The client indicated that this plan could and would be readily implemented.

Of the past 16 mo., then, the client has been free of the sadistic fantasies for 7 mo., the other 9 mo. involving what he terms a willful return for sexual stimulation while masturbating. Constant throughout this follow-up period has been the relief which he derived from finding himself able to respond sexually to conventional sexual stimuli. Additional gains are his dating activities, which, it will be recalled, were not in evidence while the writer was in direct contact with him.

Still aware of the limitations of these case-study data, it does seem noteworthy and possibly quite important that the client's self-initiated partial "relapse" took place in a step-wise fashion, that is, without a *gradual* reorientation to the sadistic fantasies: he reported himself almost immediately excited by them once he had made the decision to become so. This sudden shift raises questions as to whether "aversive counterconditioning" underlay the indifference to the fantasies which was effected during therapy. This surprising finding also underlines the probable importance of other-than-conditioning variables in the treatment.

REFERENCES

Bandura, A. *Principles of behavior modification.* New York: Holt, Rinehart & Winston, 1969.

Blakemore, C. B., Thorpe, J. G., Barker, J. C., Conway, C. G., & Lavin, N. I. The application of faradic aversion conditioning in a case of transvestism. *Behaviour Research and Therapy*, 1963, *1*, 29–34.

Cautela, J. R. Treatment of compulsive behavior by covert sensitization. *The Psychological Record*, 1966, *16*, 33–41.

Davies, B., & Morgenstern, F. A case of cysticercosis, temporal lobe epilepsy, and transvestism. *Journal of Neurological and Neurosurgical Psychiatry*, 1960, *23*, 247–249.

Davison, G. C. Relative contributions of differential relaxation and graded exposure to in vivo desensitization of a neurotic fear. *Proceedings of the 73rd annual convention of the American Psychological Association*, 1965, 209–210.

Davison, G. C. Differential relaxation and cognitive restructuring in therapy with a "paranoid of schizophrenic" or "paranoid state." *Proceedings of the 74th annual convention of the American Psychological Association*, 1966, *2*, 177–178.

Davison, G. C. Systematic desensitization as a counterconditioning process. *Journal of Abnormal Psychology*, 1968, *73*, 91–99.

Feldman, M. P. Aversion therapy for sexual deviations: A critical review. *Psychological Bulletin*, 1966, *65*, 65–79.

Feldman, M. P., & MacCulloch, M. J. The application of anticipatory avoidance learning to the treatment of homosexuality: I. Theory, technique and preliminary results. *Behavior Research and Therapy*, 1965, *2*, 165–183.

Freund, K. Some problems in the treatment of homosexuality. In H. J. Eysenck (Ed.), *Behaviour therapy and the neurosis*. London: Pergamon, 1960. Pp. 312–326.

Glasser, W. *Reality therapy: A new approach to psychiatry*. New York: Harper & Row, 1965.

Grossberg, J. M. Behavior therapy: A review. *Psychological Bulletin*, 1964, *62*, 73–88.

Guthrie, E. R. *The psychology of learning*. New York: Harper, 1935.

Kalish, H. I. Behavior therapy. In B. B. Wolman (Ed.), *Handbook of clinical psychology*. New York: McGraw-Hill, 1965. Pp. 1230–1253.

Lang, P. J., & Lazovik, A. D. Experimental desensitization of a phobia. *Journal of Abnormal and Social Psychology*, 1963, *66*, 519–525.

Lang, P. J., Lazovik, A. D., & Reynolds, D. J. Desensitization, suggestibility, and pseudotherapy. *Journal of Abnormal Psychology*, 1965, *70*, 395–402.

Lavin, N. I., Thorpe, J. G., Barker, J. C., Blakemore, C. B., & Conway, C. G. Behavior therapy in a case of transvestism. *Journal of Nervous and Mental Disease*, 1961, *133*, 346–353.

Lazarus, A. A. New methods in psychotherapy: A case study. *South African Medical Journal*, 1958, *33*, 660–663.

Lazarus, A. A. Group therapy of phobic disorders by systematic desensitization. *Journal of Abnormal and Social Psychology*, 1961, *63*, 504–510.

Lazarus, A. A., & Abramovitz, A. The use of "emotive imagery" in the treatment of children's phobias. *Journal of Mental Science*, 1962, *108*, 191–195.

Levy, L. H. *Psychological interpretation*. New York: Holt, Rinehart & Winston, 1963.

Maher, B. A. *Principles of psychopathology: An experimental approach*. New York: McGraw-Hill, 1966.

Mainord, W. A. A therapy. *Research Bulletin*, Mental Health Research Institute, Ft. Steilacom, Washington, 1962, *5*, 85–92.

Paul, G. L. *Insight vs. desensitization in psychotherapy: An experiment in anxiety reduction*. Stanford: Stanford University Press, 1966.

Paul, G. L., & Shannon, D. T. Treatment of anxiety through systematic desensitization in therapy groups. *Journal of Abnormal Psychology*, 1966, *71*, 124–135.

Rachman, S. Sexual disorders and behaviour therapy. *American Journal of Psychiatry*, 1961, *118*, 235–240.

Rachman, S. Studies in desensitization—III: Speed of generalization. *Behaviour Research and Therapy*, 1966, *4*, 7–15.

Raymond, M. J. Case of fetishism treated by aversion therapy. *British Medical Journal*, 1956, *2*, 854–857.

Schubot, E. The influence of hypnotic and muscular relaxation in systematic desensitization of phobias. Unpublished doctoral dissertation, Stanford University, 1966.

Thorpe, J. G., Schmidt, E., Brown, P. T., & Castell, D. Aversion-relief therapy: A new method for general application. *Behaviour Research and Therapy*, 1964, *2*, 71–82.

Thorpe, J. G., Schmidt, E., & Castell, D. A comparison of positive and negative (aversive) conditioning in the treatment of homosexuality. *Behaviour Research and Therapy*, 1963, *1*, 357–362.

Ullmann, L., & Krasner, L. P. (Eds.) *Case studies in behavior modification.* New York: Holt, Rinehart & Winston, 1965.

Wolpe, J. *Psychotherapy by reciprocal inhibition.* Stanford: Stanford University Press, 1958.

Wolpe, J., & Lazarus, A. A. *Behavior therapy techniques.* New York: Pergamon, 1966.

Wolpin, M., & Raines, J. Visual imagery, expected roles and extinction as possible factors in reducing fear and avoidance behavior. *Behaviour Research and Therapy,* 1966, *4*, 25–37.

Zeisset, R. M. Desensitization and relaxation in the modification of psychiatric patients' interview behavior. Unpublished doctoral dissertation, University of Illinois, 1966.

Chapter 22

Punishment Procedures

This case involved a life-or-death situation for the client, a nine-month-old male infant. The problem for this little boy was continual ruminative vomiting following every meal, which, of course, resulted in severe weight loss and could have led to death. The behavior therapists were turned to only as a last resort, after many other attempts were made to stop the vomiting. Since the vomiting occurred only after the child had finished eating, the therapists decided on an aversive-conditioning technique to punish and inhibit the vomiting behavior. Electric shock applied to the infant's leg was the method by which the behavior was punished. It may seem cruel and unusual to shock a small child, but it must be remembered that this was done to save his life. It should also be noted that after the second session only very brief shocks were necessary to stop the vomiting. After this behavior had been eliminated entirely, which took a relatively short period of time, the therapists noted an increase in responsiveness to people by the child. These new interactions with adults may, of course, have been caused by a number of factors not directly related to the behavior modification procedures.

Case Report

Avoidance Conditioning Therapy of an Infant with Chronic Ruminative Vomiting[1]

PETER J. LANG and BARBARA G. MELAMED[2]

A variety of techniques have been used in the treatment of persistent vomiting in infants and children. In general these therapies are tailored to the known or hypothesized causes of the disorder. Thus, the presence of functional disturbance in the intestinal tract would encourage the use of pharmacologic agents—"tranquilizers," antinauseants, or antiemetics. If gastric, anatomical anomalies can be diagnosed, their surgical removal often proves to be the most effective treatment. Animal studies suggest that surgical manipulation of the central nervous system may also become a vehicle for emesis control (Borison, 1959).

When diagnosis excludes obvious, organic antecedents, both the etiology and treatment of the disorder appear less certain. However, clinical workers have described an apparently "psychosomatic" vomiting in children which is generally accompanied by a ruminative rechewing of the vomitus. In reviewing the syndrome, Richmond, Eddy, and Green (1958) adhere to the widely held psychoanalytic hypothesis that it results from a disruption in the mother-infant relationship. They suggest that the condition is brought about by the inability of the mother to fulfill an adult psychosexual role which is reflected in marital inadequacy. She is unable to give up her own dependent needs and is incapable of providing warm, comfortable, and intimate physical care for the infant. This lack of comfort from without causes the infant to seek and recreate such gratification from within. Thus, in attempting to regain some satisfaction from the feeding situation, he regurgitates his food and retains it in his mouth. The recommended treatment is the interruption in the mother-infant relationship by hospitalization and the provision of a stimulating, warm environment with a substitute mother figure. This method achieved success in the four cases reviewed. Berlin, McCullough, Lisha, and Szurek (1957) offer a similar psychoanalytic interpretation in reporting a case study of a 4-yr.-old child hospitalized for 8 mo. at Langley-Porter Clinic. Psychotherapy, involving concomitant counseling to improve the relationship between the parents, led to an alleviation of the child's vomiting reaction.

From the point of view espoused by learning theorists, emesis and rumination may be learned habits. In point of fact, vomiting has been clearly demonstrated as a conditioned response in at least three independent studies (Collins & Tatum, 1925; Kleitman & Crisler, 1927; Pavlov, 1927). This prompts the corollary hypoth-

From *Journal of Abnormal Psychology*, 1969, 74(1), 1–8. Copyright 1969 by the American Psychological Association. Reprinted by permission.

[1] This study was supported in part by a grant (MH-10993) from the National Institute of Mental Health, United States Public Health Service.

[2] The authors wish to thank David Kass, the physician in immediate charge of the present case, for giving the authors the opportunity to explore this treatment method and for his assistance during its application. The authors are also indebted to Charles Lobeck, Chairman of the Department of Pediatrics of University Hospitals, Madison, Wisconsin, who made facilities available for use, and to the assigned nursing staff without whose help and cooperation the present result could not have been accomplished. The authors also express their appreciation to Norman Greenfield and Richard Sternbach of the Department of Psychiatry, University of Wisconsin, for the loan of a polygraph, and to Karl G. Stoedefalke of Physical Education for providing additional EMG preamplifiers.

esis that such behavior could be eliminated directly by counterconditioning procedures.

A number of case reports indicate that considerable success may be achieved in modifying alimentary habits in the clinic setting. Both Bachrach, Erwin, and Mohr (1965) and Meyer[3] successfully treated adult anorexic patients by making various social and physical reinforcers contingent on eating behavior or weight gain. Lang (1965) described the therapy of a young adult patient who became nauseous and vomited under social stress. In this case, counterconditioning methods increased the patient's tolerance of formerly aversive social situations, and thus markedly reduced the frequency of nausea and emesis.

The only study reviewed, attempting to apply conditioning methods specifically in the treatment of ruminative vomiting was reported by White and Taylor (1967). Electric shock was applied to two mentally retarded patients (23-yr.-old female, 14-yr.-old male) whenever throat, eye, or coughing gestures signaled rumination. They suggest that the shock served to distract the patient and he engaged in other activities rather than ruminating. Significant improvement occurred after 1 wk. of treatment, and gains were maintained at a 1-mo. follow-up.

The following case report illustrates the efficacy of aversive conditioning in reversing the vomiting and rumination of a 9-mo.-old infant whose life was endangered by this behavior. The case is of general interest because of the extreme youth of the patient, the speed of treatment, and the fact that conditioning procedures were undertaken only after other treatments had been either ruled out by diagnostic procedures, or had been given a reasonable trial without success. These data also have further implications for

[3] Meyer, V. Personal communication, 1964.

the understanding of aversive conditioning procedures in clinical practice.

HISTORY OF PROBLEM AND FAMILY BACKGROUND

A. T. at the age of 9 mo. was admitted to the University Hospital for failure to retain food and chronic rumination. This infant had undergone three prior hospitalizations for his persistent vomiting after eating and failure to gain weight. Born in an eastern state after an uneventful 39-wk. pregnancy, the patient was bottle fed and gained steadily from a birth weight of 9 lb. 4 oz. to 17 lb. at 6 mo. of age. Vomiting was first noted during the fifth month, and increased in severity to the point where the patient vomited 10–15 min. after each meal. This activity was often associated with vigorous thumb-sucking, placing fingers in his mouth, blotchiness of the face, and ruminating behavior. The mother remarked that the start of vomiting may have coincided with her indisposition due to a broken ankle which forced the family to live with maternal grandparents for several weeks. Some friction was reported between the patient's mother and her own adoptive mother concerning care of the child. The patient's father is a part-time college student and the family received financial assistance from the paternal grandfather, a successful dentist. At the time of the most recent hospitalization, the social worker's report suggested that the parents were making a marginal marital adjustment.

Three brief periods of hospitalization which included medical tests (gastrointestinal fluoroscopy, EEG, and neuropsychological testing) failed to find an organic basis for this persistent regurgitation. An exploratory operation was performed and a cyst on the right kidney removed, with no discernible effect on his condition. The patient had no history of head trauma. One previous incident of persistent vomiting in a paternal uncle was noted to be of very short duration. The paternal grandfather and two uncles are reported to suffer ulcers.

Several treatment approaches were applied without success. Dietary changes (Pro-Sobee, skim milk), the administration of antinauseants, and various mechanical maneuvers to improve the feeding situation (different positions, small amounts at each feeding, burping) gave short-lived, if any, relief. As thumb sucking often preceded the response, restraints were tried. However, this did little to reduce the frequency of emesis. An attempt had been made to initiate intensive nursing care "to establish and maintain a one-to-one relationship and to provide the child with warm, friendly, and secure feelings [nurse's chart]." This had to be abandoned because it was not inhibiting the vomiting and some observers felt that it increased the child's anxiety and restlessness.

At the time the present investigators were called in, the infant was in critical condition, down to a weight of 12 lb., and being fed through a nasogastric pump. The attending physician's clinical notes attest that conditioning procedures were applied as a last attempt, "in view of the fact that therapy until now has been unsuccessful and the life of the child is threatened by continuation of this behavior."

THERAPEUTIC PROCEDURE AND RESULTS

The patient was given a private room, continuous nursing care, and assigned a special graduate nurse to assist in the conditioning procedures. The authors closely observed the infant for 2 days during and after normal feeding periods. He reliably regurgitated most of his food intake within 10 min. of each feeding and continued to bring up small amounts throughout the day. Observers on the hospital staff suggested that vomiting was originally induced by thumb pressure at the back of the throat. However, at this stage thumb manipulations were not a necessary part of the vomiting sequence. He did protest, however, if hand restraint was enforced. His frail appearance and general unresponsiveness, made him a pathetic looking child as seen from a photograph taken just prior to treatment (Figure 1).

In an attempt to obtain a clearer picture of the patterning of his response, electromyograph (EMG) activity at three sites was monitored on a Gilson Polygraph. Responses leading up to and into the vomiting sequence reliably coincided with the nurse's concurrent description of the sequence of behavior. Figure 2 illustrates the typical response pattern. The uppermost channel of information represents muscle potentials recorded just under the chin, and shows the sucking behavior which usually preceded vomiting; the lowest channel is an integrated record taken from the throat muscles of the neck; the center channel which monitors the upper chest region is largely EKG artifact. It can be noted from this segment that the onset of vomiting is clearly accompanied by vigorous throat movements indicated by rhythmic, high-frequency, high-amplitude activity, in contrast with quiescent periods and periods where crying predominated.

The authors were concerned with eliminating the inappropriate vomiting, without causing any fundamental disturbance in the feeding behavior of the child. Fortunately, the child did not vomit during feeding, and the sucking and vomiting could be distinguished readily on the EMG. After 2 days of monitoring, conditioning procedures were initiated. The aversive conditioning paradigm called for brief and repeated shock (approximately 1 sec. long with a 1-sec. interpulse in-

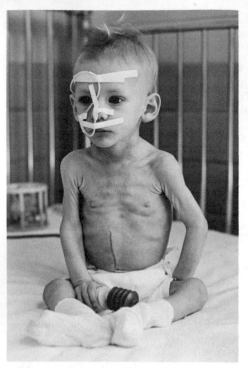
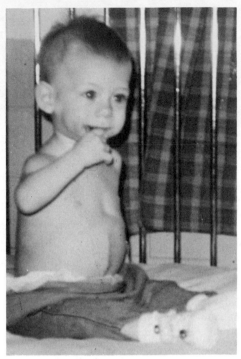

Figure 1. The photograph at the left was taken during the observation period just prior to treatment. (It clearly illustrates the patient's debilitated condition—the lack of body fat, skin hanging in loose folds. The tape around the face holds tubing for the nasogastric pump. The photograph at the right was taken on the day of discharge from the hospital, 13 days after the first photo. The 26% increase in body weight already attained is easily seen in the full, more infantlike face, the rounded arms, and more substantial trunk.)

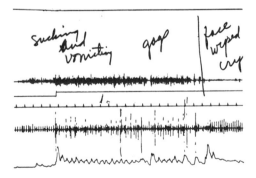

Figure 2. Three channels of EMG activity are presented. (The nurse observer's comments are written just above the first channel. The intense muscle activity on this line is associated with sucking behavior, recorded from electrodes on the underside of the chin. The second channel is just below the one pulse per second, timing line, and was taken from electrodes on the upper chest, at the base of the throat. The EKG dominates this channel, with some local muscle activity. Electrodes straddling the esophagus yielded the lowest line, which in this integrated record clearly shows the rhythmic pulsing of the vomiting response.)

terval) as soon as vomiting occurred, continuing until the response was terminated. An effort was made to initiate shock at the first sign of reverse peristalsis, but not during the preceding sucking behavior. The contingency was determined from the nurse's observations of the patient and the concurrent EMG records. In general, the nurse would signal as soon as she thought an emesis was beginning. If EMG confirmed the judgment, shock was delivered. Occasionally, the EMG would initiate this sequence, with the observational judgment following.[4] Shock was delivered by means of a Harvard Inductorium to electrodes placed on the calf of the patient's leg. A 3,000-cps tone was temporarily coincident

[4] Particular thanks are due to Mary Kachoyeanos, the nurse who assisted at all the therapy sessions.

with each shock presentation.[5] Sessions were chosen following feeding to insure some frequency of response. Each session lasted less than 1 hour.

After two sessions shock was rarely required. The infant would react to the shock by crying and cessation of vomiting. By the third session only one or two brief presentations of shock were necessary to cause cessation of any vomiting sequence. Figure 3 illustrates the typical sequence of a conditioning trial.

The course of therapy is indicated in Figure 4. Few shocks were administered after the first day of treatment, and both the time spent vomiting and the average length of each vomiting period were abruptly reduced. After only two sessions it seemed that the infant was anticipating the unpleasant consequences of his behavior. He would begin to suck vigorously using his thumb, and then he would remove his thumb and cry loudly.

The data graphed (Figure 4) for the second treatment session represent those reinforcers that the authors are certain were delivered. Early in this session, it became obvious that the infant was not

[5] Shock level was first determined by applying the electrodes to the *E*s, who judged it to be quite painful and unpleasant. Intensity was incremented slightly during the first and second sessions on the basis of the patient's response, but was subsequently unchanged. The inductorium does not permit for exact or wholly reliable measures of current level. However, under the conditions of treatment described here, the average current was within a range of from .10 to .30 ma., with a cycle frequency of approximately 50 cps. It should be borne in mind that pulses from an inductorium vary widely in amplitude, and the authors' instrument produced some spikes over 10 ma. Electrodes were first applied to the ball of the foot and then moved to the calf for reasons stated in the text. The accompanying tone was generated by a Hewlett-Packard signal generator and administered by a small oval speaker in a free field. The intensity was loud but not painful (approximately 80–95 db.), and varied considerably because of spontaneous changes in the infant's position. It was employed in order to increase the density of the reinforcer and on the possibility that the therapists might employ it alone, if shock proved to have negative side effects.

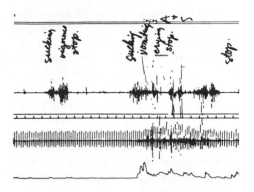

Figure 3. The electrode positions are the same as in Figure 2. (The top line shows the point at which two brief shocks were administered. It may be noted that they follow closely on the first pulse of the vomiting response and that the rhythmic regurgitation observed in Figure 2 never gets underway.)

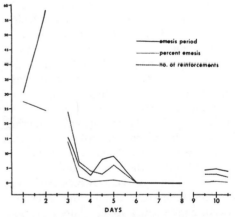

Figure 4. The abscissa describes successive days (morning and afternoon) on which observation or treatment was accomplished. ("Emesis period" is the length of any continuous period of vomiting. "Percentage of emesis" is the total time spent vomiting divided by the time observed. Sessions varied from 16 min. to 60 min. Treatment began on Day 3 which included two unshocked emesis periods. In Session 10 tone alone was presented on one trial. It is of interest to note that following therapy, nursing staff reported that they could now block the very rare vomiting periods with a sharp handclap.)

receiving the majority of the administered shocks. The electrodes were at that time attached to the plantar surface of the foot.

Observation suggested that the patient had learned to curl his foot, either coincident with emesis or at the first sensation of shock, so as to lift the electrodes off the skin and thus avoid the painful stimulus. At this point, the electrodes were relocated on the calf, and conditioning proceeded normally. If the shock administrations prior to procedural change are added to those on the graph, Day 3, afternoon figures for emesis period, percentage of emesis, and shock, respectively are 11 sec., 21.6% and 77.

By the sixth session the infant no longer vomited during the testing procedures. He would usually fall asleep toward the middle of the hour. Figure 5 indicates the sequence of response demonstrating the replacement of vigorous sucking with what the nursing observers described as a "pacifier" use of the thumb.

To vary the condtions under which learning would take place, thereby providing for transfer of effects, the sessions were scheduled at different hours of the day, and while the infant was being held, playing on the floor, as well as lying in bed. Nursing staff reported a progressive decrease in his ruminating and vomiting behavior during the rest of the day and night, which paralleled the reduction observed across therapy sessions.

After three sessions in which there was no occurrence of vomiting, the procedure was discontinued. Two days later there was some spontaneous recovery, which included some vigorous sucking, with a little vomiting and rumination. Three additional sessions were initiated to maintain the reduced frequency of the response (see Figure 4). Except for a brief slackening prior to these trials, there was a steady, monotonic increase in his weight as shown in Figure 6. In general, his activity level increased, he became more interested in his environment, enjoyed playroom experience, and smiled and reached out to be held by the nurse and other visitors.

The mother was reintroduced the day

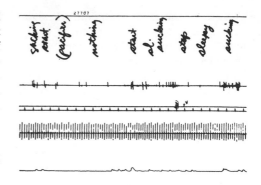

Figure 5. The above segment is representative of behavior near the end of a conditioning session. (Only mild sucking activity is apparent in the upper EMG channel. The electrode positions are the same as in Figure 2.)

following the last conditioning trial. She took over some of the patient's caretaking needs, including feedings. There was no marked change in his ruminating behavior at this time. The mother responded well and her child reciprocated her attention. He was discharged from the hospital 5 days later, after exhibiting almost no ruminating behavior. The remarkable contrast in his physical appearance is noted in a photograph taken on the day of discharge (Figure 1).

FOLLOW-UP

Correspondence with the mother indicated that there was no further need for treatment. A. T. was eating well and gaining weight regularly. She reported that any thumbsucking or rumination was easily arrested by providing him with other forms of stimulation. He was beginning to seek attention from other people and enjoyed the company of other children. One month following discharge from the hospital, he was seen for a physical check-up. He appeared as a healthy looking 21-lb. child and, aside from a slight anemic condition, was found fully recovered by the attending physician. His local physician reported on a visit 5 mo. later when his

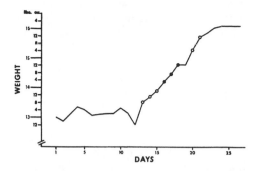

Figure 6. The infant's body weight as determined from the nursing notes is plotted over time, from well before conditioning therapy was instituted to the day of discharge from the hospital. (Days on which conditioning sessions occurred are marked by circles on the curve. Reinforcers were delivered only on days marked by open circles. The decline in body weight in the few days just prior to therapy was probably occasioned by the discontinuance of the nasogastric pump, in favor of normal feeding procedures. The marked weight gain from Day 13 to 18 is coincident with the first 6 days of therapy. The temporary reduction in weight increase, associated with a resumption of emesis, is apparent at Day 19. The additional conditioning trials appear to have acted immediately to reinstate weight gain.)

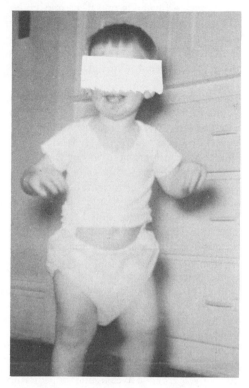

Figure 7. The patient 5 mo. after treatment.

weight was 26 lb., 1 oz. "His examinations were negative for any problems. . . . He was eating quite well . . . no vomiting had recurred. He was alert, active and attentive." A snapshot taken by the mother a few weeks before this examination is reproduced in Figure 7. One year after treatment he continues to thrive. Mother and father are both pleased with his development, and no further treatment is indicated.

DISCUSSION

The rapid recovery of this 9-mo.-old male infant following brief aversive conditioning therapy, argues for the effectiveness of behavioral modification in the treatment of this type of psychosomatic disorder. The vomiting and ruminating were treated as maladaptive behavior patterns, and electric shock was used to inhibit a previously well-established response sequence. Elimination of the response was accompanied by increase in the infant's responsiveness to people, as well as substantial weight gains, and physiological improvement.

Treatment was undertaken without analysis of the disorder's antecedants. Nevertheless, the family history of the infant could be construed as consistent with other cases in the literature. One clinical worker suggested that a feeling of hostility dominated this infant's home. It is true that the parents' wedding was attended by difficulties and the subsequent birth of the patient occurred before the parents were fully prepared for this responsibility. Furthermore, the mother later expressed anxiety about her marriage and complained of the problem of balancing the separate demands of father and child. She also reported her feeling that her own step-mother had not provided a good maternal model. As a consequence she felt inadequate herself and uncertain in the role.

The caseworker's notes are thus rich in "dynamics," and while one is unable to establish the relative accuracy or significance of these statements, it is clear that this case is interpretable within traditional personality theories. Nevertheless, therapies generated by this orientation were not successful in the present case. In deference, it should also be noted that "one-to-one" care was not maintained as long or as consistently as in many cases reported in the literature, and despite evidence of some marital discord, no extensive counseling of the parents was undertaken. However, like many psychiatric treatments, the above are expensive of professional personnel and prolonged in duration. The aversive conditioning procedures used here achieved success in little more than a week, and considering the developing danger to the child's life, speed was of more than usual importance.

No evidence of "symptom substitution" was observed following treatment. On the other hand, positive social behavior increased coincident with the sucessful conditioning therapy. The infant became more responsive to adults, smiled more frequently, and seemed to be more interested in toys and games than he had been previously. An analogous improvement in social behavior was noticed in the defective adults treated by White and Taylor (1967), Lovaas, Freitag, Gold, and Kassorla (1965) and Lovaas, Schaeffer, and Simmons (1965) have cited similar effects following the avoidance conditioning of tantrum behavior in autistic children. The latter investigators suggest that the *Es* attained secondary reinforcing value because of their association with shock reduction. This provides the basis for training the children to exhibit affec-

tionate patterns toward adults. In the present case this contingency was very imprecise, and it is not clear that the above mechanism mediated change. What could be called normal infant behavior increased regularly, as the emesis decreased. The social environment appeared simply to replace ruminating as the infant's focus of attention.

Aversive conditioning has been applied widely in adult therapy as well as with autistic children. Eysenck and Rachman (1965) and Feldman (1966) describe its use in treating alcoholic and sexual disorders. However, one hesitates to interpret these findings in a straightforward manner. Adult patients may submit to aversive conditioning procedures from a variety of motives, and cognitive factors may blunt the impact or distort the meaning of aversive stimuli. The present case is of particular interest because these procedures were successful in treating an apparently normal child. Furthermore, the absence of language and the limited cognitive development achieved at this age permit one to interpret this change as avoidance conditioning, unmitigated by the above factors.

Finally, it should be noted that the present case represents a productive use of psychophysiologic recording in therapy. Not only did the EMG provide extensive documentation of the response, but concurrent recording was of considerable help in guiding the treatment effort. Specifically, these records confirmed in an objective manner external observations of mouth and throat movements which seemd to precede emesis. Furthermore, they extended these observations, helping the authors to specify those aspects of the response which were unique to the vomiting sequence, thus assuring that shock was never delivered following noncontingent behavior. Finally, observation of the recordings during therapy probably reduced the latency of reinforcement, particularly during the early trials when the validity of external signs seemed less certain, and provided the clearest indicator of the end of the response when shock was promptly terminated. While the importance of this information to the results obtained cannot be unequivocally established, it certainly increased the confidence of the therapists in their method, and, in turn, the speed and precision with which they proceeded. The further exploration of physiological analysis in the therapeutic setting is encouraged.

REFERENCES

Bachrach, A. J., Erwin, W. J., & Mohr, J. P. The control of eating behavior in an anorexic by operant conditioning techniques. In L. P. Ullmann & L. Krasner (Eds.), *Case studies in behavior modification.* New York: Holt, Rinehart & Winston, 1965.

Berlin, I. N., McCullough, G., Lisha, E. S., & Szurek, S. Intractable episodic vomiting in a three-year old child. *Psychiatric Quarterly*, 1957, *31*, 228–249.

Borison, H. L. Effect of ablation of medullary emetic chemoreceptor trigger zone on vomiting response to cerebral intra-ventricular injection of adrenaline, apomorphine and pilocarpine in the cat. *Journal of Physiology*, 1959, *147*, 172–177.

Collins, K. H., & Tatum, A. L. A conditioned salivary reflex established by chronic morphine poisoning. *American Journal of Physiology*, 1925, *74*, 14–15.

Eysenck, H. J., & Rachman, S. *The causes and cures of neurosis.* San Diego, Calif.: Knapp, 1965.

Feldman, M. P. Aversion therapy for sexual deviations: A critical review. *Psychological Bulletin*, 1966, *65*, 65–79.

Kleitman, N., & Crisler, G. A quantitative study of the conditioned salivary reflex. *American Journal of Physiology*, 1927, *79*, 571–614.

Lang, P. J. Behavior therapy with a case of nervous anorexia. In L. P. Ullmann & L. Krasner (Eds.), *Case studies in behavior modification.* New York: Holt, Rinehart & Winston, 1965.

Lovaas, O. I., Freitag, G., Gold, V., & Kassorla, I. Experimental studies in childhood schizophrenia: Analysis of self-destructive behavior. *Journal of Experimental Child Psychology*, 1965, *2*, 67–84.

Lovaas, O. I., Schaeffer, B., & Simmons, J. Building social behavior in autistic children by use of electric shock. *Journal of Experimental Research in Personality*, 1965, *1*, 99–109.

Pavlov, I. P. *Conditioned reflexes: An investigation of the physiological activity of the cerebral cortex.* Lecture III, Oxford, England: Oxford University Press, 1927.

Richmond, J. B., Eddy, E., & Green, M. Rumination: A psychosomatic syndrome of infancy. *Pediatrics*, 1958, *22*, 49–55.

White, J. D., & Taylor, D. Noxious conditioning as a treatment for rumination. *Mental Retardation*, 1967, *5*, 30–33.

Name Index

Subject Index

416